CRITICAL SURVEY
OF
SHORT FICTION

CRITICAL SURVEY

OF

SHORT FICTION

Second Revised Edition

Volume 5

Bharati Mukherjee - Mona Simpson

Editor, Second Revised Edition

Charles E. May

California State University, Long Beach

Editor, First Edition

Frank N. Magill

SALEM PRESS, INC.

Pasadena, California   Hackensack, New Jersey

Managing Editor: Christina J. Moose
Research Supervisor: Jeffry Jensen
Acquisitions Editor: Mark Rehn
Photograph Editor: Philip Bader
Manuscript Editors: Lauren M. Mitchell
Melanie Watkins
Research Assistant: Jeff Stephens
Production Editor: Cynthia Beres
Layout: Ross Castellano

Copyright © 2001, by Salem Press, Inc.

Library of Congress Cataloging-in-Publication Data

Critical survey of short fiction / editor, Charles E. May.—2nd rev. ed.
  7 v. ; cm.
Includes bibliographical references and index.
First edition edited by Frank Northen Magill.
Includes bibliographical references and index.
  ISBN 0-89356-006-5 (set : alk. paper) — ISBN 0-89356-007-3 (v. 1 : alk. paper) —
ISBN 0-89356-008-1 (v. 2 : alk. paper) — ISBN 0-89356-009-X (v. 3 : alk. paper) —
ISBN 0-89356-010-3 (v. 4 : alk. paper) — ISBN 0-89356-011-1 (v. 5 : alk. paper) —
ISBN 0-89356-012-X (v. 6 : alk. paper) — ISBN 0-89356-013-8 (v. 7 : alk. paper)
  1. Short story. 2. Short story—History and criticism. 3. Short story—Bio-bibliography.
I. May, Charles E. (Charles Edward) 1941 -   . II. Magill, Frank Northen, 1907-1997.

PN3321 .C7 2001
809.3′1—dc21   00-046384

Fourth Printing

CONTENTS

COMPLETE LIST OF AUTHORS

Volume I

Volume II

Volume III

Volume IV

Volume V

Volume VI

CRITICAL SURVEY
OF
SHORT FICTION

BHARATI MUKHERJEE

Born: Calcutta, India; July 27, 1940

PRINCIPAL SHORT FICTION

Darkness, 1985
The Middleman and Other Stories, 1988

OTHER LITERARY FORMS

Bharati Mukherjee has written several novels, including *The Tiger's Daughter* (1972), *Wife* (1975), *Jasmine* (1989), *The Holder of the World* (1993), and *Leave It to Me* (1997); a travel memoir, *Days and Nights in Calcutta* (1977; with her husband Clark Blaise); a nonfiction critique of Canadian racism, *The Sorrow and the Terror: The Haunting Legacy of the Air India Tragedy* (1987; in collaboration with Blaise); a political treatise, *Kautilya's Concept of Diplomacy* (1976); the nonfiction studies *Political Culture and Leadership in India: A Study of West Bengal* (1991) and *Regionalism in Indian Perspective* (1992); and several essays and articles.

ACHIEVEMENTS

Bharati Mukherjee occupies a distinctive place among first-generation North American writers of Indian origin. She has received a number of grants from the Canada Arts Council (1973-1974, 1977), the Shastri Indo-Canadian Institute (1976-1977), the John Simon Guggenheim Memorial Foundation (1978-1979), and the Canadian government (1982). In 1980, she won first prize from the Periodical Distribution Association for her short story "Isolated Incidents." In 1981, she won the National Magazine Award's second prize for her essay "An Invisible Woman." Her story "Angela" was selected for inclusion in *The Best American Short Stories 1985*, and "The Tenant" was included in *The Best American Short Stories 1987*. Her second collection of short stories *The Middleman and Other Stories* won the National Book Critics Circle Award in 1988.

BIOGRAPHY

Bharati Mukherjee was born into a well-to-do, tra-

ditional Bengali Brahman family in the Calcutta suburb of Ballygunge on July 27, 1940. Her Hindu family's affluence buffered them from the political crises of independence and partition that engulfed the Indian subcontinent in the 1940's, and by the end of that troubled decade her father, Sudhir Lal Mukherjee, a chemist and the proprietor of a successful pharmaceutical company, had moved the family first to London (1948-1950) and then to Switzerland (1951) before returning them to India. Accordingly, Mukherjee explains, she and her two sisters (one older, one younger) "were born both too late and not late enough to be real Indians." Her educational experiences abroad had made her fluent in English at an early age, so that once back in India she began attending Calcutta's Loreto Convent School, an elite institution for girls run by Irish Catholic nuns, where she occasionally glimpsed Mother Teresa early in her ministry to the city's poor. At the time, Mukherjee herself followed the habits of her caste and preferred to turn away from the misery on the streets around her rather than question or reflect upon it.

Neither did she consciously plan to deviate very far from the traditional path of Indian womanhood expected of her; even her early interest in becoming a writer, fed by an ever-expanding fascination with the European novels to which her travels and education had exposed her, was tolerated because she was female—such impractical aspirations would have been quickly discouraged in a son, she believes. She has praised her mother for her courageous insistence that she receive a top-flight English education so that she "would not end up, she said, as chattel to a traditional Bengali husband." Although her father intended to have his middle daughter marry a bridegroom of the family's choosing from within their own strictly defined social class, he encouraged her intellectual aspirations in the meantime, and so Mukherjee earned an honors B.A. in English from Calcutta University in 1959 and a master's degree in English and ancient Indian culture in 1961 from the University of Baroda. She then joined "the first generation of Indians who

Bharati Mukherjee (Tom Victor)

even thought of going to the United States rather than automatically to England" when she accepted a Philanthropic Educational Organization International Peace Scholarship to the University of Iowa Writers' Workshop, receiving an M.F.A. in 1963. During that time she also met Clark Blaise, an American writer of Canadian descent, whom she married on September 13, 1963, in an action that, she explains, "cut me off forever from the rules and ways of upper-middle-class life in Bengal, and hurled me into a New World life of scary improvisations and heady explorations." The couple would have two sons, Bart and Bernard, and would, over the course of their long marriage, collaborate on a number of book projects, most strikingly *Days and Nights in Calcutta* (1977), a travel journal of their respective observations during a trip together to India.

Having already taught at Marquette University and the University of Wisconsin at Madison, in 1966 Mukherjee moved with Blaise to Montreal, Canada, where she assumed a teaching position at McGill University, which she held until 1978. She completed

a Ph.D. in English at the University of Iowa in 1969 and published her first novel, *The Tiger's Daughter* (1972), soon thereafter. In 1972 Mukherjee became a Canadian citizen but quickly grew disenchanted with her new country as she experienced the persistent racial discrimination and harassment suffered by Indians and other immigrants of color; she registered her protest in a celebrated article entitled "An Invisible Woman" and in several short stories.

After fourteen years in Canada, a period during which she published a second novel, *Wife*, along with *Days and Nights in Calcutta*, Mukherjee and Blaise brought their family to the United States and became permanent residents in 1980. In 1976-1977 she served as director of the Shastri Institute in New Delhi, India. She became writer-in-residence and distinguished professor of English at the University of California, Berkeley. In later years she and Blaise jointly published *The Sorrow and the Terror: The Haunting Legacy of the Air India Tragedy* (1987), which pointedly documents what she regards as Canada's refusal "to renovate its national self-image to include its changing complexion." In 1987 Mukherjee became a naturalized U.S. citizen. Over the course of her career she has taught in numerous American universities, including Emory University, Skidmore College, Columbia University, Queens College, and the University of Iowa Writers' Workshop. Since the 1980's Mukherjee has regarded herself squarely as an "American" writer (categorically eschewing hyphenated Asian- or Indian-American labels) and describes her geographic relocation as the seminal moment in her artistic maturation. In Canada she had come to view herself, for the first time in her life, as

> a late-blooming colonial who writes in a borrowed language (English), lives permanently in an alien country, and is read, when read at all, in another alien country, the United States.

That multilayered dispossession ended in the United States as she found herself moving "away from the aloofness of expatriation to the exuberance of immigration." The ideological legitimacy of the immigrant story in American culture has in fact become one of her central literary themes, one in which she explores "America" as "an idea" and "a stage for transformation." Her impressive literary production since arriving in the United States has included a number of critically acclaimed novels centered on strong-willed American or Americanized heroines (*Jasmine*, *The Holder of the World*, and *Leave It to Me*) and several expansive short-story collections (*Darkness* in 1985 and *The Middleman and Other Stories* in 1988, the latter the recipient of the National Book Critics Circle Award). Her enthusiasm has not blinded her to political backlash against America's most recent newcomers; in 1997 she warned in *Mother Jones* magazine against a spreading "cultural crisis" wherein "questions such as who is an American and what is American culture are being posed with belligerence, and being answered with violence." Because she sees such polarization as having "tragic" consequences not only for its victims but also for the unique "founding idea of 'America'" itself, which rejected "easy homogeneity" for a "new version of utopia," she urges instead, "We must think of American culture and nationhood as a constantly re-forming, transmogrifying 'we' that works in the direction of both the newcomer and the culture receiving her."

ANALYSIS

Bharati Mukherjee has herself become one of the literary voices whose skillful depictions of the contemporary non-European immigrant experience in the United States she credits with "subverting the very notion of what the American novel is and of what American culture is." In Canada she kept her "Indianness" smugly intact despite—or because of—a painful awareness of her displacement in the West. She consciously regarded other immigrants, as she notes in the introduction to *Darkness*, as "lost souls, put upon and pathetic," in contrast to the more ironically sophisticated postcolonials with whom she identified: people "who knew all too well who and what they were, and what foul fate had befallen them," and who therefore escaped the emotional turmoil of divided loyalties or assimilationist incongruities. Once in the United States she found herself drawn toward those same immigrant "outcasts" she once pitied—

and not just the ones from the subcontinent. In Mukherjee's two critically acclaimed short-story collections she sets out to "present a full picture, a complicated picture of America," one in which evil as well as good operates and where "we, the new pioneers, who are still thinking of America as a frontier country . . . are improvising morality as we go along." While she unblinkingly paints the bigotries that bedevil her protagonists, she resists casting them as victims

> because they don't think of themselves as victims. On the contrary, they think of themselves as conquerors. We have come not to passively accommodate ourselves to someone else's dream of what we should be. We've come to America, in a way, to take over. To help build a new culture . . . with the same guts and energy and feistiness that the original American Pilgrims had.

DARKNESS

Mukherjee's first collection of short fiction is something of a transitional work in documenting the shift in sensibility that occurred when she left Canada for the United States. Three of its twelve stories reveal a lingering bitterness about Canadian prejudice toward its Indian citizens and concern themselves with the problems that prejudice generates in the lives of individuals still wrestling with the question of whether they believe themselves to be in voluntary exile or hopeful self-transformation. The stories set in the United States, by way of contrast, regard the immigrant experience more dynamically and offer "a set of fluid identities to be celebrated" as a result of Mukherjee's having personally "joined imaginative forces with an anonymous, driven underclass of semi-assimilated Indians with sentimental attachments to a distant homeland but no real desire for permanent return." In this new context her own "Indianness" functions less "as a fragile identity to be preserved against obliteration" than as "a metaphor, a particular way of partially comprehending the world." The U.S.-based Indian protagonists of *Darkness* generate stories "of broken identities and discarded languages, and the will to bond oneself to a new community, against the ever-present fear of failure or betrayal."

In an interview published in *The Canadian Fiction Magazine*, Mukherjee stated, "My stories center on a new breed and generation of North American pioneers." The "new pioneers" inhabiting her fictional world include a wide variety of immigrant characters—most of them India-born and others, increasingly, from Third World countries—who pull up their traditional roots and arrive in the New World with dreams of wealth, success, and freedom. Her first collection of short stories, *Darkness*, focuses on immigrant Indians in North America and deals primarily with the problems of expatriation, immigration, and cross-cultural assimilation. Of the twelve stories in this collection, three reflect on the Canadian situation and the rest are set in the United States. Mukherjee calls the Canadian stories "uneasy stories about expatriation," as they stem from the author's personal encounters with racial prejudice in Canada.

Among the Canadian pieces, a notably painful and uneasy story about expatriation and racial prejudice, "The World According to Hsu," explores the diasporic consciousness of Ratna Clayton, an Indian woman married to a Canadian professor of psychology at McGill University, Montreal. Her husband, Graeme Clayton, has been offered the chair at the University of Toronto. Ratna dreads the thought of moving to Toronto: "In Toronto, she was not Canadian, not even Indian. She was something called, after the imported idiom of London, a Paki. And for Pakis, Toronto was hell." Hoping that a vacation would be the ideal setting to persuade his wife to move, Graeme arranges a trip to a beautiful African island. Upon their arrival, they find themselves caught in the midst of a revolution and constrained by a night curfew. The threat of violence unleashes memories of Toronto in Ratna's mind:

> A week before their flight, a Bengali woman was beaten and nearly blinded on the street. And the week before that an eight-year-old Punjabi boy was struck by a car announcing on its bumper: KEEP CANADA GREEN. PAINT A PAKI.

At the dinner table, when her husband reads her an article by Kenneth J. Hsu about the geological collision of the continents, Ratna wonders why she had to move to Toronto to experience a different kind of collision—racial and cultural. Finally, she brings herself to accept her situation when she realizes that "no matter where she lived, she would never feel at home again."

Another story, "Tamurlane," depicts the lives of Indian émigrés at the opposite end of the class hierarchy from the one Ratna occupies. It dramatizes the precarious situation of illegal aliens who, lured by the dream of a better life, are smuggled into Canada, where they are forced to lead an anonymous, subhuman, underground existence, sleeping in shifts and living in constant fear of being raided by immigration authorities. "Was this what I fled Ludhiana for?" poignantly asks the narrator, an illegal Indian working as a waiter at a dingy Indian restaurant in Toronto. The title of the story (alluding to Tamerlane, a lame Mongol warrior) refers to the restaurant's chef Gupta, who had been maimed six years earlier when he was thrown on the subway tracks. During a raid on illegals at the restaurant, Gupta orders the Mounties to leave. When they refuse and threaten to use force against him, he picks up a cleaver and brings it down on the outstretched hand of one of the policemen. He then defiantly holds his Canadian passport in front of his face. "That way," the story ends, "he never saw the drawn gun, nor did he try to dodge the single bullet."

The immigrant experience dramatized in the American stories is less about the humiliations inflicted on the newcomer by New World intolerance than about the inner struggles of that newcomer in mediating between the pull of old cultural loyalties and the pressures to assimilate to the new context. Dr. Manny Patel, in "Nostalgia," is an Indian psychiatrist working at a state hospital in Queens, New York. His American Dream has come true; he lives in an expensive home, drives a red Porsche sports car, is married to an American nurse, and sends his son to school at Andover. Counting his manifold acquisitions and blessings, he regards himself as "not an expatriate but a patriot." Yet he knows that, despite becoming a U.S. citizen, he will forever continue to hover between the Old World and the New. Being the only child of his parents, he feels it is his duty to return to India and look after them in their old age. Caught in a mood of remorse and longing, he drives one day into Manhattan, is smitten by the beauty of an Indian saleswoman, Padma, and invites her on a date, which she readily accepts. They go to an Indian restaurant for dinner and then to bed at an expensive hotel. The whole experience makes him so nostalgic that he wishes "he had married an Indian woman" and "had any life but the one he had chosen." At the end of their tryst, Padma's uncle enters the hotel room with a passkey and accuses Dr. Manny of the rape of his minor niece. Shocked and humiliated, Dr. Manny discovers that "the goddess of his dreams" was nothing more than a common prostitute in collusion with her uncle-pimp to deceive him for profit. The uncle extorts not only seven hundred dollars but also a physician's note on hospital stationery to secure immigration for a nephew. Afterward Dr. Manny defecates into the bathroom sink, squatting as he had done in his father's home, and writes "WHORE" on the bathroom mirror and floor with his excrement, now become "an artist's medium." Just before dawn he drives home, doubly chastened by having succumbed so foolishly to the siren's song of a culture to which he no longer truly belongs and whose gilded memories he now sees for what they are. As he approaches his home he finds the porch light still on, "glow[ing] pale in the brightening light of morning," and he decides to take his wife on a second honeymoon to the Caribbean, in effect repledging his troth to the tangible reality of America itself.

The conflict between Old World and New World takes a different form in "A Father." Mr. Bhowmick, a traditional Bengali, works as a metallurgist with General Motors and lives in Detroit with his American-ized wife and a twenty-six-year-old engineer daughter. He worships the goddess Kali in his home shrine, believes in the sanctity of Hindu superstitions, and lives in constant awe of the unseen powers he believes govern his destiny. Every day he finds himself making frequent compromises between his beliefs and the American pragmatism that surrounds him. When he discovers, to his horror, that his unmarried daughter is pregnant, his first reaction is that she should get an abortion to save the family honor. He blames his wife for this unhappy situation because coming to the United States was her idea. Then he tries to be reasonable. He pities the double life between conflicting values that his daughter must live; he hopes that maybe she has already married secretly; he prays that his hypothetical son-in-law turns out to be a white American. He even secretly enjoys the thought of having a grandson (for he is sure, in this rosier scenario, that the child must be a male).

Thus he reconciles himself to this new situation without resorting to the draconian measures a father in India would be expected to take, only to be confronted with an even more contemporary twist: His daughter reveals that she was impregnated by artificial insemination and with all the fury of Kali herself bluntly counters her parents' revulsion at the "animality" of such calculated procreative behavior with assurances that she has secured a sperm donor who meets all the standard bourgeois criteria for a good mate, just as they would have done in arranging a "good" marriage for her were they still in India: "You should be happy—that's what marriage is all about, isn't it? Matching bloodlines, matching horoscopes, matching castes, matching, matching, matching." Her caustic deflation of the traditions he still venerates defeats his effort to rise to the challenges of modernity, and he strikes out at her, hitting her swelling belly with the rolling pin he has just taken away from his wife. The story ends with Mrs. Bhowmick forced into an unthinkable violation of family honor: She calls the police, thus relying on outsiders to intervene publicly in the self-destruction of her family. In the ways it pulls the reader's sympathies back and forth inconclusively among its characters, "A Father" simulates the actual see-sawing of loyalties characteristic of the multigenerational acculturation process itself.

THE MIDDLEMAN AND OTHER STORIES

While *Darkness* focuses primarily on the experience of immigrants from the Indian subcontinent, Mukherjee's second collection, *The Middleman and Other Stories*, is broader in range and scope, as it explores the American experience of immigrants from across the developing world, including India, Afghanistan, Iraq, the Philippines, Sri Lanka, Trinidad, Uganda, and Vietnam. Moreover, four of the eleven stories in this volume have white American protagonists who offer another perspective on the contemporary immigrant situation. (It is worth noting, however, that the concluding piece, "The Management of Grief," once more returns to Mukherjee's deep animus toward the special form of bigotry suffered by Asians in Canada; it renders fictively the same subject with which she and Blaise have dealt in *The Sorrow and the Terror*.)

Virtually all of the stories examine the compromises, losses, and adjustments involved in the process of acculturating newcomers to American life and remaking American culture to reflect their presence: In fact, the volume virtually hums with the hustle of modern American cultural diversity played out across an equally various set of U.S. locations ranging from Atlanta to Detroit to Miami to Iowa. Most of the "new pioneers" in this collection are, in a metaphoric sense, middlemen and women caught between two worlds and cultures (and sometimes more), as even a brief sampling of the cast of characters suggests: an Amerasian child reunited with her veteran father; a Trinidadian "mother's helper"; a fully assimilated third-generation Italian American and her Afghan lover; an Iraqi Jew being chased by police in Central America; a Filipino makeup girl. Such international pedigrees bespeak the widespread political breakdowns that on a shrinking planet increasingly link people who once inhabited completely different worlds. She consistently uses the cross-cultural romance as locus for the societal frictions and emotional barriers that exemplify and exacerbate the problems of communication across culturally constructed differences. The faith of the newest aspirants to the American Dream is frequently contrasted with the decadent malaise of "ugly Americans," who no longer have to travel abroad to betray or defile peoples of other lands. The vigorous immediacy of the American vernacular (to which Mukherjee confesses a delighted addiction) penetrates the speech of these characters, many of whom speak directly to the reader in the first person, and conveys the volatile excitement of the dreams ignited in them by what Mukherjee calls "the idea of America."

The volume's title story is narrated by Alfred Judah from Baghdad, an individual regularly mistakenly for an Arab or an Indian. When not on the job, he lives in Flushing, Queens, and he was once married to an American, but he nonetheless feels like an eternal outsider, for "there are aspects of American life I came too late for and will never understand." As such he remains on the margins by working for an illicit border-jumper, gun smuggler Clovis T. Ransome. In this story Judah's job is as middleman delivering contraband weapons, when the armed uprising in the Central American country where they had been operating in callous indifference to the politics of their customers violently ends their exploitative enterprise and leaves Judah (through the casual intervention of Ransome's bloodthirsty mistress and his own recent lover Maria) to negotiate his way back to "civilization" by drawing yet again upon his basic repertoire of survival in the New World: "There must be something worth trading in the troubles I've seen."

Similarly, in "Danny's Girls," a young Ugandan boy living in Flushing works as a middleman for a hustler, Danny Sahib (originally "Dinesh," a Hindu from northern India), whom the boy calls "a merchant of opportunity." Danny started out selling tickets for Indian concerts at Madison Square Garden, then for fixed beauty contests, and eventually went into the business of arranging green cards through proxy marriages for Indians aspiring to become permanent U.S. residents. The latter launched a business of mail-order brides, with Danny in partnership with the African boy's aunt, Lini, in selling Indian and other Asian girls to American men eager for reputedly "compliant" wives. The young narrator has always looked up to Danny and has wanted, like his hero, to attain financial independence in the big world of the United States. When he falls in love with a Nepali girl for whom Danny had arranged a green card, however, he determines to liberate both of them from Danny's clutches, accepting the challenge of becoming his own man by resisting Danny's commodifying ethic—surely American opportunity should mean more.

"Jasmine" is the story of an ambitious Trinidadian girl of that name, who, through a middleman, illegally enters Detroit over the Canadian border at

Windsor. She finds a job cleaning and keeping the books at the Plantations Motel, a business run by the Daboo family, Trinidadian Indians also trying to remake their destinies in Michigan. In picaresque fashion Jasmine later goes to Ann Arbor and works as a live-in domestic with an easygoing American family: Bill Moffitt, a biology instructor, Lara Hatch-Moffitt, a performance artist, and their little girl, Muffin. When Lara goes on the road with her performing group, Jasmine is happily seduced by her boss, and as they make love on the Turkish carpet, she thinks of herself as literally reborn, "a bright, pretty girl with no visa, no papers, and no birth certificate. No nothing other than what she wanted to invent and tell. She was a girl rushing wildly into the future." The story in many ways presages the improvisational Indian heroine of Mukherjee's full-length novel *Jasmine*, published in 1989.

Not all of *The Middleman and Other Stories* deals with characters struggling to move from the margins into the mainstream of American opportunity: "A Wife's Story" and "The Tenant" focus on well-educated Indian women. In the first, Mrs. Panna Bhatt, married to the vice president of a textile mill in India, has come to New York on a two-year scholarship to get a Ph.D. in special education. Haunted by memories of the oppressive gender roles imposed on her mother and grandmother, she believes that she is making something new of her life; her choice of special education as a field of study provocatively mirrors the kind of intervention in her own constricted development that she is undertaking with her radical experiment abroad. She even develops a friendship with a married Hungarian man with whom she attends the theater. When an actor makes obscene jokes about Patel women, however, she feels insulted:

> It's the tyranny of the American dream that scares me. First, you don't exist. Then you are invisible. Then you are funny. Then you are disgusting. Insult, my American friends will tell me, is a kind of acceptance. No instant dignity here.

Yet when her husband comes for a short visit, as a reminder of the more decorous world she misses, she must feign enthusiasm for him. She tries to make up

to him for her years away, pretending that nothing has changed, but finally she refuses to return to India with him. When forced to choose between the vulgar freedoms of the United States and the repressive if "safe" institutions of her homeland, she realizes she has already crossed over to another country psychologically.

"The Tenant" goes to the other extreme by showing how an attractive, middle-class, young Bengali woman becomes vulnerable when she breaks with her traditional ways and tries to become part of mainstream America. Maya Sanyal from Calcutta came to the United States ten years earlier, at age nineteen. In smooth succession she received a Ph.D., married an American, became a naturalized citizen, got divorced, and now teaches comparative literature in Cedar Falls, Iowa. During that time she has indiscriminately slept with all kinds of men, except Indians, in a seemingly ambivalent repudiation of the constrictive gender mores of her homeland. Now, afraid that her bachelor landlord might make sexual advances toward her, she calls the other Bengali professor on campus, Dr. Chatterji, and secures an invitation to tea. The traditional atmosphere of his life prompts a newly awakened longing for her homeland, even as his pathetic attempt at seduction leaves her embarrassed. Tired of the fact that her unattached status makes her vulnerable to the lust of every passing male and newly nostalgic for her homeland traditions, she responds to an *India Abroad* matrimonial advertisement from a countryman seeking "the new emancipated Indo-American woman" with "a zest for life," "at ease in USA [sic]," but still holding on to values "rooted in Indian tradition." To her surprise, as she meets Ashoke Mehta at the Chicago airport, she suddenly feels as if a "Hindu god" is descending to woo her—a handsome Indian man who has indeed merged his two cultures in ways that seem to make them destined for each other. Yet witnessing his seamless acculturation also erodes her own self-confidence:

> She feels ugly and unworthy. Her adult life no longer seems miraculously rebellious; it is grim, it is perverse. She has accomplished nothing. She has changed

her citizenship but she hasn't broken through into the light, the vigor, the hustle of the New World. She is stuck in dead space.

More to the point is their mutual recognition that each carries a complicated romantic history to this moment—a history that makes each wary of the other and precludes Ashoke's contacting her again for several months. During that time she resumes her life in Cedar Falls and, when her landlord abruptly marries, moves to a new room rented to her by an armless man named Fred, whose lover she soon becomes, "two wounded people" who "settle into companionship." She also recognizes uncomfortably that this liaison speaks to some sense of her own deficiency as an rootless émigré in flight from her own past: "She knows she is strange, and lonely, but being Indian is not the same, she would have thought, as being a freak." When at last Ashoke calls and obliquely concedes the entanglements that had kept him from committing to her, she knows she will accept his invitation to join him out East—each has made peace with the contradictory emotions about their shared legacy they arouse in each other.

The Middleman and Other Stories, like *Darkness* before it, contains many melodramatic situations and a pronounced streak of violence. Mukherjee does not always provide sufficient context for the behaviors and attitudes of her characters. Nevertheless, she imparts a potent voice to these "new pioneers" and sheds light on the dynamic world of America's newest wave of self-inventors—people often invisible to those in the mainstream. Many of them suffer from racism and prejudice; others seem welcome only in the shady underworlds of sex, crime, and drugs; and some merely scramble for a living in their struggle for survival. To adapt to their new milieu, even professional men and women have to make compromises and trade-offs between their old belief systems and the New World ethos. In the process, many suffer cultural disorientation and alienation and undergo traumatic changes—psychological, cultural, linguistic. Yet Mukherjee appears to have no doubt that such a break is desirable. As she has told journalist Bill Moyers,

America is a total and wondrous invention. Letting go of the old culture, allowing the roots to wither is natural; change is natural. But the unnatural thing is to hang on, to retain the old world . . . I think if you've made the decision to come to America, to be an American, you must be prepared to really, emotionally, become American and put down roots. . . . In doing that, we very painfully, sometimes violently, murder our old selves. . . . I want to think that it's a freeing process. In spite of the pain, in spite of the violence, in spite of the bruising of the old self, to have that freedom to make mistakes, to choose a whole new history for oneself, is exciting.

Admittedly, the new selves that emerge from her stories are not always models of virtue, but "pioneering does not necessarily equate with virtue. . . . I like to think my characters have that vigor for possessing the land," with all the mother wit, ruthlessness, and tenacity of their predecessors. Yes, she admits,

the immigrant's soul is always at risk. . . . I have to make up the rules as I go along. No one has really experienced what the nonwhite, non-European immigrants are going through in the States. We can't count on the wisdom and experience of the past of the old country; and we can't quite fit into the traditional Eurocentric experiences of Americans.

In telling their stories, then, she regards herself as "writing a fable for the times. I'm trying to create a mythology that we can live by as we negotiate our daily lives."

OTHER MAJOR WORKS

LONG FICTION: *The Tiger's Daughter*, 1972; *Wife*, 1975; *Jasmine*, 1989; *The Holder of the World*, 1993; *Leave It to Me*, 1997.

NONFICTION: *Kautilya's Concept of Diplomacy*, 1976; *Days and Nights in Calcutta*, 1977 (with Clark Blaise); *The Sorrow and the Terror: The Haunting Legacy of the Air India Tragedy*, 1987 (with Blaise); *Political Culture and Leadership in India: A Study of West Bengal*, 1991; *Regionalism in Indian Perspective*, 1992.

BIBLIOGRAPHY

Alam, Fakrul. *Bharati Mukherjee*. New York: Twayne,

1996. Looks at India, women, and East Indian Americans in literature. Includes a bibliography and index.

Ascher, Carol. "After the Raj." Review of *The Middleman and Other Stories*, by Bharati Mukherjee. *Women's Review of Books* 6, no. 12 (1989): 17, 19. Using illustrative detail from six of the eleven short stories in this collection, Ascher shows how in dealing with the immigrant experience "the strategy of short stories has served [Mukherjee] well."

Bowen, Deborah. "Spaces of Translation: Bharati Mukherjee's 'The Management of Grief.'" *Ariel* 28 (July, 1997): 47-60. Argues that in the story, the assumption of moral universalism is a crucial precursor to the problems of negotiating social knowledge. Mukherjee addresses questions of cultural particularization by showing how inadequately translatable are institutionalized expressions of concern.

Drake, Jennifer. "Looting American Culture: Bharati Mukherjee's Immigrant Narratives." *Contemporary Literature* 40 (Spring, 1999): 60-84. Argues that assimilation is portrayed as cultural looting, cultural exchange, or a willful and sometimes costly negotiation in her stories; notes that Mukherjee rejects the nostalgia of hyphenated "Americans" and their acceptable stories and portrays instead settlers, Americans who want to be American—not sojourners, tourists, guest workers, or foreigners.

Ispahani, Mahnaz. "A Passage from India." Review of *Darkness*, by Bharati Mukherjee. *The New Republic* 14 (April, 1986): 36-39. Ispahani believes that the short stories in this collection "treat the classical theme of diaspora—of exile and emigration." She singles out five stories for analysis to demonstrate her point. The review includes a brief comment on Mukherjee's style.

Mukherjee, Bharati. "American Dreamer." *Mother Jones*, January/February, 1997. Depicted literally as wrapped in an American flag while standing in a cornfield, Mukherjee speaks to her passionate sense of herself as an American writer and citizen.

_____. "Immigrant Writing: Give Us Your Maximalists." *The New York Times Book Review*, August 28, 1988, 1, 28-29. An enthusiastic celebration of those American writers who eschew minimalism to paint the dynamic picture of an increasingly diverse populace and culture.

_____. "Interview." In *Speaking of the Short Story: Interviews with Contemporary Writers*, edited by Farhat Iftekharuddin, Mary Rohrberger, and Maurice Lee. Jackson: University Press of Mississippi, 1997. Mukherjee discusses the origins of her stories and the process by which they are composed. She criticizes Marxist and other social critics who reduce stories to sociology and anthropology.

_____. "An Interview with Bharati Mukherjee." Interview by Geoff Hancock. *The Canadian Fiction Magazine* 59 (1987): 30-44. In this important interview, Mukherjee discusses her family background, formative influences, and work. She provides illuminating comments on her fictional characters, themes, and voice.

_____. "Mother Teresa." *Time*, June 14, 1999, 88-90. Commentary on Calcutta's most famous citizen by another child of that city, whose impressions of Mother Teresa changed over time from those of bemusement to skepticism to profound admiration.

Nazareth, Peter. "Total Vision." *Canadian Literature: A Quarterly of Criticism and Review* 110 (1986): 184-191. Nazareth analyzes Mukherjee's first collection of short stories, *Darkness*, to show how she has distinguished herself by becoming "a writer of *the other America*, the America ignored by the so-called mainstream: the America that embraces all the peoples of the world both because America is involved with the whole world and because the whole world is in America."

Nelson, Emmanuel S., ed. *Bharati Mukherjee: Critical Perspectives*. New York: Garland, 1993. A critical study of Mukherjee's fiction. Includes a bibliography and an index.

Sant-Wade, Arvindra, and Karen Marguerite Radell. "Refashioning the Self: Immigrant Women in Bharati Mukherjee's New World." *Studies in Short*

Fiction 29 (Winter, 1992): 11-17. An analysis of "The Tenant," "Jasmine," and "A Wife's Story" as stories in which immigrant women refashion themselves and are reborn. In each story the women's sense of possibility clashes with a sense of loss, yet their exuberant determination attracts the reader to them and denies them the power of pity.

Scheer-Schäzler, Brigitte. "'The Soul at Risk': Identity and Morality in the Multicultural World of Bharati Mukherjee." In *Nationalism vs. Internationalism: (Inter)National Dimensions of Literature in English*, edited by Wolfgang Zach and Ken L. Goodwin. Tübingen: Stauffenburg, 1996. Discusses Mukherjee's approach to identity and morality, a common theme of immigration literature. Discusses the tensions between the monocultural self and its multiculturally transformed versions in her writing.

Sivaramkrishna, M. "Bharati Mukherjee." In *Indian English Novelists: An Anthology of Critical Essays*, edited by Madhusudan Prasad. New Delhi: Sterling, 1982. Sivaramkrishna offers a perceptive analysis of the theme of disintegration and displacement in Mukherjee's first two novels, *The Tiger's Daughter* and *Wife*. Her protagonists, he argues, "are victims of life which is visionless because it is voiceless."

Vignisson, Runar. "Bharati Mukherjee: An Interview." *Span* 3-4 (1993). An expansive discussion covering Mukherjee's childhood, her experiences in Canada and the United States, her evolution as a writer, her views on feminism, and some of the ideas informing her novel *Jasmine*.

Chaman L. Sahni, updated by
Barbara Kitt Seidman

ALICE MUNRO

Born: Wingham, Ontario, Canada; July 10, 1931

PRINCIPAL SHORT FICTION

Dance of the Happy Shades, 1968
Something I've Been Meaning to Tell You: Thirteen Stories, 1974
Who Do You Think You Are?, 1978 (U.S. edition, *The Beggar Maid: Stories of Flo and Rose*, 1979)
The Moons of Jupiter: Stories, 1982
The Progress of Love, 1986
Friend of My Youth: Stories, 1990
Open Secrets: Stories, 1994
Selected Stories, 1996
The Love of a Good Woman: Stories, 1998

OTHER LITERARY FORMS

The line between long and short fiction is sometimes blurred in Alice Munro's work. Although principally a writer of short fiction, she has also published a novel, *Lives of Girls and Women* (1971), which she prefers to view as a group of linked stories. On the other hand, some reviewers, including author John Gardner, have suggested that the stories in *The Beggar Maid* are so intricately related that the book could be viewed as a novel. Most critics, however, treat it as short fiction.

ACHIEVEMENTS

Alice Munro has gained recognition as a consummate writer, principally of short, psychological fiction. She received the Governor General's Award (Canada's highest literary award) for *Dance of the Happy Shades*, *The Beggar Maid*, and *The Progress of Love*. Her novel *Lives of Girls and Women* won the Canadian Booksellers Association Award in 1972, as did *Open Secrets* in 1995. In 1990 the Canada Council awarded her the Molson Prize for her contribution to Canada's cultural and intellectual life. In 1977 and 1994 she received the Canada-Australia Literary

Prize, and in 1995 *Open Secrets* won the W. H. Smith and Son Literary Award for the best book published in the United Kingdom. Munro received the National Book Critics Circle Award from the United States in 1999 for *The Love of a Good Woman.*

BIOGRAPHY

Alice Munro was born July 10, 1931, in Wingham, Ontario, Canada, where her father raised silver foxes. A scholarship covering the years 1949-1951 to the University of Western Ontario led to her bachelor's degree in 1952. Her marriage to bookstore owner James Munro produced three daughters. After a 1976 divorce, Munro married geographer Gerald Fremlin; they established homes in Clinton, Ontario, and Comox, British Columbia.

ANALYSIS

Alice Munro has been compared to Ernest Hemingway in the realism, economy, and lucidity of her style, to John Updike in her insights into the intricacies of social and sexual relationships, to Flannery O'Connor and Eudora Welty in her ability to create characters of eccentric individualism, and to Marcel Proust in the completeness and verisimilitude with which she evokes the past. She is an intuitive writer, who is less likely to be concerned with problems of form than with clarity and veracity. Some critics have faulted her for a tendency toward disorganization or diffusion—too many shifts in time and place within a single story, for example. On her strengths as a writer, however, critics generally agree: She has an unfailing particularity and naturalness of style, an ability to write vividly about ordinary life and its boredom without boring her readers, an ability to write about the past without being sentimental, a profound grasp of human emotion and psychology. Chief among her virtues is her great honesty: her refusal to oversimplify or falsify human beings, emotions, or experience. One of her characters states, "How to keep oneself from lying I see as the main problem everywhere." Her awareness of this problem is everywhere evident in her writing, certainly in the distinctive voices of her narrator-protagonists, who are scrupulously concerned with truth. Finally, her themes—

Alice Munro (©Jerry Bauer)

memory, love, transience, death—are significant. To explore such themes within the limitations of the short-story form with subtlety and depth is Munro's achievement.

"DANCE OF THE HAPPY SHADES"

One of Alice Munro's recurring themes is "the pain of human contact . . . the fascinating pain; the humiliating necessity." The phrase occurs in "The Stone in the Field" and refers to the narrator's maiden aunts, who cringe from all human contact, but the emotional pain that human contact inevitably brings is a subject in all of her stories. It is evident in the title story of her first collection, "Dance of the Happy Shades," in which an elderly, impoverished piano teacher, Miss Marsalles, has a "party" (her word for recital) for a dwindling number of her students and their mothers, an entertainment she can ill afford. The elaborate but nearly inedible refreshments, the ludicrous gifts, and the tedium of the recital pieces emphasize the incongruity between Miss Marsalles's serene pleasure in the festivities and the grim suffering of her unwilling but outwardly polite guests. Their anxieties are intensified by the mid-party arrival of Miss Marsalles's newest pupils, a group of mentally disabled children from a nearby institution. The other pupils and their mothers struggle to maintain well-bred composure, but inwardly they are repelled, particularly when one of the mentally disabled girls gives the only accomplished performance of a sprightly piece called "The Dance of the Happy Shades." The snobbish mothers believe that the idea of a mentally disabled girl learning to play the piano is not in good taste; it is "useless, out-of-place," in fact very much like Miss Marsalles herself. Clearly, this dismal affair will be Miss Marsalles's last party, yet the narrator is unable at the end to pity her, to say, "Poor Miss Marsalles." "It is the Dance of the Happy Shades that prevents us, it is the one communiqué from the other country where she lives." The unfortunate Miss Marsalles is happy; she has escaped the pain she would feel if she could know how others regard her, or care. She is living in another country, out of touch with reality; she has escaped into "the freedom of a great unemotional happiness."

"THE PEACE OF UTRECHT"

Few of Munro's characters are so fortunate. In "The Peace of Utrecht," for example, the inescapable emotional pain of human contact is the central problem. Helen, the narrator, makes a trip with her two children to Jubilee, the small town where she grew up, ostensibly to visit her sister Maddy, now living alone in their childhood home. The recent death of their mother is on their minds, but they cannot speak of it. Maddy, who stayed at home to look after their "Gothic Mother," has forbidden all such talk: "No exorcising here," she says. Yet exorcism is what Helen desperately needs as she struggles with the torment that she feels about her sister's "sacrifice," her mother's life, and her own previous self, which this return home so vividly and strangely evokes. Mother was a town "character," a misfit or oddity, even before the onset of her debilitating and disfiguring illness (she seems to have died of Parkinson's disease). For Helen, she was a constant source of anxiety and

shame, a threat to Helen's own precarious adolescent identity. (Readers who know Munro's novel *Lives of Girls and Women* will find a strong resemblance of Helen's mother to Del Jordan's bizarre mother. She also appears as recognizably the same character in the stories "The Ottawa Valley," "Connection," "The Stone in the Field," and perhaps "The Progress of Love.") Recalling the love and pity denied this ill but incorrigible woman, Helen experiences raging guilt, shame, and anger that she and her sister were forced into "parodies of love." Egocentric, petulant, this mother

> demanded our love in every way she knew, without shame or sense, as a child will. And how could we have loved her, I say desperately to myself, the resources of love we had were not enough, the demand on us was too great.

Finally, Helen and her sister withdrew even the pretense of love, withdrew all emotion:

> We took away from her our anger and impatience and disgust, took all emotion away from our dealings with her, as you might take away meat from a prisoner to weaken him, till he died.

Still, the stubborn old woman survived and might have lived longer except that Maddy, left alone with her mother and wanting her own life, put her in the hospital. After she tried to run away, restraint became necessary; she did not survive long after that.

Some critics believe that Munro's strongest works are those which draw on her own small-town origins in western Ontario, stories of Jubilee, Tuppertown, Hanratty, Dalgleish. Munro has confessed in an interview that "The Peace of Utrecht" is her most autobiographical story and thus was difficult to write. Perhaps its emotional power derives in part from its closeness to her own experience, but it exhibits those qualities for which her writing has been praised: the effortless clarity of style, the psychological penetration of character, the evocation of time and place, the unfailing eye and ear which convey an impression of absolute authenticity—these are the hallmarks of Munro's finest fiction, and they are evident even in her earliest stories. For example, in "The Peace of

Utrecht," Helen's visit to two memorable residents of Jubilee, her mother's sisters, Aunt Annie and Auntie Lou, demonstrates a deftness of characterization and a sureness of touch which are remarkable but typical of this writer at her best. Helen finds them

> spending the afternoon making rugs out of dyed rags. They are very old now. They sit in a hot little porch that is shaded by bamboo blinds; the rags and the half-finished rugs make an encouraging, domestic sort of disorder around them. They do not go out any more, but they get up early in the morning, wash and powder themselves, and put on their shapeless print dresses trimmed with rickrack and white braid.

Later, after tea, Aunt Annie tries to press on Helen a box of her mother's clothing (painstakingly cleaned and mended), seemingly oblivious to Helen's alarm and pain at the sight of these all-too-tangible reminders of her mother. To Aunt Annie, things are to be used up; clothes are to be worn. Yet she is not insensitive, nor is she a fool. Revealing to Helen (who did not know) the shameful facts about her mother's hospitalization against her will, her pitiful, frantic attempt to escape one snowy January night, the board that was subsequently nailed across the bed to immobilize her, and Maddy's indifference to it all, Aunt Annie begins "crying distractedly as old people do, with miserable scanty tears." Despite the tears, however, Aunt Annie is (as Helen is not), emotionally tough, "an old hand at grief and self-control." Just how tough she is is conveyed by Aunt Annie's final, quietly understated words: "'We thought it was hard,' she said finally. 'Lou and I thought it was hard.'"

Helen and Maddy, with less emotional resilience, try to come to terms with their own complex anguish through evasion, rationalization, and finally, admonishment—"don't be guilty"—but Munro is too honest to imply that they can be successful. In the final lines of the story, Helen urges her sister to forget the past, to take hold of her own life at last. Maddy's affirmation, "Yes I will," soon slips into an agonized question: "But why can't I, Helen? *Why can't I?*" In the "dim world of continuing disaster, of home," there is no peace of Utrecht, not for Munro's characters, perhaps not for Munro.

The preoccupation in Munro's fiction with family, usually as a "continuing disaster," is striking. Assorted eccentric aunts, uncles, and cousins appear and reappear; a somewhat miscreant brother appears in "Forgiveness in Families" and "Boys and Girls." Sometimes the family portraits are warmly sympathetic, as in the case of the grandmother in "Winter Wind" or especially the gentle father who calmly prepared for his death in "The Moons of Jupiter." Even the neurotic mother and father in "The Progress of Love" are treated sympathetically. There, the mother's fanatical hatred of her own father leads her to burn the desperately needed money she inherits from him at his death. Clearly, for Munro, family origins matter, sometimes as the source of humor and delightful revelation but more dependably as the source of endless mystery and pain. This is particularly true of "the problem, the only problem," as stated in "The Ottawa Valley": mother. At the story's conclusion, the narrator confesses that

> she is the one of course that I am trying to get; it is to reach her that this whole journey has been undertaken. With what purpose? To mark her off, to describe, to illumine, to celebrate, to *get rid*, of her; and it did not work, for she looms too close, just as she always did. . . . She has stuck to me as close as ever and refused to fall away, and I could go on, and on, applying what skills I have, using what tricks I know, and it would always be the same.

Some relationships, some kinds of "fascinating pain," can be recorded or analyzed but not exorcised. Clearly, these may become the inspiration for significant literature. In Munro's fiction, the view of the emotional entanglements called "family" is unflinchingly honest, unsentimental, but always humane, at times even humorous.

"BARDON BUS"

Another important dimension of Munro's short stories is sexual relationships, particularly in the "feelings that women have about men," as she stated in an interview. In "Bardon Bus," the narrator, a woman writer spending time in Australia, meets an anthropologist (known as "X") and begins a deliberately limited affair, asking only that it last out their short time in Australia. Later, when both have returned to Canada, she is miserable, tortured by memory and need: "I can't continue to move my body along the streets unless I exist in his mind and in his eyes." Finally, she realizes her obsession is a threat to her sanity and that she has a choice of whether to be crazy or not. She decides she does not have the stamina or the will for "prolonged craziness," and further that

> there is a limit to the amount of misery and disarray you will put up with, for love, just as there is a limit to the amount of mess you can stand around a house. You can't know the limit beforehand, but you will know when you've reached it. I believe this.

She begins to let go of the relationship and finds "a queer kind of pleasure" in doing this, not a "self-wounding or malicious pleasure," but

> pleasure in taking into account, all over again, everything that is contradictory and persistent and unaccommodating about life. . . . I think there's something in us wanting to be reassured about all that, right alongside—and at war with—whatever there is that wants permanent vistas and a lot of fine talk.

This seeming resolution, however, this salvation by knowing and understanding all, is subtly undercut by the conclusion of the story. The narrator's much younger friend, Kay, happens to mention her involvement with a fascinating new "friend," who turns out to be X. The story ends there but the pain (presumably) does not.

"TELL ME YES OR NO"

The female protagonist of "Tell Me Yes or No" is also sifting through the emotional rubble of an adulterous affair, which has ended, perhaps because of the death of her lover, or perhaps it has merely ended. In this story, it is difficult to distinguish reality from fantasy, and that may be the point. The other lives and other loves of her lover may be real, or they may be a fantasy (as defense mechanism) of the protagonist, but the central insight is the realization of how

> women build their castles on foundations hardly strong enough to support a night's shelter; how women deceive themselves and uselessly suffer, being exploit-

able because of the emptiness of their lives and some deep—but indefinable, and not final!—flaw in themselves.

For this woman, none of the remedies of her contemporaries works, not deep breathing, not macramé, and certainly not the esoteric advice of another desperate case: to live "every moment by itself," a concept she finds impossible to comprehend, let alone practice. The irony of her difficulty is evident, considering Munro's passionate concern throughout her fiction for "Connection" (the title of one of her stories). Here, it seems that there is some connection between past choice and present desolation:

> Love is not in the least unavoidable, there is a choice made. It is just that it is hard to know when the choice was made, or when, in spite of seeming frivolous, it became irreversible. There is no clear warning about that.

"LABOR DAY DINNER"

Munro's clear-eyed, self-aware narrators are never easy on themselves. They are constantly requiring themselves to face reality, to be aware of and responsible for the consequences of their own choices. In "Labor Day Dinner," the narrator, forty-three-year-old Roberta, has for the past year been living on a run-down farm with George, a younger man and former art teacher. His ambitious plan is to restore the farm and create a studio in which do to his sculpture. Roberta's daughters Angela, seventeen, and Eva, twelve, are spending the summer with her. The atmosphere is emotionally charged, prickly, and tense. George does not approve of the way Roberta indulges her daughters, allowing them to practice ballet instead of doing any work. George does not approve of Roberta, who seems to be indulging herself with tears and moody idleness. On the other hand, Roberta (weeping silently behind her sunglasses) does not approve of George's cooling ardor, his ungallant awareness of her age as evidenced by his request that she not wear a halter top to his cousin's Labor Day dinner because she has flabby armpits. So far, this sounds like the unpromising stuff of the afternoon soaps. (In fact, some of Munro's short stories first were published in popular magazines.) The difference is in what Munro is able to do with her material, the way in which she prevents her characters from deteriorating into stereotypes or her theme into cliché.

Roberta (who has reduced her waist only to discover that her face now looks haggard) reflects mournfully:

> How can you exercise the armpits? What is to be done? Now the payment is due, and what for? For vanity. . . . Just for having those pleasing surfaces once, and letting them speak for you; just for allowing an arrangement of hair and shoulders and breasts to have its effect. You don't stop in time, don't know what to do instead; you lay yourself open to humiliation. So thinks Roberta, with self-pity—what she knows to be self-pity—rising and sloshing around in her like bitter bile. She must get away, live alone, wear sleeves.

The self-awareness, the complex mingling of humor and pathos, the comic inadequacy of the solution, to wear sleeves (rivaling Prufrock's momentous decision to wear his trousers rolled), these lend to the character and to the story a dimension which is generally missing in popular fiction.

Roberta's daughters are close observers of as well as participants in this somewhat lugubrious drama. Angela, watching the change in her mother from self-reliant woman to near wreck and viewing George as a despot who hopes to enslave them all, records in her journal, "If this is love I want no part of it." On the other hand, sensitive Eva, watching her older sister develop the unpleasant traits of a typical adolescent, wants no part of that—"I don't want it to happen to me."

They all nearly get what they want, a way out of the emotional trauma in which they find themselves. On the way home from the Labor Day dinner, the pickup truck in which they are riding (the girls asleep in the back) comes within inches of being hit broadside by a car that came out of nowhere traveling between eighty and ninety miles an hour, no lights, its driver drunk. George did not touch the brake, nor did Roberta scream; they continue in stunned silence, pull into their yard and sit, unable to move.

> What they feel is not terror or thanksgiving—not yet. What they feel is strangeness. They feel as strange, as

flattened out and borne aloft, as unconnected with previous and future events as the ghost car was.

The story ends with Eva, waking and calling to them, "Are you guys dead?" and "Aren't we home?"

The ending shocks everything in the story into a new perspective, making what went before seem irrelevant, especially Roberta's and George's halfhearted playing at love. For Munro, it seems that the thought of the nearness, the omnipresence, and the inevitability of death is the only thing which can put lives and relationships into true perspective, but this (as Munro states at the conclusion of "The Spanish Lady") is a message which cannot be delivered, however true it may be.

THE LOVE OF A GOOD WOMAN

Munro continues at the top of her form in *The Love of a Good Woman*, where the pain of human contact, in its various guises, remains her central theme. In the title novella, Enid, a middle-aged, practical nurse finds herself attending the dying Mrs. Quinn. Lonely, kind Enid strives to do good, resisting her dislike of the sick woman. As an intruder in a household that cannot function without her, she is unaware of her attraction to the husband, a former classmate, until his wife implicates him in the death of a local optometrist. If the dying woman's story is true, Enid must decide whether to confront the husband or to believe in his innocence as she begins to lose hers. This complex, loosely structured work ends ambiguously, as do most of the stories, with Enid hesitating between motion and stillness.

"Cortes Island" is the most troubling story of this group, perhaps because of its ambiguity, perhaps because human lives have gone terribly wrong A newly-wed couple rents a basement apartment from the elderly Gorries. When the young woman needs a job, Mrs. Gorrie asks her to sit with her wheelchair-bound husband. A stroke has rendered Mr. Gorrie virtually speechless, but by grunts he can make himself understood. He wants her to read scrapbook articles from Cortes Island, where long ago a house burned to the ground, a child escaped, and a man died. What happened on Cortes Island, where Mr. Gorrie operated a boat? Was the death an accident, suicide, murder?

This story is so subtly written that events are not immediately clear. Typically, Munro offers only hints, although the young woman realizes that the Gorries once had an intense relationship. With harsh noises, the crippled Mr. Gorrie demands, "Did you ever think that people's lives could be like that and end up like this? Well, they can." This marriage is a wreck of love, a ruin.

As always, Munro exhibits masterful use of irony. In "Jakarta," two young wives argue over D. H. Lawrence's assertion that a woman's happiness lies in a man and that her consciousness must be submerged in his. Kath is a proper Canadian wife and mother, but Sonje, her pot-smoking, commune-dwelling friend, is an American. Over the years, conservative Kath breaks away from her stuffy marriage to become strong and self-reliant. Sonje, who has routinely accepted her husband's wish to switch sexual partners, remains faithful to him even after he disappears in Jakarta.

In other stories, a daughter seeks to ease a strained relationship with her abortionist father by revealing the birth of her child, but she is talking to a dead man. A young girl realizes that she is completely, utterly alone. In the best kind of horror story, one that will chill any parent's blood, a woman tries to entertain her grandchildren with a game that turns sinister as she glimpses the danger, as well as the pain, implicit in any human contact.

Munro has stated in an interview that her need and desire to write

> has something to do with the fight against death, the feeling that we lose everything every day, and writing is a way of convincing yourself perhaps that you're doing something about this.

Despite her characteristic concern for honesty and her determination to tell only the truth, it seems in this passage that she may be wrong about one thing: It seems clear that Alice Munro's writing is destined to last for a very long time.

OTHER MAJOR WORKS

LONG FICTION: *Lives of Girls and Women*, 1971.

BIBLIOGRAPHY

Blodgett, E. D. *Alice Munro.* Boston: Twayne, 1988. This volume provides a general introduction to Munro's fiction. Supplemented by a useful critical bibliography.

Canitz, A. E. Christa, and Roger Seamon. "The Rhetoric of Fictional Realism in the Stories of Alice Munro." *Canadian Literature*, no. 150 (Autumn, 1996): 67-80. Examines how Munro's stories portray and enact the dialectic between legend-making and demythologizing; discusses techniques that Munro uses to adapt the opposition between fiction and reality to the expectations and ethical beliefs of her audience.

Carrington, Ildikó de Papp. *Controlling the Uncontrollable: The Fiction of Alice Munro.* DeKalb: Northern Illinois University Press, 1989. A good critical study of Munro's fiction. Includes a bibliography.

_____. "Talking Dirty: Alice Munro's 'Open Secrets' and John Steinbeck's *Of Mice and Men.*" *Studies in Short Fiction* 31 (Fall, 1994): 495-606. Discusses Munro's foregrounding of language in three categories: spoken language, written language, and body language, primarily in "Open Secrets." Analyzes Munro's use of deferent kinds of language to interpret what has happened and to conceal secret, dirty meanings under innocuous surfaces. Traces the story's allusions to Steinbeck's Lennie in *Of Mice and Men* (1937).

Clark, Miriam Marty. "Allegories of Reading in Alice Munro's 'Carried Away.'" *Contemporary Literature* 37 (Spring, 1996): 49-61. Shows how the stories in Munro's *Friend of My Youth* and *Open Secrets* dismantle the foundations of realist narrative, figuring or disclosing the many texts in the one and so refiguring the linked practices of writing and reading; claims that "Carried Away" addresses allegorically the politics of the library and the ethics of reading.

Crouse, David. "Resisting Reduction: Closure in Richard Ford's 'Rock Springs' and Alice Munro's 'Friend of My Youth.'" *Canadian Literature*, no. 146 (Autumn, 1995): 51-64. Discusses how Ford and Munro deal with the problem of realistic closure and character growth in their short stories by manipulating time. Shows how they use various narrative devices to give more interpretive responsibility to the reader.

Goldman, Marlene. "Penning in the Bodies: The Construction of Gendered Subjects in Alice Munro's 'Boys and Girls.'" *Studies in Canadian Literature* 15, no. 1 (1990): 62-75. This essay presents a study of conflict between the adult voice and the child's idealistic perception of reality.

Heble, Ajay. *The Tumble of Reason: Alice Munro's Discourse of Absence*. Toronto: University of Toronto Press, 1994. Includes a bibliography and an index.

Hiscock, Andrew. "'Longing for a Human Climate': Alice Munro's *Friend of My Youth* and the Culture of Loss." *The Journal of Commonwealth Literature* 32 (1997): 17-34. Claims that in this collection of stories, Munro creates complex fictional worlds in which character, narrator, and reader are involved in the business of interpreting versions of loss, tentatively attempting to understand their function and status in a mysteriously arranged reality.

Martin, Walter. *Alice Munro: Paradox and Parallel*. Edmonton: University of Alberta Press, 1987. An analysis of Munro's use of narrative techniques and language. Complemented by an excellent bibliography of her writings.

Mayberry, Katherine J. "'Every Last Thing . . . Everlasting': Alice Munro and the Limits of Narrative." *Studies in Short Fiction* 29 (Fall, 1992): 531-541. Discusses how Munro's characters use narrative as a means of coming to terms with the past, how they manage their pain by telling. Argues that most of Munro's narrators come to realize the imperfections of narrative because of the incongruence between experience and the story's effort to render it.

Murphy, Georgeann. "The Art of Alice Munro: Memory, Identity, and the Aesthetics of Connection." In *Canadian Women: Writing Fiction*, edited by Mickey Pearlman. Jackson: University Press of Mississippi, 1993. Discusses a number of recurring characters, themes, and concerns in Munro's short stories, such as writing as an act of magical transformation, familial connection, death as a violent upheaval, and sexual connection inflicting psychic pain.

Noonan, Gerald. "The Structure of Style in Alice Munro's Fiction." In *Probable Fictions: Alice Munro's Narrative Acts*, edited by Louis MacKendrick. Downsview, Ont.: ECW Press, 1983. A study of Munro's stylistic evolution from *Dance of the Happy Shades* to *Who Do You Think You Are?*

Nunes, Mark. "Postmodern 'Piecing': Alice Munro's Contingent Ontologies." *Studies in Short Fiction* 34 (Winter, 1997): 11-26. A discussion of Munro's postmodernist focus on narrative strategies. Argues that quilting and piecing in the stories are metaphors for narrative. Instead of suggesting a disruptive postmodernism, quilting in women's writing functions as an icon for the recuperation of fragmented traditions into a healed whole.

Rasporich, Beverly. *Dance of the Sexes: Art and Gender in the Fiction of Alice Munro*. Edmonton: University of Alberta Press, 1990. A very interesting analysis focusing on male/female contrasts and relationships in Munro's fiction. Augmented by a critical bibliography.

Sheldrick Ross, Catherine. "'At Least Part Legend': The Fiction of Alice Munro." In *Probable Fictions: Alice Munro's Narrative Acts*, edited by Louis MacKendrick. Downsview, Ont.: ECW Press, 1983. A study of the way in which Munro's characters perceive legendary qualities in real life experiences.

Smythe, Karen E. *Figuring Grief: Gallant, Munro, and the Poetics of Elegy*. Montreal: McGill-Queen's University Press, 1992. A generic study of Munro's stories based on the premise that her fiction, with its emphasis on loss and the importance of story telling as a way of regaining knowledge of the past, enacts a poetics of elegy.

Karen A. Kildahl, updated by
Kenneth W. Meadwell and Joanne McCarthy

N

VLADIMIR NABOKOV

Born: St. Petersburg, Russia; April 23, 1899
Died: Montreux, Switzerland; July 2, 1977

OTHER LITERARY FORMS

Vladimir Nabokov's fifty-year career as a writer includes—besides his short stories—novels, poetry, drama, memoirs, translations, reviews, letters, critical essays, literary criticism, and the screenplay of his most famous novel, *Lolita* (1955). After his death, three volumes of lectures on literature that he had delivered to students at Wellesley, Stanford, and Cornell were scrupulously edited by Fredson Bowers and published as *Lectures on Literature: British, French, and German* (1980), *Lectures on Russian Literature* (1981), and *Lectures on Don Quixote* (1983).

ACHIEVEMENTS

Vladimir Nabokov occupies a unique niche in the annals of literature by having become a major author in both Russian and English. He wrote nine novels, about forty stories, and considerable poetry in Russian before migrating to the United States in 1940. Thereafter, he not only produced eight more novels and ten short stories in English but also translated into English the fiction that he had composed in his native language, sometimes with the collaboration of his son, Dmitri. Reversing his linguistic field, he translated his *Lolita* into Russian.

Nabokov's work has received considerable critical acclaim; a modern master, he has influenced such diverse literary figures as Anthony Burgess, John Barth, William Gass, Tom Stoppard, Philip Roth, John Updike, and Milan Kundera. Nabokov's fiction is never intentionally didactic or sociological; he detested moralistic, message-ridden writing. Instead, he delighted in playing self-consciously with the reader's credulity, regarding himself as a fantasist, a Prospero of artifice. He manipulates his characters as so many pieces on a chessboard, devising problems for absorbing, intricate games of which he and Jorge Luis Borges are the acknowledged modern masters. His precision of language, lexical command of multilingual allusions, and startling imagery have awed, delighted, but also sometimes irritated critics and readers. Few writers have practiced art for the sake of art with such talent and discipline. Nabokov's advice to students suggests the best approach to his own fiction:

> In reading, one should notice and fondle details. . . . We must see things and hear things, we must visualize the rooms, the clothes, the manners of an author's people . . . above all, a great writer is always a great enchanter, and it is here that we come to the really exciting part when we try to grasp the individual magic of his genius and to study the style, the imagery, the pattern of his novels or poems.

BIOGRAPHY

Vladimir Vladimirovich Nabokov's life divides neatly into four phases, each lasting approximately twenty years. He was born on Shakespeare's birthday in 1899 to an aristocratic and wealthy family residing

Vladimir Nabokov (Library of Congress)

in St. Petersburg. His grandfather was State Minister of Justice for two czars; his father, Vladimir Dmitrievich, a prominent liberal politician, married a woman from an extremely wealthy family. Vladimir Vladimirovich, the first of two sons, was reared with much parental love and care, eloquently evoked in his lyrical memoir, *Conclusive Evidence: A Memoir* (1951), later expanded and retitled *Speak, Memory: An Autobiography Revisited* (1966).

In 1919, the October Revolution forced the Nabokovs to flee Russia. Vladimir, who had learned both French and English from governesses during his childhood, enrolled in the University of Cambridge, took a degree in foreign languages in 1923, and published two volumes of poetry the same year. Meanwhile, his father and the other family members settled in Berlin. There, Vladimir Dmitrievich was assassinated in 1922 by two right-wing extremist Russian expatriates who had intended their bullets for another victim. Vladimir took up residence in Berlin in 1923, and in 1925 he married a Jewish émigrée, Véra Slonim, with whom he maintained a harmonious union. Between 1924 and 1929, he published, in Russian-language exile newspapers and periodicals,

twenty-two short stories. Many were collected in a 1930 book *Vozvrashchenie Chorba* (the return of Chorb), whose contents were later translated into English and distributed among several collections of Nabokov's short stories.

To avoid confusion with his well-known father, the younger Nabokov assumed the pen name "V. Sirin," after a mythological, multicolored bird featured in ancient Russian literature; he used this name until leaving Europe in 1940. The Nabokovs stayed in Berlin until 1937, even though Vladimir never learned German and usually drew his German fictive personages unfavorably. In his writings during these years, he dramatized the autobiographical themes of political exile from Russia, nostalgia, grief, anguish, and other variations of vagrant rootlessness. His most important novels during the 1920's and 1930's are commonly judged to be *Zashchita Luzhina* (1929; *The Defense*, 1964) and *Dar* (1937-1938, 1952; *The Gift*, 1963).

Nabokov's third life-stage began in 1940, when, after a three-year stay in Paris, he was glad to escape the Nazi menace by emigrating to the United States. After a one-term lectureship at Stanford University, he distributed his time for the next seven years between teaching at Wellesley College and working as a research fellow in entomology at Harvard's Museum of Comparative Zoology, pursuing his passion for lepidoptera. During these years, he began to establish himself as an American writer of note and, in 1945, became a naturalized citizen. He published two novels, *The Real Life of Sebastian Knight* (1941) and *Bend Sinister* (1947); a brilliant but eccentric study of the Russian writer who had most deeply influenced him, *Nikolai Gogol* (1944); a number of stories and poems; and sections of his first autobiography. In 1948, Cornell University lured him away from Wellesley by offering him a tenured professorship. He became a celebrated ornament of the Ithaca, New York, campus for ten years, specializing in a course called Masters of European Fiction, alternately charming and provoking his students with witty lectures and difficult examinations.

Nabokov wrote *Lolita* during his summer vacations in the early 1950's, but the book was refused publication by several American firms and was first issued in 1955 by Olympia Press, a Parisian English-language publisher that usually featured pornography. By 1958, the work had become celebrated as well as notorious, and Putnam's issued it in New York. It became the year's sensational best-seller, and Nabokov, taking an abrupt midyear leave from Cornell, thereupon moved to an elegant hotel on the banks of Switzerland's Lake Geneva for what were to prove nineteen more fecund years.

During this last arc of his career, Nabokov basked in the aura of worldwide recognition as an eminent writer yet continued to labor diligently: He revised his autobiography; resurrected his Russian long and short fiction in English translations; produced a four-volume translation of and commentary on Alexander Pushkin's novel in verse, *Yevgeny Onegin* (1833; Nabokov's English translation, *Eugene Onegin*, appeared in 1964); and wrote several new novels, including two—*Pale Fire* (1962) and *Ada or Ardor: A Family Chronicle* (1969)—worthy of consideration among the twentieth century's leading literary texts. Despite many losses and difficulties in his arduous life, Nabokov never yielded to self-pity, let alone despair. His career demonstrated not only artistic resourcefulness but also the personal virtues of resolution, resilience, and capacity for renewal.

ANALYSIS

Vladimir Nabokov's early stories are set in the post-czarist, post-World War I era, with Germany the usual location, and sensitive, exiled Russian men the usual protagonists. Many are nascent artists: wistful, sorrowful, solitary, sometimes despairingly disheartened. Many evoke a Proustian recollection of their Russian pasts as they try, and often as not fail, to understand an existence filled with irony, absurdity, and fortuity. These tales display Nabokov's abiding fascination with the interplay between reality and fantasy, between an outer world of tangs, scents, rain showers, sunsets, dawns, butterflies, flowers, forests, and urban asphalt, and an inner landscape of recondite, impenetrable, mysterious feelings. He loved to mix the disheveled externals of precisely described furnishings, trappings, and drab minutiae with memo-

ries, myths, fantasy, parody, grandeur, hilarity, masks, nostalgia, and, above all, the magic of artistic illusion. He celebrates the unpredictable permutations of the individual imagination over the massive constraints of the twentieth century's sad history. He is the supreme stylist, dedicated to forging his vision in the most dazzling verbal smithy since James Joyce's.

"THE RAZOR"

One of his first stories, "Britva" ("The Razor"), is a clever adaptation of motifs used in Gogol's "Nos" ("The Nose") and Pushkin's "Vystrel" ("The Shot"). A White Russian émigré, Colonel Ivanov, now a barber in Berlin, recognizes a customer as the Red officer who had condemned him to death six years before. He toys with his victim, terrorizing him with caustic, cruel remarks, comparing his open razor to the sharp end of a sword, inverting the menace of their previous confrontation in Russia. Yet he shaves his former captor gently and carefully and finally releases him unharmed. By doing so, Ivanov also releases himself from his burning desire for vengeance. Nabokov uses the multivalent symbol of the razor compactly and densely: The acerbic Ivanov both sharpens and encases his razorlike temperament.

"THE DOORBELL"

In "Zvonok" ("The Doorbell"), Nabokov delineates a tragic encounter between past and present in a complex tale fusing realism and symbolism. A son, Galatov, has been separated from his mother for seven years, during which time he has fought in the post-1917 Russian Civil War and wandered over Africa, Europe, and the Canary Islands. He learns that his mother's second husband has died and left her some real estate in Berlin. He searches for his mother there, meets her dentist, and through him obtains her address. Structurally, Galatov's visits to the dentist, a Dr. Weiner, anticipate his reunion with his mother: This Weiner is not Galatov's childhood dentist, yet he does happen to be his mother's. When Galatov finally meets his mother, he learns that she, too, is not the mother of his childhood: He meets, in the Berlin apartment, not the faded, dark-haired woman he left seven years earlier but an aged courtesan awaiting the arrival of a lover who is three years younger than her son. Galatov realizes that her fervent greeting of him had been intended for her paramour. When the doorbell announces the latter's arrival, Galatov learns, observing his mother's distraction and nervousness, that her new déclassé circumstances leave no room for him. He hurriedly departs, vaguely promising to see her again in a year or thereabouts. He knows now that not only has the mistress supplanted the mother but also his mother may never have cherished him as dearly as his previous need for her had deluded him into believing. The story's structural symmetry between memory and new reality is impressively achieved.

"A MATTER OF CHANCE"

"Sluchainost" ("A Matter of Chance") is one of Nabokov's most poignant tales. Its protagonist, Aleksey Luzhin—whose surname reappears five years later as that of the hero of *The Defense*—is a Russian exile who, like Galatov, has traveled to many places and worked many jobs. Currently, he is a waiter on a German train; having had no news of his wife, Elena, for five years, he is deeply depressed and has become addicted to cocaine. He plans his suicide for the night of August 1, the ninth anniversary of his wedding and the day of this story. On this particular trip, an old Russian princess, Maria Ukhtomski, is joined in her compartment by a young woman who arrived in Berlin from St. Petersburg the previous day, Elena Luzhina, who is seeking her lost husband. The story's rising action is full of suspense: Will the unsuspecting spouses find each other on the train? Luzhin sniffs cocaine in the toilet, on the day he has resolved to make his last. The princess has known the Luzhin family and recalls its former aristocratic opulence. Ironically, when the now plebeian Luzhin announces the first seating for dinner, his cocaine-rotted mind can only dimly note the princess; he cannot connect her to his elegant past.

The links between the two plots never interlock. Elena, disturbed by a rudely aggressive fellow passenger, decides to forgo the dinner in the dining car where she would probably have met her husband. She loses her prized golden wedding ring in the vestibule of the train's wagon; it is discovered by another waiter as Luzhin leaves the wagon and jumps to his

death before another train: "The locomotive came at him in one hungry bound." Missed chances abound—perhaps too many: Nabokov's uses of coincidence and his insistence of the malignity of haphazard events strain credulity.

"THE SCOUNDREL"

Perhaps Nabokov's most accomplished story of the 1920's is "Podlets" ("The Scoundrel," retitled by the author "An Affair of Honor" for its English publication). In his foreword to the English translation, Nabokov explains that "'An Affair of Honor' renders, in a drab expatriate setting, the degradation of a romantic theme whose decline had started with Chekhov's magnificent story 'The Duel' (1891)." Nabokov situates the duel within the traditional love triangle. The husband, an affluent banker named Anton Petrovich, returns home early from a business trip to find an arrogant acquaintance, Berg, nonchalantly getting dressed in his bedroom while his wife, Tanya, whom the reader never sees, is taking an interminable bath. Anton Petrovich challenges Berg to a duel. He pulls off his new glove and tries to throw it at Berg. Instead, it "slapped against the wall and dropped into the washstand pitcher." The ludicrous failure of Anton Petrovich's challenge sets the farcical, burlesque tone for the tale.

Anton Petrovich is a loving, tender, hardworking, amiable fellow whose major fault—abject cowardice—becomes his undoing. Chekhov would have treated him gently and compassionately; Nabokov handles him disdainfully and absurdly, emphasizing his fondness for his shiny fountain pen, expensive shoes and socks, and monocle which "would gleam like a foolish eye on his belly." A duel is arranged but does not actually take place. Anton Petrovich, who has never fired a weapon, shakes with increasing fear at the prospect of confronting a former White Army officer who boasts of having killed hundreds. Before entering the woods where the combat is to occur, he and his caricatured seconds stop at a tavern for a round of beers. Anton Petrovich thereupon runs into the bar's backyard, slides and slips ridiculously down a slope, stumbles his way back to a train, and thence rides back to Berlin. He fantasizes that his craven flight will have been overshadowed by Berg's even earlier change of mind about dueling and that his wife will leave Berg and return to him, filled with love, delighted to satisfy him with an enormous ham sandwich.

Abruptly, Anton Petrovich awakens from his fiction. "Such things don't happen in real life," he reflects. He realizes that his reputation, his career, and his marriage are now ruined. He orders a ham sandwich and, animalistically, "grabbed the sandwich with both hands, immediately soiled his fingers and chin with the hanging margin of fat, and grunting greedily, began to munch." Nabokov has here begun to command the art of grotesquerie, precisely observed, relentlessly rendered, contemptuously concluded. Anton Petrovich would serve as a model for Albinus Kretschmar, cuckolded lover and failed artist in the novel *Kamera obskura* (1932; *Camera Obscura*, 1936; revised as *Laughter in the Dark*, 1938). Kretschmar in turn is a prototype for *Lolita*'s Humbert Humbert.

"THE ADMIRALTY SPIRE"

An amusing as well as saddening early exercise in playing mirror games, which were to become more and more convoluted in Nabokov's fiction, is his 1933 story "Admiralteyskaya Igla" ("The Admiralty Spire"). Its narrator addresses a trashy Soviet female writer who uses the pseudonymous male name Sergey Solntsev. He asserts that her cheap romantic novel, *The Admiralty Spire*, is a vulgar version of his first love affair, sixteen years earlier, with a young woman named Katya, whom the writer has renamed Olga. He accuses her of "pretentious fabrication" and of having "encroached with astonishing insolence on another person's past!" The letter proceeds to lecture the writer on the correct, nostalgic use of the sentimental past, but in the process of recall, the writer admits his distaste for Katya's "mendacity, her presumption, her vacuity" and deplores her "myopic soul" and the "triviality of [her] opinions." He did, however, once love her. The narrator ends with the speculation that the mediocre novelist he is addressing is probably Katya herself, "who, out of silly coquetry, has concocted a worthless book." He hopes against the odds that his presumption is erroneous. The atmosphere of overlapping di-

mensions of reality established here was to be splendidly employed in such later novels as *Pale Fire* and *Ada or Ardor*.

"CLOUD, CASTLE, LAKE"

In "Oblako, ozero, bashnya" ("Cloud, Castle, Lake"), the protagonist, a timid, intellectual bachelor, Vasili Ivanovich, wins a pleasure trip at a charity ball for Russian expatriates in Berlin. He is the kind, meek, saintly soul familiar in Russian literature since Gogol's stories. He does not really want to take the journey but is intimidated by bureaucratic mazes into doing so. Obstacles thwart him persistently: Trying to settle down with a volume of Russian poetry, Vasili is instead bullied by a squadron of husky German fellow travelers, with monstrous knapsacks and hobnailed boots, into forced communal games that prove witless and humiliating. When the group pairs off, no one wants to romance him: He is designated "the loser and was forced to eat a cigarette butt." Unexpectedly, they come upon "a pure, blue lake," reflecting a large cloud and adjoining "an ancient, black castle." Overjoyed, Vasili wishes to surrender to the beautiful prospect and remain the rest of his life in the inn from which he can delight in this tableau. Unfortunately for Vasili, the group insists on dragging him back and beats him furiously during the return journey.

The tale is manifestly an allegory mourning the defeat of individuality and privacy in an ugly world determined to enforce total conformity. "Oh, but this is nothing less than an invitation to a beheading," protests Vasili as the group grimly denies him his room with a view. By no accident, Nabokov would soon write his novel, *Priglashenie na kazn'* (1938, 1935-1936; *Invitation to a Beheading*, 1959), whose main character, Cincinnatus C., is condemned to death for not fitting into a totalitarian culture. Nabokov may have occasionally presented himself as an arrogant, coldhearted puppeteer lacking any world-mending concerns, but he does clearly condemn all cultures of regimentation and authoritarianism.

"SPRING IN FIALTA"

"Vesna v Fialte" ("Spring in Fialta") was to become the title work of a collection of Nabokov's short stories; some critics regard it as the masterpiece among his stories, although others prefer "Signs and Symbols." The narrator of "Spring in Fialta," Victor, is a Russian émigré businessman who, over the course of fifteen years, has had sporadic meetings with a charmingly casual, pretty, vital woman named Nina. These encounters are sometimes sexual but never last more than a few hours and occur outside their continuing lives and separate marriages. "Again and again," Victor notes, "she hurriedly appeared in the margin of my life, without influencing in the least its basic text." So, at least, he believes. He has his respectably bourgeois world "in which I sat for my portrait, with my wife, my young daughters, the Doberman pinscher." Yet he finds himself also drawn to Nina's world of carefree sexuality mixed with "lies . . . futility . . . gibberish." This tension that Victor experiences is common in both life and literature, and Nabokov's characters are not immune. Although Nabokov appears to admire uxoriousness, as in the marriages of the Shades in *Pale Fire* or the Krugs in *Bend Sinister*, his protagonists are also mesmerized by *belles dames sans merci*—Margot (renamed Magda) in *Laughter in the Dark*, Lolita, Ada, and many more.

Nina is married to a gifted but repulsive Franco-Hungarian writer, Ferdinand; she also travels with the equally offensive but far less talented writer, Segur. Both men are artist figures: selfish, artificial, buoyant, heartless. Nina, while adaptable and "loyally sharing [Ferdinand's] tastes," is not really his muse: rather, she represents life's vulnerability, and her attempt to imitate Ferdinand's world proves fatal. When the car in which the three of them ride crashes into a truck, Ferdinand and Segur, "those invulnerable rogues, those salamanders of fate . . . had escaped with local and temporary injury . . . while Nina, in spite of her long-standing, faithful imitation of them, had turned out after all to be mortal." Life can only copy art, not replace it.

"SIGNS AND SYMBOLS"

In "Signs and Symbols," Nabokov wrote his most sorrowful story. An elderly, poor Russian émigré couple intend to pay a birthday visit to their son, institutionalized in a sanatorium, afflicted with "referential mania," in which "the patient imagines that every-

thing happening around him is a veiled reference to his personality and existence." On their way to the sanatorium, the machinery of existence seems to malfunction: The subway loses its electric current between stations; the bus is late and crammed with noisy schoolchildren; they are pelted by pouring rain as they walk the last stretch of the way. Finally, instead of being able to see their son, they are informed that he has again attempted suicide and should not be disturbed. The couple return home with the present that they cannot give him, wordless with worry and defeat, the woman close to tears. On their way they see "a tiny, half-dead unfledged bird . . . helplessly twitching in a puddle."

After a somber supper, the husband goes to bed, and the wife reviews a family photo album filled with the faces of mostly suffering or dead relatives. One cousin is a "famous chess player"—Nabokov's oblique reference to Luzhin of *The Defense*, who commits suicide. In his previous suicide attempt, the son had wanted "to tear a hole in his world and escape." In the story's last section, the time is past midnight, the husband is sleepless and in pain, and the couple decide to bring their boy home from the institution; each parent will need to spend part of each night with him. Then the phone rings: a wrong number. When it rings a second time, the wife carefully explains to the same caller how she must have misdialed. After a while the phone rings for the third time; the story ends. The signs and symbols in all likelihood suggest that the last call is from the sanatorium, to announce that the son has succeeded in escaping this world.

Artistically, this story is virtually flawless: intricately patterned, densely textured, remarkably intense in tone and feeling. For once, Nabokov the literary jeweler has cut more deeply than his usual surfaces; for once, he has entered the frightening woods of tragic, unmitigated grief; for once, he has forsaken gamesmanship and mirror-play, punning and parody and other gambits of verbal artifice to face the grimmest horrors of a sometimes hopeless world.

OTHER MAJOR WORKS

LONG FICTION: *Mashenka*, 1926 (*Mary*, 1970); *Korol', dama, valet*, 1928 (*King, Queen, Knave*, 1968); *Zashchita Luzhina*, 1929 (serial), 1930 (*The Defense*, 1964); *Podvig*, 1932 (*Glory*, 1971); *Kamera obskura*, 1932 (*Camera Obscura*, 1936; revised as *Laughter in the Dark*, 1938); *Otchayanie*, 1934 (serial), 1936 (*Despair*, 1937; revised 1966); *Dar*, 1937-1938 (serial), 1952 (*The Gift*, 1963); *Priglashenie na kazn'*, 1935-1936 (serial), 1938 (*Invitation to a Beheading*, 1959); *The Real Life of Sebastian Knight*, 1941; *Bend Sinister*, 1947; *Lolita*, 1955; *Pnin*, 1957; *Pale Fire*, 1962; *Ada or Ardor: A Family Chronicle*, 1969; *Transparent Things*, 1972; *Look at the Harlequins!*, 1974.

PLAYS: *Smert'*, pb. 1923; *Dedushka*, pb. 1923; *Polius*, pb. 1924; *Tragediya gospodina Morna*, pb. 1924; *Chelovek iz SSSR*, pb. 1927; *Sobytiye*, pr., pb. 1938; *Izobretenie Val'sa*, pb. 1938 (*The Waltz Invention*, 1966).

SCREENPLAY: *Lolita*, 1962.

POETRY: *Stikhi*, 1916; *Dva Puti*, 1918; *Gorny put*, 1923; *Grozd'*, 1923; *Stikhotvorenia, 1929-1951*, 1952; *Poems*, 1959; *Poems and Problems*, 1970.

NONFICTION: *Nikolai Gogol*, 1944; *Conclusive Evidence: A Memoir*, 1951; *Drugie berega*, 1954; *Speak, Memory: An Autobiography Revisited*, 1966 (revision of *Conclusive Evidence* and *Drugie berega*); *Strong Opinions*, 1973; *The Nabokov-Wilson Letters, 1940-1971*, 1979; *Lectures on Literature: British, French, and German*, 1980; *Lectures on Russian Literature*, 1981; *Lectures on Don Quixote*, 1983; *Vladimir Nabokov: Selected Letters, 1940-1977*, 1989.

TRANSLATIONS: *Anya v strane chudes*, 1923 (of Lewis Carroll's novel *Alice's Adventures in Wonderland*); *Three Russian Poets: Translations of Pushkin, Lermontov, and Tiutchev*, 1944 (with Dmitri Nabokov); *A Hero of Our Time*, 1958 (of Mikhail Lermontov's novel, with Dmitri Nabokov); *The Song of Igor's Campaign*, 1960 (of the twelfth century epic *Slovo o polki Igoreve*); *Eugene Onegin*, 1964 (of Alexander Pushkin's verse novel).

BIBLIOGRAPHY

Alexandrov, Vladimir E. *Nabokov's Otherworld*. Princeton, N.J.: Princeton University Press, 1991. Alexandrov argues that "The central fact of both Nabokov's life and his art was something that could be described as an intuition about a transcendent realm of being." Showing how an awareness of this "otherworld" informs Nabokov's works, Alexandrov focuses on *Speak, Memory: An Autobiography Revisited* and on six of Nabokov's novels, but his study illumines Nabokov's short fiction as well, correcting the widely accepted view of Nabokov as an aloof gamesman preoccupied with verbal artifice for its own sake. Includes notes, a secondary bibliography, and an index.

Boyd, Brian. *Vladimir Nabokov: The Russian Years*. Princeton, N.J.: Princeton University Press, 1990.

_____. *Vladimir Nabokov: The American Years*. Princeton, N.J.: Princeton University Press, 1991. In the course of the two volumes of this critical biography, Boyd discusses virtually all Nabokov's stories. Boyd generally provides a brief summary of each story, relating it to Nabokov's development as an artist and noting recurring themes. Each volume includes illustrations, extensive notes, and an exceptionally thorough index.

Field, Andrew. *Nabokov: His Life in Art*. Boston: Little, Brown, 1967. Field singles out several of Nabokov's stories for analysis. Of particular interest is his discussion of "The Potato Elf," which he describes as "a classic instance of a brilliantly executed short story whose compressed action is an essential function of its success." In Field's judgment, "The Potato Elf" is "Nabokov's greatest short story."

Nicol, Charles. "'Ghastly Rich Glass': A Double Essay on 'Spring in Fialta.'" *Russian Literature Triquarterly*, no. 24 (1991): 173-184. One of two pieces devoted to Nabokov's short fiction in this special Nabokov issue, Nicol's article on "Spring in Fialta" has two concerns: "First, a consideration of the plot structure . . . and second, a further perspective on the vexed question of whether this story has any autobiographical relevance or personal reference to its author."

Nicol, Charles, and Gennady Barabtarlo. *A Small Alpine Form: Studies in Nabokov's Short Fiction.* New York: Garland, 1993. Contains sixteen essays on Nabokov's stories from a variety of critical points of view. The essays discuss themes, sources, parallels, and symbols in such stories as "Spring in Fialta," "Signs and Symbols," and several others.

Parker, Stephen Jan. *Understanding Vladimir Nabokov.* Columbia: University of South Carolina Press, 1987. An introductory guide to Nabokov for students and nonacademic readers. After an introductory chapter on the self-reflexive aspects of Nabokov's narrative technique, the book focuses on individual analyses of five Russian novels and four American novels. The section on the short stories provides brief summary analyses of "Spring in Fialta," "Cloud, Castle, Lake," "Signs and Symbols," and "The Vane Sisters."

_____. "Vladimir Nabokov and the Short Story." *Russian Literature Triquarterly*, no. 24 (1991): 63-72. Parker worked with Nabokov and Véra Nabokov in the early 1970's to establish a precise chronology of Nabokov's short stories in Russian and to discuss possible titles for the English translations. Listed here are the results of their conversation and correspondence. Also included is a previously unpublished interview (conducted by mail) centering on the short story as a genre, with some characteristically provocative responses from Nabokov.

Shrayer, Maxim D. "Mapping Narrative Space in Nabokov's Short Fiction." *The Slavonic and East European Review* 75 (October, 1997): 624-641. Discusses the figurations of space in Nabokov's stories; emphasizes rendering three-dimensional space on an atomistic scale and the way in which a whole narrative serves as a travel guide to its own space; compares Nabokov's method of rendering the narrative space with that of his Russian predecessors.

_____. *The World of Nabokov's Stories.* Austin: University of Texas Press, 1999. A detailed analysis of Nabokov's mastery of the short-story form and his worldview. Traces Nabokov's literary practice from the early 1920's to the 1930's; focuses on Russian stories, such as "The Return of Chorb" and "Cloud, Castle, Lake." Also discusses Nabokov's relationship to Anton Chekhov and Ivan Bunin.

Gerhard Brand

RABBI NAHMAN OF BRATSLAV

Born: Medzibezh, Poland (now in Ukraine); April 4, 1772

Died: Uman, Ukraine, Russian Empire; October 15, 1811

PRINCIPAL SHORT FICTION

Sipure Ma'asiyot, 1815 (*The Tales*, 1956)

OTHER LITERARY FORMS

Rabbi Nahman's scribe, Nathan Sternhartz of Nemirov, wrote a biography, edited two volumes of the Rabbi's sermons and ethical teachings and a collection of his prayers, and transcribed his stories. Nahman had ordered that his writings be destroyed in 1808; his disciples refer to this as *The Burned Book.*

ACHIEVEMENTS

Rabbi Nahman's achievement lies in the faith that his stories inspired. Powerfully spiritual, his work became the guiding force for the Bratslav sect of the Hasidim. As writer Howard Schwartz noted, Rabbi Nahman's view was that "every act, no matter how small, held potentially great significance." In many cases, Rabbi Nahman's work was not original; rather, it was often adapted from much older Russian and Ukrainian folklore. His quest was to create religious allegories that would hold deep significance to the ordinary human condition. As he wrote in the introduction to his story "The Losing of the King's Daughter," "I told this story . . . and everyone who heard it had thoughts of repentance." Ultimately, Rabbi Nahman's literary success stemmed from his use of major theological issues to stimulate thought while disguising them as entertainment.

BIOGRAPHY

Little is known about the first twenty-six years of Rabbi Nahman's life except that he was shy, ascetic, morbidly obsessed with his own sinfulness, endowed with visions, and given to praying fervently on the grave of his great-grandfather, the Baal Shem Tov, who had been the founder of Hasidism. Married at thirteen to Sosia, he lived in his father-in-law's house in Usyatin until 1790, and then they moved to Medvedevka, in the province of Kiev, where he was established a zaddik (a charismatic leader of a group of Hasidim, literally "a righteous one"). In 1798, he left his wife and three daughters to undertake an arduous pilgrimage to the Holy Land with one of his disciples, Simeon. From 1800 he was the center of continual controversy, but he interpreted these rejections as signs of his messianic mission. Shortly before his own death from tuberculosis at the age of thirty-nine, during the period of his deepest personal tragedies—the death of his only son in 1806, and of his wife in 1807—he began to tell his stories.

ANALYSIS

The critical theory presented in the introduction to *The Tales*, culled from Rabbi Nahman's sermons, defends storytelling as a redemptive act. By engaging their imaginations, storytelling awakens listeners from their spiritual slumber. It lifts them up out of their fallen state, inspiring them to participate in the world's salvation. The interpretive strategies to be used for these charming fairy tales are anagogic; the plots are really revelations of the dynamics of the universe. The characters are figurations of the sefirot, the

emanations of God, by means of which the world was created. The story form garbs these truths which would, in their naked form, blind and dazzle the mind, so they are "clothed" as tales.

The Lurianic myth which gives the tales coherence tells how the fall and the creation were simultaneous. God was originally coextensive with the universe. In order to clear space for the world, He contracted Himself (this is called the "tzimtzum"), and in that void where God was absent, the earth was created. In the stories this empty space is represented by a desert. The next stage of creation is called the "shevirah," the shattering of the vessels. The Divine emanations were too overwhelming to be contained in the earthly forms into which They had been infused, so these exploded into shards and fragments ("klippot"). In the universal cataclysm, the Divine Sparks became mixed with mundane evil. It becomes human beings' task to lift up these fallen sparks by good deeds so that the cosmos can once again be restored to its primordial harmony. Until this reparation ("tikkun") occurs, all mankind remains in a state of exile. The redemption is figured as a cosmic marriage because the lowest of the ten Divine Emanations, the Shekina, was expelled into the world by the violence of the "tzimtzum" and must remain in exile until the messiah, who is destined to be her bridegroom, brings salvation. This is the plot of the first of Rabbi Nahman's tales, "The Lost Princess."

"THE LOST PRINCESS"

In this tale, a king is deeply grieved that his beloved daughter has been banished from his kingdom. A viceroy offers to seek her out and bring her back. His search leads him to a desert, "the empty spot" devoid of God's presence, where she is being held captive. She tells him that he must "yearn for her mightily" and fast. He fails. Repeating Adam's sin, he is smitten with such a great craving for an apple that he cannot resist and falls into a deep sleep. She forgives him for having yielded to the evil impulse and gives him a second chance to redeem her. This time, she says, he must not drink or he will again fall into a spiritual stupor. Once again he succumbs to temptation as a spring gushes forth that looks red and smells like wine. By repeating Noah's drunkenness he is condemned to seventy years of sleep. Sadly the princess tries to rouse him, but although she shakes him vigorously, he will not arise. So she unbinds the kerchief from her head and writes on it with her tears that she is being taken to an even more inaccessible place, to a pearly castle on a golden mountain.

Now determined to find her, the viceroy wanders many years through desert places, encountering, one after another, three giants. The first, who says he controls all the animals, insists that there is no pearly castle and summons the animals to testify to this; but the viceroy's faith is undaunted, and he persists, even though the second giant summons all the birds to swear that they have never seen a golden mountain. His faith remains unshaken in spite of this evidence. The more obstacles he encounters, the more convinced he is that he will ultimately find the princess. Even when the third giant summons all the winds to witness, he does not give up. Just as the giant is reproving him—"Don't you see that they have told you nonsense?"—a final wind blows in all out of breath. It apologizes for being late because it had to carry a princess to a pearly castle on top of a golden mountain. The story does not stipulate how the viceroy finally finds the lost princess because their reunion will not occur until the redemption of the world, which is not yet. Prophecy is characteristically open-ended, and the prophetic mode usually ends with a rhetorical question. The declined closure implies that the listeners must participate in shaping the desired ending and suggests that the conclusion is up to them. The tale is meant to move them to act.

The Bratslaver Hasidim, who worship in the synagogue in the Mea Shearim sector of Jerusalem beneath a sign inscribed with Rabbi Nahman's motto, "Jews, never despair!," say that "The Lost Princess" shows that they must sustain their faith in spite of all obstacles. In spite of gigantic doubts, offered with the marshaling of evidence, offered with such certitude and with such an appearance of reason, even if everything that swims, slithers, walks, and flies should testify to the contrary, the Jew must persist in his belief.

What is so fascinating about this narrative structure is the way in which content, rhetoric, and plot all mirror one another. Narratology and theology are

self-reflexive. Furthermore, the language is so full of trance-inducing repetitions that it becomes numinous. Martin Buber's 1906 German translation deleted these numinous repetitions in the interest of smoother reading that would be more appealing to impatient twentieth century readers; Meyer Levin's 1932 rendering into English also took liberties with this aspect of the text; and Elie Wiesel's 1972 version "recreates" the original to speed up the pace. Only the translation of Arnold J. Band in 1978 pretends to be faithful to the slowness and repetitiousness of the orally transmitted Yiddish story as it was actually told.

For example, here is the contact with the first giant, totally structured in an excruciating number of reiterations:

> The giant said to him: "Surely it does not exist at all." He rebuffed him and told him that they had deluded his mind with nonsense, that it surely did not exist at all. And the viceroy began to weep bitterly and said, "It surely, definitely exists somewhere." The wild man rebuffed him again saying that they surely had deluded him with nonsense. And the viceroy said that it surely exists.

The effect of the syntactic structures is also hypnotic. The repeated paratactic clauses with their endless chain of *and*'s is incantatory. Thus syntax, plot, and theme conspire to cast a spell upon the mind of the listener. The language, which twentieth century translators felt should be linear and forward-driving to sustain interest, is exposed as circular, mind-numbing, and repetitive, like the slow-moving circular dances to a wordless tune ("niggun") with which the Hasidim closed their worship services.

"THE MASTER OF PRAYERS"

"The Master of Prayers" describes the role of the zaddik. Through his ability to ascend to the upper worlds like Elijah, Moses, and Enoch, he must lead men along the true path. He must be able to assume the guise of what each individual values most, to encounter him on his own terms, to speak with him in his own language so that he can appeal to him to seek the King. Then follows a long satirical saga on the capitalist world, which, having lost touch with the King, has begun to worship money. With Swiftian satire the Master of Prayers forces them to recognize the stench of money. Appalled by its revolting smell, they roll, gasping and choking on the ground. In horror they exclaim that it stinks like excrement—an association that Sigmund Freud was to make a century later.

As a story within this story there appears a cabalistic cosmogony in retrospective flashback. The Holy Community was scattered by a great storm. At the tempest following the tzimtzum, the King, the Queen, the Princess, and her miraculous son were all dispersed, along with the Warrior and the Master of Prayers. These represent all the sefirotic attributes of the Lord sundered during the cataclysmic shattering of the vessels. They must be reunited by the power of the zaddik, who inspires men to this great work of reparation, the tikkun, after which universal harmony will be restored. The story ends: "The Master of Prayer gave them prayers of repentance and he cleansed them. And the King became ruler of the whole world, and the whole world returned to God and all engaged only in Torah, prayer, repentance, and good deeds. Amen. May it be His will."

One of Rabbi Nahman's innovations as zaddik was to stress the "cleansing" of his Hasidim. In "The Master of Prayers," he valorizes the practice of confession, both as an initiation ritual and at periodic intervals. Other autobiographical elements appear in this tale as well, showing how deeply Nahman internalized his messianic mission so that his role and his life were no longer distinguishable. For example, the fact that at the time that he told "The Master of Prayers" he was already dying of tuberculosis is reflected in the story when the King shows the Warrior a marvelous, two-edged sword:

Through one edge all enemies fall and through the other they are afflicted with consumption. They become thin and their bodies waste away just like in the plague. Heaven help us! And with a sweep of the sword, the enemies are afflicted by the two edges and their powers, defeat and consumption.

"THE TALE OF THE SEVEN BEGGARS"

The most famous of all the stories is the last one, "The Tale of the Seven Beggars." The opening epi-

sode tells of a King who wanted to transfer his power during his own lifetime to his son. The Prince is told at the coronation ceremonies that he must always remain joyous, but he becomes learned in philosophy and is plunged into despair by his rational knowledge. It comes to pass as a result that there is a mass dispersion, and everyone flees. These are the first two steps of the cosmogonic process overlaid with Hasidic ideology. The "Ayn Sof," the primordial nothingness that is God without attributes, the ineffable cosmic substance which cannot be apprehended, wills the world into being. By contracting Itself (the tzimtzum), the transfer of power is effected. Man, who is God's heir, is instructed to worship ecstatically; but instead of dancing joyously to the hymn of praise sung by the whole of creation, man studies gloomy philosophical texts. The cataclysm which follows the transfer of power from the infinite core of pure being into the material world is the "shevirah" which causes a scattering.

The second episode tells of two children who are lost in the forest and crying with hunger. Seven beggars bring them bread. The first is blind, the second deaf, the third stutters, the fourth has a twisted neck, the fifth is hunchbacked, the sixth is handless, and the seventh is legless. Each of these apparent defects turns out to be a virtue, and each beggar, after feeding the children, blesses them with the same wish: "May you be as I am." The children are later married and each beggar comes in turn to the wedding feast to tell a marvelously intricate story showing the power inherent in his illusory defect and endowing the wedding couple with that same magical power. Thus each tale becomes a wedding gift to celebrate the tikkun, the cosmic marriage that takes place "in the pit" of this world which restores the rejoicing in heaven.

First, the blind beggar tells them a complicated narrative revealing that his vision can penetrate through the illusions of this world into the secrets of infinity. His sight is so keen that it can pierce the delusory outer shape into the essence. He remembers the nothingness that preexisted creation, and he bestows upon them the same power of vision. Then the deaf beggar wishes upon them his power of hearing.

All the noises of this world are complaints, arguments, obscenities, and quarrels. Let their ears not be afflicted with these.

Then comes the third beggar to prove that he is not a stutterer except for worldly words which are not praises of the Holy One. He proves himself an extraordinary orator who can recite marvelous riddles and poems and songs. It is his enigmatic lyric about the spring and the heart which is excerpted and reprinted in every Hasidic anthology. In the poised tension of its oppositions lies the vision of balanced contraries which sustains the universe. Each sefirah is yearning for its opposite. Turbulence and disorder would follow if either submitted to the pull of the other. The cosmos is energized by the flow of longing from one to the other; the spring at one end of the world is always longing for the heart which is at the other end. The passage, too long to quote in its entirety, ends:

> And if the heart will no longer look upon the spring, its soul will perish, for it draws all its vitality from the spring. And if the heart would expire, God forbid, the whole world would be annihilated, because the heart has within it the life of everything.

The fourth beggar proves that his twisted neck enables him to throw his voice and mimic any sound. He tells how he demonstrated his gift to a group of skeptics. He imitated the sound of a door opening and shutting and being locked with a bolt. "Then I shot a gun and sent my dog to retrieve what I had shot. And the dog struggled in the snow." The scoffers looked for all these things and saw nothing.

The fifth and sixth beggars bring their gifts of wondrously wrought tales and prove themselves also master raconteurs. Only the seventh beggar does not appear. Following the pattern of paradoxical reversals that have been established by his predecessors, he, presumably, would have danced at the wedding, since he was legless. Either Nahman was obeying the principle of declined closure he had established in his first tale about the lost princess in this last one, or else, because the consummation of the sacred marriage has not yet been realized, he preferred to defer it.

The most stunning artistry links each of these fabulations with the frame narrative which encloses them. Each beggar relates another instance whose paradoxicality defies reason. This joyous sequence of illogical, irrational wonder tales to which the Prince listens should heal his melancholy.

Arnold J. Band dedicated his volume on Nahman to "the Seventh Beggar, the marvelous legless dancer who never appeared at the wedding feast, but whom we all still await."

OTHER MAJOR WORKS

NONFICTION: *Likkutei Moharan*, 1806; *Likkutei Moharan Tinyana*, 1811; *Sefer Hamidot*, 1821 (*The Aleph-Bet Book: The Book of Attributes*, 1986); *Likkutei Tefillot*, 1821-1827; *Ma'gele Zedek*, 1846; *Haye Moharan*, 1874; *Yemei Moharan*, 1876; *Rabbi Nachman's Teachings*, 1973; *Rabbi Nachman's Wisdom*, 1973.

BIBLIOGRAPHY

Green, Arthur. *Tormented Master: A Life of Rabbi Nahman of Bratslav.* University: University of Alabama Press, 1979. This text is widely acknowledged as the definitive biographical work on Rabbi Nahman. It includes a chronology of his life and a special section, entitled "Excursus II: The Tales," on the stories. Green includes detailed notes, including the schema he used for the transliteration of Hebrew and Yiddish. A useful glossary is helpful for non-Yiddish or non-Hebrew speakers. Both the primary and the secondary bibliographies are extensive, and an index is included.

Kaplan, Aryeh. *Until the Mashiach: Rabbi Nachman's Biography: An Annotated Chronology.* Edited by Dovid Shapiro. Jerusalem, Israel: Breslov Research Institute, 1985. An extensive biography of Nahman, with indexes.

Liebes, Yehuda. *Studies in Jewish Myth and Jewish Messianism.* Translated by Batya Stein. Albany: State University of New York Press, 1993. Rabbi Nahman is examined in the volume, part of the SUNY Series in Judaica. Includes bibliographical references and an index.

Nahman of Bratslav. *Nahman of Bratslav: The Tales.* Edited by Arnold J. Band. New York: Paulist Press, 1978. This edition of Rabbi Nahman's stories is invaluable for the accompanying commentary and biography provided by Band. The commentary goes story by story, and Band is scrupulous in his translations and interpretations, making this text a good English version to consult. A brief bibliography and a detailed index are included.

Polsky, Howard W., and Yaella Wozner. *Everyday Miracles: The Healing Wisdom of Hasidic Stories.* Northvale, N.J.: Jason Aronson, 1989. Polsky and Wozner present the cultural and theoretical background to Hasidic short fiction, including the role of the stories in Hasidic society. They use a multitude of different Hasidic stories to illustrate their points. Contains an appendix on the linguistic foundation of Hasidic stories, a glossary, a trans-literation guide, references, a title list of the stories used, and an index.

Wiesel, Elie. *Souls on Fire.* New York: Random House, 1972. Wiesel devotes a complete chapter to Rabbi Nahman, including in it biographical details and examples of his work. Wiesel evaluates the tales from a religious, mystical perspective within the context of Hasidism. Includes a synchronology of all the Hasidic masters profiled in the book as well as some historical background notes.

Wiskind-Elper, Ora. *Tradition and Fantasy in the Tales of Reb Nahman of Bratslav.* Albany: State University of New York Press, 1998. Examines the themes of fantasy and tradition in the short fiction. Provides bibliographical references and an index.

Ruth Rosenberg,
updated by Jo-Ellen Lipman Boon

R. K. NARAYAN

Born: Madras, India; October 10, 1906

PRINCIPAL SHORT FICTION

Malgudi Days, 1941 (1982, expanded to include eight new stories as well as stories from other collections)
Dodu and Other Stories, 1943
Cyclone and Other Stories, 1944
An Astrologer's Day and Other Stories, 1947
Lawley Road: Thirty-two Short Stories, 1956
Gods, Demons, and Others, 1964
A Horse and Two Goats and Other Stories, 1970
Old and New, 1981
Under the Banyan Tree and Other Stories, 1985
Salt and Sawdust: Stories and Table Talk, 1993
The Grandmother's Tale and Selected Stories, 1994

OTHER LITERARY FORMS

A prolific writer, R. K. Narayan has published—besides the collections of short stories cited above—more than a dozen novels, a shortened prose version of each of the two famous Indian epics, *The Ramayana* and *The Mahabharata*, several travel books, volumes of essays and sketches, a volume of memoirs, and numerous critical essays. His novel *The Guide* (1958) was made into a successful motion picture, both in English and in Hindi.

ACHIEVEMENTS

R. K. Narayan, an internationally recognized novelist and the grand patriarch of Indo-Anglian writers (writers of India writing in English), has received a number of awards and distinctions. In 1961, he received the National Prize of the Indian Literary Academy (Sahitya Akademi), India's highest literary honor, for his very popular novel *The Guide*. His other honors include India's Padma Bhushan Award for distinguished service of a high order, 1964; the United States' National Association of Independent Schools Award, 1965; the English-speaking Union Award, 1975; the Royal Society of Literature Benson Medal, 1980; and several honorary degrees. In 1982, Narayan was made an honorary member of the American Academy and Institute of Arts and Letters. He was named a member of India's nonelective House of Parliament, the Rajya Sabha, in 1989.

Narayan invented for his oeuvre the town of Malgudi, considered by critics a literary amalgam of Mysore, where he has lived for several decades, and Madras, the city of his birth. He gently asserts that "Malgudi has been only a concept but has proved good enough for my purposes." In its imaginative scope, Narayan's Malgudi is similar to Faulkner's Yoknapatawpha County, but whereas Faulkner's vision is complex and dark-hued, Narayan's vision is simpler, ironic, sad at times, yet ultimately comic.

BIOGRAPHY

Rasipuram Krishnaswami Narayan was born in Madras, South India, on October 10, 1906. Until the family moved to Mysore, he remained in Madras with his grandmother, who supervised his school and college education. In his autobiography, *My Days* (1974), Narayan admits his dislike of education: he "instinctively rejected both education and examinations with their unwarranted seriousness and esoteric suggestions." Nevertheless, in 1930, he was graduated from Maharaja's College (now the University of Mysore).

In 1933, he met a woman by the name of Rajam and immediately fell in love with her. In 1935, after overcoming almost insurmountable difficulties (to begin with, their horoscopes did not match), Narayan and Rajam were married. She was a great help in his creative work, but she lived to see publication of only three novels. She died of typhoid in 1939. Narayan's fourth novel, *Grateful to Life and Death* (1953), dedicated to his dead wife, centers on the trauma of this loss and on a hard-won sense of reconciliation.

Rajam is portrayed in some detail as Sushila in that novel and, later, as Srinivas's wife in *The Printer of Malgudi* (1957).

Narayan had not begun his career as a writer without some false starts. Indeed, only after having worked at a number of jobs without satisfaction and success—he worked for a time in the civil service in Mysore, taught for a while, and served as a correspondent for *Madras Justice*—did Narayan finally embark upon writing as a full-time career. In the beginning, many of his writings were rejected—a traumatic experience which he bore with fortitude. He was firm in his resolve to make his living as a writer. Experiencing bitter dejection when several British publishers rejected his first novel, *Swami and Friends* (1935) Narayan instructed a friend not to mail the manuscript back to him in India but to throw it into

R. K. Narayan (Library of Congress)

the Thames. Instead, his friend took the manuscript to Graham Greene, who was successful in finding a publisher for the novel. Thus, from a frustrating experience began the literary career of an eminent Commonwealth writer whose books are known throughout the world. Narayan settled in Mysore, India, and his involvement with Indian Thought Publications led to the publication of several of his works.

Narayan continued to write and publish well into his nineties, concentrating on short fiction and essays. He experimented with "table talk," a new form of his own devising, which he described as a loosely structured reflection on any subject.

ANALYSIS

R. K. Narayan has said that he found English the most rewarding medium to employ for his writing because it came to him very easily: "English is a very adaptable language. And it's so transparent it can take on the tint of any country." Critics frequently praise the unaffected standard English with which Narayan captures the Indian sensibility, particularly the South Indian ambience. His unpretentious style, his deliberate avoidance of convoluted expressions and complicated grammatical constructions, his gentle and subtle humor—all this gives his writing an elegant, unforced simplicity that is perfectly suited to the portrayal of ordinary life, of all classes and segments of Indian society—household servants, herdsmen, saints, crooks, merchants, beggars, thieves, hapless students.

Narayan is essentially an old-fashioned storyteller. With Addisonian wit, Twainian humor, and Chekhovian irony, he depicts everyday occurrences, moments of insight; while some of his stories are essentially sketches, quite undramatic, others feature the ironic reversals associated with O. Henry. While Narayan's characters are imbued with distinctively Indian values, their dilemmas are universal.

MALGUDI DAYS

Among the nineteen stories in Narayan's first collection, *Malgudi Days*, there are two stories, "Old Bones" and "Neighbours' Help," that are laced with supernatural elements. This volume includes such memorable stories as "The Gold Belt," "The White

Flower," "An End of Trouble," and "Under the Banyan Tree." Some of the stories may be viewed as social criticism; Narayan looks with a satiric eye on various aspects of traditional South Indian society, particularly the dowry system and the powerful role of astrology and other forms of superstition.

One of the finest stories in the collection, "The Mute Companions," centers on the ubiquitous Indian monkey, a source of meager income for poor people and a source of delight for children. Adopting the omniscient point of view yet without moralizing or judging, Narayan portrays the life of Sami the dumb beggar, whose "very existence depended on the behavior of the monkey." Having taught the monkey several tricks, Sami is able for a time to subsist on the earnings of the clever creature, who is his "only companion." This brief story is an excellent specimen of Narayan's art, revealing his ability to portray a segment of society that typically goes unnoticed. The story emphasizes the passiveness characteristic of the poor Indian, his acceptance of his Karma, or fate. Narayan's gentle social criticism, too, emerges: "Usually he [Sami] avoided those big places where people were haughty, aloof, and inaccessible, and kept formidable dogs and servants." As in many of his stories, Narayan in "The Mute Companions" blends humor and sadness.

Malgudi Days, it should be noted, is also the title of a later collection, published in the United States in 1982. Eight of the thirty-two stories in this collection—"Naga," "Selvi," "Second Opinion," "Cat Within," "The Edge," "God and the Cobbler," "Hungry Child," and "Emden"—were previously uncollected; the remaining stories were selected from Narayan's two earlier volumes, *An Astrologer's Day* and *Lawley Road*.

DODU AND OTHER STORIES

In his second collection, *Dodu and Other Stories*, Narayan focuses on themes related to motherly love, South Indian marriages, the financial and economic frustrations of the middle class, and childhood. Among the outstanding pieces in this volume of seventeen stories are "Dodu," "Gandhi's Appeal," "Ranga," "A Change," "Forty-five a Month," and "The One-Armed Giant." (Originally published in

The Hindu, a Madras newspaper, as most of his stories have been, "The One-Armed Giant" was the first story that Narayan wrote.) The title story, "Dodu," satirically focuses on adult attitudes toward children. "Dodu was eight years old and wanted money badly. Since he was only eight, nobody took his financial worries seriously. . . . Dodu had no illusions about the generosity of his elders. They were notoriously deaf to requests." One of the significant contributions of Narayan is his uncanny ability to portray children—their dreams, their mischief, their psychology. "Ranga," an early tale, is a moving story of a motherless child developing into a disillusioned youth. "Forty-five a Month" is a simple and tender story of the relationship of a father and his family—his wife and their young daughter. The conflict between economic security and the little pleasures of life is evocatively and movingly delineated; indeed, this depiction of a white-collar worker eking out his dreary existence reflects the experience of an entire generation in modern India.

LAWLEY ROAD

In *Lawley Road*, as in most of his fiction, Narayan is concerned more with character than with plot. He notes that he discovers "a story when a personality passes through a crisis of spirit or circumstances," but some stories present flashes of significant moments in characters' lives without any dramatic circumstances; others simply show "a pattern of existence brought to view." Many of the pieces in this collection have a reportorial quality—there are sketches and vignettes, character studies and anecdotes. Of the twenty-eight stories gathered here, fourteen are reprinted from previous collections. The title story is delightful. Named after a typical thoroughfare in the fictitious city of Malgudi, the story recounts how Kabir Lane is renamed as Lawley Road. The narrator is one of Narayan's most engaging recurring characters, whom the people of Malgudi have nicknamed the "Talkative Man," or TM for short, who lends distance and historicity to the story. In another strong story, "The Martyr's Corner," the focus is on a humble seller of *bondas, dosais* (South Indian snacks), and *chappatis* (wheat-flour pancakes) rather than on the violent action. It is the character of the vendor—his dreary and drab life and his attitude toward existence—that holds the interest of the reader.

A HORSE AND TWO GOATS AND OTHER STORIES

A Horse and Two Goats and Other Stories comprises five stories with illustrations by Narayan's brother R. K. Laxman. The title story deals with Muni, a village peasant, and his meeting with a "red man" from the United States. The language barrier is responsible for confusion about a statue and a pair of goats, with hilarious results. The second story, "Uncle," is a masterpiece; it slowly unfolds the mystery that teases a growing boy about his benevolent but inexplicably sinister "uncle." "Annamalai" and "A Breath of Lucifer" deal with two simple, hardworking, faithful servants. Annamalai is an eccentric gardener who attaches himself to a reluctant master. Sam in "A Breath of Lucifer," with an autobiographical preface, is a Christian male nurse. In the end, both Annamalai and Sam, governed by their own impulses, unceremoniously leave their masters. "Seventh House," perhaps a continuation of "The White Flower" in *Lawley Road*, dealing in astrology and superstitions, touchingly explores a husband's tender devotion to his sick wife. Each of the five stories is a character study; all the stories are embellished with picturesque native customs. The dominant tone throughout the collection is casual, understated.

UNDER THE BANYAN TREE AND OTHER STORIES

Under the Banyan Tree and Other Stories is a superb retrospective collection of twenty-eight tales, published specifically for American readers; almost all the stories are drawn from earlier volumes. When the collection appeared on the American scene, several glowing reviews were published in the leading weeklies and periodicals. This collection further confirms Malgudi's place as a great imaginary landscape. The title story, fittingly taken from Narayan's first collection, reaffirms storytelling as a central human activity. The villagers of Somal "lived in a kind of perpetual enchantment. The enchanter was Nambi the story-teller." Yet, having regaled his audience for several years with his tales, Nambi spends the rest of his life in "great consummate silence."

THE GRANDMOTHER'S TALE AND SELECTED STORIES

The Grandmother's Tale and Selected Stories (titled *The Grandmother's Tale and Other Stories* in the paperback edition) was the first collection of Narayan's fiction that attempted to give a comprehensive overview of his more than fifty years of productivity. Many of the stories, including "A Horse and Two Goats" and "Lawley Road," have been widely anthologized for many years. Others, including "Salt and Sawdust" and the title story, make their first North American appearance in this collection. Many of the stories are based on humble but complex characters engaged in daily life in India. As a collection, they demonstrate the richness of Indian life, which blends ancient tradition with Western technological modernity, but Narayan's stories do not call attention to the setting. Rather, they focus on the characters, showing with gentle humor the wonderful absurdity that makes one human and the ironic twists that shape one's life.

In "Salt and Sawdust," for example, Narayan presents a childless housewife who cannot cook—her sense of taste is so bad that she cannot tell the difference between salt and sawdust. Her poor husband is forced to take over the cooking, while his wife occupies herself with writing a novel. However, when the novel is finally completed, the publisher advises the wife to turn it into a cookbook. Narayan is a master of the small details that make domestic scenes seem true and important. Although the wife is made fun of in "Salt and Sawdust," she is a fully rounded character. The humor is good-natured, and Narayan's respect for humans with all their flaws never wavers.

"The Grandmother's Tale" is adapted from a tale Narayan's mother told him about his own great-grandmother. The story is narrated in a winding fashion by a young boy who is sent to live with his strict grandmother. Although he resents his new situation at first, he gradually comes under the spell of the story she tells him, in bits and pieces, about her own grandmother's life. The grandmother's story is set firmly in India. The heroine is married in a traditional ceremony at the age of seven, but her husband abandons her to take a new wife. The landscape she crosses to reclaim her husband is clearly the Indian subcontinent. Ironically, regaining her husband costs her her independence. "The Grandmother's Tale" is unlike many of Narayan's stories in having a strong and admirable central female character. The framing device of the boy narrator reinforces the timelessness and universality of the grandmother's story, which is equally powerful to a young Indian boy in a small village and to adult readers around the world.

As an old-fashioned storyteller, Narayan has sought to convey the vitality of his native India, a land that is full of humanity, oddity, poverty, tradition, "inherited culture," picturesqueness. Narayan realizes

> that the short story is the best medium for utilizing the wealth of subjects available. A novel is a different proposition altogether, centralized as it is on a major theme, leaving out, necessarily, a great deal of the available material on the periphery. Short stories, on the other hand, can cover a wider field by presenting concentrated miniatures of human experience in all its opulence.

Narayan's concern is the heroic in the ordinary Indian. John Updike affirms that "all people are complex, surprising, and deserving of a break: this seems to me Narayan's moral, and one hard to improve upon. His social range and his successful attempt to convey, in sum, an entire population shame most American authors, who also, it might be charged, 'ignore too much of what could be seen.'" With dignified simplicity, honesty, and sincerity, Narayan infuses his stories with charm and spontaneous humor; he guides the reader through his comic and ironic world with an unobtrusive wit.

OTHER MAJOR WORKS

LONG FICTION: *Swami and Friends*, 1935; *The Bachelor of Arts*, 1937; *The Dark Room*, 1938; *The English Teacher*, 1945 (also known as *Grateful to Life and Death*, 1953); *Mr. Sampath*, 1949 (also known as *The Printer of Malgudi*, 1957); *The Financial Expert*, 1952; *Waiting for the Mahatma*, 1955; *The Guide*, 1958; *The Man-Eater of Malgudi*, 1961; *The Sweet-Vendor*, 1967 (also known as *The Vendor of Sweets*); *The Painter of Signs*, 1976; *A Tiger for Malgudi*, 1983; *Talkative Man: A Novel of Malgudi*, 1987; *The World of Nagaraj*, 1990.

NONFICTION: *Mysore*, 1944; *My Dateless Diary*, 1960; *Next Sunday: Sketches and Essays*, 1960; *My Days*, 1974; *Reluctant Guru*, 1974; *The Emerald Route*, 1977; *A Writer's Nightmare: Selected Essays, 1958-1988*, 1988.

TRANSLATIONS: *The Ramayana: A Shortened Modern Prose Version of the Indian Epic*, 1972 (of Vālmīki); *The Mahabharata: A Shortened Prose Version of the Indian Epic*, 1978.

MISCELLANEOUS: *A Story-Teller's World*, 1989 (stories, essays, and sketches).

BIBLIOGRAPHY

Bery, Ashok. "'Changing the Script': R. K. Narayan and Hinduism." *Ariel* 28 (April, 1997): 7-20. Argues that Narayan often probes limitations and contradictions in Hindu worldviews and identities; analyzes the ways Narayan challenges Hindu doctrines, particularly those that teach that the individual self and the phenomenal world are unimportant; although Hinduism is indispensable to Narayan, it is not unchallengeable.

Holstrom, Lakshmi. *The Novels of R. K. Narayan*. Calcutta: Writers Workshop, 1973. An early study of Narayan's first ten novels in terms of his themes and narrative technique. It attempts to place him in the tradition of Indian fiction. Includes a bibliography.

Kain, Geoffrey, ed. *R. K. Narayan: Contemporary Critical Essays*. East Lansing: Michigan State University Press, 1993. A collection of essays, mostly on the novels, including feminist, cultural, postcolonial, and other contemporary approaches. Other essays focus on irony, satire, transcendence, self-reflexivity, and mythmaking in Narayan's fiction.

Knippling, Alpana Sharma. "R. K. Narayan, Raja Rao, and Modern English Discourse in Colonial India." *Modern Fiction Studies* 39 (Spring, 1993): 169-186. Using Michel Foucault's notion that discourse does not necessarily implicate human intention, Knippling contends that Narayan is not heavily influenced by English discourse and therefore not culpable in the whole Westernizing process.

Naik, M. K. *The Ironic Vision: A Study of the Fiction of R. K. Narayan*. New Delhi: Sterling, 1983. A perceptive study of Narayan's fiction demonstrating his use of irony, in its various forms, to portray human character and situations and to project his total vision of life. Devotes a chapter to the short stories and contains references, a layout of Malgudi and its surroundings, a select bibliography, and an index.

Sundaram, P. S. *R. K. Narayan*. New Delhi: Arnold-Heinemann, 1973. This volume's only aim, according to the author, "is to acquaint the Common Reader with the works of an outstanding writer and to suggest what makes the writing outstanding." Contains a brief thematic study of Narayan's short stories and notes the thematic connections between many of the stories and the novels. Supplemented by notes and references, a select bibliography, and an index.

Urstad, Tone Sundt. "Symbolism in R. K. Narayan's 'Naga.'" *Studies in Short Fiction* 31 (Summer, 1994): 425-432. Discusses Narayan's basic technique of juxtaposing scenes from modern life with the exploits of gods, demons, and heroes in the short story "Naga." Argues that in this story Narayan creates a mythic framework in which humans act out age-old patterns and conflicts.

Venugopal, C. V. *The Indian Short Story in English: A Survey*. Bareilly, India: Prakash Book Depot, 1975. The chapter on R. K. Narayan provides a useful overview of his short fiction. Complemented by references, a select bibliography, and an index.

Walsh, William. *R. K. Narayan*. London: Longman, 1971. A booklet in the British Council Writers and Their Work series, it gives a general critical appraisal of Narayan as a novelist. Walsh discusses Narayan's novels as "comedies of sadness" and argues that "his work is an original blend of Western method and Eastern material." Includes a select bibliography.

S. S. Moorty, updated by Chaman L. Sahni and Cynthia A. Bily

GÉRARD DE NERVAL
Gérard Labrunie

Born: Paris, France; May 22, 1808
Died: Paris, France; January 26, 1855

PRINCIPAL SHORT FICTION

Les Illuminés, 1852
Les Filles du feu, 1854 (*Daughters of Fire*, 1922)

OTHER LITERARY FORMS

In both his collections and other writings, Gérard de Nerval alternates between autobiography and fiction. His lengthy travel narrative, *Voyage en Orient* (1851; *Journey to the Orient*, 1972), contains elements of fiction, and *Aurélia* (1855; English translation, 1932) recounts his own mental illness. Nerval is best known, however, as a poet, especially for his sonnet sequence, *Les Chimères* (1854; English translation, 1965; also known as *Chimeras*, 1966).

ACHIEVEMENTS

Gérard de Nerval maintained close friendships with principal writers in Parisian literary circles, exchanging influences with Théophile Gautier, Heinrich Heine, and others. Since his death he has been influential through the poems of *Les Chimères* that draw on the nineteenth century interest in pagan religions compared to Christianity and that anticipate the poetic symbolism of Charles Baudelaire.

BIOGRAPHY

Except for some foreign travel, Gérard de Nerval spent his entire life in Paris, where he was born Gérard Labrunie, son of a medical doctor, in 1808. He assumed the name "de Nerval" and is often referred to simply as "Gérard."

The deaths of two women marked Nerval's life. His mother died when he was two years old. Then as a young man he was passionately attracted to Jenny Colon, an actress who married another man in 1838 and died in 1842. Nerval never married but continued to fantasize about an ideal but inaccessible woman.

Mental illness also tormented Nerval. After an attack of what may have been schizophrenia, he was treated at a clinic in Montmartre. His doctor there found him well enough to leave but not cured. Nerval's father suggested that a warmer climate might help him. Thus Nerval made an extended trip to Egypt, the Holy Land, and Constantinople in 1843.

After his trip, Nerval suffered frequent recurrences of his illness. He continued to be active, wrote extensively, traveled within Europe, and enjoyed the support of the most important writers in Paris at the time. Still, in 1855, he was found hanged in a Paris street, an apparent suicide.

ANALYSIS

The definition of Gérard de Nerval's style as a short-story writer involves distinguishing reality from fiction. In a variety of first-person narratives, Nerval alternates between autobiography and fantasy while concentrating, in both modes, on similar themes concerning a connection with a mythic past and the pursuit of an idealized woman.

Because of his mental illness, Nerval himself may not have separated his life from his fantasies. The exploitation of madness for literary inspiration follows readily from the views of the Romantic poets, both in France and in England, who tended to see their work as a result of inspired visions. Nerval, in turn, closely parallels usages of the French Symbolists. Arthur Rimbaud especially, both in poetry in "The Drunken Boat" and in prose in *Une Saison en enfer* (1873; *A Season in Hell*, 1932), described an unreal world he claimed to have derived from a "deranging of his senses."

Because an element of madness was so closely associated with genius, Nerval found both personal and professional support and even governmental appointments that sponsored his travel. While he was fascinated by the Orient and invoked its ancient gods in the poems of *Les Chimères*, the prose turns more frequently to material from the early history of France.

Nerval felt he had a deep connection to noble ancestors who had lived heroic lives. The references to traditional songs and dances as well as the descriptions of old manor houses and antique furniture that decorate his stories are all reminders of this mythic past.

The sense of continuity with the past underlines the stories of *Les Illuminés. Daughters of Fire*, presenting a series of idealized female characters, shows aspects of the eternally elusive woman who is separated from Nerval variously by marriage to another, by social constraints, or even by having lived in the past.

"LES CONFIDENCES DE NICOLAS"

"Les Confidences de Nicolas" typifies the collection *Les Illuminés*, to which Nerval gave the subtitle "Precursors of Socialism." These are stories based on actual figures from the seventeenth and eighteenth centuries but highly fictionalized with the creation of subordinate characters and considerable dialogue.

This is the story of the eighteenth century author Nicolas-Edmé Restif de la Bretonne, usually referred to as "Restif" but whom Nerval familiarly calls "Nicolas" through most of the story. The name is significant both in that it separates the fiction from historical passages where Nerval uses "Restif" and in that the alliteration with Nerval's own name parallels a link of his beloved Jenny Colon to the "Jeannette" of the story.

The plot follows the loves of Nicolas for a series of women: first an actress he admires; then Jeannette, from whom he is separated by a scandal; Madame Parangon, who is already married; Agnès, who abandons him as soon as they are married; Zéfire, who helps him recover but whom he is not free to marry; and Sara, who is married off for money. Finally late in life, he is reunited with Jeannette and marries her. Despite the late happy ending, the emphasis is on the impossibility of happiness in love.

"ANGÉLIQUE"

Published as part of *Daughters of Fire*, "Angélique" is also linked to "L'Abbé de Bucquoy," one of the stories of *Les Illuminés*. Angélique de Longueval was the abbé's great aunt. Nerval freely adapts her life as he found it in the family archives into an independent story.

Gérard de Nerval (Library of Congress)

The narrative is presented as a series of twelve letters to an anonymous correspondent, but Angélique's story begins only in the fourth letter. It is enclosed in an account of Nerval's adventures in various libraries as he attempts to find records of the family. This and numerous other digressions give rise to a comic element with several asides to the reader in contrast to the essentially serious story.

Angélique fell in love with a man her father found unacceptable for marriage. She eloped with him to Italy, but they lacked money and encountered numerous problems. Although Angélique eventually returned home, she ended her life in poverty because her family rejected her. This is again a story of unhappy love, but the distance separating Nerval himself from Angélique involves his difficulties in the archives, thus giving importance to the enclosure story.

"SYLVIE"

"Sylvie" is the best known of Nerval's stories with an organized plot and relatively few digressions. Sylvie is a country girl from the Valois region, which was home to Nerval's family. She loves the narrator, who, like Nerval, is living in Paris and is smitten by an actress. He returns home to the Valois just in time for a traditional festival that he attends with Sylvie. At the festival, he is drawn to Adrienne, a beautiful woman who sings an enchanting song, allows him to crown her with flowers, and disappears. She is reported to have entered a convent and never reappears. The narrator still loves Sylvie but cannot escape the enchantment of Adrienne. Sylvie finally will not wait for him and marries another man. Years later, when he visits Sylvie and her children, she tells him that Adrienne died shortly after entering the convent. Thus, he learns he spent his life longing for a woman who no longer existed.

In addition to incorporating Nerval's motif of the inaccessible woman, this story highlights the beauty of rural France, which symbolized for Nerval the past glory of his family. In a key scene, while visiting Sylvie's aunt, the couple dress in old-fashioned clothes, thus assuming traditional identities, but later Sylvie prefers to replace the antique furniture that represented her link with the past.

"THE TALE OF THE QUEEN OF THE MORNING AND SOLIMAN THE PRINCE OF THE GENII"

Nerval inserted this story, "La Reine du Matin et Soliman, Prince des Génies" ("The Tale of the Queen of the Morning and Soliman the Prince of the Genii"), into his *Journey to the Orient* as a tale he supposedly heard from a professional storyteller in Constantinople. The story outgrows its context just as "Angélique" dominates its enclosure, and the pattern of the inaccessible woman marks it as Nerval's.

This is really the story of Adoniram, who serves the Asian prince of the title by building palaces for him. As in the biblical story of Solomon, the prince wants an impressive palace for a visit from the Queen of Sheba. Adoniram meets the queen, who admires his work, thus making the prince jealous. Adoniram and the queen love each other, but she plans to marry the prince, and Adoniram will leave for a job in another country. At the end, the queen calls off the marriage, but too late, as Adoniram has died. Again, love has been thwarted.

Adoniram shares many attributes with Nerval. Early in the story there are hints of his mysterious background, and he eventually impresses the queen by telling her of his true nobility. Then after a work

accident, Adoniram becomes unconscious and has a lengthy dream that constitutes a descent into hell, much as Nerval described his episodes of madness.

OTHER MAJOR WORKS

POETRY: *Elégies nationales*, 1826; *Poésies allemandes*, 1830 (translation); *Petits Châteaux de Bohème*, 1853 (includes poetry and prose); *Les Chimères*, 1854 (English translation, 1965; also known as *Chimeras*, 1966); *Fortune's Fool: Selected Poems*, 1959.

PLAYS: *Faust*, pb. 1827, pb. 1840 (translation of Johann Wolfgang von Goethe's play); *Piquillo*, pb. 1837 (with Alexandre Dumas, *père*); *Alchemiste*, pb. 1839 (with Dumas, *père*); *Chariot d'enfant*, pb. 1850 (with Joseph Méry); *L'Imagier de Harlem*, pr. 1851.

NONFICTION: *Voyage en Orient*, 1851 (*Journey to the Orient*, 1972); *Promenades et souvenirs*, 1854-1856; *Aurélia*, 1855 (English translation, 1932).

BIBLIOGRAPHY

Behdad, Ali. "Orientalist Desire, Desire of the Orient." *French Forum* 15, no. 1 (January, 1990): 37-51. This article provides useful background on the psychological implications of Nerval's fascination with the East. The story of Adoniram is discussed in relationship to its context in the storytelling tradition of Constantinople. The veiled women of the East symbolize another aspect of the separation between Nerval and the woman who represents his ideal, and the author sees this concealment as increasing desire.

Dubruck, Alfred. *Gérard de Nerval and the German Heritage*. The Hague: Mouton, 1965. This study of German influences in Nerval's work cites E. T. A. Hoffmann, Johann Wolfgang von Goethe, and Heinrich Heine. Chapter 2, "The Fantastic Tale," traces the evolution of stories featuring illusions and dreams which, partly because of Hoffmann's influence, became popular in France and encouraged Nerval's use of fantasy and doubled characters.

Dunn, Susan. "Nerval and Money: The Currency of Dreams." *Nineteenth-Century French Studies* 19, no. 1 (Fall, 1990): 54-64. This discussion of

"Sylvie" relates money to the distinctions of social class that separate the characters. Nerval's own attitude is described as ambivalent in that he is torn between a bohemian disdain for money and a regard for its importance in conferring status. This dualism distinguishes the narrator of "Sylvie" from Nerval himself. The article also comments on money in "Angélique" and "La Pandora."

Jones, Robert Emmet. *Gérard de Nerval*. New York: Twayne, 1974. This volume situates Nerval within the Romantic movement in France. The section on Nerval's prose begins with an analysis of the *Journey to the Orient* including elements from the story of Adoniram that parallel those of Nerval's life. "The Eternal Woman" discusses stories from *Daughters of Fire*, and "Quest, Dreams and Transcendence" discusses the psychology revealed in *Aurélia*.

Knapp, Bettina L. *Gérard de Nerval: The Mystic's Dilemma*. University: The University of Alabama Press, 1980. Organized as a biography, Knapp's study includes chapters on Nerval's principal stories. Chapter 13, "The Queen of Sheba and Adoniram," shows how Nerval modified the original biblical story of Solomon. Chapters 17 through 19, "Angélique," "Sylvie," and "Isis, the Cult of the Madonna," trace mythic elements in *Daughters of Fire* and ways in which Nerval used them and identified with them. Chapter 21, "Aurélia," traces parallels with Nerval's illness.

Lokke, Kari. *Gérard de Nerval: The Poet as Social Visionary*. Lexington, Ky.: French Forum, 1987. This thematic study uses Nerval's stories to define the nature of his hallucinations and his concept of "the other." Chapter 2, "Woman: The Other as Sister," draws chiefly on the stories of *Daughters of Fire*.

Rhodes, S. A. *Gérard de Nerval 1808-1855: Poet, Traveler, Dreamer*. New York: Philosophical Library, 1951. This biography offers useful background on Jenny Colon and how Nerval linked her to the Queen of Sheba. Chapter 13 treats the story of Adoniram as a minor part of Nerval's trip to the East. Chapters 21 through 25 go into more detail on the stories of *Daughters of Fire* in the context of Nerval's mental state.

Rinsler, Norma. *Gérard de Nerval*. London: Athlone Press, 1973. This volume begins with a brief biography. Chapter 5 summarizes plots and discusses structures in *Daughters of Fire*. Chapter 6 on "La Pandora" considers separately this story that Nerval had thought to include in the previous collection. Both chapters stress Nerval's relationships with women. Chapter 7, on *Aurélia*, shifts to an emphasis on his illness.

Strauss, Jonathan. "Death-Based Subjectivity in the Creation of Nerval's Lyric Self." *Espirit Créateur* 35, no. 4 (Winter, 1995): 83-94. Strauss focuses on Nerval's lyric poetry, specifically his most famous sonnet, "El Desdichado," in the context of the influence of Georg Wilhelm Friedrich Hegel. This discussion raises issues of the author's alienation from himself that illuminate the use of doubled characters in the short stories.

_____. *Subjects of Terror: Nerval, Hegel, and the Modern Self*. Stanford, Calif.: Stanford University Press, 1998. Despite the mention of Georg Wilhelm Friedrich Hegel in the title, this is a book about Nerval. The first two chapters deal with Hegel and other influences in order to put Nerval's madness in context in chapter 3, ending with an overview of *Daughters of Fire*. Chapter 4 focuses on "Les Faux Saulniers," an extract from "L'Abbé de Bucquoy" from *Les Illuminés*.

Dorothy M. Betz

ANAÏS NIN

Born: Paris, France; February 21, 1903
Died: Los Angeles, California; January 14, 1977

PRINCIPAL SHORT FICTION
 Under a Glass Bell and Other Stories, 1944
 Delta of Venus: Erotica, 1977
 Waste of Timelessness and Other Early Stories,
  1977
 Little Birds: Erotica, 1979

OTHER LITERARY FORMS

Anaïs Nin's published works include fiction, auto-biography, literary criticism, essays, speeches, and interviews. She is best known for her monumental diary, which, in edited versions, comes to eleven volumes. Seven volumes form the first series of the diary, which is entitled *The Diary of Anaïs Nin*. The other four volumes constitute the second series, entitled *The Early Diary of Anaïs Nin*. Of Nin's nine novelettes and novels, the major work is the "continuous novel," *Cities of the Interior* (1959), which comprises five interrelated works: *Ladders to Fire* (1946), *Children of the Albatross* (1947), *The Four-Chambered Heart* (1950), *A Spy in the House of Love* (1954), and *Solar Barque* (1958).

ACHIEVEMENTS

Anaïs Nin holds a unique place as a twentieth century writer. Widely admired and criticized all of her life, she began her literary career at the age of eleven when she jotted down observations in her diary, a practice she would continue all of her life. In point of fact, although she had written a number of fictional works to a small, discerning public, it would be the publication of her diaries spread over many volumes that would finally earn Nin the wide recognition she always sought. Ironically, Nin was initially opposed to their publication despite entreaties from her closest friends to have them published. Nin's greatest literary achievement was the multifaceted self-portrait to be found explicitly in her diaries and to a lesser degree in her experimental fiction. Nin's most liberating in-

fluences were the therapy she underwent with Sigmund Freud's disciple Otto Rank and her acquaintance and subsequent love affair with Henry Miller. Nin's involvement with Miller and his wife were the subject of a controversial motion picture, *Henry and June* (1990), based on her unexpurgated memoirs. Honors came to Nin late in life. In 1971, she was awarded France's Prix Sevigne and two years later she received an honorary doctorate in art from the Philadelphia College of Art. One year before her death in 1977 at age seventy-three, she was elected to the National Institute of Arts and Letters and Dartmouth College saluted her with an honorary doctorate.

BIOGRAPHY

The Nin family broke up in Spain, and in 1914 Rosa Culmell-Nin and her three children, of whom Anaïs was the oldest, left Barcelona for New York City. In 1918 Anaïs, age fifteen, left school, and in 1923 she married Hugh P. Guiler (known as engraver and filmmaker under the name of Ian Hugo). Nin returned to New York City in 1934 from Paris, where she had been living with her husband, to practice psychotherapy briefly under the supervision of Otto Rank. Then, in 1935, she returned to France until 1939, when the approaching war caused yet another removal to the United States. After nearly thirty years of publishing her works without much acclaim, Nin in 1966 began to receive national and international recognition with the publication of *The Diary of Anaïs Nin: 1931-1934* (1966). There followed a decade of public appearances and other forms of recognition until her death from cancer in January, 1977.

ANALYSIS

The posthumous publication of erotica that Anaïs Nin wrote during the late 1930's and early 1940's to help her friend Henry Miller has, ironically, made Nin's name known to a broad commercial market. Near the end of her life Nin agreed to publish these stories, providing a preface to *Delta of Venus* as well

Anaïs Nin (Christian Du Bois Larson)

as a postscript. Written four months before her death, the postscript explains: "I finally decided to release the erotica for publication because it shows the beginning efforts of a woman in a world that has been the domain of men." *Delta of Venus* and its sequel *Little Birds* contain sexual fantasies expressed with a delicate explicitness; they are tender, understanding, and elegant, entirely lacking in vulgarity. Both books are suffused with emotion. *Delta of Venus* and *Little Birds* are, however, tangential to the main body of Nin's writings and do not represent the subtle psychological perceptions and the bold and ingenious imagery of her best short stories, which are found in *Under a Glass Bell and Other Stories*.

In 1977, Magic Circle Press published a slim collection of Nin's early stories titled *Waste of Timelessness and Other Early Stories*. The sixteen pieces represent the author's apprentice work. In a short preface Nin warns that "This is a book for friends only"; however, *Waste of Timelessness and Other Early Stories* is remarkable for its humor, verbal adventurousness, and "first hints of feminism."

UNDER A GLASS BELL AND OTHER STORIES

Nin's major achievement in short fiction, *Under a Glass Bell and Other Stories* is a result of thoughtful artistry; the thirteen individual pieces were written during the late 1930's and early 1940's and printed by the author herself in 1944 on a pedal-operated press. This edition bore the images of fantastic creatures engendered by the fantasy of engraver Ian Hugo, and it is a valuable discovery for contemporary book collectors. Oliver Evans, author of the first book-length study of Nin's writings, claims *Under a Glass Bell and Other Stories* as "one of the most distinguished short-story collections published in this country in the forties." He reports that Nin herself said: "When people ask me what book of mine they should begin by reading, I invariably reply *Under a Glass Bell*. If I had to choose one book by which I would like to be remembered, it is this one."

The second of Nin's published fictional works, *Under a Glass Bell and Other Stories* presents a series of eccentric protagonists who are imprisoned in protective but airless enclosures. All the stories are expressed with admirable stylistic virtuosity. The central unifying metaphor is, naturally, the glass bell which isolates those inside it, able to observe but not to participate in the life beyond the fetid atmosphere of their luxurious prison. The title story is a family portrait of an aristocrat named Jeanne and her two brothers, who are bound together in a triangle of psychological incest. Their castle is beautiful but they cannot escape from it: "The light from the icicle bushes threw a patina over all objects, and turned them into bouquets of still flowers kept under a glass bell." At the end of this story the string of Jeanne's guitar breaks mysteriously as she prophesies her own decay "in the tomb."

The theme of threatened decay and death, caused by unconquered fear, appears in most of the thirteen stories. "Houseboat" conveys the reader on an occasionally merry but ultimately sordid voyage along the Seine. The boat is finally condemned to exile in a boatyard filled with "rotting skeletons of barges, piles of wood, rusty anchors, and pierced water tanks." In "The Mohican" a European astrologer is terrified by the very system on which he depends to endow life with meaning: the planets, especially the recently discovered Pluto. The Mohican takes refuge in the stacks of the Bibliothèque Nationale, but his sanctuary is invaded by the German military; he is then arrested as a "celestial saboteur." This image, which swiftly penetrates and exposes the tragic absurdity of Nazi paranoia, is a good example of Nin's magical fusion of the marvelous with the mundane. In "Je suis le plus malade des Surrealistes" Nin drew a compassionate portrait of her friend Antonin Artaud. This brilliant man's prison was madness, exacerbated by drugs. By letting him speak in the imagery of sharp contrast, Nin captures the terror of his exile from reason. When asked why he "has many enemies," Pierre (Artaud) replies: "Because when one is white like the white phoenix and the others are black one has enemies."

Both "The Labyrinth" and "Through the Streets of My Own Labyrinth" are explorations of Nin's ambivalent feelings about her diary, the massive work that she started as a child to persuade her father to rejoin the family by traveling to New York. The diary was a spiritual and emotional haven in which she could live in safety; yet at times her obsessive need for it threatened to bar Nin from entering life as she yearned to do. This particular prison, which might be thought of as a soothing fantasy or subjective creation, is actually an articulated dream, as well as a mirror in which one sees a usually inflated and even perfected image of the self. The snapshots of lonely, frightened men in "The All-Seeing" and "The Eye's Journey" are further additions to the portrait album of self-imprisoned dreamers.

"RAGTIME"

The dream is central, as well, to "Ragtime," but in this whimsical fantasy a more positive view emerges, as Nin elaborates a modern-day allegory of the process of transformation. "Ragtime" suggests comparison to the forbidden art of alchemy, through which base and worthless metals were transformed into the most valuable of all substances, gold. The story begins by creating a nightscape in which the ragpicker, who represents the artist, wanders through a garbage dump selecting irresistible debris to pack in his swelling bag. The dreamer herself enters this mysterious landscape as a passenger on the hump of a camel that is itself only the ragpicker's shadow. These images stress the power of imagination. Later, as she strolls through the wreckage of shacks, gypsy wagons, and trash, the dreamer grows depressed. Fearing that she herself may come apart and disintegrate into worthless fragments, she begins to clutch various parts of her body. She now stumbles upon discarded parts of herself. First appears an old dress, once a favorite; but the dreamer has grown; she can no longer "stay inside of it" (note, again, the imagery of the imprisoning enclosure and the need to expand beyond its confines). Next she finds castoff parts of her body: a wisdom tooth, her shorn long hair. Naturally, the dreamer is disturbed by the reappearance of these parts of her former self. Do they mean that it is impossible to get rid of the old self, to shed one's skin? "Can't one throw anything away forever?" The ragpicker answers this wistful question by leading his colony of vagabonds in the "serpentine song":

> Nothing is lost but it changes
> into the new string old string
> in the new bag old bag
> in the new pan old tin
> in the new shoe old leather
> in the new silk old hair
> in the new hat old straw
> in the new man the child
> and the new not new
> the new not new
> the new not new

With this reassuring lullaby in her ears, the dreamer falls asleep again (in her own dream), only to be picked up along with other odds and ends of scrap and stashed away inside the ragpicker's bag.

"BIRTH"

The seductive nature of enclosure and retention is more directly and more powerfully presented in "Birth" than in the other pieces collected in *Under a Glass Bell and Other Stories*. This story, whose "real life" version can be read in the concluding pages of Nin's diary covering the years 1931 to 1934, has often been reprinted, perhaps because it is closer to realism than Nin's other stories. Against a background of routine medical indifference, the narrator attempts to expel from her body a stillborn six-month infant. "Birth" begins with the doctor's statement that "The child is dead." During the narrator's excruciating struggle to push out the baby, one of the nurses comments: "Mine passed through like an envelope through a letter box." Angry at his patient, the doctor threatens her with scalpels and hypodermic needles. Finally, it is the woman's retaliatory anger, her instinctual return to a primitive self-reliance that saves her. She has come to experience the dead child inside as "a demon strangling her." This dead thing within cannot be allowed to kill her. With a formidable act of will the woman wrests control of the birth process away from the doctor. She demands that he and the nurses leave her alone. Then, very gradually, by drumming on her abdomen with the tips of her fingers, she succeeds in inducing a trancelike state of relaxation. After a terrifying final exertion the baby passes through the birth canal, expelled at last.

"Birth" closes *Under a Glass Bell and Other Stories*. In spite of its rage, its anguish, and its prevailing note of physical suffering, this story offers an image of consoling growth that counters the sadness with which the houseboat goes to its graveyard in the book's opening selection. In a way that becomes characteristic of her later work, Nin interprets the expulsion of the dead baby as a release for the mother, almost as an exorcism. Most of the stories in *Under a Glass Bell and Other Stories* explore the stultifying effects of remaining at the safe childish stages of life, of remaining inside one's cocoon or womb. In "Birth" the new life is not that of the baby, obviously, but that of the woman who has succeeded in expelling the infantile version of herself, so that she can aspire to a more mature level of existence. *Under a Glass Bell and Other Stories* ends with an image of consolation, for the "Birth" tale confirms the terrible reality of suffering, but it also portrays the transformative power of the act of creation.

OTHER MAJOR WORKS

LONG FICTION: *Winter of Artifice*, 1939; *Winter of Artifice: Three Novelettes*, 1945 (contains *Winter of Artifice*, "Stella," and "The Voice"); *This Hunger*, 1945; *Cities of the Interior: A Continuous Novel*, 1959 (contains *Ladders to Fire*, 1946, *Children of the Albatross*, 1947, *The Four-Chambered Heart*, 1950, *A Spy in the House of Love*, 1954, *Solar Barque*, 1958); *Seduction of the Minotaur*, 1961; *Collages*, 1964.

NONFICTION: *D. H. Lawrence: An Unprofessional Study*, 1932; *The House of Incest*, 1936; *Realism and Reality*, 1946; *On Writing*, 1947; *The Diary of Anaïs Nin: 1931-1934*, 1966; *The Diary of Anaïs Nin: 1934-1939*, 1967; *The Novel of the Future*, 1968; *The Diary of Anaïs Nin: 1939-1944*, 1969; *The Diary of Anaïs Nin: 1944-1947*, 1971; *Paris Revisited*, 1972; *The Diary of Anaïs Nin: 1947-1955*, 1974; *A Photographic Supplement to the Diary of Anaïs Nin*, 1974; *A Woman Speaks: The Lectures, Seminars, and Interviews of Anaïs Nin*, 1975; *The Diary of Anaïs Nin: 1955-1966*, 1976; *In Favor of the Sensitive Man and Other Essays*, 1976; *Linotte: The Early Diary of Anaïs Nin: 1914-1920*, 1978; *The Diary of Anaïs Nin: 1966-1974*, 1980; *The Early Diary of Anaïs Nin, Volume Two: 1920-1923*, 1982; *The Early Diary of Anaïs Nin, Volume Three: 1923-1927*, 1983; *The Early Diary of Anaïs Nin, Volume Four: 1927-1931*, 1985; *Henry and June: From the Unexpurgated Diary of Anaïs Nin*, 1986; *A Literate Passion: Letters of Anaïs Nin and Henry Miller, 1932-1953*, 1987.

BIBLIOGRAPHY

Blair, Deirdre. *Anaïs Nin: A Biography*. New York: G. P. Putnam's Sons, 1995. A definitive biography that attempts to separate the lies from the reality in Nin's journals; argues that Nin will always be considered a major/minor writer, one of the first to write about sex, the self, and psychoanalysis.

Evans, Oliver. *Anaïs Nin*. Carbondale: Southern Illinois University Press, 1968. A solid and widely admired first study of Nin's work. The only major weakness is the limited examination of the diaries, most of which were not yet published.

Fitch, Noel Riley. *Anaïs: The Erotic Life of Anaïs Nin*. Boston: Little, Brown, 1993. As the subtitle suggests, Fitch is concerned with tracing Nin's erotic relationships and close friendships with male and female writers. A biographer of Sylvia

Beach and an expert on Paris, Fitch writes with verve and expertise.

Franklin, Benjamin V., and Duane Schneider. *Anaïs Nin: An Introduction.* Athens: Ohio University Press, 1979. A well-balanced study of Nin's work, better than most, that carefully and separately examines her fiction, six volumes of diaries, and her critical and nonfiction work. This study attempts to redress critical neglect of the author and gives her due recognition for her literary achievements.

Hinz, Evelyn J., ed. *A Woman Speaks: The Lectures, Seminars, and Interviews of Anaïs Nin.* Chicago: Swallow Press, 1975. This collection of thirty-eight recorded tapes by Nin from 1966 to 1973 chronicles her interviews, conversations, commencement addresses, and lectures. Provides an interesting look at Nin's public persona.

Jason, Philip K., ed. *The Critical Response to Anaïs Nin.* Westport, Conn.: Greenwood Press, 1996. A selection of essays examining Nin's works. Includes bibliographical references and an index.

Knapp, Bettina L. *Anaïs Nin.* New York: Frederick Ungar, 1978. An appreciative examination of Nin's work that explores the psychological depths of her diaries and fiction. Complemented by a chronology.

Lawrence, Charles. "Her Life Was Her Masterpiece." *The Ottawa Citizen,* July 27, 1998, p. D3. Discusses Nin's creation of an elaborate set of lies in order to maintain relationships with two men at the same time; focuses primarily on her relationship with one of her husbands, Rupert Pole; reports the results of an interview with Pole about his relationship with Nin.

Nin, Anaïs, *A Literate Passion: Letters of Anaïs Nin and Henry Miller.* Edited by Gunther Stuhlmann. New York: Harcourt Brace Jovanovich, 1987. A highly interesting, readable, and fascinating account of the passionate friendship and literary romance that flowered for more than two decades between two great writers, Henry Miller and Anaïs Nin. The excellent biographical notes describe the major individuals mentioned in their correspondence.

Pierpont, Claudia Roth. "Sex, Lies, and Thirty-five Thousand Pages." *The New Yorker* 69 (March 1, 1993): 74-80. Discusses the publication of the second volume of Nin's Diary; notes that the diaries show that Nin's deceptions gained her a long list of lovers, allowed her to present her unintelligible writing style as a form of surrealism, won her undeserved public acclaim as a pioneer of "female writing," and provided a saintly gloss on her manipulative character.

Scholar, Nancy. *Anaïs Nin.* Boston: Twayne, 1984. A good critical introduction to Nin. The first chapter offers an overview of her life, and succeeding chapters examine the diaries, short stories, prose pieces, and novels. Scholar believes Nin's diaries hold the key to understanding the artist and her work. Supplemented by a useful chronology and a select bibliography.

Sharon Spencer, updated by
Terry Theodore

FRANK NORRIS

Born: Chicago, Illinois; March 5, 1870
Died: San Francisco, California; October 25, 1902

PRINCIPAL SHORT FICTION

A Deal in Wheat and Other Stories of the New and Old West, 1903
The Joyous Miracle, 1906
The Third Circle, 1909
Frank Norris of "The Wave," 1931 (Oscar Lewis, editor)

OTHER LITERARY FORMS

Frank Norris is best known for his novels *Vandover and the Brute* (1914), *McTeague* (1899), *The Octopus* (1901), *The Pit* (1903), and three others. There have been film versions of *Moran of the Lady Letty* (1898; with Rudolph Valentino), *The Pit* (along with a play and a board game), and *McTeague* (*Life's Whirlpool* in 1915 and Erich Von Stroheim's famous *Greed* in 1924). His story "The Guest of Honour" has twice been adapted for the stage. Norris has also achieved a considerable reputation as a literary critic. Nearly all of his early criticism appeared during his tenure (1896-1898) on the San Francisco weekly, *The Wave*, where he also wrote news articles, theater and book reviews, interviews, football reports, editorials, features, translations, and short fiction. Earlier in his career he wrote several poems (including his first book, *Yvernelle: A Tale of Feudal France*, 1892), a play (the junior farce for 1892 at the University of California), stories, and essays.

ACHIEVEMENTS

Frank Norris was the first full-blown practitioner of Zolaesque naturalism in America. Like the nineteenth century French writer Émile Zola, Norris often analyzed the effects of heredity, biological instincts, social and cultural influences, and the physical environment on individuals—a strategy that champions a less metaphysical and more scientific approach to looking at life. Although these naturalistic novels are usually considered to be Norris's best writing, his reputation primarily grew during his lifetime because of his productivity and versatility (he wrote six novels and approximately three hundred essays, book reviews, short stories, literary pieces, interviews, and poems). When Norris made the economics of American agriculture the subject of his unfinished trilogy—*The Octopus* deals with the struggle between the wheat growers and the railroad owners, *The Pit* depicts speculators and the Chicago wheat exchange, and *The Wolf* (never written) was to focus on the dispersal of wheat in Europe—he contributed to the muckraking movement at the beginning of the twentieth century. The unfinished trilogy also helped establish the realistic tradition in twentieth century American fiction.

BIOGRAPHY

Although invariably associated with San Francisco and naturalism, Benjamin Franklin Norris, Jr., was actually born in Chicago, the son of a wealthy wholesale jeweler and a former actress (his parents were divorced in 1894). The family moved to Oakland in 1884 and across the bay the following year. Norris's education was desultory, all the more so because of his unwillingness to follow in his father's footsteps as a businessman. From 1887 to 1889 he was enrolled in the Atelier Julien in Paris but had little success as an art student and never did begin the huge painting of the Battle of Crecy he had planned. From 1890 to 1894 he pursued the literary course at the University of California but, owing to a deficiency in mathematics, did not graduate. The next year was more fruitfully spent at Harvard where, as a student in Lewis E. Gates's writing class, he began two novels, first *Vandover and the Brute* and then *McTeague*. In the winter of 1895 to 1896, he took a Richard Harding Davis jaunt to South Africa and became involved in the abortive Uitlander Rebellion. He served on the staff of *The Wave* from April, 1896, to February, 1898, much of the time as its subeditor. His serialized *Moran of the Lady Letty* brought him to the attention of the editor and publisher S. S.

Frank Norris (Library of Congress)

McClure, for whom he worked two years, including a brief stint as a correspondent during the Spanish-American War. In 1900, Norris, with four novels already in print, became a manuscript reader at Doubleday, Page & Company, his new publisher. That same year he married Jeannette Black of San Francisco and "discovered" and championed (unsuccessfully) Theodore Dreiser's novel *Sister Carrie* (1900). *The Octopus*, published the next year, was Norris's first financially successful book. Following the birth of a daughter in February, 1902, and the completion of *The Pit* in July, he began planning the sea cruise which would be part of his research for *The Wolf*, the projected third part of his "The Epic of the Wheat." While in San Francisco, however, Norris was stricken with appendicitis and died on October 25.

ANALYSIS

Except for Jeanette Gilder, in her review of the posthumous collection *The Third Circle*, no one has been so bold as to prefer Frank Norris's short fiction to his novels. In fact, a number of his critics seem to agree with Warren French, who, in a chapter of his *Frank Norris* (1962) entitled "Stubble," decries the fact that the stories have been "undeservedly rescued from the obscurity of the periodicals in which they first appeared." Most believe that Norris wrote the stories as potboilers or, in the case of the stories published in *The Wave*, as apprentice pieces (this despite the fact that drafts of *Vandover and the Brute* and *McTeague* had already been written) and that their value lies solely in whatever light they shed on his longer fiction. It is true that in his literary essays of 1901 and 1902 Norris did equate the short story with money and the novel with truth; moreover, in distinguishing between literature as construction and the more important literature as exploration, he did cite short-story writers Edgar Allan Poe, Frank R. Stockton, and Rudyard Kipling as examples of the former and novelists Gustave Flaubert, Thomas Hardy, and George Eliot as examples of the latter. Norris also contended (in May, 1902) that the continued increase in the publication of short fiction in American magazines, particularly the new low-priced magazines such as *McClure's*, would result in a decrease in the public's demand for short-story collections and ultimately would cause the short story to degenerate to the level of magazine ephemera.

During his *The Wave* period, however—that is to say, during the time prior to his success as a novelist—Norris showed a much greater interest in the possibilities of short fiction. In May, 1897, he wrote that San Francisco is a true story city, where "things can happen"; although it is, he claimed, not yet settled enough for the purposes of the novelist, the city abounds with material for the writer of short stories. A few months earlier, in "The Decline of the Magazine Short Story," he had lamented the "absolutely stupid," "deadly dull" fiction published in the major American magazines. Echoing Hjalmar Boyesen's remarks concerning the "Iron Madonna," he charged that "It is the 'young girl' and the family center table that determine the standard of the American short story." Seeking to challenge this standard, Norris adopted various stylistic elements of those writers, such as Kipling, whom he distinguished from the writers of "safe" fiction. His failure to find a publisher for a collection of these stories does, to some extent, reflect upon their quality (and, as Norris suggests in his semiautobiographical novel *Blix*, 1899, their being commercially out of fashion); but his persistence during late 1897 and 1898 in trying to secure the collection's publication reflects his more-than-passing interest in these writings.

"THE THIRD CIRCLE"

One of the best of his *The Wave* pieces is "The Third Circle." Norris's use of a Chinatown setting in this story and of San Francisco and California locales for nearly all of the fiction of this period evidences the realist method of direct observation. He was less in the tradition of the nostalgic local colorists than of Stephen Crane investigating New York's demimonde and even more of Kipling and Davis depicting settings that were both primitive and foreign to their readers. Basically, the story is a study in limited perception; in it Norris attempts to expose his readers to what he liked to call (in *The Octopus*) the "larger view." The first half of the story concerns an engaged couple from the East and their "lark" in San Francisco's Chinatown. First they "discover" a quaint Chinese restaurant and then invite to their table a Chinese fortune-teller who turns out to be a Kanakan tattooist. Miss Harriet Ten Eyck thinks it would be "awfully queer and original" to have a tattoo, but her fiancé, young Hillegas, reminds her that their "lark" is one thing and the society in which they move quite another: "Let him do it on your finger, then. You never could wear an evening dress if it was on your arm." Once the tattoo is completed—"a grotesque little insect, as much butterfly as anything else"—Hillegas goes off to find their waiter, leaving Harriet alone. Instead of the waiter he finds a Chinese silk merchant to whom he at first speaks condescendingly. Much to his surprise, this "Chinaman" is articulate and cultured. "Here was a side of Chinese life he had not seen, nor even suspected." There is another side as well, as Hillegas discovers when he returns to find his fiancé gone: "He never saw her again. No white man ever did." This is that part of Chinatown Norris terms "the third circle," the part "no one ever hears of."

The second half of the story is set in the late 1890's, twenty years after Miss Ten Eyck's disappearance into white slavery. Here the narrator is no longer simply the teller of the tale, as in the first half, but a participant as well. Like the hapless Eastern couple, he too makes a foray into Chinatown's third circle, but unlike them he has a guide, a "bum" and opium addict "who calls himself Manning." To a degree, the rest of the story follows a predictable course. The narrator tells Manning the story the reader has just read. Manning adds several details and mentions that there is a white slave, Sadie, who works in the opium joint he frequents who might know something further about Miss Ten Eyck. The debased Sadie, an alcoholic and opium addict, without the least desire to escape either her degradation or her addiction, is Harriet Ten Eyck, as the reader figures out long before Norris's rather unsurprising surprise ending: "She thrust out her left hand, and I saw a butterfly tattooed on her little finger."

Despite its unsatisfactory ending, the story does succeed as a study in perception, if not as a tale of suspense. As Norris (by way of Hamlet) points out in the opening sentence, "There are more things in San Francisco's Chinatown than are dreamed of in heaven and earth." Just as young Hillegas discovers aspects of life he had never before suspected and at first entirely misunderstands, so too does Norris's narrator; and readers—specifically the middle- and upper-middle-class readers of *The Wave* for whom the story was written—discover aspects of their own immediate surroundings about which most San Franciscans had, like the Easterner Hillegas, little or no knowledge. Although some readers will be offended by how readily Norris accepted the popular theory of the Chinese as a depraved and inferior race, he does describe the violence, slave trade, and opium traffic then to be found in Chinatown in convincing detail. More important, he makes clear that this depravity extends to the white population itself and that not even a proper middle-class woman such as Harriet Ten Eyck, or, Norris implies, the readers of *The Wave*, are entirely safe from its dangers.

"A REVERSION TO TYPE"

A similar vulnerability is also evident in Norris's more conventionally naturalistic stories. In "A Reversion to Type," for example, Paul Schuster, a forty-one-year-old floorwalker in a San Francisco department store, suddenly bolts from his "sober, steady, respectable life" and for a month lives as an outlaw in the California mining district where he murders the superintendent of the Little Bear mine. Schuster then returns to San Francisco and resumes his commonplace life. On his deathbed, he confesses his crimes but is not believed. A man of his character and steady habits, it is assumed, could not lapse into such criminal behavior. Norris's point is that Schuster's criminality is very much in character—in his hereditary character. As a prison official at San Quentin explains to the narrator (who has just told him Schuster's story), Schuster's grandfather was a "bad egg," a convicted highway robber. "A Case for Lombroso" (which Norris at one time considered titling "A Story for Max Nordau") develops along the same lines. When two young people, Cresencia Hromada and the allegorically named Stayne, become sexually attracted to each other, her pride and morbid passion—both inherited characteristics—and his failure of will combine to turn their love into a perverse and ultimately destructive relationship.

NORRIS'S ROMANTICISM

Norris's interest in these and other rather unsavory subjects derives not from any personal morbidity but instead from his literary theory. Despite his admiration for the novels of William Dean Howells, Norris was impatient with realism's "teacup tragedies." Realism, he maintained, "confines itself to the type of normal life. . . . It notes only the surface of things." Romance, on the other hand, explores "the unplumbed depths of the human heart, and the mystery of sex, and the problems of life, and the black unsearched penetralia of the soul of man." Whereas realism aimed for accuracy, romance went after truth. In such early writings as the stories "The Jongleur of Taillebois" and "Lauth" and the poem *Yvernelle: A Tale of Feudal France*, Norris did write superficially romantic works. Later, however, he developed his theory of naturalism, combining Romanticism's high drama and emphasis on variations from commonplace life with realism's contemporaneity and careful attention to detail.

NORRIS AND THE SHORT FORM

Norris's naturalistic style was more appropriate to his novels, in which the romantic and realistic elements could complement each other, than to his stories, in which his very definition of the genre worked to restrict his generally expansive imagination. Like many other critics of the late nineteenth century, Norris propounded an evolutionary theory of literature. Magazines of the 1890's, he maintained, had only "limited space" for fiction; as a result, the short story was, of necessity, "reduced in some cases to the relation of a single incident by itself, concise, pungent, direct as a blow." (As an unfortunate corollary to this theory of extreme brevity, Norris held that the short-story writer must resort to various "tricks," such as surprise endings.) For the writer of short fiction the chief "difficulty lies not so much in the actual writing, in the condensing and suggesting, etc., as it does in the invention or selection . . . of the original idea, the motive." Taken to the limit, Norris's definition leads to the literary sketch, a form in which he worked often and with much success—for example, the thrice-weekly themes he submitted while a student in Lewis E. Gates's class at Harvard and the "Western City Types" series of 1896. In "Little Dramas of the Curbstone," Norris catenated three sketches into a single work, a technique he later used, with some modification, in one of his finest and best-known stories, "A Deal in Wheat."

"A DEAL IN WHEAT"

Written concurrently with *The Pit*, the second part of his epic trilogy, "A Deal in Wheat" is typical of Norris's work in three respects; its richly detailed portrayal of a phase of American life, its dramatic interest, and its emphasis on the "larger view." The first of the story's five parts (or sketches), "The Bear—Wheat at Sixty-Two," concerns the failure of one small Kansas farmer, Sam Lewiston. When, owing to the machinations of a "bearish" wheat trader in Chicago, the price of wheat plummets well below the cost of raising it, Lewiston is forced to sell his farm and, ironically, find employment in Chicago. In "The Bull—Wheat at a Dollar-Ten," the "bear," Truslow, having forced the price down too far, loses his hold on the market to a "bull," Horung, who for no particular reason and against the advice of his broker chooses not to gore "the Great Bear to actual financial death." That decision turns out to be costly—although not ruinous—for Horung. In "The Pit," a lively account of actual trading in the wheat pit at Chicago's Board of Trade, an unknown bear begins to unload wheat on Horung. In "The Belt Line," a private detective named Cyrus Ryder (also a character in Norris's Three Crows stories of 1901-1902) explains that the wheat Horung has been forced to buy in order to keep the price artificially high does not in fact exist; Truslow has simply routed the same carloads around the city on the railroad belt line he owns, selling the same wheat over and over in order to make up the money he lost when Horung destroyed his corner some months earlier. The ploy merely amuses Horung, who, to cut his own losses, boosts the price to two dollars. In the fifth section, "The Bread Line," Sam Lewiston reappears. Now out of work and temporarily separated from his family, he is seen waiting outside a bakery at midnight, one of the growing number of unemployed forced to depend upon charity. That night there is no free bread, however, only a sign informing the men of the high price of wheat.

Like Hamlin Garland's "Under the Lion's Paw," a story it much resembles, "A Deal in Wheat" vividly dramatizes a social condition about which Norris clearly felt deep concern. Norris is especially successful in evoking sympathy for Sam Lewiston and the economic class he represents. Unfortunately, in the final three paragraphs, Norris abandons objective dramatization and becomes much more openly partisan. Lewiston, the reader learns in Norris's summing up, manages to secure a job and even to do modestly well in the city; in the newspapers, he reads about Truslow's and Horung's deals in wheat and so attains a "larger view" which Norris chooses to make didactically overt rather than dramatically suggestive.

"PERVERTED TALES"

Among Norris's more than eighty-five works of short fiction, there are no truly great stories. His repeated preference for "life, not literature" virtually ensured a certain indifference to aesthetic craftsmanship, an indifference painfully apparent in his melodramatic passages and frequent overwriting. This is

not to say Norris had no understanding of the fine points of literary style, as his borrowings and his six "Perverted Tales," in particular his Stephen Crane parody "The Green Stone of Unrest," make clear. What chiefly characterizes his short fiction are his wide range of subjects and literary forms and his remarkable enthusiasm for writing itself. The works discussed above are certainly his most significant, although there are others which will repay a reader's careful attention: "His Sister" and "Dying Fires," dealing with writers very much like Norris; "A Memorandum of Sudden Death," written in the form of a recovered journal; "This Animal of a Buldy Jones," "Buldy Jones, *Chef de Claque*," and especially "The Associated Un-Charities" (mistitled "The Dis-Associated Charities" in *The Third Circle*) for their slapstick comedy. Finally, there are several nonfiction pieces, such as "Dago Conspirators" and "'A Lag's Release," which are narratively so well constructed that they rise well above the level of the news report to the status of journalistic art.

OTHER MAJOR WORKS

LONG FICTION: *Moran of the Lady Letty*, 1898; *McTeague*, 1899; *Blix*, 1899; *A Man's Woman*, 1900; *The Octopus*, 1901; *The Pit*, 1903; *Vandover and the Brute*, 1914.

POETRY: *Yvernelle: A Tale of Feudal France*, 1892; *Two Poems and "Kim" Reviewed*, 1930.

NONFICTION: *The Responsibilities of the Novelist*, 1903; *The Surrender of Santiago*, 1917; *The Letters of Frank Norris*, 1956; *The Literary Criticism of Frank Norris*, 1964.

MISCELLANEOUS: *The Complete Edition of Frank Norris*, 1928.

BIBLIOGRAPHY

Boyd, Jennifer. *Frank Norris Spatial Form and Narrative Time*. New York: Peter Lang, 1993. Chapters on all of Norris's novels, with discussions of his pictorialism, his relationship to Zola and naturalism, and the structures of his longer fictional works. Includes notes and bibliography.

Dillingham, William. *Frank Norris: Instinct and Art*. Lincoln: University of Nebraska Press, 1969. This study comprises a biographical sketch and a survey of Norris's work. Dillingham argues that certain attitudes of the academicians, such as hard work and close observation, influenced Norris's conception of painting and writing. Stresses naturalism. Includes an annotated bibliography.

Graham, Don, ed. *Critical Essays on Frank Norris*. Boston: G. K. Hall, 1980. A collection of reviews and essays aimed at presenting Norris as a vital and still undefined writer. Among the contributors are Norris's contemporaries William Dean Howells, Willa Cather, and Hamlin Garland. Literary critics include Donald Pizer and William Dillingham.

_____. *The Fiction of Frank Norris: The Aesthetic Context*. Columbia: University of Missouri Press, 1978. This volume is one of the few studies concerning itself with the aesthetics of Norris's work. Much attention is given to his four most literary novels—*Vandover and the Brute, McTeague, The Octopus*, and *The Pit*. Includes an excellent bibliography.

McElrath, Joseph R., Jr. "Beyond San Francisco: Frank Norris's Invention of Northern California." In *San Francisco in Fiction: Essays in a Regional Literature*, edited by David Fine and Paul Skenazy. Albuquerque: University of New Mexico Press, 1995. A discussion of the romantic transformation of the San Joaquin Valley in Norris's local-color sketches, as well as his treatment of San Francisco in some of his novels.

_____. *Frank Norris: A Descriptive Bibliography*. Pittsburgh: University of Pittsburgh Press, 1992.

_____. *Frank Norris Revisited*. New York: Twayne, 1992. An updating and rewriting of a volume that first appeared in 1962 under the authorship of Warren French. This introductory study includes a chapter on the "novelist in the making," followed by subsequent chapters that discuss each of Norris's novels. Includes a chronology, notes, and an annotated bibliography.

Marchand, Ernest. *Frank Norris: A Study*. Stanford, Calif.: Stanford University Press, 1942. The first full-length critical study of Norris, this overview situates Norris's work against a social and intellectual, as well as a literary, background. Considers a wide variety of critical opinions about Norris's fiction. Excellent bibliography.

Marut, David. "Sam Lewiston's Bad Timing: A Note on the Economic Context of 'A Deal in Wheat.'" *American Literary Realism* 27 (Fall, 1994): 74-80. Provides the economic and political context for Norris's story about how grain traders manipulate the market at the expense of the working class in Norris's best-known story.

Walker, Franklin. *Frank Norris: A Biography*. New York: Russell & Russell, 1932. The first full-length biography of Norris, this study is uncritical of its subject. Extraordinarily detailed. Contains personal interviews with Norris's family and friends.

Robert A. Morace, updated by Cassandra Kircher

O

JOYCE CAROL OATES

Born: Lockport, New York; June 16, 1938

OTHER LITERARY FORMS

Joyce Carol Oates is remarkable for the volume and breadth of her literary output. In addition to hundreds of short stories published in collections and various literary journals and popular magazines, Oates produced several volumes of poetry, plays, numerous novels, and edited texts. Furthermore, through interviews, essays, editorship of anthologies and journals, and positions at the University of Windsor and then Princeton University, she engaged in an ongoing dialogue with the North American literary community.

ACHIEVEMENTS

Joyce Carol Oates received National Book Award nominations in 1968 and 1969; she won the award in 1970, for her novel *them* (1969). Other honors include O. Henry Awards in 1967, 1973, and 1983 for her short stories, John Simon Guggenheim Memorial Foundation and Rosenthal Fellowships, and election to the American Academy and Institute of Arts and Letters. She won the Heidemann Award for one-act plays and the Rea Award, both in 1990. Oates was nominated for a National Book Critics Circle Award and a Pulitzer Prize for *Black Water* (1992), and she was nominated for the Nobel Prize in Literature in 1993. She was a Pulitzer finalist again in 1995. In 1996 she won the Bram Stoker Award for Horror and the Fisk Fiction Prize for *Zombie* (1995).

BIOGRAPHY

Joyce Carol Oates was born on June 16, 1938, in Lockport, New York, a small city outside Buffalo. Her father was a tool and die designer, and her childhood was spent in a rural town where she attended a one-room schoolhouse. From earliest memory, she wanted to be an author. As a small child, she drew pictures to tell stories; later, she wrote them, sometimes producing handwritten books of up to two hundred pages, with carefully designed covers. Her youth was simple and happy, and she developed a closeness to her parents that flourished in her adult years.

In 1956, Oates graduated from Williamsville Central High School, where she had written for the school newspaper, and she entered Syracuse University under a New York State Regents Scholarship. During her freshman year, a tachycardiac seizure dur-

Joyce Carol Oates (©Norman Seeff)

ing a basketball game profoundly affected her view of life by bringing her face to face with her mortality. She continued writing, and in 1959 was selected cowinner of the *Mademoiselle* college fiction award for "In the Old World." An excellent student, she was elected Phi Beta Kappa and graduated in 1960 at the top of her class.

She received a Knapp Fellowship to pursue graduate work at the University of Wisconsin, where she met Ph.D. candidate Raymond Joseph Smith. She and Smith were married on January 23, 1961. After receiving her M.A., Oates and Smith moved to Texas, where he taught in Beaumont and she began doctoral work at William Marsh Rice University in Houston. With one of her stories appearing on the Honor Roll of Martha Foley's *Best American Short Stories*, however, Oates decided to devote herself to writing.

Her first collection of stories, *By the North Gate*,

appeared in 1963, followed a year later by her first novel, *With Shuddering Fall* (1964). In 1967, *A Garden of Earthly Delights* appeared as the first novel in a thematic trilogy exploring the American obsession with money. The last of the trilogy, *them* (1969), earned Oates the 1970 National Book Award.

Oates taught at the University of Detroit from 1961 to 1967; then she and Smith moved to the University of Windsor in Ontario, Canada. A prolific author, Oates continued publishing stories in such periodicals as *The Literary Review* and *Cosmopolitan* and produced a steady flow of novels, stories, and poetry. Various other writings—essays, plays, reviews—add to the unusual breadth of her oeuvre.

In 1978, Oates became the Roger S. Berlind Distinguished Professor of Creative Writing at Princeton University in New Jersey. From their home, she and Smith edited *The Ontario Review* and ran a small publishing company. As her body of work grew, so did its formal and thematic diversity. *Bellefleur* (1980), *A Bloodsmoor Romance* (1982), and *Mysteries of Winterthurn* (1984) are experimental ventures into the genres, respectively, of the family chronicle, the romance, and the gothic mystery. In the later 1980's, her work turned toward a modern naturalism.

Oates traveled and lectured widely, and in December, 1987, she was among a group of artists, writers, and intellectuals invited to greet Mikhail Gorbachev, then president of the Soviet Union, at the Soviet Embassy in Washington, D.C. During the 1990's, Oates produced a succession of works that were varied in format. From the novel *Foxfire: Confessions of a Girl Gang* (1993), about the members of an adolescent girl gang, to the gothic short stories in *Haunted: Tales of the Grotesque* and *The Collector of Hearts*, Oates continued to display her versatility and maintain her position as one of the world's most eminent authors. In 1998, she moved into the children's market with *Come Meet Muffin*, an imaginative tale of a brave, adventuresome cat. Her extensive expression as a writer, thinker, and teacher ensured Oates's role as a respected and vigorous participant in the United States' intellectual and literary life from the 1960's onward.

ANALYSIS

Joyce Carol Oates is a very American writer. Early in her career, she drew comparisons with such predecessors as Flannery O'Connor and William Faulkner. The chiefly rural and small-town milieu of her earlier work expanded over the years, as did her vision of passion and violence in the United States in the twentieth century.

It is difficult to separate Oates's short fiction from her novels, for she consistently produced volumes in both genres throughout her career. Unlike many writers who produce both long and short fiction, Oates never subordinated her stories to her novels: They represent in sum a no less considerable achievement, and Oates is by no means a novelist who sometimes writes stories, nor for that matter a storyteller who sometimes writes novels. Both forms figure centrally in her overall work. In many cases, her stories are crystallized versions of the types of characters and dramatic moments found in larger works; over the years, the themes and stylistic approaches in the two genres maintained a parallel progression.

Oates concerns herself with the formulation of the American Dream and how it has changed and even soured through the decades of American prosperity and preeminence. Her characters are often prototypes of the nation, and their growth from naïveté to wisdom and pain reflect aspects of the national destiny that she sees in the evolving society around her. In her short stories, the naïveté is often the innocence of youth; many stories focus on adolescent girls becoming aware of the potential of their own sexuality and the dangers of the adult world. Like the United States, however, such characters retain an unbounded youthful enthusiasm, an arrogant challenge to the future and the outside world.

An individual's relationship to the world around him or her is key to many of Oates's stories. Her fascination with images of the American Dream and the power of belief and self-creation implied therein translates to an awareness of her characters' self-perceptions, and, equally, their self-deceptions. Many of her characters have a built-in isolation: That is not to say that they are not involved with other people, but that their perceptions are necessarily limited, and that they

are aware, though not always specifically, of those limits. Oates often establishes their subjectivity with remarkable clarity, allowing the reader to bring wider knowledge and perspective to the story to fill it out and complete the emotional impact. Isolation, detachment, and even alienation create the obstacles that her characters struggle to overcome, and while Oates has been criticized for the darkness of her writing, as often as not her characters find redemption, hope, and even happiness. Neither the joy, however, nor the tragedy is ever complete, for human experience as Oates sees it is always a complex and mixed phenomenon.

Such complexity naturally emerges from human relationships, especially from those between the sexes. As a female writer, Oates had to deal with the "sexual question" merely in the act of sitting down at the typewriter, and her writing reveals a keen sensitivity to the interactions of men and women. While some of her works toward the end of the 1980's manifest a more explicitly feminist outlook, Oates has never been a feminist writer. Rather, her feminism—or humanism—is subsumed in her refusal to write the kind of stories and novels that women have traditionally written or to limit her male and female characters to typically male and female behaviors, attitudes, emotions, and actions. Oates does not make the sexes equivalent but celebrates the differences and examines feminine and masculine sexual and emotional life without preconceived assumptions. Thus, reading an Oates story is peering into a vision of the world where almost anything is possible between men and women. While they are eminently recognizable as the men and women of the contemporary United States, at the same time they are wholly independent and capable of full response to their inner lives.

Those inner lives often contain ugly possibilities. One of the major complaints that Oates faced, especially early in her career, regards the violence—often random, graphic, even obsessive—that characterizes much of her work. In 1981, in an essay in *The New York Times Book Review* entitled "Why Is Your Writing So Violent?" Oates branded such criticism as blatantly sexist and asserted the female novelist's right to depict nature as she knows it. She clearly sees the United States as a nation where violence is a fact of life. In her novels, such violence takes the form of assassinations, mass murders, rapes, suicides, arsons, autopsies, and automobile accidents. In her short stories, the same events are treated with greater economy and precision but with no less commitment to the vivid portrayal of truth. She shies away from neither the physical details of pain and atrocity nor the psychological realities that accompany them. Even when the violence of her stories is a psychological violence performed by one character upon another, with no effusion of blood and guts, the effects are no less visceral. Oates's stories are deeply felt.

Violence, however, is never the ultimate point of an Oates story. Rather, the violence acts as either catalyst or climax to a dramatic progression: Through violent events, characters undergo inevitable transformations, and the suddenness of violence or the sharpness of pain, either felt or observed, jolts characters into a greater appreciation of life. Frequently, the violent event or action is very peripheral to the protagonist or prime action of the story. Rather, it is often anonymous, perpetrated by unseen hands for unknown reasons, presenting mysteries that will never be solved. Violence becomes an emphatic metaphor for the arbitrary hand of fate, destiny, chance, God—or whatever one wishes to call it. Oates generally portrays it without naming or quantifying it: For her, it is simply the way things are.

Beneath the passion, deep feeling, and violence of her stories, there is a meticulously intellectual mind that is evident, looking at the larger picture, in the wide array of approaches and devices that Oates employs over the range of hundreds of stories. She uses first-, second-, and third-person viewpoints, both male and female. Sometimes dialogue predominates; at other times, the prose is richly descriptive. Some of her stories turn on the use of imagery, tone, or rhythm, and plot is all but nonexistent; others are journalistically rich in event and sparse in stylistic embellishment. Some stories approach the length of novels, others are mere brush strokes, several pages or even a single paragraph to express the crux of a character or dramatic situation. Some stories adhere to the traditional unity and structure of the short story, recounting a single event from beginning to end; others meander, circle in upon themselves, travel backward in time, or derive unity not from the narrative but from character or mood. In brief, Oates uses stories to explore the various tools available to her as a writer. As novelist John Barth noted, "Joyce Carol Oates writes all over the aesthetical map."

In addition, while each story has integrity as a complete work of fiction, Oates devoted great attention to the composition of her collections, and each is unified structurally or thematically and forms an artistic whole as well as an anthology of smaller parts. For example, the stories in Oates's first collection, *By the North Gate*, are largely set in rural, small-town America and show individuals seeking to find order in their lives. *The Wheel of Love* consists of stories exploring varieties of love, and those in *The Goddess and Other Women* are all about women. The volume entitled *Marriages and Infidelities* contains reworkings of popular stories by such masters as Anton Chekhov, Henry James, Franz Kafka, and James Joyce; not only do the stories deal with married people and marital issues, but also the literary approach itself suggests a "marriage" between Oates's tales and the originals on which they are modeled. The collection *The Hungry Ghosts* is unified by the stories' academic settings (places not unlike Oates's own University of Windsor and Princeton) and the vein of satire that runs throughout. The stories in *The Poisoned Kiss* were, according to a prefatory note by Oates, written by a certain Ferdinand de Briao and deal with the exotic, rustic, and more authentically European material that such a gentleman—Oates's own imaginary creation—would naturally devise. *Night-Side* and *The Seduction* contain stories that involve darker, psychologically ambiguous, sometimes surrealistic situations, and the stories in *Last Days* focus on individuals in upheaval and crisis, on the verge of emotional or physical breakdown. Many of the pieces in *Crossing the Border* are linked together by characters—Renee, Evan, Karl, Jake, Cynthia—who appear throughout, and many of those in *Raven's Wing* are set in small towns on the New Jersey coast.

"THE CENSUS TAKER"

A small rural town in mythical Eden County, based loosely on the region of western New York where Oates grew up, is the setting of "The Census Taker," one of the notable stories from *By the North Gate*. It is a simple story involving four relatively anonymous characters—a census taker, a boy, a girl, and a mother—and it is told in simple prose against a hazy, fairy-tale-like landscape. A census taker comes to a remote home to ask questions, but instead of finding the father who can give him the facts that he needs and send him on his way, he is faced with a pair of relentlessly inquisitive children who peel away the layers of his protective delusion in an effort to bring order to their young existence. Eventually, they wear away his confidence in the meaning of any answers, factual or existential, and he leaves without having taken the simplest measure of their household. At heart is the profound mystery of life which, if not confronted with courage, will drive one to seek refuge in madness, blindness, or obsession.

"IN THE REGION OF ICE"

One of Oates's early triumphs in the short story, also dealing with obsession and madness, is a piece entitled "In the Region of Ice." First published in *The Atlantic Monthly* in 1965, and later in *The Wheel of Love*, it was an O. Henry Award-winner for 1967. The protagonist of "In the Region of Ice" is Sister Irene, a Shakespeare lecturer at a small Catholic university. For all practical purposes, she lives "in the region of ice"—a region void of feeling and passion. Perfectly comfortable in front of a class, she is otherwise timid and essentially incapable of developing meaningful human contact.

Into her insulated existence comes Allen Weinstein, a brilliant but emotionally disturbed Jewish student. Obsessed with the reality of ideas, he comes to dominate one of Irene's classes, inspiring the hatred of his classmates but awakening intellectual and emotional life in the professor herself. The story, narrated through Irene's viewpoint, charts the emotional journey that she travels in response to Allen's erratic behavior. Their relationship, through her perception, becomes a dance of intellectual passion and spiritual magnetism.

Allen, however, stops coming to class and, after a prolonged absence, contacts Irene from a sanatorium with a plea that she intervene with his father. The

Christian awakening and power that Irene feels as she approaches the Weinstein home disappear when she is faced with Allen's hateful, exasperated, unsympathetic father. Later, released from the sanatorium, Allen comes to Irene for emotional and financial support, but she painfully and inarticulately denies him, incapable of establishing a meaningful connection. While Allen is clearly on the edge of sanity, Irene's situation is more pathetic, for she is knowingly trapped within the trivial limits of her own selfhood. At the story's end, even the inevitable news of Allen's suicide provokes only a longing for feeling but no true emotional response.

"WHERE ARE YOU GOING, WHERE HAVE YOU BEEN?"

Another story that details the effects of a male intruder into the life of a female protagonist and the difficulty of connection between two very different people is "Where Are You Going, Where Have You Been?," one of Oates's most anthologized early stories. This tale of confused adolescence, based on a true story of a serial killer in Tucson, Arizona, is about Connie, a fifteen-year-old who abhors her parents, haunts suburban malls, and passes the hot summer nights with her equally precocious girlfriends. Through it all, however, she privately harbors innocent dreams of ideal love. One day, while home alone, she is approached by a strange man ominously named Arnold Friend, who is determined to seduce her and take her away. Rather than use force, Friend insinuates his way into Connie's mind and subdues her vulnerable and emerging sexuality. In the end, it is clear that he is leading her to some sort of death, spiritual or physical, and that his love is empty, but she is powerless against him.

Oates tells the story naturalistically but includes dreamy and surrealistic passages that suggest allegorical interpretation. The title implies both the uncertainty of adolescence and the changelessness of feminine behavior, or, possibly, the slow pace of social progress in improving women's lives. Subtly crafted and typically Oatesian, "Where Are You Going, Where Have You Been?" is in some ways a precursor to many later Oates stories. "How I Contemplated the World from the Detroit House of Correction and Began My Life Over Again" is a first-person account of a wayward adolescent girl in search of love and self-definition; the much later "Testimony" portrays a teenage girl who is so devoted to her older boyfriend that she serves as his accomplice in the abduction, rape, and murder of her perceived "rival"; and "April" is a simple sketch of two young adolescents rebelling against maternal authority. These four, and many others, portray moments in time when youth teeters on the brink of adulthood, when innocence is subtly transformed into sophistication, and when desire and love become stronger than life itself.

"THE SCREAM"

The struggles with desire, rebellion, and identity are subtler but no less intense in a story entitled "The Scream." It is a mood piece, in which little happens; the emotional impact is found in the images and the tension of stillness. The protagonist is a woman named Renée who, like many of the characters in the volume *Crossing the Border*, is an American living across the border in Canada. Floundering in a loving but lifeless marriage, she has been having an affair with a man for whom she feels passion but little trust.

The narrative of the story follows Renée as she wanders through an art museum, intentionally absent from an appointed rendezvous with her lover. An old man approaches her; she eavesdrops on talkative tourists; she peruses the art; she ruminates on her marriage, her affair, and her various uninteresting options. One photograph especially catches her attention: that of an Indian woman holding out a dead child, her face frozen in an anguished shriek. After gazing a long while at the photograph, losing herself in it, Renée swiftly leaves the museum and goes to meet her lover. The story ends as she stands outside their meeting place, no more determined to enter than when she started.

The power of the story lies in the photograph as an image. On one hand, the Indian woman's scream touches Renée's own internal anguish, which is magnified by the relative paltriness of her particular discontent. On the other hand, the static quality of the photographic image—the scream does not vanish when Renée looks away and back again—figures her own emotional paralysis. She can see and feel the in-herent contradiction of her quandary—frozen in anguish—and through the experience at the museum can only barely begin to take action for self-liberation.

"IN THE AUTUMN OF THE YEAR"

An even more mature woman is at the center of "In the Autumn of the Year," which received an O. Henry Award in 1979, a year after its first publication in *The Bennington Review*, and which is included in the collection *A Sentimental Education*. Eleanor Gerhardt is a Pulitzer Prize-winning poet, an articulate spinster who has come to a small New England college to accept an award. Her host for the visit is Benjamin Holler, a man she knew when he was a boy in Boston when she was his father's mistress. She was never married, and her passion for Edwin Holler and the dramatic dissolution of their relationship form a memory that she sustains, though she had not seen him in the decades before his death. Upon meeting Benjamin, her consciousness shifts back and forth from the uneventful present to the tumultuous and deeply felt past. Oates here uses balance to create powerful emotional dynamics. The juxtaposition of immediate experience and memory communicates the dislocation with which Eleanor perceives her existence in the "autumn" of her life.

The second half of the story comes suddenly and unexpectedly. In a seemingly casual conversation, Benjamin expresses accumulated anger and hatred at Eleanor and his father. Confronted with the sordidness of their affair and their responsibility for the emotional misery of his childhood, Eleanor's sentimental vision of the past is shattered. Benjamin offers her the love letters and suicide threats that she sent to Edwin upon their separation, but she cannot face them and denies their authenticity. In the end, alone, she tosses the unopened letters in the fire, as if so doing will alleviate her guilt and folly. Benjamin's brutal honesty, however, has provided a missing piece to the puzzle of her life. Without the delusions by which her past drained her present of meaning, she is forced to face the past honestly and, recognizing its mixed qualities, to let go of it. Through this encounter, she can begin to take responsibility for her continued existence and her continued potential to think, feel, do, and live. As so often in Oates's stories, small encounters bring great transformations, and in pain there is redemption.

"RAVEN'S WING"

"Raven's Wing," a story in the volume of the same title, first appeared in *Esquire* and was included in *The Best American Short Stories, 1985*. It is a subtle story that portrays a rather ordinary marriage and lacks the violence and passion of much of Oates's other work. Billy and Linda have been married for barely a year. Though Linda is five months pregnant, Billy treats her with indifference; Linda, in turn, baits, teases, and spites him. A horse-racing enthusiast, Billy becomes fascinated with a prize horse named Raven's Wing after it is crippled during a race. He finds a way to visit Raven's Wing in Pennsylvania, where it is recovering from major surgery, and, eye to eye with the animal, feels a connection, an implicit mixture of awe, sympathy, and trust. The story ends soon thereafter in two brief scenes: Billy gives Linda a pair of delicate earrings and finds excitement in watching her put them on, and, weeks later, as he talks on the phone, Linda comes to him warmly, holding out a few strands of coarse black hair—a souvenir from Raven's Wing—and presses close against him.

In "Raven's Wing," rather than stating the characters' true feelings, of which they themselves are only hazily aware, Oates suggests them through the details of external reality. This is a story about perception—about how things appear differently through the blurring lens of familiarity and routine. Billy's fascination with the crippled horse betrays an unconscious awareness of his own crippled psyche, and the enormous, beautiful, and priceless creature's inevitable consignment to a stud farm is an ironic reminder of Linda's pregnancy and the very human power that a man and woman share to love, to support, and to create.

THE ASSIGNATION

The collection *The Assignation* is stylistically noteworthy, as Oates departs from standard forms and offers a variety of stories, character sketches, mood pieces, and other experiments in short fiction. Many of the pieces are deceptively short; lacking in plot information and often anonymous regarding character, they portray an emotional situation, interaction, or moment through the economic uses of detail and action. The first piece, "One Flesh," is no more than a paragraph suggesting the richly sensual relationship shared by an old couple. In "Pinch," a woman's fleeting emotions during a breast examination create a tense picture. In "Maximum Security," a woman's tour of a prison invokes a disturbing sense of isolation while invigorating her appreciation of nature and freedom. "Quarrel" and "Ace" are about how events of random violence affect, respectively, a homosexual couple's communication and a young street tough's sense of identity. In all these pieces, Oates provides the essentials of a fuller story and invites the reader's imagination to go beyond and within the story. The characters are no less unique, the prose no less picturesque, and the situations no less compelling; the economy with which Oates evokes these tales is testament to the depth of her craft.

WILL YOU ALWAYS LOVE ME?

Will You Always Love Me? is a collection of twenty-two narratives based upon childhood memories, suffering, and reason for hope. Oates cuts to the core of everyday life, revealing the truth about what people know but are not willing to admit. She portrays a profound commentary on the human condition by acting as a witness in describing the needs, cruelty, and violence displayed by humankind. Three of the stories, "You Petted Me, and I Followed You Home," "The Goose-Girl," and "Mark of Satan," won O. Henry Awards.

A lost dog is a central figure in "You Petted Me, and I Followed You Home," a story that first appeared in *TriQuarterly*. Dawn, who fears the erratic behavior and sudden violent acts of her husband Vic, pets a little lost dog, which subsequently follows her and Vic home. Oates skillfully unveils how Dawn's feelings of fear for what lies ahead—of betrayal by loved ones and a terrible sense of lost feeling—parallel the feelings of the dog. By treating the dog with care and kindness, Dawn relays to Vic the need for similar consideration.

Oates examines some of the consequences that result from unbridled thoughts of passion in "The Goose-Girl," which first appeared in *Fiction*. Lydia, a respected suburban mother, helps her son Barry humiliate their new neighbor, Phoebe Stone. Phoebe, who reminds Lydia of the goose-girl in the fairy tales of the Brothers Grimm, propositions Barry at a neighborhood party. Struggling with deep feelings of guilt, Barry eventually reveals the incident to his mother and pleads with her to call Phoebe. After allowing Barry time to worry, Lydia finally makes the call and wittingly embarrasses Phoebe over the proposed sexual encounter with her son.

In "Mark of Satan," which first appeared in *Antaeus*, Oates brings protagonist Flash to a renewed definition of self, even a renewal of spirit. During a visit from Thelma, a female missionary, Flash attempts to seduce her by drugging her lemonade. Thelma instinctively avoids the ploy and tells Flash that Satan is present in his home. Ironically, after Thelma leaves, she returns and prays for Flash. Finally, he realizes that someone cares about him, even though he does not deserve it.

Included in *The Best American Stories, 1996*, "Ghost Girls" emerged from Oates's childhood image of a small country airport isolated between cornfields. Ingrid Boone, the child narrator, is intrigued by the mysterious lives led by her parents. Because she cannot fully comprehend or do anything about the strange adult world that surrounds her, Ingrid's life, influenced by the example of her attractive mother and her frequently absent father, eventually spirals down into a tale of grotesque horrors. "Ghost Girls" is the seed of Oates's *Man Crazy* (1997), a novel of many stark images.

Perhaps the most concise articulation of the Oatesian aesthetic can be found in a story entitled "Love. Friendship.," from *The Assignation*. In recollecting a friendship with a sensitive man who became obsessed with her marriage, the narrator Judith reflects:

> Our lives are narratives; they are experienced in the flesh, sometimes in flesh that comes alive only with pain, but they are recollected as poems, lyrics, condensed, illuminated by a few precise images.

Such descriptive narratives—long, short, lyrical, violent, experienced, recollected, full of precise images portraying real-life situations filled with deep heartfelt emotions—form the bulk of Oates's short fiction.

OTHER MAJOR WORKS

LONG FICTION: *With Shuddering Fall*, 1964; *A Garden of Earthly Delights*, 1967; *Expensive People*, 1968; *them*, 1969; *Wonderland*, 1971; *Do with Me What You Will*, 1973; *The Assassins: A Book of Hours*, 1975; *Childwold*, 1976; *The Triumph of the Spider Monkey*, 1976; *Son of the Morning*, 1978; *Unholy Loves*, 1979; *Cybele*, 1979; *Bellefleur*, 1980; *Angel of Light*, 1981; *A Bloodsmoor Romance*, 1982; *Mysteries of Winterthurn*, 1984; *Solstice*, 1985; *Marya: A Life*, 1986; *Lives of the Twins*, 1987 (as Rosamond Smith); *You Must Remember This*, 1987; *American Appetites*, 1989; *Soul/Mate*, 1989 (as Smith); *Because It Is Bitter, and Because It Is My Heart*, 1990; *I Lock My Door Upon Myself*, 1990; *Nemesis*, 1990 (as Smith); *The Rise of Life on Earth*, 1991; *Black Water*, 1992; *Snake Eyes*, 1992 (as Smith); *Foxfire: Confessions of a Girl Gang*, 1993; *What I Lived For*, 1994; *Zombie*, 1995; *You Can't Catch Me*, 1995 (as Smith); *We Were the Mulvaneys*, 1996; *First Love*, 1996; *Man Crazy*, 1997; *My Heart Laid Bare*, 1998; *Broke Heart Blues*, 1999; *Starr Bright Will Be with You Soon*, 1999 (as Smith); *Blonde*, 2000.

PLAYS: *Miracle Play*, pr. 1974; *Three Plays*, pb. 1980; *In Darkest America: Two Plays*, pb. 1991; *I Stand Before You Naked*, pb. 1991; *Twelve Plays*, pb. 1991; *The Perfectionist and Other Plays*, pb. 1995; *New Plays*, pb. 1998.

POETRY: *Women in Love*, 1968; *Anonymous Sins*, 1969; *Love and Its Derangements*, 1970; *Angel Fire*, 1973; *The Fabulous Beasts*, 1975; *Women Whose Lives Are Food, Men Whose Lives Are Money*, 1978; *Invisible Woman: New and Selected Poems, 1970-1982*, 1982; *The Luxury of Sin*, 1984; *The Time Traveler*, 1987; *Tenderness*, 1996.

NONFICTION: *The Edge of Impossibility: Tragic Forms in Literature*, 1972; *The Hostile Sun: The Poetry of D. H. Lawrence*, 1973; *New Heaven, New Earth: The Visionary Experience in Literature*, 1974; *Contraries: Essays*, 1981; *The Profane Art: Essays and Reviews*, 1983; *On Boxing*, 1987; *(Woman) Writer: Occasions and Opportunities*, 1988; *George Bellows: American Artist*, 1995.

CHILDREN'S LITERATURE: *Come Meet Muffin*, 1998.

EDITED TEXTS: *Scenes from American Life: Contemporary Short Fiction*, 1972; *The Best American Short Stories 1979*, 1979 (with Shannon Ravenel); *Night Walks: A Bedside Companion*, 1982; *First Person Singular: Writers on Their Craft*, 1983; *The Best American Essays*, 1991; *The Oxford Book of American Short Stories*, 1992; *American Gothic Tales*, 1996.

BIBLIOGRAPHY

Bastian, Katherine. *Joyce Carol Oates's Short Stories: Between Tradition and Innovation*. Frankfurt: Verlag Peter Lang, 1983. Bastian surveys the Oatesian short story, providing occasional insights into theme and character. The focus is to place Oates in the tradition of the genre and find her links with its other masters.

Creighton, Joanne V. *Joyce Carol Oates*. Boston: Twayne, 1979. A penetrating exploration of the themes that dominate Oates's work, such as self-definition, isolation, and violent liberation. Creighton devotes a chapter to the experimentalism of five short-story collections. Includes chronology, notes, and an annotated bibliography.

Easterly, Joan. "The Shadow of a Satyr in Oates's 'Where Are You Going, Where Have You Been?'" *Studies in Short Fiction* 27 (Fall, 1990): 537-543. Interprets the character Arnold Friend as a satyr, a demigod from Greek and Roman mythology. Presents a number of arguments about the imagery and structure of the story to support this claim. Asserts Friend is the embodiment of dream, symbolizing the freedom of the imagination as opposed to the discipline of culture and intellect.

Johnson, Greg. "A Barbarous Eden: Joyce Carol Oates's First Collection." *Studies in Short Fiction* 30 (Winter, 1993): 1-14. Discusses Oates's *By the North Gate* as a microcosm of her entire career in fiction. Focuses on her Faulknerian mythmaking, her view of love as a violent force through which characters strive for power, and the similarity of her stories to those of Flannery O'Connor.

_____. *Invisible Writer: A Biography of Joyce Carol Oates*. New York: Penguin Putnam, 1998. Johnson provides a thorough analysis of Oates's work and life in this full-length authorized biography. Draws on a variety of sources, including Oates's private letters and journals.

_____. *Joyce Carol Oates: A Study of the Short Fiction*. New York: Twayne, 1994. After a general introduction to Oates's contribution to the short story, devotes separate chapters to feminism, the gothic, and postmodernism in several of Oates's short-story collections. Includes a number of comments by Oates on the short story, as well as brief excerpts from seven other critics.

_____. *Understanding Joyce Carol Oates*. Columbia: University of South Carolina Press, 1987. Geared to the general reader, this volume examines both Oates's major novels and some of her best-known stories. The focus is more on specific works than on Oates's overarching concerns. Easy to read, with a biography and bibliography.

Wagner, Linda, ed. *Critical Essays on Joyce Carol Oates*. Boston: G. K. Hall, 1979. A good collection of twenty-eight reviews and essays, some on particular works, others on general themes or stylistic considerations. The short stories receive less attention than the novels and even, surprisingly, the poetry. Extensive and evenhanded, with a chronology and bibliography, and a short but refreshing preface by Oates herself.

Wesley, Marilyn. *Refusal and Transgression in Joyce Carol Oates's Fiction*. Westport, Conn.: Greenwood, 1993. A feminist analysis, this work focuses on the family as portrayed in Oates's fiction. Wesley contends that the young protagonists of many of Oates's stories and novels commit acts of transgression that serve as critiques of the American family. Wesley maintains that the acts indict the society that produces and supports these unstable, dysfunctional, and often violent, families.

Barry Mann, updated by Alvin K. Benson

EDNA O'BRIEN

Born: Tuamgraney, Ireland; December 15, 1930

PRINCIPAL SHORT FICTION

The Love Object, 1968
A Scandalous Woman and Other Stories, 1974
Mrs. Reinhardt and Other Stories, 1978 (pb. in
    U.S. as *A Rose in the Heart*, 1979)
Seven Novels and Other Short Stories, 1978
Returning, 1982
A Fanatic Heart, 1984
Lantern Slides, 1990

OTHER LITERARY FORMS

Besides short stories, Edna O'Brien has written dramas (including screenplays and teleplays), poetry (*On the Bone*, 1989), children's literature (*The Dazzle*, 1981), and novels such as *A Pagan Place* (1970), *Night* (1972), *The Country Girls Trilogy and Epilogue* (1986), *House of Splendid Isolation* (1994), *Down by the River* (1996), and *Wild Decembers* (1999). She has also published nonfiction, including autobiographical travel books such as *Mother Ireland* (1976), newspaper articles, and biographical and literary criticism such as *James and Nora* (1981), and *James Joyce* (1999). She has also edited the anthology *Some Irish Loving* (1979).

ACHIEVEMENTS

After a strong start in the early 1960's with three splendid short novels in the *Bildungsroman* tradition of maturation and escape (*The Country Girls*, 1960, winner of the Kingsley Amis Award; *The Lonely Girl*, 1962, reprinted as *Girl with Green Eyes*, 1964; and *Girls in Their Married Bliss*, 1964), Edna O'Brien established herself publicly in a variety of television appearances. She became a most articulate spokeswoman for a not overly romantic view of Ireland, for women trapped in an eternal mother-daughter conflict, and for some feminists. The last-mentioned achievement is reached paradoxically in O'Brien's fictions by her frequent exploration and exploitation of an unsympathetic woman in the leading role—the Caithleen (Kate) of the early novels. O'Brien has very few male leads or narrators. Her Kate-women often are whiners and losers who make poor choices in their liaisons with men (often already married), which inevitably bring grief. Her depiction of character, setting (particularly in Ireland—Philip Roth has praised her sense of place), and conflict is, however, so strong, so graphic, and often in such memorable language, appealing to all the senses, that the negative point is made: This is not how a woman, or indeed any person, seeking happiness should go about the search "for love or connection."

At her best, O'Brien has another counterbalancing woman present as a foil, such as the ebullient Baba, the other heroine with Kate in her early novels; this confident voice is particularly strong in *Girls in Their Married Bliss* and *Night*, an extended "Baba" monologue in the fashion of Joyce's Molly Bloom in *Ulysses* (1922). O'Brien's achievement is to take her readers some distance along the road to realizing what it is to be an integrated, and therefore a happy, person. She is at her best when the setting of her fictions is rural Ireland, not the jet-setters' London or Mediterranean. O'Brien is most popular in the United States, where she gives frequent readings of her work. She is a gifted re-creator of the sights, smells, tastes, and feel of Ireland—with a vivid way of capturing what people might say, at their colorful best.

BIOGRAPHY

As the youngest child in a Roman Catholic family that included a brother and two sisters, Josephine Edna O'Brien was born on December 15, 1930, and grew up on a farm in the west of Ireland. She was educated at the local parochial school in Scarriff and was a boarder in the Convent of Mercy, Loughrea, County Galway. She went to Dublin to study pharmacy in the apprentice system then in vogue and began contributing to the *Irish Press*. In 1954, O'Brien married writer Ernest Gebler, author of *Plymouth Adventure*, 1950; they had two sons, Carlo and Sasha.

The family moved to London, where O'Brien es-

Edna O'Brien in 1990 (©1990, Terry O'Neill)

tablished her permanent residence and wrote *The Country Girls* in her first month there. She followed it quickly with the other parts of the trilogy, *The Lonely Girl* and *Girls in Their Married Bliss*. Though O'Brien and Gebler have argued in print over just how much help he gave her with the trilogy (the marriage was dissolved in 1964), O'Brien was launched on a successful, high-profile career. *The Lonely Girl* was made into a film, *Girl with Green Eyes*, starring Rita Tushingham.

Based in London, very successfully bringing up her sons on her own, O'Brien had two most prolific decades of work, in a variety of genres. The novels accumulated: *August Is a Wicked Month* (1965); *Casualties of Peace* (1966); *A Pagan Place*, her favorite work; *Zee and Co.* (1971); *Johnny I Hardly Knew You* (1977); and, after what was for O'Brien a long hiatus, *The Country Girls Trilogy and Epilogue* (1986), *The High Road* (1988), and other contemporary-setting novels including *Wild Decembers* (1999). Between

novels, she published short stories in a variety of magazines (*The New Yorker* in particular), the best of which have been collected. Along with prose fiction, journalism, and travel books, O'Brien also continued her interest in drama: *A Cheap Bunch of Nice Flowers* (1962), *Time Lost and Time Remembered* (1966), *X, Y, and Zee* (1971), and *Virginia* (1980).

O'Brien's biography provides the raw material for her fictions. "All fiction is fantasized autobiography," she affirms in the introduction to *An Edna O'Brien Reader* (1994). In 1984 and 1986, she published in New York a pair of matched volumes: *A Fanatic Heart*, largely from the best of her previously collected stories, and, what many would consider her best work, *The Country Girls Trilogy and Epilogue*, of which a twenty-one-page last section is entirely new. For a while, it seemed that the well of inspiration was exhausted. In 1988, however, she was back again in New York with *The High Road*, published after a ten-year novel-writing hiatus. She also presented a reading in New York in 1990 of "Brother," from her short-story collection *Lantern Slides* and autographed her poem *On the Bone* (1989).

Analysis

Edna O'Brien has written short stories throughout her long career. "Come into the Drawing Room, Doris" (retitled "Irish Revel" in *The Love Object* collection) first appeared in *The New Yorker*, on October 6, 1962. "Cords," published as "Which of Those Two Ladies Is He Married To?" in *The New Yorker*, on April 25, 1964, adumbrates many of the aspects of loss and missed connections, which are O'Brien's constant themes. The missed connections are most frequently between mothers and daughters, and between women and men. O'Brien is at her most persuasively graphic when her protagonists are clearly Irish women, at home, in a vanished Ireland whose society as a whole she re-creates and often increasingly indicts most convincingly.

"Cords"

The question above, which forms the original title of "Cords," is posed in the story by Claire's scandalized, rural, Irish mother on a London visit to her sexually active, editor, lapsed Catholic, poet-daughter.

The dinner guests are a husband, his pregnant wife Marigold, and his mistress Pauline—which grouping elicits the mother's question. The newer title, "Cords," more aptly focuses attention on the constrictive mother-daughter bond, which is at the center of this story. The conflict is effectively rendered; no final judgment is made on who is to blame. The Catholic, self-sacrificing mother, who masochistically sews without a thimble, is a spunky traveler. The rather precious daughter, with her "social appendages" but no friends, "no one she could produce for her mother [or herself] and feel happy about," for her part means well. The two similarly looking women are deftly shown to be on a collision course, not just with their umbrellas or their differences over food. The detailed parts of the story all function smoothly. The mother looks at herself in a glass door; Claire sees herself reflected in a restaurant's mirrors. Each woman is herself and an image projected elsewhere. The constraint between them is vividly rendered from their moment of meeting until they are at the airport again, where both "secretly feared the flight number would never be called."

In the background here, in Claire's thoughts, is the father, "emaciated, crazed and bankrupted by drink," with whom the mother's unhealthy, symbiotic relationship continues: "She was nettled because Claire had not asked how he was." In "Cords," then, are many of the perennial, rush-of-memory themes: the family feuding, the malevolent church influence, the searing, almost flawlessly detailed exposé of the tie that binds many mothers and daughters. All is rendered here with the saving grace of good humor, and even old jokes are recalled, such as those about good grazing on the Buckingham Palace lawns, about Irish planes being blessed and therefore never crashing, and about an overly heavy suitcase—"Have you stones in it?"Claire asks.

"A SCANDALOUS WOMAN"

"A Scandalous Woman" sets the tone for O'Brien's second collection, named after it, and reveals an increasingly gloomy view of the female predicament, whether in Ireland or elsewhere. The story, published in 1974, concludes, "I thought that ours indeed was a land of shame, a land of murder, and a land of strange, [to which is added in the stronger *A Fanatic Heart* version, 'throttled'] women." Here is an indictment of a family, its church, and society, very like that in *A Pagan Place*, and to be seen again in "Savages." The anonymous narrator leads the reader through Eily's life from early courtship days until the moment when the narrator, now no longer a young girl but a mother herself, seeks out her childhood friend, to find her much changed: "My first thought was that they must have drugged the feelings out of her . . . taken her spark away." "They" and their "strange brews" are part of the "scandalous" environment of this pagan place.

The anonymous narrator graphically describes how, as a young girl, she admired and sought the company of Eily, who was a few years older and had the "face of a madonna." The narrator tells how she loved Eily and visited her home each Tuesday, even though this meant that she had to play, in the hospital game, the patient to Eily's sister's surgeon. Lying on the kitchen table, she saw "the dresser upside down" in a world whose values are far from upright either. It is Eily, however, who is hollowed out at the story's end: Her playing Juliet to her Protestant Romeo, a bank clerk named Jack, ends in Eily's sniveling at a shotgun wedding. The young narrator had acted as lookout and cover so Eily could meet her lover, "Sunday after Sunday, with one holy day, Ascension Thursday, thrown in." When Jack attempts to throw Eily over, the narrator reveals in herself the same confusion of pagan and Christian values of the others:

> I said . . . that instead of consulting a witch we ought first to resort to other things, such as novenas, putting wedding cake under our pillows, or gathering bottles of dew in the early morning and putting them in a certain fort to make a wish.

The combined forces of the family, church, and community, in a profusion of animal imagery, move events along to the marriage solution.

This is a dense, beautifully put together story, packed with details of the repressive effects of parents, school, and church on a lively girl, who is cowed into submission. From the symbolism of the upside-down world observed by the child on the kitchen table to the loaded "Matilda" term for the female genitalia (between "ma" and "da," there "I" am), everything in this story contributes to the indictment and ironic redefinition of what is "scandalous."

MRS. REINHARDT AND OTHER STORIES

O'Brien's pessimism about much of the female condition shows little alleviation in the *Mrs. Reinhardt and Other Stories* collection, heavily though erratically edited and renamed *A Rose in the Heart* in the American edition. The stories overall continue to chronicle the depressing, unsuccessful search of O'Brien's heroines for happiness in, but more often out of, marriage. Other perennial themes such as loss, isolation, motherhood, and bigotry are not neglected, especially when the setting is Ireland. The gothic story "Clara" has a rare male narrator.

The stories "Number Ten" and "Mrs. Reinhardt" fit together and were in fact dramatized as a unit in a 1981 drama prepared for the British Broadcasting Corporation. Tilly, in a failing marriage with her art-dealer husband, Harold, sleepwalks her way into misery. For the normally self-centered O'Brien woman who lives, especially when in England, in an economic and social vacuum (very unlike O'Brien's own successful career), Tilly's two afternoons a week teaching autistic children is unusual and helps her credibility. In her dreams, she sees the perfect "nest"—an apartment, with one entire bedroom wall a mirror, where she and her husband can come together at night. The apartment, surreally, does exist, she discovers, and her husband uses it in the daytime with another woman. It is a rending, no-communication stand-off; the unhappy O'Brien woman remains "an outsider looking in."

In the second tale, Mrs. Reinhardt heads off to color-splashed Brittany for a trial separation, determined to somnambulate no more. She resolves to forget the past and to "get even with life" by taking advantage of a brash Iowan in his mid-twenties whom she meets by the sea. It is an ugly picture that O'Brien paints of Tilly's sexual conduct, which is as predatory as that of the lobsters she observes in their tank. In this bleak tale, neither the love of the old patron at the hotel nor the arrival of Tilly's husband

does much to alleviate: "What then does a Mrs. Reinhardt do? . . . One reaches out to the face that is opposite . . . for the duration of a windy night. And by morning who knows? Who knows anything anyhow?" Such is the pessimistic conclusion to this fiction; O'Brien's aging heroine's search continues.

RETURNING

O'Brien's sharp study of a certain kind of female psychology continues in the collection *Returning*, where the external topography in all nine stories is the west of Ireland and the craggy community there. A young girl is present in all the collection's stories, either as the ostensible narrator or as the subject of mature reflection on the part of the now-experienced woman. This then-and-now tension between the innocence of childhood and the experience of fifty years, Philip Roth, in his introduction to *A Fanatic Heart*, isolates as the spring for these stories' "wounded vigor." There is no title story of the same name, but in a very real sense each of the tales here represents a return for O'Brien, a going home.

"Savages," in this collection, represents O'Brien, often accused of careless, awkward, and too-rapid writing, at her careful, three-times-reworked best. The theme bears distinct similarities to "A Scandalous Woman" in its indictment of the community. The story deals with Mabel McCann's search for love in her village community, her false pregnancy, and ostracism. The three published versions of the story that exist (the version published in *The New Yorker*, January 18, 1982; the English edition; and the version in *A Fanatic Heart*) help reveal O'Brien's artistic development, which, though it is by no means a straight-line progression, nevertheless represents work and progress. A noticeable distancing and maturing in the narrator can be seen from the first version to the second one, where she is no longer a precocious twelve-year-old. The second version introduces the five-hundred-word addition of a lugubrious scene between a deaf-and-dumb brother and sister to underscore the gothic qualities of the environment. While all is not unequivocal, there is artistic progress in this second version, where Mabel is called a "simpleton" in the conclusion. In the third and final version, this term, removing her from the world of choices, is wisely dropped; readers are left to work out for themselves what happened. This emendation is a final improvement in the best overall version of an excellent story. The collection also includes the sensory-rich "Sister Imelda," which received the accolade of inclusion in the 1986 *Norton Anthology of English Literature.*

A FANATIC HEART

A Fanatic Heart includes twenty-five O'Brien stories previously anthologized and a quartet of *The New Yorker,* heretofore uncollected works, in a splendidly produced volume introduced by Roth. The quartet is typical of O'Brien's writing when she is on the brittle high road outside Ireland and is generally much less satisfactory. The shallow, codependent Irish woman of these stories moves in three of them through bitter, first-person musings on a current, seemingly doomed affair of the heart with a married family man. Only in the second story, "The Call," is she looked at in the third person as she does not answer the ringing telephone. It is time to cease to be strangers, she muses in "The Plan." In a later version of this tale, though, O'Brien cut the pessimistic note that follows immediately, "Though of course we would always be strangers." The "blue" narrator takes a geographical cure to forget, but that does not work, and readers are left with her wondering in "The Return" how much longer she will be able to endure.

"ANOTHER TIME"

In "Another Time," in the collection *Lantern Slides,* the narrator, a single parent and glamorous former television announcer, gets away to her home in the west of Ireland. After a series of sharply observed encounters with and flashbacks to places and people, Nelly Nugent comes to terms with the present: "She felt as if doors or windows were swinging open all around her and that she was letting go of some awful affliction." At her best, O'Brien has the capacity in her fictions to give this release to her readers. The mirrors that appear so often in her work serve then to alert not only her recurring characters but also her readers to the roller-coaster realities of love, loss, and endurance. This work was selected for *The Best New Yorker Stories of 1989,* in which magazine four others of the dozen stories in this collection also appeared.

"LOVE'S LESSON"

Whatever the question is, O'Brien's answer is love; this story, then, which appeared in *Zoetrope* (Summer, 1998) closes out a decade in which no collection appeared after *Lantern Slides.* The varieties-of-love theme continued in the 1990's to dominate O'Brien's short fictions, beginning with "No Place" (*The New Yorker,* June 17, 1991) where her well-off, ageless, lonely, Irish protagonist, her two boys still in boarding school, waits "on love" in North Africa; her man fails to show up from London's rougher-trade side. Still, in *The New Yorker* (July 11, 1994), a now aging, lonely widow, the love of her children growing "fainter and fainter," her husband's "unloving love" now a memory, shows herself in "Sin" to be far from well as she pictures her paying guests' incestuous relations with their daughter: "What reached her ears could not be called silence."

In "Love's Lesson" a jagged, uneven, disconnected, at times overwritten letter from an Irish woman in New York City reviews the course of her affair with a celebrated architect. Her relationship with him has magnified her feeling of being an outsider. Cosmopolitan and international in her experiences and sympathies, she is yet setting out for home, the mysteries of love still mysterious: "Now we will never know for sure." The lessons taught here by "love" in its various manifestations send the protagonist home to freedom, "to give up the habit of slavery." Freedom has its costs, too. Nor is there any free love as the narrator discovers, reviewing her violent relationship with the architect, which she wishes was just physical. She shares her lesbian relationship with her friend Clarissa, who is greatly troubled by thoughts of her dead mother, as is the nameless narrator. People she meets and observes, all with their "connection" problems, cause her to book her flight home.

Given the personal-journal format here, reinforced by O'Brien's ongoing admiration for and work on master wordsmith James Joyce, the stream-of-consciousness technique is to be expected. O'Brien's best prior example of this technique is her *Night.* Here, in "Love's Lesson," she continues her alliterative reaching for metaphorical, verbal epiphanies through all the senses to establish the mood. Sometimes she is successful, sometimes not: "Skeins of sound sweetening the air." Here then O'Brien's Irish heroine, alone, courageously as ever, confronts life and the varieties and manifestations of love. The constraints of the Roman Catholic Church and rural society have no place here, but family pressures are not absent, nor is the gallant hope with which her secular heroines view life as they must live it.

OTHER MAJOR WORKS

LONG FICTION: *The Country Girls*, 1960; *The Lonely Girl*, 1962 (reprinted as *Girl with Green Eyes*, 1964); *Girls in Their Married Bliss*, 1964; *August Is a Wicked Month*, 1965; *Casualties of Peace*, 1966; *A Pagan Place*, 1970; *Zee and Co.*, 1971; *Night*, 1972; *Johnny I Hardly Knew You*, 1977 (pb. in U.S. as *I Hardly Knew You*); *The Country Girls Trilogy and Epilogue*, 1986; *The High Road*, 1988; *Time and Tide*, 1992; *An Edna O'Brien Reader*, 1994; *House of Splendid Isolation*, 1994; *Down by the River*, 1996; *Wild Decembers*, 1999.

PLAYS: *A Cheap Bunch of Nice Flowers*, pr. 1962; *A Pagan Place*, pr. 1972; *The Gathering*, pr. 1974; *Virginia*, pr. 1980; *Flesh and Blood*, pr. 1985.

SCREENPLAYS: *Girl with Green Eyes*, 1964; *Time Lost and Time Remembered*, 1966 (with Desmond Davis); *Three into Two Won't Go*, 1969; *X, Y, and Zee*, 1971.

TELEPLAYS: *The Wedding Dress*, 1963; *Nothing's Ever Over*, 1968; *Mrs. Reinhardt*, 1981; *The Country Girls*, 1983.

POETRY: *On the Bone*, 1989.

NONFICTION: *Mother Ireland*, 1976; *Arabian Days*, 1977; *James and Nora*, 1981; *Vanishing Ireland*, 1986; *James Joyce*, 1999.

CHILDREN'S LITERATURE: *The Dazzle*, 1981; *A Christmas Treat*, 1982; *The Expedition*, 1982; *The Rescue*, 1983; *Tales for the Telling: Irish Folk and Fairy Stories*, 1986.

EDITED TEXT: *Some Irish Loving*, 1979.

BIBLIOGRAPHY

Dunn, Nell. "Edna." In *Talking to Women*. London: Macgibbon and Kee, 1965. In this thirty-eight-page, wide-ranging talk with O'Brien, the topics discussed range from the difficulties facing a single-parent writer to aging. O'Brien in this revealing, autobiographical interview, shares her thoughts on family, love, and relationships. Contains no bibliography, index, or chronology.

Eckley, Grace. *Edna O'Brien*. Lewisburg, Pa.: Bucknell University Press, 1974. This excellent, eighty-eight-page study is the first such on O'Brien. The themes perceptively discussed in O'Brien's extremely personal work include preeminently love and loss.

Gillespie, Michael Patrick. "(S)he Was Too Scrupulous Always." In *The Comic Tradition in Irish Women Writers*, edited by Theresa O'Connor. Gainesville: University Press of Florida, 1996. Discusses how O'Brien's humor is distinguished from that of Irish male writers; shows the relationship between her humor and that of James Joyce, particularly the relationship between her short stories and those in *Dubliners* (1914).

Guppy, Shusha. "The Art of Fiction: Edna O'Brien." *The Paris Review* 26 (Summer, 1984): 22-50. The topics discussed include how O'Brien got started on her writing career; the writers, such as James Joyce, Marcel Proust, and Anton Chekhov, whom she admires; feminism, into which O'Brien fits uneasily; religion; Ireland; and other areas, such as theater and film, in which O'Brien has worked. At fifty-four, O'Brien affirms that she is putting the themes of love, loss, and loneliness behind her. She recommends *A Pagan Place* as her best book.

O'Brien, Edna. "Interview." *Paris Review* 26 (Summer, 1984): 22-50. O'Brien discusses the influence of Chekhov on her stories, the animosity of feminists to much of her writing, the theme of Ireland in her stories, and her focus on sexuality in many of her stories.

_____. "The Pleasure and the Pain." Interview by Miriam Gross. *The Observer* (April 14, 1985): 17-18. A provocative interview, interesting also in that, two weeks later, it draws from Ernest Gebler, O'Brien's former husband, a detailed rebuttal of her statements about him (*The Observer*, April 28, 1985) and an incendiary interview with him (*Sunday Independent*, April 28, 1985, 7).

_____. *Publishers Weekly* 239 (May 18, 1992): 48-49. O'Brien discusses her relationship with her mother, her calling to become a writer, her interest in the Gospels and the writings of Catholic mystics, and her relationship with her editors.

O'Brien, Peggy. "The Silly and the Serious: An Assessment of Edna O'Brien." *The Massachusetts Review* 28 (Autumn, 1987): 474-488. An overview of O'Brien's work, discussing her central themes and critiquing critical reception of her stories. Argues that her obsession with a father figure makes her portray sexually insatiable women in disastrous relationships with hurtful men.

O'Hara, Kiera. "Love Objects: Love and Obsession in the Stories of Edna O'Brien." *Studies in Short Fiction* 30 (Summer, 1993): 317-326. Discusses O'Brien's characters' obsession with love, which stands in the way of love's attainment. Discusses "Irish Revel" from her 1969 collection *The Love Object* as the birth of the obsession and the title story of her 1990 collection *Lantern Slides* as the epitome of it.

Shumaker, Jeanette Roberts. "Sacrificial Women in Short Stories by Mary Lavin and Edna O'Brien." *Studies in Short Fiction* 32 (Spring, 1995): 185-197. Examines sacrificial women in two stories by Lavin and two by O'Brien; claims that in the stories, female martyrdom engendered by the Madonna myth has different forms, from becoming a nun to becoming a wife, mother, or "fallen woman."

Woodward, Richard B. "Edna O'Brien: Reveling in the Heartbreak." *The New York Times Magazine* (March 12, 1989): 42, 50, 52. An up-close and unsympathetic portrait, with a color photo, of O'Brien, whom Woodward, after several meetings and much research, calls "a poet of heartbreak." This careful essay shows an off-putting, publicity-hunting, and difficult side of the deliberately apolitical O'Brien. Woodward does not find that *The High Road* breaks any new ground, in contrast to the affirmation of Shusha Guppy; he finds her short fiction more accomplished.

Archibald E. Irwin

FITZ-JAMES O'BRIEN

Born: County Limerick, Ireland; c. 1828
Died: Cumberland, Maryland; April 6, 1862

PRINCIPAL SHORT FICTION

The Poems and Stories of Fitz-James O'Brien, 1881
The Diamond Lens, with Other Stories, 1885
What Was It? and Other Stories, 1889
The Fantastic Tales of Fitz-James O'Brien, 1977

OTHER LITERARY FORMS

Fitz-James O'Brien's "Oh: Give a Desert Life to Me" in the Irish nationalist newspaper *The Nation* (1845) was the first of hundreds of his poems published in Irish, English, and American newspapers, journals, and literary magazines. Many poems can be read with pleasure by the modern reader; "The Finishing School," a long satiric poem on Madame Cancan's New York School for women, is one example. O'Brien wrote at least six plays; *A Gentleman from Ireland* (1854), a two-act comedy, is the best known, having been staged at Wallack's Theatre in New York during his lifetime. He also wrote innumerable essays, dramatic reviews, articles on varied subjects, and narratives for periodicals, including *Atlantic Monthly, Knickerbocker, Putnam's Magazine, Harper's New Monthly Magazine, Harper's Weekly, Vanity Fair, The American Whig Review, Lantern,* and *Home Journal.*

ACHIEVEMENTS

Although Fitz-James O'Brien was born in Ireland and began his literary career there and in England before emigrating to the United States, his short stories are more within the American than the Irish tradition of that genre. Some critics have labeled O'Brien a minor Edgar Allan Poe. A figure of New York's bohemian literary scene in the 1850's, he wrote much poetry, several plays, and a number of short stories that appeared in many of the popular newspapers and magazines of the day. Although one of his plays was produced as late as 1895 and his verse was widely published in his own lifetime, his literary reputation had declined even before his death. Several of his short stories, however, possibly influenced later writers such as Ambrose Bierce and Guy de Maupassant, and the application of his gothic imagination to science and pseudoscience, placed within a realistic setting, has influenced such modern practitioners of science fiction and fantasy as H. P. Lovecraft and Abraham Merritt.

BIOGRAPHY

Fitz-James O'Brien was the only child of an Irish attorney who died when Fitz-James was twelve years old. He lived better than most Irishmen. Educated at the University in Dublin, he never caught the rising political fever of his day, although he did contribute to *The Nation*. In 1849, on reaching twenty-one, he inherited his father's estate and emigrated to London. By 1851, he sailed to New York after squandering his fortune; in New York City he established himself as a journalist, a poet, and a soldier. O'Brien never married. In 1861, he joined the New York Seventh Regiment sent to the defense of Washington. Following a duel with a Confederate Colonel in 1862, he died from tetanus after six weeks of intense pain.

ANALYSIS

The judgment of Fitz-James O'Brien's friends that "The Wondersmith" and "The Diamond Lens" were remarkable stories and pacesetters for other writers was a sound one; the two stories represent the best of O'Brien's short tales. The plots move quickly as the human characters interact with fantastic creatures,

Fitz-James O'Brien (Library of Congress)

demons, and spirit mediums. Murder and mystery heighten the degree of horror evoked in the reader. The stories do not carry a message, moral, or meaning by which man is to pattern his life, although messages, morals, and meanings are evident. Written to entertain the readers of the *Atlantic Monthly*, these stories satisfied the desire for fictional horror. O'Brien held his audience by unfolding the plot through a series of dramatic episodes. By fusing fact with fiction, a blend of science and pseudoscience and good with evil, he created another world which came to life through vivid descriptive passages.

"THE DIAMOND LENS"

"The Diamond Lens," set in New York, is narrated by the protagonist, Linley, a master of deceit and cunning. This first deception involves his studying optics while telling his family that he is studying medicine. Setting up a laboratory in his apartment, he is a true scientist, experimenting, investigating, and theorizing about optics. Simon, a young French Jew then introduces the pseudoscientific element—Mrs. Vulpes, a spirit medium. She conjures up the spirit of Leeuwenhoek, which instructs Linley on the mechanics of the perfect microscope. He learns that a one-hundred-and-forty-carat diamond is necessary to construct the universal lens for the perfect microscope. Coincidentally, Simon has such a diamond. Linley murders him, rationalizing that his act is a service to mankind, although when the perfect microscope is made, it is to serve him.

When Linley examines a common drop of water, the reader is hardly prepared for the vision he sees: a gaseous globule infused with supernatural light with clouds and forests of unbelievable hues. Through the colored clouds, a perfect female form emerges which Linley calls Animula—the "divine revelation of perfect beauty"—and he promptly falls in love with the phantom figure. The impossible nature of the relationship is later recognized by the lover, who tries to break the spell to no avail.

Linley, frustrated by Animula's inability to return his passion, seeks the company of Signorina Caradolce, the most beautiful and graceful woman in the world; but he finds her ugly and her movements grotesque, and he hurries home. There he finds Animula suffering, convulsed in pain, her beauty fading; her multichromatic fantasy world is growing dim, and she is dying. Linley checks the water drop; it has evaporated. Haunted by his memories, he goes mad. Even in his madness, he shows no hint of repentance of his deeds; he only weeps for his lost love. The author leaves the reader to discover a moral for his tale.

"THE WONDERSMITH"

O'Brien's skill is again apparent in "The Wondersmith," which describes a deeper level of evil, cruelty, and terror than that seen in "The Diamond Lens." The story revolves around murder, science, pseudo-science, and an unusual love story, along with rituals which demonstrate that demonology is not dead. Everything takes place on Golosh Street, a ghetto off Chatham Street in New York. To the passerby, Herr Hippe and Madame Filomel are ordinary residents of Golosh Street. He is the wondersmith, a maker of lifelike toys, and she is a run-of-the-mill gypsy fortune-teller. In reality, they are bohemians; O'Brien uses the words gypsy and bohemian interchangeably,

but there is no doubt that these bohemians are special gypsies. Hippe is Duke Balthazar of Lower Egypt, possessor of the secrets of the ages; Filomel is one of his followers.

Hippe and Filomel are of a lower cast than Philip Brann of another tale, "The Bohemian." English by birth, Brann is a mesmerizer and operates alone. Confident of his supernatural powers, Brann chides Edgar Allan Poe, whom he identifies as a bohemian. Instead of using his powers, Poe simply writes about them. According to Brann, Poe should dig up buried treasures, as does Brann, rather than merely describe such things.

The Duke and the hag Filomel are joined by Kerplonne, a French gypsy, and Oaksmith, another English gypsy, to plan the slaughter of millions of innocent Christian children. By magical incantation, Madame Filomel, upon uncorking a black bottle of souls, animates a series of puppets, each of which, carrying a sword or dagger of some type, is an image of evil. A practice session is first arranged for the "Lilliputian assassins," during which they slaughter a roomful of caged birds. O'Brien describes this scene with vivid passages of blood and gore.

Counterbalancing this scene, O'Brien introduces a strange love affair between Solon, a hunchbacked bookseller of Golosh Street, and Zonela, Hippe's daughter (she is not really his daughter, having been kidnapped from a Hungarian nobleman). When Hippe accidentally discovers the lovers conversing in Zonela's room, he almost goes mad with rage against the cripple who dared to comfort his captive. Another unequal fight ensues, which O'Brien compares to the battle between Jove and the Titan; it ends when Hippe whiplashes the young man and binds him. Solon's life is spared so he can be the human target for the diminutive demonic army.

In another dramatic episode, the four gypsies meet in a religious rite for the anointing of the swords and daggers with a mysterious poison. Afterward, they drink to celebrate the success of their mission; but they drink too much wine and fall into a deep sleep. Solon, having been helped in his escape by Zonela, like his Classical namesake, wisely looks through the keyhole of Hippe's door before planning any action.

What he sees horrifies him. The black bottle falling from Filomel's pocket activates the manikins. With malice and pleasure, the incarnate fiends swarm over the sleeping bodies, stabbing as they move from one region of the body to another. Hippe, the first to awaken, emits a frightful shriek. His body swollen and discolored, he is covered with his creations; the bodies of his followers are also grotesque masses. All four grab handfuls of the horde and fling them into the fire; but some of the puppets escape and run around the room, igniting it. All perish in the flames as Solon and Zonela flee into the night.

"WHAT WAS IT?"

In "What Was It?," Harry and Dr. Hammond are two opium smokers, living in a Twenty-sixth Street boardinghouse which is supposedly haunted. One night Harry is attacked by an invisible assailant. Hammond, discovering him in combat with the air, thinks he is experiencing an opium vision; but Harry is not hallucinating, as Hammond quickly discovers. Both men grapple with "The Thing," finally getting it controlled by tightly lacing it with rope. Although to the eye it appears as though the rope is encasing an empty space, a scientific investigation determines its weight and height. Physiologically, it breathes, has a pulsating heart, struggles to be free, and has a will and a human form. The men, curious to learn about the elemental being, have it chloroformed so that a plaster of paris mold can be cast. They are terrified by what they discover: It is a hideous ghoul capable of feeding on human flesh.

The fiend, actually starving to death because the pair cannot find the proper food for its survival, remains in Harry's room for a few weeks. Nobody knows what to do with it. When it dies, they bury it in the garden and give the cast to Doctor X as a memento of the link with the other world. To make the tale more credible, O'Brien introduces an interesting dialogue between Harry and Hammond in which Hammond recalls the voices in Charles Brockden Brown's *Wieland* (1798) and the pictures of terror in Henry Bulwer-Lytton's *Zanoni* (1842). Both the American and the British novelist were caught up in the nineteenth century's preoccupation with the occult, which by that time had become a literary prop.

DUKE HUMPHREY'S DINNER

Not all of O'Brien's tales depict the transformation that mysticism and magic underwent in his lifetime when ancient science became a pseudoscience. His dramatic comic sense, for example, dominates in *Duke Humphrey's Dinner*, which was produced at Wallack's Theatre in 1856. A starving couple with a vivid imagination pretend that they are dining with Duke Humphrey, enjoying the finest delicacies of the world. Fortunately, they are rescued by an old friend of the young husband and live happily ever after.

O'Brien's lasting fame rests upon his adherence to the Romance tradition, writing of the confrontation of the material world with its counterpart. Magic, the macabre, malevolent spirits, ritual, psychological phenomena, witchcraft, and spiritualism in its broadest definition are inherent parts of his fiction. Overall, there is more disharmony than harmony between mankind and the realm of the spirit. Modern science had not yet ordered the chaos, according to these tales, but the human spirit is not vanquished. On the contrary, it appears anxious to face the challenge and ready for the combat.

OTHER MAJOR WORKS

PLAYS: *My Christmas Dinner*, pr. 1852; *A Gentleman from Ireland*, pr. 1854; *The Sisters*, pr. 1856; *Duke Humphrey's Dinner*, pr. 1856; *The Tycoon; Or, Young America in Japan*, pr. 1860 (with Charles G. Rosenberg).

POETRY: *Sir Basil's Falcon*, 1853.

MISCELLANEOUS: *The Poems and Stories of Fitz-James O'Brien*, 1881.

BIBLIOGRAPHY

Franklin, H. Bruce. *Future Perfect*. 2d ed. New York: Oxford University Press, 1978. Franklin, in his introduction to "The Diamond Lens," stresses O'Brien's great inventiveness as his major quality in becoming one of the seminal figures in the early era of science-fiction writing. He also discusses "How I Overcame My Gravity" and "What Was It?," which he argues influenced later stories by Ambrose Bierce, Guy de Maupassant, and H. P. Lovecraft's "The Color Out of Space."

Hoppenstand, Gary. "Robots of the Past: Fitz-James O'Brien's 'The Wondersmith.'" *Journal of Popular Culture* 27 (Spring, 1994): 13-30. Discussion of the way O'Brien blends realistic immigrant fiction with nineteenth century German fairy tale; notes how O'Brien parodies romantic conventions; suggests that O'Brien helped to establish the robot as an important literary motif.

Moskowitz, Sam. *Explorers of the Infinite*. Cleveland: World Publishing, 1963. In a work that discusses writers of fantasy and science fiction from Cyrano de Bergerac to the mid-twentieth century, the author devotes one chapter to O'Brien, titled "The Fabulous Fantast—Fitz-James O'Brien." In Moskowitz's opinion, O'Brien was not only one of the significant early figures in the genre of fantasy but also one of the most important short-story writers of the nineteenth century.

Tremayne, Peter, ed. *Irish Masters of Fantasy*. Dublin: Wolfhound Press, 1979. In his introduction to O'Brien's "The Wondersmith," Tremayne discusses several of O'Brien's most important stories, including "The Diamond Lens," "Jubal the Ringer," "What Was It?," and "From Hand to Mouth." He also comments upon O'Brien's influence on Ambrose Bierce and Guy de Maupassant.

Wentworth, Michael. "A Matter of Taste: Fitz-James O'Brien's 'The Diamond Lens' and Poe's Aesthetic of Beauty." *American Transcendental Quarterly*, n.s. 2 (December, 1988): 271-284. Analysis of one of O'Brien's most famous stories, arguing that it manifests the transcendent theory of beauty articulated by Edgar Allan Poe in his aesthetic theory.

Wolle, Francis. *Fitz-James O'Brien: A Literary Bohemian of the Eighteen Fifties*. Boulder: University of Colorado, 1944. The first full biography of O'Brien's short but eventful life. Originally a doctoral dissertation, this study's approach and emphasis, which include a scholarly discussion of all O'Brien's writings, is suggested in the book's subtitle. Supplemented by a bibliography.

Eileen A. Sullivan, updated by Eugene S. Larson

TIM O'BRIEN

Born: Austin, Minnesota; October 1, 1946

PRINCIPAL SHORT FICTION

The Things They Carried, 1990

OTHER LITERARY FORMS

Tim O'Brien often blurs the boundaries between genres. He began his career as a journalist, and sections of reporting are often mixed with his fiction. He develops novels, such as *Going After Cacciato* (1978), around successful short stories. He interlocks short fictions so closely that collections can be read as novels, although their components are published individually as short stories, as with *The Things They Carried*. He also often walks with one foot in fiction and one foot in autobiography, as in his early work *If I Die in a Combat Zone, Box Me Up and Ship Me Home* (1973; revised 1979), to which he refers as a war memoir rather than a novel. His essay "The Vietnam in Me," was the cover story for *The New York Times Magazine* of October 2, 1994. He has also written the novels *In the Lake of the Woods* (1994) and *Tomcat in Love* (1998).

ACHIEVEMENTS

Tim O'Brien's short stories have been honored by the National Magazine Award and included in *The Pushcart Prize*, *Prize Stories: The O. Henry Awards*, and *The Best American Short Stories* collections. He was awarded the National Book Award in 1979 for *Going After Cacciato*. His collection of interrelated stories *The Things They Carried* won the *Chicago*

Tribune Heartland Prize, the Melcher Book Award, and France's Prix du Meilleur Livre Étranger. His novel *In the Lake of the Woods* (1994) holds the Society of American Historians' James Fenimore Cooper Prize for best historical novel. He has received awards from the National Endowment for the Arts, the John Simon Guggenheim Memorial Foundation, and the Vietnam Veterans of America.

BIOGRAPHY

William Timothy O'Brien was born in Minnesota in 1946 and lived there until he graduated summa cum laude from Macalester College in 1968. He was immediately drafted and, despite deep ambivalence, was inducted into the U.S. Army. The former student body president of a radical college, O'Brien served in Vietnam, first as a foot soldier and then as a typist. He was honorably discharged from the Army in 1970 with seven medals, among them the Purple Heart. He disapproved of the Vietnam War before he was drafted, while he was fighting it, and after he returned home.

Although O'Brien had done some scattered writing before the war (while he was still in college, he produced a novel that he did not publish), his real career as a writer began with Vietnam. During the summer after he was drafted, while he grappled with his conscience about serving in the war, he began to write intensely. "That horrible summer made me a writer," he recalls. O'Brien sent home accounts of the fighting in Vietnam that were first published in Minnesota newspapers and later recycled into his books.

After the war, O'Brien studied government at Harvard University and worked for *The Washington Post*. The first book he published, the 1973 war memoir *If I Die in a Combat Zone, Box Me Up and Ship Me Home*, was well received, opening the door for him to set aside both journalistic and political aspirations to build a full-time literary career.

ANALYSIS

Tim O'Brien is in essence a writer of the Vietnam War, but his relationship with that war is not simple. It is his setting, the geographical and historical reality in which his best stories are played out. It is his story,

Tim O'Brien in 1979 (AP/Wide World Photos)

his material, the subject matter of his telling. It is also the reason he must write—because he went to Vietnam, certain things happened to him that require him to write, trying, as he says "to save Timmy's life with a story. . . ."

Vietnam also defines for him a constituency. The three and a half million people who served in Southeast Asia between 1964 and 1975 constitute the group to which he is responsible, the men and women for whom and to whom he speaks in his best work. He is sharply aware of his responsibility to this audience, which requires him to tell the truth about Vietnam—to shun oversimplifying, moralizing, or taking the easy way out. Scrupulous honesty about Vietnam—a situation where confusion, mystery, fear, uncertainty, and moral ambiguity reigned supreme—require O'Brien to shun straightforward narrative techniques, easy moralizing, or self-protective authorial distance.

Out of this need to be faithful to the deep truth about the Vietnam War experience, O'Brien developed his way of building a story like a jigsaw, out of a set of interlocking pieces. Books are built of story-pieces; stories are built of moment-pieces. In the spaces between the pieces, there is room for interpretation, for uncertainty, for mystery. It is because of this structure built up from fragments that it is impossible to categorize some of O'Brien's work as either a unitary novel or a collection of short stories, either fiction or nonfiction: He has deliberately abandoned the security of categories.

"GOING AFTER CACCIATO"

This story, which was selected for *The Best American Short Stories 1977* and *The Pushcart Prize* (and also grew into the novel *Going After Cacciato*), deals with the Vietnam draftee's terrible ambivalence about the war—the passionate desire to be someplace else, balanced against the utterly unthinkable act of leaving. O'Brien writes about this conflict in a number of his works. In this story, the two sides of the issue are embodied by the deserter Cacciato, on the one hand, and the obedient soldiers pursuing him, on the other.

Cacciato is a fool. His simplemindedness frees him to think simple, direct thoughts and take simple, direct action. His foolishness liberates him from the weight of duty, propriety, inertia, and expectation that chains the more "mature" soldiers to the war. When he wants to be elsewhere, he simply goes. His going is a radical act that threatens the whole conceptual structure of the war, because he enacts the possibility of saying no. The entire war mentality, as seen by O'Brien, depends on individual men finding it unthinkable to say no in such a way. Thus, Cacciato, always seen in the distance (like a wishing star or a mirage), becomes the image of unthinkable possibilities to the obedient soldiers still caught in the war. As one of them puts it, "Can't hump away from a war, isn't that right sir? The dummy has got to learn you can't just hump your way out of a war."

THE THINGS THEY CARRIED

Throughout his career, O'Brien continued to write short pieces for a number of magazines. One of these, his prizewinning "The Things They Carried," he later developed into a full-length book which was published in 1990 under the same title. It is a related sequence of short pieces about the experience of a foot soldier in Vietnam. The vignettes range from one to twenty-five pages in length. In them, O'Brien mixes the techniques of the action/adventure war story with the self-doubting exploration of a contemplative. He intersplices war memories with present reflection, fact with fiction, novel with short story. This is his most successful book, telling the particular story of one soldier's war but also turning its attention to the universal questions of the nature of war, truth, healing, and courage.

O'Brien's craft in *The Things They Carried* is often compared to that of Ernest Hemingway and Joseph Heller, two other twentieth century American writers who shared the project of telling "a true war story." Like them, O'Brien creates a carefully controlled net of unstated meaning. Through understatement, oddities of style, and the juxtaposition of superficially unrelated information, O'Brien "shows" and does not "tell." Much is implied. By cooperatively reconstructing the implicit material, the reader actively participates in co-creating the story. Because of this, readers may experience themselves as more engaged, more immediately involved, than with other, more explicit, texts.

Another way in which O'Brien strives to "tell a true war story" is in his attention to physical details, the details that make up the life of a soldier. The rain, the mud, the fungus that grows in the socks, the jungle rot that attacks the skin, the precise physical sensation of bowel-loosening terror—these are the facts of a soldier's life, and these are the details that enrich the texture and reality of *The Things They Carried*. Through careful sensory detail, O'Brien attempts the impossible task of telling the true story of Vietnam so clearly that even those who were not there may stand in witness.

"THE THINGS THEY CARRIED"

The physical details of the experience of a soldier are primary in this story, which is structured as if it were a simple list of what infantrymen carried on their backs, with the exact weight added to underscore the reality of the load. It is almost as if the author had set himself a memory assignment of writing a straightforward inventory of a soldier's pack and found that the physicality of the list opened out into story, because each item is needed for a reason. Those reasons tell the daily lives of the soldiers. (He also used the list format to powerful effect in "What They Didn't Know" in *Going After Cacciato*.) Some things they all carry, some things are particular to certain roles in the group, reflecting the shared and uniquely personal experience of war. As the list develops, it begins to include the psychological and spiritual loads the men carry, things like fear and responsibility, until it becomes a full catalog of the weight that crushes humans at war.

"LOON POINT"

Published in 1993, this story is an example of an O'Brien work that does not implicitly or explicitly refer to the Vietnam War. However, much of the same confusion, mystery, fear, uncertainty, and moral ambiguity that rule his work about the war also dominate his work about the intimate conflicts between men and women. In this story, a married woman lies to her husband in order to go on a romantic getaway with her lover. During their interlude, her lover drowns before her eyes, and she returns to her husband with a wall of lies spoken and unspoken between them.

"Loon Point," like *The Things They Carried*, reflects on the simultaneous necessity and impossibility of telling the truth about the important things—love, war. Truth is necessary in order to heal, to mend the damaged heart, but it is also impossible because the inscrutable Other (the partner, the enemy) is so mysterious and the truth is so complex that putting it into words would require an oversimplification so gross as to constitute a lie. The wife elects silence because "there is nothing she could say that was entirely true"—which could also be a condensed statement of why O'Brien's work about the truth of both war and relationships is veiled in fiction, implicitness, and ambiguity.

OTHER MAJOR WORKS

LONG FICTION: *Northern Lights*, 1975; *Going After Cacciato*, 1978, revised 1989; *The Nuclear Age*, 1981, 1985; *In the Lake of the Woods*, 1994; *Tomcat in Love*, 1998.

NONFICTION: *If I Die in a Combat Zone, Box Me Up and Ship Me Home*, 1973, revised 1979; "The Vietnam in Me," 1994.

BIBLIOGRAPHY

Herzog, Tobey C. *Tim O'Brien*. Boston: Twayne, 1997. Critical biography addressed to informed readers from advanced high school students to university professors. Covers O'Brien's work from *If I Die in a Combat Zone, Box Me Up and Ship Me Home* through *In the Lake of the Woods*. Includes bibliography.

Kaplan, Steven. *Understanding Tim O'Brien*. Columbia: University of South Carolina Press, 1994. Scholarly interpretation and criticism of O'Brien's work from *If I Die in a Combat Zone, Box Me Up and Ship Me Home* through *In the Lake of the Woods*. Includes bibliography.

Lee, Don. "About Tim O'Brien." *Ploughshares* 21 (Winter, 1995-1996): 196-201. A concise and sensitive sketch of O'Brien's life and work through 1994, written on the occasion of O'Brien's guest editorship (with Mark Strand) of a volume of the literary review *Ploughshares*.

Tegmark, Mats. *In the Shoes of a Soldier: Communication in Tim O'Brien's Vietnam Narratives*. Uppsala: Ubsaliensis, 1998. This is a good study of problematic communication in O'Brien's writings on Vietnam. Includes a bibliography and index.

Donna Glee Williams

FLANNERY O'CONNOR

Born: Savannah, Georgia; March 25, 1925
Died: Milledgeville, Georgia; August 3, 1964

PRINCIPAL SHORT FICTION
A Good Man Is Hard to Find, 1955
Everything That Rises Must Converge, 1965
The Complete Stories, 1971

OTHER LITERARY FORMS

In addition to writing thirty-one short stories, Flannery O'Connor wrote two short novels, *Wise Blood* (1952) and *The Violent Bear It Away* (1960). A collection of her essays and occasional prose entitled *Mystery and Manners* (1969) was edited by Robert and Sally Fitzgerald, and a collection of letters entitled *The Habit of Being* (1979) was edited by Sally Fitzgerald. More correspondence is collected in *The Correspondence of Flannery O'Connor and Brainard Cheneys* (1986), edited by C. Ralph Stephens. O'Connor also wrote book reviews, largely for the Catholic press; these are collected in *The Presence of Grace* (1983), which was compiled by Leo J. Zuber and edited by Carter W. Martin.

ACHIEVEMENTS

The fiction of Flannery O'Connor has been highly praised for its unrelenting irony, its symbolism, and its unique comedy. O'Connor is considered one of the most important American writers of the short story, and she is frequently compared with William Faulkner as a writer of short fiction.

For an author with a relatively small literary output, O'Connor has received an enormous amount of attention. More than twenty-five books devoted to her have appeared beginning in the early 1960's, when significant critics worldwide began to recognize O'Connor's gifts as a fiction writer. Almost all critical works have emphasized the bizarre effects of reading O'Connor's fiction, which, at its best, powerfully blends the elements of southwestern humor, the southern grotesque, Catholic and Christian theology and philosophy, atheistic and Christian existential-

ism, realism, and romance. Most critics have praised and interpreted O'Connor from a theological perspective and noted how unusual her fiction is, as it unites the banal, the inane, and the trivial with Christian, though fundamentally humorous, tales of proud Georgians fighting battles with imaginary or real agents of God sent out to shake some sense into the heads of the protagonists.

As an ironist with a satirical bent, O'Connor may be compared with some of the best in the English language, such as Jonathan Swift and George Gordon, Lord Byron. It is the comic irony of her stories that probably attracts most readers—from the orthodox and religious to the atheistic humanists whom she loves to ridicule in some of her best fiction. Thus, as a comedian, O'Connor's achievements are phenomenal, since through her largely Christian stories, she is able to attract readers who consider her beliefs outdated and quaint.

In her lifetime, O'Connor won recognition, but she would be surprised at the overwhelming response from literary critics that her fiction has received since her death. O'Connor won O. Henry Awards for her stories "The Life You Save May Be Your Own," "A Circle in the Fire," "Greenleaf," "Everything That Rises Must Converge," and "Revelation." *The Complete Stories*, published posthumously in 1971, won the National Book Award for Fiction. O'Connor received many other honors, including several grants and two honorary degrees.

BIOGRAPHY

Flannery O'Connor's relatively short life was, superficially, rather uneventful. O'Connor was born on March 25, 1925, in Savannah, Georgia, to Regina Cline and Edward Francis O'Connor, Jr. She was their only child. O'Connor's father worked in real estate and construction, and the family lived in Savannah until 1938, when the family moved to Atlanta. In that year, Edward O'Connor became a zone real estate appraiser for the Federal Housing Administration (FHA). Shortly thereafter, O'Connor and her mother moved to Milledgeville, Georgia, and her father became so ill that he had to resign from his job in Atlanta and move to Milledgeville. On February 1, 1941, Edward O'Connor died.

In her youth, O'Connor was diagnosed with the same disease that had killed her father when she was almost sixteen. Her short life would end tragically from complications related to disseminated lupus, a disease that attacks the body's vital organs. From the fall of 1938 until her death, O'Connor spent most of her life in Milledgeville, except for brief hiatuses. After graduating from the experimental Peabody High School in 1942, O'Connor entered Georgia State College for Women (subsequently renamed Georgia College) in Milledgeville, where she majored in sociology and English and was graduated with an A.B. degree in June, 1945. While in college, she was gifted both in drawing comic cartoons and in writing. In September, 1945, O'Connor enrolled at the State University of Iowa with a journalism scholarship, and in 1946, her first story, "The Geranium" (later revised several times until it became "Judgement Day," her last story), was published in *Accent*. In 1947, she received the master of fine arts degree and enrolled for postgraduate work in the prestigious Writers' Workshop. She was honored in 1948 by receiving a place at Yaddo, an artists' colony in Saratoga Springs, New York.

Planning never to return to the South, O'Connor lived briefly in New York City in 1949 but later moved to Ridgefield, Connecticut, to live with Robert and Sally Fitzgerald. Robert Fitzgerald is best known as a classics scholar and a translator of such works as the *Odyssey* and *The Theban Plays*. City life was too much for O'Connor, but she became quickly acclimated to life in slower-paced Ridgefield. In January, 1950, she underwent an operation while visiting her mother during Christmas. She remained in Milledgeville until she returned to Ridgefield in March.

In December, 1950, O'Connor became extremely ill en route to Milledgeville for Christmas. At first, it was believed that she was suffering from acute rheumatoid arthritis, but in February, after being taken to Emory University Hospital in Atlanta, O'Connor was diagnosed with disseminated lupus erythematosus.

Flannery O'Connor (Joe McTyre)

As a result of her illness, O'Connor would remain under the care of her mother for the rest of her life, and in March, 1951, she and her mother moved from the former governor's mansion in Milledgeville to Andalusia, the Cline family's farm, which was on the outskirts of town. O'Connor's mother, a Cline, was part of a family who had played a significant part in the history of the town of Milledgeville and the state of Georgia. Like many O'Connor protagonists, her mother, using hired help probably very often similar to the "white trash" and black field hands of O'Connor fiction, ran Andalusia as a dairy farm.

Meanwhile, O'Connor continued to write when she was not too weak. During the rest of her lifetime, she wrote fiction and befriended many people, some, such as the woman referred to in the collected letters as "A," through correspondence, others through frequent trips to college campuses for lectures, and still others through their visits to see her at Andalusia. Though her illness restricted her life considerably, she was able to achieve greatness as a writer, with a literary output that had already become a permanent part of the canon of American literature since World War II.

Physicians were able to control the effects of lupus for years through the use of cortisone and other drugs, but in early 1964, O'Connor, suffering from anemia, was diagnosed with a fibroid tumor. The operation to rid her of the tumor reactivated the lupus, and O'Connor died of kidney failure in August, 1964. In her last months, most of which were spent in hospitals, O'Connor worked slowly but conscientiously on the fiction that was to appear in her second (and posthumous) collection of short stories, *Everything That Rises Must Converge*.

Throughout her life, O'Connor remained faithful to her Catholic and Christian beliefs. Although her letters and fiction indicate frequent humor and self-mockery over her illness, it seems clear that O'Connor did not wish to be treated like an invalid, and she did not fear death, because she held to the Christian belief in immortality. While some critics recognize elements of anger, bitterness, and frustration in the fiction, perhaps it was through her craft that she was able to vent her feelings in a more fruitful way. Friends and acquaintances admired her for her wit, her intelligence, and her sharpness of tongue, but they also admired her for her courage.

ANALYSIS

Flannery O'Connor is uncharacteristic of her age. In writing about the pervasive disbelief in the Christian mysteries during contemporary times, O'Connor seems better suited to the Middle Ages in her rather old-fashioned and conventional Catholic and Christian conviction that the central issue in human existence is salvation through Christ. Perhaps the recognition that such conviction in the postmodern world is rapidly fading and may soon be lost makes O'Connor's concerns for the spiritual realm, what she called the "added dimension" in her essay entitled "The Church and the Fiction Writer," more attractive for a dubious audience.

Although O'Connor completed thirty-one short stories and two novels, she is best remembered for nearly a dozen works of short fiction. These major stories may be classified as typical O'Connor short stories for a number of reasons. Each story concerns a proud protagonist, usually a woman, who considers herself beyond reproach and is boastful about her own abilities, her Christian goodness, and her property and possessions. Each central character has hidden fears that are brought to surface through an outsider figure, who serves as a catalyst to initiate a change in the protagonist's perception. O'Connor's primary theme, from her earliest to her last stories, is hubris—that is, overweening pride and arrogance—and the characters' arrogance very often takes on a spiritual dimension.

Closely connected with the theme of hubris is the enactment of God's grace (or Christian salvation). In an essay entitled "A Reasonable Use of the Unreasonable," O'Connor states that her stories are about "the action of grace in territory held largely by the devil" and points out that the most significant part of her stories is the "moment" or "action of grace," when the protagonist is confronted with her own humanity and offered, through an ironic agent of God (an outsider) and, usually through violence, one last chance at salvation. O'Connor's protagonists think so highly of themselves that they are unable to recognize their own fallenness because of Original Sin, so the characters typically are brought to an awareness of their humanity (and their sinfulness) through violent confrontations with outsider figures.

"THE GERANIUM"

O'Connor's six earliest stories first appeared in her thesis at the University of Iowa. The most memorable in terms of O'Connor's later themes are "The Geranium," her first published story, and "The Turkey." "The Geranium," an early version of O'Connor's last story, "Judgement Day," deals with the experience of a southerner living in the North. In the story, an old man is treated as an equal by a black man in his apartment building but longs to return home to the South. More modernist in its pessimistic outlook than the later, more characteristic (and religious) O'Connor works, "The Geranium" shows the effects of fading southern idealism and resembles O'Connor's later stories concerned with home and displacement—other central themes of her fiction.

"THE TURKEY"

"The Turkey" describes an encounter between a young boy named Ruller and a turkey. Receiving little recognition from home, Ruller manages to capture the turkey, only to be outwitted by a leathery confidence woman, a forerunner of O'Connor's later outsider figures. Thematically, the story concerns the initiation of Ruller into adult consciousness and paves the way for O'Connor's later concern with theological issues. Ruller, who resembles the prophetlike figures of the novels and several stories, blames God for allowing him to catch the turkey and then taking it away from him.

A GOOD MAN IS HARD TO FIND

The first collection of O'Connor's fiction, *A Good Man Is Hard to Find*, consists mostly of previously published short stories and a short novella, *The Displaced Person*. The title story, which may be O'Connor's most famous, deals with a Georgia family on its way to Florida for vacation. As the story opens, the main character, the grandmother, tries to convince her son, Bailey, to go to east Tennessee because she has just read about an escaped convict, The Misfit, who is heading to Florida. The next day, the family, including the nondescript mother, a baby, the other children, John Wesley and June Star, and Pitty Sing, the grandmother's cat, journeys to Florida. They stop at Red Sammy's Famous Barbeque, where the proprietor discusses his views of the changing times, saying "A good man is hard to find" to the grandmother, who has similar views.

The seemingly comic events of the day turn to disaster as the grandmother, upsetting the cat, causes the family to wreck, and The Misfit and two men arrive. The grandmother recognizes The Misfit, and as a result, brings about the death of the entire family. Before she dies, however, the grandmother, who has been portrayed as a self-centered, judgmental, self-righteous, and hypocritical Protestant, sees the humanity of The Misfit and calls him "one of my babies." This section of the story represents what O'Connor calls "the action or moment of grace" in her fiction. Thematically, the story concerns religious hypocrisy, faith and doubt, and social and spiritual arrogance. The Misfit, who strikes comparison with

Hazel Motes of *Wise Blood* (1952), is a "prophet gone wrong" (from "A Reasonable Use of the Unreasonable"), tormented by doubt over whether Christ was who he said he was.

"THE LIFE YOU SAVE MAY BE YOUR OWN"

Another important story, "The Life You Save May Be Your Own," portrays a drifter named Tom T. Shiftlet, a one-armed man who covets the automobile of a widow named Lucynell Crater and marries her daughter, a deaf-mute, in order to obtain it. He tells the mother that he is a man with "a moral intelligence." Shiftlet, who is searching for some explanation for the mystery of human existence, which he cannot quite comprehend, reveals himself to be just the opposite: one with amoral intelligence. An outsider figure who becomes the story's protagonist, Shiftlet leaves his wife, also named Lucynell, at a roadside restaurant, picks up a hitchhiker, and flies away to Mobile as a thunderstorm approaches. The story's epiphany concerns the irony that Shiftlet considers the hitchhiker a "slime from this earth," when in reality it is Shiftlet who fits this description. In rejecting his wife, he rejects God's grace and, the story suggests, his mother's valuation of Christianity.

"THE ARTIFICIAL NIGGER"

The next major tale, "The Artificial Nigger," is one of O'Connor's most important and complex. It has been subjected to many interpretations, including the suggestion by some critics that it contains no moment of grace on the part of Mr. Head and Nelson, the two main characters. The most Dantesque of all O'Connor stories, "The Artificial Nigger" concerns a journey to the city (hell), where Nelson is to be introduced to his first black person. As O'Connor ridicules the bigotry of the countrified Mr. Head and his grandson, she also moves toward the theological and philosophical. When Nelson gets lost in the black section of Atlanta, he identifies with a big black woman and, comparable to Saint Peter's denial of Christ, Mr. Head denies that he knows him. Nevertheless, they are reunited when they see a statue of an African American, which represents the redemptive quality of suffering and as a result serves to bring about a moment of grace in the racist Mr. Head. The difficulty of this story, other than the possibility that some may see it as racist itself, is that O'Connor's narrative is so ironic that critics are unsure whether to read the story's epiphany as a serious religious conversion or to assume that Mr. Head is still as arrogant and bigoted as ever.

Of all O'Connor's stories—with the possible exceptions of "The Life You Save May Be Your Own" and "Good Country People"—"The Artificial Nigger" most exemplifies the influence of the humor of the Old Southwest, a tradition that included authors such as Augustus Baldwin Longstreet, Johnson Jones Hooper, and George Washington Harris. In "The Artificial Nigger," the familiar motif of the country bumpkin going to the city, which is prevalent in Southwestern humor in particular and folk tradition in general, is used.

"GOOD COUNTRY PEOPLE"

The next important story, "Good Country People," is preceded by two lesser stories, "A Circle in the Fire" and "A Late Encounter with the Enemy," the former being a successful story about a woman's inability to comprehend the true nature of evil, and the latter being the only O'Connor portrayal of the South's attitude toward the Civil War. "Good Country People," which is frequently anthologized, concerns another major target of O'Connor's satirical fictions: the contemporary intellectual. O'Connor criticizes modern individuals who are educated and who believe that they are capable of achieving their own salvation through the pursuit of human knowledge. Hulga Hopewell, a Ph.D. in philosophy and an atheistic existentialist, resides with her mother, a banal woman who cannot comprehend the complexity of her daughter, because Hulga has a weak heart and has had an accident that caused her to lose one leg.

Believing herself to be of superior intellect, Hulga agrees to go on a picnic with a young Bible salesman and country bumpkin named Manley Pointer, hoping that she can seduce him, her intellectual inferior. Ironically, he is a confidence man with a peculiar affection for the grotesque comparable to characters in the humor of the Old Southwest. As he is about to seduce Hulga, he speeds away with her wooden leg and informs her, "I been believing in nothing since I was born," shattering Hulga's illusion that she is sophisti-

cated and intelligent and that her atheism makes her special. As the story ends, Hulga is prepared for a spiritual recognition that her belief system is as weak and hollow as the wooden leg on which she has based her entire existence. Pointer, whose capacity for evil has been underestimated by the logical positivist Mrs. Hopewell but not by her neighbor Mrs. Freeman, crosses "the speckled lake" in an ironic allusion to Christ's walking on water.

THE DISPLACED PERSON

The final piece in the collection, a novella entitled *The Displaced Person*, portrays the most positive of O'Connor's outsider figures, Mr. Guizac, a Pole. The story is divided into two sections. In the first part, to escape incarceration in the refugee camps after World War II, Mr. Guizac agrees to work for Mrs. McIntyre, a widow who runs a dairy farm. Unknown to him, Mr. Guizac arouses jealousy and fear in the regular tenant farmers, the Shortleys, and the black field hands. Because Mr. Shortley is lazy and lackadaisical, he particularly resents the productivity of Mr. Guizac. The story moves toward the spiritual dimension when Mrs. Shortley, who considers herself a model Christian, begins to see Mr. Guizac and his family as agents of the devil. After Mrs. Shortley learns that her husband is to be fired the next morning, the Shortleys drive away, and Mrs. Shortley dies of a stroke and sees her "true country," which is defined in one of O'Connor's essays as "what is eternal and absolute" ("The Fiction Writer and His Country"). At the time of her death, Mrs. Shortley, displaced like the poor victims of the Holocaust, which she has witnessed in newsreels, is redeemed through displacement and enters her spiritual home.

The story's second part concerns Mrs. McIntyre's growing fear of outsiders. Mr. Shortley reappears after his wife's death and learns that Mr. Guizac is arranging a marriage for, and taking money from, Sulk, a Negro field hand, so that Mr. Guizac's niece can earn passage to the United States. The southern racial taboos are portrayed as fundamentally inhumane when confronted with the reality of human suffering, as seen in the niece, who is in a refugee camp. Father Flynn, the priest who has arranged for Mr. Guizac and his family to come to the United States to work for Mrs. McIntyre, tries to teach Mrs. McIntyre the importance of Christian charity and the fine points of Catholic theology. Unconcerned with these matters, which she considers unimportant, Mrs. McIntyre becomes neurotic about Mr. Guizac's inappropriateness and overlooks the spiritual for the material. Throughout the novella, O'Connor links the peacock, a symbol of Christ's Transfiguration, with Mr. Guizac, and in the end, Mr. Shortley "accidentally" allows a tractor to run over Mr. Guizac while Mrs. McIntyre and the other field hands watch. As the human race is complicit in the persecution and crucifixion of Christ, so are Mrs. McIntyre and the others in the death of Mr. Guizac, a Christ figure. At the story's end, Mrs. McIntyre, losing her dairy farm and all the material possessions in which she has put so much faith all of her life, becomes displaced, as do the others who have participated in the "crucifixion" of Mr. Guizac.

EVERYTHING THAT RISES MUST CONVERGE

The second collection of O'Connor's short fiction, *Everything That Rises Must Converge*, shows the author's depth of vision as she moved away from stories rooted primarily in the tradition of Southwestern humor to heavily philosophical, though still quite humorous, tales of individuals in need of a spiritual experience. Most apparent is the influence of Pierre Teilhard de Chardin, the French paleontologist and Catholic theologian, on the title story as well as the vision of the entire collection. Teilhard de Chardin argued that through the course of time, it was inevitable, even in the evolution of the species, that there was a process moving toward convergence with God.

"EVERYTHING THAT RISES MUST CONVERGE"

This idea, though perhaps used ironically, appears as the basis for "Everything That Rises Must Converge," which is considered one of O'Connor's greatest works. O'Connor once said that this story was her only one dealing with the racial issue; even so, the tale still transcends social and political commentary. The main character, Julian, is another typical O'Connor protagonist. Arrogant and unjust to his more conventional southern and racist mother, the adult college graduate Julian angrily hopes that his mother will be given a lesson in race relations by having to sit next to a black woman wearing the same hat that she is wearing. Outwardly friendly to the black woman's child, Julian's mother, with characteristic O'Connor violence, converges with the oppressed black race after she offers a penny to Carver, the child. After the black woman hits Julian's mother with her purse, Julian is as helpless, lost, and innocent as Carver is. He recognizes that his mother is dying and enters the world of "guilt and sorrow." Through this story, O'Connor reflects on the rising social status of blacks and connects this rise with a spiritual convergence between the two races.

"GREENLEAF"

"Greenleaf," also a major work, portrays still another woman, Mrs. May, attempting to run a dairy farm. Her two ungrateful bachelor sons refuse to take her self-imposed martyrdom seriously when she complains of the Greenleafs and their bull, which, at the beginning of the story, is hanging around outside her window. The Greenleafs are lower-class tenant farmers whose grown children are far more productive and successful than the bourgeois Mrs. May's. O'Connor moves to pagan mythology as she characterizes the bull as a god (compared to Zeus) and unites the Greenleaf bull symbolically with peculiarly Christian elements. The coming of grace in this story is characteristically violent. Mrs. May is gored by a bull, who, like the ancient Greek gods, is both pagan lover and deity (although a Christian deity).

"THE LAME SHALL ENTER FIRST"

The next significant story in the collection, "The Lame Shall Enter First," strikes comparison with the novel *The Violent Bear It Away*, for the main character, Rufus Johnson, a sociopathic teenage criminal, reminds readers of Francis Marion Tarwater, the hero of the novel. There is also Sheppard, the intellectual social worker who, like Tarwater's Uncle Rayber, is a secular humanist and believes that if he takes away the biblical nonsense that the adolescent protagonist has been taught, he will be saved.

Ironically, Sheppard spends all of his time trying to analyze and improve Rufus while at the same time neglecting his own son, Norton. While Rufus is clearly a demonic figure, he nevertheless believes in God and the Devil and convinces the child that he can be with his dead mother through Christian conversion. The child, misunderstanding, kills himself, and Sheppard is left to recognize the emptiness of his materialist philosophy. O'Connor's attitude toward the secular humanist is again satirical; without a divine source, there can be no salvation.

"REVELATION"

O'Connor's last three stories, according to most critics, ended her career at the height of her powers. "Revelation," one of the greatest pieces of short fiction in American literature, is O'Connor's most complete statement concerning the plight of the oppressed. While her fiction often uses outsiders, she seldom directly comments on her sympathies with them, but through Ruby Turpin's confrontation with the fat girl "blue with acne," who is named Mary Grace, O'Connor is able to demonstrate that in God's Kingdom the last shall be first. Mary Grace calls Mrs. Turpin, who prides herself on being an outstanding Christian lady, a "wart hog from hell," a phrase that Mrs. Turpin cannot get out of her mind. Later, Mrs. Turpin goes to "hose down" her hogs, symbols of unclean spirits, and has a vision of the oppressed souls entering heaven ahead of herself and her husband (Claud). Critical disagreement has centered largely on whether Mrs. Turpin is redeemed after her vision or whether she remains the same arrogant, self-righteous, bigoted woman she has been all of her life.

"PARKER'S BACK"

"Parker's Back" is one of the most mysterious of O'Connor's stories. Obadiah Elihue Parker, a nonbeliever, marries Sarah Ruth, a fundamentalist bent on saving her husband's soul. After a mysterious accident in which he hits a tree, Parker gradually experiences religious conversion and, though tattooed all over the front of his body, is drawn to having a Byzantine tattoo of Christ placed on his back, thinking that his wife will be pleased. She is not, however, accusing him instead of idolatry. In reality, she is the heretic, for she is incapable of recognizing that Christ was both human and divine. Beating welts into her husband's back, Sarah Ruth fails to recognize the mystical connection between the suffering of her husband and that of the crucified Christ. By this point in her career, O'Connor was using unusual symbols to convey her sense of the mystery of God's redemptive power.

"JUDGEMENT DAY"

O'Connor's last completed story, "Judgement Day," is a revised version of her first published story, "The Geranium." The central character, a displaced southerner living with his daughter in New York City, wishes to return home to die. Tanner, while an old and somewhat bigoted man, remembers fondly his relationship with a black man and hopes to befriend a black tenant in his daughter's apartment building. This story concerns Tanner's inability to recognize differences in southern and northern attitudes toward race, and, as with earlier O'Connor stories, "home" has more than a literal meaning (a spiritual destiny or heaven). Unlike almost all other O'Connor works, this story portrays racial relations as based on mutual respect. Also, Tanner, while attacked violently by the black tenant, is portrayed as a genuine believer and is sent to his eternal resting place (heaven), the destiny of a Christian. By the end of her life, O'Connor considered a return to a heavenly home much more significant than any other subject.

OTHER MAJOR WORKS

LONG FICTION: *Wise Blood*, 1952; *The Violent Bear It Away*, 1960.

NONFICTION: *Mystery and Manners*, 1969; *The Habit of Being: Letters*, 1979; *The Presence of Grace*, 1983; *The Correspondence of Flannery O'Connor and Brainard Cheneys*, 1986.

MISCELLANEOUS: *Collected Works*, 1988.

BIBLIOGRAPHY

Asals, Frederick. *Flannery O'Connor: The Imagination of Extremity*. Athens: University of Georgia Press, 1982. In one of the best books on O'Connor's fiction, Asals focuses on the use of the *Doppelgänger* (double) motif in the novels and short fiction, the most thorough and intelligent treatment of this subject. Asals also concentrates on O'Connor's religious extremity, which is evident in her fiction through her concern with polarities and extremes. Contains extensive endnotes and a good bibliography.

_____. *"'A Good Man Is Hard to Find'": Flannery O'Connor*. New Brunswick, N.J.: Rutgers University Press, 1993. A casebook in the Women Writers: Texts and Contexts series that includes critical essays on O'Connor's story from a variety of critical perspectives. Critics discuss the pros and cons of O'Connor's shift in point of view from the grandmother to The Misfit, the nature of grace in a materialistic world, and the theological significance of the story's concluding confrontation.

Bacon, Jon Lance. *Flannery O'Connor and Cold War Culture*. New York: Cambridge University Press, 1993. Reads O'Connor's stories in relation to social issues of their milieu. Discusses the context of Cold War politics, popular culture, media, and consumerism that form the backdrop to O'Connor's stories.

Desmond, John F. *Risen Sons: Flannery O'Connor's Vision of History*. Athens: University of Georgia Press, 1987. Desmond's argument is that O'Connor's fictions reenact Christian history and Catholic theology through an art O'Connor herself saw as an "incarnational act." Discussing several major stories and the two novels, the book focuses on the metaphysical and the Christian historical vision as observed through reading O'Connor's fiction and emphasizes that *The Violent Bear It Away* represents the fullest development of her vision. Includes an extensive bibliography and useful endnotes.

Feeley, Kathleen. *Flannery O'Connor: Voice of the Peacock*. New Brunswick, N.J.: Rutgers University Press, 1972. A useful though somewhat early study of O'Connor's fiction from a theological perspective. Contains analyses of almost all the stories and novels and focuses on the connection between the books in O'Connor's library and her works. Feeley's primary fault is that the works are sometimes oversimplified into religious messages without enough emphasis on the humor, the sarcasm, and the satire. A bibliography of primary and secondary works is included, as is a list of some possible sources of O'Connor's fiction found in her library.

Hendin, Josephine. *The World of Flannery O'Connor*. Bloomington: Indiana University Press, 1970. Although this study is an early one in O'Connor scholarship, Hendin's case that O'Connor may be read in other than religious ways makes the book worth consideration. Hendin offers effective analyses of most of the major O'Connor stories. While her interpretations should be approached with caution, they are nevertheless convincing as they attempt to show that O'Connor was an artist rather than a polemicist. Select bibliography and rather useful endnotes.

Orvell, Miles. *Flannery O'Connor: An Introduction*. Jackson: University Press of Mississippi, 1991. Chapters on the novels as well as explorations of O'Connor's treatment of the South, of belief, of art, of the American romance tradition, of prophets and failed prophets, and of comedy. Appendices include a chronological list of the fiction, book reviews by Flannery O'Connor, notes, and bibliography.

Paulson, Suzanne Morrow. *Flannery O'Connor: A Study of the Short Fiction*. Boston: Twayne, 1988. A useful resource for the beginner. Paulson's book includes primary and secondary material on O'Connor's fiction and concentrates on the predominant issues, themes, and approaches to O'Connor's fiction. Paulson divides O'Connor's stories into four categories: death-haunted questers, male/female conflicts, "The Mystery of Personality" and society, and good/evil conflicts. Supplemented by a chronology of O'Connor's life and a bibliography of primary and secondary works.

Rath, Sura P., and Mary Neff Shaw, eds. *Flannery O'Connor: New Perspectives*. Athens: University of Georgia Press, 1996. The new perspectives illustrated in this collection of essays are primarily feminist and Bakhtinian, with one essay using discourse theory and one focusing on race and culture. Stories discussed include "A View from the Woods," "The Artificial Nigger," and "The Crop."

Spivey, Ted R. *Flannery O'Connor: The Woman, the Thinker, the Visionary*. Macon, Ga.: Mercer University Press, 1995. Attempts to understand O'Connor first as a southerner, then as a modernist intellect, and finally as a visionary thinker. Argues that O'Connor reflects the personal and social issues of the last decades of the twentieth century.

Walters, Dorothy. *Flannery O'Connor*. Boston: Twayne, 1973. This effective but early introduction to the works of O'Connor includes analyses of the short fiction and the novels. Walters argues perceptively and conventionally that O'Connor is predominantly a religious writer whose works can be classified as Christian tragicomedy. Walters also makes some useful observations about O'Connor's connections with earlier literary traditions. Includes a chronology of O'Connor's life, useful endnotes, and a select bibliography.

Westling, Louise Hutchings. *Sacred Groves and Ravaged Gardens: The Fiction of Eudora Welty, Carson McCullers, and Flannery O'Connor*. Athens: University of Georgia Press, 1985. A useful book for those interested in critical perspectives other than religious readings of O'Connor's fiction as well as for those curious about O'Connor's relationship with Eudora Welty and Carson McCullers, two of her rivals as masters of short fiction. This book is the first feminist study of O'Connor's fiction. Westling discusses the female characters and emphasizes that O'Connor often shows female protagonists as victims of male antagonists. Contains an extensive bibliography as well as useful endnotes.

D. Dean Shackelford

FRANK O'CONNOR
Michael Francis O'Donovan

Born: Cork City, Ireland; 1903
Died: Dublin, Ireland; March 10, 1966

PRINCIPAL SHORT FICTION

Guests of the Nation, 1931
Bones of Contention and Other Stories, 1936
Crab Apple Jelly, 1944
Selected Stories, 1946
The Common Chord, 1947
Traveller's Samples, 1951
The Stories of Frank O'Connor, 1952
More Stories, 1954
Stories by Frank O'Connor, 1956
Domestic Relations, 1957
My Oedipus Complex and Other Stories, 1963
Collection Two, 1964
A Set of Variations, 1969
Collection Three, 1969
Collected Stories, 1981

OTHER LITERARY FORMS

Frank O'Connor was a prolific writer who wrote in nearly every literary genre. His published books include poems, translations of Irish poetry, plays, literary criticism, autobiographies, travel books, and essays. His two novels—*The Saint and Mary Kate* (1932) and *Dutch Interior* (1940)—are interesting complements to the many short-story collections, for which he is best known.

ACHIEVEMENTS

Frank O'Connor was a masterful short-story writer. He was a realist who closely observed his characters and their world. He was not a pitiless realist, however, but he always seemed to have great sympathy for his characters, even those who insisted on putting themselves in absurd situations. It follows that one of his major techniques was humor. There is a place for humor in nearly all of his works, including

Frank O'Connor (Library of Congress)

those that border on tragedy. His stories tend to deal with a domestic rather than a public world, and the characters make up what he has called a "submerged population."

Structurally, the stories are simple. O'Connor likes to use a sudden reversal to bring about the necessary change in the plot. The plots tend to be simple and the reconciliation of the conflict is always very clear. One of the special devices he employed to give the stories some distinction is his use of a narrator. Whether the narrator is a child or an old priest, there is always a distinctive voice telling the reader the story. This voice has some of O'Connor's special qualities: warmth, humor, sympathy, and a realistic appraisal of the circumstances.

BIOGRAPHY

Educated at the Christian Brothers College, Cork, Frank O'Connor (Michael Francis O'Donovan) joined the Irish Volunteers and participated on the Republican side in the Irish Civil War (1922-1923), for which activity he was imprisoned. He supported

himself as a librarian, first in Cork, and later in Dublin, where he met George (Æ) Russell and William Butler Yeats, and began his literary career on Æ's *Irish Statesman*. He was until 1939 a member of the Board of Directors of the Abbey Theatre. From 1940 he coedited *The Bell*, a literary journal, with Seán O'Faoláin. In addition to his editorial work, O'Connor was writing the stories that ensured his fame. From *Guests of the Nation* on, O'Connor wrote a number of superb collections of short stories. In recognition of this feat, O'Connor was invited to teach at a number of prestigious American universities. In 1939 he married Evelyn Bowen, with whom he had two sons and a daughter. During part of World War II he lived in London, working for the Ministry of Information. In 1951 he took up a creative writing position at Harvard, was divorced in 1952, and remarried in 1953 (Harriet Randolph Rich, with whom he had one daughter). He returned to Ireland permanently in 1961. He received a Litt.D. from Dublin University in 1962, where for a time he held a Special Lectureship. He died in Dublin on March 10, 1966.

ANALYSIS

Although widely read in Western literature, Frank O'Connor's literary character is most profoundly influenced by tensions within the literature and life of Ireland, ancient and modern. He was a dedicated student of the literature of Ireland's native language, a keen observer of the life of the folk, intimately familiar with Ireland's topography, and an active participant in its revolutionary and literary politics. These interests shaped his art. His literary vocation, however, like so many others of his generation, begins with Yeats's literary nationalism and continues through a dialectic between his perceptions of that poet's idealism and Joyce's early naturalism. O'Connor's predominantly realistic fiction attempts a fusion of these two influences, while also recalling the popular origin—in the oral art of the *shanachie*—of the short story. He found that Yeats and Joyce were too "elitist" for the "common reader"; and with O'Faoláin, he is associated with the development of the realistic Irish short story, the most representative art of the Irish Literary Revival.

"GUESTS OF THE NATION"

"Guests of the Nation," the title story of O'Connor's first collection, is probably his single finest work. All the stories in this volume reflect his involvement in the War of Independence; and this one distinguishes itself by its austere transcendence of the immediate circumstances, which in the rest of the stories here trammel the subjects with excessive patriotic enthusiasm. During the War of Independence, the protagonist's (Bonaparte's) cadre of Volunteers has been charged with the task of holding hostage two British soldiers, Belcher and Hawkins; during their captivity, the forced intimacy of captors, and hostages leads to a reluctantly admitted mutual respect which develops through their card-playing, arguments, and sharing of day-to-day chores. As the reader observes the exchanges of sympathy, idiom, and gesture between Irish and English soldiers, the two Englishmen become distinct from their roles, and from each other. The narrative develops the issues of religion, accent, and political allegiances as only superficially divisive, so that when the order arrives from headquarters to execute the hostages in military reprisal, the moral conflict is joined.

The story nicely dramatizes the contrasting reactions to this order among the various figures, captors and hostages: Donovan's giving grim precedence to national duty over "personal considerations"; Noble's pious reflections, which short-circuit his comprehension of the enormity of his actions; and Bonaparte's reflective agony. The change in the attitudes of the Englishmen, once they know the truth of the directive, poignantly reveals new dimensions in these men's characters. The argument to the last of Hawkins, the intellectual, dramatizes the limitations of rational discussion; but the stoicism of the more effective Belcher, his unflappability in the face of his own annihilation, drives the story to its height of feeling, a height to which only Bonaparte is equal. Noble's moral earnestness and Donovan's objectivity provide contrasts and contexts for Bonaparte's tragic anagnorisis.

O'Connor achieves the inimitable effects of the fine conclusion by a combination of devices: the shreds of partisan argument about religion and politics, the range of attitudes embodied by the various characters, the carefully modulated speaking voice of the narrator—steady, intelligent, slightly uncouth, bitter—the spare use of images (ashes, spades, light and dark), and the figure of the old woman who observes the whole affair. This woman, at once a representative of the "hidden powers" of the universe, the irrationality behind the appearances of coherence, and also a representative of the affinity between such forces in the human psyche and the justifiable cause of Mother Ireland, gives the story both historical and universal resonances. Thus as one considers the story as a tragic examination of the theme of duty (to self, friends, institutions, nation, God), and of the tension between the claims of individual conscience and communal obligation, between commitments to the personal and the abstract, developed with psychological accuracy in a modern setting, one notes its roots in the soil of Irish literature and tradition. The political situation, the various elements of local color, the allusively named characters, the figure of the old woman, the precedence of the ancient Celtic ritual of bog-burial, and the echoes of the tension in Celtic society between the obligations to provide hospitality to strangers and at the same time to protect the clan's rights through the insurance of hostage-taking: All these elements blend the modern with the archaic. Taken in combination, they achieve the result of casting these English soldiers as "guests" of the nation as an imaginative entity.

The restrained lyricism of the last paragraph, coming as it does on the heels of a rather colloquial narrative, shows how moved is the storyteller by his recollections. The bathetic solecism of the summary comment, however—"And anything that happened to me afterwards, I never felt the same about again"—certifies that the narrator's education is unfinished. This sentence mirrors the dislocation of his feelings, while it also nicely preserves the integrity of O'Connor's characteristic fictional device, the speaking voice.

"IN THE TRAIN"

The story "In the Train" (*Bones of Contention and Other Stories*) dramatizes the reactions of a group of South-of-Ireland villagers toward an accused murderer in their midst, as they all return homeward by train from the Dublin criminal court. They have all conspired to prevent the woman's conviction, planning to punish her in their own manner when they return home. By a series of interconnected scenes, observed in a sequence of compartments of the train as it traverses the dark countryside, the story develops the theme of the villagers' common opposition to the law of the state and, by implication, their allegiance to the devices of their ancient community. From the bourgeois pretensions of the sergeant's wife to the dialogue that reveals the tensions and boredom among the policemen, to the stoicism of the peasants, to the huddled figure of the accused herself, the focus narrows from the humor of the opening scenes to the brooding interior monologue of the isolated woman in the final scene. The various parts of the story are interconnected by the characters' common motion west, their agreed attitude toward the legal apparatus of the Free State, by the Chaplinesque rambling drunk, and by the fated, defiant pariah. The story proceeds by indirection: Its main action (the murder and trial) is over and revealed only in retrospect; and its focus (the accused) is not fully identified until the final section. O'Connor develops these suspensions, however, in a resourceful manner, by focusing on the secondary tension in the community occasioned by the presence of the sergeant's carping wife, and by having the shambling drunk lead the reader to the transfixed woman.

The apparent naïveté of the narrator's voice—colloquial, amused, relishing the folksy scenes—is belied by the complex structure of the piece. Moreover, the narrative is rich with echoes of Chekhov, touches of melodrama and vaudeville, devices from folktales and folkways, as it portrays the residue of the ancient legal unit of Celtic society, the *derb-fine*, persisting under the "foreign" order of the Irish Free State. In these contexts, the ambiguities of the sergeant's position and that of the local poteen manufacturer are richly developed, while we discern that the woman's guilt is never firmly established. The story ends with a choric circle around the tragic complaint of the woman, whose community has preserved her only to impose their own severe penalty: ostracism from the only community she knows. O'Connor shares and enlarges her despair. The initial amusement of his story yields to chagrin at the loss both of the ideals of the Irish revolution in the Free State, and of humaneness in the dying rural communities of Ireland.

"THE LONG ROAD TO UMMERA"

"The Long Road to Ummera" concerns an old woman's conflict with her son over her desire for burial in the ancestral ground in the remote West Cork village of Ummera. Abby, Batty Heig's daughter, has followed her son Pat to the city of Cork, but feeling the approach of death, desires to be returned to Ummera, not by the modern highway, but by the ancient "long road." A tragicomic test of wills between mother and son ensues, pitting against each other the desires for established ritual against modern efficiency, uncouth rural mannerisms and polite town manners, homage to ancestors, and modern progressivism. Because of her son's insensitivity, the old woman is forced to engage in comic subterfuge to achieve her last wish, and by grotesque turns of events involving a cobbler, a jarvey, and a priest, she has her way in all its details: Her body is transported along the prescribed road and announced ritually to the desolate countryside.

This is a moving portrait of an old woman, dignified by a lively sense of the presence of the dead and by lyrical evocations of the scenery of West Cork. In contrast to these qualities is the philistinism of her businessman son. The story itself has ritual quality, woven as it is with repeated phrases, scenes, arguments, events, recurrent images of death, various addictions, and the rehearsals of rituals themselves. The story represents O'Connor's criticism of bourgeois Ireland and the triumph of profit and respectability, major themes of his sweet-and-sour stories from the 1930's and 1940's contained in this, perhaps his best collection, *Crab Apple Jelly*. Although the speaking voice remains the norm, the tone here is more knowing than in the earlier stories. O'Connor, like Abby, is keeping promises to ancient values, including the language, family loyalty, community, and rootedness. If the old woman's loyalty to her circuitous way is bypassed by Ireland's new one, however, the narrator's sad lyricism suggests that he can tread neither.

"FIRST CONFESSION"

Of O'Connor's childhood stories, "First Confession," "My Oedipus Complex," and "The Drunkard," developed over the 1940's, are his most famous, although not his most distinguished, works. The much-anthologized "First Confession" humorously exploits the mildly exotic Catholic rite, as the little boy finds that the image of religion fostered by his female educators is not borne out in the encounter with the priest-confessor. Hearing that the boy's chief sin is his desire to murder his ill-mannered grandmother, the priest humors the impenitent child by having him articulate the fantasy and sends him back to the sunny street. The idiom of an Irish child carries the narration here, although with the injection of some adult irony directed at the boy's naïve literalism. The story might be faulted for its slapstick and cuteness, as if O'Connor indulges too liberally in the mood of his creation. Many of O'Connor's stories portray insensitive and repressive priests, but not this one. Rather, it is the women who are the agents of terrifying, dogmatic religiosity, in contrast with the priest's personification of a paternal, forgiving, and humorous God.

"MY OEDIPUS COMPLEX" AND "THE DRUNKARD"

"My Oedipus Complex" and "The Drunkard" are charming examples of O'Connor's mastery of the narrator-as-child. In them, the themes of marital tension, domestic evasiveness, and the dependence of Irish males on their mothers are treated with light irony. By means of an unexpected turn of events, the severe social controls on incest and alcoholism are toyed with as the jealous conspiracies of women; thus moral awareness commences with male bonding. In each of these three childhood stories, the antagonist at first appears as male—priest, bed-rival, drunken father—until the possessiveness of women emerges as the substantial moral antagonist. In these much-revised stories, O'Connor has refined the instrument of the speaking voice to a point that is perhaps too ingratiating, too calculatedly smooth, so that the spontaneity of the "rough narrative voice" is lost, and with it, some of his cold and passionate isolation. The attraction of these stories, however, is readily apparent in their author's recorded versions, which he narrates with considerable relish.

"A STORY BY MAUPASSANT"

O'Connor's tendency to reread his own work with disapproval led to constant revisions, so that there are two, three, or more variants of many of his most popular works. A case in point is "A Story by Maupassant," which first appeared in *The Penguin New Writing* (No. 24, 1945) and in a significantly revised version in *A Set of Variations*. This story of the corruption of an Irish intellectual, observed by his more concrete-minded friend, climaxes when Terry Coughlan admits to the narrator that his appreciation of Maupassant's grasp of "what life can do to you" came during a sleepless night in the bed of a Parisian prostitute. A comparison of the two versions shows several changes: He expands the proportion of more precise and graphic details and reduces dialectal, self-conscious, and repetitive elements; he achieves a more complex ironic effect by a stronger investment in double perspective; he condemns more forthrightly the hypocrisy of the Catholic school, as he renders more deft the function of religious metaphor; he enlarges the sympathy for Terry Coughlan by an enlargement of oblique cultural references and a softening of the narrator's moralizing. O'Connor's own view of Maupassant—that the mainspring of his art lay in the mixture of creative and destructive tendencies interacting as perversity—is brought to bear on the bitter conclusion of the story: Maupassant, at least, has not abandoned these self-destructive characters. In his revisions, O'Connor strengthens Maupassant's perspective, focusing in the end on the prostitute's baby, a symbol of the naïveté of new life. O'Connor bitterly notes that nature, like Maupassant's fiction, without an ideal that is informing, seeks the lowest level. Here is a story that, by the intervention of O'Connor's matured hand, gains considerably in power and perspective, subtlety and professionalism.

"INTROVERTED" IRELAND

The general subject of O'Connor's fiction is a critique of the "introverted religion" and "introverted politics" of bourgeois Ireland—sectarian obscurantism, the abuses of clerical power, class snobbery, family rivalries, disingenuous piety, Anglophobia, and thwarted idealism—although these criticisms are usually modified by warm portraits of energetic children, humane clerics, and unpretentious peasants. His central object in these stories is "to stimulate the moral imagination" by separating his characters from their assumed social roles and having them stand, for a moment, alone. In many of his most distinguished works, and indeed throughout his whole career as a writer of short fiction, one may discern such a movement from the depiction of the comfortably communal to that of the isolated, enlightened individual. He proposes a nexus between such a contrast of perspectives and the short-story form.

THE LONELY VOICE

In his study entitled *The Lonely Voice* (1963), O'Connor holds as central that "in the short story at its most characteristic [there is] something we do not often find in the novel—an intense awareness of human loneliness." This collection of essays on selected practitioners of the modern short story (Ivan Turgenev, Anton Chekhov, Rudyard Kipling, James Joyce, Katherine Mansfield, D. H. Lawrence, Ernest Hemingway, A. E. Coppard, Isaac Babel, and Mary Lavin) draws on seminar notes from O'Connor's classes at various universities in the 1950's. The discussions are genial, opinionated, and not academic, and afford brilliant comments on individual artists and works, although they suffer from diffuseness and overextension at certain points in the argument. The study rests on the theory that the distinction of the short story from the novel is less a formal than an ideological one: It is the expression of "an attitude of mind that is attracted by submerged population groups . . . tramps, artists, lonely idealists, dreamers, and spoiled priests . . . remote from the community—romantic, individualistic, and intransigent."

From this position, O'Connor argues that "the conception of the short story as a miniature art is inherently false," holding that, on the contrary, "the storyteller differs from the novelist in this: he must be much more of a writer, much more of an artist . . . more of a dramatist." From the same vantage point he evaluates his selected authors as they severally identify with some "submerged population group," finding that as each author compromised or found less

compelling the vision of his subjects as outsiders or social or political minorities, he either failed as a short-story writer or found another form more expressive of his vision.

While O'Connor's claims for these theories are maintained in the face of easily adduced contrary evidence, they have limited, and in some ways startling, application to certain authors and works. As a critic, O'Connor possessed brilliant intuitions, although he did not have the power to systematize. In *The Lonely Voice* his remarks on Joyce's and Hemingway's rhetorical styles, his contrasting Chekhov and Mansfield, his accounting for Kipling's artistic failure, and, in *The Mirror in the Roadway* (1956), his discussion of Joyce's "dissociated metaphor" have useful application to the contribution of each of these authors to the literature of the short story.

From various accounts by former students and colleagues, as well as from these critical works, it is quite clear that O'Connor was a brilliantly successful teacher of fiction-writing. His seminars were guided with authority and seriousness, and he placed great emphasis on the perfection of technique. He trained his students to begin with a "prosaic kernel" which the "treatment" takes to its crisis. The finished work takes its power from the cumulation of the drama, poetry, and emotion developed throughout the narrative, finally resolving itself in universalizing mystery. The short story is not concerned with the passage of time or with particularities of character; ideally it is based on an incident and a briefly stated theme, which technique elaborates to the final formula; it should not proceed on technique alone (Hemingway's fault) or follow a preconceived symbolic pattern (Joyce's fault), but ideally it is a fusion of the opposites of naturalism and symbolism.

OTHER MAJOR WORKS

LONG FICTION: *The Saint and Mary Kate*, 1932; *Dutch Interior*, 1940.

PLAYS: *In the Train*, pr. 1937 (with Hugh Hunt); *The Invincibles: A Play in Seven Acts*, pr. 1937 (with Hunt); *Moses' Rock*, pr. 1938 (with Hunt); *The Statue's Daughter: A Fantasy in a Prologue and Three Acts*, pr. 1941.

POETRY: *Three Old Brothers and Other Poems*, 1936.

NONFICTION: *Death in Dublin: Michael Collins and the Irish Revolution*, 1937; *The Big Fellow*, 1937; *A Picture Book*, 1943; *Towards an Appreciation of Literature*, 1945; *The Art of the Theatre*, 1947; *Irish Miles*, 1947; *The Road to Stratford*, 1948; *Leinster, Munster, and Connaught*, 1950; *The Mirror in the Roadway*, 1956; *An Only Child*, 1961; *The Lonely Voice*, 1963; *The Backward Look: A Survey of Irish Literature*, 1967; *My Father's Son*, 1968.

TRANSLATIONS: *The Wild Bird's Nest*, 1932; *Lords and Commons*, 1938; *The Fountain of Magic*, 1939; *Lament for Art O'Leary*, 1940; *The Midnight Court: A Rhythmical Bacchanalia from the Irish of Bryan Merryman*, 1945; *Kings, Lords, and Commons*, 1959; *The Little Monasteries*, 1963; *A Golden Treasury of Irish Poetry*, 1967 (with David Greene).

BIBLIOGRAPHY

Alexander, James D. "Frank O'Connor in *The New Yorker*, 1945-1967." *Eire-Ireland* 30 (1995): 130-144. Examines how O'Connor changed his narrative style during the twenty years he was writing for *The New Yorker*—contracting the presence of a narrator to a voice and developing a double-leveled view of "experienced innocence" in his young boy stories. Argues that O'Connor created a genial persona in his stories that diverted attention from his more serious subject matter of Irish social problems.

Bordewyk, Gordon. "Quest for Meaning: The Stories of Frank O'Connor." *Illinois Quarterly* 41 (Winter, 1978): 37-47. Discusses O'Connor's concern with fundamental qualities of everyday life and his sense of wonder in the mundane in four major groups of stories of war, religion, youth, and marriage. Examines how the search for meaning changes the lives of characters in these four groups.

Davenport, Gary T. "Frank O'Connor and the Comedy of Revolution." *Eire-Ireland* 8 (Summer, 1973): 108-116. Davenport analyzes some of O'Connor's early stories on the Irish Civil War and points out the persistence of comedy even in tragic situations. He claims that O'Connor sees revolution as farcical.

Evans, Robert C., and Richard Harp, eds. *Frank O'Connor: New Perspectives*. West Cornwall, Conn.: Locust Hill Press, 1998. Fresh, thoughtful interpretations of O'Connor's works.

McKeon, Jim. *Frank O'Connor: A Life*. Edinburgh: Mainstream Publishing, 1998. A brief, readable life of O'Connor; comments on the biographical sources of some of the short stories; discusses O'Connor's literary career.

Matthews, James H. *Frank O'Connor*. Lewisburg, Pa.: Bucknell University Press, 1976. This book is an excellent introduction to O'Connor's fiction since it deals with the social context of the stories and the critical theory underlying them. Part of the Irish Writers series.

Neary, Michael. "The Inside-Out World in Frank O'Connor's Stories." *Studies in Short Fiction* 30 (Summer, 1993): 327-336. Discusses O'Connor's use of smallness to accent the collision between the world of the self and the vast world outside. Discusses "The Story Teller" as the most emphatic embodiment of this tension in O'Connor's stories, for the protagonist confronts characters who refuse to take her quest for magic and meaning seriously.

Renner, Stanley. "The Theme of Hidden Powers: Fate vs. Human Responsibility in 'Guests of the Nation.'" *Studies in Short Fiction* 27 (Summer, 1990): 371-378. Argues that the story's moral design emphasizes the existence of mysterious "hidden powers" or forces of chance and fate that control human lives. Suggests that the moral judgment of the story is against the protagonist-teller Bonaparte, who contributes to the world's brutality by mistakenly believing people have no choice.

Steinman, Michael. *Frank O'Connor at Work*. Basingstoke: Macmillan, 1990. A study of O'Connor's life and works.

Tomory, William M. *Frank O'Connor*. Boston: Twayne, 1980. An introductory book on O'Connor that briefly sketches his life and then gives an overview of his work. Tomory touches on a few stories, but most of the analysis is on themes and character types.

Wohlgelernter, Maurice. *Frank O'Connor: An Introduction.* New York: Columbia University Press, 1977. The fullest critical study on O'Connor's fiction available. The author is especially good at articulating O'Connor's theory of the story and in applying those concepts to individual short stories.

Cóilín Owens, updated by James Sullivan

KENZABURŌ ŌE

Born: Ōse, Shikoku, Japan; January 31, 1935

PRINCIPAL SHORT FICTION

"Kimyo na shigoto," 1957

"Shisha no ogori," 1957 ("Lavish the Dead," 1965)

Miru mae ni tobe, 1958

"Shiiku," 1958 ("The Catch," 1966; "Prize Stock," 1977)

Kodoku na seinen no kyuka, 1960

"Sebuntin," 1961 ("Seventeen," 1996)

"Seiji shonen shisu," 1961

Seiteki ningen, 1963

Warera no kyōki o ikinobiru michi o oshieyo, 1969, 1975 (*Teach Us to Outgrow Our Madness: Four Short Novels,* 1977)

Gendai denikshu, 1980

"Ame no ki" o kiku on natachi, 1982

"Rein tsurī" o kiku onnatachi, 1982

Ika ni ki o korosu ka, 1984

Kaba ni kamareru, 1985

Boku ga hontō ni wakakatta koro, 1992

OTHER LITERARY FORMS

Although Kenzaburō Ōe first gained attention through his short stories, which are included in many anthologies of postwar Japanese writing, he has also written many novels, such as *Kojinteki na taiken* (1964; *A Personal Matter,* 1968) and *Man'en gannen no futtoboru* (1967; *The Silent Cry,* 1974). *Pinchi rannā chōso* (1976; *The Pinch Runner Memorandum,* 1994), *Jinsei no shinseki* (1989; *An Echo of Heaven,* 1996), and *Shizuka na seikatsu* (1990; *A Quiet Life,* 1996) are also powerful novels that have been translated into English. In addition, Ōe has published many essays on literature and politics, the latter reflecting his political activism. Much of this nonfiction work has been collected in *Aimai na Nihon no watakushi* (1995; *Japan, the Ambiguous, and Myself,* 1995). Ōe's memoir of his life with his mentally disabled son, *Kaifuku suru kazoku* (1995; *A Healing Family,* 1996), includes beautiful watercolor paintings by his wife Itami Yukari.

ACHIEVEMENTS

Kenzaburō Ōe emerged in the late 1950's as one of the leading figures of the postwar generation of writers. His short story "The Catch" received the coveted Akutagawa Prize in 1958. *A Personal Matter* won the 1964 Shinchōsha Literary Prize and *The Silent Cry* won the Tanizaki Jun'ichirō Prize in 1967. As Ōe's novels continued to win major Japanese literary awards, such as the Noma Literary Prize in 1973, the Yomiuri Prize in 1982, and the Ito Sei Literary Prize in 1990, his reputation began to attract international attention.

The European community awarded Ōe the Europelia Prize in 1989, and he won the Italian Mondelosso Prize in 1993. Ōe's high standing in world literature was fully recognized in 1994, when he won the Nobel Prize in Literature. Indicative of Ōe's inner conflict with what he called the antidemocratic cult of the Emperor at home in Japan, he immediately declined Japan's Imperial Order of Culture, which he received days after the Nobel Prize.

Kenzaburō Ōe, Nobel Laureate for Literature in 1994
(©The Nobel Foundation)

BIOGRAPHY

Kenzaburō Ōe was born on January 31, 1935, in a small village on Shikoku, the smallest of Japan's four main islands. The third son of seven children, he was only six when World War II erupted; he lost his father. Ōe was ten when Hiroshima and Nagasaki were destroyed by atomic attack as the war ended. He entered prestigious Tokyo University in 1954, studying French literature, and burst upon the literary scene while still a student there, publishing a short story, "Shisa no ogori" ("Lavish the Dead"), in the magazine *Bungakukai* in 1957. It attracted attention, and his talent was widely recognized when he received the prestigious Akutagawa Prize in 1958 for "The Catch," which draws upon his experience as a boy in a remote rural village during World War II.

After his graduation, Ōe married Itami Yukari, the daughter of screenwriter Itami Mansaku, in February, 1960. In May of that year he was a member of the Japan-China Literary Delegation, which met with Mao Zedong. The next year he traveled in the former Soviet Union and Western Europe, where he met Jean-Paul Sartre.

Drawing upon his childhood, Ōe dealt in his early works with alienation and those on the fringes of society, as well as political issues, contemporary society, and sexual mores. In the summer of 1963, however, his first son was born with serious brain damage, leading him to a new stage in his writing, in which he affirmed hope arising from despair. In five works written between 1964 and 1976, Ōe used the persistent theme of a father dealing with a disabled son: *A Personal Matter* and "Sora no kaibutsu Agui" ("Aghwee the Sky Monster") are notable examples.

In 1965, Ōe traveled to the United States, returning there for another visit in 1968. He also visited Australia, and in 1970 he toured Southeast Asia. He made frequent literary appearances and in 1975 took part in a two-day fast protesting the treatment of Korean writer and poet Kim Chi Ha. In 1976, Ōe met the Mexican writer Gabriel García Márquez after teaching for a semester at the Collegio de Mexico. Impressed by García Márquez's work, Ōe returned to Japan and published *Shosetsu no hoho* (1978; methodology of the novel), which promotes the Western literary theory of structuralism to revive Japanese writing. Indeed, many of Ōe's next writings show his fascination with structuralism and marginal existence.

Often traveling to Europe after 1980, Ōe visited the Soviet Union, where he attended a 1987 Conference on Peace in Moscow. Ōe also publicly debated authors: Germany's Günter Grass in 1990 and France's Michel Tournier in Paris in 1991.

Winning the Nobel Prize in Literature in 1994 came as a joyful surprise for Ōe. In his acceptance speech in Stockholm on December 7, 1994, Ōe claimed the prize in part on behalf of other dissident Asian writers, and he indirectly explained why he had immediately declined Japan's Imperial Order of Culture as belonging to a feudalistic past.

Back in Japan, Ōe told a stunned public that he would stop writing novels now that his mentally disabled son Hikari Ōe had become a successful composer of music. In 1997, Ōe's ongoing political involvement led to his participation in protests against French nuclear testing in the Pacific. Having settled in Tokyo with his wife and family, Ōe gave literary lectures around the world and continued to spend time with close friends.

ANALYSIS

Prewar Japanese writers such as Jun'ichirō Tanizaki and Yasunari Kawabata, who continued to build their literary reputations after the war, focused on the introspective (notably in the so-called I-novel), but New-Left writers emerging after the war, such as Kenzaburō Ōe, are as indebted to Western literary traditions as they are to those of Japan. Like his contemporary Kōbō Abe, Ōe writes about alienation from modern society and the loss of identity in modern Japan. He does so by using as themes his childhood in a small village, the war and subsequent occupation by Americans, and the personal tragedy of his son's birth defect.

One of the most prolific and popular writers in Japan, Ōe clearly reflects the concerns of the postwar generation, a generation that saw the fall of old symbols such as the Emperor. The war and defeat of Japan left a void in which his characters try to find themselves, groping for meaning. In "The Catch," the harmony of rural Japan is shattered as a young boy is disillusioned by the adults around him. In "The Day He Himself Shall Wipe My Tears Away," a boy sees his father's death as a sacrifice to the old values. This same hero appears in Ōe's later writing—older, but trying to escape through sex and deviant behavior. *Teach Us to Outgrow Our Madness* is a powerful tale of the importance of telling the truth, even when doing so can be painful. Ōe's unique style, heavily influenced by Western traditions and directness, is fresh and controversial, undergirding the issue addressed in most, if not all, of his fiction: the cultural disharmony that his generation has experienced as a result of World War II and its aftermath. In writing about his own personal crisis, Ōe deals with the larger themes of modernity and meaning in Japan. Like the hero in his favorite novel, Mark Twain's *Adventures of Huckleberry Finn* (1884), Ōe sees life as a quest for adventure, whether in Africa or in the back streets of Tokyo—a quest for truth.

"THE CATCH"

In "The Catch," the boy-narrator is combing the

village crematory looking for bone fragments with friends when an American plane roars overhead at treetop level. The next morning, the children awaken to an ominous silence. The adults are out searching for downed American airmen. They return late in the day from the mountains, leading an enormous black man. The boy is reminded of a boar hunt as the hunters silently circle around the captive, who has the chain from a boar trap around his legs.

The enemy excites both fear and curiosity among the children. He is put into the cellar of the communal storehouse and a guard is posted. The storehouse is a large building, and the boy and his young brother live on the second floor with their father, an impoverished hunter. The boy is excited at the thought of sleeping in the same building as the exotic prisoner who has fallen into their midst.

At first the captive is treated as a dangerous animal. The boy goes with his father to town to report the capture. He is uncomfortable in the town, aware of his poverty and dirtiness. The local officials refuse to take the prisoner until they receive orders from the prefecture offices. The boy and his father return to the village at sunset with the unwelcome news.

The boy carries food down into the dark cellar, guarded by his father with shotgun ready. At first the captive only stares at the food, and the boy realizes in shame that the poor dinner might be rejected, but the black man suddenly devours the meal. Gradually the boy loses his fear of the American as they bring him food every day. The children begin to take a proprietary interest in the captive. As time passes, the adults return to fieldwork, and the children are left with the American. Noticing that the man's leg is wounded from the boar trap, the boy and his friend release him with trepidation, but they find him well behaved. Even the adults in the village accept the idea that the black man is human, coming to trust him.

Eventually the children let the captive out of the cellar to walk through the village. The adults come to accept this, and he is even allowed to wander around the village alone. The women lose their fear and give him food from their own hands. The children take him to the village spring, where they all strip naked and splash in the water. The boy considers the man a splendid animal, an animal of great intelligence.

Trust and respect evaporate, however, when an official appears on a rainy day. As the adults assemble, the prisoner senses that he is about to be taken away, and he grabs the boy and drags him to the cellar, locking the door behind them. The boy is shocked and hurt as he realizes his sudden danger and sees the airman reverting to the dangerous beast he was when first captured. The grown-ups break into the cellar, and the boy's father plunges a hatchet into the prisoner's skull. They plan to cremate the black man but are ordered to keep the body for identification.

The story ends in irony. Paying another visit, the village official notices the children using the lightweight tail of the American plane as a sled on the grass. In a playful mood, he decides to give it a try, but he hurtles into a rock and is killed. He will be cremated with the wood that villagers collected to cremate the American captive.

Although the story is set during the war years and the events occur in the context of unusual hardship, its major theme, a youth's coming-of-age, is a universal one: The young boy finds his childhood innocence and trust betrayed by the black captive and the adults who rush to rescue him in a frenzy of hatred. There are echoes of *The Adventures of Huckleberry Finn* in this story: in the young boys' spirit of adventure, in their unaffected wonder and curiosity, and in their rejection of adult attitudes. (It is not surprising that, during his trip to the United States in 1965, Ōe visited Hannibal, Missouri, the birthplace of Mark Twain.) The coming-of-age theme also underscores another major concern in the story: man's (as opposed to boy's) inhumanity to man. Ōe uses juxtaposition to create a realistic yet somehow absurd view of the world; the young narrator allows him to introduce humorous elements of childish enthusiasm that make the final tragedy all the more appalling.

"AGHWEE THE SKY MONSTER"

In the short story "Aghwee the Sky Monster," a young father is haunted by an imaginary baby that flies down from the sky, reminding him of his own baby, whom he killed in the false belief that it had a malignant brain tumor. The story is told through a young college student, who is hired to take care of a banker's son. The student is told that the son, a composer, is having delusions and requires supervision. Needing the money, the student agrees to act as a chaperon, to help keep the son's mind off his delusions. The student accompanies the composer on trips about Tokyo, wary of the possibility that his charge may, at any moment, be joined by the imaginary Aghwee.

He learns that Aghwee is a fat baby, dressed in a white nightgown, who is as big as a kangaroo. From time to time, the composer believes that he sees Aghwee flying down to his side; this naturally alarms the student chaperon, who worries about a possible suicide attempt. In time, the student learns to step aside to leave room for the imaginary baby as they make excursions to bars, motion-picture theaters, and swimming pools, where they invariably turn back without entering the water. When the composer gets his chaperon to take a message to a former lover in Kyoto, the student learns that the lovers were in bed together in a hotel room when a call came from the hospital informing them of the death of the baby, who had uttered only one sound, "Aghwee."

Then disaster strikes. While walking on the Ginza on Christmas Eve with the composer and Aghwee, the student is shocked as they are mysteriously pitched forward into the path of a truck; the student escapes serious harm, but the composer is fatally injured. Visiting the dying composer in the hospital later that day, the student admits that he was about to believe in Aghwee, and the composer smiles. He dies the next day.

Ten years later, the student is suddenly attacked by rock-throwing children who have been mysteriously provoked. One of the rocks hits him in the eye, and he suddenly senses a large white being the size of a kangaroo: Aghwee. He has completed his identification with the dead composer's fantasy.

"THE DAY HE HIMSELF SHALL WIPE MY TEARS AWAY"

In his lengthy short story "Mizu kara waga namida o nuguitamau hi" ("The Day He Himself Shall Wipe My Tears Away"), Ōe again writes about a man who is trying to grasp the reality of his youth, this time in an isolated farm village as World War II was ending. It is difficult and sometimes frustrating work, and the background of the story is only gradually revealed as the protagonist shifts from the present to a mythical reconstruction of events.

The story opens in a hospital room where the man is dying, or imagines he is dying (this is never resolved), of cancer. What is clear is that the narrator is grappling with a lifetime struggle to free himself from his mother's harsh and stifling influence. He is dictating a history of the events leading to his father's bizarre death in a futile uprising on August 16, 1945, the day after the Japanese surrender in World War II. He attempts to shut his mother and the rest of the contemporary world out by wearing his father's old goggles, which are masked with green cellophane. His identification with his father and his reconstruction of events that he only dimly understood as a six-year-old boy are meant to challenge his mother's sarcastic realism and allow him to relive the most important moment in his life.

The boy's father apparently was involved in right-wing political activities with the military in Manchuria in Northeastern China. After Japan's military fortunes took a turn for the worse at Midway and Guadalcanal, the father was involved with an underground group that was against Prime Minister Tōjō. Their plans to change policy failed, for the father suddenly appeared in the valley on January 1, 1943, going straight into seclusion in the storehouse.

The boy's elder stepbrother was sent to war and became the valley's first war casualty. Even though he was not her own son, the narrator's mother took the death as a failure of the father and his politics. Thereafter, his name was never spoken in the family; throughout the story he is referred to as "a certain party," who lived by himself in a shed behind the main house. His mother also shut herself off from all contact with the neighbors in the valley, ignoring everyone thereafter.

The valley was not a peaceful childhood sanctuary for the young boy, for he was subject to ridicule and hazing by the village children at school. When school bullies taunted him for his impoverished appearance, he stabbed himself in the hand with a hand sickle and

threatened to slit his own throat if they attempted to harm him. Confused and appalled, the gang backed off because the boy did not react normally: "He's like a *kamikaze* pilot that didn't get to die!" In the same fashion, the narrator, now thirty-five years old, hopes to upstage his elderly mother by dying of real or imagined cancer.

He was still psychologically wounded by her actions when she caught him attempting suicide when he was almost out of high school. She took his suicide note, stole into the mimeograph room of the school, printed it, and distributed it to all of his teachers and classmates to reveal his weakness. To complete his humiliation, she noted all the incorrect characters he had written in the sentimental will. By making him the fool, she made it impossible for him to consider suicide in the future. Now he believes that cancer can get her attention.

As a boy he both feared and admired his father, wanting to be recognized and accepted, but he was ignored. His father was repugnantly fat, spending his days in semidarkness, sitting in a barber chair, wearing the green goggles. While in Manchuria he had acquired the habit of eating meat, and he had sent the boy to town to buy the only meat Japanese would not eat, oxtails and pig feet. Acquiring his loathsome burden, the boy also had had to visit Korean forest workers to ask for some garlic to flavor the stew his father was going to make. His father had emerged from his dark room to cook the meat outdoors but collapsed on the boy, venting blood and urine. The doctor had been summoned and had diagnosed cancer of the bladder. From that time, the summer of 1944, his father had remained inside the storehouse, his disease slowly progressing.

The critical incident in the story is the appearance in the valley of ten soldiers who had deserted their unit when the surrender of Japan was announced. They came to the house to enlist the support of the former political activist but also to get the funds that the boy's mother had inherited. That night, the soldiers made plans to go to the city the next day to get money from the bank; they hoped to capture some army planes, disguise them as American planes, and somehow fly to Tokyo and crash them into the Imperial Palace in a final attempt to get the Japanese people to rise up against the invaders. They drank sake and listened over and over to an old German record on the phonograph, a Bach cantata with the line, "His Majesty the Emperor wipes my tears away with his own hand, Death, you come ahead, you brother of Sleep you come ahead, his Majesty will wipe my tears away with his own hand. . . ." It is from this evocation of the prewar imperial ethos that Ōe chose his title.

The next morning, the ten soldiers pulled the father in a hand-built cart to a truck they had stolen and drove to town. The boy's father was bleeding from his terminal cancer and was in considerable pain, but he agreed to lead the quixotic band. The group vowed *junshi*, or death, as a sign of allegiance to the emperor. As they emerged from the bank—it was not clear whether they had robbed it or made a withdrawal on the mother's account—they encountered another band of soldiers who opened fire on them, killing all of them except the young boy.

Just as the narrator gets to this crux of the story, the mother suddenly speaks from the corner of the hospital room. She may have been there all along, taking it all in. His mother narrates a different account, describing in cynical terms the soldiers who came after the money and the futility of the make-believe uprising. She shatters the mythical reconstruction the narrator has been trying to build, once again dominating his life and reducing him to a madness that only death will relieve.

Teach Us to Outgrow Our Madness

For a contemporary American reader, Ōe's recurrent concern with the issue of mental disability, which is also at the core of his novella *Teach Us to Outgrow Our Madness*, sheds an interesting light on another culture's handling of the subject. Yet here, while Ōe illuminates aspects of the traditional fear of disability as possibly hereditary and shameful in Japan, his fiction outspokenly opposes this view and argues for a positive attitude of compassion for the disabled. Thus, the story's father, referred to only as "the fat man," refuses to kill his love for his disabled four-year-old son, even in the face of severe social prejudice.

The story unfolds as the father gradually recovers from nearly being thrown into the pool of the polar bear exhibit at the Tokyo Zoo. As he lies in his bed alone, in a moment of existential self-introspection typical for Ōe's characters, he mentally recounts a conflict with his mother. Recently, she has unjustly accused him of having contracted syphilis in China, a sexually transmitted disease which, if not treated, can lead to brain damage and was believed to be transmitted to one's children. Thus, she viciously insists on a link between her husband, the "fat man's" father, whom she calls mad for admiring the Chinese and mysteriously secluding himself in a storehouse for years before dying with a blood-curdling scream, and her "mad" son who passed on his illness to her grandson.

Gradually, Ōe deconstructs this convenient belief of the mother, who uses the term "madness" to explain anything which does not fit in her traditional views. She thus becomes a stand-in for those parts of traditional Japanese culture which Ōe himself felt he rejected when he declined Japan's Imperial Order of Culture in 1994. For as the story reveals, the "fat man's" father confined himself because he let down his friends who tried to kill the Emperor during World War II as a protest against Japan's war on China.

The "fat man's" probing for details about his father's actions is rejected by his mother as a mere symptom of syphilitic madness, for to acknowledge the validity of his quest would lead the mother to confront the fact of Japanese atrocities against the Chinese in the war, an issue which had met with near-unanimous silence in the Japanese postwar political debate until the 1990's. The false excuse of syphilis also serves to exonerate the mother from any societal blame for her own genes when it comes to her grandson's disability.

The "fat man" comes to repudiate all this, and Ōe offers an exquisite description of his loving, emphatic relationship with his son Mori. The father named him so after the Japanese word for forest, in an allusion to his being a child of nature rather than intellect. Betraying the influence of Western writing on the author, the father also calls his son affectionately

Eeyore, the name of the little donkey in A. A. Milne's English story *Winnie-the-Pooh* (1926).

In the end, the "fat man's" love for his son causes his mother to renounce the false story of her son's alleged syphilis, and to tell the truth about her husband. As Ōe's story implies, the "fat man's" love finally leads his family to outgrow their real madness of lying.

OTHER MAJOR WORKS

LONG FICTION: *Memushiri kouchi*, 1958 (*Nip the Buds, Shoot the Kids*, 1995); *Warera no jidai*, 1959; *Yoru yo yuruyaka ni ayume*, 1959; *Seinenno omei*, 1960; *Okurete kita seinen*, 1962; *Sakebigoe*, 1963; *Kojinteki na taiken*, 1964 (*A Personal Matter*, 1968); *Nichyoseikatsu no boken*, 1964; *Man'en gannen no futtoboru*, 1967 (*The Silent Cry*, 1974); *Nichijo seikatsu no boken*, 1971; *Kōzui wa waga tamashii ni oyobi*, 1973; *Pinchi rannā chōsho*, 1976 (*The Pinch Runner Memorandum*, 1994); *Atarashii hito yo mezameyo*, 1983; *Atarashii hito yo mezameyo*, 1983; *Natsukashii toshi e no tegami*, 1987; *Jinsei no shinseki*, 1989 (*An Echo of Heaven*, 1996); *Chiryōtō*, 1990; *Shizuka na seikatsu*, 1990 (*A Quiet Life*, 1996); *Chiryōtō wakusei*, 1991; *Moeagaru midori no ki*, 1993-1995 (includes *"Sukuinushi" ga nagurareru made*, 1993; *Yureugoku "vashireshon,"* 1994; *Ōinaru hi ni*, 1995).

NONFICTION: *Sekai no wakamonotachi*, 1962; *Hiroshima nōto*, 1965 (*Hiroshima Notes*, 1982); *Genshuku na tsunawatari*, 1965; *Jisokusuru kokorozashi*, 1968; *Kowaremoto to shite no ningen*, 1970; *Kakujidai no sōzōryoku*, 1970; *Okinawa nōto*, 1970; *Dōjidai to shite no sengo*, 1973; *Bungaku noto*, 1974; *Jōkyō e*, 1974; *Kotoba ni yotte*, 1976; *Shōsetsu no hōhō*, 1978; *Ōe Kenzaburō dojidaironshu*, 1981; *Sengo bungakusha*, 1981; *Kaku no taika to "ningen" no koe*, 1982; *Atarashii bungaku no tame ni*, 1988; *Bungaku sainyūmon*, 1992; *Aimai na Nihon no watakushi*, 1995 (*Japan, the Ambiguous, and Myself*, 1995); *Kaifuku suru kazoku*, 1995 (*A Healing Family*, 1996); *On Politics and Literature: Two Lectures*, 1999.

EDITED TEXT: *Nan to moshirenai mirai ni*, 1985 (*The Crazy Iris and Other Stories of the Atomic Aftermath*, 1985).

BIBLIOGRAPHY

Cargas, Harry James. "Fiction of Shame." *The Christian Century* 112 (April 12, 1995): 382-383. Brief biographical sketch, commenting on Ōe's theme of guilt over Japanese attraction to Western customs and rejection of their own traditions and guilt over the sneak attack on Pearl Harbor, which violates the samurai code of honor.

Ōe, Kenzaburō. "Kenzaburō Ōe: After the Nobel, a New Direction." Interview by Sam Staggs. *Publishers Weekly* 242 (August 7, 1995): 438-439. Ōe talks about his decision to discontinue writing fiction; discusses his lifestyle and his relationship with Jean-Paul Sartre.

Remnick, David. "Reading Japan." *The New Yorker* 70 (February 6, 1995): 38-44. Recounts a meeting with Ōe, in which the writer talks about his life and art. Discusses Ōe's obsession with his mentally disabled son in several of his stories and his place in modern Japanese culture and literature.

Swain, David L. "Something Akin to Grace: The Journey of Kenzaburō Ōe." *The Christian Century* 114 (December 24-31, 1997): 1226-1229. Brief profile, discussing Ōe's sense of native place, his sense of marginalization, and his literary cosmopolitanism; briefly discusses *An Echo of Heaven* and *A Healing Family*.

Wilson, Michiko Niikuni. "Kenzaburō Ōe." *The Georgia Review* 49 (Spring, 1995): 331-350. A biographical sketch, including a bibliography of Ōe's work that has been translated into English. This article also includes the text of Ōe's 1994 Nobel Prize lecture, in which he discusses the influence of Mark Twain and Yasunari Kawabata on his work and comments on contemporary Japanese culture and literature. Ōe also used this vehicle to make his famous announcement that he would stop writing fiction.

_____. *The Marginal World of Ōe Kenzaburō: A Study in Themes and Techniques*. Armonk, N.Y.: M. E. Sharpe, 1986. An attempt at dealing with the weird, grotesque, and perverse imagination of Ōe by showing—or attempting to show—how two short stories and three novels present the relationship of a corpulent father and his mentally disabled son by establishing a unity of theme, a chronological development, and an ironic turn of events.

Yamanouchi, Hisaaki. "In Search of Identity: Abe Kōbō and Ōe Kenzaburō." In *The Search for Authenticity in Modern Japanese Literature*. New York: Cambridge University Press, 1978. Draws parallels between Abe and Ōe respecting their treatment of themes and mutual concern in the search for identity. The ideas of identity, authenticity, and alienation that Ōe attempts to use are Western themes stemming from the existentialist philosophy of Martin Heidegger and Jean-Paul Sartre. Ōe seeks to graft these themes onto a Japanese culture that, although it has been rapidly modernized, still manages to maintain some strong traditions. Yet Ōe insists on using antisocial characters, whether juvenile delinquents, sexual perverts, or vicious criminals, whom he treats as "fallen angels," while he himself dreams of a "pastoral community."

Yoshida, Sanroku. "Kenzaburō Ōe: A New World of Imagination." *Comparative Literature Studies* 22 (Spring, 1985): 80-96. Ōe is presented as the lead-

ing Japanese literary reformer, who, rejecting literary elitism and high art, holds that literature should be democratic and should appeal to the masses in didactic terms. Ōe sees literature under the obligation to protest against social evils, which, in his view, have only political solutions. Hence he believes that political ideology has a legitimate place in literature.

_____. "Kenzaburō Ōe's Recent Modernist Experiments." *Critique: Studies in Modern Fiction* 26 (Spring, 1985): 155-164. A general view of Ōe's innovative narrative techniques, including his characterizations, his recurrent themes, and his stylistic practices. Stylistically he is said to have attempted to wed the structure of the Japanese language to Indo-European structure. He also indulges widely in grotesque and animal imagery. His narrative techniques include scrambled chronologies and spatial narrative structure. His characterizations feature a voiceless narrator, switched identities, and a character who turns out to be the author's *Doppelgänger*.

Richard Rice, updated by Richard P. Benton and R. C. Lutz

SEÁN O'FAOLÁIN
John Francis Whelan

Born: Cork, Ireland; February 22, 1900
Died: Dublin, Ireland; April 20, 1991

PRINCIPAL SHORT FICTION

Midsummer Night's Madness and Other Stories, 1932

A Purse of Coppers, 1937

Teresa and Other Stories, 1947

The Man Who Invented Sin and Other Stories, 1948

The Finest Stories of Seán O'Faoláin, 1957

I Remember! I Remember!, 1961

The Heat of the Sun: Stories and Tales, 1966

The Talking Trees and Other Stories, 1970

Foreign Affairs and Other Stories, 1976

The Collected Stories of Seán O'Faoláin, 1980-1982 (3 volumes)

OTHER LITERARY FORMS

Seán O'Faoláin's literary production includes novels, biographies, travel books, social analysis, and literary criticism. He wrote a number of well-received novels and several biographies of prominent Irish political figures. O'Faoláin's most notable work

Seán O'Faoláin in 1954 (AP/Wide World Photos)

of literary criticism is his study of the short story, *The Short Story*, published in 1948. O'Faoláin also wrote a memorable autobiography, *Vive Moi!* (1964).

ACHIEVEMENTS

Seán O'Faoláin is one of the acknowledged Irish masters of the short story. His stories are realistic and closely dissect the social world of the ordinary Irishman of the twentieth century. His protagonists are usually forced to accept the limitations and defeats that life in modern Ireland enforces. O'Faoláin, however, is not a social critic or satirist. Such an accommodation with society is often seen as welcome and necessary. The central theme in many of O'Faoláin's stories is the defeat of rigid principle and idealism by social and individual compromise. O'Faoláin seems to resist any appeal to pure principle and to celebrate a healthy realism and recognition of the limits that life imposes.

Seán O'Faoláin's most important structural device is the reversal, in which a character's situation is sud-

denly altered. These reversals may be embarrassing or even humiliating, but O'Faoláin often softens the ending to show something human and positive even in the defeat that the reversal effects. O'Faoláin progressed as a writer of short fiction from his early autobiographical stories, focusing on the Irish troubles and civil war to stories dealing with a variety of Irish people in different sections and social situations. The autobiography became a more flexible and distanced art as O'Faoláin approached the ideal of his master, Anton Chekhov.

BIOGRAPHY

Seán O'Faoláin was born as John Francis Whelan in the city of Cork, Ireland, in 1900. His parents led an untroubled conventional life; his father was a constable for the Royal Irish Constabulary and his mother a pious Roman Catholic. By the time that John grew up, however, the problems of Ireland and England were becoming acute. The 1916 uprising in Dublin declared an Irish Republic, and a war broke out between Irish revolutionaries and British soldiers. John Whelan knew on which side he had to be and joined the Irish Volunteers in 1918 and later the Irish Republican Army. He changed his name to its Gaelic form of Seán O'Faoláin in 1918 to signal his new identity.

During the Irish troubles, O'Faoláin was educating himself; he received his B.A. and M.A. from University College, Cork, and a fellowship to Harvard University in 1928. In 1932, he published his first collection of short stories, *Midsummer Night's Madness and Other Stories*. After that O'Faoláin became a prolific writer, as he produced novels, travel books, biographies, and studies of the national character of Ireland. Above all, however, he was a masterly writer of short stories.

O'Faoláin's *Midsummer Night's Madness and Other Stories* contains a number of stories dealing with the Irish Civil War. Most of these treat broken promises and the destruction of idealism and romantic dreams. The later collections contain a considerable amount of irony, as the ordinary Irishman, with little hope of engaging in a historic event, tries to find some distinction in a bleak society. O'Faoláin, however, often modulates his irony and finds some compensatory victory even in defeat.

After having found his style and subject matter, O'Faoláin published a number of excellent collections of stories, culminating in *The Collected Stories of Seán O'Faoláin*. O'Faoláin has become one of the finest Irish writers of the twentieth century and a master in his chosen genre, the short story.

ANALYSIS

Seán O'Faoláin's stories are varied. The earliest ones deal with the immediate political concerns of the Irish Civil War. Others use irony, although the irony tends to be gentle rather than harsh. O'Faoláin never merely mocked or made fun of his characters; there is always affection and sympathy for those he created. Another group of stories expose idealism or abstract principles. O'Faoláin had little use for such general principles; he was consistently on the side of the specific case and the demands of realism and life. The later stories deal with sexuality and relationships between man and woman, especially the problems of husbands and wives.

A few constants do exist, however, in the stories. O'Faoláin's strength is in the portrayal and development of character and world. Each of his major characters fully exists in a well-defined environment. Ireland, as portrayed by O'Faoláin, is nearly a character in the story, and the limitations created by that world are significant. Whether it be religion or a narrow-minded social system, Ireland often restricts in various ways the opportunities for expression and a fuller and freer life.

"THE OLD MASTER"

"The Old Master," from *A Purse of Coppers*, is an early story that punctures the claims of a character to a privileged position; it uses a sudden and surprising reversal to bring about its resolution. The use of irony in this story is direct and amusing, if not very sophisticated. The protagonist, John Aloysius Gonzaga O'Sullivan, spends his time mocking the provincialism and lack of culture in his small Irish town. He has a sinecure as a law librarian and refuses to practice law; he spends his time, instead, berating the locals for their lack of sophistication. He is "the only man

left in Ireland with a sense of beauty . . . the old master deserted in the abandoned house."

One day, the Russian Ballet comes to town, and he is ecstatic. A conflict arises, however, from the presence of the Russian Ballet. When O'Sullivan attempts to see a performance, he is stopped by men from the Catholic Church who oppose "Immoral Plays." O'Sullivan holds his sinecure from the county council, and he can lose his job if he offends the Catholic Church. Therefore, he compromises and walks away from the door; he has apparently failed to live up to his ideals. He tries, however, to make amends by sneaking in the back way and reassuring the Russian performers that he is with them.

O'Sullivan returns to the front of the theater and is immediately involved in a march against the ballet company. If he is seen by the people at the courthouse, he will be ruined, but if he is seen abandoning the march, he may lose his job. He tries to resolve his conflict by escaping to an outhouse and cursing the local leaders, as he has done so often in the past. He remains in the outhouse all night and catches pneumonia from this exposure and soon dies. The people in the town had seen him earlier as a "public show" and only at his death did they see him as a "human being." "The Old Master" is a typical O'Faoláin story. The unnatural idealism and pomposity of the main character have to be exposed. He is not mocked, however, for his fall; he has instead joined a fallible human community and rid himself of false pretensions.

"CHILDYBAWN"

"Childybawn" was published in *The Finest Stories of Seán O'Faoláin*, and it is a delightful study of the Irish character in which O'Faoláin reverses the usual view of the Irishman's dominance by his mother. The story is simple in its structure, and its effect depends on a reversal of expectations. O'Faoláin is not really a comic writer in the traditional sense; in later stories, the humor is much more subtle and becomes a part of the story, not the only element as it is here. The plot begins when Benjy Spillane's mother receives an anonymous note telling her that her son, fat and forty, is carrying on with a bank teller. Her strategy to retain the dedication and presence of her son is to remind him incessantly of Saint Augustine's love for his mother, Monica. This has little effect until Benjy becomes seriously ill and begins to read religious texts and change his life.

Suddenly the relationship is reversed; the religious Benjy begins complaining about the drinking and excessive betting of his mother. His mother now wishes that he would get married and leave her alone. The climax of the story is another reversal, as Benjy returns to his riotous ways and finally gains the promise of the bank clerk to wed him. There is a five-year engagement until his mother dies. After all, Benjy notes, "a fellow has to have *some* regard for his mother!"

"Childybawn" is a comic story and plays on many Irish stereotypes. There is the dominating mother and the middle-aged son who worships his mother. O'Faoláin gives the story and the types an original twist when he shows what would happen if a middle-aged son actually behaved the way a mother wished him to behave. Mrs. Spillane realizes that she has not had a peaceful moment since her son took up religion; she longs for the old, irreverent, and natural relationship that works on conflict and confrontation.

"THE FUR COAT"

"The Fur Coat" is a poignant story taken from *The Man Who Invented Sin and Other Stories*. It is concerned with social class, a somewhat unusual area for an O'Faoláin story. Most of his characters seem to live in a static environment, and such social change in Ireland is very different from the earlier stories. The plot is very simple, since it emphasizes character rather than action. Paddy Maguire receives an important promotion, so his wife, Molly, immediately determines that she must have a fur coat to go with her new status. She immediately becomes defensive over such a purchase, however, asking her husband if he thinks that she is "extravagant." The conflict grows between husband and wife as they discuss the fur coat, but it is really within Molly. Her own doubts about such a purchase are projected onto her husband, and they end up fighting, with her accusing him of being "mean." The climax of the story comes when Paddy gives Molly a check for £150 and she rips it

up. She wants the coat desperately, but she cannot afford it. "I couldn't, Paddy. I just couldn't." The story ends with Paddy asking her why she cannot purchase what she most desires and receiving the despairing answer, "I don't know."

"The Fur Coat" is a social story as well as a character study. The sudden rise in class and position leaves Molly between the old ways that have sustained her and the new ones that she cannot embrace. O'Faoláin has found a new subject for Irish fiction. The focus is no longer the enduring and unchanging peasant but an urban middle-class character who must deal with changes in his or her social position and personal life.

"THE SUGAWN CHAIR"

"The Sugawn Chair," from *I Remember! I Remember!*, is a perfect example of O'Faoláin's gentle irony; the story pokes fun at the illusions of an ideal rural life with economy and humor. O'Faoláin seems dedicated to exposing the various illusions that are endemic in Ireland. The chair, as the story opens, is abandoned and without a seat in the attic of the narrator. He associates the chair with memories of a yearly sack of apples that would be delivered, smelling of "dust, and hay, and apples. . . ." The sack and the chair both signify another world, the country.

The chair also has a history. It was an object of comfort in which "my da could tilt and squeak and rock to his behind's content." One night while rocking, his father went through the seat of the chair, where he remained stuck and cursing, much to the amusement of his wife and son. The father decides to repair his chair with some straw that he bought in a market. He enlists the aid of two of his country comrades. They soon, however, begin to argue about the different regions that they came from in rural Ireland. These arguments subside, but a new argument erupts about the type of straw needed to repair the chair. One claims that this straw is too moist, while another says that it is too short. Finally, they abandon the project and return to their earlier pursuits.

The story ends with the father symbolically admitting defeat by throwing a potato back into the sack and sitting on one of the city-made "plush" chairs. The Sugawn chair remains as it had been, shattered without a seat. The narrator comes upon the chair one day when he is cleaning out the attic after his mother has died. It recalls to his mind not only the country smells but also his mother and father embracing and "laughing foolishly, and madly in love again." "The Sugawn Chair" modulates its irony at the very end, so that the mocking at the illusions of an ideal rural life are tempered by the real feelings and memories that they share. O'Faoláin is by no means a James Joyce who fiercely indicts the false dreams of his Dubliners. O'Faoláin has a place even in his irony for true affections and relationships.

"DIVIDENDS"

"Dividends," from *The Heat of the Sun: Stories and Tales*, is a more ambitious story than many of the earlier ones, and it shows both a greater tolerance for the foibles of the characters and a subtlety in structure. Its primary subject is the clash between principle and reality, a favorite O'Faoláin theme. The story begins with the narrator's Aunt Anna coming into a legacy of £750. The narrator advises her to invest her legacy in secure stocks, so that she will receive a steady income. An old friend of the narrator, Mel Meldrum, arranges the transaction. The conflict arises when Aunt Anna sells her shares and continues to demand her dividends from Mel. Mel finally gives in and pays her the money, even though it is against his principles.

In order to resolve the dispute, the narrator is forced to return to Cork from Dublin. He finds that Mel is very well situated, with a country cottage and a beautiful young girl as a servant. Mel reveals that Aunt Anna has sold the shares not for a chair and some masses for her soul but for a fancy fur coat. Mel now refuses to compromise and pay Anna her dividends. This intensifies the conflict as the narrator urges Mel to be his old self and take a chance on life, abandon his principles, pay Aunt Anna the dividends, and marry the young girl. Mel, however, is unable to change; if he marries the girl, he may be unhappy; if he pays the dividends, he is compromised and is no longer his ideal self.

Mel resolves the problem by abandoning his relationship with the young girl and hiring Aunt Anna as a servant. He will remain logical and consistent.

The ending of the story, however, is not an indictment of Mel's principled consistency but a confession by the narrator that he has done something terrible by demanding that Mel remain the Mel that he had known as a boy at school. He had "uncovered his most secret dream and destroyed it by forcing him to bring it to the test of reality." He also has been narrow-minded in demanding a consistency of character and exposed a life-giving illusion no less than Mel had. "Dividends" is a complex narrative and a psychological study of how characters live upon illusions rather than principles. There is no neat exposure of illusions as in "The Old Master" but instead an unmasking of those who are all too eager to uncover dreams.

"HYMENEAL"

"Hymeneal" is a story from O'Faoláin's latest period, and it is one of the fullest explorations of marriage, as O'Faoláin scrutinizes the relationship between husband and wife. "Hymeneal" covers the many years of a couple's marriage, but it focuses on the period of retirement. It is one of O'Faoláin's best plotted stories, with a sudden and surprising reversal. It begins peacefully, detailing the enduring relationship of a married couple, Phil and Abby Doyle, who have been rooted in one spot in the North Circular section of Dublin. They have lived in this section for some thirty-five years. Phil, however, is to retire in a year, and he knows that Abby needs some help with the house, but he cannot afford it on his pension. He then decides—without consulting his wife—to sell their house and move to West Clare, where he can hire a servant and have the peace and time to write the book that he has been planning to write for years, which will expose the Education Department and Ministry.

The conflict between Phil and Abby develops quickly. She hates the isolation of West Clare, especially since it means moving away from her Dublin-based sister, Molly. Phil is also unhappy, although he refuses to admit it. He does none of the things that he has talked about for years; he does not fish or hunt, and he makes no progress on his book, although he continues to talk about it. Phil talks incessantly about exposing the department, where he has worked for such a long time, and the current minister, Phelim Quigley, the husband of Molly, Abby's sister. He sees Phelim as the perfect example of a man who has sacrificed principle to sentiment and convenience. When Phelim refuses to fire a teacher who drinks and quarrels with his wife, Phil Doyle is outraged at this lack of action. The book will reveal all.

The plot turns when Phelim Quigley suddenly dies in a car crash and Phil and Abby return to Dublin to console Molly and set her affairs in order. Phil assigns himself to work alone to sort out Phelim's papers. In those papers, Phil finds a number of surprising documents that alter his life. First of all, he finds that Phelim has acquired a decent sum of money and has recently purchased Phil's old house in Dublin. He then finds a sequence of poems that Phelim has written about his love for Abby rather than his wife, Molly. Phil is enraged at this soiling of his own love for Abby. Phil changes once more, however, when he comes upon some letters of Abby to Phelim that tell of Phelim's advice to Abby to stick to Phil and not divorce or leave him. Phelim also praises Phil's great ability as a civil servant; it is just those rigid qualities, however, that have made it so difficult to live with him. The whole tone and attitude of the last part of the story changes. The weather changes from stormy to sunny and clear. Molly announces that she would like to rent the Dublin house that she and Phelim had bought recently to Phil and Abby. Phil has become more accommodating. He will abandon his book and his inhuman principle for a fuller and less rigid life.

"THE PATRIOT"

O'Faoláin's fiction shows clear lines of development. The early stories that focus on the Irish Civil War are filled with bitterness at the failure of leaders to live up to the republican ideal. They also tend to lack the smooth narrative surface, and some, such as "The Patriot," are quite simple and undemanding in their structure. The collections that followed showed an increasing mastery of the short-story form. They also avoid the simple structure and tiresome bitterness at the failures of ideals. "The Old Master," for example, shows an exposure of ideals that can deepen a character's humanity.

By the time of *I Remember! I Remember!*, O'Faoláin had mastered the short story; the stories from this period demonstrate a subtlety of characterization, plot, and theme that was not found in the earlier works. In addition, O'Faoláin changes his attitude toward the world of his fiction. He now was able to distance himself and find amusement in the dreams of his characters, as "The Sugawn Chair" makes clear. The last phase of O'Faoláin's development can be seen in the stories of *The Heat of the Sun: Stories and Tales* and *The Talking Trees and Other Stories*. He began more fully to investigate the place and role of sexuality in Ireland. Stories such as "One Man, One Boat, One Girl" and "Falling Rocks, Narrowing Road, Cul-de-Sac Stop" are humorous explorations of human relationships. The Irishman's fear of women is handled with grace and sympathy, while at the same time acknowledging its absurdity. One other aspect of human relationships in O'Faoláin's fiction needs to be mentioned. "Hymeneal" is a haunting portrayal of marriage in which the main character's illusions are punctured so that he might re-create and strengthen his relationship with his wife.

OTHER MAJOR WORKS

LONG FICTION: *A Nest of Simple Folk*, 1933; *Bird Alone*, 1936; *Come Back to Erin*, 1940; *And Again?*, 1979.

PLAY: *She Had to Do Something*, pr. 1937.

NONFICTION: *The Life Story of Eamon De Valera*, 1933; *Constance Markievicz: Or, The Average Revolutionary*, 1934; *King of the Beggars: A Life of Daniel O'Connell*, 1938; *An Irish Journey*, 1940; *The Great O'Neill: A Biography of Hugh O'Neill, Earl of Tyrone, 1550-1616*, 1942; *The Story of Ireland*, 1943; *The Irish: A Character Study*, 1947; *The Short Story*, 1948; *A Summer in Italy*, 1949; *Newman's Way*, 1952; *South to Sicily*, 1953 (published in the United States as *An Autumn in Italy*, 1953); *The Vanishing Hero*, 1956; *Vive Moi!*, 1964.

EDITED TEXT: *The Silver Branch*, 1938.

BIBLIOGRAPHY

Bonaccorso, Richard. *Seán O'Faoláin's Irish Vision.* Albany: State University of New York Press,

1987. An excellent study that places O'Faoláin and his work in a social and literary context. His readings of the stories are thorough and ingenious, if not always convincing.

Butler, Pierce. *Seán O'Faoláin: A Study of the Short Fiction*. New York: Twayne, 1993. An introduction to O'Faoláin's short fiction in which Butler claims that O'Faoláin shifts from an early focus on individuals in conflict with repressive Irish forces to more universal human conflicts. Examines O'Faoláin's realistic style and narrative voice as it changes throughout his career. Includes O'Faoláin's comments on the short story, some contemporary reviews, and three previously published critical studies.

Davenport, Guy. "Fiction Chronicle." *The Hudson Review* 32 (1979): 139-150. In a review article, Davenport has high praise for O'Faoláin's ability as a writer of short fiction. He finds the central themes of the stories to be the Irish character and Irish Catholicism.

Doyle, Paul A. *Sean O'Faoláin*. New York: Twayne, 1968. A life and works study of O'Faoláin in the Twayne series. It is good on the novels and the literary context in which O'Faoláin wrote but only adequate on the short fiction.

Hanley, Katherine. "The Short Stories of Seán O'Faoláin: Theory and Practice." *Eire-Ireland* 6 (1971): 3-11. An excellent introduction to O'Faoláin's stories. Hanley briefly sketches the theoretical base of the stories and then traces the development of O'Faoláin from the early romantic stories to the more sophisticated ones.

Harmon, Maurice. *Seán O'Faoláin*. London: Constable, 1994. Harmon first analyzes O'Faoláin's biographies on Irish figures to provide a social context and then examines briefly each book of short stories. Useful for an understanding of the Irish political and social scene.

Neary, Michael. "Whispered Presences in Seán O'Faoláin's Stories." *Studies in Short Fiction* 32 (Winter, 1995): 11-20. Argues that O'Faoláin confronts his Irishness in his stories in a way that refuses closure or the comfort of the telling detail. Asserts that many of his stories create a feeling of characters being haunted by some event from the past that cannot be made sense of.

James Sullivan

CHRIS OFFUTT

Born: Rowan County, Kentucky; August 24, 1958

PRINCIPAL SHORT FICTION

Kentucky Straight, 1992
Out of the Woods, 1999

OTHER LITERARY FORMS

Less than a year after the publication of his first collection of short stories, Chris Offutt published *The Same River Twice: A Memoir* (1993). His first novel, *The Good Brother*, was published in 1997.

ACHIEVEMENTS

Chris Offutt was named one of *Granta*'s Best Young American Fiction Writers. He has received a Whiting Writers Award, the Jean Stein Award from the American Academy of Arts and Letters, a fellowship from the National Endowment for the Arts, and a John Simon Guggenheim Memorial Foundation Fellowship. His work has been anthologized in *The Picador Book of American Short Stories* and in *The Best American Short Stories 1994*.

BIOGRAPHY

Chris Offutt was born in 1958 in Rowan County, Kentucky, near the tiny town of Haldeman, an area he once described as "a zip code with a creek," to his mother, Mary "Jody" Jo McCabe, a teacher, and his

Chris Offutt (©Miriam Berkley)

father, Andrew Jefferson Offutt, a teacher-turned-science-fiction-writer. Before earning a B.A. in theater arts from Morehead State University (also in Rowan County), Offutt hitchhiked around the country, working at odd jobs. Among his more colorful jobs was a stint in Alabama with a circus, where he tended the elephants and got a role in one of the animal acts dressed as a walrus. While in Boston he met Rita Lily, who later became his wife. After their plans to move back to Rowan County fell through, Offutt was accepted into the writing program at the University of Iowa, where he earned an M.F.A. in 1990. He and Rita lived in a small rented house on the Iowa River until they migrated to Albuquerque then to Montana before they completed the circle by returning to Rowan County, Kentucky, where Offutt took a job teaching creative writing at Morehead State University.

ANALYSIS

The one ubiquitous character throughout the fiction of Chris Offutt is the hill country of eastern Kentucky. It is not just a location or a backdrop for stories, as it has so often been for other Kentucky

writers, such as James Lane Allen and Jesse Stuart. Offutt's hills are living, breathing things that hold people and, within the workings of the story, often become like a deuteragonist, the character who most heavily influences and motivates the protagonist. In his early fiction, eastern Kentucky, wounded, suspicious, and recovering from the damages of the coal and steel companies, which, in earlier generations, stripped it and its people of physical and spiritual worth, leaving nothing but wounds and scars, is entering a new age. New roads and new forms of communication are forcing connections with the rest of the world, allowing the people to move, in the words of Terry Heller in his review of *Kentucky Straight*, Offutt's first collection of stories, "from subsistence living to consumerism." Offutt deals with the growing pains of these changes without derision or mockery. He does not create stereotypical hillbillies or subhuman families that breed only within their own family. He deals with incest and other subjects often associated with the area in real, honest, and accurate ways.

Offutt's more recent fiction is rife with the power of those same hills to project a siren's call for the return of those who have gone away. These later stories deal more with human feelings of isolation, alienation, and disorientation; whereas the earlier stories concentrate more on the protagonists' feelings of belonging, of being connected by some mystic or metaphorical umbilical cord.

"SAWDUST"

One recurring theme in Offutt's stories is the imposing notion in eastern Kentucky that a person should never try to rise above his or her peers or elders. At the beginning of "Sawdust," Junior, the boy who serves as first-person narrator, says, "Neighbors say I think too much." When Junior makes known his intention to take an equivalency test and thus earn a high school diploma, his family acts as if they are ashamed of him, and his brother refuses to talk to him at all. When a group of boys, after hearing about his ambition, beat him, Junior's older brother, Warren, retaliates to save the family honor. He seems to accept Junior's claim that he wants the diploma for the same reason Warren wants a battery-powered television—"To sit and look at." Once he has it, the diploma is much more than that to Junior. It is proof that his father, a lunatic who hanged himself with his belt because he was unable to heal a puppy's broken leg, was wrong when he said "a smart man wouldn't bother with town." Junior knows that he "can go there anytime." He knows that his boundaries are expandable.

"THE LEAVING ONE"

In "The Leaving One" Offutt explores the bond with the mountains felt by the natives of eastern Kentucky and the equally mysterious and mystic power of that area to call its people back to it. Vaughn, a boy who lives with his mother, meets a strange old man in the woods who claims to be Vaughn's maternal grandfather, Elijah "Lije" Boatman—a name that foreshadows the mystical journey through which he will lead Vaughn. Lije, who left the mountains to serve as a chaplain in World War I, lost his three sons to World War II and abandoned the civilized world to live in the mountains for more than forty years, until workers captured him and his daughter, Vaughn's mother, and had him committed to an asylum. Lije has returned to the mountains to die and to find his grandson and train him to replace him as mountain mystic. Lije gives Vaughn a stone that he has worn around his neck since Lije's "pa-paw" gave it to him just before he died, a talisman that identifies the wearer as the inheritor and as the keeper of the old ways of the hills. Lije says to Vaughn, "You be the Boatman now." At the heart of this story of maturation and succession are the beliefs, still shared by many people native to eastern Kentucky, that the hills themselves are alive and actually communicate with people who can listen to them. It is also a story of preservation and of the need to integrate mystical and empirical knowledge.

"BLUE LICK"

"Blue Lick" is another of Offutt's stories narrated by a boy whose intelligence and powers of perception put him at odds with his fellow mountain folk. All of Offutt's stories are, to some extent, about limits on people's freedom, limits imposed by the land itself, by other people, or by traditions—all, at least to some extent, self-imposed. The father in this story goes to prison for car theft but is released early because his wife, who felt imprisoned by her family, ran off with the owner of the car her husband was falsely accused of stealing. With the mother gone, the father's elderly mother is saddled with the job of raising two boys she cannot possibly handle, especially because one of the boys, nicknamed Little Elvis because he makes up songs, is mentally disabled and thus requires constant supervision. When a neighbor makes cruel fun of his son and shoots his dog, the father feels that his new freedom is negated by the restrictions of his parole. His interpretation of the mountain code of manly behavior demands revenge, so he steals the man's car, takes it apart piece by piece, is caught throwing the pieces into the Blue Lick River, and is sent back to prison. Little Elvis becomes a ward of the state, and our young, unnamed narrator is left to battle his guilt. The great irony of the story is that he blames himself for his mother's leaving because he walked in on her while she was having sex with her lover. He suffers the burden of responsibility for the breakup of his family.

"NINE BALL"

It is certainly no accident that "Nine Ball" is the last story in Offutt's collection *Kentucky Straight*. Each story in this collection has as one of its themes the power of the Appalacian Mountains of eastern Kentucky to keep the people born there from abandoning them. Everett, the protagonist of "Nine Ball," may be the only major character in the book to successfully escape. He and his father make their living by raising hogs on the slop from the cafeteria of a school built fifty years ago by the Works Progress Administration. The state has announced that it will close the school the next summer. This marks the beginning of the end of their way of life, and Everett, with seemingly no plan in mind, starts severing other ties that have kept him bound there. He has a passion for the game of pool and this leads him into a game that allows him to win enough money to leave. The sweetest part of this victory is that he wins most of the money from the local thug that has bullied him most of his life. Another tie he severs is with his sister. Although it angers him that she has sex with virtually every man she meets, in his last moments with her he regrets that he had never had sex with her himself. "He'd missed something that everyone knew more about than him." Because his decision to leave the mountains comes at the very end of the story, it makes a perfect ending for the entire book.

OUT OF THE WOODS

Out of the Woods, Offutt's second collection of short stories, seems like a very logical outgrowth of his first collection, *Kentucky Straight*. Whereas the nine stories in *Kentucky Straight* focus on the difficulties people have in escaping the mountains, the eight stories in *Out of the Woods* deal primarily with people who have left the hills of Kentucky but still feel the almost undeniable call to return to their mountain homes. The title story, the first story in the collection, eases us into this notion with two characters whose return is already built into the plot. The first to leave was Ory, one of five brothers and the only one in the family to ever move away. At the beginning of the story he has been gone for ten years, and the family has just received word that he has been shot and is in a hospital in Wahoo, Nebraska. Kay, the brothers' only sister, voices an opinion predominant in the hills of Kentucky: "Him leaving never made sense. . . . He hadn't done nothing and nobody was after him." As a means of becoming more accepted by Kay's family, her husband Gerald, the newcomer to the family, agrees to bring Ory home. By the time he gets there Ory is dead, and he has to cut a deal with the local police to claim the body and, in a journey reminiscent of William Faulkner's *As I Lay Dying* (1930), take it back to Kentucky. The seven stories that follow explore the insecurities and phobias many hill folk experience when they move to places where the sky, without the mountains to limit their vi-

sion of it, is disorienting, and the horizon is so far away that the distance keeps them in a fluctuating state of anxiety.

OTHER MAJOR WORKS

NONFICTION: *The Same River Twice: A Memoir*, 1993.

LONG FICTION: *The Good Brother*, 1997.

BIBLIOGRAPHY

Balee, Susan. Review of *Out of the Woods*, by Chris Offutt. *Hudson Review* (Spring, 1999): 170.

Beattie, L. Elisabeth, ed. "Chris Offutt." In *Conversations with Kentucky Writers*. Lexington: University Press of Kentucky, 1996. Extensive biographical information that reveals volumes about the sources of Offutt's stories.

Halpern, Sue. "A Zip Code with a Creek." Review of *The Same River Twice* and *Kentucky Straight*, by Chris Offutt. *The New York Times Book Review* 142 (January 31, 1993): 10. Halpern describes Offutt as an exquisite storyteller. She discusses his ear for dialect and his connection to Appalachia.

Palmer, Louis H., III. "Chris Offutt Comes Home." *Appalachian Journal: A Regional Studies Review* 26, no. 1 (Fall, 1998): 22-31.

Rooke, Leon. "His Old Kentucky Home." Review of *Out of the Woods*, by Chris Offutt. *The New York Times Book Review* 104, no. 10 (March 7, 1999): 16. Rooke addresses Offutt's characterization and use of language, summarizing that *Out of the Woods* is a "magical book," with not one weak story.

Edmund August

LIAM O'FLAHERTY

Born: Gort na gCapell, Aran Islands, Ireland; August
28, 1896
Died: Dublin, Ireland; September 7, 1984

PRINCIPAL SHORT FICTION

Spring Sowing, 1924
Civil War, 1925
Darkness, 1926
The Terrorist, 1926
The Tent and Other Stories, 1926
The Mountain Tavern and Other Stories, 1929
The Ecstasy of Angus, 1931
The Short Stories of Liam O'Flaherty, 1937
Two Lovely Beasts and Other Stories, 1948
Dúil, 1953
The Stories of Liam O'Flaherty, 1956
The Pedlar's Revenge and Other Stories, 1976
The Wave and Other Stories, 1980

OTHER LITERARY FORMS

Liam O'Flaherty wrote four regional novels, of
which *Thy Neighbour's Wife* (1923), *The Black Soul*
(1924), and *Skerrett* (1932) are set on Inishmore, the
largest of the Aran Islands; the fourth, *The House of
Gold* (1929), is set in Galway City. Four novels of
Dublin city life are *The Informer* (1925), *Mr.
Gilhooley* (1926), *The Assassin* (1928), and *The Puritan* (1931). *The Return of the Brute* (1929) concerns
O'Flaherty's World War I experiences in trench warfare; *The Martyr* (1933), *Famine* (1937), *Land*
(1946), and *Insurrection* (1950) are Irish historical
novels for the years 1845-1922. O'Flaherty wrote
three books of autobiography, *The Life of Tim Healy*
(1927), several essays on social conditions and on literature, poems, and stories in Gaelic.

ACHIEVEMENTS

The source of many of Liam O'Flaherty's achievements is his birthplace off the coast of the west of Ireland. The Aran Islands' remoteness and stark natural
beauty, the dependence of their scattered population
on the vagaries of wind and sea, the inhabitants' preservation of the Irish language as their primary means
of communication, and the virtually mythological
status accorded such phenomena by leading figures
in the Irish Literary Revival such as William Butler
Yeats and John Millington Synge, all exerted a crucial influence on the development of O'Flaherty's
work.

Both his short fiction and novels are noteworthy
for their unsentimental treatment of island life, the
vivid directness of their style, and their attention to
natural detail. While by no means all, or even all the
best, of O'Flaherty's work draws on his Aran background, the marked degree to which all of his work
emphasizes the spontaneity and volatility of all living
things is the product of his formative exposure to the
life forces of Aran. One of the consequences of this
background's influence is plots that deal with the
problematical socialization of natural energy. These
plots tend to take on a melodramatic or expressionis-
tic coloration that can mar the overall balance and objectivity of the work. Such coloration also, however,
unwittingly reveals O'Flaherty's essential opposition
to the aesthetic and cultural codes of the Irish Literary Revival and lends his work an often overlooked
but crucial, critical dimension.

O'Flaherty won the James Tait Black Memorial
Prize in 1926 for his novel *The Informer*. That same
novel won him several other awards and honors in
France and England, including two Academy Awards
in 1935. O'Flaherty was honored with a doctorate in
literature from the National University of Ireland in
1974, and with the Irish Academy of Letters Award
for literature in 1979.

BIOGRAPHY

Liam O'Flaherty was educated in seminaries and
at University College, Dublin, from which in 1915 he
joined the British army. He served in France and Bel-
gium and, shell-shocked, became an invalid in 1918.
He traveled to the United States and Canada and
returned to Ireland in 1920 and became a Communist
and Socialist activist. Forced to escape to England in

Liam O'Flaherty (AP/Wide World Photos)

1922, he began writing steadily. He married Margaret Barrington in 1926 but they separated in 1932, the same year he helped to found the Irish Academy of Letters. During World War II he lived in Connecticut, the Caribbean, and South America. Despite his controversial participation in the Irish struggle for independence and the general political militancy of his twenties, and despite his active contribution to the establishment of the Irish Academy of Letters, O'Flaherty absented himself from public involvement for virtually the last forty years of his life. Unlike most Irish writers of his generation, O'Flaherty did not continue to develop. The widespread public congratulations that greeted his eightieth birthday in 1976 and the republication of many of his best-known novels during the last decade of his life did nothing of significance to break the immense silence of his later years.

ANALYSIS

To experience the full range of Liam O'Flaherty's stories, one must deal with the exceptions in the collection *The Stories of Liam O'Flaherty*, notably "The Mountain Tavern," which, like his historical novels, treats the revolutionaries in the 1920's, and "The Post Office," a humorous account of visitors' attempts to send a telegram from a small Irish town. The bulk of his stories, however, deal with nature and with people close to nature. In his publication entitled *Joseph Conrad* (1930), O'Flaherty distinguishes himself from Conrad and other novelists, saying, "I have seen the leaping salmon fly before the salmon whale, and I have seen the sated buck horn his mate and the wanderer leave his wife in search of fresh bosoms with the fire of joy in his eye." Such firsthand observance characterizes twelve of the forty-two stories in the collection, for all twelve are animal stories with little or no intrusion of a human being.

The raw guts of nature, its tenderness and its viciousness, appear in these stories, with both wild and domesticated animals. A cow follows the trail of its stillborn calf to where it has been thrown over a cliff, the maternal instinct so strong that, when a wave washes the calf's body away, the cow plunges to her death in pursuit. A rockfish fights for its life against a fisherman's hook, winning the battle by leaving behind a torn piece of its jaw. A proud black mare overruns a race and falls to her death; a huge conger eel tears up a fisherman's net in making his escape; a wild goat, protecting its kid, attacks and kills a marauding dog. In "Birth," the people watch through the night for a newborn calf. Among several bird stories, a blackbird, proud of his song, barely escapes the claws of a cat; a baby seagull conquers fear and learns to fly; a wild swan's mate dies and, forlorn and desperate, he woos, fights for, and flies away with another mate. A wounded cormorant, outcast from its flock, tries to gain acceptance, but the others tear at it and destroy it. A hawk captures a lark to feed his mate and by his very presence, drives peaceful birds out of the territory; but then the hawk loses his life in attacking a man climbing up to his nest, and the man captures the mate and takes the eggs.

Yet the objective study of nature, impassioned

alike with tenderness and viciousness, yields a delicate study of erotica. The laws of nature are so closely observed in primitive living conditions and so necessary to the barren efforts of survival that any slight aberration seems marked by a higher intelligence. In O'Flaherty's stories, this phenomenon seems to take two directions. Ordinary living conditions become bound by rigid customs so that anything not traditional, the peasants say, has "the law of God" against it. Some creatures, however, respond to a different divinity. In these cases the law of nature may permit more individuality than does social custom or the Church. Caught between these baffling natural and socioreligious forces, the people may switch their allegiances with remarkable speed and use the same kind of logic to support two different kinds of action. Some of O'Flaherty's best stories—"The Fairy Goose," "The Child of God," "Red Barbara," "Two Lovely Beasts"—deal with the reaction of the people not so much to adversity as to difference. "The Red Petticoat" and "The Beggars" deal with people who are different.

"THE FAIRY GOOSE"

The title creature of "The Fairy Goose" from before its birth evokes undue emotion; sitting on the egg with two others, an old woman's pet hen dies. Of the three eggs, only one hatches, into a scrawny, sickly thing obviously better off dead. The woman's husband intervenes with his admonition of "the law of God" not to kill anything born in a house. So unlike a goose is its subsequent behavior that the people begin to treat it as a fairy, adorn it with ribbons, and bestow other favors. Regarding it as sacred, O'Flaherty writes, "All the human beings in the village paid more respect to it than they did to one another." On the basis of its supernatural powers, its owner becomes a wise woman sought far and near, but jealousy intervenes: A woman who herself casts spells informs the local priest. He destroys the goose's nest and calls its admirers idolaters. Confronted with the powers of the Church, the former adherents of the goose now denounce it and threaten to burn the old woman's house. Only those villagers hitherto unconcerned manage to restrain the threatened violence, but eventually young men during the night approach

and kill the goose. The old woman's only defense, a traditional curse, seems to linger in the air, for thereafter the villagers become quarrelsome drunkards.

"THE CHILD OF GOD"

No doubt based on his own disaffection with the Church, O'Flaherty's stories do not present priests as dispensers of benevolence or wisdom. For the people themselves, religion, custom, and superstition equally comprise the law of God. Tradition, moreover, curbs the active intelligence and promotes baleful ironies; a thing may be blessed and cursed in rapid succession. Such is the career of Peter O'Toole in "The Child of God." The farmer O'Toole and his wife, in their forties, have an embarrassing "late from the womb" child. The baby's uncommon ill health provokes the first accusation that he is a fairy child, but the mother maintains that he is a child of God. The wife's unusual attention to the child seems in itself to be a miracle and alters the conduct of the father, who gives up his drinking bouts. The mother believes the child will bring prosperity to the house, and she makes the older children take jobs and save. At age ten, as if to confirm the mother's faith, Peter announces his ambition to become a priest—an honor higher than his parents could have dreamed for him. After six years, however, with the family driven into debt to support his education, Peter is expelled because, as he explains later, he does not believe in God. Further, they learn upon his return home at age nineteen that he has become an artist. To their horror, his books of pictures show "naked women . . . like French postcards." Peter's difference becomes a threat, and the artist, like the satirists of old, becomes feared for his sketching the people in unflattering poses.

After some six months, an "orgy" occurs at a wake. It would be bad enough for Peter as a participant, but it is much worse for him when the people discover that he is stone sober. As if spellbound, they watch while he sketches the entire shameful scene; afterward outraged, they call his art sacrilege and threaten to stone him. His mother now believes he has brought a curse with his birth, and his father believes God will strike all of the villagers dead for what Peter has done. The priest intervenes and dispels a stone-throwing mob; but, exhibiting no more compassion, benevolence, or enlightenment than do the people, he denounces Peter for having brought a curse on the parish and banishes him. The mother, left alone, weeps for her lost child, not aware of the irony that her son's creativity indeed makes him a child close to God.

"RED BARBARA"

Between the alternatives of a blessing or a curse, one who thrives—provided he is not too different—surely must be blessed. So Barbara's second husband in "Red Barbara," although a weaver and a flower grower, gains acceptance until his marriage proves unfruitful; then he proves himself limited to the prevailing viewpoint. Barbara, accustomed to beatings and violent lovemaking by a frequently drunken husband, shrinks from Joseph's gentle touch and soon despises him as a "priestly lecher." Sharing the people's belief in the importance of a family, he grows fearful of his own failure to father a child, becomes strange, solitary, and emaciated, and eventually dies deranged. Barbara returns to her wild ways with her third husband, and Joseph is remembered only as "a fable in the village."

"TWO LOVELY BEASTS"

So closely knit is a small Aran community that the owner of a cow shares its milk, free, with his neighbors. Thus a crisis occurs in "Two Lovely Beasts" when Colm Derrane consents to buy a motherless calf from a poor widow and feed it alongside his own calf. The widow, Kate Higgins, assures Colm that he is different from everybody else. The difference in his decision to raise a calf on the people's milk definitely breaks the law of God and of the community, and the family becomes outcast. Kate herself cannot find another cow to buy, uses the sale money to feed her children, and turns against Colm with the accusation that his money was cursed. Forcing his family to live frugally in order to feed both calves, Colm beats his wife into submission; this evidence of male sanity restores her confidence in him. Hereafter all the children work hard to save, the tide of public opinion turns as the family prospers, and now the people say that God has blessed the family's efforts to rise in the world.

Two of the Higgins children die without proper nourishment; the distraught mother, removed to an asylum, leaves behind a plot of grassland which Colm rents through a difficult winter. He demands of his starving and threadbare family another year of sacrifice while the two beasts grow into bullocks and he can save money to open a shop. At last, with the community's belief that God blesses those who prosper, the shop brings financial success, and the calves become champions on fair day. Envy intrudes, also, but as Colm and his family drive away to open a shop in the town, he appears unaware of the people's hostility and derision. "Two Lovely Beasts" in this way shows the possible rise of a merchant class, who as money lenders became known as the hated gombeen men—those who live off the peasants by buying their produce at low prices and selling it elsewhere for a profit, a topic O'Flaherty treated in *The House of Gold*.

"THE RED PETTICOAT"

Most of the stories, however, relate the peasants' situation at home—their contention with the forces of nature, their primitive living conditions, and their sensitivity to social order and ideals. Often conditions seem to be fixed at the close of a story, but occasionally good wit or good fortune alters the circumstances, at least temporarily, as in "The Red Petticoat" and "The Beggars." The ankle-length skirt of red or blue wool called a petticoat is a colorful part of the native costume of women of the Aran Islands. Often paired with a heavy, long shawl, it stands out against a somber background of rocks and grey houses. "The Red Petticoat" begins with Mrs. Mary Deignan and her four children, with no food in the house, trying to think of a way to obtain provisions. This unusual family does not work consistently, although all work valiantly when they have work; they enjoy laughing together and composing poems, some of them satires against their enemies. Unlike most residents of Aran, they can laugh in the midst of near-starvation. Out of such a background and the family's rehearsals come the expediency that Mrs. Deignan contrives to relieve their want—a melodrama spawned in her own brain, using the stock character of a witch or "wise woman," and acted out against the village storekeeper.

Mrs. Deignan, known as "Mary of the bad verses" because her poems are "scurrilous and abusive, and at times even indecent and in a sense immoral," is not powerless when she sets forth wearing her shawl and her new check apron to visit Mrs. Murtagh, the local storekeeper who has somewhat the character of a gombeen. In her "wise woman" role Mrs. Deignan terrifies Mrs. Murtagh with a hissing account of Mrs. Murtagh's sins in the traditional style of name-calling, out of which eventually Mrs. Deignan shoots a question: "Where is the red petticoat you were wearing last Sunday night, when you went to visit the tailor?" Tricking Mrs. Murtagh into denying it was red and admitting it was a black skirt, Mrs. Deignan now has what she wanted—the means of blackmail. Mrs. Murtagh launches into a vicious battle with Mrs. Deignan and knocks her into a corner but attracts passersby. Mrs. Deignan only pretends to be unconscious and, at the propitious moment, she changes character and becomes a pitiful beggar, blessing Mrs. Murtagh for having agreed to provide whatever she wants on six-months' credit. The neighbors understand that something is wrong, but they are totally mystified. Mrs. Deignan returns home with her shawl turned into a grocery sack slung over her shoulder; Mrs. Murtagh knows she will be subject to further blackmail but comforts herself with thoughts of spending more time with the tailor.

"THE BEGGARS"

"The Beggars" features as protagonist a blind man who with "priestly arrogance" exhorts people to beware the hour of their deaths, although he knows from experience that a church is not a place to beg alms; cemeteries and missions are better. His repeated cry, totally incongruous with his surroundings, earns him nothing near the gateway to a racetrack. Changing to angry curses when he thinks a man jeers at him, the beggar gains the sympathy and the aid of other beggars—a tipster, a singing woman, and an accordionist. The honor and generosity he finds among beggars seem sufficient to confirm his dream that he would find good fortune in a strange place on this day; but then the formerly cursed man returns to count into his hand five one-pound banknotes, part of two hundred pounds earned from an intuitive flash at the sight of the blind man and the memory of a horse named "Blind Barney."

"THE MOUNTAIN TAVERN"

In "The Mountain Tavern" O'Flaherty records some of the political upheaval caused by the Act of Partition in 1921. Three Republican revolutionaries trudge through a night snowstorm to reach a tavern and obtain aid for their wounded. When they arrive, the tavern is a smoking ruin, destroyed in a shootout between the Republicans and the Free Staters. Their incredulity on finding that the destitute survivors can do nothing for them parallels the anger of the tavern owner's wife, who tongue-lashes them for the three years she has suffered in their war. The wounded man dies and the other two are taken prisoner.

"THE POST OFFICE"

In an opposite and humorous vein, O'Flaherty in "The Post Office" assembles on old-age pension day the most traditional elements of a small Gaelic town; to them, the telephone, a newfangled gadget, complicates former lives of simplicity which relied on donkeys, carts, and rowboats. Three tourists speaking French and arriving in a New York Cadillac have a tourist's reason for sending a telegram to California—a friend's ancestor is from this town—and create great humor and confusion because the postmaster considers telegrams the bane of his existence. Even a priest forgets to be scandalized by the two women's clothing when he learns the visitors' purpose. The local old people take the male visitor to be a government spy because of his fluent Gaelic, consider that the women's painted toenails are a disease on their feet, believe the Spanish girl to be a duke's daughter, and appraise the American girl for her obvious reproductive capacities. The postmaster refuses to send a telegram in Spanish because it may be obscene, relents upon a recitation of Lorca's poetry, and tries to place the call to Galway; but he finds himself on the telephone at first cursed as a fishmonger, then receives news of a neighbor's operation and death, and finally hears a wrong-number grievance from a schoolteacher. "We are all in it," say sone native upon pronunciation of the town's name, Praiseach Gaelic for confusion, disorder, and shapelessness.

The best character, the mocking young man who has graduated from his native background, lends himself to the confusion for the humor of it, reads a letter to oblige an old soldier, and with quick wit constructs tales appropriate for the native credulity. O'Flaherty's depiction of the clash of two cultures, his ear for the local diction, and his intelligence for the local logic and laughter here show him at his very best.

OTHER MAJOR WORKS

LONG FICTION: *Thy Neighbour's Wife*, 1923; *The Black Soul*, 1924; *The Informer*, 1925; *Mr. Gilhooley*, 1926; *The Assassin*, 1928; *The House of Gold*, 1929; *The Return of the Brute*, 1929; *The Puritan*, 1931; *Skerrett*, 1932; *The Martyr*, 1933; *Hollywood Cemetery*, 1935; *Famine*, 1937; *Land*, 1946; *Insurrection*, 1950.

NONFICTION: *The Life of Tim Healy*, 1927; *Joseph Conrad*, 1930; *Two Years*, 1930; *I Went to Russia*, 1931; *Shame the Devil*, 1934.

CHILDREN'S LITERATURE: *All Things Come of Age; and, The Test of Courage*, 1984.

BIBLIOGRAPHY

Cahalan, James M. *Liam O'Flaherty: A Study of the Short Fiction*. Boston: Twayne, 1991. An introduction to O'Flaherty's stories by an expert in Irish literature. Discusses the peasant consciousness in the stories, as well as the stories' relationship to the Irish language. Comments on issues of gender and politics raised by the stories. Also includes many comments by O'Flaherty from letters and articles, as well as secondary sources.

Costello, Peter. *Liam O'Flaherty's Ireland*. Dublin: Wolfhound Press, 1996. Explores O'Flaherty's life and times, how his environment influenced his writings.

Daniels, William. "Introduction to the Present State of Criticism of Liam O'Flaherty's Collection of Short Stories: *Dúil*." *Eire-Ireland* 23 (Summer, 1988): 122-134. A summary of criticism of O'Flaherty's stories in *Dúil*. Takes issue with a number of criticisms of the stories, such as their lack of focus on setting, plot, and point of view. Argues that the stories deserve much better criticism than they have received from critics in both Irish and English.

Doyle, Paul A. *Liam O'Flaherty*. Boston: Twayne, 1972. The first comprehensive overview of O'Flaherty's life and work. The author's reading of O'Flaherty's short fiction tends to be more illuminating than that of the novels. Although superseded by later studies, this volume is still helpful as a means of orientating the newcomer to O'Flaherty's work. Contains an extensive bibliography.

Jefferson, George. *Liam O'Flaherty: A Descriptive Bibliography of His Works*. Dublin: Wolfhound Press, 1993. A useful tool for the student of O'Flaherty. Includes bibliographical references and an index.

Kelly, A. A. *Liam O'Flaherty: The Storyteller*. London: Macmillan, 1976. An exhaustive treatment of the themes and techniques of O'Flaherty's short fiction. Although somewhat disjointed in organization, this study ultimately makes a convincing case for the distinctiveness of O'Flaherty's achievements in the form. Particular emphasis is placed on the range and variety of his stories. Supplemented by an excellent bibliography.

Kilroy, James R. "Setting the Standards: Writers of the 1920's and 1930's." In *The Irish Short Story: A Critical History*, edited by James F. Kilroy. Boston: Twayne, 1984. An introduction to O'Flaherty's stories, emphasizing their ethical implications and naturalism. Discusses his simple narrative technique and style and how the short story suits his single-minded vision.

O'Brien, James H. *Liam O'Flaherty*. Lewisburg, Pa.: Bucknell University Press, 1973. A brief introduction to O'Flaherty's life and work. Its longest chapter is devoted to O'Flaherty's short stories, but the study also contains biographical information and analyses of the novels. O'Flaherty's achievements as a short-story writer are considered in the context of those of his Irish contemporaries. The stories' themes and motifs are also discussed.

Sheeran, Patrick J. *The Novels of Liam O'Flaherty: A Study in Romantic Realism*. Dublin: Wolfhound

Press, 1976. This study contains more than its title suggests. It is both a comprehensive study of O'Flaherty's novels and an investigation of their cultural context. The author's knowledge of, and original research into, O'Flaherty's background provides invaluable information about his formative experiences. The critique of O'Flaherty's longer works may be usefully adapted by students of his short fiction. In many ways, the most satisfactory study of O'Flaherty's work.

Thompson, Richard R. "The Sage Who Deep in Central Nature Delves: Liam O'Flaherty's Short Stories." *Eire-Ireland* 18 (Spring, 1983): 80-97. A discussion of the central themes in O'Flaherty's stories, focusing primarily on the moral lessons inherent in his nature stories, which urge a turning away from intellectualism.

Zneimer, John. *The Literary Vision of Liam O'Flaherty.* Syracuse, N.Y.: Syracuse University Press, 1970. An ambitious approach to O'Flaherty's work. The author sees a strong religious component in O'Flaherty's novels and stories and a tension between the two forms. The novels are said to be despairing, while the stories are claimed to offer a redemptive alternative. Some important insights do not ultimately make the author's argument persuasive.

Grace Eckley, updated by George O'Brien

JOHN O'HARA

Born: Pottsville, Pennsylvania; January 31, 1905
Died: Princeton, New Jersey; April 11, 1970

PRINCIPAL SHORT FICTION

The Doctor's Son and Other Stories, 1935
Hope of Heaven, 1938
Files on Parade, 1939
Pal Joey, 1940
Pipe Night, 1945
Hellbox, 1947
Sermons and Soda Water, 1960
Assembly, 1961
The Cape Cod Lighter, 1962
The Hat on the Bed, 1963
The Horse Knows the Way, 1964
Waiting for Winter, 1966
And Other Stories, 1968
The O'Hara Generation, 1969
The Time Element and Other Stories, 1972
Good Samaritan and Other Stories, 1974

OTHER LITERARY FORMS

John O'Hara is probably best known to American readers for his long, complex novels of manners, liberally spiced with sex and seasoned with class conflict. Most of his stories are set in that coal-mining region of Pennsylvania known as The Region by its inhabitants, an O'Hara domain which was ruled, at least fictionally, by the city of Gibbsville. He also wrote seven plays, five of them included in *Five Plays* (1961). From 1934 to 1957, he worked on treatments, adapted other fictions, and wrote original screenplays for Hollywood. He received sole credit for *Moontide* (1942) and credit in varying degrees for *I Was an Adventuress* (1939), *He Married His Wife* (1939), *Down Argentine Way* (1940), and *Best Things in Life Are Free* (1955). For the last title he wrote the original story. He also wrote a series of political columns for national syndication later collected and published as *My Turn* (1966).

ACHIEVEMENTS

Although John O'Hara was perhaps best known

during his lifetime as a novelist, his growing posthumous reputation appears to rest upon his shorter fiction, particularly upon the tales issued in collections nearly every Thanksgiving holiday during the last decade of the author's life; significantly, relatively few of the stories in such volumes as *Assembly, The Cape Cod Lighter, The Horse Knows the Way,* or *Waiting for Winter* had seen prior publication in magazines.

Following his rupture with *The New Yorker* at the end of the 1940's, O'Hara poured most of his prodigious energies into the longer fictional form, sometimes approaching but never really matching or surpassing the accomplishment of his first novel, *Appointment in Samarra* (1934). Around 1960, with a distinct—and often expressed—premonition that time was running out, O'Hara returned to the shorter form with a vengeance, often returning for the setting of his stories to the 1920's and 1930's—as if to make good use of his vivid memory while it still served him. Following a reconciliation of sorts with *The New Yorker* on the occasion of *Sermons and Soda Water,* O'Hara resumed publication there and elsewhere, particularly in the declining *Saturday Evening Post.* It was, however, in published collections quickly reissued in paperback that O'Hara's later stories would reach their widest audiences and exercise their greatest impact. Although he continued to write and publish novels, it is clear that the best of his energies—and memories—were reserved for the stories, which accounted in large measure for the Award of Merit bestowed upon him by the American Academy of Arts and Letters in 1964.

BIOGRAPHY

John Henry O'Hara was born January 31, 1905, the eldest child of Patrick O'Hara, M.D., and Katherine Delaney O'Hara of Pottsville, Pennsylvania. He was taught to read at the age of four and given a hand-printing set at age six. After he was refused permission to graduate from Niagara Prep, even though he was valedictorian, on the grounds of drunkenness, O'Hara went back to Pottsville. His father died shortly thereafter, and O'Hara found that his father's investments had been worthless; he was never able to attend college. His first job was on the *Pottsville*

John O'Hara (Library of Congress)

Journal; in 1927, he worked his way to Europe, and the next year he was in New York, working for the *Herald-Tribune.* He sold his first story to *The New Yorker* in 1928 and was published by that magazine continuously until 1949, when a review by Brendan Gill (which, James Thurber passed the word, had been written by Wolcott Gibbs) ended O'Hara's association with the magazine, and as it turned out, interrupted his career as a short-story writer for eleven years. After 1960, O'Hara made collections of stories he liked and sent them to Albert Erskine at Random House, where they were published without the intermediation of magazine editing and publication; this accounts for the greater length of the post-1960 stories.

O'Hara did most of his work in Hollywood between 1929 and 1931, before he had ever published a novel; in 1931, he married Helen R. Petit. Although he achieved some success in the next two years, O'Hara became a hard drinker, was divorced, and eventually became the victim of despair—which became an almost suicidal mood he dispelled only by locking himself in a hotel room in New York in 1933 to write *Appointment in Samarra* (1934). In the next three years he worked again in Hollywood, published his first collection of short stories, the novel *Butterfield 8* (1935), one story in *Scribner's* and eleven in *The New Yorker*, and in 1938 married Belle Mulford Wylie of New York and Quogue, Long Island, to which he subsequently returned as a summer resident every year of his life. In the next few years he consolidated his reputation as a short-story writer and saw *Pal Joey* produced on Broadway with music and lyrics by Richard Rodgers and Lorenz Hart. O'Hara became a regular contributor to *Newsweek* and reviewed theater and motion pictures for that publication for the next two years. In 1944, he served as a war correspondent for *Liberty* after resigning from OSS because he did not, as he told his superiors, want to have the responsibility for killing anyone. Wylie Delaney O'Hara, his only child, was born in 1945, and in 1949 the family moved to Princeton, where he wrote *A Rage to Live* (1949).

In 1953, O'Hara almost died after his gastric ulcer hemorrhaged, and the next year his wife died after a congenital heart defect worsened; but O'Hara made both a physical and an emotional recovery from these disasters. He quit drinking and in 1955 he remarried, to Katharine (Sister) Barnes Bryan.

O'Hara published *Ten North Frederick* in 1955 and received membership in the National Institute of Arts and Letters two years later. The events were connected: Now his peers recognized that O'Hara was master of the large canvas as well as the small, of the sweep of history as well as of the social value of one neighborhood. In the next six years, O'Hara produced *Ourselves to Know* (1960), a novel; *Sermons and Soda Water*, three novellas; *Assembly*, twenty-six stories; *Five Plays*; *The Cape Cod Lighter*, twenty-three stories; *Elizabeth Appleton* (1963), a novel; and *The Hat on the Bed*, twenty-four stories. In 1964, he received the Award of Merit for the Novel from the American Academy of Arts and Letters, an honor

which then had been given to only four other novelists, and only two Americans—Ernest Hemingway and Theodore Dreiser. The next year he published *The Lockwood Concern*, remarkable for its gothic atmosphere and for the linguistic and architectonic wizardry which beguiles the reader into accepting that atmosphere. He then published two novels and two short stories. He finished *The Ewings* (1972) in February of 1970 and had written seventy-four pages of a sequel when he died quietly in his sleep on April 11, 1970. He left behind an enormous achievement.

"ANDREA"

John O'Hara's "Andrea" is a wintry story first published in the collection *Waiting for Winter* (1966). Andrea Cooper is the woman whose life is chronicled by Phil, the narrator, who met Andrea at a country club dance when she was sixteen and he was in the University of Pennsylvania law school. She is beautiful, truthful, and a little aggressive (in the fine old tradition of O'Hara women), and he "did not often hear Andrea use a line that was not her own." During an interlude, they go out to his car. She wants to come to see him at his apartment in Philadelphia and make love to him. The dialogue that resolves this and moves the story on to all its other plateaus, indeed through its progressions from brightness to darkness and from eroticism to melodrama to tragedy, is vintage O'Hara. Over the decades, they become a couple, with Phil the responsible member. Their relationship lasts through Andrea's marriages and through Phil's rise in the legal profession. Andrea cannot stay married; Phil will not marry. Andrea is naïve about everything but sex; Phil is savvy, but perhaps not about sex. The temptation to make it neat by making him only an average lover is perhaps too overwhelming, but the implicit accusation is there in the way O'Hara presents his character.

At the end of the story, Phil goes back to Gibbsville, where they met, to try to head off expensive litigation in a complicated mineral rights case. Andrea's father, an unscrupulous businessman who is ruining the store he manages so that the owners will sell to a chain that has made a deal with him, has also ruined her financial security. Phil also finds out that she has had another abortion, this one performed by the man she was going to marry, a doctor, to whom she had come about the pregnancy before that. Phil has made her pregnant. The night before the child was conceived, they had had an argument—superficially about her marriages but really an attempt on her part to get him to marry her—and she had thrown a heavy glass at him. It made him realize how old he was when he did not catch it; and he had been a "sensible" lover that night.

Now, on his visit to Gibbsville, she tries to pretend that she is in love with her homosexual business partner, and he soberly refuses to believe it and tells her she could have killed herself with the abortion and, for the first time in their long relationship, offers immediate marriage. She gets angry at him and he leaves, for the first time without their making love. He rationalizes her promiscuity by thinking to himself that "it was her nature to pass herself around among men and she would have done so whether I was in her background or not." The problem is that Andrea is calling out for a stabilizing influence. He does not really know how to become one, although now an old bachelor set in his ways, and he continually, partly by design and partly because of unadmitted jealousy, knocks down in Andrea's estimation the other men to whom she reaches out for stability.

Phil goes abroad and in Brussels avails himself of a tall blonde call girl and takes to heavy drinking. Four months pass and he has to go back to Gibbsville to try again to resolve the mineral rights case. He goes out to supper with the members of the local bar association and then reminisces with a few until midnight, returns to his hotel room, and falls asleep with the lights on. Andrea comes to see him at three o'clock in the morning. At first, she is annoyed; then he is impotent. They finally make love and, afterward, when they remember that they have been together for twenty years, Andrea says "Then it certainly isn't love. . . . Although it certainly is." Then, after inviting him to her apartment for dinner that night, she opens the windows and tells him to get some sleep. Then their affair and Phil's life as well as hers end:

"Then she went to the other window and opened it, and I don't know what happened next because I was not watching. But when I did look she was not there, and I did not believe that until I heard a most awful scream. Then I believed it and it is all I have left to believe."

"YOU CAN ALWAYS TELL NEWARK"

"You Can Always Tell Newark" also belongs to the post-1961, book-publication-only group of short stories. The story begins with two middle-aged men watching a singles match between two young men; the outcome of both the plots run concurrently in the story, through the help of exposition which seems to be (but is not) flashback. One of the handsome young men keeps making *sotto voce* comments to Nance, an attractive, pregnant young woman watching them. Williams, one of the older men, offers her a seat up on the row where the spectators' backs are supported by the wall. She refuses, a little huffily. Williams and Smith, who is Williams's foil in their little expository scene, watch the young man who has been addressing Nance lose; and then they go to the clubhouse, where Williams is even more sympathetic to the girl because he has found out that she is the daughter of his old flame. He says as much and the girl wonders why her mother did not marry him—there is a kind of empathy between them, a powerful feeling of alikeness. Then Williams figures out that Nance is probably his daughter; and Smith tells him that Nance's husband, Bud, is a brilliant medical student but that she has been having an affair with Rex Ivers. Williams recalls that Nance's mother *wanted* to marry him, but that he was not "very reliable in those days" and her present husband was.

Williams finds himself on the seven o'clock to New York with Ivers, and they begin talking. Ivers is a little high and Williams's curiosity about Nance is consuming him. Ivers talks about his affair with her, not using her name. He then says that "his girl" cannot leave her husband because he depends on her. Williams tells him he knows the girl he is describing, and Ivers tells him what has been worrying him: that Nance wants to divorce her husband, have the child, and marry him. Rex asks him for advice. Then a wonderfully ironic scene begins. Williams says:

"Well I have an ethical problem too. My ethical problem is whether to advise you one way or the other. As a matter of fact, Rex, my problem is really more difficult than yours." Rex finally, in the process of thinking out loud, which is really what he has wanted to do all along, but in the presence of someone who could be trusted to hear it, says, "It never will work out," and says that he does not want to sink the other man or be responsible for a kid growing up without a father, as he had to after his father was killed in the war.

Williams then asks him if it would make a difference if the child she was carrying was his (earlier in the story the reader learns that Nance's mother never told Williams that Nance was his child, and Smith agrees that she would probably never admit it to him). "No. It would make things tougher for me, but as long as she didn't tell Bud, her husband, she and the baby are better off." "Thank you," Williams says, and then the story is allowed to die in small talk. It is a wonderful story and shows what irony, sympathy, and drama-without-melodrama O'Hara was capable of even in the shortest stories and with the most dangerous materials—materials which could have become soap opera in the hands of anyone less magisterially in control of the story, the characters, and the style.

"THE DOCTOR'S SON"

"The Doctor's Son," which is a very long story by the standards of the 1930's and which carried his first collection, is important to look at as part of a great writer's first efforts. The story is autobiographical, or seems to be, which is never a disadvantage for an American short story, and especially at that time, when sincerity was more highly prized as one of the minor virtues, and the examined life, particularly the first parts of it, was interesting to people who had just discovered psychoanalysis. The story is told by James Malloy, a young man, and not yet very experienced; in fact, he is fifteen. The year is 1919 and the world is being decimated by influenza, an apocalyptic event in O'Hara's own life. Like James Malloy, who is his fictional alter ego, his father was a doctor, and O'Hara spent a great deal of time driving him on his rounds.

Malloy's father is hit by the "flu" and has to call in Dr. Myers, a senior in medical school. James Malloy has a crush on Edith Evans, daughter of the local mine superintendent. Young Dr. Myers starts an affair with Mrs. Evans; and much of the interest of the story comes from the two little romances, one adult and one adolescent, that serve as counterpoint to the realistic scenes of how doctoring was done in the Polish and Irish bars of The Region. The plot and its subplot and theme are joined when Mr. Evans comes to see Dr. Myers at a Polish bar and makes some ambiguous remarks about the doctor's having seen his wife in the Evans home. Finally, they leave the bar following Evans in the Malloy Ford. Malloy's problem is that he is trying to make Edith feel better about the affair between the adults, which both know about, and to keep the community from having to do without the services of a doctor either because Evans has killed Dr. Myers or Dr. Malloy has beaten him up and sent him back to Philadelphia.

Nothing is wrong, apparently, and Dr. Malloy calls the Evans house telling Dr. Myers to come to the Malloys. All is cordiality at the Malloy residence and Dr. Myers is sent off with many thanks. In the meantime, James has tried to kiss Edith and she has put him off. The doctor and his son go all over the back roads visiting patients, arguing and mumbling and visiting the Poles and the Irish. Then they hear that Mr. Evans has died. Earlier in the story, when Evans comes into the Polish bar, he says things O'Hara constructed in such a way they were totally ambiguous, and only to be feared by the guilty—Dr. Myers and Malloy. He does not want a drink, but when Dr. Myers both refuses to step outside with him—fearing this is an excuse to get him alone and beat him up—and comforts Evans about his wife's condition, he takes a drink from the bottle that the sick miners have been passing around.

Dr. Myers should appeal to him as an educated person and a family man and a leader of the community not to take a drink, but he—and Malloy—are so relieved (both sigh audibly) that they do not. Evans dies, Dr. Myers leaves town, the affair between the two adolescents sours, Dr. Malloy mourns a good friend, and ramification piles upon ramification, irony upon irony. Young Malloy thinks: "I thought of the bottle that he had shared with Steve and the other Hunkies, and Mrs. Evans's illness and Doctor Myers. It was all mixed up in my mind." The education of Malloy has begun. A perfect story is thoroughly realized and ended—sometimes the hardest part for a writer—with great restraint.

OTHER MAJOR WORKS

LONG FICTION: *Appointment in Samarra*, 1934; *Butterfield 8*, 1935; *A Rage to Live*, 1949; *The Farmer's Hotel*, 1951; *Ten North Frederick*, 1955; *A Family Party*, 1956; *From the Terrace*, 1958; *Ourselves to Know*, 1960; *The Big Laugh*, 1962; *Elizabeth Appleton*, 1963; *The Lockwood Concern*, 1965; *The Instrument*, 1967; *Lovey Childs: A Philadelphian's Story*, 1969; *The Ewings*, 1972.

PLAYS: *Five Plays*, pb. 1961; *Two by O'Hara*, pb. 1979.

SCREENPLAY: *Moontide*, 1942.

NONFICTION: *Sweet and Sour*, 1954; *My Turn*, 1966; *A Cub Tells His Story*, 1974; *An Artist Is His Own Fault*, 1977.

BIBLIOGRAPHY

Bruccoli, Matthew J. *The O'Hara Concern*. New York: Random House, 1975. A carefully researched scholarly biography that reconstructs O'Hara's life and career in scrupulous detail, showing the evolution of his talent and thematic interests. Particularly authoritative in its account of O'Hara's break—and eventual reconciliation—with *The New Yorker*, and the impact of both events on his approach to short fiction. Bruccoli's biography is useful also for its exhaustive primary and secondary bibliography.

Eppard, Philip B. *Critical Essays on John O'Hara*. New York: G. K. Hall, 1994. A collection of essays on O'Hara's fiction, including some of his more than four hundred short stories. The essays range from reviews to formal academic studies of O'Hara's themes and narrative techniques.

Farr, Finis. *O'Hara*. Boston: Little, Brown, 1973. Written by a journalist of O'Hara's own generation, Farr's was the first O'Hara biography and, indeed, the first book to be written about O'Hara after his death, including discussion of novels and stories published during the last five years of his life. Somewhat more anecdotal in tone and scope than Bruccoli's biography, Farr's book, intended for the general reader, nevertheless includes penetrating readings of selected novels and stories, together with a brief but useful bibliography.

Goldleaf, Steven. *John O'Hara: A Study of the Short Fiction*. New York: Twayne, 1999. An excellent introduction to O'Hara's short stories. Includes bibliographical references and an index.

Grebstein, Sheldon Norman. *John O'Hara*. New Haven, Conn.: College & University Press, 1966. The first full-length study of O'Hara's narrative prose, prepared somewhat too soon to take in the full range of the author's later short fiction. Grebstein's volume discusses at length O'Hara's ongoing problems with the critical establishment; although Grebstein strives to achieve objectivity, it is clear that he tends to share the establishment's skeptical view of O'Hara's accomplishments. Grebstein does, however, provide good "readings" of such stories as were then available to him.

Grimes, William. "The John O'Hara Cult, at Least, Is Faithful." *The New York Times*, November 9, 1996, p. 17. An account of a panel discussion on O'Hara by five of his most ardent fans; the group chose O'Hara's *Appointment in Samarra*, as the best introduction to O'Hara's work.

MacShane, Frank. *The Life of John O'Hara*. New York: E. P. Dutton, 1980.

_____. Introduction to *Collected Stories of John O'Hara*. New York: Random House, 1984. MacShane, author of a somewhat sensational, if academically sound, biography of O'Hara, is perhaps most notable for his carefully prepared anthology of the author's shorter fiction, preceded by a most perceptive introduction. No small part of MacShane's accomplishment is the selection itself, covering the full length of O'Hara's career, yet subtly—and quite justifiably—weighted toward the stories written after 1960.

Quinn, Joseph L. "A Cold-Weather Journey with

John O'Hara." *America* 169 (December 18-25, 1993): 17-21. Points out that throughout his career, O'Hara was preoccupied with the harsh winters and small-town atmosphere of Pottsville, Pennsylvania, the industrial coal-mining community where he was raised; discusses his links to F. Scott Fitzgerald and Ernest Hemingway.

John Carr, updated by David B. Parsell

BEN OKRI

Born: Minna, Nigeria; March 15, 1959

PRINCIPAL SHORT FICTION
Incidents at the Shrine, 1986
Stars of the New Curfew, 1988

OTHER LITERARY FORMS

Besides his collections of short fiction, Ben Okri has written several novels, including *Flowers and Shadows* (1980), *The Landscapes Within* (1981), *The Famished Road* (1991), and *Infinite Riches* (1998). He has also published the nonfiction work *A Way of Being Free* (1997).

ACHIEVEMENTS

Ben Okri has impressed his readers with his colorful, vibrant use of the English language, the power of his words and imagery, and his control over structure and motif. He received the Commonwealth Writer's Prize for Africa and *The Paris Review* Aga Khan Prize for Fiction in 1987. He also received the Booker McConnell Prize for *The Famished Road* in 1991.

BIOGRAPHY

Ben Okri was born in Minna, Nigeria, in 1959, the son of Silver Oghekeneshineke Loloje Okri and Grace Okri, both of the Urhobo ethnic group of southwestern Nigeria. His father was an executive officer with the Nigerian Post and Telecommunications. After finishing his secondary education in 1972, three months before his fourteenth birthday, Okri moved to Lagos. He is the first Nigerian writer to have won the Booker McConnell Prize and the first to have chosen self-expatriation; he settled in London, England. He has been poetry editor of the magazine *West Africa* and a broadcaster for the British Broadcasting Corporation (BBC).

ANALYSIS

The settings in Ben Okri's stories are for the most part African, specifically Nigerian. More significantly, the attitudes expressed, toward society and the natural world, seem consistent with an African cosmology. That is to say, Okri presents a world wavering between order and chaos, an ambiguous and mysterious world, of which human beings are but a part and over which they have little control. Whatever differences may exist between Okri and his two famous countrymen Chinua Achebe and Wole Soyinka in their styles or subjects, he shares with these two writers both the awe and the comic bemusement with which they face the human condition. While offering guidance, they do not presume to offer solutions. While calling to account instances of irresponsible behavior, they do not expect it to cease or promise peace if it does. While not being fatalists, they accept a certain inevitability in human affairs. Like Achebe and Soyinka, Okri takes Africa as his primary subject but humanity as his theme. What his Nigerians do in exaggerated gestures, all people do in some measure.

Acknowledging the limitations of human perception, Okri does not, then, insist upon absolutes. He does, however, suggest some patterns. For example, the principle of reciprocity in Soyinka's works (for example, the play *Madmen and Specialists*, pr. 1970; rev. pr., pb. 1971) is also in those of Okri: What one sows, one also reaps. The responsibility that one has toward others and toward nature seems to be fundamental in Okri's thought. If his stories are bleak and nightmarish, a cause may be the failure of individuals in society to observe this principle. The primary manifestation of this behavior in his collections of stories is the failure of characters to face reality. Okri presents this evasion as an escape into dreams (illusions) that, because false and evasive, become nightmares. The reader can hardly distinguish dream from reality because characters without warning, after a short sleep, step out of reality into dream. What people really need is honesty and the capacity for "terror and compassion" to face what honesty reveals. Because awareness is thus central to Okri's theme, "seeing" is a major motif in his collections. In fact, the most Okri seems to hope for in his characters or his readers is some conceptual breakthrough, some acknowledgment that much of life is pain and that life ends in death. Only then can one know sweetness and beauty.

Ben Okri (Archive Photos)

INCIDENTS AT THE SHRINE

Okri's collection opens with a story about a child being initiated into reality during the Nigerian Civil War. The nameless ten-year-old boy who narrates "Laughter Beneath the Bridge" (in *Incidents at the Shrine*) has not as yet begun to evade reality but instead offers an objective if naïve account of what he sees and feels. He, along with two other boys, abandoned at school because of the war, survives by foraging and stealing. His mother, a member of "the rebel tribe," accompanies him on a harrowing journey home in a crowded truck; they must speak only the father's language at the barricades. The soldiers physically and mentally abuse them, partly because the boy refuses to speak at all. The boy sees, apparently for the first time, the terrors of war, as the illiterate, lascivious, and repulsive soldiers rape and kill suspicious passengers. Only the boy's sudden urge to defecate, spoken in the safe language, allows them to continue their journey. Once home, he continues to face the repulsiveness and danger of war. Beneath the bridge outside town, dead bodies begin to dam the river. His childhood girlfriend, Monica, acts even more strangely than usual. The soldiers have killed her brother, Ugo. She has been spending her time, the boy soon learns, sitting on the bank above the river, contemplating the spot where the soldiers threw his body. At that moment the boy has an epiphany: "The things on the water suddenly looked different, transformed." He "saw them as they were." The soldiers above the bridge laugh; then Monica "started to laugh. I had never heard that sort of twisted laughter before." Then he hears something unearthly: "I thought it was all the swollen corpses that were laughing."

At this point, the world of the boy begins its transition into the frenetic world of the adult, but he has not yet blocked out the reality of death and pain. During a mock Egungun (ancestral) dance, he and Monica defy the soldiers. Seizing the occasion, the soldiers take her away to be raped and killed, as the elders of the town exult because they have cleared the bloated bodies that were polluting the town's air and clogging the river. The child's awakening to death contrasts with the elders' blind, inadequate victory over pollution. The narrator cannot explain why he recalls this period in his life as "a beautiful time," but the reader speculates that beauty is in the clarity and purity of the child's seeing.

In the title story, "Incidents at the Shrine," Anderson in a daze exits a museum through "the Department of Antiquities" and "the ancestral stoneworks in the museum field." He has just been fired. His resulting paranoia—people seem to be pointing at him—increases after a sleep in which he dreams of "his dead parents." The very goats in the marketplace stare at him, and a fire that breaks out seems "intent upon him because he had no power to protect himself." People call out his names, not only his English one, Anderson, but also the ones out of his past. Two rusty nails give him tetanus. Quack doctors give him injections and medicines. After three days, he has "the gaunt face of a complete stranger." At this point, he returns to his home village.

The emphasis in the first part of the story on Anderson's personal and cultural past and on an obsessive insecurity that has no observable cause suggests by juxtaposition that a cure or an answer demands a return to origins. This is the only story in the collection that holds out any such hope. What follows is a dreamlike sequence, a psychological or spiritual recovery of archetypal experiences. Each dream or trance carries him further back into the inner recesses of the self and its cultural history.

As he approaches the village on foot, "three rough forms" chase him, calling out his names and causing him to abandon his box of clothes, medicines, and gifts. He thus enters the village empty-handed. He does not recognize Mr. Abas, and the town itself seems changed. Ants carry him in a dream into the pool office, where he eventually recognizes his uncle who, Mr. Abas tells him, is the Image-maker, and who guides Anderson through this ancestral world. As the uncle grows "raw and godlike" in Anderson's mind, he utters words of wisdom and parabolic riddles: "The more you look, the less you see" and "The world is the shrine and the shrine is the world." The two men walk through "irregular rows of soapstone monoliths" (like those at the museum), which according to the uncle "were originally decorated with pearls, lapis lazuli, amethysts and magic glass which twinkled wonderful philosophies. But the pale ones from across the seas came and stole them." Clearly the uncle's cure for this "afflicted 'son of the soil'" is

to reintroduce him to his African heritage. Anderson enters the shrine, where he finds "the master Image" still sporting its jewels, in order to undergo a grotesque yet symbolic initiation. After the purification, the Image-maker assures him (what the pragmatic dreamer wants to hear) that he can with confidence collect the salary the museum owes him and can find another job. The shrine, he explains, is a meeting place for "spirits from all over the world," who come to discuss "everything under the sun." Anderson himself "must come home now and again," for it is at home that he will "derive power," whose ultimate source, a strange voice warns him, is awareness of self and the world. In his final dream, he eats of the ever-replenished master Image. He recognizes as he walks out of the village that "There is hunger where I am going" and understands Mr. Abas's parting words: "Suffering cannot kill us." The rough forms that chased him into the village, the threats of death, no longer frighten him. He continues the journey of life with a "new simplicity." This symbolic dream experience, in fact, proposes a simple solution to the nightmarish complications of modern society: an acceptance of the human condition. What the story gives, however, it also takes away. The solution comes in a dream, and dreams are not reliable. The stories that follow show little promise that human beings in a waking state are likely to be so lucid and bold.

The final story, "The Image-Vendor," with its emphasis on dreams, anticipates the second collection of stories, *Stars of the New Curfew*. The main character, Ajegunle Joe, is not only a victim but also a seller of dreams. After taking "Correspondence Courses in psychology and salesmanship," he is reborn as a mystic and publishes pamphlets describing his visions—that is, quack solutions to life's problems. After two years at this job, however, he loses confidence. When he becomes sexually impotent, he himself visits a quack and undergoes a grotesque ritual cure. In his most intriguing dream, a midget offers him a gift, but when he looks, it flies away. It is wisdom, he learns. The midget then offers him a second gift, which Joe pockets on faith. When the midget returns in a later dream to reclaim the gift, Joe learns that he has been carrying around "bad luck." The midget's ironic advice is that Joe should keep his eyes open. With eyes open or closed, Joe apparently cannot win. The Image-maker has already warned Anderson, one remembers, that "the more you look, the less you see." Okri thus ends this collection on a not unexpectedly ambiguous note. Joe and his friend Cata-cata (confusion) try to escape temporarily by fishing off a pier "washed by the August rain." Joe sums up his life as "one long fever" and thinks now that he is "getting well." Yet he still believes that "a man must fly," and the only vision he can muster is another quack pamphlet, "Turning Experience into Gold." This final story calls into question the efficacy and reliability of the lesson learned in the title story at the African shrine. The god of confusion, Eshu, will not permit definitive answers.

STARS OF THE NEW CURFEW

In *Stars of the New Curfew*, dream becomes nightmare. In the opening story, "In the Shadow of War," Okri once again starkly contrasts a child's innocence with the brutality of war. Repulsive soldiers again contaminate the environment with their crude manners and disrespect for human life. The boy watches them abuse and kill a woman suspected of being a spy, as corpses float down a river. Yet the soldiers, with some gentleness, carry the boy back to his father, who speaks apologetically to the soldiers when the son tries to explain what has happened. The son's delirium sets the tone and theme for the remaining stories.

In "Worlds That Flourish," a nightmarish parody of the title story in the first collection, the main character, now nameless, also loses his job and his way in the world. Soldiers falsely arrest him for burglarizing his own house. His neighbors gradually disappear around him, though he does not notice until one reclusive neighbor chastises him for not "seeing." In a daze, he begins to see handwriting on faces. Then the neighbor disappears, and a two-day rainstorm turns the city into chaotic ruins. His escape, unlike Anderson's, is "without a destination." His frenzied, dreamlike journey seems to move him in circles; his car drives him. An old man at a service station warns him against going "that way": "Stay where you can be happy." As he continues into the forest, people attack

his car; blood and flesh cling to broken glass. The car crashes into an anthill. If what has been happening to him is "real," he now has what might be called an out-of-body experience. His spirit enters a traditional village, where objects are upside down, where people move backward and walk through mirrors. Oddly, they have been expecting him for some three months. Both his reclusive neighbor and his dead wife are among those welcoming him to the land of the dead. He passes the shrine, where a huge statue of a god has only holes for eyes. This is not the same sanctifying image that Anderson encounters. He escapes by running backward. Pursued to the boundary, he finds his car, reenters his body, extricates himself from the wreckage, and tries to find the old man before dying. Like Anderson, he has faced death—he had not been willing before to accept his wife's death—but Okri does not suggest any spiritual purification. At most, the nameless man has achieved awareness. His last words are a warning to another young man traveling in the same direction he had taken.

"In the City of Red Dust" and "Stars of the New Curfew" are likewise bleak extensions of a story in *Incidents at the Shrine*. In the former, two men, Emokhai and Marjomi, and a woman, Dede, are even further trapped in the world of nightmare than their counterparts in "The Dream-Vendor's August." The men survive by selling their blood to a hospital and by picking pockets. Against the suggestive background of Adamic red dust and Egyptian plagues, the military governor, hiding his "secret physical corruptions" and "his monstrosities," celebrates his fiftieth birthday with a parade and an air show. A plane crashes, causing havoc and death. Raped by five soldiers, Dede attempts suicide. The only redeeming grace is Emokhai's protective care of Dede in the hospital and of Marjomi sleeping in his room deep in the ghetto. In that room, Emokhai finds a "confusion of books" on the occult—including the one Joe contemplates writing at the end of "The Dream-Vendor's August." While Joe and Cata-cata escape by fishing, Emokhai and Marjomi smoke marijuana stolen from the governor's secret farms. In the latter story, "Stars of the New Curfew," the narrator and main character, Arthur, is a vendor not of visionary pamphlets but of mind-altering drugs. As the drugs become more powerful in their promise to cure a multitude of ills, he and his customers enter deeper into nightmare. He is responsible for a bus accident killing seven people. His escape to his past yields only petty quarrels and struggles for power and sexual advantage. His escape to his home village traps him in a confrontation between two wealthy power seekers, an ugly satire on Nigeria's political corruption. When he returns to the city at the end, he is aware enough to know that life is a nightmare, but he would prefer to dream and continues to sell drugs.

Okri closes this second collection with a poignant love story and a farcical allegory. "When the Lights Return" traces the fate of a young singer whose vanity, insensitivity, and neglect lead to the death of the woman he should have loved. As he watches her die, he sings like Orpheus of those victimized by life. He truly sees her, however, only after she dies, and then her image gives way to a midget girl who yells "thief," as market women stone him to death. In "What the Tapster Saw," death is again the teacher. Forewarned by a dream, the tapster falls from a tree and wakes up in the land of the dead. In this allegory, reminiscent of the fiction of Amos Tutuola, the death experience combines wisdom and nonsense, comic inversions, talking animals, and teasing proverbs— for example, "your thoughts are merely the footsteps of you tramping round the disaster area of your own mind." The herbalist who claims credit for the tapster's seven days in death had never had "a better conversation." The god of chaos does indeed rule in death, in dreams, and among the living. While Okri's language is sometimes accusatory, his tone is not, and his final utterance is a laugh.

OTHER MAJOR WORKS

LONG FICTION: *Flowers and Shadows*, 1980; *The Landscapes Within*, 1981; *The Famished Road*, 1991; *Songs of Enchantment*, 1993; *Astonishing the Gods*, 1995; *Birds of Heaven*, 1996; *Dangerous Love*, 1996; *Infinite Riches*, 1998; *Mental Flight*, 1999.

POETRY: *An African Elegy*, 1992.

NONFICTION: *A Way of Being Free*, 1997.

BIBLIOGRAPHY

Bissoondath, Neil. "Rage and Sadness in Nigeria." Review of *Stars of the New Curfew*, by Ben Okri. *The New York Times Book Review* (August 13, 1989): 12. Bissoondath calls Okri "a natural storyteller" and especially appreciates his social commentary "on a variety of issues," including politics in Nigeria. The stories respond sensitively to conditions not only in Africa but also, by inference, in the Third World generally. Only the final story, being totally imaginative rather than based in reality, is pointless and disappointing.

Hawley, John C. "Ben Okri's Spirit Child: Abiku Migration and Postmodernity." *Research in African Literatures* 26 (Spring, 1995): 30-39. Addresses Ben Okri's use of the abiku, or child-spirit, narrator; discusses the background of the *abiku* in Nigerian culture and analyzes how Ben Okri uses the figure as a spokesman for two worlds.

Henry, Andrea. "More Magic than Realism." Review of *Infinite Riches*, by Ben Okri. *The Independent*, August 29, 1998, p. 15. Comments on its use of fantasy and folklore; comments on the novel's strong anticolonial message; suggests that the fantastic sense of the magical in the book is not always satisfying.

Kakutani, Michiko. "Brave New Africa Born of Nightmare." Review of *Stars of the New Curfew*, by Ben Okri. *The New York Times*, July 28, 1989, p. C25. Kakutani interprets the stories as surreal commentary on contemporary Africa, where "social realities . . . resemble our worst dreams" and the "people live in a state of suspended animation." While the style is "fiercely lyrical," Okri's "voice . . . needs only to expand its narrative territory to fulfill its bright promise."

Olshan, Joseph. "Fever Dreams from Nigeria's Troubled Soul." Review of *Stars of the New Curfew*, by Ben Okri. *Chicago Tribune*, July 16, 1989, p. 6. In this review, Olshan calls *Stars of the New Curfew* a "magnificent" collection depicting Nigeria in a state of crisis. He notes Okri's "feverishly poetic" language, frenetic characters "living on the edge of extinction," and incidents hovering between nightmare and reality.

Quayson, Ato. *Strategic Transformations in Nigerian Writing: Orality and History in the Work of Rev. Samuel Johnson, Amos Tutuola, Wole Soyinka, and Ben Okri*. Bloomington: Indiana University Press, 1997. This critical study compares the work of these Nigerian writers and includes a discussion of the Nigerian oral tradition and the Yoruba peoples. Includes a bibliography and an index.

Ryan, Alan. "Ben Okri's Modern Fetishes." Review of *Stars of the New Curfew*, by Ben Okri. *The Washington Post*, August 7, 1989, p. 602. Ryan emphasizes the "deeply Nigerian and universal" qualities of the stories, as they depict a world without stability, where a city, without communal traditions, is a forest, and "demons dig potholes" for human travelers.

Smith, Ali. "A Treasure Beyond Dreams." A review of *Infinite Riches*, by Ben Okri. *The Scotsman*, August 22, 1998, p. 15. Suggests that the story is a masterpiece of narrative slippage, a book full of disintegration and divisions; comments on the book's allusions to bygone English literature.

Thomas, Maria. Review of *Stars of the New Curfew*, by Ben Okri. *Los Angeles Times Book Review*, September 24, 1989, p. 3. Thomas sees in Ben Okri "an updated [Amos] Tutuola," who presents "an Africa of its own myths, thronged and bewitched." Despite his black humor, Okri can be wonderful and hilarious; despite the corruption, terror, and despair, he registers hope through an indestructible "vitality."

Thomas Banks

TILLIE OLSEN

Born: Omaha, Nebraska; January 14, 1913

PRINCIPAL SHORT FICTION

Tell Me a Riddle, 1961

OTHER LITERARY FORMS

Besides her short stories and the novel *Yonnondio: From the Thirties* (1974), Tillie Olsen is the author of "A Biographical Interpretation," the afterword published in Rebecca Davis's *Life in the Iron Mills* (1972), which she edited, and *Silences* (1978), a collection of essays about women and writing. She has edited two books: *Mother to Daughter, Daughter to Mother, Mothers on Mothering: A Daybook and Reader* (1984), a collection of excerpts, and *Mothers and Daughters, That Special Quality: An Exploration in Photographs* (1987). In addition, she has written uncollected magazine articles on women and writing and many uncollected poems, several of which appeared in *Partisan Review*, *Prairie Schooner*, *New World Writing*, *Ms.*, *Harper's*, and *College English*.

ACHIEVEMENTS

Even though Olsen secured her literary reputation on the strength of one collection of short fiction, her voice as a humanist and feminist extends her influence beyond this small output. Olsen writes about working-class people who, because of class, race, or sex, have been denied the opportunity to develop their talents. Frequently she focuses on the obstacles women have experienced. She understands them well. She herself was exactly such a victim of poverty during the 1930's, and then she worked and raised a family for more than twenty years until she could begin writing. Both her fiction and her nonfiction deal with the problem women face: developing individual talents while combating socially imposed views.

Olsen is also known as a leading feminist educator. Her courses have introduced students to forgotten writings, such as journals, to teach them about women's lives. The reading lists she developed have provided models for other women's studies' courses throughout the United States. Besides the O. Henry Award for the best American short story of 1961 for

Tillie Olsen (Leonda Fiske)

"Tell Me a Riddle," Olsen has also won the Award for Distinguished Contribution to American Literature from the American Academy and the National Institute of Arts and Letters. Her other awards include a John Simon Guggenheim Memorial Foundation Fellowship in 1975-1976, an honorary doctorate from the University of Nebraska in 1979, a Ministry to Women Award from the Unitarian Women's Federation in 1980, a Bunting Institute Fellowship from Radcliffe College in 1985, and a Rea Award for the short story in 1994. Her short fiction appears in more than one hundred anthologies, including *The Best American Short Stories* for 1957, 1961, and 1971, and *Fifty Best American Stories, 1915-1965*.

BIOGRAPHY

The daughter of Russian-Jewish immigrant par-

ents, Tillie L. Olsen spent her youth in Nebraska and Wyoming. Her parents were active union members, so political commitment as well as economic pressures accompanied her early years. Her father served as state secretary in the Socialist Party. In 1933, she moved to California, where, in 1936, she married printer Jack Olsen. Because she raised four daughters and worked at full-time clerical jobs, she did not publish her first book until she was in her late forties. She worked as a pork trimmer in meat-packing houses, a hotel maid, a jar-capper, and a waitress. Then, with the help of a Stanford University Creative Writing Fellowship and a Ford grant in literature she put together *Tell Me a Riddle*, the title story of which received the O. Henry Award for the best American short story of 1961. There followed a fellowship at the Radcliffe Institute for Independent Study, grants from the National Endowment for the Arts, and a Guggenheim Fellowship. A grant from the MacDowell Colony allowed her to complete *Yonnondio: From the Thirties*, a novel she began in the 1930's which was originally published in 1934 in the *Partisan Review*. After its revision and publication in 1974, Olsen continued writing essays and articles as well as editing collections of women's writings. In addition, she has taught at Amherst College, Stanford University, the Massachusetts Institute of Technology, and the University of Minnesota, among others. In her nonfiction book *Silences* (1978), Olsen writes in her dedication, "For our silenced people, century after century, their beings consumed in the hard everyday essential work of maintaining human life. Their art, which still they made–anonymous; refused respect, recognition; lost." She was twice arrested for her activism.

ANALYSIS

Tillie Olsen's *Tell Me a Riddle* contains four stories arranged chronologically in the order in which they were written: "I Stand Here Ironing," "Hey Sailor, What Ship?," "O Yes," and "Tell Me a Riddle." All but the first story contain, as major or minor characters, members of the same family, whose parents emigrated from Russia. The characters in the first story could also belong to the same family, although there is no evidence to prove it and the names of the children are different; nevertheless in "I Stand Here Ironing" characters, situation, and tone are similar to those found in the other three stories. A difference between "I Stand Here Ironing" and the remaining stories in the volume is that the former story is told in the first person, being a kind of interior monologue (actually an imagined dialogue), whereas "Hey Sailor, What Ship?," "O Yes," and "Tell Me a Riddle" are told in varieties of the third person.

"I STAND HERE IRONING"

Exterior action in "I Stand Here Ironing" is practically nonexistent, consisting of a woman moving an iron across an ironing board. Interior action is much more complicated, being a montage of times, places, and movements involving a mother in interaction (or lack of interaction) with her firstborn, a daughter, Emily. Questions arise as to whether the montage can define or even begin to define the daughter; whether the mother or anyone else can help the daughter or whether such help is needed; whether the daughter will continue to be tormented like the mother, who identifies herself with the iron moving inexorably back and forth across the board; or whether, as the mother hopes, the daughter will be more than the dress on the ironing board, "helpless before the iron." "She will leave her seal," the mother says, the only words spoken aloud in the story; but the words could express only the mother's fervent hope for the well-being of a daughter born to a mother of nineteen, impoverished, alone, distracted, in an age of depression, war, and fear.

"HEY SAILOR, WHAT SHIP?"

"Hey Sailor, What Ship?" introduces Lennie and Helen and their children, Jeannie, Carol, and Allie; but the story is not so much about them as it is about Whitey (Michael Jackson, a sailor and friend of the family who seems more lost at sea than at home in any port or ship). Filtering through Whitey's consciousness, the story explores his frustrations and anger, pain and despair. At the same time, however, the living conditions of Lennie and Helen and their children and the relationships among the family and between various members of the family and Whitey are carefully delineated.

Whitey is a mariner, a perpetual wanderer whose only contact with family life is with Lennie, a boyhood friend. As the story opens, Whitey is drunk, a condition he finds himself in more and more, and with almost nothing left of his pay. His anguish, born of his desire to be with Lennie and the family and his reluctance to bear the pain of such a visit, is evident from the beginning, as is also the shame and degradation he feels associated with his lifestyle. What had started out as a dream, a life of adventure on the sea, with comrades who shared the good and the bad, has become a parade of gin mills and cathouses, clip joints, hock shops, skid rows, and lately hospitals. Lennie's dreams, however, have also been frustrated. Lennie is a worn likeness of his former self; Helen is graying and tired from holding a job as well as caring for house and home. They live in poverty in cramped quarters. Still, as Helen explains to her oldest daughter Jeannie, this house is the only place Whitey does not have to buy his way. The tragedy is that he feels he does. He comes bearing presents, distributing dollars and at the same time too drunk to share in meaningful interaction with the family he loves, where he is brother, lover, and father to a family not his own.

"O YES"

"O Yes" picks up the family several years later when Carol, the second daughter, is twelve and about to experience the pain of parting with a close friend, Parry, a black girl. Carol and her mother, Helen, have accompanied Parry and her mother, Alva, to a black church to witness Parry's baptism. Carol is uncomfortable, however, both with the surroundings and with Parry, who is growing away from her. As the services rise to a crescendo of passion, Carol asks her mother to take her home and then faints. Later Alva tries to explain to Carol that the religion is like a hope in the blood and bones and that the music offers a release to despair, but Carol will not listen.

Later Jeannie tries to explain to her mother that Carol and Parry are undergoing an inevitable "sorting out" process, a sorting out demanded by the culture—their environment, their peers, their teachers—a sorting out that "they" demand. The separation is hard on both girls. Nevertheless, Parry seems better equipped to handle the crisis, while Carol continues to suffer and question. Helen knows that Carol, too, has been baptized, immersed in the seas of humankind, and she suffers with her daughter. The irony is that white people have no means of catharsis through their religion; they are unable to cry "O Yes."

"TELL ME A RIDDLE"

The most haunting story in the collection *Tell Me a Riddle* is the title story. Longer than the other stories, this one focuses on Lennie's mother and father while at the same time it brings to a culmination themes Olsen explores in the other stories: the frustration of dreams unrealized; the despair of never having enough money; the anger and hostility of women who have had to cope with too much with too little and who have lost themselves in the process; the search for meaning and explanation; the continuing hope of the young in spite of the tensions around them; the pain of mortality. If the story has a fault, it may be that it is too painful as it grasps the reader and pulls him or her too close to raw feeling. "Tell me a riddle, granny," a grandchild demands. "I know no riddles, child," the grandmother answers; but she knows, and the reader knows, that the riddle is of existence itself. Why claw and scratch; why hold on? Aged and consumed by cancer, the grandmother's body will not let go.

Russian emigrants of Jewish extraction who have fled persecution to come to the American land of promise, the grandfather and grandmother have been married forty-seven years and have reared seven children, all of whom are married and have families of their own. Now the grandfather wants to sell the house and move to The Haven, a retirement community, where he will have freedom from responsibility, from fretting over money, and will be able to share in communal living, to fish or play cards or make jokes with convivial companions. The grandmother refuses, however, countering every argument her husband puts forth. She was the one who worked eighteen hours a day without sufficient money to keep the house together. Not once did he scrape a carrot or lift a dish towel or stay with the children. He is the one who needs companions; she lived a life of isolation. "You trained me well," she tells him. "I do not need

others to enjoy." She is adamant: "Never again to be forced to move to the rhythms of others." The argument between them erupts continually, fanned by his desires and her anger and resentment.

The children do not understand. How can people married forty-seven years and now at a time of life when they should be happy get themselves into a power struggle that threatens to pull them apart? Unknowingly the children take their father's side, considering their mother to be unreasonable or sick. They advise him to get her to a doctor. The doctor finds nothing seriously wrong and advises a diet and a change in lifestyle—"start living like a human being." The grandmother continues to deteriorate; more and more she keeps to herself, stays in bed, and turns her face to the wall. One night she realizes that although the doctor said she was not sick, she feels sick, and she asks her husband to stay home with her. He refuses, once again bringing up the old argument, and as he leaves she sobs curses at him. When he returns he finds that she has left their bed and retired to a cot. They do not speak to each other for a week until one night he finds her outside in the rain singing a love song of fifty years ago. The husband and the children bring her to a son-in-law who is a physician, and during surgery he finds cancer. The children advise their father to travel with her and visit all the children; and now begins an exodus of pain. She does not yet realize she is terminally ill and the constant movement causes her utter despair when all she wants is to be at home. From house to house they carry her and she refuses to participate, will not touch a baby grandchild, and retreats finally to sit in a closet when they believe she is napping. Once a granddaughter, herself upset, hauls her little body into the closet and finds her grandmother there—"Is this where you hide, too, Grammy?"

Finally the grandfather brings her to a new apartment close to a seaside resort, dismal in off season and filled with the impoverished aged. The grandmother, ill in bed for several days, is tended by her granddaughter, Jeannie, daughter of Lennie and Helen, and now a visiting nurse. When she is better, the grandmother wants to go by the sea to sit in the sand. More and more now she loses control of her conscious self, sings snatches of songs, remembers pieces of quotations, tries in herself to find meaning while noticing that death, decay, and deterioration are all around her. Then she realizes that she, too, is dying and knows that she cannot tell her husband of her realization because a fiction is necessary to him; and she wants to go home.

One day Jeannie brings her a cookie in the shape of a real little girl who has died and tells her of a Spanish custom of partying at funerals, singing songs, and picnicking by the graves. From this interaction Jeannie draws solace, from what she takes to be a promise from her grandmother that at death she will go back to when she first heard music, to a wedding dance, where the flutes "joyous and vibrant tremble in the air." For the others there is no comfort. "Too late to ask: and what did you learn with your living, Mother, and what do we need to know?"

OTHER MAJOR WORKS

LONG FICTION: *Yonnondio: From the Thirties*, 1974.

NONFICTION: *Silences*, 1978.

EDITED TEXTS: *Life in the Iron Mills*, 1972; *Mother to Daughter, Daughter to Mother, Mothers on Mothering: A Daybook and Reader*, 1984; *Mothers and Daughters, That Special Quality: An Exploration in Photographs*, 1987 (with others).

BIBLIOGRAPHY

Aiken, Susan Hardy, Adele Marie Barker, Maya Koreneva, and Ekaterina Stetsenko. *Dialogues/ Dialogi: Literary and Cultural Exchanges Between (Ex)Soviet and American Women*. Durham, N.C.: Duke University Press, 1994. In this series of essays/dialogues, Susan Aiken's feminist reading of Olsen's "Tell Me a Riddle" focuses on home as a site of repression that relegates women to domestic work and child care. Argues that Olsen creates for her protagonist a free discursive space in which preestablished categories are redefined; by so doing, she contests the larger political forces of repression that divide people from themselves.

Bauer, Helen Pike. "'A Child of Anxious, Not Proud, Love': Mother and Daughter in Tillie Olsen's 'I Stand Here Ironing.'" In *Mother Puzzles: Daughters and Mothers in Contemporary American Literature*, edited by Mickey Pearlman. Westport, Conn.: Greenwood, 1989. Analyzes the story as a dialogue between a number of opposites in which the basic issues are how much of the past determines the daughter's future, how much of the mother is in the daughter, and how much responsibility the mother has for her daughter's passivity and repression.

Cardoni, Agnes Toloczko. *Women's Ethical Coming-of-Age: Adolescent Female Characters in the Prose Fiction of Tillie Olsen*. Lanham, Md.: University Press of America, 1998. A survey of Olsen's adolescent female characters, comparing and contrasting their milieux. Includes a bibliography and an index.

Coiner, Constance. *Better Red: The Writing and Resistance of Tillie Olsen and Meridel Le Sueur*. New York: Oxford University Press, 1995. Compares these two authors' activism and writing styles. Includes a bibliography and an index.

Faulkner, Mara. *Protest and Possibility in the Writing of Tillie Olsen*. Charlottesville: University Press of Virginia, 1993. Examines the themes of motherhood, relationships between men and women, community, and language in Olsen's fiction.

Frye, Joanne S. *Tillie Olsen: A Study of the Short Fiction*. New York: Twayne, 1995. One of the most extensive discussions of the four stories in *Tell Me a Riddle* and "Requa." Frye contends that Olsen's readings are embedded in history—both cultural and personal. The book also contains a long conversation Frye had with Olsen about her five short stories.

Jacobs, Naomi. "Earth, Air, Fire, and Water in *Tell Me a Riddle*." *Studies in Short Fiction* 23 (Fall, 1986): 401-406. Jacobs analyzes the plot of Olsen's story by showing the development of a series of images derived from the four basic elements. Jacobs then relates this interpretation to Olsen's theme of spiritual rebirth.

Martin, Abigail. *Tillie Olsen*. Boise, Idaho: Boise State University, 1984. Martin sees Olsen as a writer in the Western tradition because, by advocating a change in how men and women are perceived, Olsen placed herself on a frontier in thinking. Martin interprets Olsen's work in terms of the obstacles she overcame to become a writer and compares her with Virginia Woolf. A part of the Western Writer series, this book contains a select bibliography and a list of Olsen's poems.

Nelson, Kay Hoyle, and Nancy Huse, eds. *The Critical Response to Tillie Olsen.* Westport, Conn.: Greenwood Press, 1994. A collection of the most important articles, reviews, and parts of books about Olsen, arranged in chronological order; includes essays from a variety of approaches on the stories "I Stand Here Ironing," "Tell Me a Riddle," and "O Yes."

Niehus, Edward L., and Teresa Jackson. "Polar Stars, Pyramids, and *Tell Me a Riddle.*" *American Notes and Queries* 24 (January/February, 1986): 77-83. Niehus and Jackson analyze one incident recalled by Eva, the dying woman, by relating it to a pole or center of life, an idea that derives from basic astronomy and late nineteenth century pyramidology. The authors explore how Olsen handles this theme when circumstances change so that the pole does not remain stable.

Olsen, Tillie. Interview by Lisa See. *Publishers Weekly* 226 (November 23, 1984): 76. Interviewed when she was almost seventy-two, Olsen focuses on her two haunting concerns, motherhood and writing, and how society continues to misunderstand these topics.

Pearlman, Mickey, and Abby H. P. Werlock. *Tillie Olsen.* Boston: Twayne, 1991. A general introduction to Olsen's life and work that tries to redress previous critical neglect and to suggest new directions for further study of her work. Includes an interview and extensive discussions of the four stories in Olsen's *Tell Me a Riddle*, especially "I Stand Here Ironing" and the title story.

Staub, Michael. "The Struggle for 'Selfness' Through Speech in Olsen's *Yonnondio.*" *Studies in American Fiction* 16 (Autumn, 1988): 131-139. Staub sees *Yonnondio*, like James Agee and Walker Evans's *Let Us Now Praise Famous Men* (1941), as part of the 1930's literature that attempts to raise society's consciousness about the working classes. Staub examines Olsen's focus on the right of women to develop selfness so they can speak freely. He explores how Olsen develops this theme by revealing character strength through dramatic speech and silences, rather than through action.

Mary Rohrberger, updated by Louise M. Stone and
Nika Hoffman

JUAN CARLOS ONETTI

Born: Montevideo, Uruguay; July 1, 1909
Died: Madrid, Spain; May 30, 1994

PRINCIPAL SHORT FICTION

Un sueño realizado y otros cuentos, 1951
Los adioses, 1954 (novella; *Goodbyes*, 1990)
Una tumba sin nombre, 1959 (novella; better
    known as *Para una tumba sin nombre*; *A Grave
    with No Name*, 1992)
La cara de la desgracia, 1960 (novella; *The Image
    of Misfortune*)
El infierno tan temido, 1962
Tan triste como ella, 1963 (novella)
*Jacob y el otro: Un sueño realizado y otros
    cuentos*, 1965
La novia robada y otros cuentos, 1968
Tiempo de abrazar, 1974
Tan triste como ella y otros cuentos, 1976
Goodbyes and Other Stories, 1990

OTHER LITERARY FORMS

Juan Carlos Onetti first gained recognition with
the publication of his novels, particularly *El astillero*
(1961; *The Shipyard*, 1968) and *Juntacadáveres*
(1964; *Body Snatcher*, 1991), which confirmed his
role as an international literary figure. He has also
published the novels *Dejemos hablar al viento* (1979;
Let the Wind Speak, 1997) and *Cuando ya no importe*
(1993; *Past Caring?*, 1995). In addition to his short
stories and novels, Onetti has published a number of
novellas, including *The Image of Misfortune* in 1960
and *Tiempo de abrazar* in 1974. In 1975, a number of
his literary essays were collected in the volume
Réquiem por Faulkner (1975).

ACHIEVEMENTS

Among Juan Carlos Onetti's many awards is the
Premio National de Literature, Uruguay's most prestigious literary prize, which he received in 1962. He
received the William Faulkner Foundation Certificate
of Merit that same year for his novel *The Shipyard*.
His novel *Body Snatcher* was a finalist for the presti-

gious Rómulo Gallegos Prize, given only once every
five years to the author of the best Spanish-language
novel. In 1980, Onetti was nominated for the Nobel
Prize in Literature and was awarded the Premio
Miguel de Cervantes Prize.

BIOGRAPHY

Juan Carlos Onetti was born in Montevideo, Uruguay, on July 1, 1909, the son of a customs official.
Onetti did not complete high school or attend a university; he earned a living in his early years by taking
on a number of menial jobs. In 1930, he married his
cousin and left for Buenos Aires to accept a job as a
salesman of calculators. In the late 1930's his first
marriage broke up, and he married his wife's sister.

Onetti published his first short story in 1933, and
in 1939 he helped found, and became chief editor of,
Marcha, which developed into an influential cultural
weekly in Latin America. After the publication of *El
pozo* (1939; *The Pit*, 1991) he began working for the
British news agency Reuters and edited several periodicals. His best-known novel *La vida breve* (1950; *A
Brief Life*, 1976) established him as a significant literary figure in Latin America.

In 1973, when the civilian government in Uruguay
was overthrown by the military, *Marcha* was closed
down and many journal archives were burned; historical research was forbidden, and many European and
U.S. writers were banned. Because Onetti was a
judge for a literary prize awarded to a work critical of
the military regime, he was put in prison, soon to be
released because of public outcry and poor health.
Later after he was refused permission to leave Uruguay to receive an award, he escaped to live in Madrid, Spain, where he stayed in exile until his death in
1994.

ANALYSIS

Frequently compared to William Faulkner, both
for his elaborate prose style and for his creation of a
postage-stamp fictional world, Juan Carlos Onetti is
often praised for his modern focus on alienated hu-

man beings and his postmodern experiments with self-reflexive metafictions. Many of his characters, facing old age and death, desire to find a way to retreat into the past or to escape to an ideal fictional creation to regain what is lost. As a result, his stories often focus on the power of the imagination and feature characters who are writers, actors, and dramatists. Ultimately, this emphasis compels Onetti to examine the nature of fictionality and playacting, which, finally, forces many of his stories into a realm somewhere between fantasy and reality, where the nature of reality itself is questioned.

"A DREAM COME TRUE"

The narrator of the title story of Onetti's first collection is a theater producer asked by a woman to stage a play for her. The woman has in mind a single scene featuring herself, a man, and a girl who comes out of a shop to give the man a glass of beer. When pressed for a title, the woman says she will call it "A Dream Come True." She is willing to pay to see the scene enacted once for her alone. Even though the producer thinks the woman is crazy, he has had a bad season and needs the money to escape to Buenos Aires; he thus contracts an actor he knows and makes the arrangements.

The woman has a mythical ageless quality about her; although she appears to be fifty, she has a girl's air from another century "as if she had fallen asleep and only awakened now, her hair in disarray, hardly aged but seemingly at any moment about to reach her own age all of a sudden and then shatter in silence." In the dramatized scene, she sits on a curb beside a green table next to which a man sits on a kitchen stool. When the man crosses the street to get a beer the girl has carried out, she fears he will be hit by a car. The woman lies on the sidewalk as if she were a child, and the man leans over and pats her on the head. The woman wants the scene enacted because she has dreamed it; during the dream she felt happy, and she wants to recapture that feeling.

During the enactment of the scene, while the woman lies on the stage being patted on the head by the actor, she dies, and the story ends with the producer concluding that he finally understands what it was all about, what the woman had been searching for. "I understood it all clearly, as if it were one of those things that one learns once and for all as a child, something that words can never explain." Indeed, the woman's desire is not as enigmatic as it may first appear, for by actualizing a dream, she fulfills a common human fantasy, after which she can happily die.

"HELL MOST FEARED"

The story focuses on a reporter who reports horse racing for a newspaper. After the reporter is separated from his actress-wife, he begins to receive intimate photographs of her with other men. The first two photographs create in him a feeling that is neither hate nor pain, a feeling that he cannot name, but which is "linked to injustice and fate, to the primal fears of the first man on earth, to nihilism and the beginning of faith." He thinks that although he can understand and even accept his wife's act of revenge, there is some "act of will, persistence, the organized frenzy with which the revenge was being carried out" that is beyond his comprehension.

When the estranged wife begins to send photographs to other people, even the man's young daughter in a convent school, he begins to understand, but he is no longer interested in knowing what it is that he understands. The story ends with the man, blaming himself for mistakes in his relationship and in his life, killing himself. In sending the photographs, the wife seems to be searching for her husband's weakness, until, finally, by sending a pornographic photo of herself to the husband's daughter she has found the place where he is most vulnerable.

"WELCOME, BOB"

In this early Onetti story, popular with anthologists, a middle-aged narrator gets a sadistic pleasure from observing the aging of Bob; it is his revenge for Bob's preventing his marriage several years earlier to his sister Inez, because he was too old for her. At that time Bob told the narrator that he was a finished man, washed up, "like all men your age when they're not extraordinary." Bob tells the narrator that the most repulsive thing about old age, the very symbol of decomposition, is to think in terms of concepts formed by second-rate experiences. For the old, Bob says, there are no longer experiences at all, only habits and repetitions, "wilted names to go on tagging things with and half make them up."

After the sister rejects the narrator and Bob grows older, the narrator begins a friendship with him so that he can more closely watch Bob's aging process. He delights in thinking of the young Bob who thought he owned the future and the world as he watches the man now called Robert, with tobacco-stained fingers, working in a stinking office, married to a fleshy woman. "No one has ever loved a woman as passionately as I love his ruin," says the narrator, delighting in the hopeless manner in which Bob has sunk into his filthy life. The story ends with the narrator's final sad and ironic triumph: "I don't know if I ever welcomed Inez in the past with such joy and love as I daily welcome Bob into the shadowy and stinking world of adults."

OTHER MAJOR WORKS

LONG FICTION: *El pozo*, 1939, 1965 (*The Pit*, 1991); *Tierra de nadie*, 1941; *Para esta noche*, 1943 (*No Man's Land*, 1994, also known as *Tonight*, 1991); *La vida breve*, 1950 (*A Brief Life*, 1976); *El astillero*, 1961 (*The Shipyard*, 1968); *Juntacadáveres*, 1964 (*Body Snatcher*, 1991); *La muerte y la niña*, 1973; *Dejemos hablar al viento*, 1979 (*Let the Wind Speak*, 1997); *Cuando ya no importe*, 1993 (*Past Caring?*, 1995).

NONFICTION: *Réquiem por Faulkner*, 1975.

MISCELLANEOUS: *Obras completas*, 1970; *Onetti*, 1974 (articles, interview).

BIBLIOGRAPHY

Adams, M. Ian. *Three Authors of Alienation: Bombal, Onetti, Carpentier.* Austin: University of Texas Press, 1975. Includes an extended discussion of Onetti's novella *The Pit*; shows how Onetti's artistic manipulation of schizophrenia creates a sensation of participating in an alienated world.

Deredita, John F. "The Shorter Works of Juan Carlos Onetti." *Studies in Short Fiction* 8 (Winter, 1971): 112-122. Surveys Onetti's short fiction, focusing on the two ages of man—naïve youth and the age of conformity—in such stories as "Welcome, Bob" and "A Dream Come True."

Harss, Luis, and Barbara Dohmann. "Juan Carlos Onetti or the Shadows on the Wall." In *Into the Mainstream: Conversations with Latin-American Writers.* New York: Harper & Row, 1967. Claims that in Onetti's middle-aged protagonists there is a yearning for vanished youth and innocence. Discusses *Un sueño realizado y otros cuentos*, Onetti's Faulknerian style in *Goodbyes*, and his pessimism.

Lewis, Bart L. "Realizing the Textual Space: Metonymic Metafiction in Juan Carlos Onetti." *Hispanic Review* 64 (Autumn, 1996): 491-506. Discusses four Onetti works in terms of his use of metonymy as a metafictional device. Argues that the plasticity of *Goodbyes* gives it a composed, pictorial quality absent from his other works. Discusses the relationship between story and storytelling.

Maio, Eugene A. "Onetti's *Los adioses*: A Cubist Reconstruction of Reality." *Studies in Short Fiction* 26 (Spring, 1986): 173-181. Shows how Onetti's novella has affinities with the aesthetic goals and structures of cubism. Argues that his narrative style has much in common with the aesthetics of contemporary art in general and cubism in particular.

Millington, Mark. *Reading Onetti: Language, Narrative and the Subject.* Liverpool, England: Francis Cairns, 1985. Discusses the development of Onetti's work under the "hegemony of international modernism." Drawing on stylistics, narratology, and post-structuralism; Millington focuses on the status of Onetti's fiction as narrative discourse. Discusses how *Goodbyes* problematizes the act of reading.

_____. "No Woman's Land: The Representation of Woman in Onetti." *MLN* 102 (March, 1987): 358-377. Discusses the function of the wife, prostitute, girl, and mad woman in Onetti's fiction; argues that the subjection of women is one of the major impasses of Onetti's thinking.

Murray, Jack. *The Landscapes of Alienation: Ideological Subversion in Kafka, Céline, and Onetti.* Stanford, Calif.: Stanford University Press, 1991. In his discussion of alienation in Onetti's fiction,

Murray provides some background about how Uruguay has affected Onetti's ideological unconscious.

Richards, Katherine C. "Playing God: The Narrator in Onetti's *Los adioses*." *Studies in Short Fiction* 26 (Spring, 1989): 163-171. Argues that the narrator has a will to power that conflicts with his role as witness-observer; says his special knowledge contradicts the reader's experience of reality and literary convention.

Sullivan, Mary-Lee. "Projection as a Narrative Technique in Juan Carlos Onetti's *Goodbyes*." *Studies in Short Fiction* 31 (Summer, 1994): 441-447. Argues that Onetti's novella is designed to draw on the projective capacity of readers. Suggests that by leaving inexplicable gaps in the narrator's version of the story, Onetti elicits readers' desires and fears within the creative space of the text.

Charles E. May

OVID
Publius Ovidius Naso

Born: Sulmo, Roman Empire (now Sulmona, Italy); March 20, 43 B.C.E.

Died: Tomis on the Black Sea (now Constantsa, Romania); 17 C.E.

PRINCIPAL SHORT FICTION

Metamorphoses, c. 8 C.E. (English translation, 1567)

OTHER LITERARY FORMS

Ovid survives in his poetry (his tragedy *Medea* is lost), the most important of which, in probable order of composition, are: *Amores* (c. 20 B.C.E.; English translation, 1597); *Heroides* (before 8 C.E.; English translation, 1567), a collection of fifteen imaginary letters from heroic women to their lovers, a form Ovid claimed to have invented; *Ars amatoria* (c. 2 B.C.E.; *Art of Love*, 1612), a tongue-in-cheek manual for philanderers; *Remedia amoris* (before 8 C.E.; *Cure for Love*, 1600), the companion poem to *Ars amatoria*, with "cures" for excessive passions; *Metamorphoses, Fasti* (c. 8 C.E.; English translation, 1859), which deals with the origins of and the legends associated with the first six months of the calendar of Roman festivals; and two collections of verse letters from exile, *Tristia* (after 8 C.E.; *Sorrows*, 1859) and *Epistulae ex Ponto* (after 8 C.E.; *Letters from the*

Black Sea, 1639). All Ovid's poetry except the *Metamorphoses* are in elegiac meter.

ACHIEVEMENTS

The most classical of Latin poets, Ovid has had an influence "almost coterminous with the history of education" in the West. While the earlier "Middle Ages" reflected a greater predominance to Vergil, Charles Martindale observed that "from the twelfth century onwards Ovid has had a more wide-ranging impact on the art and culture of the West than any other classical poet." This significance, however, was minimized in the eighteenth and nineteenth centuries, as classical scholarship rediscovered many other authors. At the same time, Puritan and Anglican sentiments turned against not only "paganism" in general but also the apparent "laxity in sexual matters" thought to be apparent in Ovid's works in particular.

In the twentieth century, however, there was renewed interest in Ovid's work. The International Congress of Ovidian Studies was held at his birthplace on May 20-24, 1958, and it celebrated the bimillenary with a spate of scholarly articles by "fifty-two scholars from ten countries in five languages." To these articles can be added numerous other writings that were published in Romania that same year, also in commemoration of Ovid. This re-

Ovid

newed impetus stemming therefrom, while not exclusively focused on the *Metamorphoses*, has allowed this "most difficult major poem" of the Greco-Roman world to gain for its 11,995 lines renewed attention. Such intensive investigation not only brings Ovid back to the center of classical studies but also makes him significant to the study, for example, of women, or of rape and related pathologies of human sexuality. As Leo C. Curran has remarked, Ovid "exhibits a sympathy for women and an effort to understand, as well as a man can, women's intellectual and emotional life rivaled by no male author of antiquity other than Euripides." This may well be the *Metamorphoses*' greatest achievement.

BIOGRAPHY

Born of an aristocratic family and educated at Rome and Athens, Ovid began a political career, but he soon abandoned it for poetry. He moved in the highest circles of Augustan society until he was abruptly banished by the Emperor to a remote settlement for reasons that remain obscure. Together with his third wife, he remained in exile on the Black Sea from C.E. 8 until his death in C.E. 18. His output as we have it is larger than the extant works of Vergil, Lucretius, Horace, and Catullus combined.

ANALYSIS

Ovid never published any prose, and the *Metamorphoses* (the transformations) is his only thoroughly narrative work; in the telling of its manifold but continuous stories, however, the poem exemplifies a range of narrative techniques which has had inestimable influence on the history of short fiction.

METAMORPHOSES

The verse form of the poem (dactylic hexameter), the invocation to the gods, and the opening statement of theme all indicate from the outset that this is Ovid's epic:

> My spirit moves me to tell of forms changed into new bodies. Gods, since you made these changes, favor my attempt and from the first beginning of the world to my own time spin out an uninterrupted song.

The ambitious scope of the project is reflected in its sheer size alone; with fifteen books of about eight hundred lines each, the *Metamorphoses* is longer than either the *Aeneid* (c. 29-19 B.C.E.) or *Paradise Lost* (1667). It has more in common with the Greek poet Hesiod than with the Homeric tradition of epic from which Vergil and John Milton drew inspiration, and it is odd enough in its subject and particularly in its tone that some commentators have called it an antiepic.

The poem appears to tell of the world's progress from an original chaos of matter to Creation and the Golden Age, then of a decline through four ages to the Flood; from there, it recounts the vicissitudes in the life of humans and gods, first in a mythological epoch and then in the historical period from the founding of Troy to the reign of Augustus Caesar. Underlying the narrative is a sense of the continuous war between order and disorder, cosmos and chaos, integrity (in every sense of the word) and disintegration. Thus, the poem that begins with the transformation of shapeless chaos into an ordered but unstable universe climaxes with Augustus's imposition of order on Rome's political chaos after the death of Julius Caesar. It ends with the anticipated death and metamorphosis of its own author:

> And now my work is done, which neither Jove's wrath nor fire nor sword nor gnawing tooth of time can destroy. Let that day which has power over nothing but this body come when it will and end my uncertain span of years. Yet the best of me will be borne up, everlasting, above the lofty stars, and my name will be imperishable. Wherever Roman power extends over conquered lands I shall be read aloud by the people; famous through all ages, if there be any truth to the poets' presentiments, I shall live.

The *Metamorphoses*, however, is not in any rigorous sense a philosophical poem (such as Lucretius's *On the Nature of Things*, first century B.C.E.) or a politico-religious poem (such as the *Aeneid*). It is secular and above all literary, and the issues that most engage its author are primarily artistic ones. Indeed, to say that Ovid weaves stories from Greek and Latin mythology into an unbroken narrative of transformations is to characterize the three major aesthetic problems that the poet sets for himself; it is his resourceful solutions to these problems that have been of most value to subsequent writers of fiction.

First, it is clear that Ovid was not, like William Blake or J. R. R. Tolkien, trying to devise a mythology; but while his stories are traditional, it would be a mistake to conceive him as compiling a handbook like Thomas Bulfinch's *The Age of Fable* (1855). Although it is all too often used like a handbook or reference work, the *Metamorphoses* is a literary work of great originality and personality, a sophisticated and even skeptical handling of myth by a characteristic narrative voice. Although Ovid occasionally made a point of telling a little-known story ("Pyramus and Thisbe" is presented in this way, although thanks to Ovid and one of his most assiduous readers, it is very familiar to the modern audience), he expected his audience on the whole to know the stories he told and so to be most interested in how he transformed the old familiar songs in the voice, perspective, and detail of his particular telling. This intention is certainly apparent in the poet's choosing to end with the apotheosis of himself, or, more strictly speaking, of his narrative voice. (The closest modern equivalents to Ovid's interplay between a tale and its narration would be Thomas Mann's in *Joseph and His Brothers*, 1933-1943, or John Barth's in *Chimera*, 1972.)

When, for example, Ovid came to tell the story of Medea (book 7: lines 1-424), he was addressing an audience familiar with Euripides' tragedy, and perhaps also with his own lost tragedy, *Medea*. There may be resemblances between Ovid's own two versions; the story of Daedalus in *Metamorphoses* (8:152-235) reuses a number of lines from the poet's earlier account of the same material in *Ars Amatoria* (2:21-96). In any case, these circumstances afford a poet considerable freedom, because in a sense he can take the plot for granted. The story, therefore, begins with the major events relegated to a subordinate clause:

> While the Argonauts were approaching King Aeetes and asking for the Golden Fleece, and while the King was imposing his monstrous conditions, his daughter was seized by an overpowering passion. . . .

This is immediately followed by a long interior monologue by Medea—an almost operatic struggle with her passion that, like an overture, firmly fixes the character as the center of attention in this version of the story. She finally yields to her love and provides Jason with the herbs and spells he will need to survive the trials imposed by the king. Ovid dwells on one of these, the sowing of the serpent's teeth to produce an army that must be defeated, perhaps because the motif recalls the second "creation" after the Flood when Deucalion and Pyrrha sow stones to repopulate the world. With the help of Medea's magic, the dragon that guards the Fleece is entranced and Jason carries off both the prize and the princess to Thessaly. Once there, Medea uses her powers to rejuvenate Jason's father Aeson in an elaborately detailed ritual. She then exacts vengeance from Aeson's usurping brother Pelias by offering to restore his youth by the same magic. She pretends to repeat the ceremony but instead tricks Pelias's daughters into butchering their father. She escapes in her dragon chariot to Corinth, where the best-known part of her story, the substance of Euripides' tragedy, is passed over in a single sentence: "But after the new wife had been set afire by Colchian poisons and the two seas had seen the king's house burning, an impious sword was drenched in the blood of her sons and, having wickedly avenged herself, the mother fled Jason's weapons." This escape is to Athens, where an unsuccessful attempt to poison Theseus initiates the transition to another tale.

"MEDEA"

In "Medea" as elsewhere, Ovid successfully shifts the reader's attention from the inherited tale to its present telling. Medea's opening monologue, her prayer to Hecate (the model for Prospero's speech abjuring magic in *The Tempest*, 1611), and vivid descriptions of her rituals take up close to half of the entire narrative. Ovid made the tale his own by the resulting emphasis on the psychological dimension of her love and jealousy, and on the rare power of the witch, unlike most mortals, to cause transformations rather than to suffer them.

The second challenge Ovid sets for himself is that of maintaining "uninterrupted song." This creates, above all, an opportunity to demonstrate virtuosity in the art of transition, and the display begins almost at once. In book 1, for example, when the story moves from the primeval to the mythological epoch, the spot is marked with a complex and ornate transition. The world has been progressively formed out of chaos, culminating in upright humans; but then a decline leads to the Flood, described as a kind of second chaos, with fish in the trees and everything out of place. New creations emerge from the discordant harmony of heat and moisture in the fertile mud, one of which is the monstrous Python, which the archer Apollo has to kill with thousands of arrows. To commemorate his triumph, the god established the Pythian games, in which the winning athletes were crowned with oak leaves. Ovid's audience, however, knew that the Pythian victors were in fact crowned with laurel, so the transition continues: "There was not yet any laurel (*laurus*), so any tree served to pro-

vide the garland that crowned the flowing locks of Phoebus. His first love was Daphne, daughter of Peneus the river god. This came about not by sheer chance, but through the wrath of Cupid."

"PYTHON" AND "DAPHNE"

There are actually three facets to this transition from "Python" to "Daphne." One is naïvely narrative: The exploits of the young god are seen first in war, then in love. A second transition is via the name Daphne, which a Roman literary audience would recognize as Greek for "laurel," and the *absence* of laurel in the preceding story. (Transition by way of some missing element is frequent in the *Metamorphoses*; in fact, the story of Daphne also ends with one, leading to the story of Io: When the other rivers come to console Daphne's father, one is missing because he is worried about the disappearance of his own daughter.) What actually causes Apollo's infatuation, however, is his condescending to Cupid as a direct result of his victory over the monster. Apollo taunts Cupid that a bow is a weapon for a warrior, not a boy; but Cupid replies, "Your bow strikes everything, but mine will strike you," and promptly shoots Apollo with a love dart that sends him chasing the nymph.

Although the narrative of the *Metamorphoses* is in principle chronological, the long mythological section generally replaces temporal sequence with some formal symmetry. Stories are grouped around a place (Athens, Crete, Troy); a person (Theseus, Orpheus); or a theme (unrequited love, the amours of the gods). The handling of two stories about Daedalus is typical. The story of how Icarus flew too high on his manmade wings ends in his burial, at which is present a partridge who (as readers come to expect) is the subject of the following story. The relation between the two tales is more complex than it appears, however, for the bird is Perdix, a nephew of Daedalus, who as an apprentice was so precocious that his uncle in envy hurled him from a temple of Minerva. As he fell, the goddess turned him into a bird that bears his name—one that stays close to the ground and seems to fear high places, as the poet tells us. Thus, the nephew is too bright and saved from death by being transformed into a bird; the son is not bright enough and dies pretending to be a bird; and Daedalus, who loves his son and hates his nephew, is responsible for the fall of both.

Ovid's chief model for the short narrative units of his poem was what has come to be called the *epyllion*. It was a type of narrative poem, usually of a few hundred lines, developed by the Hellenistic Greeks (particularly Callimachus and Theocritus), and characterized by *ekphrasis* (densely detailed scene-setting), recounted speech, and often the insertion of another loosely related story. This other story was a digression, told or sung by one of the characters, depicted on a tapestry, vase, or similar invention within the original story. Typical of the method of epyllion is Ovid's insertion of "Pan and Syrinx" into the narrative about Io: It is the tale in which Mercury finally puts to sleep the last of the hundred eyes of Argus. This technique helps the poet avoid monotony, but it also makes possible more extensive effects than could be managed in a mere sequence of transformation stories. Apparently taking his cue from the epyllion, Ovid frequently has characters tell or sing stories to one another as a way of passing time during their own stories. So Theseus and his companions swap tales while waiting for flood waters to subside (8:546ff.), and the garrulous Nestor tells stories of heroes during a truce in the Trojan War (12:146ff.).

In the story of Minyas's daughters (4:1-415), Ovid develops this device into something like a miniature *Decameron* (1353). The women of Thebes, dressed in animal skins and dancing to the music of flutes, drums, and cymbals, are in the streets celebrating the orgiastic festival of Bacchus (Dionysius). The daughters of Minyas, however, denying the divinity of Bacchus, remain indoors, demurely working at the loom and telling tales in the service of Minerva. Three of the sisters' stories are recounted. The first, after sketching three stories, finally decides to tell the little-known "Pyramus and Thisbe." The third sister similarly passes over five tales before telling that of "Hermaphroditus and Salmacis." While these two stories are of virtually equal length, the story told in the center by the second sister is about the mutual cruelties of Apollo (as the Sun) and Venus. Although shorter than the stories that surround it, this is a double story. The first part is familiar and involves no transformation—the Sun revealing the infidelity of Venus with Mars to her husband Vulcan so that he can catch them in a web of bronze chain. The second part, about the revenge of Venus, is very unfamiliar and probably Ovid's own invention. It ends with two transformations: The Persian princess, seduced by Apollo and buried alive by her father, is turned into an incense shrub; and the nymph Clytie, who informed on the princess because Apollo spurned her and who gazed at the sun with unrequited love until she pined away, is turned into a heliotrope. The storytelling ends at dusk, when the power of Bacchus overcomes the impious sisters. Amid the smoke and unearthly music of the bacchanal, the god of wine turns their looms into grape vines and the sisters themselves into bats.

This group of stories is held together not only by its frame but also by a number of repeated motifs that unify and balance the composition. For example, Thisbe's blood-dyed veil, the brazen mesh forged by Vulcan, and Salmacis ensnaring Hermaphroditus like ivy on a tree trunk or a squid about its prey all recall the tapestry being woven by the narrators. In them the ingenuity of Minerva is combined with the dark passions associated with Bacchus, and this is confirmed in the end when the cloth being woven in her honor is preempted by Bacchus and turned into vines. Thus, the deeper underpinning of these stories is the tension between Bacchus and Minerva, the god of riot and intoxication who had two mothers, versus the goddess of wisdom, ingenuity, and weaving who was born directly from the brain of her father Jupiter. This antithesis, loosely related to that of chaos and cosmos, is also mirrored in the central story here, in the antipathy of Apollo and Venus.

The third artistic challenge that Ovid faces is the avoidance of tedium in the telling of hundreds of stories, all of which end in metamorphosis. It is a problem which Ovid shared with anyone dealing in repetition and already-known formulaic denouements, and his solutions resemble those of the literary pornographer. In this regard he mobilized all of the opulent devices that endeared him to the Renaissance and helped shape the style of the Baroque. Varied narrative pace, the subordination of some stories to others, and high and low relief in the modeling of details and personalities all contribute to obscure the repeated denouement of transformation by creating the illusion of a dense and varied world. The strong presence of a narrator is another factor here; a good-humored, humane, mildly ironic sensibility behind the shaping and selection of detail is felt, but what the narrator selects above all is the language of his telling. It was in his management of the subtle tension between the immediate pleasure of poetic language and the ongoing pressure of narrative that Ovid was most inventive. His mobile and sensuous descriptions of how one form changes into another are impressive, and the impression is visible, for example, throughout Dante's *The Divine Comedy* (c. 1320). Even more notable is a pioneering use of simile and metaphor to anticipate transformation.

The story of Tereus, Procne, and Philomela (6:424-674) is almost a showcase of this technique. Tereus marries Procne and she bears him a son, Itys. After five years, Procne asks her sister Philomela to visit, but when Tereus goes to fetch her, he falls in love. When she steps onto his ship and so into his power, Ovid compares him to an eagle with a hare in its claws. When he rapes her, she is like a timid lamb or a dove. When she threatens to tell what has happened, he cuts out her tongue, and it writhes on the ground like a snake. Mute and confined, she manages to weave her story into a tapestry and sends it to her sister. Under cover of another festival of Bacchus, Procne frees her sister and together they plan revenge. Finally, Procne, murmuring, "how like his father he is," drags Itys off "like some tigress on the Ganges bank," butchers him, and feeds him to Tereus. When he has eaten, Philomela appears with the bloody head of Itys, and the story ends like this: "Drawing his sword, he was rushing in pursuit of Pandion's daughters, when it almost seemed that the girls' bodies were hovering in the air, raised up on wings; in fact, they were hovering on wings." All three have been transformed into birds. Throughout the story, similes have been appearing at moments of passion, each potentially an actual transformation, but the conclusion emphasizes the fine line between being like a beast, and becoming one. At the same time it also invites the reader to see every figure of speech as a sort of metamorphosis.

"Orpheus"

At more than eight hundred lines, "Orpheus" (10:1-11:84) is the longest single episode in the *Metamorphoses* and stands as a concluding example of Ovid's narrative craft. Only the first seventy lines are devoted to the story of Orpheus and Eurydice, probably because that tale had provided the climax of Vergil's *Georgics* (c. 37-29 B.C.E.) a generation earlier. Instead, the emphasis is on the power of a poet (Ovid himself as much as Orpheus) to create and transform worlds; thus 650 lines reproduce his songs. After the loss of Eurydice, there is only a single setting, a hilltop once barren that has been transformed as birds, animals, and trees gather to hear Orpheus sing. The subject of the songs is love: first the successful love of Jupiter for Ganymede, balanced by the failed love of Apollo for Hyacinthus. These tales of divine infatuation are contrasted with two brief tales of the hatred of Venus for the Propoetides and the Cerastae. The Propoetides are turned to stone, and their story is followed by that of Pygmalion, the sculptor whose statue is turned into a woman by the power of his love. Pygmalion and the former statue are wed, and their grandson Cinyras is the subject of the next story. Cinyras's own daughter Myrrha falls in love with him; after tortured monologues, she attempts suicide, and then, with the connivance of an old nurse, she succeeds in sleeping with Cinyras until he discovers her identity. She flees, turns into a myrrh tree, and only afterward gives rather complicated birth to Adonis, who is the subject of the next story, and, as Ovid points out, is grandson (in a manner of speaking) to Cinyras. Venus falls in love with Adonis, and, by way of warning him to avoid wild beasts, tells him the story of Atalanta and Hippomenes, who end transformed into fierce lions. Immediately after the warning, however, Adonis is killed by a wild boar and Venus can only memorialize him in the frail anemone. Then, immediately after this song, Orpheus is interrupted by the bacchants who kill him. Unlike Adonis, he can charm wild beasts, but he has no power over humans acting like beasts. When his music is drowned in their charivari, its spell is broken.

Orpheus, like Medea, pointedly suffers no changes of form. Throughout the *Metamorphoses*, men lose their form, when, through fear, grief, or wickedness, they lose their human individuality; but Orpheus is a model of self-possession. At the second death of Eurydice, Ovid tells the reader that he was stunned "not unlike" a man turned to stone at the fearful sight of Cerberus, but he is not turned to stone; he remains himself. So too at the end, Orpheus simply dies, to be reunited with his wife; but he is surrounded by transformations he has induced, not only the landscape he has created by his singing, but also a snake turned to stone by Apollo as it tried to bite the poet's severed head, washed up on the shore. The bacchic women are also transformed; for acting like beasts, they are turned to trees, but, in describing the process, Ovid compared them to birds:

> Just as a bird, finding its foot caught in the snare of a cunning fowler flaps its wings when it feels it is caught, and tightens the bonds by its fluttering, so each of these women, as she became rooted to the ground, with mad fear vainly tried to flee.

Ovid gathered birds and trees in his verse, as Orpheus did on his hilltop.

The *Metamorphoses* is an anomaly, a poem that has contributed to the development of modern short fiction from its beginnings. It offers a vast array of stories that can be retold or can inspire new invention. At the same time, it is a compendium of narrative strategies. Ovid brought to narrative the virtues of poetry—speed, economy, vividness. He invited new ways of thinking about the use of detail in narrative, continuing to employ the symbolic or functional detail of earlier narration but experimenting broadly with the *effect* of detail, whether homely, sensuous, or grotesque, in establishing an illusion of reality. When the stick with which Medea stirs her cauldron turns green and leafy, then suddenly is laden with fat olives; when Deucalion and Pyrrha after the flood go to pray by the banks of a stream whose waters are not yet clear; or when Pygmalion brings little presents of shells and flowers to his beloved statue, Ovid was adding to the resources by which all fiction creates not merely an exemplary fable, but a world of its own.

Ovid deemphasized plot and "moral"; for him, the art of fiction had to do with matters of tone, setting, and characterization. His psychological interest leads to Giovanni Boccaccio and the later development of the novella, and thus ultimately to short fiction of the Jamesian sort, in which plot is altogether contingent on character. Perhaps most influential to short fiction is Ovid's unabashed presence in his own book, felt not only explicitly, in authorial intrusions, self-conscious anachronisms, and the like but also felt more pervasively in the poem's language and in its self-consciousness about language, in the wit and irony of its surface, and in its profound humanity. What the *Metamorphoses* tells the reader through its hundreds of transformations is that to be human is an achievement, and an achievement never definitively won. Each upright person is like the universe, a crossing point of chaos and cosmos. In self-possession, one can go wrong in the manner of Narcissus, his sympathy meaning dissolution; when most moved one can lose one's grip and cease to be oneself. If "metamorphosis" is the name for the mechanics of a universe generated in the paradox is "love." This is what the *Metamorphoses* endlessly celebrates: a disruptive force which is yet the source of all aspiration; a chthonic passion that brings down each of the gods in turn, yet makes possible an apotheosis of what it is to be mortal; an emotion that breathes life into its object, and, although nothing can defeat death, manages somehow to immortalize by cherishing.

OTHER MAJOR WORKS

POETRY: *Amores*, c. 20 B.C.E. (English translation, 1597); *Ars amatoria*, c. 2 B.C.E. (*Art of Love*, 1612); *Heroides*, before 8 C.E. (English translation, 1567); *Metamorphoses, Fasti*, c. 2-7 (*Calendar of Festivals*, 1640); *Remedia amoris*, c. 8 (*Remedy of Love*, 1636); *Epistulae ex Ponto*, 8-17 (*Letters from Pontus*, 1639); *Tristia*, 11-17 (*Complaints*, 1633).

BIBLIOGRAPHY

Barsby, John. *Ovid*. Oxford, England: Clarendon Press, 1978. In a noted series by the Classical Association of Great Britain, planned in collaboration with the Joint Association of Classical

Teachers of London, Barsby summarizes the latest in research on Ovid. Devised for student use, this study focuses on the author and his variety of works, with generous notes and principal bibliographical references.

Curran, Leo C. "Rape and Rape Victims in the Metamorphoses." *Arethusa* 11 (1978): 213-241. This highly significant essay considers the avoidance of the topic of rape in most commentaries on, and retellings of, Ovid's stories.

Gertz, Sun Hee Kim. "Echoes and Reflections of Enigmatic Beauty in Ovid and Marie de France." *Speculum* 73 (April, 1998): 372-396. Examines Ovid's and Marie de France's fascination with the subject of beauty and its relation to love; compares Ovid's tale of Narcissus and Echo in the *Metamorphoses* with Marie's *Lai Guigemar.*

Hughes, Ted. "On Ovid's 'Metamorphoses.'" *The New York Review of Books* 44 (July 17, 1997): 18. Suggests that it is a mystery why Ovid's versions of Romanized Greek myths and legends in *Metamorphoses* have been so influential; argues that Ovid is of little use as a guide to the historic and original forms of the myths he adapts in that he takes up only those tales that catch his fancy and engages with each only until it liberates his own creativity.

Kenney, E. J. Introduction to *Metamorphoses.* Translated by A. D. Melville. New York: Oxford University Press, 1987. Kenney, the principal contemporary editor of the Latin text, provides an introduction and notes to the *Metamorphoses.* Kenney has teamed up with Melville, who is noted for his capacity to render Ovid into English by using blank verse that captures the fluent style, to provide a translation for modern times.

Mack, Sara. *Ovid.* New Haven, Conn.: Yale University Press, 1988. The "Hermes Books" are intended to provide an adequate introduction to a major classical author by one who loves literature, perceives contemporary life, and writes with clarity and eloquence. "Ovid Today" precedes Ovid in his own time and through his own poetry, with *Metamorphoses* receiving central place. Contains a brief appendix on Latin meter for the general reader, a bibliography, and an index.

Martindale, Charles, ed. *Ovid Renewed: Ovidian Influences on Literature and Art from the Middle Ages to the Twentieth Century.* Cambridge, England: Cambridge University Press, 1988. Fourteen members of the Faculty Latin Reading Group of the University of Sussex, in memorial to L. P. Wilkinson, survey in successive chapters the most important influences of Ovid. Extensive notes, bibliography, indexes, plus sixteen plates.

Solodow, Joseph B. *The World of Ovid's Metamorphoses.* Chapel Hill: University of North Carolina Press, 1988. While the *Metamorphoses* is based on the transmission of a vast repertoire of "mythological material," the significance and unity lie not in that material itself but in Ovid as transmitter. Solodow covers successively the "structures" of the poetry, the narrator, the "mythology," a comparison of narratives with the *Aeneid* of Vergil, before coming to the work as literature "without morality" and as art.

Spencer, Richard A. *Contrast as Narrative Technique in Ovid's "Metamorphoses."* Lewiston, N.Y.: Edwin Mellen Press, 1997. A good discussion of Ovid's style and use of narrative. Includes bibliographical references and an index.

Syme, Ronald, Sir. *History in Ovid.* New York: Oxford University Press, 1978. Syme is a major historian known for his studies of the revolution that terminated the Republic and of Tacitus who narrated the emerging Empire. Syme employs Ovid and his prosopographical connections to understand the era of Augustus, and the legislation, morals, and poetry of the Augustan Age to understand Ovid and his exile.

Tissol, Garth. *The Face of Nature: Wit, Narrative, and Cosmic Origins in Ovid's "Metamorphoses."* Princeton, N.J.: Princeton University Press, 1997. The three themes of the subtitle are examined in-depth in this volume.

Wheeler, Stephen Michael. *A Discourse of Wonders: Audience and Performance in Ovid's "Metamorphoses."* Philadelphia: University of Pennsylvania Press, 1999. A thoughtful book of criticism and interpretation of *Metamorphoses.*

Wilkinson, Lancelot Patrick. *Ovid Recalled.* Cambridge, England: Cambridge University Press, 1955. The "major general work on Ovid in English" from which all subsequent discussion of his study proceeded. This book brought Ovid back into focus from nineteenth century neglect, with

chapters on his life, his influence, and each portion of his poetry: *Metamorphoses* receives nearly one hundred pages of discussion. Ample references, bibliography, and indexes.

Laurence A. Breiner, updated by
Clyde Curry Smith

AMOS OZ
Amos Klausner

Born: Jerusalem, Israel; May 4, 1939

PRINCIPAL SHORT FICTION

Artsot hatan, 1965, rev. ed. 1976 (*Where the Jackals Howl and Other Stories*, 1981)
Ahavah me'uheret, 1971 (*Unto Death*, 1975)
Har ha'etsah ha-ra'ah, 1976 (*The Hill of Evil Counsel: Three Stories*, 1978)

OTHER LITERARY FORMS

Amos Oz has written several novels, among them the well-known *Mikha'el sheli*, 1968 (*My Michael*, 1972)—the basis of an esteemed feature film of that title—*Kufsah shehorah* (1987; *Black Box*, 1988), which received worldwide attention when it was published, and *Al tagidi lailah* (1994; *Don't Call It Night*, 1995). He has also written a children's novel, *Sumkhi* (1978; *Soumchi*, 1980). His many nonfiction books range from collections of essays on history, politics, and society, as in *Po va-sham be-Erets-Yisra'el bi-setav* (1982; *In the Land of Israel*, 1983) and *Mi-mordot ha-Levanon: Ma'amarim u-reshimot* (1987; *The Slopes of Lebanon*, 1989), to essays mixing autobiography, philosophy, literary criticism, and sociopolitical analysis, as in *Be-or ha-Techelet ha-azah: Ma'amarim ve-reshimot* (1979; *Under This Blazing Light: Essays*, 1995) and *Israel, Palestine, and Peace: Essays* (1994), to focused literary criticism in *Shetikat ha-shamayim* (1993; *The Silence of Heaven*, 2000) and *Mathilim sipur* (1996; *The Story Begins: Essays on Literature*, 1999).

ACHIEVEMENTS

With Avraham Yehoshua and Aharon Appelfeld, Amos Oz is one of the select group of the most highly regarded writers in the earliest of the new waves in Israeli fiction. However, he has won not only prestigious literary prizes (Holon Prize, 1965; Brenner Prize, 1978; Bialik Prize, 1986; French Prix Femina, 1988; Israel Prize for Literature, 1998) but also political awards (Frankfurt Peace Prize, 1992; French Legion of Honor, 1997), which reflect his liberal philosophy and leadership in the Peace Now movement in Israel. His books consistently have been translated into not only English but also most Asian and European languages in worldwide publication.

BIOGRAPHY

Born Amos Klausner, Amos Oz left his Jerusalem home at age fifteen, breaking with the right-wing politics and Eurocentrism of his family, changed his surname to one with biblical overtones—as many settlers in Israel have done—and joined Kibbutz Hulda. Subsequently, he has been a kibbutz agricultural field hand, kibbutz teacher, member of an Israeli army tank crew in the 1967 and 1973 wars, writer, globetrotting lecturer, visiting professor at Oxford University in England and Colorado Springs College in the United States, and the Agnon Professor of Literature at Ben Gurion University in the Negev.

The varied experiences of Oz's life are revealed in much of his fiction. The emphasis in the three interlinked novelettes of *The Hill of Evil Counsel* on a young boy's growing up in Jerusalem on the eve of Israel's war of independence in 1948, also paralleled in Oz's novel *Panter ba-martef* (1994; *Panther in the Basement*, 1997), reflects Oz's own experience. The kibbutz settings of five of the eight stories in *Where the Jackals Howl and Other Stories* reflect Oz's personal knowledge of this way of life; the many soldiers and military characters in his short fiction likewise reflect Oz's life experiences—indeed, main character Sergei Unger in "Late Love" (*Unto Death*) acquires a book about Israeli tank warfare. The many intellectuals and ideologues in Oz's short fiction reflect not only people Oz encountered on the kibbutz but also intellectual European immigrants to Israel, political activists, teachers such as Oz himself, and even some of Oz's own family, including his father and grandfather.

ANALYSIS

Amos Oz's short fiction focuses on the Jewish experience, especially in his homeland. It has, collectively, an impressive historical sweep from biblical times to the decades following the 1948 founding of the state of Israel. The main character in "Upon This Evil Earth," in *Where the Jackals Howl and Other Stories*, is the biblical Jephthah (Judges 11-12); the main characters in "Crusade," in *Unto Death*, are the aggressively anti-Semitic members of the medieval retinue of the Count Guillaume of Touron on their way from Europe to the Holy Land in a crusade of the year 1095; the characters in the three interlinked novelettes of *The Hill of Evil Counsel* are Jerusalem inhabitants concerned about the imminent end of the British mandate and subsequent war of liberation in 1948; finally, "Late Love," in *Unto Death*, and the stories in *Where the Jackals Howl and Other Stories*, except "Upon This Evil Earth," are set on the kibbutz, an Israeli military base, or in the cities of Jerusalem or Tel Aviv in Israel in the decade or two after the 1948 founding of the state. In all of these works, a main concern is the contrast between belonging and not belonging, between being an insider and an outsider, to the land, culture, or society.

Other themes and subjects that pervade Oz's short and long fiction are, especially as connected to

Amos Oz (©Miriam Berkley)

sociopolitical conditions, nostalgia for European culture and ideas in the midst of harsh Middle Eastern realities, the dangers of obsession and extremism, the interrelation between humanity and the natural world, the injuries done to romantic love and marriage by a harsh physical and political environment, the problems of the parent-child relationship, the contrast between one generation and the next, and the power of language and art.

These themes are expressed in articulated form. The short stories—not shorter than twenty pages—and novelettes all have numbered sections as well as subsections indicated by spacing. The only exception is "Longing" (in *The Hill of Evil Counsel*), which is epistolary: eight letters of Dr. Emanuel Nussbaum to his former sweetheart, Dr. Hermine ("Mina") Oswald, from September 2 to September 10, 1947. Also distinctive—beyond Oz's shifts in point of view (particularly in and out of the first-person plural mode), symbolism, figurative language, pervasive personifications, and sentence fragment notation of details—is his frequent biblical allusion. Writing in the very language of the Hebrew Bible, Oz is alert to and makes thematic use of biblical references and overtones in his stories' titles, characters' names, imagery, and plot parallels. He even has his own expanded version of a biblical narrative.

Where the Jackals Howl and Other Stories

Damage done to marriage and, consequently, the parent-child relationship by the pioneering life in a new, hard land, permeated by threats, is a theme of four of the stories of *Where the Jackals Howl and Other Stories*, as well as "The Hill of Evil Counsel," "Mr. Levi," and "Longing" in *The Hill of Evil Counsel*. In "Where the Jackals Howl," what appears to be the luring of the beautiful Galila to an attempted lover's tryst in his kibbutz bachelor's quarters by the ugly workman Matityahu Damkov, using Galila's interest in art—painter's supplies gotten by Damkov from South America—turns out to be the surprising revelation by Damkov to Galila that he is her father. Her father is not her mother's husband, Sashka, one of the kibbutz intellectuals.

Reader and child are likewise surprised at the end of "Strange Fire" (note the title's overtones of perversity from Leviticus 10:1). Lily Dannenberg has not, spurred by her Eurocentric unhappiness with Israeli culture, capriciously broken an appointment with the father of her daughter's fiancé Yosef in order to make a pass at her future son-in-law Yair Yarden. She instead pressures Yair into taking a walk around Jerusalem with her to reveal to him his father's secret: Yosef had long ago been married for several months to Lily.

The title "Way of the Wind"—with allusions to Genesis and Ecclesiastes—suggests the caprice of the father, Shimshon Sheinbaum, who to be strong, like his similarly unshorn biblical namesake Samson, in his devotion to country and to political writing has abandoned his wife and son Gideon. He lives apart from them on the kibbutz. The allusive title also forecasts Gideon's tragic attempt to live up to his own heroic biblical namesake to please Shimshon. The result is his becoming fatally tangled in power lines on the kibbutz when his army paratroop unit makes a jump

and the wind shifts. Gideon ironically enacts his nickname, "Pinocchio," by literally hanging from lines. Furthermore, an unpleasant though athletic youngster attempts to rescue him and is surprisingly revealed at the story's end to be a half brother, one of Shimshon's rumored but unacknowledged children on the kibbutz.

In "Before His Time," the unrelenting adversities of the new land—its heat, barrenness, Arab theft or attack—are the background for Dov Sirkin's desertion of his wife and young children. Poring over maps, a recurrent symbol in Oz's short fiction, Sirkin lives in Jerusalem, leaving his family behind on the kibbutz. The story's title refers to Dov's premature desertion, the death in combat of his estranged military-hero son, and the slaughter of the kibbutz prize stud bull, Samson. Although still healthy, the bull was impotent from the bite of a poisoned jackal. Jackals are recurrent symbols in Oz's short fiction of the untamed, sometimes savage land, in which a struggle for possession and belonging is continual.

In "The Hill of Evil Counsel" the unhappy, Eurocentric Ruth Kipnis, in contrast to her biblical namesake, deserts her husband and young son, Hillel. She begins an affair, at the ominously named geographical site of the story's title, with a British officer and second world war hero and leaves Israel with him. Hillel, in contrast to his self-possessed Talmudic namesake, is so upset that he eventually has to be placed on a kibbutz while his father continues to live in Jerusalem.

Another displaced boy is young Uriel ("Uri") Kolodny, in "Mr. Levi" and "Longing," who has a series of surrogate parents as he grows up. This situation partly results from his mother being somewhat incapacitated by life in the new land, while his father struggles with making a living, helping his wife, and dealing with British oppression. Uri's surrogate parents include Ephraim, a young repairman and underground agent, who is obsessed with developing a secret weapon—another recurring motif in Oz's short fiction; the old poet, Nehamkin, who speaks the obsessive language of biblical prophecy; and the seriously ill Dr. Emanuel Nussbaum, whose beloved, Mina Oswald, has left him and Israel behind.

Four other stories in *Where the Jackals Howl and Other Stories* illustrate how, in the context of pioneering in an often hostile environment, obsession and alienation may impair romantic love. This theme is also exemplified in the stories "Crusade" and "Late Love," in *Unto Death*, and Oz's uncharacteristically brief (ten-page) "Setting the World to Rights," included in *The Penguin Book of Jewish Short Stories* (1979, edited by Emanuel Litvinoff).

In "Nomad and Viper," Geula's natural, unfulfilled sexuality and the negative relations between Israeli settlers and native Arabs cause her to have conflicting emotions about a young Arab goatherd to whom she is drawn. She meets him in an orchard, which, with the garden, is a recurrent, often biblical symbol in Oz's short fiction. When the young goatherd—friendly, polite, but nervous—is frightened off by her intensity, her conflict is resolved into hatred toward Arabs and the delusion of an attempted rape.

"The Trappist Monastery" ends with the ironic revelations that the main character, Itcheh, passionately cares about Bruria, despite his exaggeratedly apparent indifference toward her. His show results from the strains of combat and maintaining his image as legendary military hero. Instead, he really is just a Romanian immigrant who plans to retire from the army as soon as he can to join a soccer team or head a bus service. Unfortunately, Bruria begins to carry on affairs with other men. While pursuing Bruria on an erroneous chase, Itcheh's Jeep breaks down in Arab territory, near the landmark of the story's title, with implied fatal disaster for Itcheh and his malevolent passenger, Nahum, a military medic jealous of Itcheh.

Death in combat permanently severs the romantic relationship between central character Batya Pinski and her husband, Abraham, in the story "A Hollow Stone." Abraham's fervor about socialism in Israel and Spain began his emotional drift from his wife even before he went to fight and die in the Spanish Civil War of the 1930's. This makes Abraham yet another deserter in Oz's short fiction. The placid existence of the fish in Batya's aquarium, a repeated symbol in the story, where the hollow stone of the title is located, differs greatly from that of the people on Batya's kibbutz.

The fifty-page novelette "Upon This Evil Earth" has a complex intertwining of themes like many of Oz's stories—the term "story" being what Oz prefers, or "prose narrative," following the Hebrew language, instead of the term "fiction." Gilead the Gileadite lives in the hard country between the fertile lands of the Ammonites and the tribe of Ephraim. Both his external surroundings and internal temperament lead to an almost existentialist alienation that is shared by his son Jephthah. As a result of this alienation, neither Gilead nor Jephthah is capable of true romantic love. Jephthah's inability to love is aggravated by his being the son of a concubine (reflecting the biblical account) from Ammon (not in the biblical account), making him only the half brother of the sons from Gilead's proper Israelite wife. Jephthah repeatedly asserts that he does not feel complete allegiance either to the Israelites or to the Ammonites, much as a liberal modern Israeli might feel when caught between obsessed Israelis and obsessed Arabs, neither willing to acknowledge the vision and values of the other.

Sergei Unger in "Late Love" represents the Israeli obsessed by an enemy, in Unger's case the Russian Communists. He is so obsessed that he frankly confesses he has given up romantic love. The story shows how he has missed his chance for this love in a constant companion on the lecture tour for much of his life, Liuba Kaganovskaya. Unger's parallel opposite in "Crusade" is the medieval Count Guillaume of Touron, whose name suggests the pride of a tower and the monument from the Crusades explained in "The Trappist Monastery": "Latrun," from "Le Touron des Chevaliers—The Tower of the Knights." The Count is an anti-Semite obsessed with exterminating Jews in general and, in particular, the Jew whom he repeatedly and paranoically imagines has infiltrated his Crusader band. Only at the end of "Crusade," when the Count has suffered tremendously, learned to empathize with all other human beings, and killed himself as a symbol of equating himself to a Jew, does he finally return to the long lost feelings of love for his wife.

Sadly, the central character of "Setting the World to Rights," whose very anonymity, being never named, is symbolic of his commonness, never modifies the mainspring of his being: his hatred of all things he is obsessively sure are wrong. He has magnified his kibbutz occupation of repairman to monstrous proportions, thinking everything in the world needs repairing but, ironically, is unable to repair himself. A bachelor, he lives alone, unable to find love or let it into his life, and at the story's end he hangs himself in the kibbutz orchard. An orchard or the Garden of Eden represents the possibilities of life, growth, and love, making the setting an ironically symbolic opposite of the repairman's suicide and life's work.

OTHER MAJOR WORKS

LONG FICTION: *Ma'kom a'her*, 1966 (*Elsewhere, Perhaps*, 1973); *Mikha'el sheli*, 1968 (*My Michael*, 1972); *Laga 'at ba-mayim, laga 'at ba-ruah*, 1973 (*Touch the Water, Touch the Wind*, 1974); *Menuhah nekhonah*, 1982 (*A Perfect Peace*, 1985); *Kufsah shehorah*, 1987 (*Black Box*, 1988); *La-da'at ishah*, 1989 (*To Know a Woman*, 1991); *Matsav ha-shelishi*, 1991 (*Fima*, 1993); *Al tagidi lailah*, 1994 (*Don't Call It Night*, 1995); *Panter ba-martef*, 1994 (*Panther in the Basement*, 1997).

NONFICTION: *Be-or ha-Techelet ha-azah: Ma'amarim ve-reshimot*, 1979 (*Under This Blazing Light: Essays*, 1995); *Po va-sham be-Erets-Yisra'el bi-setav*, 1982 (*In the Land of Israel*, 1983); *Mi-mordot ha-Levanon: Ma'amarim u-reshimot*, 1987 (*The Slopes of Lebanon*, 1989); *Shetikat ha-shamayim*, 1993 (*The Silence of Heaven: Agnon's Fear of God*, 2000); *Israel, Palestine, and Peace: Essays*, 1994; *Mathilim sipur*, 1996 (*The Story Begins: Essays on Literature*, 1999); *Kol ha-tikvot: Mahashavot 'al zehut Yisre'elit*, 1998.

CHILDREN'S NOVEL: *Sumkhi*, 1978 (*Soumchi*, 1980).

MISCELLANEOUS: *Oto ha-yam*, 1999 (stories and poems).

BIBLIOGRAPHY

Aschkenasy, Nehama. "On Jackals, Nomads, and the Human Condition." *Midstream* 29 (January, 1983): 58-60. One of the more extended reviews of *Where the Jackals Howl and Other Stories*.

Balaban, Avraham. *Between Good and Beast: An Examination of Amos Oz's Prose*. University Park: Pennsylvania State University Press, 1993. Chapter 2, "Introduction to Oz: The Early Stories," is a forty-six page detailed analysis of *Where the Jackals Howl and Other Stories*, including some Hebrew stories left out of the revised Hebrew edition and the English translation. The novelette collections receive much less attention in the book.

Bargad, Warren. "Amos Oz and the Art of Fictional Response." *Midstream* (November, 1976): 61-64. An article focusing on *Unto Death*.

Dickstein, Morris. Review of *The Hill of Evil Counsel*, by Amos Oz. *The New York Times Book Review*, May 28, 1978, 5. The lengthiest review, surpassing by several hundred words, in its 1850 words, the review in the *New York Review of Books* (July 20, 1978) and *The New Yorker* magazine (August 7, 1978).

Fuchs, Esther. *Israeli Mythogynies: Women in Contemporary Hebrew Fiction*. Albany: State University of New York Press, 1987. A six-page subsection of chapter 4, "Amos Oz: The Lack of Conscience," focuses on *Where the Jackals Howl and Other Stories*, analyzed from the feminist perspective of the presentation of women from the sometimes biased male view; the other two sections discuss the image of women in Oz's novels *Elsewhere Perhaps* and *My Michael*.

Jacobson, David. *Modern Midrash: The Retelling of Traditional Jewish Narratives by Twentieth-Century Hebrew Writers*. Albany: State University of New York Press, 1987. A nine-page subsection of chapter 7, "Uses and Abuses of Power in Ancient and Modern Israel: Nissim Aloni, Moshe Shamir, and Amos Oz," examines "Upon This Evil Earth" in *Where the Jackals Howl and Other Stories* as "midrash," a commentary and expanded parable based on biblical material.

McElroy, Joseph. Review of *Unto Death*, by Amos Oz. *The New York Times Book Review*, October 26, 1975, 4. The lengthiest review, surpassing, by several hundred words, in its 1100 words, the substantial review in *The New Republic* (November 29, 1975).

Mojtabai, A. G. Review of *Where the Jackals Howl and Other Stories*, by Amos Oz. *The New York Times Book Review*, April 26, 1981, 3. The lengthiest contemporary review, 2200 words long, about a thousand words longer than the substantial reviews to be found in *The New Republic* (June 27, 1981), the *Times Literary Supplement* (September 25, 1981), *Studies in Short Fiction* (1982), or *World Literature Today* (1982).

Yudkin, Leon. *1948 and After: Aspects of Israeli Fiction*. Manchester, England: University of Manchester Press, 1984. The fourteen-page chapter 10, entitled "The Jackal and the Other Place: The Stories of Amos Oz," is devoted to an analysis of Oz's principal short fiction collections of 1965, 1971, and 1976.

Norman Prinsky

CYNTHIA OZICK

Born: New York, New York; April 17, 1928

PRINCIPAL SHORT FICTION

The Pagan Rabbi and Other Stories, 1971
Bloodshed and Three Novellas, 1976
Levitation: Five Fictions, 1982
The Shawl, 1989
The Puttermesser Papers, 1997

OTHER LITERARY FORMS

Cynthia Ozick is the author of poems, articles, reviews, and essays, as well as short stories. She has also published several novels, including *Trust* (1966), *The Cannibal Galaxy* (1983), and *The Messiah of Stockholm* (1987). Her poems have appeared in journals such as *Epoch*, *Commentary*, *The Literary Review*, and *Judaism*. Her other short works have been published frequently in journals such as those mentioned above and also in a wide variety of others.

ACHIEVEMENTS

Often characterized as difficult and involved in syntax and idea, Cynthia Ozick's works have, nevertheless, received many awards. The short fiction especially has been judged prizeworthy, winning for her such prestigious awards and honors as the Best American Short Stories award (several times), the National Book Award, the American Academy of Arts and Letters Award for Fiction, the O. Henry Award, the PEN/Faulkner Award, and the Jewish Book Council Award. Immediately consequent to the publication of "Rosa," one of her prizewinning stories, Ozick was invited to deliver the Phi Beta Kappa oration at Harvard University, and she became the first person to receive the Michael Rea Award for career contribution to the short story. She has received a number of honorary degrees from schools like Adelphi University, Williams College, Brandeis University, and Skidmore College as well as Yeshiva University, Hebrew Union College, and the Jewish Theological Seminary.

BIOGRAPHY

Born of Russian immigrants who took up residence in the Bronx borough in New York, Cynthia Ozick and her parents and siblings worked in the family drugstore, which kept them in comfort and relative prosperity even through the years of the Great Depression. As a female child, Ozick was not marked for extensive education by her family and community. Nevertheless, she was enrolled at the age of five and a half in a Yiddish-Hebrew school, so she could take religious instruction, and her family insisted that she be allowed to stay. The rabbi giving the instruction soon found that she had what he called a "golden head." Successful as she was in religious instruction, however, her public school experiences were difficult and humiliating. It was not until her entrance into

Cynthia Ozick (Julius Ozick)

Hunter College High School in Manhattan that she was once again made to feel part of an intellectual elite. Her years at New York University, where she earned a B.A. in 1949, were followed by attendance at Ohio State University, where she received her M.A. in 1951.

In 1952, she married Bernard Hallote. One daughter, Rachel, was born in 1965. Early in her career, Ozick became interested in the Jewish textual tradition, and over the years she became an expert in it. In fiction and nonfiction, she has argued with passion concerning the vital role Judaism has played in Western culture, and she has become for many a spokesperson for the importance of art and artists in the Jewish tradition and for the role of women in Jewish culture.

ANALYSIS

Cynthia Ozick's thesis for her M.A. degree was titled "Parable in the Later Novels of Henry James," an exercise that she later thought of as a first step in an act of devotion that resulted in her belief in the exclu-

sivity of art. In effect, as a result of studying James, she became, she believed, a worshiper at the altar of art, a devotee of the doctrine of art for art's sake. This idea—one that many believe places art before life, form before content, beauty before truth, aesthetic enjoyment before moral behavior—became the belief system that led Ozick to conclude that to worship art is to worship idols—in effect, to break the Mosaic law. This kind of understanding led Ozick to study the Jewish textual tradition and the role of Judaism in Western culture.

In the 1980's, Ozick began to realize that creative writers needed to use the highest powers of imagination to posit an incorporeal god, as exists in the Jewish faith, and to put forth a vision of moral truth rooted in the history, traditions, and literature of the Jewish people. Ozick's success in this endeavor is manifested not only in her identification as a Jewish American author but also in the number of awards she has received from representatives of the Jewish people. Perhaps most important, however, is her own satisfaction that in her writing she is serving and has continued to serve the cause of moral truth according to Mosaic law.

A highly serious approach to art as embodying moral imperatives, however, is not necessarily one that eschews metafictional techniques, repetitions, reworkings, and story sequences. Happily, in her use of self-referential devices and other dazzling postmodern presentations of the fantastic, the irreverent, and the grotesque, Ozick's techniques are relevant to the traditions and teachings of Judaism, where magic, dreams, and fantastic occurrences are ways to embody and convey truth.

"THE PAGAN RABBI"

"The Pagan Rabbi" is a case in point. It is the story of Isaac Kornfeld, a pious and intelligent man who one day hangs himself from the limb of a tree. Isaac's story is told by a friend who has known Isaac since they were classmates in the rabbinical seminary and who is a parallel character to Isaac. In the same way that the narrator and Isaac are counterparts, the fathers of both men are set up as opposites who agree on one thing only—that philosophy is an abomination that must lead to idolatry (the worship of false gods). Though the fathers are rivals, the sons accept the apparent differences in their own personalities and remain friends. In time, their different ambitions and talents separate them. The narrator leaves the seminary, marries a Gentile, and becomes a furrier; Isaac continues his brilliant career in the seminary and achieves the peak of his renown at the time of his death, when he has almost reached the age of thirty-six. The narrator, now a bookseller separated from his wife, learns that Isaac has hanged himself with his prayer shawl from a tree in a distant park. Immediately, the narrator takes a subway to the site of the suicide; Isaac's behavior seems totally alien to his character and personality.

In the remainder of the story, Ozick attempts to explain the odd circumstances of Isaac's death, and, by means of the parallelisms, inversions, and doublings, point to the ramifications of leaving the intellectual path for the mysteries and seductions of the unknown world of fantasy, magic, and dream. Apparently Isaac, shortly after his marriage, began to seek different kinds of pleasure that may have been associated with the marriage bed and the beautiful Scheindel. In line with marriage customs, Scheindel covers her lustrous black hair after the wedding ceremony and subsequently bears Isaac seven daughters, one after another. As he fathers each daughter, Isaac invents bedtime stories for each, relating to such aberrations as speaking clouds, stones that cry, and pigs with souls. At the same time, Isaac shows an inordinate interest in picnics in strange and remote places.

As Isaac behaves in odder and odder ways for a rabbi, exhibiting unhealthy (because excessive) interest in the natural world, Scheindel becomes more and more puzzled and estranged, since she has no interest in old tales of sprites, nymphs, gods, or magic events. Scheindel's refusal to countenance anything magical is in counterpoint to her escape from the electrified fences of the concentration camp, which seemed a miracle of chance. Isaac's notebook offers little explanation for his behavior, though it is filled with romantic jottings, quotations from lyric poets, and a strange reference to his age, using the means of counting rings as for a tree. Below this unusual computation, Isaac has written a startling message: "Great Pan lives."

The narrator begins to understand more as Scheindel reads a letter written by Isaac and left tucked in his notebook. The letter makes clear that Isaac has eschewed deeply held Jewish beliefs to accept a kind of animism or pantheism, where all matter has life and, moreover, soul, although all matter except for human beings can live separate from their souls and thus are able to know everything around them. Humans cannot live separate from their souls and thus are cursed with the inability to escape from their bodies except through death. Isaac concludes that there may be another route to freedom—exaltation and ecstasy by means of coupling with a freed soul. The idea, once conceived, needs a trial, and Isaac's efforts are subsequently rewarded by the appearance of a dryad, the soul of a tree. The dryad's lovemaking brings Isaac to marvels and blisses that no man, it is said, has experienced since Adam. Isaac errs, however, in trying to trap the dryad into his own mortal condition. In so doing, he loses his own soul. His soul free, Isaac's body is doomed to death. More important, however, the soul retains the visage of the rabbi, who has been and will be the one who walks indifferently through the beauties of the fields, declaring that the sound, smells, and tastes of the law are more beautiful than anything to be found in the natural world.

Scheindel's repugnance toward, and lack of charity for, her husband's folly surprises the narrator and turns him away from her. The narrator is able to appreciate the subtlety of the rabbi's thinking and the bravery of the pursuit, but Scheindel is one who guarded the Mosaic law with her own wasted body during the Holocaust, and Scheindel is the issue here—not intellectual subtlety—she who seemed doomed to death when she was seventeen years old, she who traded her youth and vitality for marriage to a Jewish rabbi. After his conversation with Scheindel, and as an ironic afterthought, the narrator goes home to clear his house of his three paltry houseplants. His gesture next to Isaac's forthright penetration into the forest, however, indicates something of the struggle of every Jew seduced by the pleasures of the beautiful but charged to interpret and guard the laws instead.

"THE SHAWL"

By the time of the publication of "The Shawl" in *The New Yorker* and "Rosa," also in *The New Yorker*, Ozick had come to articulate fairly clearly her recognition that imagination need not be a negative, leading to idolatry, but a positive, allowing Jews to imagine a god without image. These stories are of exceptional importance and significance in the Ozick canon. In them, Ozick deals directly with the horror of the Holocaust. Rosa is the focal character of both stories, each of which exists as a separate entity coherent in itself, but also, when juxtaposed as in a diptych or modified story sequence, each takes on added significance as the two parts interact with each other.

In "The Shawl," Rosa is a young woman with a baby in her arms wrapped in a shawl that serves not only to shelter the child, called Magda, but also to hide it, to muffle its cries, and to succor it. With Rosa is her young niece, Stella, who is jealous of Magda and craves the shawl for her own comfort. Deprived of her shawl, the baby begins to cry and crawl around on the ground. Rosa's dilemma must be excruciatingly painful. She understands that her adolescent niece took the shawl, trying to cling to her own life, and she understands that if she chances getting the baby without the shawl to cover it up, she is likely to lose both her life and Magda's. She chooses to go after the shawl first, and the fatal moment arrives too soon. A German officer finds the child wandering around and hurls her against the electrified fence.

Complicating the issue is the question of who is Magda's father. Early in the story, it is suggested that the father is no Jew, since Magda has blue eyes and blond hair and seems a pure Aryan, a situation that causes Stella to react even more bitterly. As in any nightmare, the dreaded occurs. Stella steals the shawl; the baby cries, wanders about, and is killed. Rosa survives the horrible ordeal as she has survived others, including repeated rapes by German soldiers. She knows that any action will result in her death, so she stuffs the shawl in her own mouth and drinks Magda's saliva to sustain herself.

"ROSA"

For "Rosa," Ozick won four awards. On the basis of the story's publication, she was named one of three best short-story writers in the United States. Because the story does not proceed chronologically, a brief plot summary is helpful. After Rosa and Stella are rescued from the camps, Rosa brings Stella to the United States, where Stella gets a job and Rosa opens an antique shop. The action takes place some thirty-five years after the occurrences described in "The Shawl." Rosa is still very angry with Stella for her role in Magda's death, and she is able to get little personal satisfaction from her activities in the antique shop. Apparently, her customers do not want to listen to the stories she has to tell, and one day, extremely angry and apparently insane, Rosa destroys her shop. To escape institutionalization, she agrees to move to what appears to be a poverty-stricken retirement hotel in Miami Beach. Life is difficult for her. The intense heat makes it hard for her to get out into the sunlight in order to shop. When she does eat, she scavenges or makes do with tiny portions, such as a cracker with grape jelly or a single sardine. The condition of her clothes seems to indicate that she has nothing to wear. One morning, however, Rosa makes her way to a supermarket, and there, she meets Simon Persky. Persky is not a person in the ordinary mold. He notices Rosa on a personal level and insists that she respond to him. While Rosa's relationship with Simon Persky is developing, Ozick establishes two parallel plot lines having to do with Rosa's request of Stella that she send Magda's shawl and a request from a Dr. Tree asking Stella to help him conduct research on Rosa's reaction to her imprisonment and ill treatment.

These three plot lines weave about one another, providing the matrices for the action. Rosa is responsible for saving Stella's life in the concentration camp and bringing her to the United States, and Stella is indirectly responsible for Magda's death, perhaps the single most horrible thing that happened to Rosa in a life full of horrors—the internment, the death of family and friends, assaults and rape by brutal Nazis, near starvation, and finally Magda's execution by electric shock. Since Magda's death, Rosa has teetered on the brink of insanity, managing to hold herself together by working and by the creative act of writing letters to an imaginary Magda who, in Rosa's fantasy, has survived and become a professor of Greek philosophy at Columbia University. Stella too has survived in Rosa's imagination in another guise. She is a thief, a bloodsucker, evil personified, and the Angel of Death. To Magda, Rosa writes letters in perfect Polish, literary and learned. To Stella, Rosa writes in crude English, a language she never bothered to learn. To Stella, Rosa admits that Magda is dead; to Magda, Rosa explains that Stella is unable to accept and cannot be told the truth.

The shawl, which Stella agrees to send to Rosa and which finally arrives, acted in Poland during the worst years as an umbrella covering the three people—Rosa, prepubescent Stella, and baby Magda—and providing sustenance and security, even though illusionary. After Magda's death, the shawl becomes for Rosa an icon; "idol," "false god," Stella says, since Rosa worships it and prays to it.

Dr. Tree is another threat to Rosa; he is a kind of parasite, living to feed off the horrors attached to other people's lives. He wants to interview Rosa for a book that he is writing on Holocaust survivors. His letter to Rosa calling her a survivor is replete with jargon, with clinical terms naming the horrible conditions with neutral language and hiding the grotesque reality under the name of his own Institute for Humanitarian Context. Rosa objects to being called a "survivor" because the word dehumanizes her and every other person on the planet. Persky, on the other hand, offers Rosa an actual friendship, a human relationship in concrete, not abstract, terms. Thus he emerges as winner of Rosa's attention, with Dr. Tree dismissed and memories of Magda put on hold for a while.

THE PUTTERMESSER PAPERS

The Puttermesser Papers consists of a series of five previously published short stories about Ruth Puttermesser. In the stories, it is often difficult to distinguish between what actually happens to her and what she fantasizes. In the first story, "Puttermesser: Her Work History, Her Ancestry, Her Afterlife," for example, she visits her Uncle Zindel for Hebrew lessons, but the narrator says that Uncle Zindel died before Puttermesser was born. In the second story, "Puttermesser and Xanthippe," Puttermesser creates a female golem, a person made of clay, from the dirt in the flowerpots in her apartment. The golem, named Xanthippe, helps Puttermesser get elected mayor of New York City and helps Puttermesser transform New York into a kind of paradise. The golem discovers sex, however, and as a result destroys all of the wonderful things she has helped Puttermesser achieve.

In each story, Puttermesser is a loser. She tries to achieve some kind of ideal and ends up with an unpleasant reality. In the long run, things never go right for her. In the third story, "Puttermesser Paired," she finds someone she considers to be a true soul mate, Rupert Rubeeno, a copyist. Rubeeno and Puttermesser share a love of literature, especially an interest in the British authors and lovers George Eliot, the novelist, and George Lewes, the essayist. Eventually they marry, but Rubeeno leaves her on their wedding night, apparently without consummating the marriage.

In the fourth story, "Puttermesser and the Muscovite Cousin," one of her relatives in the Soviet Union calls her and asks her to save the relative's child. The child, Lidia Klavdia Girshengornova, turns out to be a grown woman interested in making a fortune in America. Eventually, she returns to the Soviet Union to rejoin her boyfriend. The final section, "Puttermesser in Paradise," is probably the saddest of all. In it, Puttermesser is killed by a man who rapes her after she is dead. She enters a Paradise in which all things seem to go well for her, but in Paradise, she ultimately finds no happiness, for even there, "nothing is permanent." She discovers the secret meaning of Paradise: "It too is hell." Each thing she enjoys there disappears in turn, leaving her longing to be back on earth in spite of earth's having also been in many ways unpleasant for her.

Discussions of Cynthia Ozick's fiction often include the descriptors "uncompromising," "demanding," "difficult"—characteristics that can diminish a writer's popularity and, consequently, status. For Ozick, however, no such diminution has taken place. Indeed, her reputation has grown steadily and strongly, her writings gaining more attention and Ozick herself more recognition. The phenomenon is not, after all, that surprising. If her protestations are stronger than those of other Jewish American writers, her demands are based more clearly in moral imperatives of the Jewish tradition; yet there is another tradition as truly her own—one commentators sometimes forget—an American literary heritage, with Nathaniel Hawthorne, Herman Melville, Edgar Allan Poe, William Faulkner, those writers who clearly work like Ozick in a realm where the "power of blackness" wrestles with us all.

OTHER MAJOR WORKS

LONG FICTION: *Trust*, 1966; *The Cannibal Galaxy*, 1983; *The Messiah of Stockholm*, 1987.

PLAY: *Blue Light*, pr. 1994 (based on *The Shawl*).

POETRY: *Epodes: First Poems*, 1992.

NONFICTION: *Art and Ardor*, 1983; *Metaphor and Memory: Essays*, 1989; *What Henry James Knew, and Other Essays on Writers*, 1993; *Fame and Folly: Essays*, 1996; *Portrait of the Artist as a Bad Character, and Other Essays on Writing*, 1996; *Quarrel and Quandary: Essays*, 2000.

MISCELLANEOUS: *A Cynthia Ozick Reader*, 1996.

BIBLIOGRAPHY

Alkana, Joseph. "'Do We Not Know the Meaning of Aesthetic Gratification?' Cynthia Ozick's *The Shawl*, the Akedah, and the Ethics of Holocaust Literary Aesthetics." *Modern Fiction Studies* 43 (Winter, 1997): 963-990. Argues that Ozick takes a stance against universalism in the two stories, the tendency to level human suffering under an all-inclusive existential or theological quandary.

Bloom, Harold, ed. *Cynthia Ozick: Modern Critical Views*. New York: Chelsea House, 1986. An excellent collection of essays, including brief book reviews as well as lengthy articles. Much of value for both the beginning student and a scholarly audience involved in an examination of complications of idea and form.

Burstein, Janet Handler. "Cynthia Ozick and the Transgressions of Art." *American Literature: A Journal of Literary History, Criticism, and Bibliography* 59 (March, 1987): 85-101. One of a number of articles on Ozick appearing in major scholarly journals. Concludes that Ozick is the most provocative of contemporary Jewish American voices. Her intelligence and stature provide her with an authoritarian voice as she speaks of literature and art and the didactic moral purpose art must display.

Cohen, Sarah Blacher. *Cynthia Ozick's Comic Art: From Levity to Liturgy*. Bloomington: Indiana University Press, 1994. Places Ozick in the context of the Jewish comic tradition but argues that levity in her fiction must serve a higher purpose than laughter for laughter's sake, usually the satiric purpose of attacking vices, follies, and stupidities.

Fisch, Harold. "Introducing Cynthia Ozick." *Response* 22 (1974): 27-34. A very early article concentrating on analyses of the novel *Trust* and the story "The Pagan Rabbi." Tries to show connections between theme and techniques in both genres.

Friedman, Lawrence S. *Understanding Cynthia Ozick*. Columbia: University of South Carolina Press, 1991. A critical study of Ozick, which includes a bibliography and an index.

Kauvar, Elaine M. *Cynthia Ozick's Fiction: Tradition and Invention*. Bloomington: Indiana University Press, 1993. Examines the sources and contexts of Ozick's fiction, focusing on tensions between Hebraism and Hellenism, Western culture and Judaism, artistic imagination and moral responsibility; discusses Ozick's relationship to psychoanalysis, feminism, and postmodernism.

Lowin, Joseph. *Cynthia Ozick*. New York: Twayne, 1988. This excellent overview of Ozick's canon includes an annotated bibliography and full notes. Most valuable for beginning students whose knowledge of Holocaust literature and Ozick is limited. Offers perceptive and lucid analyses of all the major works.

_____. "Cynthia Ozick, Rewriting Herself: The Road from 'The Shawl' to 'Rosa.'" In *Since Flannery O'Connor: Essays on the Contemporary American Short Story*, edited by Loren Logsdon and Charles W. Mayer. Macomb: Western Illinois University Press, 1987. Contends Ozick paints not the thing itself but, like the French Symbolists, the effect produced by the thing; each of the three characters in the story uses the shawl as a life preserver.

Ozick, Cynthia. "An Interview with Cynthia Ozick." Interview by Elaine M. Kauvar. *Contemporary Literature* 26 (Winter, 1985): 375-401. Contains references to Ozick's religion, history, intelligence, feminism, postmodern techniques, and philosophy of art. A good introduction to her views, personality, and level of intelligence.

_____. "An Interview with Cynthia Ozick." *Contemporary Literature* 34 (Fall, 1993): 359-394. Ozick discusses Jewish culture, other Jewish writers, her own fiction, and the Holocaust with her friend Elaine M. Kauvar.

Pinsker, Sanford. *The Uncompromising Fiction of Cynthia Ozick*. Columbia: University of Missouri Press, 1987. A brief analysis of major works, including several of the more important short stories. Excellent for a reader new to Ozick's fiction. Emphasizes postmodern aspects of Ozick's work, particularly self-referential elements and the use of fantasy.

Strandberg, Victor. *Greek Mind, Jewish Soul: The Conflicted Art of Cynthia Ozick*. Madison: University of Wisconsin Press, 1994. Argues that Ozick's work derives from her conflict between hating Western civilization and taking pride in the Jewish foundation of that civilization. Claims that she is an Orthodox Jewish feminist who reveres the ancient law but demands an equal rights amendment to the Torah.

Mary Rohrberger, updated by
Richard Tuerk

P

GRACE PALEY

Born: New York, New York; December 11, 1922

OTHER LITERARY FORMS

In addition to her short fiction, Grace Paley has published the poetry collections *Leaning Forward* (1985), *New and Collected Poems* (1992), and *Begin Again: Collected Poems* (2000), the nonfiction works *Conversations with Grace Paley* (1997) and *Just as I Thought* (1998), and, along with the staff of the New Americas Press, edited *A Dream Compels Us: Voices of Salvadoran Women* (1989). She has also contributed short stories to *The New Yorker* and essays on teaching to various journals.

ACHIEVEMENTS

Grace Paley received a John Simon Guggenheim Memorial Foundation Fellowship, a National Council on the Arts grant, and a National Institute of Arts and Letters Award for short-story writing. She was elected to the American Academy of Arts and Letters in 1980, and in 1988 and 1989 she received the Edith Wharton Award. In 1993, she was awarded the Michael Rea Award for the short story and the Vermont Governor's Award for excellence in the arts. In 1994, she was a nominee for the National Book Award and a finalist for the Pulitzer Prize. In 1997, she was awarded the Lannan Foundation Literary Award.

BIOGRAPHY

The daughter of Russian immigrants, Grace Paley was born and raised in New York City. Both her parents, Mary (Ridnyik) Goodside and Isaac Goodside, M.D., were political exiles in their early years and passed on their political concerns to their daughter. At home they spoke Russian and Yiddish as well as English, exposing their daughter to both old and new cultures. She studied in city schools and after graduation attended Hunter College in 1938 and later New York University. Paley, however, was not interested in formal academic study and dropped out of college. She had begun to write poetry and in the early 1940's studied with W. H. Auden at the New School for Social Research. In 1942 she married Jess Paley, a motion-picture cameraman. The couple had two children and separated three years later, although they were not legally divorced for twenty years. In the 1940's and 1950's, Paley worked as a typist, while raising her children and continuing to write. At this time she began her lifelong political involvement by participating in New York City neighborhood action groups.

After many rejections, her first collection of eleven stories, *The Little Disturbances of Man*, was published in 1959. Even though the book was not widely reviewed, critics admired her work, and Paley's teaching career flourished. In the early 1960's, she taught at Columbia University and Syracuse University and also presented summer workshops. She also began writing a novel, a project which she did not complete. She increased her political activism, participating in nonviolent protests against prison conditions in New York City and the government's position on the war in Vietnam. A prominent member in the peace movement, she was a member of a 1969 mission that went to Hanoi to negotiate for the release of prisoners of war. In 1973, she was a delegate to the World Peace Conference in Moscow. In 1974, her second collection of stories appeared. It received sporadic condemnation from reviewers, partially because of her political views but also because the writing was deemed uneven in quality.

In the 1970's and 1980's, Paley continued her political activism as well as her writing and teaching. She joined with other activists in condemning Soviet repression of human rights, was a leader in the 1978 demonstrations in Washington, D.C., against nuclear weapons, and in 1985, along with campaigning against American government policy in Central America, visited Nicaragua and El Salvador. This trip resulted in *A Dream Compels Us: Voices of Salvadoran Women*, published in 1989. Her stories have appeared in *The Atlantic, Esquire, Accent*, and other magazines. Paley settled in Greenwich Village in New York City, with her second husband, poet, playwright, and landscape architect Robert Nichols. In the 1990's Paley continued to teach in the New York City area, particularly at Sarah Lawrence College, but she retired by the end of the decade. She divided her time between her place in Vermont and the Greenwich Village apartment that was so often a backdrop for her fiction.

Grace Paley (©Dorothy Marder)

ANALYSIS

Despite her small literary output, Grace Paley's innovative style and the political and social concerns she advocates in her work have enabled her to generate significant critical attention. Her stories treat traditional themes, focusing on the lives of women and the experiences of love, motherhood, and companionship that bind them together. She presents these themes, however, in inventive rather than traditional structures. Her stories are frequently fragmented and open-ended, without conventional plot or character development, structural innovations that make her work more true to life. The stories gain their vitality by Paley's use of distinctive language—the voice, idiom, tone, and rhythms of the New York City locale. She writes best when rendering the razor-tongued Jewish American urban female, with an ironic wit, who does not hesitate to voice her opinions.

To speak out is a basic theme in Grace Paley's stories, and it reflects her own life and political principles. The women in her stories are like her; they are political activists who speak on nuclear energy, on the environment, and on all conditions that affect the world into which their children are born. This intermingling of politics and art brought Paley mixed reviews, but she has continued to stretch the limits of the short story, in both form and content.

THE LITTLE DISTURBANCES OF MAN

"Goodbye and Good Luck," the first story in Grace Paley's first collection, *The Little Disturbances of Man*, shows her characteristic style and theme. The story begins, "I was popular in certain circles, says Aunt Rose. I wasn't no thinner then, only more stationary in the flesh." Aunt Rose knows what her sister—Lillie's "mama"—does not, that time rushes by relentlessly, that the old generation is quickly forgotten as the new generation supplants it, and that mama's life of stodgy domesticity (the "spotless kitchen") has meant little to her or anyone else as her life slips away. Mama, however, feels sorry for "poor Rosie" because Aunt Rose has not married or led a virtuous life.

As a young girl, Rose cannot stand her safe but boring job in a garment factory and takes instead a job selling tickets at the Russian Art Theatre, which puts on Yiddish plays. The man who hires her says "Rosie Lieber, you surely got a build on you!" These attributes quickly gain the attention of the Yiddish matinee idol Volodya Vlashkin, "the Valentino of Second Avenue."

Although he is much older than she and has a wife and family elsewhere, he sets her up in an apartment. Their affair continues on—and off—over the years while he has many other lovers, but Rose is not lonely herself when he is gone. She never complains but worships him when she has him and is philosophical about his infidelities: An actor needs much practice if he is to be convincing on the stage. While she never asks anything from him, "the actresses . . . were only interested in tomorrow," sleeping lovelessly with wealthy producers for advancement. They get their advancement: Now they are old and forgotten. Vlashkin himself is old and retired, Aunt Rose fat and fifty, when his wife divorces him for all his past adulteries. He comes back to Rosie, the only woman who never asked anything of him, and they decide to get married. She has had her warm and love-filled life, and now she will have a bit of respectability, a husband— and, "as everybody knows, a woman should have at least one before the end of the story."

The theme is seen most clearly when Rose contrasts her life with her own mother's. Her mother had upbraided her when she moved in with Vlashkin, but her mother had "married who she didn't like. . . . He never washed. He had an unhappy smell . . . he got smaller, shriveled up little by little, till goodbye and good luck." Rosie, therefore, "decided to live for love." No amount of respectability, no husband, advancement, or wealth will save one from imminent change, decay, and death; so live for love, Aunt Rose would say, and you will have the last laugh.

The characters and tone may change in other stories, but the theme remains the same. In "The Pale

Pink Roast" Anna sees her former husband and asks him to help her move into her new apartment. He is in "about the third flush of youth," a handsome, charming, but "transient" man. In the midst of hanging her curtains, he stops and makes love to her. Then, admiring her fancy apartment and stylish clothes, he asks archly who is paying for it. "My husband is," she responds. Her former husband is furious with her. The new husband, she tells him, is a "lovely" man, in the process of moving his business here. Why did you do it, then, her former husband wants to know: "Revenge? Meanness? Why?" "I did it for love," she says.

Over and over the female characters must choose between the safe but boring man and the charming but worthless lover. In "An Interest in Life," the girl has her secure but dull boyfriend yet dreams of the husband who deserted her. In "Distance," Paley tells the same story over again, but this time from the point of view of another character in the story, a bitter old woman full of destructive meanness. She was wild in youth, but then opted for the safe, loveless marriage, and it has so soured her life that she has tried to force everyone else into the same wrong pattern. Her own very ordinary son is the analogue of the boring boyfriend from "An Interest in Life." At heart, the bitter old woman understands the young girl, and this is her redeeming humanity.

In a slight variation of theme, "Wants" demonstrates why the love relationship between man and woman must be transitory. The desirable man wants everything out of life; the loving woman wants only her man. "You'll always want nothing," the narrator's former husband tells her bitterly, suggesting a sort of ultimate biological incompatibility between the sexes. The result assuredly is sadness and loneliness, but with islands of warmth to make it endurable. In "Come On, Ye Sons of Art," Kitty is spending Sunday morning with her boyfriend ("Sunday was worth two weeks of waiting"). She is pregnant by him and already has a houseful of children by other fathers. She takes great pleasure in the fine morning she can give her boyfriend. The boyfriend, a traveling salesman, delights in his skill as a salesman. He only regrets he is not more dishonest, like his sister who, ignoring human relationships, has devoted herself to amassing an immense fortune by any means. Kitty's boyfriend wistfully wishes he too were corrupt, high, and mighty. They are listening to a beautiful piece of music by English composer Henry Purcell on the radio, which the announcer says was written for the queen's birthday; in reality, the music was not written for the queen, but rather for Purcell's own delight in his art, in the thing he did best, and no amount of wealth and power equals that pleasure.

In her later stories, Paley has been striking out in new directions, away from the inner-city unwed mothers and the strongly vernacular idiom, to sparse, classical, universal stories. The theme, however, that there is no safe harbor against change and death, and that the only salvation is to live fully, realistically, and for the right things, has not changed. "In the Garden" has, essentially, four characters who appear to be in some country in the West Indies. Lush gardens of bright flowers and birds surround them, suggesting a particularly bountiful nature. One character is a beautiful young woman whose children were kidnapped eight months earlier and now are certainly dead, but she cannot face this fact, and her talk is constantly about "when they come home." Her husband is a rich landlord, who did not give the kidnappers their ransom money; he shouts constantly in a loud voice that everything is well. There is a vacationing communist renting one of the landlord's houses, who, out of curiosity, asks the neighbors about the case. He learns that the landlord had once been poor but now is rich and has a beautiful wife; he could not believe that anything had the power to hurt his luck, and he was too greedy to pay the ransom. It is known that it was "his friends who did it." There is an elderly neighbor woman who is dying of a muscle-wasting disease. She had spent much time with the beautiful woman listening to her talk about when the children would return, but now she is fed up with her and cannot stand the husband's shouting. For a while, since she is too wasted to do much more, she follows with her eyes the movements of the communist, but "sadly she had to admit that the eyes' movement, even if minutely savored, was not such an adventurous jour-

ney." Then "she had become interested in her own courage."

At first it may appear that nothing happens in the story, but it is all there. The garden is the world. The young woman with her beauty has won a rich husband; the landlord, through aggressiveness, has clawed his way to the top. Both these modes—beauty and aggressiveness—have succeeded only for a while, but inevitably whatever is gained in the world is lost because human beings are all mortal. The communist—by being a communist, "a tenderhearted but relentless person"—suggests someone who will try to find a political way to stave off chance and mortality, but in fact he merely leaves, having done nothing. The old woman, who realizes the fecklessness of trying to help, and who has found mere observation of process insufficient, becomes more interested in the course of her own courage in facing up to inevitable change. She and her husband are the only ones who admit to change, and this seems the right position, the tragic sense of life which makes life supportable.

THE COLLECTED STORIES

The Collected Stories gathers over thirty years of stories from Paley's previous collections, allowing the reader to track the development of Paley's feminism and pacifism, as well as her depiction of urban family life. *The Collected Stories* also brings with it an opportunity to examine one of Paley's most enduring fictional characters, a major figure in thirteen stories, and a minor figure in several more. This character, Faith Darwin, first appeared in the "The Used Boy-Raisers," where it was clear that she served as her author's alter ego, so that Faith, like Paley, is of Jewish descent, lives in Greenwich Village, has married, divorced and remarried, has two children, and is also a writer.

In addition to paralleling Paley's own life to some degree, the Faith Darwin stories track the various political movements in which Paley has been involved. For instance, in "Faith in a Tree," Faith s personal life is refrained in the light of her political principles, indicated by a demonstration against the war in Vietnam. In "Dreamer in a Dead Language," Faith's father, whom she had loved and admired uncritically, is critically reassessed in the light of her growing feminism. In later stories, however, Faith herself is subjected to criticism and revaluation. In "Listening," Faith is confronted by her lesbian friend Cassie, who accuses her of ignoring her in her fiction. Faith is also criticized by other characters in "Friends," "Zagrowsky Tells," and "Love," the latter story detailing the breaking up of friendships over disagreements concerning the Soviet Union.

In these later stories, Faith must deal with changing times. In "The Long-Distance Runner" Faith faces her own aging process by returning to the old Jewish neighborhood in which she and her parents had once lived, and which is now populated by - African Americans. When Faith decides to live in her old apartment for three weeks with four African American children and their mother, Mrs. Luddy, she discovers that, despite their differences, they share a sense of sisterhood because they are both women and mothers. The centrality of motherhood in the life of women is a continuing theme in the Faith Darwin stories, beginning with "The Used Boy Raisers" and emerging again in such stories as "The Long Distance Runner" and "The Exquisite Moment."

Stories such as "The Long-Distance Runner," with its African American family, and "The Exquisite Moment," involving a Chinese houseguest, also remind the reader of the multicultural element in Paley's fiction. Faith's own neighborhood—a Greenwich village community of artists, left-wing political activists, and people from minority ethnic and racial groups—is different from what is considered mainstream America, but at the same time it reminds the reader that this world, too, is part of the American scene. This urban community, which blends and mixes ethnicities, religions, and radical politics, along with her role as a fictional version of Paley herself, makes Faith Darwin's stories a particularly representative aspect of Grace Paley's collected work.

OTHER MAJOR WORKS

POETRY: *Leaning Forward*, 1985; *New and Collected Poems*, 1992; *Begin Again: Collected Poems*, 2000.

NONFICTION: *Conversations with Grace Paley*, 1997; *Just as I Thought*, 1998.

EDITED TEXT: *A Dream Compels Us: Voices of Salvadoran Women*, 1989.

MISCELLANEOUS: *Long Walks and Intimate Talks: Stories and Poems*, 1991 (with paintings by Vera Williams).

BIBLIOGRAPHY

Aarons, Victoria. "Talking Lives: Storytelling and Renewal in Grace Paley's Short Fiction." *Studies in American Jewish Literature* 9 (1990): 20-35. Asserts that Paley empowers her characters through their penchant for telling stories. In telling their stories, her characters try to gain some control over their lives, as if by telling they can reconstruct experience.

Arcana, Judith. *Grace Paley's Life Stories: A Literary Biography*. Urbana: University of Illinois Press, 1993. A biography of Paley which includes a bibliography and an index.

Bach, Gerhard, and Blaine Hall, eds. *Conversations with Grace Paley*. Jackson: University Press of Mississippi, 1997. A collection of interviews with Paley from throughout her career as a writer, in which she comments on the sources of her stories, her political views, her feminism, and the influences on her writing.

Baumbach, Jonathan. "Life Size." *Partisan Review* 42, no. 2 (1975): 303-306. Baumbach approaches *Enormous Changes at the Last Minute* by concentrating on the innovative narrative voice and how it enhances the themes that run throughout the stories.

DeKoven, Marianne. "Mrs. Hegel-Shtein's Tears." *Partisan Review* 48, no. 2 (1981): 217-223. Grace Paley wanted to tell about everyday life but in story forms that were not the traditionally linear ones. DeKoven describes how innovative structures enable her to achieve uncommon empathy with her subjects.

Iannone, Carol. "A Dissent on Grace Paley." *Commentary* 80 (August, 1985): 54-58. Iannone states that Paley's first collection of stories reveals talent. Her second, however, written when she was deeply involved in political activity, shows how a writer's imagination can become trapped by ideologies, not able to rise above them to make sense of the world. Iannone's comments on the intermingling of politics and art result in interesting interpretations of Paley's stories.

Isaacs, Neil D. *Grace Paley: A Study of the Short Fiction*. Boston: Twayne, 1990. An introduction to Paley's short fiction, strong on a summary and critique of previous criticism. Also contains a section of Paley quotations, in which she talks about the nature of her fiction, her social commitment, and the development of her narrative language. Emphasizes Paley's focus on storytelling and narrative voice.

Marchant, Peter, and Earl Ingersoll, eds. "A Conversation with Grace Paley." *The Massachusetts Review* 26 (Winter, 1985): 606-614. A conversation with novelist Mary Elsie Robertson and writer Peter Marchant provides insights into Paley's transition from poetry to short stories, her interest in the lives of women, and the connection between her subject matter and her politics.

Meyer, Adam. "Faith and the 'Black Thing': Political Action and Self-Questioning in Grace Paley's Short Fiction." *Studies in Short Fiction* 31 (Winter, 1994): 79-89. Discusses how Paley, through the character of Faith, examines someone very much like herself while distancing herself from that person's activities.

Paley, Grace. "Grace Paley: Art Is on the Side of the Underdog." Interview by Harriet Shapiro. *Ms.* 11 (May, 1974): 43-45. This interview about Paley's life and politics succeeds in presenting her as a unique personality.

Schleifer, Ronald. "Grace Paley: Chaste Compactness." In *Contemporary American Women Writers: Narrative Strategies*, edited by Catherine Rainwater and William J. Scheick. Lexington: University Press of Kentucky, 1985. As Schleifer puts it, "Both little disturbances and enormous changes are brought together at the close of [Paley's] stories to create a sense of ordinary ongoingness that eschews the melodrama of closure."

Taylor, Jacqueline. *Grace Paley: Illuminating the Dark Lives*. Austin: University of Texas, 1990. Taylor focuses on what she calls Paley's "woman centered" point of view. Asserts that "Conversation with My Father" allows discussion of many of the narrative conventions her fiction tries to subvert. The story reveals the connection between Paley's recognition of the fluidity of life and her resistance to narrative resolution.

Norman Lavers, updated by Louise M. Stone and
Margaret Boe Birns

EMILIA PARDO BAZÁN

Born: La Coruña, Spain; September 16, 1852
Died: Madrid, Spain; May 12, 1921

PRINCIPAL SHORT FICTION

La dama joven, 1885
Cuentos escogidos, 1891
Cuentos de Marineda, 1892
Cuentos nuevos, 1894
Circo iris, cuentos, 1895
Novelas cortas, 1896
Cuentos de amor, 1898
Cuentos sacro-profanos, 1899
Un destripador de antaño, 1900
A Galician Girl's Romance, 1900
En tranvía, cuentos dramaticos, 1901
Cuentos antiguos, 1902
Cuentos de la patria, 1902
Cuentos de Navidad y Reyes, 1902
Novelas ejemplares, 1906
El fondo del alma, cuentos, 1907
Cuentos actuales, 1909
Belcebú, novelas cortas, 1912
Cuentos trágicos, 1912
Cuentos de la tierra, 1923
Great Stories of All Nations, 1927

OTHER LITERARY FORMS

Emilia Pardo Bazán began her literary career with a critical study of the eighteenth century scholar and essayist Feijóo y Montenegro and soon thereafter published her first novel. These were the two domains to which she devoted the bulk of her writing: literary criticism and fiction. The criticism took the form of journalistic articles, as well as book-length studies, and included one influential polemic, the book in defense of literary realism which she called *La cuestión palpitante*. Her fiction included not only novels and short stories but also several intermediate-sized works which she called *novelas cortas* and which might be called novellas. Several collections of travel pieces were published in her lifetime, and essays on social and political issues appeared in jour-

nals and were collected in book form as well. She also wrote some half dozen plays, a biography of Saint Francis of Assisi, and a two-volume work on Spanish cuisine.

ACHIEVEMENTS

Emilia Pardo Bazán was the most prolific short-story writer of nineteenth century Spain. She achieved renown not only for the quantity of her work—publishing at least 579 short stories—but also for the art and skill with which she wrote, and she was made a *condesa* (countess) in 1907 in recognition of her literary achievements. Pardo Bazán worked tirelessly in the field of literary criticism as well. from 1891 to 1893, she wrote and edited a monthly literary review, *Nuevo teatro critico*. In 1906, she became the first woman president of the Ateneo, the literary intellectual circle of Madrid, and in 1916 she earned the title of chair of romance literature at the Central University of Madrid. It was Pardo Bazán's willingness to champion the cause of equal educational, economic, and career rights for women, however, which gave her the widest influence she achieved throughout her career. Her genuine devotion to this crusade was recognized by her appointment as adviser to Spain's ministry of education in 1910. Her strong interest in the status of women was also expressed in many polemical articles and in the founding of a book series, "Biblioteca de la mujer" ("Women's Library").

BIOGRAPHY

Emilia Pardo Bazán was born into a prominent, but not aristocratic, family. Her father was active in politics and something of an intellectual, and it was he who encouraged his daughter to extend her education and to develop ambitions beyond the conventional limits accepted by young girls of that era. In spite of her liberal upbringing, however, Emilia found herself party to an arranged marriage before she had quite turned seventeen, and she eventually had three children, so that all the conventional obligations and

Emilia Pardo Bazán (Library of Congress)

ties stood in her way when she began to feel the stirrings of literary ambition as she neared her thirtieth birthday. By the time she was thirty-five, she had made a name for herself with several novels and some polemical literary criticism, and she had separated from her husband.

After the publication of *Los Pazos de Ulloa* (1886; *The Son of a Bondwoman*, 1908), generally regarded as her best novel, Pardo Bazán became a dominant and active figure in the literary world, not only in Madrid but also abroad, particularly in Paris, where she had made several visits and met the major writers of the day. She was well read in French literature and knew Italian and English as well, enabling her to bring into Spain many new literary ideas imported from the rest of Europe. She was perhaps the most cosmopolitan literary presence in Spain during the final decades of the nineteenth century. Her literary activism consisted not only of publishing novels, short stories, literary criticism, social commentary, and travel pieces in a steady stream but also of editing and publishing her own journal, giving public lectures, and campaigning for admittance into the all-male stronghold, the Royal Academy.

Following the turn of the century there was more lecturing, more travels to other parts of Europe, some unsuccessful efforts to write for the theater, and still the steady production of respected novels and the always welcome short stories. In 1907 the king of Spain conferred upon her the aristocratic title of Countess in recognition of her achievements. She undertook a study of the modern French novel, which had wide influence in the early decades of the twentieth century in Spain, and in 1916, she broke a major barrier for women when she became a professor of literature at the Central University of Madrid. She died shortly before her seventieth birthday, much honored and genuinely mourned, even though in her final years she had tended to look back upon her active but controversial life as somewhat disappointing because of the failure of some of her most cherished projects of literary and social reform. In spite of those failures, however, she was, at the time of her death, Spain's most successful woman writer, one of her country's best novelists, and without doubt the greatest short-story writer the country had ever produced.

ANALYSIS

The sheer number and variety of Emilia Pardo Bazán's works must obviously defy any efforts of systematic analysis that scholarship can provide. At best, one can note certain recurrent themes in her fiction and illustrate by example her most successful techniques.

"A DESCENDANT OF EL CID"

Of the overall evolution of her practices in short-story writing, one can say first that she wrote relatively few short stories during the 1880's, her first decade as a serious writer, and perhaps half of those were in the form of sketches, of *cuadros de costumbres*—observations of her native Galicia—rather than plotted narratives. The best-known story of that period, "Nieto del Cid" ("A Descendant of El Cid"), shows Pardo Bazán about halfway along in her development from *costumbrista* to story-teller. "A Descendant of El Cid" is an account of an old village curate's resistance to a band of robbers who invade his sanctuary in search of money. First with his hunting rifle, then with a common table knife, the curate puts up a fierce fight until he is killed by the thieves. The story begins with a neutral-voiced description of the curate, his nephew, and two servants having a frugal evening meal together in the tiny kitchen of the sanctuary. There is no preliminary "frame," no indication of any identity of the implied narrator, or of the occasion for which the account has been set down. The beginning has the impersonal tone of a daily newspaper article. Fully half the story consists of a description of the setting and the generalized analysis of the tough and courageous character of the old curate. Until the invasion of the robbers begins, the story is indistinguishable from a *cuadro de costumbres*—that is, it is a portrait of the curate as a local type in Galicia. Once the action begins, however, the narrative moves swiftly to its violent conclusion, without description or analysis, and with the unblinking realism of gruesome detail. In a somewhat awkward concluding paragraph, the narrator suddenly uses the first person pronoun for the first time to say that he was told by a police sergeant, who arrived after the incident was over, what the curate's body looked like when the thieves had finished with him.

It is the unbalanced division between description and action and the awkward handling of narrative technique in "A Descendant of El Cid" that reveals the still tentative grasp the author had, in the 1880's, on the short-story form. That story is nevertheless powerful and deserves the popularity it has enjoyed. By the end of the 1880's, Pardo Bazán had read the best work of Guy de Maupassant in French and had written admiringly of his mastery of the art of the short story; it is to Maupassant's influence that one may attribute the fact that the 1890's saw a great increase in the number of stories Pardo Bazán was publishing and a corresponding elevation in the level of her control of the medium. An impressive collection of tales about her birthplace, La Coruña—to which she gave the fictitious name Marineda—was the first clear indication that she had attained understanding and mastery of this rather new genre.

"THE WHITE LOCK OF HAIR"

Cuentos de Marineda (tales about Marineda) appeared in 1892 and won for Pardo Bazán her first

wide notice as a short-story writer. A deeply probing story of a woman's private suffering, called "El mechón blanco" ("The White Lock of Hair"), is a fine example of the degree of mastery Pardo Bazán was able to demonstrate in that collection of hometown tales. The white lock of hair of the title belongs to a woman of striking beauty but reserved demeanor, the rest of whose hair is ebony black in color. She is the wife of the commandant of the military garrison in Marineda and the object of the most attentive curiosity in the town, both because of her provocative beauty and bearing, and because she and her husband had managed to give different explanations for the existence of that shock of white hair. The story thus opens with a mystery and concludes with its true explanation—an explanation which reveals fully the sorrow which had thus marked the commandant's wife. Accused of unfaithfulness by her husband, she had sworn her innocence on the life of their baby daughter. Almost immediately thereafter, the child died of meningitis, and when the mother next appears in public, her jet-black hair is scarred with the single lock of white hair on her forehead. What gives the explanation its power to move the reader deeply is that it is made, almost offhandedly, by a stranger visiting Marineda who knows the story because it occurred in his town. The skillful management of the narrative sequence, the creation of the air of mystery, and the casual, almost accidental, revelation at the end especially show the sophisticated control of the short-story which Pardo Bazán, inspired by the example of Maupassant, had attained by 1892.

Later in the same decade Pardo Bazán published a new group of stories which demonstrated that she was extending her skills beyond the Galician subject matter into new domains. *Cuentos de Amor* (tales of love) explores with penetrating insight the vagaries of the sex drive and the unexpected patterns of behavior it occasions. Both the settings and tones of these stories are varied. It is a pleasure, for example, to come upon "La última ilusión de Don Juan" ("Don Juan's Last Illusion"), which rings a most amusing change on the traditional Don Juan legend and does so in a merry tongue-in-cheek style which is a refreshing contrast to the author's usual seriousness. Pardo

Bazán had little gift of comic invention, but in this tale she imagined a Don Juan who is the center of a comic situation. Weary of the single-minded pursuit of sexual conquest, which he feels women always require of him, he has found respite and new delight in the conversation and correspondence he has lately struck up with a cousin, because it is all spiritual and intellectual, with never a mention of physical love. At last Don Juan—at heart a dreamer and idealist—feels he has found the perfect basis for a relationship with the opposite sex until he is rudely disillusioned by a letter from the lady announcing her intention to marry and therefore to end all further correspondence with him.

"THE REVENGE"

A story in the same collection, "Desquite" ("The Revenge"), returns the reader to the more usual tone of dark suffering characteristic of the author; but it is equally unconventional in its perspective, for none of the stories in this collection can be called a "traditional" love story, of the sentimental, or even of the star-crossed, variety. "Desquite" examines the dark soul of a young man whose congenitally malformed body has forced him to grow up with the realization that he is universally regarded as too repulsive to women to be dangerous company for well-brought-up young ladies. He has become a successful music teacher precisely because parents do not fear to trust him in intimate contact with their daughters. His "revenge" is to "seduce" one of his pupils, using passionate letters and an elaborate disguise, until she tearfully confesses that she loves him, whereupon he takes her home again without the slightest physical gesture in her direction and without explanation. He has satisfied his need for vengeance by enabling himself to make the truthful claim, henceforth, that he too has been loved by a beautiful woman. The most remarkable feature of the story is its profound understanding of the twisted bitterness in the psychology of a victim of physical deformity. Only in a most painfully ironic sense is it a "tale of love."

The first decade of the twentieth century was a time of even more fertile productivity in the domain of the short story for Pardo Bazán; during this time, she wrote many dozens of narratives, publishing them in the best Spanish periodicals, in several Spanish American journals which sought to print her work to enhance their own prestige, and even in certain French periodicals. By that time she had attained recognition as Spain's finest writer of short stories, and she turned her talents to many new subject areas: fantasy, ancient legends, religion, patriotism, even social and economic problems. She continued to write about Galicia but focused more and more on the violence and brutality of peasant life in her native region. Amid all the variety of topics, however, the dominant interest her stories display in the 1900's, as in the 1890's, is in the analysis of the awesome complexity of human motivation. Above all else she was fascinated by the way people behave toward one another, and her tales tended to become subtle dissections of instances of apparently incomprehensible conduct.

"THE LOCKET" AND "THE REVOLVER"

Two fine examples in this vein are "El guardapelo" ("The Locket"), which appeared in a collection called *En tranvía cuentos dramáticos* (dramatic tales), and "El revólver" ("The Revolver"), which is contained in a volume called *Interiores*. In "The Locket," a bizarre case of suppressed jealousy is analyzed: A husband is uneasy about the locket his wife always devotedly wears and has doubts about her explanation that it contains, as a remembrance, a lock of her father's hair. He doggedly pursues information about the color of his father-in-law's hair, learns it was black, then demands to see the hair in the locket. When he sees it is blond, however, he quickly finds reason to believe his wife is not lying because he loves her too much. "The Revolver" concerns an extreme instance of marital terror and its effects. It is the story of a woman who marries an older man and is subjected to a kind of psychological terror by a device the husband invented to calm his natural fear of being cuckolded by his pretty young bride: He tells her that she is free to come and go as she pleases, at all times and without question from him, but that if she ever betrays him and he finds out, he will instantly kill her with the revolver he is keeping in a drawer for that very purpose. He then shows her the revolver. From that moment on, the wife lives in a constant and intense state of terror, which continues after her husband's accidental death and reduces her to a trembling creature, old before her time and unable to take any further pleasure in living.

These glimpses of the dark inner life of human beings are both what is best and what is most characteristic of Pardo Bazán's short-story art. She developed a brilliant technique of compression and concentration in structure, a vivid, direct, unadorned style of narration, and a whole arsenal of technical devices for framing a story and controlling its point of view and its tone. That skill was applied in the service of her finest talent: the analysis and understanding of the human heart when subjected to intense social pressure. Inevitably, the quality of her stories is uneven; she wrote too many of them for it to be otherwise. Her best short stories, however, have contributed the finest jewels of their kind to be found in Spain's literary treasury.

OTHER MAJOR WORKS

LONG FICTION: *Pascual López*, 1879; *Un viaje de novios*, 1882 (*A Wedding Trip*, 1891); *La tribuna*, 1883; *El cisne de Vilamorta*, 1885 (*The Swan of Vilamorta*, 1891; also as *Shattered Hope: Or, The Swan of Vilamorta*, 1900); *Los pazos de Ulloa*, 1886 (*The Son of the Bondwoman*, 1908); *La madre naturaleza*, 1887; *Insolación*, 1889 (*Midsummer Madness*, 1907); *Morriña*, 1889 (*Morriña: Homesickness*, 1891); *Una cristiana*, 1890 (*A Christian Woman*, 1891); *La prueba*, 1890; *La piedra angular*, 1891 (*The Angular Stone*, 1892); *Doña Milagros*, 1894; *Memorias de un solterón*, 1896; *Adán y Eva*, 1896 (includes *Doña Milagros* and *Memorias de un solterón*); *El saludo de las brujas*, 1897; *El tesoro de Gastón*, 1897; *El niño de Guzman*, 1898; *Misterio*, 1903 (*The Mystery of the Lost Dauphin: Louis XVII*, 1906); *La quimera*, 1905; *La sirena negra*, 1908; *Dulce dueño*, 1911.

PLAYS: *Cuesta abajo*, pb. 1906; *Verdad*, pb. 1906.
POETRY: *Jáime*, 1881.

NONFICTION: *Ensayo crítico de las obras del Padre Feijóo*, 1876; *Reflexiones científicas contra el darwinismo*, 1878; *San Francisco de Asís*, 1882; *La cuestión palpitante*, 1883; *Apuntes autobiográficos*, 1886; *La revolución y la novela en Rusia*, 1887 (*Russia: Its People and Its Literature*, 1890); *De mi tierra*, 1888; *La romería*, 1888; *Al pie de la torre Eiffel*, 1890; *El Padre Luis Coloma*, 1890; *El nuevo teatro crítico*, 1891-1893; *Polémicas y estudios literarios*, 1892; *Los poetas épicos cristianos*, 1895; *Por la España pintoresca*, 1895; *Vida contemporánea*, c. 1896; *Cuarenta días en la exposición*, 1900; *Por la Europa católica*, 1902; *Lecciones de literatura*, 1906; *Retratos y apuntes literarios*, 1908; *Literatura francesca moderna*, 1910-1914; *La cocina española antigua*, 1913; *Hernán Cortés y sus hazañas*, 1914.

MISCELLANEOUS: *Obras completas*, 1891-1912 (41 volumes).

BIBLIOGRAPHY

Brown, D. F. *The Catholic Naturalism of Pardo Bazán*. Chapel Hill: University of North Carolina Press, 1957. Situates Pardo Bazán within the literary movement of Catholic naturalism and discusses her connection with French naturalist author Émile Zola's theory and practice. Emphasis is placed on Pardo Bazán's novels.

Feeny, Thomas. "Pardo Bazán's Pessimistic View of Love as Revealed in *Cuentos de amor*." *Hispanófila* 22 (1978): 6-14. An excellent treatment and analysis of the lack of love in the forty-three stories contained in the collection *Cuentos de amor*. Contains some untranslated Spanish passages.

Goldin, David. "The Metaphor of Original Sin: A Key to Pardo Bazán's Catholic Naturalism." *Philological Quarterly* 64 (Winter, 1985): 37-49. Analysis of Pardo Bazán's depiction of sex in her fiction; comments on the myth of the fall of man motif in Pardo Bazán's work and relates it to her Catholic naturalism.

González-Arias, Francisca. *Portrait of a Woman as Artist: Emilia Pardo Bazán and the Modern Novel in France and Spain*. New York: Garland, 1992. A thorough volume of interpretation of Pardo Bazán. Includes bibliographical references.

Hemingway, Maurice. *Emilia Pardo Bazán: The Making of a Novelist*. Cambridge, England: Cambridge University Press, 1983. Traces the literary development of Pardo Bazán. Provides a detailed analysis of the novels written between 1890 and

1896, which have all but been forgotten by literary critics. Offers a limited biographical sketch.

Hilton, Ronald. "Pardo Bazán and the Literary Polemics About Feminism." *Romanic Review* 44 (1953): 40-46. Chronicles Pardo Bazán's strong feminist career and the resistance with which her stance was met.

Pattison, Walter. *Emilia Pardo Bazán*. New York: Twayne, 1971. A good biography and examination of the intriguing personality of Emilia Pardo Bazán. Discusses her most important naturalistic novels. Chapter 9 deals with her short stories.

Scarlett, Elizabeth A. *Under Construction: The Body in Spanish Novels*. Charlottesville: University Press of Virginia, 1994. Deals with feminist issues in Pardo Bazán.

Murray Sachs, updated by Mary F. Yudin

DOROTHY PARKER

Born: West End, New Jersey; August 22, 1893
Died: New York, New York; June 7, 1967

PRINCIPAL SHORT FICTION

Laments for the Living, 1930
After Such Pleasures, 1933
Here Lies: The Collected Stories, 1939
The Portable Dorothy Parker, 1944
The Penguin Dorothy Parker, 1977

OTHER LITERARY FORMS

Dorothy Parker's principal writings, identified by Alexander Woolcott as "a potent distillation of nectar and wormwood," are short stories and verse—not serious "poetry," she claimed. Her poetic volumes include *Enough Rope* (1926), *Sunset Gun* (1928), and *Death and Taxes* (1931)—mostly lamentations for loves lost, never found, or gone awry. She wrote witty drama reviews for *Vanity Fair* (1918-1920), *Ainslee's* (1920-1933), and *The New Yorker* (1931); and terse, tart book reviews for *The New Yorker* (1927-1933) and *Esquire* (1959-1962). "Tonstant Weader Fwowed Up," her provoked, personal reaction to A. A. Milne's *The House at Pooh Corner* (1928), typifies her "delicate claws of . . . superb viciousness" (Woolcott). Parker's major plays are *The Coast of Illyria* (about Charles and Mary Lamb's tortured lives) and *The Ladies of the Corridor* (1953; three case studies of death-in-life among elderly women).

ACHIEVEMENTS

Dorothy Parker's career flashed brilliantly out in the 1920's and early 1930's and then faded equally quickly as the world she portrayed in her stories and poems disappeared into the hardships of the Depression. Her stories are sharp, witty portraits of an age when social and sexual conventions were changing rapidly. Her dramatic monologues, usually spoken by unself-confident women, her sharp social satires, and her careful delineations of scenes and situations reveal the changing mores of the 1920's. They also, however, portray the attendants of rapid social change: anxiety, lack of communication, and differing expectations of men and women on what social and sexual roles should be. These problems continue into contemporary times, and Parker's incisive writing captures them well. Her writings are like herself—witty and sad.

Her stories, verse, and reviews appeared in, and helped to set the tone of, the newly founded *The New Yorker*, which began publication in 1925, and she remained an occasional contributor until 1955.

BIOGRAPHY

Educated at Miss Dana's School in Morristown, New Jersey, Dorothy Rothschild Parker wrote fashion blurbs and drama criticism for *Vanity Fair*, short stories for *The New Yorker* irregularly, Hollywood screenplays at intervals (1934-1954), and *Esquire*

Dorothy Parker (Library of Congress)

book reviews (1959-1962). Her marriage to Edwin Pond Parker (1917-1928) was succeeded by two marriages to bisexual actor-writer Alan Campbell (1934-1947; 1950-1963, when Campbell died). Campbell, Lillian Hellman, and others nurtured Parker, but they could not control her drinking and her worsening writer's block that kept her from finishing many of her literary attempts during her last fifteen years.

ANALYSIS

Dorothy Parker's best-known stories are "The Waltz," "A Telephone Call," and her masterpiece, "Big Blonde," winner of the O. Henry Memorial Prize for the best short story of 1929.

"THE WALTZ"

"The Waltz" and "A Telephone Call," both dramatic monologues, present typical Parker characters, insecure young women who derive their social and personal acceptance from the approval of men and who go to extremes, whether sincere or hypocritical, to maintain this approbation. The characters, anonymous and therefore legion, elicit from the readers a mixture of sympathy and ridicule. They evoke sympathy because each is agonizing in an uncomfortable situation which she believes herself powerless to control. The waltzer is stuck with a bad, boorish dancer—"two stumbles, slip, and a twenty-yard dash." The other woman is longing for a telephone call from a man she loves who does not reciprocate her concern: "Please, God, let him telephone me now, Dear God, let him call me now. I won't ask anything else of You. . . ."

These predicaments are largely self-imposed as well as trivial and so they are ludicrous, unwittingly burlesqued through the narrators' hyperbolic perspectives. Both women are trapped in situations they have permitted to occur but from which they lack the resourcefulness or assertiveness to extricate themselves. The waltzer not only accepts the invitation to dance but also hypocritically flatters her partner: "Oh, they're going to play another encore. Oh, goody. Oh, that's lovely. Tired? I should say I'm not tired. I'd like to go on like this forever." These cloying words mask the truth, which she utters only to herself and to the eavesdropping audience: "I should say I'm not tired. I'm dead, that's all I am. Dead . . . and the music is never going to stop playing. . . ." Enslaved by an exaggerated code of politeness, therefore, she catches herself in the network of her own lies: "Oh, they've stopped, the mean things. They're not going to play any more. Oh, darn." Then she sets herself up for yet another round of hypocritical self-torture: "Do you really think so, if you gave them twenty dollars? . . . Do tell them to play this same thing. I'd simply adore to go on waltzing."

"A TELEPHONE CALL"

Like the waltzer, the narrator in "A Telephone Call" is her own worst enemy. Suffering from too much time on her hands—she is evidently not occupied with a job or responsibility for anyone but herself—she can afford the self-indulgence to spend hours focused exclusively on the dubious prospect of a phone call. She plays games with God; her catechism is a parody: "You see, God, if You would just let him telephone me, I wouldn't have to ask You . . . for anything more." She plays games with herself:

"Maybe if I counted five hundred by fives, it might ring by that time. I'll count slowly. I won't cheat." She is totally preoccupied with herself and her futile efforts to fan the embers of a dying love; having violated the social code by phoning her former admirer at his office, by the monologue's end she is desperately preparing to violate it again by calling him at home. Nevertheless, she is ludicrous rather than pathetic because her concern is so superficial (although her concentration on the anticipated phone call is also a barrier against the more serious reality of the estrangement); her calculations so trivial ("I'll count five hundred by fives, and if he hasn't called me then, I will know God isn't going to help me, ever again"); and the stakes for which she prays so low (attempting to manipulate God's will in such a minor matter). She, like the waltzer, envisions a simplistic fairy-tale solution dependent on the agency of another.

Thus the plots of these slight stories are as slender as the resources of the monologist narrators, for whom formulaic prayers or serial wisecracks ("I'd like to [dance] awfully, but I'm having labor pains. . . . It's so nice to meet a man who isn't a scaredy-cat about catching my beri-beri") are inadequate to alter their situations. Such narratives, with their fixed perspectives, exploitation of a single, petty issue, and simple characters, have to be short. To be any longer would be to add redundance without complexity, to bore rather than to amuse with verbal pyrotechnics.

"BIG BLONDE"

Although "Big Blonde" shares some of the features of the monologues, it is far more complex in narrative mode and in characterization. Rather than anatomizing a moment in time, as do the monologues, "Big Blonde" covers an indefinite span of years, perhaps a dozen. The story moves from comedy into pathos as its protagonist, Hazel Morse, moves from genuine gaiety to forced conviviality, undergirded by the hazy remorse that her name connotes.

Hazel, "a large, fair," unreflective, voluptuous blonde, has been, in her twenties, by day a "model in a wholesale dress establishment," and for "a couple of thousand evenings . . . a good sport among her [nu-merous] male acquaintances." Having "come to be more conscientious than spontaneous" about her enjoyment of men's jokes and drunken antics, she escapes into what she unthinkingly assumes will be a stereotype of marriage, isolation from the outer world *à deux*, but what instead becomes a travesty. She revels in honesty—the freedom to stop being incessantly cheerful and to indulge in the other side of the conventional feminine role that is her life's allotment, the freedom to weep sentimental tears over various manifestations, large and small, of "all the sadness there is in the world."

Her husband, Herbie, is "not amused" at her tears and impersonal sorrows: "crab, crab, crab, that was all she ever did." To transform her from "a lousy sport" into her former jocular self he encourages her to drink, "Atta girl! . . . Let's see you get boiled, baby." Having neither the intellectual, imaginative, nor domestic resources to hold her marriage together any other way, Hazel acquiesces, even though she hates "the taste of liquor," and soon begins to drink steadily. Herbie, however, is as barren of human resources as is his wife, and alcohol only ignites their smoldering anger, despite Hazel's "thin and wordless idea that, maybe, this night, things would begin to be all right." They are not; Herbie fades out of Hazel's alcohol-blurred existence as Ed merges into it. He, too, insists "upon gaiety" and will not "listen to admissions of aches or weariness." Nor will Ed's successors, Charley, Sydney, Fred, Billy, and others, to whom Hazel responds with forced cordiality through her alcoholic haze in which the days and year lose "their individuality."

By now perpetually "tired and blue," she becomes frightened when her "old friend" whiskey fails her, and she decides, having no ties, no talents, and no purpose in living, to commit suicide by taking twenty sleeping pills—"Well, here's mud in your eye." In her customary vagueness she fails again, however, causing the impersonal attendants, a reluctant doctor and housemaid, more annoyance than concern. She concludes that she might as well live, but with a paradoxical prayer of diabolic self-destructiveness: "Oh, please, please, let her be able to get drunk, please keep her always drunk."

Although in both "Big Blonde" and the monologues Parker satirizes vapid, unassertive women with empty lives, her work carries with it satire's inevitable message of dissatisfaction with the status quo and an implicit plea for reform. For in subtle ways Parker makes a feminist plea even through her most passive, vacuous characters. Women ought to be open, assertive, independent; they should think for themselves and act on their own behalf, because men cannot be counted on to do it for them. They should be their own persons, like Geoffrey Chaucer's Wife of Bath, "wel at ease," instead of allowing their happiness to depend on the waxing and waning affections and attentions of inconstant men.

To the extent that Dorothy Parker was a satirist she was also a moralist. In satirizing aimless, frivolous, or social-climbing lives, she implied a purposeful ideal. In ridiculing self-deception, hypocrisy, obsequiousness, and flattery, she advocated honesty in behavior and communication. In her epigrams, the moralist's rapiers, she could hone a razor-edge with the best. In her portraits, cameos etched in acid, the touchstone of truth shines clear.

OTHER MAJOR WORKS

PLAYS: *Nero*, pr. 1922 (with Robert Benchley); *Close Harmony*, pr. 1924 (with Elmer Rice); *The Coast of Illyria*, pr. 1949 (with Ross Evans); *The Ladies of the Corridor*, pr., pb. 1953 (with Arnaud d'Usseau).

SCREENPLAYS: *Business Is Business*, 1925 (with George S. Kaufman); *Here Is My Heart*, 1934 (with Alan Campbell); *One Hour Late*, 1935 (with Alan Campbell); *Mary Burns, Fugitive*, 1935; *Hands Across the Table*, 1935; *Paris in Spring*, 1935; *Big Broadcast of 1936*, 1935 (with Alan Campbell); *Three Married Men*, 1936 (with Alan Campbell); *Lady Be Careful*, 1936 (with Alan Campbell and Harry Ruskin); *The Moon's Our Home*, 1936; *Suzy*, 1936 (with Alan Campbell, Horace Jackson, and Lenore Coffee); *A Star Is Born*, 1937 (with Alan Campbell and Robert Carson); *Woman Chases Man*, 1937 (with Joe Bigelow); *Sweethearts*, 1938 (with Alan Campbell); *Crime Takes a Holiday*, 1938; *Trade Winds*, 1938 (with Alan Campbell and Frank R. Adams); *Flight into Nowhere*, 1938; *Five Little Peppers and How They Grew*, 1939; *Weekend for Three*, 1941 (with Alan Campbell); *The Little Foxes*, 1941; *Saboteur*, 1942 (with Alan Campbell, Peter Viertel, and Joan Harrison); *A Gentle Gangster*, 1943; *Mr. Skeffington*, 1944; *Smash-Up: The Story of a Woman*, 1947 (with Frank Cavett); *The Fan*, 1949 (with Walter Reisch and Ross Evans); *Queen for a Day*, 1951; *A Star Is Born*, 1954.

POETRY: *Enough Rope*, 1926; *Sunset Gun*, 1928; *Death and Taxes*, 1931; *Not So Deep as a Well*, 1936.

BIBLIOGRAPHY

Calhoun, Randall. *Dorothy Parker: A Bio-bibliography*. Westport, Conn.: Greenwood Press, 1993. A helpful guide for the student of Parker. Includes bibliographical references and an index.

Freibert, Lucy M. "Dorothy Parker." In *Dictionary of Literary Biography: American Short Story Writers, 1910-1945*, edited by Bobby Ellen Kimbel. Vol. 86. Detroit: Gale Research, 1989. Freibert's excellent entry on Dorothy Parker provides some general biographical information and close readings of some of her most important stories. Includes a bibliography of Parker's work and a critical bibliography.

Keats, John. *You Might as Well Live: The Life and Times of Dorothy Parker*. New York: Simon & Schuster, 1970. Keats's book was the first popular biography published on Parker and it is quite thorough and readable. Supplemented by a bibliography and an index.

Kinney, Arthur F. *Dorothy Parker, Revised*. New York: Twayne, 1998. Argues that what appears monotonal in Parker's work is a compound of complicated voices, for her work is dialogic and polyvocal. Traces influences and sources of her work and assesses her achievements. Provides a summary survey of Parker's short-story collections, including publishing history and critical reception.

Meade, Marion. *Dorothy Parker: What Fresh Hell Is This?* London: Heinemann, 1987. Meade has produced a good, thorough biography that relates events in Parker's fiction to situations in her life.

Nevertheless, Meade's focus is biographical and the discussion of Parker's work is mostly in passing. Includes notes and an index.

Melzer, Sondra. *The Rhetoric of Rage: Women in Dorothy Parker*. New York: Peter Lang, 1997. Explores Parker's representation of female characters in her works.

Simpson, Amelia. "Black on Blonde: The Africanist Presence in Dorothy Parker's 'Big Blonde.'" *College Literature* 23 (October, 1996): 105-116. Claims that "Big Blonde" exposes the way race and gender are mutually constitutive and how blackness contests and constructs the privilege of white-

ness; argues that three seemingly unimportant African figures are the key to this narrative about the subjugation of white women in America.

Walker, Nancy A. "The Remarkably Constant Reader: Dorothy Parker as Book Reviewer." *Studies in American Humor*, n.s. 3, no. 4 (1997): 1-14. A discussion of Parker's book reviews for *The New Yorker* from 1927 to 1933 and for *Esquire* from 1957 to 1962 as a reflection of her literary sensibility.

Lynn Z. Bloom, updated by Karen M. Cleveland Marwick

BORIS PASTERNAK

Born: Moscow, Russia; February 10, 1890
Died: Peredelkino, U.S.S.R.; May 30, 1960

PRINCIPAL SHORT FICTION

"Pisma iz Tuly," 1922 ("Letters from Tula," 1945)
"Deststvo Liuvers," 1923 ("The Childhood of Luvers," 1945)
Rasskazy, 1925
Sochineniya, 1961 (*Collected Short Prose*, 1977)

OTHER LITERARY FORMS

Primarily a lyric poet, Boris Pasternak also wrote epic poems upon revolutionary themes and translated English and German classics into Russian. Besides several pieces of short fiction, he wrote two prose autobiographies and an unfinished play, *Slepaya Krasavitsa* (1969; *The Blind Beauty*, 1969), intended as a nineteenth century prologue to his single novel, *Doktor Zhivago* (1957; *Doctor Zhivago*, 1958), the first major Russian work to be published only outside the Soviet Union. Pasternak won the Nobel Prize in Literature in 1958, but Soviet governmental pressure forced him to refuse it. His lyric "The Nobel Prize" describes him "caught like a beast at bay" in his homeland.

ACHIEVEMENTS

Boris Pasternak is best known in his native country for his poetry and abroad for his novel *Doctor Zhivago*. In both of these genres he ranks among the best in Russian literature. His short fiction, though not on the same level of excellence as his poetry and the novel, is still appreciated. Pasternak was also an accomplished translator into Russian, especially of William Shakespeare's works and of Georgian poetry. An equally important achievement on his part was his ability to project himself as an ultimate artist in the Soviet environment notably hostile to free art. During the last four decades of his life, he was able to preserve the dignity of a free individualist and to write his works according to the dictates of his conscience. It was this courageous attitude, in addition to the artistic merits of his works, that won him the Nobel Prize in 1958.

BIOGRAPHY

The eldest son of the celebrated Russian Jewish painter Leonid Pasternak and his wife, the musician Rosa Kaufman, Boris Leonidovich Pasternak abandoned an early interest in music for the study of philosophy at the Universities of Moscow and later Mar-

Boris Pasternak, Nobel Laureate for Literature in 1958 (CORBIS/ Bettmann)

burg, where he remained until returning to Russia at the outbreak of World War I, at which time he began to write seriously. From his literary debut in 1913 to 1914 with "The Story of a Contraoctave" and a collection of lyrics, "A Twin in the Clouds," Pasternak devoted the whole of his creative life to literature. Most of his short fiction and both long epic poetry and shorter lyrics, headed by the collection *Sestra moia zhizn'* (1922; *My Sister, Life*, 1964), occupied him for the next fifteen years. His first autobiography, *Okhrannaya gramota* (1931; *A Safe-Conduct*, 1945) foreshadowed his personal and artistic survival through the Stalinist purges of the 1930's, when a new moral direction became evident in his work, demonstrated in fragments of a novel he never finished. Although he again wrote lyric poetry during World War II, Pasternak answered Soviet postwar restrictions on creativity by mainly supporting himself with his translations, producing versions of works by Johann Wolfgang von Goethe, Friedrich von Schiller,

and William Shakespeare. He also began the novel that he eventually considered his finest achievement, *Doctor Zhivago*, in which he discussed and analyzed the disintegrative reality of Russia's conversion to Communism. At the end of 1946 he met his great love, Olga Ivinskaya, the model for the heroine of the novel, and although the Soviet authorities imprisoned her in an attempt to silence Pasternak's apolitical praise of Christian values, he nevertheless completed the novel and allowed it to be published in 1957 in Italy. The Soviet regime retaliated by forcing Pasternak to refuse the Nobel Prize awarded him in 1958, the year his 1957 autobiography, *Avtobiograficheskiy ocherk* (1958; *I Remember: Sketch for an Autobiography*, 1959), appeared in the West. Crushed by depression and fear for those he loved, Pasternak died of leukemia in early 1960, and two months later, as he had dreaded, Ivinskaya was rearrested and sentenced again to prison.

ANALYSIS

All Boris Pasternak's fiction illustrates the tragic involvement of a poet with his age. Just prior to World War I, Russian literature was dominated by the figure of Vladimir Mayakovsky, who embodied a strange combination of symbolist mythmaking with the fierce futurist rejection of traditional forms. Bordering on the theatrical, Mayakovsky's self-dramatization pitted the gifted literary artist's elevated emotions and extreme sensitivity against his supposedly dull and unappreciative or even hostile audience, an artistic tendency which Pasternak recognized and from which he tried to liberate himself in his early stories.

"THE STORY OF A CONTRAOCTAVE"

"The Story of a Contraoctave," written in 1913, stems from Pasternak's Marburg years and his exposure there to German Romanticism. Centered upon a German organist who, caught up in a flight of extemporaneous performance, unknowingly crushes his son to death in the instrument's works, this story exhibits the Romantic artist's "inspiration," his lack of concern for ordinary life, and the guilt that society forces upon him. Pasternak's first published story, "Apellesova Cherta" ("The Mark of Apelles"), written in

1915 at the height of his admiration for Mayakovsky, explores the problem of Pasternak's simultaneous attraction to, and dismay with, the neo-Romantic posture. In this story, two writers agree to a literary competition which quickly spills over into real life when one, clearly named for Heinrich Heine, the German nineteenth century poet whose irony punctured the naïve bubble of Romantic idealism, outdoes the heavy-handed idealistic fantasy of his opponent Relinquimini by arousing and responding to genuine love in Relinquimini's mistress. A similar pair of antagonists forms the conflict in "Bezlyube" ("Without Love"), written and published in 1918 and originally intended as part of an unfinished longer work, although it actually furnished material for *Doctor Zhivago*. "Without Love" paradoxically shows an activist living in a peculiar never-never land, while a lyric dreamer's adherence to the truth of remembered experience illustrates Pasternak's inability to adapt his artistic inspiration to political service.

"LETTERS FROM TULA"

"Letters from Tula," written in 1918, again juxtaposes reality and art, but here the Russia of Pasternak's own time provides his setting. A powerful contrast develops between the reactions of a young poet and an old retired actor to a film crew working near the town of Tula. The poet, passing through on the train, is in the grasp of a violent passion for his distant lover. The mediocrity of the vulgar filmmakers appalls him, but as he tries to write to his beloved, he becomes even more disgusted with his own self-consciously arty efforts at conveying his emotion. On the other hand, the aged actor, who wholeheartedly detests the philistine cinema and the loss of tradition it caused, uses his own successful artistic representation. Made grindingly aware by them of his age and his loneliness and most of all of his need for "the human speech of tragedy," the old man returns to his silent apartment and re-creates a part of one of his performances, which in turn calls up a valid response of healing memory.

In *A Safe-Conduct*, his first autobiography, Pasternak wrote, "In art the man is silent, and the image speaks." The young poet's silence in "Letters from Tula" would eventually foster his creativity, but it had to be purchased at the sacrifice of his youthful arrogance and the painful achievement of humility. The old actor attains his creative silence because he is the only one in the story who could make another speak through his own lips. Thus the humble willingness to serve as the vehicle of art, allowing experience to speak through him, becomes an important stage in Pasternak's artistic development, enabling him to move beyond romantic self-absorption toward an art that needs no audience.

"THE CHILDHOOD OF LUVERS"

Pasternak wrote one of his masterpieces, "The Childhood of Luvers," from 1917 to 1919, intending it originally as the opening of a novel but finally publishing it by itself in 1923. This long short story shares the childlike innocence of *My Sister, Life*, the height of Pasternak's lyric expression, also appearing that year. In the first section of the story, the world of childhood impressions becomes a part of Zhenya Luvers's experience. Little by little, the shapes, colors, smells—all the sensory images to which the young child responds so eagerly—impinge upon her consciousness, are assimilated, and finally arrange into an order which becomes more coherent as she grows older. Zhenya's impressions of her surroundings also gradually give place to her emotional impressions of people and situations, as the child's apprehension of "things" progressively is able to grasp more complex relations between them. Zhenya's world is at first markedly silent, as is the world of the angry young lover and the old actor in "Letters from Tula"; Pasternak's impressionistic technique allows few "realistic" details, preferring to let lovely and strange combinations of images flood the child's developing awareness of her life.

In the second part of this story, Pasternak shifts his attention from Zhenya's instinctive grasp of emotions through images given to her by the bewildering world of adulthood. As Zhenya matures, she begins to respond to the essential sadness of things by assuming, as children do, that she herself has committed some sin to cause her misery. When Zhenya's household is turned upside down by her mother's miscarriage and she is sent to the home of friends, she learns how to deal with adult condescension and cruelty. At the moment that Zhenya realizes her own participation in the body of humankind, her simultaneously Christian and singularly Russian consciousness of shared suffering, her childhood abruptly ceases.

One of the pervasive themes of Pasternak's work, the suffering of women, is thus treated in "The Childhood of Luvers," reflecting Pasternak's anguish at being "wounded by the lot of women" that underlay his fascination with the tragic Mary, Queen of Scots. Zhenya Luvers, however, evokes the growth into recognition of adult responsibility that is basic to the human condition, extending from fragments of sense impressions into the ability to make the only sense of her world a Christian knows: the participation in its suffering. For Pasternak, Zhenya Luvers also marks the childhood of the girl whom his great love Olga Ivinskaya called "the Lara of the future," the woman at the heart of *Doctor Zhivago*. The capacity to grow and mature through the experience of suffering makes Zhenya the personification of Pasternak's betrayed Russia, trusting and defenseless in the grip of the godless aggression that followed the 1917 Communist Revolution.

"THE STORY"

All Pasternak's works of the 1920's reveal his growing awareness of the poet's responsibility to humankind, continuing to lead him from his earlier lyric expression of romantic self-absorption toward the epic presentation of his moral impulse. "Three Chapters from a Story" and "Vozdushnye puti" ("Aerial Ways"), as well as his long narrative poetry of the decade, also illustrate Pasternak's attempt to come to grips with the cannibalistic tendency of revolutions to devour the very forces that unleashed them. By 1929, in another long short story titled simply "Povest" ("The Story"), Pasternak reached a new manifestation of his creative position. His young hero Seryosha comes to visit his sister, exhausted and dismayed by the chaos around him in the turmoil of 1916, when Russia's contribution to the struggle against Germany was faltering because of governmental ineptitude and social tensions. Pasternak's impressionistic glimpses of the disorder swirl around Seryosha like nightmarish, demonic scenes, until he lies down on a shabby cot to rest, losing himself in memories of the bittersweet prewar years when his artistic vocation had come to him.

Seryosha had been a tutor to a well-to-do family, but he saw his real mission as saving the world through art. Pasternak's "suffering women," here a sympathetic prostitute and later a widowed Danish governess trapped in poverty, awaken Seryosha's compassion and lead him to begin a story within "The Story," the tale of "Y$_3$," a poet and musician who intends to alleviate the suffering of some of his fellow men by selling himself at auction. As Seryosha's retrospective experiences flash through his tired mind, he suddenly becomes distressingly aware of his own failure in those earlier years. At the very time when he was self-consciously creating his gloriously idealistic artistic work, he was overlooking the genuine self-sacrifice of a young acquaintance being called into the army, ignoring the man so completely that he could not even remember his name, and now, miserable himself, guilt overcomes Seryosha.

"The Story" employs Pasternak's early impressionistic technique of unprepared-for, disruptive shifts in plot, setting, and time, but at the same time, its portraiture and characterization are both more intimate and more realistic than those he had previously created. The element Pasternak had added to Zhenya Luvers's recognition of the necessity of shared suffering was now Seryosha's guilty realization of the need for self-sacrifice, a distinct shift from a passive to an active participation in the fate of Russia. By setting "The Story" in the context of the gathering revolution, whose true meaning the oblivious "artist" cannot grasp until it has swept him up, Pasternak establishes the grounds for his subsequent opposition of creative moral man to deathly political machine. "The Story" unmistakably illustrates Pasternak's growing preference for longer and more realistic prose forms, and thematically it demonstrates his tendency, increasing steadily during the period just before the Stalinist purges of the 1930's, to integrate his own experience with that of his suffering fellows, a distinct foreshadowing of the life and poems of Yuri Zhivago that Pasternak was later to create.

SECOND BIRTH

For many of Russia's artists, Mayakovsky's suicide in 1930 marked the end of faith in the ideals of the 1917 revolution. The title of Pasternak's collection of verse *Vtoroye rozhdeniye* (1932; *Second Birth*, 1964) reflects his new orientation, for in one of the poems an actor speaks: "Oh, had I known when I made my debut that lines with blood in them can flood the throat and kill!" During the decade of terror, Pasternak inclined still further toward a realistic novel of the revolution, although only six fragments of it remain, the last short pieces of fiction he wrote. "A District in the Rear" and "Before Parting," both written in the late 1930's, treat autobiographical motifs from 1916, the strange prelude to the revolution, with none of Pasternak's earlier swift flashes of impression nor any penetration of the creating artist's consciousness. "A District in the Rear," however, links family love with the stirrings of the artistic impulse, since the hero senses the feelings of his wife and children as "something remote, like loneliness and the pacing of the horse, something like a book," as he approaches the decision to leave them and sacrifice his life "most worthily and to best advantage" at the front.

The four remaining story fragments, "A Beggar Who Is Proud," "Aunt Olya," "Winter Night," and "The House with Galleries," do not involve the events of 1917 but rather Pasternak's childhood reminiscences of the 1905 revolution, possibly because in the late 1930's he was as yet unable to deal fully with the poet's relation to the Communist movement and its aftermath. Only after he had lived through World War II and met Olga Ivinskaya could Pasternak express his experiences through the fictional perspective of Doctor Zhivago, binding the moral and the creative, the personal and the objective, the loving and the sacrificial elements of human life into an organic whole. While all Pasternak's short fiction are steps toward that goal, each piece also independently reflects successively maturing phases of his recognition, as he wrote toward the end of his life, that to be a great poet, writing poetry was not enough; that it was essential to contribute in a vital way to his times by willingly sacrificing himself to a lofty and lovely destiny. Accordingly, the personae of Pasternak's short fiction—the romantic poet, the lyric dreamer, the aging actor, the maturing girl, the suffering woman, the self-sacrificing husband and father—all finally coalesced into the figure of his Christian "Hamlet":

> The noise is stilled. I come out on the stage . . .
> The darkness of the night is aimed at me
> Along the sights of a thousand opera glasses.
> Abba, Father, if it be possible,
> Let this cup pass from me. . . .

OTHER MAJOR WORKS

LONG FICTION: *Doktor Zhivago*, 1957 (*Doctor Zhivago*, 1958).

PLAY: *Slepaya krasavitsa*, pb. 1969 (*The Blind Beauty*, 1969).

POETRY: *Bliznets v tuchakh*, 1914; *Poverkh barierov*, 1917 (*Above the Barriers*, 1959); *Sestra moia zhizn'*, 1922 (*My Sister, Life*, 1964); *Temy i variatsii*, 1923 (*Themes and Variations*, 1964); *Vysokaya bolezn'*, 1924 (*High Malady*, 1958); *Carousel: Verse for Children*, 1925; *Devyatsot pyaty god*, 1926 (*The Year 1905*, 1989); *Lyutenant Shmidt*, 1927 (*Lieutenant Schmidt*, 1992); *Spektorskiy*, 1931; *Vtoroye rozhdeniye*, 1932 (*Second Birth*, 1964); *Na rannikh poezdakh*, 1943 (*On Early Trains*, 1964); *Zemnoy prostor*, 1945 (*The Vastness of Earth*, 1964); *Kogda razgulyayetsa*, 1959 (*When the Skies Clear*, 1964); *The Poetry of Boris Pasternak, 1914-1960*, 1959; *The Poetry of Boris Pasternak, 1917-1959*, 1959; *Poems*, 1959; *Poems, 1955-1959*, 1960; *In the Interlude: Poems, 1945-1960*, 1962; *Fifty Poems*, 1963; *The Poems of Doctor Zhivago*, 1965; *Stikhotvoreniya i poemy*, 1965; *The Poetry of Boris Pasternak*, 1969; *Selected Poems*, 1983.

NONFICTION: *Pis'ma k gruzinskim*, n.d. (*Letters to Georgian Friends by Boris Pasternak*, 1968); *Okhrannaya gramota*, 1931 (*A Safe-Conduct*, 1945); *Avtobiograficheskiy ocherk*, 1958 (*I Remember: Sketch for an Autobiography*, 1959); *An Essay in Autobiography*, 1959; *Essays*, 1976; *The Correspondence of Boris Pasternak and Olga Friedenberg, 1910-1954*, 1981; *Pasternak on Art and Creativity*, 1985.

TRANSLATIONS: *Hamlet*, 1941 (by William Shakespeare); *Romeo i Juliet*, 1943 (by Shakespeare); *Antony i Cleopatra*, 1944 (by Shakespeare); *Othello*, 1945 (by Shakespeare); *King Lear*, 1949 (by Shakespeare); *Faust*, 1953 (by Johann Wolfgang von Goethe); *Maria Stuart*, 1957 (by Friedrich Schiller).

MISCELLANEOUS: *Safe Conduct: An Early Autobiography and Other Works by Boris Pasternak*, 1949; *Sochinenii*, 1961; *Vozdushnye puti: Proza raz nykh let*, 1982; *The Voice of Prose*, 1986.

BIBLIOGRAPHY

Barnes, Christopher. *Boris Pasternak: A Literary Biography, Volume One: 1890-1928*. New York: Cambridge University Press, 1990. A comprehensive biography, scholarly but also accessible.

Conquest, Robert. *The Pasternak Affair: Courage of Genius*. London: Collins and Harvill, 1961. A detailed account of Pasternak's conflict with the state on his reception of the Nobel Prize. Conquest provides much valuable information about Pasternak as a man and a writer.

De Mallac, Guy. *Boris Pasternak: His Life and Art*. Norman: University of Oklahoma Press, 1981. An extensive biography of Pasternak. The second part is devoted to De Mallac's interpretation of the most important features of Pasternak's works. A detailed chronology of his life and an exhaustive bibliography complete this beautifully illustrated book.

Erlich, Victor, ed. *Pasternak: A Collection of Critical Essays*. Englewood Cliffs, N.J.: Prentice-Hall, 1978. This skillfully arranged collection of essays covers all important facets of Pasternak's work, including short fiction, although the emphasis is on his poetry and *Doctor Zhivago*.

Gifford, Henry. *Boris Pasternak: A Critical Study*. New York: Cambridge University Press, 1977. Gifford follows the stages in Pasternak's life and discusses works written during those stages in order to establish his achievements as a poet, writer of prose fiction, and translator. This volume contains many sharp critical remarks, and chapter 6 deals with the short fiction. Supplemented by a chronological table and a select bibliography.

_____. "Indomitable Pasternak." *The New York Review of Books* 37 (May 31, 1990): 26-31. Discusses Pasternak's courage in his defense of artistic freedom under Soviet power, refusing to sign denunciations.

Ivinskaya, Olga. *A Captive of Time*. Garden City, N.Y.: Doubleday, 1978. Ivinskaya, Pasternak's love in the last years of his life, the model for Lara in *Doctor Zhivago*, and a staff member at the influential Soviet literary magazine *Novy mir*, provides a wealth of information about Pasternak, his views and works, and Russia's literary atmosphere in the 1940's and 1950's.

Mossman, Elliott. "Pasternak's Short Fiction." *Russian Literature Triquarterly* 3 (1972): 279-302. Mossman sees Pasternak's preoccupation with short fiction in the 1920's not as a diversion but as an alternative to poetry and a legitimate genre in his work. He discusses "Aerial Ways," "The Story," "The Childhood of Luvers," and "The Story of a Contraoctave" within Pasternak's development as a writer.

Rowland, Mary F., and Paul Rowland. *Pasternak's "Doctor Zhivago."* Carbondale: Southern Illinois University Press, 1967. This book-length interpretation of *Doctor Zhivago* offers many interesting attempts to clarify allegorical, symbolic, and religious meanings as, for example, the meaning of virtually every name in the novel. Although some interpretations are not proven, most of them are plausible, making for a fascinating reading.

Rudova, Larissa. *Understanding Boris Pasternak*. Columbia: University of South Carolina Press, 1997. A general introduction to Pasternak's work, including both his early poetry and prose and his later work; provides analyses of individual novels and stories.

Mitzi M. Brunsdale, updated by
Vasa D. Mihailovich

CESARE PAVESE

Born: Santo Stefano Belbo, Italy; September 9, 1908
Died: Turin, Italy; August 27, 1950

PRINCIPAL SHORT FICTION

Feria d' agosto, 1946 (*Summer Storm and Other
  Stories*, 1966)
Notte di festa, 1953 (*Festival Night and Other
  Stories*, 1964)
Racconti: Pavese, 1960
Cesare Pavese: Racconti, 1968
Told in Confidence and Other Stories, 1971
The Leather Jacket: Stories, 1980
Stories, 1987

OTHER LITERARY FORMS

Cesare Pavese's fame initially rested on his novels
published in the 1940's, including *Tra donne sole*
(1949; *Among Women Only*, 1953) and *La casa in
collina* (1949; *The House on the Hill*, 1956). Following his death in 1950, readers discovered his poetry,
short stories, and such nonfiction works as studies
of mythology and American literature. Volumes of
his letters have been published, as well as his diary,
which some critics consider his masterpiece: *Il
mestiere di vivere: Diaro, 1935-1950* (1952; *This
Business of Living: Diaries, 1935-1950*, 1961), also
known as *The Burning Brand: Diaries, 1935-1950*
(1961).

ACHIEVEMENTS

Cesare Pavese's work has received increasing attention in the decades following his death. Many
readers consider him the greatest Italian writer of the
twentieth century. Different groups admire him for
different reasons. Historians treat his writings as a record of a period marked by revolution, war, and fascist suppression. Some fans have entered him on their
roll of existential heroes, based on his literary explorations of despair and solitude and on his suicide at
the height of his power. Literary critics see him as a
master craftsman and an original talent who helped
create a new Italian literature.

Pavese wanted to free literature first from the
heavy hand of Italian literary and philosophical tradition and then from the suppressive hand of the fascist
state. His goal was to create a new literature, based
on new literary language and symbols.

BIOGRAPHY

Cesare Pavese was born on September 9, 1908, in
his family home in the village of Santo Stefano
Belbo. He grew up there and in the industrial city of
Turin, where his father, Eugenio, was a clerk in a law
court. After his father died, his mother, Consolina,
provided him with the best education available. In
high school, he was enthralled by the ideas of
Benedetto Croce and Antonio Gramsci and by the
aestheticism of Giacomo Leopardi. At the University
of Turin, he became captivated by American literature and wrote his thesis on Walt Whitman.

After his graduation in 1930, Pavese began teaching, which required him to join the Fascist party. The
Fascists, however, could no more control his mind
than could the Communists when he joined that party
in 1945. He was arrested for anti-Fascist activities
and sentenced to internal exile in rural southern Italy.
He was released in March, 1936. Pavese's conviction
ended his teaching career. After he returned from exile, he scraped out a living by writing and by working
part-time at the Einaudi Publishing House.

Depression and anguish were Pavese's constant
companions. He was emotionally devastated in 1936
by the failure of his relationship with the antifascist
activist Battistina Pizzardo. With astute self-knowledge, he wrote in his diary: "Now I see the reason
why I isolated myself until '34. Subconsciously I
knew that for me love would be a massacre." His earlier distrust and fear of women was later revived. He
wrote: "One cannot escape one's own character: a mi-
sogynist you were, and still are."

The fascist grip tightened on Italy, then World
War II brought destruction and defeat. Amid this turmoil, Pavese emerged as a leading figure in Italy's literary life. He became a major figure in the Einaudi

Publishing House, and he continued writing poetry, short stories, and a diary. Critical and public recognition came through his novels, with *Paesi tuoi* (1941; *The Harvesters*, 1961). He wrote rapidly and showed how fully he had mastered his craft in a series of novels published in the late 1940's.

Pavese's personal life, however, deteriorated. "I know an idiot," he wrote of himself, "who refused to learn the rules of the game when he was young, lost as he was in fantasies. Now the fantasies are vanishing and the game is shattering him." He refused to allow his many friends to help him with his inner struggle. At the beginning of 1950, he wrote in his diary: "I am filled with distaste for what I have done, for all my works. A sense of failing health, of physical decadence. The downward curve of the arc. . . . I find that the world is beautiful and worthwhile. But I am slipping." His last entry in his diary was on August 18, 1950: "All this is sickening. Not words. An act. I won't write anymore." He checked into a hotel in Turin and took an overdose of sleeping pills. He was found dead on August 27, 1950.

ANALYSIS

Cesare Pavese wrote most of his short stories during the 1930's and early 1940's, but few were published before his death. In them, he explores childhood, rural versus urban life, solitude and loneliness, and the difficulty of forming relationships with other people, especially women. Pavese's work is remarkably free of overt political concerns. The political undercurrent in his writing, however, is found in its inward focus, the only center of freedom in a suppressive society, and in the atmosphere of bleakness and social blight that pervades his stories.

It was in his short stories that Pavese perfected his writing style. His writing, in expressive vernacular, is always elliptical and oblique. His work is often classified as neorealistic, but his real concern is psychological processes. While his subject matter includes incest, rape, and murder, they usually occur offstage, and his style is unsensational and detached. His cool, distancing language heightens the tension and turmoil bubbling beneath the surface. Behind the ellipses and silences that characterize Pavese's writing are

Cesare Pavese (Kimberly Dawson Kurnizki)

the dramatic events to which his characters react. These events, hidden from the reader, obviously frighten and distress the characters. The event itself is slowly revealed to the reader. This technique downplays the importance of the event and emphasizes the psychological reaction of the characters. The language is flat but laden with emotional tension, with the events too explosive for the characters to describe directly.

"LAND OF EXILE"

Most of Pavese's short stories were translated into English in the collections entitled *Festival Night and Other Stories, Summer Storm and Other Stories*, and *Told in Confidence and Other Stories*. They have an autobiographical tone, since most were written in first person and deal with settings or episodes that Pavese experienced.

A turning point in Pavese's life came with his exile for antifascist activities. Several of his stories deal with exile or prison, including "Terra d'esilio" ("Land of Exile"), "L'introso" ("The Intruder"), and "Carogne" ("Gaol Birds"). The narrator in "Land of Exile" is self-exiled to a place in southern Italy much like the one to which Pavese was sent by the Fascists. The land is bleak, and the people lead harsh and empty lives. The narrator meets Ciccio, a half-witted beggar driven mad by his wife, and Otino, imprisoned for beating a soldier who had an affair with his wife. When Otino learns that his wife was murdered by her lover, he is angry because he cannot kill her himself. The narrator feels callous and degraded because he sees suffering and tragedy around him but cannot respond to it. Solitude, a constant theme in Pavese's work, is the real prison that cuts him off from others.

"THE LEATHER JACKET"

Problems with women preoccupy many of the imprisoned men, and women increasingly become central in Pavese's writing. Women are often the center of his tragedies. One of Pavese's favorite retreats was the Po River. The Po provided the backdrop for several stories, as a beautiful setting for contemplation and solitude or as an uncaring witness to horror. In "La giacchetta di cuoio" ("The Leather Jacket"), a boy, Pino, recalls his hero Ceresa, who ran a boat-dock café and lived with the spiteful and unfaithful Nora. Pino records but does not fully comprehend the tragedy that he witnesses. With the typical indirection that one finds in Pavese's stories, Pino describes Ceresa, framed in a window confronting a person whom the boy cannot see and then later in a boat, with Pino mumbling to a fish, "You're no good, either." One feels the tension mounting between Ceresa and Nora. Pino, for reasons that he does not fully understand, is repelled and frightened and stays away from his friend. Finally, he hears that Ceresa has been arrested after killing Nora and throwing her body into the Po.

"SUMMER STORM"

The detachment in "The Leather Jacket" comes through Pino's ability to describe what he cannot understand. In "Temporale d'estate" ("Summer Storm"), Pavese's powerful descriptions of nature distance the reader from human tragedy. Two young women drown in the Po, one of them raped by men who then impassively watch her die.

"WEDDING TRIP"

Many Pavese characters are monstrous experts at psychological brutality. George, the narrator in "Viaggio di nozze" ("Wedding Trip"), recalls his marriage to Cilia. He is a French teacher, trapped by his poverty and loneliness. He marries the poorly educated, adoring Cilia because he thinks that coming home to a woman will relieve the bleakness of his existence. After marriage, George's psychological brutality reduces the bright, cheerful Cilia into a dull, uncomprehending sacrifice to his own failures. She regains some hope when he takes their meager savings to pay for an overnight holiday trip to Genoa. She is bursting with excitement to be with him and to see him happy, but then he leaves her alone in their hotel room while he wanders in the streets all night. Writing after Cilia's death, George is filled with remorse not because of the way he treated Cilia but for himself, condemned again to a lonely, bleak existence.

"SUICIDES"

In "Suicidi" ("Suicides"), the narrator recalls Carlotta, a simple salesclerk who falls in love with him. The narrator had been badly hurt by a woman and avenges himself on Carlotta by humiliating and psychologically punishing her. He tells her of his boyhood friend who made a suicide pact with him. The friend killed himself (as a friend had done when Pavese was a child), and the narrator ran off and lived. The narrator breaks up with Carlotta in a humiliating and brutal fashion and later hears that she has committed suicide. The remorse he feels is not for Carlotta but for himself.

"THE FAMILY"

Pavese's narrators are saved from being dismissed as uninteresting misogynists because they usually perceive that the problem rests with themselves and not with the women. Often, they are addicted to solitude while feeling the need for human connection. In "La famiglia" ("The Family"), Pavese explores his fear of relationships with women. In this story, he expresses one of his fundamental beliefs: that a person's character never changes, although the person fully realizes that failure to change will lead to disaster.

Corradino (the diminutive of Corrado, indicating the thirty-year-old man's immaturity) meets Cate, a woman with whom he had a love affair years before, when she was young and shy. Now she is an attractive, self-possessed, charming woman, supporting herself and her child, Dino. Cate's maturity is in striking contrast to Corradino's irresponsibility and lack of direction. Corradino is again attracted to Cate and feels remorse for the way he has treated people, especially women.

Then Cate reveals to him that Dino is his son. Corradino is stunned, panicked by a feeling that his freedom is threatened and that he is faced with a responsibility that is beyond his ability to assume. Cate, knowing him well, breaks the news to him gently and wants nothing from him. Corradino withdraws into self-contemplation and self-accusation; he knows that he suffers in comparison with Cate. His self-loathing grows, but he cannot change. Cate goes on with her life. A few days later, Corradino is pursuing another woman.

As Pavese became more confident as a writer, and perhaps as his inner turmoil increased, he often used his stories to examine childhood. These stories were usually set in the country village, like that of Santo Stefano Belbo. Pavese wrote beautifully of nature, "Il mare" ("The Sea"), and of the rustic way of life, although he did not hide its hard, bleak side—"Notti di festa" ("Festival Night") and "Il campo di granturco" ("The Cornfield"). Sometimes, his narrators were thrust back into memories of early love, as in "Villa in Collina" ("The Villa on the Hill"), or of adult figures that shape their lives, as in "L'eremita" ("The Hermit"), "Mister Peter," and "Told in Confidence."

In many of these stories, the narrators try to recreate in their minds formative events of their past. Pavese believes that human nature does not change; age only flakes away the superfluous and reveals more clearly what one has always been. Children are more closely in touch with the mythic life of humanity than are adults. Formative experiences shape chil-

dren, creating personal mythic structures that control the rest of their lives.

"FREE WILL"

In "Free Will," Pavese explains his theory of human nature and perhaps reveals something of the nature of his own solipsism and his habit of indulging in harsh verbal self-laceration. Alexis, who hates children, derides the idea of free will. He is enraged to think that even while they are playing, children are forming, like a coral reef below the surface, a structure that controls their entire future. Alexis recalls that when as a child he was punished, the whole world seemed to exist only to torture him, "and the thought pleased me so keenly that I wouldn't have changed it for any comforting kisses from anyone at all." What does this mean, however, for the development of his personality? "I could feel like that then, and there was no harm in it," Alexis says. "But what if one is still doing it at fifteen, eighteen, or twenty-five? This wallowing in self-pity like a sponge soaking up water, is it harmless, or something to be ashamed of?"

The narrator, who rejects Alexis's theory that one is completely shaped and controlled by childhood events, goes to comfort his own son, whom he had earlier punished for some minor infraction. He sees in his son's aloof rejection of his comfort confirmation of Alexis's theory.

"FIRST LOVE"

In "Primo amore" ("First Love"), Pavese shows how sex and violence are forever joined in a sensitive young boy. Berto, a village boy, meets Nino, a sophisticated boy visiting from the city. They roam the countryside together, and Berto is vaguely attracted to Nino's older sisters, especially Clara. Both boys worship the handsome, macho chauffeur, Bruno. One of their vindictive companions, a blacksmith's son, takes them to an abandoned house where he tells them that they can watch two people having sex. As they look on in longing and revulsion, they realize that the naked pair is Bruno and Clara. In explosive rage, they turn on the blacksmith's son. Berto is covered with blood, and Nino has his arm broken. Sex comes to them as an expression of violence and shame, not love.

"THE END OF AUGUST"

One of Pavese's most provocative stories of childhood sheds light on his attitude toward women. In "Fine d'agosto" ("The End of August"), the narrator walks with his lover, Clara, on a warm summer evening. The pleasant breeze brings back memories of his childhood. He withdraws into solitude and loneliness. Clara, with insight into his mood, allows him to be by himself. Later, he joins her, and they sit before the window with the breeze wafting over them.

Suddenly, his affection for Clara turns to hatred: "There is something in my recollections of childhood that cannot endure the carnal tenderness of any woman, not even Clara." The narrator explains: "There was a boy (myself?) who used to stroll along the sea-shore at night, captivated by the music and the unrealistic lighting of the cafés, enjoying the wind. . . . That boy could exist without me, indeed he *did* exist without me, unaware that his delight would bloom again after so many years, incredibly, for someone else, a man." Yet between boyhood and manhood comes sexual awareness, which the man knows but the boy does not. The man cannot regain contact with the boy that dwells within him. "Clara, poor girl, loved me very much that night. She always did. . . . But by this time I could no longer forgive her for being a woman, one capable of transmuting the far-away scent of the wind into the smell of flesh."

In "The End of August," Pavese brings together his main concerns: the power and importance of nature in human life, childhood as the key to self-knowledge, and the difficulty of forming relationships with women. The tragedies that inevitably occur in life stem from the immutable fact, Pavese believes, that after childhood one's nature can never change.

OTHER MAJOR WORKS

LONG FICTION: *Paesi tuoi*, 1941 (*The Harvesters*, 1961); *La spiaggia*, 1942 (*The Beach*, 1963); *Il compagno*, 1947 (*The Comrade*, 1959); *Il carcere*, 1949 (*The Political Prisoner*, 1959); *La bella estate*, 1949 (includes *La bella estate* [*The Beautiful Summer*, 1959], *Il diavolo sulla colline* [*The Devil in the Hills*, 1954], *Tra donne sole* [*Among Women Only*,

1953]); *Prima che il gallo canti*, 1949 (includes *Il carcere* [*The Political Prisoner*, 1955], *La casa in collina* [*The House on the Hill*, 1956]); *La Luna e i falò*, 1950 (*The Moon and the Bonfire*, 1952); *Fuoco grande*, 1959 (with Bianca Garufi; *A Great Fire*, 1963); *The Selected Works of Cesare Pavese*, 1968.

POETRY: *Lavorare stanca*, 1936, 1943 (*Hard Labor*, 1976); *La terra e la morte*, 1947; *Verrà la morte e avrà i tuoi occhi*, 1951; *Poesie edite e inedite*, 1962; *A Mania for Solitude: Selected Poems, 1930-1950*, 1969.

NONFICTION: *Dialoghi con Leucò*, 1947 (*Dialogues with Leucò*, 1966); *La letteratura amiricana e altri saggi*, 1951 (*American Literature: Essays and Opinions*, 1970); *Il mestiere di vivere: Diario, 1935-1950*, 1952 (*The Business of Living: Diaries, 1935-1950*, 1961; also known as *The Burning Brand: Diaries, 1935-1950*, 1961); *Lettere*, 1966 (partially translated as *Selected Letters, 1924-1950*, 1969).

TRANSLATIONS: *Il nostro signor Wrenn*, 1931 (of Sinclair Lewis's *Our Mr. Wrenn*); *Moby-Dick*, 1932 (of Herman Melville's *Moby Dick*); *Riso nero*, 1932 (of Sherwood Anderson's *Dark Laughter*); *Il 42° parallelo*, 1935 (of John Dos Passos's *Forty-second Parallel*); *U omini e topi*, 1938 (of John Steinbeck's *Of Mice and Men*); *Tre esistenze*, 1940 (of Gertrude Stein's *Three Lives*); *Il borgo*, 1942 (of William Faulkner's *The Hamlet*).

BIBLIOGRAPHY

Biasin, Gian-Paolo. *The Smile of the Gods: A Thematic Study of Cesare Pavese's Works*. Translated by Yvonne Freccero. Ithaca, N.Y.: Cornell University Press, 1968. This excellent study focuses on the importance of mythology in Pavese's thinking and provides a guide to the major themes in his work.

Fiedler, Leslie A. "Introducing Cesare Pavese." *The Kenyon Review* 16 (Autumn, 1954): 536-553. Fiedler is credited with introducing Pavese to the American reading public. He stresses his importance to the Italian and European literary world and places him in his world literary context.

Giobbi, Giuliana. "Pavese and Joyce: Exile, Myth, and the Past." *Journal of European Studies* 21

(March, 1991): 43-53. Discusses literary parallels between James Joyce and Pavese, especially in terms of their sense of social alienation and their relationship to the past.

Lajolo, Davide. *An Absurd Vice: A Biography of Cesare Pavese*. New York: New Directions, 1983. Lajolo was a friend of Pavese and his first biographer. His friendship with Pavese gave him special insights, but later scholars distrusted some of his psychological and political speculations about Pavese.

O'Healy, Áine. *Cesare Pavese*. Boston: Twayne, 1988. This short, excellent biography clears away many of the myths about Pavese. It is an excellent place to begin a study of Pavese and his work.

Rubin, Merle. "Timeless Themes." *The Christian Science Monitor*, June 8, 1990, 15. A review of *Dialogues with Leucò*, commenting on the themes of the dialogues about Greek mythology; discusses the themes of the difference between Greek gods who have no fear of death and men and women haunted by their mortality; comments on the contrast between the old mythological era of the Titans and the new dispensation of the Olympians.

Simborowski, Nicoletta. "From 'La famiglia' to the *Tacculino* and *La casa in collina*: Pavese and the Need to Confess." *The Modern Language Review* 92 (January, 1997): 70-85. Discusses links between the author's secret notebooks and his fiction that suggest a confessional element, an admission of guilt regarding anti-activist sentiments during World War II.

Thompson, Doug. *Cesare Pavese: A Study of the Major Novels and Poems*. New York: Cambridge University Press, 1982. Thompson avoids many of the biographical myths that marred many studies of Pavese. His clear, insightful study locates the major themes that run through all of Pavese's work.

William E. Pemberton

SUSAN PERABO

Born: St. Louis, Missouri; January 6, 1969

PRINCIPAL SHORT FICTION

Who I Was Supposed to Be: Short Stories, 1999

OTHER LITERARY FORMS

In *Writers in the Schools: A Guide to Teaching Creative Writing in the Classroom* (1998), Susan Perabo provides hands-on exercises and activities for use with students in creative writing classes.

ACHIEVEMENTS

Susan Perabo's stories have been anthologized in *New Stories from the South* and in *Best American Short Stories 1996*. Her work has appeared in *Story*, *Glimmer Train*, *TriQuarterly*, and *The Black Warrior Review*. She was the 1992 winner of the Henfield/Transatlantic Review Award.

BIOGRAPHY

Susan Perabo was born on January 6, 1969, in St. Louis, Missouri. She graduated from Webster University in Missouri. Because the college did not have a women's softball team, Perabo played on the men's baseball team. Her brief career as the first woman to play NCAA baseball earned her a spot in the Baseball Hall of Fame in Cooperstown, New York. The following year she joined a women's club team. She received her master of fine arts degree in creative writing from the University of Arkansas, Fayetteville. She taught creative writing at Dickinson College in Carlisle, Pennsylvania, where she became an assistant professor and writer-in-residence. In addition to teaching fiction workshops, she teaches literature courses in contemporary fiction and serves as a faculty advisor for the Belles Lettres Literary Society and *The Dickinson Review*.

ANALYSIS

As an introduction to her collection of stories, Susan Perabo quotes these lines from James Baldwin's "Sonny's Blues":

> For while the tale of how we suffer, and how we are delighted, and how we may triumph is never new, it always must be heard. There isn't any other tale to tell, it's the only light we've got in all this darkness.

Perabo presents the reader with characters who suffer in various situations and in many cases achieve a type of triumph.

She tells these stores from different points of view, employing both male and female narrators of varying ages and circumstances. Typically, her stories begin with a short, attention-getting sentence such as this opening line from "Explaining Death to the Dog": "After the baby died, I found it imperative that my German shepherd Stu understand and accept the concept of death." Another typical device is the twist that appears at the end of a number of the stories. A woman who travels to her hometown to deal with her mother's problems discovers hope for her own life. A father, who has been so distracted by his own thoughts that he has lost touch with his family, is surprised by the actions of his twin sons. Perabo creates desperate characters who often deal in unusual ways with the hardships of everyday life. In their attempts to survive painful situations, they try to escape from reality. Sharp dialogue reveals the complicated relationships between friends, parents and children, husbands and wives. At times the snatches of dialogue add a touch of humor.

"THICK AS THIEVES"

The narrator of "Thick as Thieves," Jack, a fifty-nine-year-old Hollywood actor whose career is in a slump, is having problems with his fourth wife. The theme of alienation is dominant here as shown in Jack's failure to maintain personal relationships. His wife tells him that he makes her feel empty, and he has had very little contact with his father, a retired grocer. In an attempt to make contact with his father, Jack invites him to come for a visit. Jack has seven cars, owns paintings worth forty thousand dollars, and lives in a twenty-four-room mansion in a very

wealthy area. When the neighbors' security camera catches his father in the act of stealing jewelry, Jack makes excuses for him, saying that his father may be a victim of Alzheimer's disease. Admitting that he has done this before, the father tells Jack that he steals for the thrill of it, that it is "the purest thrill you'd ever know." He does not sell the jewelry, but gives it to the old women who live in his retirement community and bake cookies for him. When Jack returns the neighbors' jewelry, he holds back one piece, which he puts in his father's pocket. Later, when Jack attends his father's funeral, he notices that many of the old women, dressed in ordinary house dresses and worn coats, are wearing expensive jewelry. Jack recognizes some of the pieces as jewelry that belonged to his wife. This story represents one of Perabo's major themes, the desire to reinvent oneself. Just as Jack's career has allowed him to assume different identities, his father has chosen to live the life of a thief because it provides excitement. When Jack complains that he does not even know who his father is, the old man replies, "I'm anybody I want to be."

"COUNTING THE WAYS"

Joel and Katy, the young married couple in "Counting the Ways," inherit twenty-eight thousand dollars when Katy's mother dies. Although they might have used the money as a down payment on a house, Katy decides to purchase one of Princess Diana's dresses. They put the dress on a mannequin and prop it up in their bedroom. Katy is an example of another character who tries to reinvent herself by creating a fantasy life that allows her to escape from the pressures of her ordinary life. At first the dress provides a sense of excitement and pleasure for the young couple, but soon the dress begins to lose its magic. When Katy hears the news of Diana's death, the dress no longer provides a sense of joy. Joel has been caught up in the fantasy but becomes more practical when he sees a chance to make a profit on the dress, thereby enabling the couple to buy a house and have a better life. The couple has reached a turning point in their lives, but Katy, unwilling to give up her fantasy life, refuses to sell the dress.

"THE MEASURE OF DEVOTION"

The narrator of "The Measure of Devotion," David Peabody, is working as an automobile tour guide at Gettysburg when Mrs. Spencer, the mother of his high school friend, Gwen, appears with Gwen's children. Mrs. Spencer introduces David to the children with the phrase, "This is the man that should have been your daddy." During the course of the tour, Mrs. Spencer tells David of the problems Gwen has experienced with drugs and failed relationships. When David insists that he and Gwen were only friends, Mrs. Spencer says she knows that he was in love with her. The theme of alienation is evident in the relationship between Gwen and her mother and in Gwen's inability to maintain relationships. When he is alone, David reflects on the night Gwen left town with another boy, while he "just lay there dying all night long while she was getting farther and farther away." Now happily married with a beautiful wife, a home of his own, and a child, David can say to himself, "She got what she deserved." Gwen has messed up her own life along with the lives of her children, but David has managed to survive. The twist at the end of this story is David's reaction to the news of Gwen's misfortunes.

"THE ROCKS OVER KYBURZ"

In "The Rocks over Kyburz" Ray, a high school band director, is so dissatisfied with his job and his life that he escapes into dreams of the past when he was smoking pot and playing in bands. He spends his time thinking of ways he can change his life as he watches "images float by in his head like a memory that hadn't happened yet." He is so caught up in his own unhappiness that he has lost contact with his fifteen-year-old twin sons. When a neighbor confronts Ray with the accusation that his sons are smoking pot with her teenage daughter, Ray and his wife deny the charges. One night Ray follows the boys up the mountain path to a place where the family used to have picnics and discovers that both boys are having sex with the girl. The central image of the story is the mountain path with its twin rocks, each the size of a house, that balance precariously on a flat rock underneath. At one time there had been four rocks, but many years ago two had fallen, "crushing everything in their path." The story ends with the image of the rocks, as Ray thinks of the future, when "the steadiest

thing he knew" would "shift free of its roots and roll blindly toward all of them."

"THE GREATER GRACE OF CARLISLE"

"The Greater Grace of Carlisle" opens with the following line: "My mother, beside herself with loss, spent thirty-five thousand dollars on lottery tickets in nine months." Hildy, the narrator's widowed mother, is like many of Perabo's characters who act in bizarre ways in an attempt to change their lives or deal with loneliness and depression. Short snatches of dialogue between mother and daughter provide a touch of humor. Kathy, the daughter, learns that Hildy has sold her mother's silver, her husband's stock, and her car to finance her lottery purchases. When Kathy asks how much money is left, Hildy replies "Enough to buy you a plane ticket back to Phoenix." Carlisle is a small town in Illinois with a sign which reads "Home of the 3A Cross Country District Champs, 1984, Go Bees." When she goes to a Gamblers Anonymous meeting with her mother, Kathy meets Andy, a member of that 1984 team, who has remained in the hometown. As she sits with him on the bank of the pond in the park, Kathy feels a sense of hope for her own life.

OTHER MAJOR WORKS

LONG FICTION: *The Broken Pieces*, 2000.

NONFICTION: *Writers in the Schools: A Guide to Teaching Creative Writing in the Classroom*, 1998.

BIBLIOGRAPHY

Fichtner, Margaria. "*Who I Was Supposed to Be: Short Stories* by Susan Perabo." Review of *Who I Was Supposed to Be*, by Susan Perabo. *The Miami Herald*, August 4, 1999. In her review of Perabo's short-story collection Fichtner provides brief summaries of several stories and credits Perabo with keen insight into the lives of her troubled characters.

Golden, Jay. "*Who I Was Supposed to Be:* Stories by Susan Perabo." Review of *Who I Was Supposed to Be*, by Susan Perabo. *Fort Worth Star Telegram*, October 20, 1999. Sees Perabo's strength in her ability to provide twists that catch the reader off guard. Golden comments on her light touch and ironic humor and calls her stories "quirky and engaging."

"Short Stories Show Off Young Author Waiting for Growth Spurt." *Chicago Tribune*, September 10, 1999. Calling Perabo's stories "tough-minded and clever," this reviewer notes that Perabo grabs the reader's attention with intriguing first sentences. The theme that connects the stories is the characters' need for "reinvention."

"*Who I Was Supposed to Be:* Short Fictions." Review of *Who I Was Supposed to Be*, by Susan Perabo. *Publishers Weekly* 246 (July 9, 1999): 186. Points to Perabo's ability to narrate her stories from different points of view, using narrators of different ages and genders. Notes that Perabo relieves the tragic with the whimsical as she provides the reader with characters who face difficult situations.

Judith Barton Williamson

S. J. PERELMAN

Born: Brooklyn, New York; February 1, 1904
Died: New York, New York; October 17, 1979

PRINCIPAL SHORT FICTION

Dawn Ginsbergh's Revenge, 1929
Parlor, Bedlam and Bath, 1930 (with Quentin J. Reynolds)
Strictly from Hunger, 1937
Look Who's Talking, 1940
The Dream Department, 1943
Crazy Like a Fox, 1944
Keep It Crisp, 1946
Acres and Pains, 1947
Westward Ha! Or, Around the World in Eighty Clichés, 1948
Listen to the Mocking Bird, 1949
The Swiss Family Perelman, 1950
A Child's Garden of Curses, 1951
The Ill-Tempered Clavichord, 1952
Hold That Christmas Tiger!, 1954
Perelman's Home Companion, 1955
The Road to Miltown: Or, Under the Spreading Atrophy, 1957
The Most of S. J. Perelman, 1958
The Rising Gorge, 1961
Chicken Inspector No. 23, 1966

Baby, It's Cold Inside, 1970
Vinegar Puss, 1975
Eastward Ha!, 1977

OTHER LITERARY FORMS

S. J. Perelman's more than twenty-five books include essays, stories, plays, and an autobiography. He has also written screenplays for film and television, and he is best known for his work with the Marx Brothers on *Monkey Business* (1931) and *Horse Feathers* (1932).

ACHIEVEMENTS

S. J. Perelman was a highly successful and well-loved humorist whose best writing appeared in *The New Yorker* and then was collected in popular books for five decades, from the 1930's to the 1970's. He wrote the book upon which the Broadway hit *One Touch of Venus* (1943) was based, and he wrote one other acclaimed Broadway comedy, *The Beauty Part* (1961). For his contribution to *Around the World in Eighty Days*, he shared an Academy Award in 1956 and also received a New York Film Critics Award. In 1978, he received the special National Book Award for his lifetime contribution to American literature.

Perelman's influence on other writers is difficult

to measure because, although he was the leader of the "dementia praecox" school of humor closely associated with *The New Yorker*, he was not the inventor of the techniques of verbal humor he used so well, and his type of writing has been on the decline. There seem to be clear mutual influences between Perelman and several of his contemporaries: James Thurber, Dorothy Parker, Groucho Marx, and Nathanael West, his brother-in-law. French Surrealists admired his style, and contemporary black humorists often use the techniques he mastered; but one hesitates to assert direct influence on writers such as Joseph Heller and Kurt Vonnegut. Perelman's type of writing seems to have been taken over by television, film, and perhaps the New Journalism. Woody Allen admired Perelman and is often mentioned as one of his disciples. In his critiques of American style, Perelman may be a predecessor of writers such as Tom Wolfe, Hunter Thompson, and Terry Southern.

S. J. Perelman (Library of Congress)

BIOGRAPHY

Sidney Joseph Perelman was born in Brooklyn, New York, on February 1, 1904, the son of Sophia Charren and Joseph Perelman, a Jewish poultry farmer. He briefly attended Brown University, where he edited the *College Humor* magazine. After leaving the university in 1925, he began his career as a writer and cartoonist for *Judge* magazine. Following a brief time at *College Humor* and his marriage to Laura Weinstein on July 4, 1929, he began writing full time, and in 1931 became a regular contributor to *The New Yorker* and other major magazines. Their marriage produced a son and a daughter. He worked occasionally in Hollywood, writing motion-picture screenplays, but he spent most of his life in New York City and on his Pennsylvania farm. He collaborated to write several successful plays; his usual collaborator on films as well as plays was his wife, although on *One Touch of Venus*, he worked with Ogden Nash, and for a television musical, *Aladdin*, with Cole Porter.

After his wife's death in 1970, Perelman lived for two years in England but then returned to Manhattan, where he remained until his death on October 17, 1979.

ANALYSIS

Parody, satire, and verbal wit characterize S. J. Perelman's works. Most of them are very short and tend to begin as conversational essays that develop into narrative or mock dramatic episodes and sometimes return to essay. Perelman called them *feuilletons* (little leaves), "comic essays of a particular type." They seem formally related to the earliest American forms of short story, Benjamin Franklin's bagatelles and early American humor. Norris Yates best summarizes the worldview reflected in Perelman's work: Perelman values normal life, "integrity, sincerity, skepticism, taste, a respect for competence, a striving after the golden mean, and a longing for better communication and understanding among men." Yates sees Perelman's typical persona (the "I" of the pieces) as a Little Man resisting the forces of American cultural life which would "invade and corrupt his personality and impel him toward neuroses," the forces which seem determined to destroy the values Perelman holds. According to Yates, these forces manifest themselves for Perelman most decisively in "the mass media, which are, on the whole, the offspring of technology's unconsecrated marriage with Big Business."

Perelman's "autobiographical" work reveals his version of the Little Man. A favorite type of *The New Yorker* humorists, the Little Man is a caricature of a typical middle-class, early twentieth century American male, usually represented as helpless before the complexities of technological society, cowed by its crass commercialism, dominated by desperate, unfulfilled women, sustaining himself on heroic fantasies of a bygone or imaginary era. James Thurber's Walter Mitty has become the classic presentation of this character type. Perelman's personae seem related to the type, but vary in several significant ways.

ACRES AND PAINS

In *Acres and Pains*, the major collection of his adventures on his farm, he makes his persona into a city dweller who has naïvely tried to realize a romantic agrarian dream on his country estate, but who has come to see the error of his ways. Perelman uses this reversal of the rube in the city to debunk a sentimental picture of country life by exaggerating his trials. Many episodes show good country people betraying the ideal with which they are associated. Contractors, antique dealers, and barn painters rob him of purse and peace. "Perelman" differs from the Little Man type in that, although he may at any time fall victim to another illusion, he knows and admits that country life is no romance. In these sketches, he also differs from the Little Man type in his relationship to wife and family. He is not dominated by a frustrated woman. He and his wife are usually mutual victims of pastoral illusion, although often she suffers more than he.

This "Perelman" is most like the typical Little Man when he deals with machines. For example, when his water pump goes berserk during a dinner party, he handles the problem with successful incompetence: "By exerting a slight leverage, I succeeded in prying off the gasket or outer jacket of the pump, exactly as you would a baked potato. . . . This gave me room to poke around the innards with a sharp stick. I cleaned the pump thoroughly . . . and, as a final precaution, opened the windows to allow the water to drain down the slope." The major difference between this persona and Walter Mitty is that the former is competent; he escapes neurosis and resists with some success his crazy world. By splitting the narrator into a present sophisticate (a mask that often slips) and a former fool, he tends to shift the butt of humor away from the present narrator and toward the man who believes in romantic ideals and toward the people who so completely fail to live up to any admirable ideals. The latter are typified by the contractor who digs "Perelman's" pool in a bad place although he knows the best place for it. Asked why he offered his advice when the pool was dynamited rather than before it was begun, he virtuously replies. "It don't pay to poke your nose in other people's business." Implied in these tall tales of mock pastoral life are criticisms of the values which oppose those Yates lists: dishonesty, hypocrisy, greed, naïveté, incompetence, overenthusiasm, deliberately created confusion, and lying.

Looking over the full range of Perelman's first-person sketches, one sees significant variation in the presentation of the persona. In *Acres and Pains*, the narrator is much more concrete than in many other sketches in which the "I" is virtually an empty mind waiting to take shape under the power of some absurd mass-media language. Perelman is acutely sensitive to this language as a kind of oppression. Many of his sketches explore "sub-dialects" of American English in order to expose and ridicule the values that underlie them. "Tomorrow—Fairly Cloudy" is a typical example of the author's probing of a sample of American language.

"TOMORROW—FAIRLY CLOUDY"

In "Tomorrow—Fairly Cloudy," Perelman notices a new advertisement for a toothpaste which promises its users rescue from humdrum ordinary life and elevation into romance and success. In his introduction,

Perelman emphasizes the absurdity of taking such ads seriously, describes the ad in detail, then introduces a dramatic scenario by observing that this ad heralds the coming demise of a desperate industry: "So all the old tactics have finally broken down—wheedling, abuse, snobbery and terror. I look forward to the last great era in advertising, a period packed with gloom, defeatism, and frustration. . . ." In the following spectacle, the children bubble excited "adese" while father despairs over his drab life:

BOBBY—Oh, Moms, I'm so glad you and Dads decided to install a Genfeedco automatic oil burner and air conditioner with the new self-ventilating screen flaps plus finger control! It is noiseless, cuts down heating bills, and makes the air we breathe richer in vita-ray particles. . . .

MR. BRADLEY (tonelessly)—Well, I suppose anything is better than a heap of slag at this end of the cellar.

Soon the Fletchers arrive to sneer at their towels and to make the Bradleys aware of all the products they do not have. The sketch ends in apocalypse as their inferior plumbing gives way, and they all drown in their combination cellar and playroom. It remains unclear throughout whether this episode forecasts the forms of future advertising or its effects on the public.

Perelman exposes the absurdity of this language of conspicuous consumption by imagining its literal acceptance. In the world this language implies, happiness is possessing the right gadgets. If sales are to continue, it must be impossible for most people ever to have all the right things, and so impossible ever to be happy. The Bradleys have the right oil burner, but their towels disintegrate in two days, and they failed to use Sumwenco Super-Annealed Brass Pipe. This last omission costs them their lives. Not only their happiness but also their very survival depend on their ability to possess the right new product.

"ENTERED AS SECOND-CLASS MATTER"

Perelman's many sketches of this type culminate perhaps in "Entered as Second-Class Matter," which is apparently a montage of fragments lifted (and, one hopes, sometimes fabricated) from magazine fiction and advertising. The resulting silliness may be intended as a portrait of the mass feminine mind

as perceived by American magazines, 1930-1944. It ends:

We have scoured the fiction market to set before you *Three Million Tiny Sweat Glands Functioning* in that vibrant panorama of tomorrow so that *Your Sensitive Bowel Muscles Can* react to the inevitable realization that only by enrichment and guidance *plus a soothing depilatory* can America face its problems confidently, unafraid, *well-groomed mouth-happy, breaking hair off at the roots without undue stench. Okay, Miss America!*

In such pieces, Perelman's values are clearly those Yates names. Especially important in these works is the humorous attempt to clear away the garbage of American language culture through ridicule. This aim is central to the series "Cloudland Revisited," in which he reexamines the popular literature of his youth. Perelman varies this formula with attacks on absurd fashion and the language of fashion, one of the best of which is "Farewell, My Lovely Appetizer."

VERBAL WIT

Perelman is deservedly most admired for his faculty of verbal wit. In several of his more conventional stories which seem less restrained by satiric ends, his playfulness dazzles. Among the best of these are "The Idol's Eye," "Seedlings of Desire," and "The Love Decoy." Based on the sensational plots of teen-romance, "The Love Decoy" is narrated by a coed who seeks revenge on an instructor who once failed to make a pass and who later humiliated her before her classmates by accusing her of "galvanizing around nights." Her plan is to lure him to her room after hours, then expose him as a corrupter of undergraduates. This plan backfires in a *non sequitur* when a lecherous dean arrives to assault her. The reader expects the plot to complicate, but instead it is transformed when the dean is unmasked as Jim the Penman who framed the girl's father and sent him to the pen. Other identities are revealed, and the reader arrives at the end of a detective thriller. Although there is parody here of sentimental language and plot, the story seems more intent on fun than ridicule. It contains a number of Perelman's most celebrated witticisms. For example:

He caught my arm in a vice-like grip and drew me to him, but with a blow I sent him groveling. In ten minutes he was back with a basket of appetizing fresh picked grovels. We squeezed them and drank the piquant juice thirstily.

At the center of this wit is the double entendre. Multiple meanings of words suggest the multiple contexts in which they may apply. Perelman juxtaposes these contexts, makes rapid shifts between them, and sometimes uses a suggestion to imagine a new context. The effects are sometimes surreal. The double meaning of "sent" suggests a transformation from a blow to the groin to an activity such as berrying. "Groveling" gathers an imaginary context which generates a new noun, "grovels." While this reading seems most plausible, in another reading there are no transformations, and gathering grovels becomes a euphemistic way to describe the amorous instructor's reaction to her literal attack or to her unusually expressed affection.

Perelman creates this slipperiness of meaning and encourages it to reverberate in this passage and in the language and structure of the whole work. One result is a heightened alertness in the reader to the ambiguity of language and the elusiveness of meaning, a first but important step on the way to the sort of respect for language Perelman implies in his many critiques of its abuses. This concern connects Perelman most closely with James Joyce, whom he considered the greatest modern comic writer, with a number of his contemporaries, including William Faulkner and Thurber. While Perelman has not the stature of these great writers, he shares with them a consciousness of the peculiar problems of modern life and a belief that how one uses language is important to recognizing and dealing with those problems. Among *The New Yorker* humorists with whom S. J. Perelman is associated, he is probably one of the lesser lights, showing neither the versatility, the variety, nor the universality of Dorothy Parker or of Thurber. Although critical estimates of his achievement vary, there is general agreement that his best work, done mostly before 1950, shows a marvelous gift for verbal wit.

OTHER MAJOR WORKS

PLAYS: *The Night Before Christmas*, pr. 1941 (with Laura Perelman); *One Touch of Venus*, pr. 1943 (with Ogden Nash); *The Beauty Part*, pr. 1961.

SCREENPLAYS: *Monkey Business*, 1931; *Horse Feathers*, 1932; *Around the World in Eighty Days*, 1956.

NONFICTION: *The Last Laugh*, 1981; *Don't Tread on Me: Selected Letters of S. J. Perelman*, 1987.

MISCELLANEOUS: *That Old Gang O' Mine: The Early and Essential S. J. Perelman*, 1984 (Richard Marschall, editor).

BIBLIOGRAPHY

Epstein, Joseph. "Sid, You Made the Prose Too Thin." *Commentary* 84 (September, 1987): 53-60. A biographical sketch of Perelman, suggesting that his best writing occurred when he was angry, as in *Acres and Pains*, a collection of stories about an idealistic city man being taken advantage of by rural hustlers; claims that elsewhere his natural penchant for gloom, suspicion, and pessimism led him merely to make wisecracks about banal subjects or unpleasantly callous pokes at barely disguised real people.

Fowler, Douglas. *S. J. Perelman*. Boston: Twayne, 1983. This critical study examines influences on Perelman, the development of his career, his relationships with his contemporaries, his technique, and his importance. Includes a chronology, a biographical sketch, and an annotated bibliography.

Gale, Steven. *S. J. Perelman: A Critical Study*. New York: Greenwood Press, 1987. Gale examines Perelman's prose, screenplays, and plays, then studies his themes and techniques. Gale gives special attention to Perelman's background in Jewish humor and his use of clichés and allusions. The volume is supplemented by a chronology and a bibliographic essay.

_____. *S. J. Perelman: An Annotated Bibliography*. New York: Garland, 1985. This useful, annotated bibliography lists 650 Perelman publications and 380 items written about Perelman.

Gale, Steven H., ed. *S. J. Perelman: Critical Essays*.

New York: Garland, 1992. Includes two dozen essays, articles, and critiques of Perelman from academic studies, newspapers, and popular journals over a seventy-year period of his career. Gale's introduction places Perelman in the tradition of such great humorists as Sir Geoffrey Chaucer and Mark Twain.

Herrmann, Dorothy. _S. J. Perelman: A Life_. New York: Putnam, 1986. This complete biography makes use of recollections of his acquaintances to shed light on the life of a very private man. It includes select bibliographies of writing by and about Perelman.

Newquist, Roy. _Conversations_. New York: Rand McNally, 1967. In this interview, Perelman talks about the writers he most admires, such as Mark Twain, Ring Lardner, and Robert Charles Benchley.

Perelman, S. J. _Conversations with S. J. Perelman_. Edited by Tom Teicholz. Jackson: University Press of Mississippi, 1995. A collection of interviews with the author.

Plimpton, George, ed. _Writers at Work: The Paris Review Interviews, Second Series_. New York: Viking, 1963. In an interview appearing on pages 241-256, Perelman offers glimpses into his creative process and his artistic purposes.

Yates, Norris Wilson. "The Sane Psychoses of S. J. Perelman." In _The American Humorist: Conscience of the Twentieth Century_. Ames: Iowa State University Press, 1964. Though this study has to some extent been superseded by more extensive and later works, it still provides a good, brief introduction to Perelman.

Terry Heller

ISAAC LEIB PERETZ

Born: Zamość, Poland, Russian Empire; May 18, 1852
Died: Warsaw, Poland; April 3, 1915

PRINCIPAL SHORT FICTION

Bekannte Bilder, 1890
Dos shtreimel, 1896
Stories and Pictures, 1906
Bontshe the Silent and Other Stories, 1927
Peretz, 1947 (_Stories from Peretz_, 1964)
Three Gifts and Other Stories, 1947
The Three Canopies, 1948
As Once We Were: Selections from the Works of I. L. Peretz, 1951
In This World and the Next: Selected Writings, 1958
The Book of Fire: Stories by I. L. Peretz, 1960
Selected Stories, 1974

OTHER LITERARY FORMS

Although best known for his short stories—especially the quintessential tale "Bontsha the Silent"—Isaac Peretz was a noted playwright, poet, essayist, and ideologue in two languages. He wrote prolifically in Hebrew and Yiddish, and only the novel form escaped his sustained attack. In 1888, his mock-heroic poem _Monish_ (1888), published under the auspices of Sholom Aleichem, demonstrated his ability to express themes from Jewish life with the sophistication derived from secular literary pursuits. His symbolic dramas, such as _Baynakht oyfn altn mark_ (1907; night in the old marketplace), provided further proof of his ability to harmonize diverse traditions. In Warsaw, he published a literary almanac, the first volume of which was distinguished by what he called "Travel Pictures" delineating shtetl life. In the 1890's, Peretz contributed to New York Yiddish journals many poems and stories that were regarded as anticlerical and politically subversive. A subsequent change of heart led him to East European mystical lore, and his writings assumed the manner of Hasidic monologues, symbolic romances, and folkloric sketches. In allegories sometimes defying classification, he sought to penetrate the social concerns of his time, especially those impinging on international Jewish life. His writings are surviving testimony to his broad interests, which encompassed history, science, social welfare, and Jewish national survival.

ACHIEVEMENTS

Although Mendele Mokher Sefarim preceded him as "the father of modern Yiddish fiction" and Sholom Aleichem always surpassed him in popularity, Isaac Peretz's accomplishments remain unique. Sol Liptzin has called Peretz "the great awakener of Yiddish-speaking Jewry," arousing in readers the desire for emancipation from restrictions, whether imposed from without or within. Peretz did not merely console his audience or praise their endurance. He combined in his personality the realism of a successful lawyer with the romantic mysticism of a Hasidic Jew. In a style enriched by the knowledge of Polish, Russian, German, French, Yiddish, and Hebrew, and with the authority of an enlightened thinker, he spoke in a variety of literary forms. Though he did not always escape the sentimentality and self-pity to which Yiddish literature has generally been prone, he was an intellectual voice and a social conscience, his hope always mingled with skepticism. While his leading antiheroes, those Jewish sufferers such as Bontsha the Silent and Rabbi Moses Leib of Sasov were stock figures of Yiddish fiction, Peretz also pointed beyond the stereotypes, toward the schlemiel as Everyman, which would culminate in James Joyce's great character, Leopold Bloom, the Jew as modern-age Odysseus.

Peretz brought the refinements of mainstream European artistic movements—of naturalism, neo-Romanticism, and Symbolism—into a provincial literature. He endowed his writing with a psychological realism that is reminiscent of Fyodor Dostoevski's. Sholem Asch was one of the first Peretz protégés to reach beyond the shtetl or even the later "golden ghetto" of the more affluent Jewish diaspora to address the Gentile world. It was Peretz's stories that inspired Isaac Bashevis Singer to become a writer instead of a rabbi. "Gimpel the Fool" is "Bontsha" in later incarnation. Bernard Malamud has, in many of his own stories, embellished themes from Peretz, and Saul Bellow's rhetoric also echoes the Yiddish master. Peretz's influence is thus felt by thousands of fiction readers who have never heard his name.

BIOGRAPHY

Isaac Leib Peretz had a strict orthodox education in Hebrew studies. One of his neighbors was so impressed with the genius of his Talmudic interpretations that he gave Isaac the key to his library. Thus, at fifteen, Peretz read his way through the secular learning and fiction of the nineteenth century, in French, German, Polish, and English, which, with the help of dictionaries he found there, he taught himself. When he was eighteen, his father arranged a marriage for him with Sarah Lichtenfeld that ended in divorce in 1876. His father-in-law, Gabriel Yehudah Lichtenfeld, was an intellectual with whom he published a book of poetry. He began the study of law and passed the bar exam in 1877. For a decade he was a practicing attorney, but his license was revoked in 1887 by czarist authorities for alleged radical activities. In 1878 he married Helena Ringelheim and moved to Warsaw in 1889. He was sent by Jan Bloch to make a sociological survey of Jews in the outlying provinces of Poland to refute anti-Semitic charges that Jews controlled the economy. The poverty and starvation Peretz found are recorded in the bleak sketches called "Travel Pictures." From 1891 to the end of his life, he was a clerk in the Jewish Community office, recording burial dates. He was deeply involved in social reform, lecturing, teaching, and founding schools and journals to educate the poor to better their lives.

ANALYSIS

In diction, tone, and narrative perspective, Isaac Peretz valued the understated. He warned his disciples against verbosity, urging them to strip away all superfluous words. His own stories are noted for their brevity, his diction for its precision. His tone is always restrained. His prose style is laconic, virile, and unadorned, yet capable of conveying the most subtle nuances. Before he retold a folktale, he sought out all the variant versions so that he could pare away the rhetorical flourishes and restore it to its essence. The judge at Bontsha's trial is speaking for Peretz's literary philosophy when he calls out, "No metaphors, please!" and later interrupts, "Facts! Facts! Never mind the embellishments!"

Peretz's angle of narration is always strictly controlled so that the events are viewed obliquely, or at a distance, or through a fallible narrator. By thus withholding the full resolution, he intellectually engages the reader. The enigmatic and the paradoxical are inherent in the genre in which Peretz worked: the wisdom story.

Peretz quickened the pace of the Yiddish tale. Instead of leisurely, winding sentences, he used a rush of phrases punctuated by dashes, or energy-charged fragments punctuated by ellipses—for example, the nervous staccato notes in which Bontsha's stepmother is described: "She begrudged him every bite . . . moldy bread . . . gristle of meat . . . she drank coffee with cream. . . ." The ellipsis marks are impregnated with how much has been left unsaid. The very elusiveness is suggestive.

"BONTSHE THE SILENT"

Peretz's most popular story "Bontshe the Silent" is a paradigm for most of his fictions. Its central scene of a last judgment recurs, in some form, in all of his tales. The orthodox tradition in which he had been reared is permeated with the idea of human beings being called after death to account for their behavior on earth. The details of these trials in the heavenly tribunal probably derived from his ten years' experience as a successful lawyer, a decade that certainly familiarized him with court procedure.

The trial, which is dramatized, is preceded by an account of Bontshe's death, which is summarized. The folkloric quality is preserved in the simplicity of diction, in the rhythmic repetitions, in the lack of description, in the unindividuated hero who is a type rather than a character. Without any temporal or spa-

tial specificity, it is set in an unnamed locale which readers recognize as a city because there are crowds. Readers are given no distinguishing characteristics such as physical features; they do not even know what color hair or eyes Bontshe has. Peretz has honored all the folktale conventions, in which the heroes exist only to enact the plot, and any extraneous details would only distract from their function.

Bontshe's function is to enact passivity; he is, therefore, mute. His inarticulateness is stressed by implied relationships with subhuman things. His death is no more noticed than if a grain of sand had blown away; the collapse of a horse would have aroused more interest. "In his eyes there was a doglike supplication." Even nature is indifferent to his existence. His footprints have left no impression in the dust, and the wind has blown away the wooden marker over his grave. "In silence he was born, in silence he lived, in silence he died." No glasses clinked at his circumcision; no speeches were made at his Bar Mitzvah.

The uncomplaining porter, bowed down from a lifetime of bearing others' burdens, is welcomed into paradise by a blast from the great trumpet of the Messiah. Bontshe is terrified, convinced that they have mistaken him for someone else. Because of the ringing in his ears, he cannot hear his defending angel, but slowly he begins to recognize aspects of his life as they are recounted. Starved by a cruel stepmother, beaten by a drunken father, run over by the very man whose life he had saved, and abandoned by his wife after the birth of her illegitimate child whom he reared, only to have the child throw him out of his own house, Bontshe has never complained. The prosecutor says that because Bontshe has suffered so much in silence, he also will be silent. The great court of justice grows very still as the judge tells him to choose whatever reward he wishes:

"Really?" he asks, doubtful, and a little embarrassed. "Really!" the judge answers. "Really! I tell you, everything is yours. Everything in paradise is yours. Choose! Take! Whatever you want!"

After a few more protestations and repeated assurances, Bontshe finally requests a hot roll with butter.

In the appalling disparity between what he has been offered, and what he is able to imagine for himself, the story resists closure. He has been so conditioned to negate his own desires that none, beyond the bliss of daily bread, is available to him. In the inadequacy of this compensation for the injustice he has endured, the tale ambiguously ends:

> A silence falls upon the great hall, and it is more terrible than Bontshe's has ever been, and slowly the judge and the angels bend their heads in shame at this unending meekness they have created on earth. Then the silence is shattered. The prosecutor laughs aloud, a bitter laugh.

At whom is that dark laughter directed? Peretz leaves the enigma unresolved.

"THE THREE GIFTS"

An equally famous tale, "The Three Gifts" opens with the paradigmatic scene. An ordinary soul stands before the throne watching his deeds being weighed on the scale of judgment. The accuser pours out all his sins while the advocate pours out his good deeds. Because they are in exact equilibrium, he can neither be condemned to hell nor admitted to heaven, so he is consigned to earth to find three tokens of selfless martyrdom which will unbar the gates to paradise. Many ages pass before he finds the first tribute, a grain of sand. Robbers have murdered an elderly Jew for his bag of treasure, which turns out to be sanctified soil from the Holy Land he has saved to place under his head in the grave. The second gift is a bloody pin from the skirt of a rabbi's daughter. Her hair has been tied to the tail of a wild horse which dragged her through the streets of a medieval German town. The third is a skullcap which falls from the head of an emaciated youth being flogged to death by soldiers in a prison square.

Again, this is marked as a folktale by the minimal descriptions, by the anonymous types who perform the actions, and by the number three. Folktale heroes always have to perform three tasks. The ordinary soul, who had been neither good nor bad, "without evil intent or capacity for sacrifice," has been ennobled by variously participating in the communal history of persecution. He is admitted to heaven and congratulated by "the Eternal Voice" for having brought such "truly beautiful gifts." This ironic closure is as disturbing as the prosecutor's "bitter laugh." Do the heavens require such tributes?

"IF NOT HIGHER"

Peretz's most frequently anthologized Hasidic tale is "If Not Higher." He took a legend told of Rabbi Moses Leib of Sasov, who disguised himself as a peasant to bring firewood to a bedridden widow, and added a skeptical observer. This supplies the oblique angle of vision which Peretz so favors and turns it into a conversion story. Again the story opens just before the Days of Judgment when those who have made atonement will be inscribed in the book of life for another year. Since the rabbi always disappears at this time, his followers assume that he has ascended to heaven to intercede for them. A Litvak laughs scornfully at this and points to where it says in Scripture that even Moses could not ascend to heaven during his lifetime. Formidable rationalists who were learned in the legal codes, Litvaks were notoriously intolerant of Hasidic miracles. Thus, determined to discover where the rabbi went, the Litvak conceals himself under his bed.

The subsequent events are rendered in acoustic imagery. This mode of exposition simultaneously imposes unity and creates suspense. By focusing on what the eavesdropper can hear in the dark, his furtiveness and guilty anxiety are stressed. His fear is so great that "the roots of his earlocks pricked him like needles." He keeps himself awake by reciting an entire tractate of the Talmud. He knows that dawn has come when the sexton utters the call to prayer. He hears beds creaking, water splashing, doors opening and shutting. As he follows the rabbi into the street, lurking behind him in the shadows, he hears voices praying overhead. The thudding of his own heart seems to keep time with the rabbi's heavy footsteps in his peasant boots as they enter a wood. The rabbi takes out an ax. The Litvak hears a tree creak, then snap, then crash to the ground. He hears it being split into logs, then chopped into chips. Then he hears the rabbi tell a sick old widow that he is the peasant, Vassil, come to light her fire. As it is ignited, he hears the penitential prayers being recited. Having witnessed this simple good deed, the skeptical Litvak becomes a loyal disciple, and ever after, when another of his followers says that he ascends to heaven, he only adds, "If not higher."

OTHER MAJOR WORKS

PLAYS: *Baynakht oyfn altn mark*, pb. 1907; *Di goldne keyt*, pb. 1909; *In polish oyf der keyt*, pb. 1909.

POETRY: *Monish*; 1888; *Poezie*, 1892.

NONFICTION: *Mayne zikhroynes*, 1914 (*My Memoirs*, 1964).

MISCELLANEOUS: *Bilder fun a provints-rayze*, 1891; *Ale verk*, 1910-1913; *The I. L. Peretz Reader*, 1990.

BIBLIOGRAPHY

Bellow, Saul, ed. *Great Jewish Short Stories*. New York: Dell, 1969. Contains four classic Peretz stories as well as a representative assortment of tales from major Jewish writers, from biblical times to the present. Bellow's interesting introduction suggests the tradition and continuity of the material.

Frieden, Ken. *Classic Yiddish Fiction: Abramovitsh, Sholem Aleichem, and Peretz*. Albany: State University of New York Press, 1995. Compares the fiction of Shalom Abramovich and Aleichem with that of Peretz.

Howe, Irving, and Eliezer Greenberg, eds. *A Treasury of Yiddish Stories*. New York: Viking Press, 1968. Contains seven Peretz stories, along with a judicious selection of Yiddish narratives of all major types and significant authors. The editors' introduction, although concise, is the best single survey of Yiddish writing available.

Liptzin, Sol. *A History of Yiddish Literature*. Middle Village, N.Y.: Jonathan David, 1972. A comprehensive overview of Yiddish writing from its beginnings to its current practice in the Americas, South Africa, Australia, Europe, and Israel. Contains perceptive and favorable critiques of writings by Peretz and sound judgments of his position in world literature.

_____. *Peretz*. New York: YIVO Bilingual Series, 1947. An important investigation of the author's life and career, with Yiddish and English on opposite pages. Thoroughly readable, informative, and provocative. Liptzin awards Peretz higher status than do most Yiddish literary historians.

Peretz, Isaac Leib. *Selected Stories*. Edited by Irving Howe and Eliezer Greenberg. New York: Schocken Books, 1974. An essential Peretz collection because of the editorial skills of Howe and Greenberg. Like any superior anthology, this one reveals new facets of its subject's talent. Peretz is interpreted as a major writer in both Hebrew and Yiddish, who made interesting contemporary uses of traditional Jewish materials. Peretz is viewed more as the forerunner of Franz Kafka than as the disciple of Sholom Aleichem.

Roback, A. A. *Peretz, Psychologist of Literature*. Cambridge, Mass.: Sci-Art, 1935. A stimulating psychological examination of Peretz's writings by a prolific writer of psychological and literary studies.

Roskies, David G. *A Bridge of Longing: The Lost Art of Yiddish Storytelling*. Cambridge, Mass.: Harvard University Press, 1995. Discusses Peretz as the master architect of Jewish modernism who first made use of folk material to mock it, but then later changed direction, insisting that a connection with the past was essential to Jewish nationalism.

Waxman, Meyer. *History of Jewish Literature*. New York: Bloch, 1930. A complete survey of Jewish writing from the postbiblical period to the 1930's. Interesting for its attempt to place Peretz within the broader context of Jewish history, ethics, religion, and Zionist thought.

Wisse, Ruth R. *I. L. Peretz and the Making of Modern Jewish Culture*. Seattle: University of Washington Press, 1991. Explores Peretz's contributions to Jewish and non-Jewish society.

Ruth Rosenberg, updated by Allene Phy-Olsen

PETRONIUS

Gaius Petronius Arbiter

Born: Unknown; c. C.E. 20
Died: Cumae, Italy; c. 66

PRINCIPAL SHORT FICTION

Satyricon, c. 60 (*The Satyricon*, 1694)

OTHER LITERARY FORMS

The Satyricon is the only existing work attributed to Petronius.

ACHIEVEMENTS

The novel, in the sense of a long work of fiction possessing a continuous plot, was largely the creation of Petronius. Though *The Satyricon* contains elements of Menippean satire (a mixture of prose and poetry), Milesian tales (bawdy stories that usually deal with romantic conquests), ancient mime (short scenes intended for dramatic recitation or performance), and more traditional satire, nothing exactly like *The Satyricon* had ever existed in either the Greek or Roman literary traditions. Breaking new ground, *The Satyricon* is able both to ridicule and to celebrate much of the decadence seen in Rome during the age of Nero.

Petronius departed radically from the heroic and romantic characters, which had been the mainstay of classical literature until his own day. Far from the larger-than-life characters found in the *Odyssey* (c. 800 B.C.E.) or the *Aeneid* (c. 29-19 B.C.E.), the central figures of *The Satyricon* are scoundrels, petty criminals, and the nouveau riche. These individuals, though each of them is exaggerated in his or her own way, would have reminded Petronius's audience of types completely familiar to them from everyday life.

Petronius also departed from earlier authors in using not the elevated Latin of Cicero and Vergil but a language more like that spoken by ordinary Romans. In his use of slang, dialect, and colloquialisms, Petronius pioneered elements of style found in later authors such as Mark Twain, Joel Chandler Harris, and J. D. Salinger.

BIOGRAPHY

The identity of the author of *The Satyricon* was agreed upon in the late twentieth century, and very little is known about his life. Gaius Petronius was governor of Bithynia and later consul. He became a member of Nero's inner circle, where he was known as *Arbiter Elegantiae* and became responsible for keeping the Emperor amused and entertained by creating new and "elegant" diversions. Denounced by the leader of Nero's Praetorian Guard, he was detained at Cumae to await the Emperor's pleasure. His strange suicide, the only event of his life for which an account survives, is described in the *Annals* (c. 119) of Tacitus.

ANALYSIS

The Satyricon, Petronius's only extant work aside from a few poems, survives as a group of fragments which may represent as little as one tenth of the entire original. The nature of the work is difficult to characterize, not only because the story is impossible to reconstruct in full but also because *The Satyricon* is unlike anything else that comes to modern readers from antiquity. The only comparable book is *The Golden Ass* (c. 150) of Lucius Apuleius, written a century later. The book was written for Nero and his court and was probably intended for recitation. Fragments of the text were known during the Middle Ages, but it was the rediscovery in 1650 of a codex containing the most significant and coherent section of the work, the famous *Cena Trimalchionis (Dinner at Trimalchio's)* that justified renewed interest in Petronius.

THE SATYRICON

Sometimes considered the first realistic novel, *The Satyricon* describes the picaresque adventures of the narrator Encolpius and his sometime lover, the boy Giton, through the largely Greek cities of southern Italy. As usually reconstructed, the story begins with Encolpius engaged in a discussion of rhetoric with the teacher Agamemnon. He breaks away to pursue Ascyltos, his companion and rival for the affections of Giton. After various adventures during the day, the three spend a farcical night, interrupted by the priestess of Priapus, Quartilla, and her retinue. After a break in the surviving text, the three are brought to Trimalchio's banquet by Agamemnon. This is the *Cena Trimalchionis*, which is followed after another gap by a scene in which Encolpius meets the poet Eumolpus at a picture gallery. This provides an opportunity for poetic parodies and some roughshod art criticism. The two then dine together with Giton, and another rivalry develops over the boy. Encolpius and Giton pretend to attempt suicide, and at the height of the hubbub that follows, Ascyltos appears with an official, looking for Giton. The boy, however, hides himself by clinging to the underside of a mattress, similar to Odysseus under the ram of Polyphemos. Ascyltos leaves empty-handed, and Eumolpus and Encolpius are reconciled. After another gap, the reader finds Encolpius, Eumolpus, and Giton on shipboard, apparently fugitives. As it happens, the captain of the ship, Lichas, is an old enemy of Encolpius, while one of the passengers is Tryphaena, a woman with some claim on Giton (presumably both of these characters have appeared in parts of the story subsequently lost). A voyage full of intrigue, suspense, and violence climaxes in shipwreck, but the three companions survive and make for Croton, a city reportedly full of legacy hunters. Beyond this point, the story becomes increasingly fragmentary, but several episodes are concerned with Encolpius's impotence and with other mishaps that befall him amid witches, priestesses, and thieves.

Fragmentary as it is, *The Satyricon* is one of the few surviving examples of several classical genres. Along with the *Apocolocyntosis* (c. 55), attributed to Lucius Annaeus Seneca, it is the only extant example of Menippean satire, a form that mixed prose, verse, and satirical observation in an episodic narrative. The result is a kind of intellectual comedy of which the closest modern relatives might be *Candide* (1759) and *Alice's Adventures in Wonderland* (1865).

Within the Menippean framework of the book there are traces of two other all but vanished genres: Roman mime and the Milesian tale. Mime, a kind of obscene farce in colloquial language, generated out

of stock characters, seems to have influenced several episodes, such as those among the legacy hunters of Croton. The language of mime is explicitly parodied at least once, and the naturalism of the book may owe something to this and other theatrical models. Milesian tales, marked by raciness and an inclination to satire, are forerunners of the novella tradition that reached maturity in Giovanni Boccaccio's *The Decameron* (1353). Two of the best-known tales in *The Satyricon* are of this type: "The Boy of Pergamum" and "The Widow of Ephesus."

"THE BOY OF PERGAMUM"

In "The Boy of Pergamum" (chapters 85-87), Eumolpus tells how, while a guest in Pergamum, he schemes to seduce the son of his host by presenting himself as an ascetic philosopher. With the parents' approval, he accompanies the boy constantly to protect him from seducers. One night, noticing that the boy is awake, Eumolpus whispers a prayer to Venus: "If I can kiss this boy without his knowing it, tomorrow I will give him a pair of doves." Hearing this, the boy at once begins to snore loudly. Eumolpus takes his kisses and next morning produces two doves. The whispers become louder, the desires more extensive, the gifts more valuable, the boy's sleep more improbable, until on the third night Eumolpus promises a thoroughbred in return for consummation. He gets his wish, but since thoroughbreds are harder to come by than doves, the boy's impatience next morning breaks the spell: "Please sir, where's my horse?"

Later, Eumolpus attempts a reconciliation, but the boy, still piqued, warns him, "Go to sleep or I'll tell my father at once." Passion drives Eumolpus to force himself on his ward. No longer resisting, the boy even offers to do it again, to prove he is not so stingy as Eumolpus (the thoroughbred has not materialized). After being awakened three times by the boy, however, who asks, "Don't you want anything?," it is Eumolpus's turn to say, "Go to sleep or I'll tell your father at once."

This tale, really two linked tales, is like a primitive novella. The ribaldry of the anecdotes creates an impression of realism, but there is nothing real about the characters; they are interchangeable blanks. The boy, for example, can be, and has been, replaced by a girl without difficulty. These tales are above all formal inventions. Such familiar structures as the neat turnabout at the end, or the repetitions in threes, are formulas from which all kinds of stories can be generated. This is fiction aspiring to the efficiency of the joke.

"THE WIDOW OF EPHESUS"

"The Widow of Ephesus," also told by Eumolpus, is much more impressive. A woman renowned for her virtue is widowed. Not content with ceremonial grief, she keeps vigil with the corpse in its vault, accompanied only by a devoted maid to share her grief and keep the lamp lit. Unable to dissuade her, relatives and friends leave her to her fate, praising her as a paragon of faithful love. Some robbers, however, are crucified nearby, and the soldier on guard, curious about the light he sees among the tombs, comes upon the beautiful widow. He invites her to share his supper. She refuses, but eventually the maid accepts food and urges the widow to do the same, saying, "Your dead husband's body itself ought to persuade you to keep alive." Exhausted by hunger and grief, the woman gives in. Then, however, "the inducements the soldier has used to persuade the lady to go on living became part of his assault on her virtue." The widow consents to this too, and the couple spend three happy nights shut up together in the tomb while the parents of one of the crucified, finding no one on watch, take the body away for burial. Finding the cross empty the next day, the soldier resolves to fall on his sword rather than await punishment, but now it is the widow's turn to dissuade: "I would rather make use of the dead than kill the living." So the husband's body is taken from the tomb and fastened on the empty cross.

These are still stock characters, but not the narrative ciphers of "The Boy of Pergamum"; the story develops as it does *because* the woman is a widow, and *because* the man is a soldier. Milesian structural formulas are apparent here, too, in the recognition of the three nights of love and the turnabout at the end. In this tale, however, genuine human issues are raised. The nature and limits of fidelity are explored not only in the widow, once exemplary, and perhaps still so,

but also in the devoted (*fidissima*) servant. The widow's love for her husband, even dead, is strikingly reflected in the parents of the robber who dare to retrieve his corpse, while the soldier's perhaps frivolous passion for her must be weighed against the honesty of her devotion to him. The story also meditates on persuasion, resistance, and acquiescence: The widow is seen, under the pressure of events, custom, and even the other characters, eventually to take command of her own story.

Eumolpus tells this as a story from his own time, but there is an earlier version in the Aesopian *Fables* of Phaedrus, and although the story is the most influential single element in *The Satyricon*, Petronius's version became authoritative only after the discovery of the *Cena Trimalchionis* revived interest in its author. "The Widow of Ephesus" was then retold by Jean de La Fontaine, and its dramatic possibilities inspired a series of stage versions, beginning with George Chapman's *The Widow's Tears* (1612) and continuing through Christopher Fry's *A Phoenix Too Frequent* (1946) and Federico Fellini's film *Satyricon* (1969).

Like Phaedrus, Eumolpus tells this as a fable about the fickleness of women, and so it is received by the auditors in *The Satyricon*—one even thinks the woman should be crucified for distracting the soldier from his duty. In medieval versions the treatment is the same, but modern versions, without changing the narrative appreciably, have reversed the theme, presenting the widow as sympathetic and even heroic. Fellini, for example, transforms the tale into a fable about the triumph of life and love over death; to enhance that reading, he also shifts the context, so that the story is told at the tomb of Trimalchio during his mock funeral. As the variety of versions testifies, "The Widow of Ephesus" is a triumph of economy, richer than any of the morals that can be, or have been, attached to it.

CENA TRIMALCHIONIS

The Satyricon also bears traces of more familiar genres. Indications that Encolpius has somehow offended the god Priapus and as a result is afflicted with impotence suggest that the author may have intended a broad parody of epic, with the "wrath of

Priapus" as the thread connecting many episodes that seem unrelated, just as the "wrath of Poseidon" unifies the incidents of the *Odyssey* (c. 800 B.C.E.). The present state of the text, however, makes this impossible to verify. The *Cena Trimalchionis* is also to some extent imitative, a parody of Plato's *Symposium* by way of the *Satires* (35, 30 B.C.E.) of Horace. What strikes any reader, however, is not the sources of the episode, but its impressive originality. Although it hardly has a plot, the *Cena Trimalchionis* is a milestone in the craft of narration. In its cinematic wealth of detail, its control of shifting pace and perspective, it is Petronius's most sustained achievement as a writer.

The story is simple. When Encolpius, Giton, and Eumolpus arrive for dinner, the introduction to Trimalchio is by way of his appurtenances: a house cluttered with souvenirs, trophies, gaudy art, and the amulets of every superstition. Like Donald Barthelme, Petronius is master of his society's *dreck*; he knows how to make even the description of objects and settings eventful. The host finally appears after the first course, and the dinner begins in earnest. The sequence of outlandish *trompe l'œil* dishes is seasoned with monologues from Trimalchio, the conversations of his guests, and the constant traffic of innumerable servants, many of them singing while they work. After several speeches full of ignorance, pretension, and platitudes, Trimalchio excuses himself, and in his absence the guests gossip freely about him, one another, and their social world. Trimalchio returns with a little speech about constipation, and dinner continues, punctuated by the arrival of the drunken Habinnas (an episode obviously modeled on the entry of Alcibiades in the *Symposium*). Trimalchio, growing boozy, reads his will aloud; the former slave wants his own slaves to love him now "as much as they would if I were dead." This leads to a discussion of plans for his tomb, to a recital of his own career that begins to sound like a eulogy, and finally to a mock funeral, at the height of which the general uproar brings the fire brigade and the narrator slips away with his companions.

As even this summary can suggest, what controls the *Cena Trimalchionis* is not a plot or some authorial

moral stance but the dominant figure of Trimalchio, the *arriviste* at home among his kind. The insecurity of the former slave turned millionaire is reflected in the illusionism and impostures of his ambience, from the painted watchdog at his door to the deceptive dishes of his banquet: Pea hen eggs are served nestling under a wooden hen, but the eggs are actually pastries stuffed with whole birds. A roast boar is stuffed with live thrushes that fly around the room when the carving begins. An apparent roast goose turns out to be contrived entirely of pork by a cook appropriately named Daedalus. Trimalchio's aspirations to taste are sabotaged by his native vulgarity. There is a Homeric recitation, but by way of illustrating it a slave dressed as Ajax rushes in, attacks a cooked calf dressed in a helmet, and serves up the resulting slices to the applause of the guests. Trimalchio boasts of his jewelry and then has it weighed at the table to prove he is not lying. Above all, Trimalchio is preoccupied with death; the first thing readers learn about him is that he has a clock and a trumpeter in his dining room "so he'll know how much of his life has passed." At the last glimpse, he is saying to other trumpeters, "Pretend I'm dead. Play something nice." The self-made man knows that Fortune takes as readily as she gives, so in his house, in his world, nothing is stable, nothing is what it seems. The *Cena Trimalchionis* depicts a vivid circus of ill-assorted people moving among a chaos of possessions. Its lack of plot is purposeful, expressing the aimlessness of the world over which presides the monumentally vulgar, oddly sympathetic Trimalchio.

Although *The Satyricon* moves often toward satire, it is a special sort of satire: tolerant, generous, Horatian. Petronius's observations are penetrating but rarely condescending and in a way almost impartial. He makes way for his objects to reveal themselves. Critics who wish to see him primarily as a satirist of imperial decadence find themselves complaining about a lack of moral focus, of "seriousness." One of the most obvious features of the book, however, its frank impartiality in sexual matters, should be a clue to the author's underlying attitude. His primary goal is realism rather than satire; his book is preoccupied with the surfaces of society, its texture, rather than its structure. Thus for example, while the narrator regularly makes judgments about what he sees, the author makes it clear that these are self-interested and unreliable. Even the judgments are part of the milieu being depicted. As objects of satire, the characters in *The Satyricon* are extremely traditional: bad poets, *nouveaux riches*, parasites, licentious women; but at the heart of Petronius's originality is a willingness to present these types on their own terms, to let them speak for themselves and about each other. The reader sees the insecurities of the loose women, the embattled pride of the self-made man. Petronius's command of several colloquial styles enables him to provide a distinguishable idiom for each of them. As a result, *The Satyricon*'s audience comes to know ostensibly stock characters from within.

This genial realism, along with the techniques of observation and language that make it possible, is Petronius's most significant contribution to the art of short fiction. If there is any statement of artistic intention in his work, it is these lines from a poem recited by Encolpius "A kindness far from sad laughs in my pure speech;/ whatever the people do, my frank tongue reports." That candor is the hallmark of *The Satyricon*.

BIBLIOGRAPHY

Colton, R. E. "The Story of 'The Widow of Ephesus' in Petronius and La Fontaine." *Classical Journal* 71 (1975): 35-52. Examines the influence of Petronius's short fiction upon Jean de La Fontaine. Considers the degree to which La Fontaine, in his version of the story "The Widow of Ephesus," suppressed unpleasant details found in Petronius's original, added new elements, and used more refined language than that found in the Roman version of the story.

Conte, Gian Biagio. *The Hidden Author: An Interpretation of Petronius' "Satyricon."* Translated by Elaine Fantham. Berkeley: University of California Press, 1996. Offers a good discussion and analysis of the seminal work.

Corbett, Philip B. *Petronius*. New York: Twayne, 1970. A general and easily accessible introduction

touching upon nearly every aspect of Petronius's work and his literary style. Also contains a useful bibliography.

Kimball, Jean. "An Ambiguous Faithlessness: Molly Bloom and the Widow of Ephesus." *James Joyce Quarterly* 31 (Summer, 1994): 455-472. Examines the influence of Otto Rank's 1913 psychoanalytic interpretation of the tale of the "Widow of Ephesus" on Joyce's *Ulysses*; discusses the faithfulness of the wife, the triangle of characters, and the motif of the hanged man.

McMahon, J. M. "A Petronian Parody at Sat. 14.2-14.3." *Mnemosyne* 50 (February, 1997): 77-81. Suggests that one way Petronius incorporated contemporary philosophical issues into the *Satyricon* was through the parody of popular Cynic philosophy; discusses Petronius's familiarity with the exponents of Cynic philosophy and how he used them as targets of parody.

Sandy, G. N. "Petronius and the Tradition of the Interpolated Narrative." *Transactions of the American Philological Association* 101 (1970): 463-476. Examines the ways in which Petronius's interpolated short fiction allowed the author to develop a perspective toward his larger narrative. Explores how the style of Petronius's short fiction serves as an indication of the narrator's character and the imaginary audience's interests.

Slater, Niall W. *Reading Petronius*. Baltimore: The Johns Hopkins University Press, 1990. A good general introduction to *The Satyricon* and its place in Roman satire.

Sullivan, J. P. *"The Satyricon" of Petronius: A Literary Study*. Bloomington: Indiana University Press, 1968. The best general study on Petronius, examining every aspect of the author's work, including his use of humor, satire, and sexuality. Also contains a reconstruction of the lost parts of *The Satyricon*. Sullivan considers the question of the novel's authorship and includes an exhaustive bibliography. Concludes that *The Satyricon* is not sufficiently concerned with morality to be a true satire.

Walsh, P. G. *The Roman Novel*. Cambridge, England: Cambridge University Press, 1970. Traces the history and style of the Roman novel, giving particular attention to *The Satyricon* and Lucius Apuleius's *The Golden Ass*. Also includes a

lengthy bibliography containing a section devoted entirely to Petronius.

Laurence A. Breiner, updated by Jeffrey L. Buller

ANN PETRY

Born: Old Saybrook, Connecticut; October 12, 1908
Died: Old Saybrook, Connecticut; April 28, 1997

PRINCIPAL SHORT FICTION
Miss Muriel and Other Stories, 1971

OTHER LITERARY FORMS

Ann Petry has received her greatest critical recognition for her adult novels: *The Street* (1946), *Country Place* (1947), and *The Narrows* (1953). In 1949 she began a distinguished career as a writer of children's literature with the publication of *The Drugstore Cat*, to be followed by the now-classic biographical novels *Harriet Tubman: Conductor of the Underground Railroad* (1955) and *Tituba of Salem Village* (1964). She has also published a devotional work, *Legends of the Saints* (1970), in addition to various articles for small periodicals.

ACHIEVEMENTS

Ann Petry's receipt of a Houghton Mifflin Literary Fellowship in 1945 (and an award of twenty-five hundred dollars) enabled her to complete *The Street*, which went on to become the first novel by an African American woman to sell more than one million copies. In 1977 she was awarded a National Endowment for the Arts grant and in 1983 received a D. Litt. from Boston's Suffolk University. In 1992 the reissuing of *The Street* renewed Petry's reputation as an important American writer and introduced a new generation to her work. Her death in April, 1997, was eulogized publicly by Connecticut senator Christopher Dodd, and the following year MacArthur Fellow

Max Roach premiered "Theater Pieces" (December, 1998), an adaptation of Petry's tale of a jazz love triangle, "Solo on the Drums," featuring Ruby Dee and Ossie Davis along with Roach.

BIOGRAPHY

Ann Lane Petry was born to Peter Clarke Lane and Bertha James Lane on October 12, 1908, joining a family that had lived for several generations as the only African American citizens of the resort community of Old Saybrook, Connecticut. The descendant of a runaway Virginian slave, Petry admitted to never having felt herself to be a true New Englander; her cultural legacy was not that of the typical Yankee, and as a small child she came to know the isolating effects of racism after being stoned by white children on her first day of school. Nevertheless, her family distinguished itself within the community and boasted numerous professionals: Her grandfather was a licensed chemist; her father, aunt, and uncle became pharmacists; and her mother worked as a chiropodist. In 1902 Peter Lane opened a pharmacy in Old Saybrook, for which Ann herself trained. Inspired by the example of her many independent female relatives—women who had, she explained, "abandoned the role of housewife in the early twentieth century"—in 1931 Ann secured a degree in pharmacology from the University of Connecticut, the only black graduate in her class. She worked in family-owned pharmacies until 1938, when she met and married Louisiana-born George D. Petry and moved with him to his home in Harlem.

Petry had begun writing fiction seriously in high school after an antagonistic teacher grudgingly praised her work as having real potential, and she wrote steadily thereafter (although to no immediate success). With the move to New York City, her writing career began in earnest. She quickly secured jobs with various Harlem newspapers as a reporter, editor, and copywriter, working for the *Amsterdam News* and *The People's Voice* (the latter a weekly begun by African American clergyman and politician Adam Clayton Powell, Jr.). She also briefly acted in the American Negro Theatre and worked on a study conducted by the New York Foundation investigating the effects of segregation on black children.

Participation in a creative writing seminar at Columbia University greatly influenced Petry during this time. Her first published short story, "On Saturday the Siren Sounds at Noon," appeared in a 1943 issue of *The Crisis* (a magazine published by the National Association for the Advancement of Colored People) and not only earned her twenty dollars but also led to her discovery by an editor at Houghton Mifflin. He encouraged her to submit preliminary work on what would become *The Street*, for which Petry received the 1945 Houghton Mifflin Literary Fellowship and a stipend of twenty-five hundred dollars. Thus she was able to complete her novel, translating nearly a decade spent observing the difficulties of aspiring African Americans in the urban North into the powerful story of single mother Lutie Johnson and her star-crossed eight-year-old Bub. While her trenchant insights into the play of race and class as conjoined factors stifling Lutie's dreams recall Richard Wright's landmark *Native Son* (1940), Petry's recognition of the role of gender in the discriminatory equation made *The Street* a groundbreaking work on its own and another expression of the woman-centered ethic she had learned from her family. Published in 1946, *The Street* received both critical and popular acclaim and sold 1.5 million copies—at the time the largest audience ever reached by an African American woman. The fame accompanying that success overwhelmed Petry, however, and in 1948 she and George returned to the obscurity of Old Saybrook, where they bought the two-hundred-year-old house of an old sea captain and reared their daughter Elizabeth Ann.

Ann Petry in 1946 (AP/Wide World Photos)

Petry's subsequent fiction did not receive the same kind of praise accorded her first novel, despite her continued willingness to tackle difficult racial themes (*The Narrows*, 1953) and explore the terrain of small-town white America from its own assumed vantage point, a project seldom undertaken by black writers even today (*Country Place*, 1947). In 1971 she issued a collection of her short fiction, *Miss Muriel and Other Stories*. She also contributed stories and essays to numerous magazines and journals. Perhaps in response to the indifference accorded her adult fiction, she began writing for n during the time she was raising Elizabeth and produced such classics as *The Drugstore Cat*, *Harriet Tubman*, and *Tituba of Salem Village*. The latter two novels, about actual historical personages, reflect her determination to place art in the service of an honest picture of American racial history; they have become young adult classics and are perhaps more widely read than the adult fiction on which her initial reputation was built.

Petry spent the second half of her life away from the hurly-burly of publishing centers and for the most part outside the rarefied walls of the university; David Streitfeld of *The Washington Post* said that she "had little tolerance for fools or academics, two categories she regarded as essentially synonymous." She did hold a visiting professorship at the University of Hawaii in 1974-1975 and in 1977 received a grant from the National Endowment for the Arts. Boston's Suffolk University awarded her a D.Litt. degree in 1983. She had the satisfaction of seeing her daughter continue the legacy of strong female achievement by becoming an attorney.

Petry died at the age of eighty-eight in a convalescent home in the same community where she was born, still married to the man who had briefly taken her out of New England and made possible the launching of her lifelong career.

ANALYSIS

While Ann Petry's fiction typically involves African Americans struggling against the crippling impact of racism, her overarching theme involves a more broadly defined notion of prejudice that targets class and gender as well as race. Thus her aims are consistently broader than racial critique, since she regularly exposes the consequences of America's hierarchical social systems and its capitalistic materialism. That vision explains what might otherwise seem to be inconsistencies of direction in Petry's career: her decision, for example, following the potent racial protest of *The Street* to focus her next novel, *Country Place*, on a white community's postwar crises of adjustment or her movement into the realm of children's literature. Like her contemporaries, black and white alike, who came of age in the 1930's, she adopted a social realist aesthetic committed to documenting the obstacles to human fulfillment imposed on those at the margins of American prosperity. As she explained,

I find it difficult to subscribe to the idea that art exists for art's sake. It seems to me that all truly great art is

propaganda . . . [and fiction], like all other forms of art, will always reflect the political, economic, and social structure of the period in which it was created.

Her work also reveals an increasingly overt Christian existentialist vision celebrating the individual's potential for spiritual liberation, through which an entire culture might come to relinquish its crippling prejudices.

Rather than celebrating the American ideal of self-making with which her native New England is so closely associated, Petry exposes the illusions it has fostered and depicts their graphic costs to those relegated to the periphery of American possibility. Racism invites Petry's most scathing attacks, not only for the material hardship it forces upon people of color but also for the psychological and cultural distortions it produces. At her most biting, Petry lampoons the absurdist systems of human classification into which racist societies ultimately fall. Generally, her perspective is a tragic one, however, grounded in the recognition that confronting racism necessitates confronting history itself.

One of Petry's most insistent indictments of America's hypocrisy targets the class distinctions that parallel and overlap racism as forces negating individual hope for a better life, a more just world. Repeatedly she shows how Americans in quest of the material security, comfort, and status that propel middle-class striving acquiesce to soul-numbing labor and retreat into a moral inflexibility that blindly sanctions aggressive self-interest. In Petry's fiction the culture's high-flown rhetoric is belied by rigid social hierarchies that produce venal, grasping have-nots at the bottom, whose ambitions mimic the ruthless acquisitiveness of those at the top.

Petry's most important characters are those who reject the fallacy of the self-made individual existing independently of the world or the continuing legacy of the past. Though that perspective assumes certain mechanistic dimensions in her work, she does not concede full authority to deterministic necessity; the dice may be loaded against her protagonists, but the game is not inexorably mandated to play itself out to any single predetermined end. Her characters sometimes prove capable of personal growth that moves them toward a common humanity with the potential to fuel real and far-reaching change in the social order itself. Petry's narratives of personal transformation often grow from characters' chance movements across rigid cultural boundaries; the resulting crises test the spiritual flexibility of many others besides her protagonists.

Overlooked by academic critics, Petry's children's books offer tantalizing clues to her larger agenda. Their emphasis upon personal fearlessness in rethinking entrenched assumptions and disengaging from unjust systems invites comparison with numerous figures from her adult fiction. Moreover, in applying their new insights, these characters undertake subtly revolutionary actions that defy the cultural boundaries that had previously defined their lives. It takes a saint, perhaps, to challenge a predatory universe with an alternative vision of love, but having told children in *Legends of the Saints* that true sanctity is a function of bravery, Petry seems to evaluate her other fictional characters on their receptivity to grace as an antidote to hate.

MISS MURIEL AND OTHER STORIES

While Petry's reputation rests primarily on her novels, she saw herself quite differently at the start of her career:

> I set out to be a writer of short stories and somehow ended up as a novelist—possibly because there simply wasn't room enough within the framework of the short story to do the sort of thing I wanted to do.

Yet the pieces in *Miss Muriel and Other Stories*, written over the course of several decades, provide a compact and provocative introduction to her imaginative concerns, chief among them her sensitivity to racism's psychological as well as material consequences.

"LIKE A WINDING SHEET"

In the prizewinning story "Like a Winding Sheet," she depicts the physical and mental toll exacted by the nature of work in an industrial society where laborers are treated as interchangeable machines. The story dramatizes how the corrosive humiliations of prejudice, when added to work stresses, can trigger blind and catastrophic violence. A husband's inability to challenge the string of racist assaults on his dignity delivered both during and after his exhausting night shift at a World War II defense plant not only make him incapable of imagining benign white behavior (even in the face of apologies) but also cause him to respond to his wife's affectionate teasing with the beating he is forbidden to direct at his real oppressors. While racism provides the context for his rage, however (her unwitting use of the word "nigger" echoing the hostile epithet regularly used against him by the outside world), his reaction exposes the starkness of the struggle between male and female in Petry's world and the sobering betrayals it can provoke. The title image begins as the bedsheet in which he has tossed and turned all day in a futile effort to sleep, but his wife jokingly casts it as a burial linen—a reference ironically appropriate to his sense of himself as the walking dead. By story's end that reference has assumed sinister dimensions as he feels trapped by the violence he is committing but cannot control, "and he thought it was like being enmeshed in a winding sheet."

"IN DARKNESS AND CONFUSION"

"In Darkness and Confusion" fictionalizes the Harlem Riot of 1943, an event sparked by the wounding of a black soldier whose uniform provided scant protection on his own home front. The story's protagonist, William Jones, a drugstore porter who, despite endless humiliations, has worked hard all his life to secure a better world for his son Sam, suddenly loses that son to the wartime draft and the dangers of a Jim Crow world at the southern training camp to which he is sent. When Sam, who once aspired to college and his share of the American Dream, protests an order to move to the back of the bus and then shoots the aggressive military police officer who gave it, he is court-martialed and sentenced to twenty years of hard labor.

As Jones broods over this news in a Harlem bar, he watches as another uniformed black G.I., this one standing in the supposedly more egalitarian north, tries to help a black woman being beaten by a white policeman, punches the lawman, runs, and is summarily gunned down. Jones erupts into a violence ignited by grief and rage and becomes the leader of a mob. When his churchgoing wife learns of their son's fate, she too turns to retributive action with an explosive passion that kills her: Her religion proves unable to provide her with the strength to resume her burden and go on with her life. Nor is the mob's looting of local merchants legitimized, for it is produced by the intoxicating siren song of white capitalist materialism, with which the culture regularly deflects attention from matters of real social justice. The riot leaves Jones more completely bereft than he had been before, for it literally costs him his heart and soul, even as it finally allows him to understand the anomie of his disaffected teenage niece, who has baldly scorned his lifetime of exhausting effort for the whites, who in the end allow them "only the nigger end of things."

"THE NEW MIRROR"

Petry as skillfully evokes the impact of racism on the black bourgeoisie as she does on the proletariat, and in several tales she demonstrates how a lifetime of belittlement and intimidation can erode one's ability to act ethically in the world. In "Miss Muriel" and "The New Mirror," Petry creates a black family much like her own—the Layens are professionals who own the pharmacy in a small New England town. The adolescent girl who narrates these tales speaks of "the training in issues of race" she has received over the years, not only through the casual bigotries she has witnessed but also through the painful self-consciousness of respectable people like her parents, whose behavior is a continual exercise in refuting cultural stereotypes while carefully preserving proudly held racial loyalties. In "The New Mirror" the ironies are more overt, cleaner. Mr. Layen's decision to take a day off to outfit himself with a new pair of false teeth leads his unknowing wife to an excruciating encounter with police, from whom she withholds her fear that the absent Layen may have become another black man who deserts his family as a delayed response to a lifetime of indignities within the white patriarchal social order. Layen's surprising secrecy leads his daughter to realize that even securing a new set of teeth subjects a black male to humiliation, in this case taking the form of the grinning

Sambos and toothless Uncle Toms he fears his dental problems will call to mind. The child learns to use the codes by which the black middle class shields itself from white contempt—just as she shoulders her own share of the burden of always acting with an eye on the reputation of "the Race": She thus learns why "all of us people with this dark skin must help hold the black island inviolate."

"MISS MURIEL"

The title story of the volume, "Miss Muriel," operates more subtly in its exploration of the racist preoccupations inculcated within and often unwillingly relinquished by its victims. The title itself refers to a white racist joke the young narrator innocently relates to one of Aunt Sophronia's black suitors—a joke in which an African American trying to buy a Muriel cigar is upbraided for not showing the proper respect for white womanhood by asking instead for a "Miss" Muriel. The child is bluntly chastised for voicing such "nigger" put-downs in one of the many moments of confusion she suffers over the inconsistent and seemingly arbitrary management of prejudices operating among the adults around her: her aunt's unpopular courtship by Bemish, a white member of their upstate New York community; the equal dismay with which Mr. Layen regards Sophronia's other suitor, the "tramp piano player" Chink, who evokes the "low" culture of the black masses, from which the bourgeois Layen has distanced himself as part of his accommodation to a scornful white world; the contempt quietly directed against the homosexual partner of her cherished Uncle Johno; the colorist hierarchies of all the African Americans she knows (even when the lightest skinned among them eschew the opportunity to "pass"). At the end of the story, when the black men in her circle have effectively driven Bemish out of town for his persistent wooing of Sophronia, the narrator brokenheartedly confronts their hypocrisy, yelling, "You both stink. You stink like dead bats. You and your goddamn Miss Muriel." Internalizing such divisiveness as they have just enforced directly clashes with the other set of values she has been taught, and the two are starkly juxtaposed early in the story when the child muses:

If my objections to Mr. Bemish are because he's white . . . then I have been 'trained' on the subject of race just as I have been trained to be a Christian. . . .

It is one of the paradoxes of bigotry that its victims may become its emissaries, at the price of their most cherished beliefs.

"THE WITNESS"

Petry revisits this theme in a number of ways throughout the collection. Against the most aggressive forms of white hatred directed at her characters, there is no defense except a temporary abandonment of one's human dignity. "The Witness" presents the case of a retired black college professor who takes a high school teaching position in a northern white community. Called upon to assist the local pastor in counseling delinquent adolescents, he finds himself their prey as they kidnap him and force him to watch their sexual abuse of a young white woman. Having at one point coerced him to place his hand on the girl, they effectively blackmail him into complicit silence about their crime, for he is paralyzed by the specter of being publicly accused of the ultimate racial taboo. His exemplary life and professional stature cannot protect him from such sordid insinuations, and he bitterly describes himself in his moral impotence as "another poor scared black bastard who was a witness."

"THE NECESSARY KNOCKING ON THE DOOR"

In "The Necessary Knocking on the Door" a similar loss of agency is made bitingly ironic by the context in which Alice Knight's dilemma unfolds: A participant at a conference about the role of Christianity in the modern world, she finds herself unable to master her dislike for a white woman dying in the hotel room across the hall from hers—a woman who had earlier in the day refused to be seated next to a "nigger" and had thus awakened in Alice the bitterness that a lifetime of such indignities has nurtured. Her hardened heart is jolted the next day by news of the woman's death during the night—and her own guilty knowledge that she alone had heard the woman's distress but had let the hated epithet reduce her to that "animal," "outcast," "obscene" state it implies—not because it had been leveled at her but because she had let it rob her of her Christian commit-

ment to do good to those who harm her. Even her own dreams indict Alice: "The octopus moonlight" pitilessly asserts, "Yours is the greater crime. A crime. A very great crime. It was a crime. And we were the witnesses." Like other African American writers before and since, Petry warns that prejudice delivers its most sinister harm when it saps its victims' capacity for decency and compassion and enlists them in the service of a gospel of irreparable division. In these stories Petry vividly captures the spiritual anguish of discovering that one's own grievances can weaken rather than deepen one's moral courage.

"THE BONES OF LOUELLA BROWN"

Her handling of white perspectives on racism is more unyielding. The absurdities into which segregationist practices lead multiracial societies (including the pseudosciences hunting frantically for physical evidence of racial "difference") are lampooned in "The Bones of Louella Brown." The most prestigious family in Massachusetts, the Bedfords, find their plans to build a chapel for its deceased members compromised when an undertaker's assistant confuses the bones of an African American maid with the sole noblewoman in their clan and, because of the "shocking" similarities of hair, teeth, height, and bone mass between the two skeletons, cannot differentiate the two. That alone is newsworthy enough to attract a Boston reporter sniffing for scandal, but the story gets juicier when it becomes clear there is every likelihood that the segregation that has been a hallmark of the cemetery in question will be permanently breached once it can no longer guarantee that "black" bones will not commingle in the same park with "white" bones. After Mrs. Brown makes a series of ghostly visitations to principals in the story, they decide to acknowledge the truth with an epitaph explaining that either woman (or both) may lie in the crypt, along with the admission of their common humanity: "They both wore the breastplate of faith and love, and for a helmet, the hope of salvation." Here too Petry moves her reader beyond social contexts and into metaphysical ones by reminding readers that this story of dry bones (an unmistakable homage to a favorite trope of black oral tradition) is also a meditation on mortality itself, which exposes such preoccupation with earthly pecking orders for the consummate folly it is.

"THE MIGRAINE WORKERS"

"The Migraine Workers" offers another example of white protagonists brought up short in the knowledge of their moral blindness in following the unquestioned attitudes of a lifetime. Pedro Gonzalez, proud owner of a successful truck stop, suddenly finds himself staring into a trailer full of migrant laborers exuding a human misery more palpable than anything he has ever encountered. Outraged by the black driver, who blithely explains how he usually hides such scenes from public scrutiny, Pedro feeds the people with the surplus food left on his premises by other haulers. When he later discovers that an elderly man from the crew has hidden himself in the area and is living off what he can scavenge from the truckstop, his first impulse is to have the man removed by the police. It is only when his longtime assistant challenges his callousness and points to the resources they could easily spare for the man's upkeep that Pedro realizes how his own fleshy body indicts him of complicity in a system of polarized haves and have-nots: migraine-producing epiphanies indeed in the land of equal opportunity.

"MOTHER AFRICA"

Other stories in the collection evoke the mysterious private centers of grief hidden in the human heart: "Olaf and His Girl Friend" and "Solo on the Drums" show Petry's interest in African American music as an exquisite, untranslatable evocation of that pain. "Mother Africa" introduces Emanuel Turner, another of Petry's junk men, whose business indicts the acquisitive mandate of American consumer culture. Years earlier, the loss of his wife and baby in childbirth had robbed him of any further desire for self-improvement; as a junk dealer he is free from anxious adherence to other people's standards of worth or accomplishment, and because he is his own man, he is a welcome figure to those around him. All that changes when a friend blesses him with the huge sculpture of a female nude being discarded by a wealthy white woman. The statue seduces Turner back into a realm of self-conscious striving as

he tries to live up to its grandeur; in the process he loses his liberty and the easy rapport he has had with his neighbors. Convinced that she is a mythic evocation of Africa itself, he resents the prudish efforts of others to clothe her as missionaries had once done to his ancestors. Thus he is stunned to learn that this dark madonna is not a black woman at all but a white woman—the oxidized metal had misled him.

By parodying the assumed black male obsession with white women in this way, Petry implies that the real hunger at work is for authentic enunciation of the African American experience, a hunger left unsatisfied when Turner hurriedly rushes to sell the piece for scrap. In succumbing to the desire to make a world fit for his queenly companion, Turner submits himself for the first time in twenty-five years to the pressures of conformity and material acquisition. Is it love which so compromises him?—or are the statue's racial associations Petry's warnings against the lure of cultural standards derived from the spiritually bankrupt spheres of white consumer capitalism? Taken together, the stories in this collection offer tantalizing variations upon Petry's most insistent themes.

OTHER MAJOR WORKS

LONG FICTION: *The Street*, 1946; *Country Place*, 1947; *The Narrows*, 1953.

CHILDREN'S LITERATURE: *The Drugstore Cat*, 1949; *Harriet Tubman: Conductor on the Underground Railroad*, 1955; *Tituba of Salem Village*, 1964; *Legends of the Saints*, 1970.

BIBLIOGRAPHY

Bell, Bernard. "Ann Petry's Demythologizing of American Culture and Afro-American Character." In *Conjuring: Black Women, Fiction, and Literary Tradition*, edited by Marjorie Pryse and Hortense J. Spillers. Bloomington: Indiana University Press, 1985. An argument for moving Petry out of the shadow of male contemporaries like Richard Wright to permit her fiction the proper reevaluation it deserves.

Clark, Keith. "A Distaff Dream Deferred? Ann Petry and the Art of Subversion." *African-American Review* 26 (Fall, 1992): 495-505. A study of Petry's interest in the ways black women respond to the American Dream while subverting it to their own ends.

Gross, Theodore. "Ann Petry: The Novelist as Social Critic." In *Black Fiction: New Studies in the Afro-American Novel Since 1945*, edited by A. Robert Lee. New York: Barnes & Noble, 1980. A discussion of Petry's strong commitment to an aesthetic of social realism that puts art in the service of political, economic, and societal transformation and justice.

Hernton, Calvin. "The Significance of Ann Petry." In *The Sexual Mountain and Black Women Writers*. New York: Doubleday, 1987. An analysis of the relationship between Petry's fiction and that of contemporary black women writers, particularly in its wedding of social protest and violence.

Washington, Gladys. "A World Made Cunningly: A Closer Look at Ann Petry's Short Fiction." *College Language Association Journal* 30 (September, 1986): 14-29. A critical argument for tracing Petry's important themes and their evolving nuances through her understudied short stories.

Wilson, Mark. "A *MELUS* Interview: Ann Petry—The New England Connection." *MELUS* 15 (Summer, 1988): 71-84. A discussion with Petry about her early life and the first decades of her writing career.

Barbara Kitt Seidman

JAYNE ANNE PHILLIPS

Born: Buckhannon, West Virginia; July 19, 1952

PRINCIPAL SHORT FICTION

Black Tickets, 1979
How Mickey Made It, 1981
Fast Lanes, 1984

OTHER LITERARY FORMS

Although Jayne Anne Phillips's oeuvre is dominated by her short fiction, which includes contributions to numerous anthologies, she has also written novels such as *Counting* (1978), *Machine Dreams* (1984), and *Shelter* (1994). Indeed, *Machine Dreams* was such a critical and popular success that it was ultimately translated into fourteen languages.

ACHIEVEMENTS

Jayne Anne Phillips's work has been critically acclaimed throughout the world, and honors include the Pushcart Prize for her novel *Sweethearts* (1976), in 1977, as well as for several of her short stories in later years; the O. Henry Award for her short-story "Snow," in 1980; and a National Book Critics Circle Award nomination, an American Library Association Notable Book citation, and a Best Books of 1984 citation for *Machine Dreams* from *The New York Times*, all in 1984.

BIOGRAPHY

Jayne Anne Phillips was born July 19, 1952, in Buckhannon, West Virginia. Her parents were Russell R. Phillips, a contractor, and Martha Jane Phillips (née Thornhill), a teacher. On May 26, 1985, Phillips married Mark Brian Stockman, a physician.

Phillips received a B.A. (magna cum laude) from West Virginia University, in 1974, and an M.F.A. from the University of Iowa, in 1978. In 1982, she began working as adjunct associate professor of English at Boston University, and she also held the Fanny Howe Chair of Letters at Brandeis University, Waltham, Massachusetts, from 1986 to 1987. Despite her evidently academic career, however, Phillips has said that teaching does not really interest her and that she prefers to write.

Jayne Anne Phillips (©Jerry Bauer)

ANALYSIS

Jayne Anne Phillips's writing style in her short fiction varies in person and in tone. For example, in "How Mickey Made It" (first published in *Rolling Stone*, on February 5, 1981), the writing style suggests the rambling monologue that results from hearing only one side of a conversation. Phillips originally started her writing career as a poet, an influence that critics contend is apparent in her prose.

Many of Phillips's stories track the modern pursuit of happiness, which seems, for the most part, to be an unsuccessful quest: The main characters in stories such as "Fast Lanes" (first published in *Granta: More Dirt: The New American Fiction*, in the fall of 1986) and "Bess" (first published in *Esquire*, in August of 1984) are all trying to get away from their homes and families, either physically or mentally. The action often takes place around the time of the Vietnam War or soon thereafter. In "Blue Moon," the protagonist's younger brother, Billy, is told to improve his school grades, with his mother pleading, "Don't you know you'll get drafted? Vietnam is on the news every night now."

Many of Phillips's stories are drawn from observations made while traveling, during a period in the 1970's that one critic called "her rootless days on the road" wandering from West Virginia to California and back again. "Fast Lanes" concerns the travels of a pair of post-Vietnam era "dropouts," one a self-described "hippie carpenter" named Thurman and the other an unnamed, twenty-three-year-old cocaine addict who cannot face her addiction—or the consequences of her self-destructive behavior. During a conversation about their respective pasts, Thurman says about "the old days":

> People weren't stupid; they just didn't worry. The war was over, no one was getting drafted. The girls had birth control pills . . . and everything was chummy.

Yet, he then negates this lotus-land vision with a cynical "Ha."

Phillips's stories concentrate on the illusiveness of the sunny American Dream. Thurman's brother Barnes is killed in Vietnam, but his parents refuse to accept it; instead, his father believes that his eldest son's death was caused by drugs because he "wouldn't have died otherwise, he was an athlete." His mother, meanwhile, finds solace in alcohol, preferring to believe that Barnes is still alive, although she is upset that he never calls or writes.

Phillips does not accept "true love" as the panacea to these ills. In "Fast Lanes," the main character's addiction or self-destructive tendencies are too strong to allow her to accept healing in the form of love from Thurman. In "Blue Moon," the protagonist's mother is forever soured on football—she will not allow her son to play for the school team—when her first real love dies of a heart attack after a football game. Her marriage (to someone she clearly considers second best) disintegrates through the years, and she tries to break up her son's love affair with an "unsuitable" girl.

"BESS"

In "Bess," true love has become forbidden love, as it exists between a brother and a sister. It is not necessarily an incestuous love, for in this large family, each brother is described as having a favorite sister. Yet, as the main character, Bess, notes, "No love is innocent once it has recognized its own existence." For the title character in "Bess," the death of her brother Warwick ends her emotional life. She is left alone, with only memories of an event from years before to keep her company.

Many of Phillips's stories develop similar themes. In "Home," "The Heavenly Animal," "Souvenir," "Fast Lanes," and "Something That Happened," Phillips covers the problems of grown-up children and their aging parents. In "Home," a young woman comes home as an adult, forcing her mother to accept both her daughter's and her own sexuality. "The Heavenly Animal" addresses the failure that a father faces as he attempts to draw his adult daughter into his life as a senior citizen. "Souvenir" is the heartrending account of a mother dying of cancer who still can find the strength and courage to comfort her daughter. In "Fast Lanes," a son must accept the mental disintegration of his parents as age and emotional trauma take their toll. Conversely, "Something That Happened" deals with a mother who must accept the strange behavior of her daughter, who morbidly forces her mother to celebrate her wedding anniversary even though her parents have been divorced for five years. In fact, the mother, Kay, notes, "the last sound of the marriage was Richard (her soon-to-be-former-husband) being nervously sick in the kitchen sink."

"SOMETHING THAT HAPPENED"

Phillips's characters often seem on the verge of self-destruction or else eating themselves alive. The mother in "Something That Happened" has had to have half of her stomach removed because of ulcers—through stress and worry, she has chewed her way through her own stomach lining. In fact, she finally tells her children,

> Look, I can't worry for you anymore. If you get into trouble, don't call me. If you want someone to take care of you, take care of each other.

Since then, she has gradually resumed what she calls her "duties," although she still draws the line at attending any of her children's weddings. "Something That Happened" looks at the family from the perspective of a woman trapped by society. The main character, Kay, notes that a woman's fertile years are called "the Child-Bearing Years, as though you stand there like a blossomed pear tree and the fruit plops off." Ironically, her first three daughters become feminist vegetarians, but her fourth, Angela, is a throwback to the days of women in marital bondage. Of her mother's former wedding anniversary, Angela says to Kay: "The trouble with you . . . is that you don't care enough about yourself to remember what's been important in your life," conveniently ignoring the destructiveness of this "something that happened." In addition, Kay has to contend with her daughter trying to feed her, as though if she eats "surely something good will happen."

The perspective of this story is multifaceted; it shows the hurt and anger of a daughter who feels betrayed by her parents' divorce while also presenting evidence that the marriage was literally eating up Kay. Kay's former husband, Richard, comes across as a selfish, sickening sort of personality. For example, after "the fourth pregnancy and first son," Richard is satisfied; he terms the fifth baby a "miscalculation" on Kay's part. This fifth pregnancy does not go as well as the others, however, and Richard feels guilty over not wanting the baby to begin with, so "he swore his love to [Angela]," giving her anything she wanted and a diamond ring on her sixteenth birthday. It is perhaps from this unhealthy aspect of the relationship that Kay is trying most to escape. She even bluntly tells Richard that Angela is his daughter, not his fiance. The day that Richard "slipped the diamond on [Angela's] finger," Kay filed for divorce.

Dysfunctional though this family may be, it is not an obvious picture; characters are abused or degraded in very subtle ways. In fact, what Phillips writes about are the black undercurrents that slowly, inexorably drag her characters down, grinding the hope and joy out of their lives. One of the final images in "Something That Happened" is Kay's recollection of "starting oranges for ten years, piercing thick skins with a fingernail so that the kids could peel them." After a while, she continues, she "didn't want to watch the skin give way to the white ragged coat beneath."

It is this "white ragged coat" that symbolizes the raw pain inside Phillips's characters, pain that is often never resolved or ameliorated. Yet these people do not necessarily give up on life; rather, they live from day to day, surviving as best they can. Phillips's stories have a realistically gritty finish.

OTHER MAJOR WORKS

LONG FICTION: *Sweethearts*, 1976; *Counting*, 1978; *Machine Dreams*, 1984; *Shelter*, 1994; *MotherKind*, 2000.

BIBLIOGRAPHY

Carter, Susanne. "Variations on Vietnam: Women's Innovative Interpretations of the Vietnam War Experience." *Extrapolation* 32 (Summer, 1991): 170-183. This article addresses what it calls "the most representative interpretation possible for a war that still begs for definition." Carter cites Phillips as foremost among the modern innovative writers who reach "beyond the confines of realism to expand the possibilities of interpretation in their individual novels and short stories." Although this article mainly looks at *Machine Dreams*, it casts light on similar themes that recur in many of Phillips's works. Includes a list of works cited.

Edelstein, David. "The Short Story of Jayne Anne Phillips: She Transforms Isolation and Dark Obsession into Exquisite Prose." *Esquire* 104 (December, 1985): 108-112. This article gives a good biographical background, including details of Phillips's childhood and early writing career. Contains comments from one of Phillips's first writing teachers as well as information on Phillips's close relationship with her publisher, Seymour (Sam) Lawrence. Also details Phillips's wanderings across the United States before settling in Boston.

Goldberg, G. D. "The Intimacy of Mass Culture." *New Perspectives Quarterly* 7 (Winter, 1990): 58-62. In this interview, Phillips talks about the role that television plays in the minds of children, suggesting that mass-cultural images replace myth and tradition with little sense of relationship between cultures and generations.

"Jayne Anne Phillips." *Harper's Bazaar* (October, 1984): 213. A brief biographical sketch of Phillips, commenting on her collection of short stories *Black Tickets* and her first novel, *Machine Dreams*; notes that Phillips is dedicated to maintaining the quality of her art and has refused offers to write for Hollywood.

Lassner, Phyllis. "Jayne Anne Phillips: Women's Narrative and the Re-creation of History." In *American Women Writing Fiction: Memory, Identity, Family, Space*, edited by Mickey Pearlman. Lexington: University Press of Kentucky, 1989. This chapter examines Phillips's work in the context of her own comments on characters and settings in her stories. Much of the chapter is devoted to stories from the collection *Fast Lanes* and includes an in-depth discussion of Phillips's writing. Complemented by primary and secondary bibliographies. The primary bibliography is especially helpful for individual publication dates and places for stories.

Phillips, Jayne Anne. "Interview with Jayne Anne Phillips." Interview by Celia Gilbert. *Publishers Weekly* 225 (June 8, 1984): 65-67. Phillips gives her views on her writing, with details about the family stories in *Black Tickets*. Contains some biographical information as well as information on her writing career and her relationship with Seymour (Sam) Lawrence. Phillips also reveals influences on her writing and explains how she works.

Jo-Ellen Lipman Boon

LUIGI PIRANDELLO

Born: Girgenti (now Agrigento), Sicily, Italy; June
   28, 1867
Died: Rome, Italy; December 10, 1936

PRINCIPAL SHORT FICTION

Amori senza amore, 1894

Beffe della morte e della vita, 1902

Quando'ero matto . . ., 1902

Bianche e nere, 1904

Erma bifronte, 1906

La vita nuda, 1910

Terzetti, 1912

Le due maschere, 1914

Erba del nostro orto, 1915

La trappola, 1915

E domani, lunedì, 1917

Un cavallo nella luna, 1918

Berecche e la guerra, 1919

Il carnevale dei morti, 1919

A Horse in the Moon and Twelve Short Stories,
   1932

*Better Think Twice About It! and Twelve Other
   Stories*, 1933

The Naked Truth and Eleven Other Stories, 1934

Four Tales, 1939

The Medals and Other Stories, 1939

Short Stories, 1959

The Merry-Go-Round of Love and Selected Stories,
   1964

Selected Stories, 1964

Short Stories, 1964

OTHER LITERARY FORMS

In addition to 233 published short stories, Luigi
Pirandello produced several volumes of poetry, seven
novels, and forty-four plays. Through his many essays, Pirandello established himself as an influential
literary philosopher, commentator, and critic.

ACHIEVEMENTS

In 1934, Luigi Pirandello was awarded the Nobel
Prize in Literature in recognition of his lifetime
achievement in all the major literary genres.
Pirandello was the preeminent figure in the European
revolt against the pretentiousness and sentimentality
of nineteenth century Romantic literature. With compassion for the reality of human misery, he labored
through more than fifty years of creative activity to
present one central thesis: the bittersweet comedy of
life in which sorrow and joy are inextricably com-
mingled, the absurd contradictoriness of the human
condition. He appealed to generations disillusioned
by the failure of numerous revolutions designed to
bring harmony within countries terrorized by the
chaos of a truly world war and confounded by their
own inability to establish harmony even in their personal relationships with those they loved. His tragicomic view that the paradox of human reality could
be resolved only in black laughter was masterfully
presented in his seminal essay *L'umorismo* (1908, revised 1920; partial translation *On Humour*, 1966,
complete translation, 1974), a view that caught the attention of the literary world and gave rise to the literary movements that coalesced by midtwentieth century as absurdism and existentialism. Pirandello is
recognized as a key figure in the modern exploration
of the crisis of the interior life.

BIOGRAPHY

Born June 28, 1867, to wealthy parents in a small
village on the island of Sicily, Luigi Pirandello was
brought up with the expectation that he would work
in the family sulfur-mining business. From an early
age, however, he showed little interest or talent in
business matters. Instead, he began writing poetry
and short stories and, in 1886, persuaded his father
to allow him to pursue a classical education at the
University of Palermo. In 1887, he went on to the
University of Rome, transferring from there to the
University of Bonn, Germany, where he completed
his doctorate in 1891 with a dissertation in philol-
ogy: a rhetorical study of the dialect of his native Sicilian area.

At the age of twenty-seven, he entered an arranged marriage with the daughter of his father's business partner and settled in a career as a novelist and short-story writer, while teaching at a girls' academy in order to support his growing family of three children. In 1903, the emotional trauma of the failure of the family's sulfur business so affected Pirandello's wife that she became mentally unstable. For more than a dozen years, she plagued him with paranoiac jealousy, spying on his movements and raging about his every relationship both within and without the home. Pirandello devoted himself at great sacrifice to caring for her personally until, in 1919, he finally conceded to placing her in a nursing institution, where she remained until 1959.

During these same troubled years, Europe was enmeshed in the internecine destructiveness of World War I. Pirandello was torn between his dual allegiance to Germany as the land where he had so enjoyed the intellectual stimulation of his graduate studies, and his love for his homeland of Italy, which entered the war in support of France and England. His writings during the years 1903 to 1920 reflect the turmoil of his circumstances and establish his basal premise of the inability of persons to find truth and peace in an existence driven by appearances. Repeatedly, he delineated the hopelessness of his characters' willing assumption of roles to be played—of masks to be worn and so cherished that they cease to be masks at all and become the very reality of the person within.

Pirandello achieved international recognition primarily as a playwright, a genre to which he turned most seriously after 1915, when a few of his earliest plays were first performed. He founded a theater company in Rome in 1925 and managed there a sort of national theater until its financial collapse in 1928. After this, he traveled and worked extensively in Europe and the United States, writing and producing drama and even spending some time in Hollywood studying cinematic form. In December, 1936, he died in Rome and was cremated, following the austere and simple service that he had requested. The world community mourned the loss of a truly great poet, painter, novelist, critical essayist, short-story writer, and dramatist.

Luigi Pirandello, Nobel Laureate for Literature in 1934 (©The Nobel Foundation)

ANALYSIS

Luigi Pirandello's earliest short stories are tales of the insular environment of his native Sicily. Originally written in Sicilian dialect and later translated into Italian, they deal in naturalistic style with the traditions and customs of the peasant peoples. He admired the writings of the Italian Verists (realists) but moved beyond them in his view that reality is individual and psychologically determined. External realism was for Pirandello insufficient for the expression of internal states. He strove to transform naturalistic determinism into a broad philosophical commentary on the inner meaning of the human person, proclaiming that a single reality does not exist. All is illusion, experience is ambiguous, and each person lives behind a self-constructed mask, concealing one's essential nature and adapting to the environment for the protection of the fragile ego within. As his world experience grew, his stories, too, grew to be blends of philosophy and human emotion, brave attempts to express the inexpressible dilemma of humankind's inability to communicate honestly in a world of false appearances and deceitful words.

Pirandello's characters are victims of insecurity and self-doubt, combined with a great capacity for love. They live their lives as in a mirror, reaching always from behind a mask of reality for elusive and illusionary happiness. His characters move out from a core of circumstantial suffering, attempting to discover meaning and truth in the very suffering itself and discovering instead the perverse comedy of deception upon deception—of mask upon mask. Only through ironic laughter could humankind endure such contradiction. Humor, for Pirandello, is an amalgam of laughter and tears, a coming together of the power to mock with the power to sympathize. He treats his characters with pity rather than derision for their follies and with compassion for their inescapable miseries.

Pirandello's stories appeal to the intellect searching for answers to the puzzling contradictions of life. They contain frequent asides, some long disquisitions, and occasional intellectual debates with the self. Characters seem at times to be delivering speeches for the author rather than revealing themselves through action. The narrative line seems fragmented and convoluted, with the reader's interest not drawn steadily along with the unfolding plot but instead concentrated on particular discrete moments of paradox and inversion of fortune.

All of this comes to the non-Italian reader in translations that may seem tedious because of the double problem of language and cultural differences. Since he was chiefly known as a dramatist, Pirandello's stories have been overlooked, many never translated, and often even these few translations are questionable renderings of his thought rather than of his rhetoric. Nevertheless, those few tales that are available will give the thoughtful reader a sampling of the philosophy and view of life of a writer whose works provide a bridge from nineteenth century Romanticism, on through realism, to twentieth century relativism.

"SUNLIGHT AND SHADOW"

Among Pirandello's earliest short stories is "Sole e ombra" ("Sunlight and Shadow"), a tale of the suicide of an elderly gentleman, Ciunna, who has stolen money from the company for which he works in order to help his poverty-stricken son and his young family. On the day after the theft, Ciunna plans to journey to the nearby coastal town where he will throw himself into the sea, thereby escaping judgment and guaranteeing that his son may keep the stolen money.

Here, Pirandello uses the unusual technique of extended "dialogue soliloquies." Ciunna walks about the street of his village on the night of the theft, carrying on vocalized conversations with the inspector who will discover his crime the following day. He speaks also with his son, telling of his great happiness in being able to sacrifice his life for the boy. He chats also with the chemist from whom he has received a few crystals of arsenic in preparation for his suicide.

For two weeks, Ciunna has been going about the streets muttering to himself as he formed his plan, but no one has bothered to ask what is disturbing him. He feels himself an outsider among his friends, a man alienated from others and even from himself. This sense of total alienation from life is a repeated theme in Pirandello's stories and plays, and the response of suicide—or at least the contemplation of it as a possibility for escaping life's harsh realities—is the basis of some two dozen of his better known tales.

On the morning after the theft, Ciunna sets out by horse and carriage on his journey to the sea. As he goes through the countryside, he continues his "dialogue," greeting in a whisper the peasants he sees laboring long hours for a few coins, inviting them to join him on his journey. He calls out within himself "Let's be merry! Let's all go and throw ourselves into the sea! . . . Life's a beautiful thing and we shouldn't trouble it with the sight of us." The motif of life as a ridiculous journey of futility lived among strangers with whom one cannot communicate is a further common element of Pirandellian stories.

Ciunna's plan for death in the sea is foiled when he meets a young friend at the coast who spends the whole day with him. That evening, as he is returning to his village in the same carriage, he swallows the arsenic crystals and dies, alone and in agony, unnoticed even by the driver who is singing overhead.

"ADRIANNA TAKES A TRIP"

A suicide tale of a different sort is "La viaggio" ("Adrianna Takes a Trip"). Adrianna, a widow of thirteen years, lives simply with her two teenage sons in the home of her brother-in-law Cesare. It is the custom in this Sicilian mountain village that mourning for a husband is perpetual, that all widows live in seclusion and in submisiveness to some male of her own or her deceased husband's family. It was Adrianna's accepted role to live this life of repression, this pinched and narrow existence in a barren, parched land, and it was a role that she carried well.

Adrianna's marriage to her husband had been an arranged, loveless affair. He had married her to spite his older brother, who truly loved her as she had come to love him in return through the years of her widowhood. Though neither, by custom, could express their true feelings in any way, each came to understand and accommodate the masks imposed upon them by circumstances and by village expectations.

In time, Adrianna begins to experience some pain in her shoulder and chest. Local doctors advise Cesare to take her to Palermo for diagnosis. She resists the idea of such a journey, fearful of venturing beyond the village after thirty-five years of confinement there. The trip is arranged, however, and she must go despite her terror both at the newness of the experience and at the prospect of being alone with Cesare beyond the village for the first time.

After the diagnosis of a fatal tumor and the procurement of a potentially lethal medicine for her pain, Cesare prevails on Adrianna to continue their trip to the mainland for a short holiday, as is his annual custom. They journey on to Naples, Rome, and finally Venice, each city another revelation to her of the fullness of life, which can never be hers. In the course of their journey, they are at last able to express and consummate their deep love for each other. Adrianna knows, however, that they can never return to Sicily as man and wife—an action considered sacrilegious there. After a day of surrender to perfect joy

together in Venice, she sends Cesare on an errand and drinks the whole of her medicine in one draft, choosing an immediate death of the body over a return to Sicily and a lingering death of the heart.

This tale shows clearly Pirandello's insight concerning women such as Adrianna, the falseness of the life that they were forced to lead, the masks that they were required to wear to hide their true selves, the masks that in turn they forced upon those around them. Adrianna and Cesare were victims of what Pirandello frequently referred to as the "reciprocity of illusion," the mutual life-lie that each human being must assume in order to survive within the black comedy of a world filled with deception and false expectations.

"SIGNORA FROLA AND HER SON-IN-LAW, SIGNOR PONZA"

Adrianna's refusal to continue the mutual deception required by her life circumstances stands in sharp contrast to the positions of the protagonists of "La signora Frola e il signor Ponza, suo genero" ("Signora Frola and Her Son-in-Law, Signor Ponza"). One of Pirandello's most popular and typical tales, it is a highly compressed comic presentation of multiple planes of illusion and reality, a trenchant satire on pious busybodies and their rationalization of gross curiosity. More than that, however, it is his clearest statement of the ironic comedy of humankind's search for the one truth among the many truths that make up the reality of interrelationships and of the compassionate necessity of supporting one another's mutual deceits.

The plot is both simple and complex: A family of three (husband, wife, and mother-in-law) has come to a small town where their background is unknown. Local gossips are eager to solve the mystery of their past and to discover why the two women are maintained in separate households by the husband, Signor Ponza, and why he visits his mother-in-law daily but apparently does not allow her to visit with her daughter except through shouted conversations from courtyard to a third-floor window and through occasional letters. First the husband and then the mother-in-law explain their unusual arrangement, each stating that the other is mad and under a delusion concerning the true identity of the wife: Signor Ponza declares her to be his second wife, taken after the death of Signora Frola's daughter, who had been his first wife, a death that her mother has never accepted and has convinced herself never happened; Signora Frola maintains that the woman is her own daughter and Ponza's only wife, though married to him in a second ceremony after a serious illness of a year's duration during which time he convinced himself that she was dead.

Strangely, each of these two is aware of the other's version of the truth, and not only aware of it but also at pains to help maintain the other's belief in order to preserve their carefully constructed arrangement for living with their mutual tragedy. To believe either of the stories would provide an adequate explanation of the mysterious relationship among the three. To have two apparently "real" explanations, however, is not acceptable to the townspeople, who are bent on discovering "the truth"—even though both the husband and the mother-in-law beseech them to drop their investigation, as further probing can only cause deeper suffering for the little family.

Here, Pirandello illustrates the immutable failure of the desire for truth in a world where individuals know so little of themselves that they can never hope to know the full reality of others. He would have his reader accept the *construziones*, the masks that members of the family have created as a protection from the encroachment of a third reality too terrible to realize. This tale is a Pirandellian conundrum in which nothing is as it seems. Perceptions are not reality; apparent reality may be no more than perceptions. Here, as in all of his works, Pirandello holds that life itself strives to give the perfect illusion of reality. People are all make-believe. Their pretense is their reality, and that is the horror. Through such depiction of ordinary characters enmeshed in the chance circumstances of life and sharing compassionate, redeeming love, Pirandello accomplishes in his short fiction universal statements of lasting human value.

OTHER MAJOR WORKS

LONG FICTION: *L'esclusa*, 1901 (*The Outcast*, 1925); *Il turno*, 1902 (*The Merry-Go-Round of Love*,

1964); *Il fu Mattia Pascal*, 1904 (*The Late Mattia Pascal*, 1923); *Suo marito*, 1911; *I vecchi e i giovani*, 1913 (*The Old and the Young*, 1928); *Si gira . . .*, 1916 (*Shoot! The Notebooks of Serafino Gubbio, Cinematograph Operator*, 1926); *Uno nessuno, centomila*, 1925 (*One, None and a Hundred Thousand*, 1933); *Tutti i romanzi*, 1941 (collected novels).

PLAYS: *La morsa*, pb. as *L'epilogo*, 1898, pr. 1910 (*The Vise*, 1928); *Scamandro*, pb. 1909; *Lumìe di Sicilia*, pr. 1910 (*Sicilian Limes*, 1921); *Il dovere del medico*, pb. 1912 (*The Doctor's Duty*, 1928); *Se non così . . .*, pr. 1915; *All'uscita*, pr. 1916 (*At the Gate*, 1928); *Liolà*, pr. 1916 (English translation, 1952); *Pensaci, Giacomino!*, pr. 1916; *Il berretto a sonagli*, pr. 1917 (*Cap and Bells*, 1957); *Così è (se vi pare)*, pr. 1917 (*Right You Are (If You Think So)*, 1922); *La giara*, pr. 1917 (*The Jar*, 1928); *Il piacere dell'onestà*, pr. 1917 (*The Pleasure of Honesty*, 1923); *Il giuoco delle parti*, pr. 1918 (*The Rules of the Game*, 1959); *Ma non è una cosa seria*, pr. 1918; *La patente*, pb. 1918 (*The License*, 1964); *L'innesto*, pr. 1919; *L'uomo, la bestia, e la virtù*, pr., pb. 1919; *Maschere nude*, pb. 1919-1922 (4 volumes), pb. 1920-1928 (24 volumes), 1920-1929, 1929-1937 (second edition, 31 volumes), 1933-1938; *Come prima, meglio di prima*, pr. 1920; *La Signora Morli, una e due*, pr. 1920; *Tutto per bene*, pr., pb. 1920 (*All for the Best*, 1960); *Sei personaggi in cerca d'autore*, pr., pb. 1921 (*Six Characters in Search of an Author*, 1922); *Enrico IV*, pr., pb. 1922 (*Henry IV*, 1923); *L'imbecille*, pr. 1922 (*The Imbecile*, 1928); *Vestire gli ignudi*, pr. 1922 (*Naked*, 1924); *Three Plays (If You Think So)*, pb. 1922; *L'altro figlio*, pr. 1923 (*The House with the Column*, 1928); *L'uomo dal fiore in bocca*, pr. 1923 (*The Man with the Flower in His Mouth*, 1928); *La vita che ti diedi*, pr. 1923 (*The Life I Gave You*, 1959); *Each in His Own Way and Two Other Plays*, pb. 1923 (includes title play, *The Pleasure of Honesty*, and *Naked*); *Ciascuno a suo modo*, pb. 1923 (*Each in His Own Way*, 1923); *Sagra del Signore della nave*, pb. 1924 (*Our Lord of the Ship*, 1928); *Diana e la Tuda*, Swiss pr. 1926, pr., pb. 1927 (*Diana and Tudo*, 1950); *L'amica della mogli*, pr., pb. 1927 (*The Wives' Friend*, 1949); *Bellavita*, pr. 1927 (English translation, 1964); *La nuova colonia*, pr., pb. 1928 (*The New Colony*, 1958); *The One-Act Plays of Luigi Pirandello*, pb. 1928; *Lazzaro*, pr., pb. 1929 (*Lazarus*, 1952); *O di uno o di nessuno*, pr., pb. 1929; *Sogno (ma forse no)*, pb. 1929 (*I'm Dreaming, But Am I?*, 1964); *Come tu mi vuoi*, pr., pb. 1930 (*As You Desire Me*, 1931); *Questa sera si recita a soggetto*, pr., pb. 1930 (*Tonight We Improvise*, 1932); *I giganti della montagna*, act 1 pb. 1931, act 2 pb. 1934, act 3 pr. 1937 (*The Mountain Giants*, 1958); *Trovarsi*, pr., pb. 1932 (*To Find Oneself*, 1943); *Quando si è qualcuno*, pr. 1933 (*When Someone Is Somebody*, 1958); *La favola del figlio cambiato*, pr., pb. 1934; *Non si sa come*, pr. 1934 (*No One Knows How*, 1960); *Naked Masks: Five Plays*, pb. 1952.

POETRY: *Mal giocondo*, 1889; *Pasqua di Gea*, 1891; *Pier Gudrò*, 1894; *Elegie renane*, 1895; *Elegie romane*, 1896 (translation of Johann Wolfgang von Goethe's *Römische Elegien*); *Scamandro*, 1909 (dramatic poem); *Fuori de chiave*, 1912.

NONFICTION: *Arte e scienze*, 1908; *L'umorismo*, 1908, revised 1920 (partial translation *On Humour*, 1966; complete translation, 1974); *Saggi*, 1939.

MISCELLANEOUS: *Opere*, 1966.

BIBLIOGRAPHY

Bassanese, Fiora A. *Understanding Luigi Pirandello*. Columbia: University of South Carolina Press, 1997. An introduction to Pirandello's work, focusing largely on his thought and the relationship of his life to his work.

Budel, Oscar. *Pirandello*. London: Bowes & Bowes, 1966. Argues Pirandello's short stories depict human entrapment in the strange and incongruous.

Bloom, Harold, ed. *Luigi Pirandello*. New York: Chelsea House, 1989. Bloom has collected ten short selections from the best studies of Pirandello's major thought and works. These include critical articles as well as selections and full chapters from complete works. Dante della Terza's essay "On Pirandello's Humorism" will be especially useful. Contains a short chronology, a bibliography, and an index.

Caesar, Ann. *Characters and Authors in Luigi Pirandello*. New York: Clarendon Press, 1998. A good study focusing on Luigi Pirandello's characters. Includes bibliographical references and an index.

Cambon, Glauco, ed. *Pirandello*. Englewood Cliffs, N.J.: Prentice-Hall, 1967. This collection of twelve essays contains Adriano Tilgher's seminal Pirandello criticism and moves on through critical views of the 1960's, a period of intense interest in Pirandello's influence on world literature of the early twentieth century. Includes a detailed chronology and a select bibliography.

Caputi, Anthony. *Pirandello and the Crisis of Modern Consciousness*. Urbana: University of Illinois Press, 1988. Caputi is concerned with Pirandello as the source of the twentieth century's literary recognition and explication of the crisis of self-awareness. One of the few approaches to Pirandello's thought that makes equal reference to all forms of his work, not limiting itself to his plays. Supplemented by an extensive Italian and English bibliography and an index.

DiGaetani, John Louis, ed. *A Companion to Pirandello Studies*. New York: Greenwood Press, 1991. A comprehensive volume, twenty-seven essays on Pirandello's biography and work, with an excellent introduction and several appendices, including production histories and an extensive bibliography.

May, Frederick. Introduction to *Short Stories* by Luigi Pirandello. London: Oxford University Press, 1965. Argues that Pirandello's basic fiction themes are the same as those in his plays: the nature of identity, reality and illusion, and the difficulty of communication.

Radcliff-Umstead, Douglas. *The Mirror of Our Anguish: A Study of Luigi Pirandello's Narrative Writing*. Rutherford, N.J.: Fairleigh Dickinson University Press, 1978. The introductory segment on Pirandello's philosophy of literature and its role in literary history is excellent. Of particular interest is the in-depth study of his short fiction complemented by a full treatment of his rhetorical style and themes. Extensive bibliography, index.

Starkie, Walter. *Luigi Pirandello*. 3d ed. Berkeley: University of California Press, 1965. Starkie, a widely recognized Pirandello scholar, focuses on the author's position as inheritor of one literary tradition and forerunner of another. He provides one of the few extended commentaries on Pirandello's prose fiction, novels, and short stories, and does so in nontechnical style. Includes a bibliography and index.

Gabrielle Rowe

SYLVIA PLATH

Born: Boston, Massachusetts; October 27, 1932
Died: London, England; February 11, 1963

PRINCIPAL SHORT FICTION
Johnny Panic and the Bible of Dreams, 1977, 1979

OTHER LITERARY FORMS

Sylvia Plath is widely recognized as one of the strongest and most distinctive American poets of the postwar period. Her major collections include *The Colossus* (1960), a number of posthumous collections including *Ariel* (1965), *Crossing the Water* (1971), and the definitive *Collected Poems* (1981). She also wrote the best-selling novel *The Bell Jar*, which first appeared in England under the pseudonym Victoria Lucas in 1963.

ACHIEVEMENTS

Sylvia Plath's *Collected Poems* won the Pulitzer Prize for poetry in 1982. She was a Fulbright scholar in England (1955-1957) and a Phi Beta Kappan.

BIOGRAPHY

Sylvia Plath was born October 27, 1932, in Boston, Massachusetts. Her father Otto, a professor of biology and renowned entomologist, died when she was a young child, leaving Plath in the care of her mother Aurelia (née Schober). A number of instances in her writings acknowledge this event as one of the most traumatic in her life, creating in her a sense of abandonment that fueled the dark, introspective character that is prominent in her work. A distinguished academic, Plath graduated summa cum laude from Smith College in 1955. She attended Newnham College, Cambridge, on a Fulbright scholarship, receiving her M.A. in 1957. She married renowned English poet Ted Hughes in 1956.

After completing her graduate work at Cambridge, Plath returned to the United States, where she taught for a year at Smith. Shortly thereafter, she returned with Hughes to England, where she spent the last years of her life raising two children and writing. She committed suicide in early 1963.

Plath was briefly institutionalized after a breakdown and suicide attempt in 1953 that delayed the completion of her undergraduate work at Smith. She recounts this experience in the autobiographical novel *The Bell Jar*, which appeared shortly before her death in 1963. Plath's literary reputation is based primarily on the confessional, metaphorically dense poems she wrote during the late 1950's and early 1960's. However, she also wrote a number of short fiction works during this period that appeared in publications as diverse as *Sewanee Review*, *The Atlantic Monthly*, *Madamoiselle*, and *Granta*. In the decades following her death, much of this work has been rediscovered, mostly due to the 1977 appearance of *Johnny Panic and the Bible of Dreams*, a collection of Plath's more significant short prose writings.

ANALYSIS

Like her poetry, Plath's short fiction is characterized primarily by its mythic dimension. It reveals a profound fascination with dream and ritual, and their connection to artistic endeavor. Similarly, both her poetry and fiction are strikingly allusive. Regardless of its subject matter or genre, the body of Plath's work concerns the aura of mystery and myth surrounding major transitions in human life. Her stories typically concern the ambivalence people feel during transformative experiences, and they seek to characterize that ambivalence.

Ted Hughes asserts in his introduction to Plath's short fiction collection *Johnny Panic and the Bible of Dreams* that her fiction also tends to be highly autobiographical. In fact, Plath withheld much of it from publication during her lifetime, fearing the reprisals of those who might recognize themselves and disapprove of her portrayal of them in her work. Plath's protagonists are almost universally female, which also suggests that she wished to remain at the center of even her most exotic and experimental stories.

As do many fiction writers, Plath frequently recycles characters and motifs from previous works. A number of her earlier short stories in ways appear to function as prototypes for her most developed work, the later novel *The Bell Jar*. For example, both *The Bell Jar* and "Johnny Panic and the Bible of Dreams" depict traumatic experiences with electroshock therapy, although each differs significantly in style and tone. Henry in "Sunday at the Mintons'" and *The Bell Jar*'s Buddy Willard possess a similar tendency toward dogged, uninspired rationality. Both "Mothers" and *The Bell Jar* center on the experiences of a protagonist named Esther, who is often interpreted as Plath's alter ego. Similarly, Esther struggles in both works with her fears and misgivings about motherhood and female identity.

"Sunday at the Mintons'"

Plath's earliest story to merit critical attention, "Sunday at the Mintons'" reflects in prose the stylistic tendency of her early poetry toward control and order. Written in third person to heighten its pervasive sense of restraint, the story focuses on the relationship between two parentless, retired siblings—the compulsive, "fastidious" Henry and his "impertinent," daydreaming sister Elizabeth. Having been forced late in life into each other's care, the pair confront their many differences in personality and per-

Sylvia Plath in 1955 (The Sophie Smith Collection, Smith College)

spective during an evening meal and stroll by the ocean.

Plath's discipline as a poet becomes markedly evident in this story, particularly toward its conclusion. In the climactic scene, Elizabeth loses a treasured brooch, given to her by her deceased mother, while leaning absently into the evening tide. When Henry treads stiffly but dutifully into the water to retrieve it, he is leveled by an unexpectedly strong "black" wave. Elizabeth, unable to deny the humor in the situation, takes the opportunity to muse lyrically about her brother, whom she compares to "Neptune sitting regally on a wave with his trident in his hand and the crown on his blown white hair." Henry, the unlikely object of her mythic fantasy, returns from the sea dripping wet, brooch in hand. His gesture underscores the story's awareness of the tension between rigidity and spontaneity in human experience.

"Johnny Panic and the Bible of Dreams"

Brazenly satirical and consciously allegorical, "Johnny Panic and the Bible of Dreams," written in 1958, differs markedly in approach from Plath's other fiction. The story was composed around the same time as *The Bell Jar* and is akin to the novel in subject matter. Like *The Bell Jar*, "Johnny Panic" concerns Plath's deep fear of electroshock therapy, with which she had a number of horrific experiences in her life-long battle with depression. However, while the depiction of her experiences with the therapy in the novel is primarily straightforward, in "Johnny Panic" it is woven into an allegorical tapestry that is decidedly more surrealistic and Kafkaesque. The story's unnamed narrator, a clerical worker in a psychiatric ward, is caught by one of her supervisors, a psychiatrist, copying accounts of patients' dreams into a secret notebook, which she fancifully calls "Johnny Panic's Bible of Dreams." A self-proclaimed "lover of dreams," she seeks what, to her mind, is a clearer understanding of the collective unconscious through these stolen dream accounts. She describes the unconscious as a "lake" into which "people's minds run at night . . . the sewage farm of the ages."

The narrator is promptly whisked away by the doctor into electroshock therapy, which she chides as an attempt "to unseat Johnny Panic from his own throne." The story ends with her first treatment, the narrator left "shaken like a leaf in the teeth of glory," her namesake Johnny Panic beckoning her in "a nimbus of arc lights on the ceiling overhead." The story's ambiguous, irresolute ending reflects the narrator's own ambivalence toward both the shame and sanctimoniousness of her illness. At points she flaunts her condition playfully before the reader like a badge of honor; at others she hides it self-consciously like her purloined book of dreams.

"THE FIFTEEN-DOLLAR EAGLE"

Written in 1959, "The Fifteen-Dollar Eagle" contains some of Plath's boldest experiments with subject matter, description, and characterization. Written in first person, but with relatively little interpretive intrusion on the part of the narrator, the story meticulously describes the inner workings of a tattoo shop. On the insistence of her "steady man" Ned Bean, the narrator visits the shop of Carmey, a colorful and matter-of-fact tattoo artist, where she furtively explores the part-ritualistic, part-clinical exhibition of Carmey's craft.

The narrator tentatively observes Carmey as he tattoos two men—one a seasoned sailor, the other a naïve schoolboy. Each man's unique reaction to this exotic, seminal experience sets up the story's central dynamic, which involves the tension between the pride and fear associated with this archetypal but enigmatic ritual. Plath describes the ritual memorably, in a story rich and perceptive in its passion for detail and description.

"MOTHERS"

Plath's last completed story, "Mothers," written in 1962, deals with two of the most prevalent motifs in her fiction, hypocrisy and motherhood. The story concerns Esther, a young mother who, having recently moved to the English countryside, seeks to involve herself in her new community by attending a "Mothers' Union" meeting at the local church. Through a litany of disillusioning experiences with superficial and self-important "church people," Esther eventually establishes a more satisfying, meaningful relationship with Mrs. Nolan, an outspoken, endearing divorcée. Ironically, Mrs. Nolan has been summarily excluded from the Mothers' Union because of the church's disapproval of divorce. Still, she forges an unlikely but intimate bond with Esther, who shares her sense of alienation and innate sense of being tagged an "outsider."

"Mothers" is among Plath's most pointedly autobiographical stories. Written at a time when marital frictions between her and husband Ted Hughes had led to their separation, the story likewise has Esther and husband Tom "arguing loudly and freely" as the story begins. Similarly, "Mothers" presents an almost pathological preoccupation with hypocrisy. This is portrayed primarily in the character of the absent-minded, solicitous village rector, who embodies the fundamental lack of sincerity and conviction Esther regards as endemic to organized religion. "Mothers" clearly reflects the struggles Plath herself endured late in her life as she fought to forge a new identity in the wake of marital conflict, single parenthood, religious skepticism, and depression.

OTHER MAJOR WORKS

LONG FICTION: *The Bell Jar*, 1963.

POETRY: *The Colossus and Other Poems*, 1960; *Three Women*, 1962; *Ariel*, 1965; *Crossing the Wa-*

ter: *Transitional Poems*, 1971; *Crystal Gazer*, 1971; *Fiesta Melons*, 1971; *Lyonesse*, 1971; *Winter Trees*, 1971; *Pursuit*, 1973; *The Collected Poems*, 1981; *Selected Poems*, 1985.

NONFICTION: *Letters Home*, 1975; *The Journals of Sylvia Plath*, 1982 (Ted Hughes and Frances McCullough, editors).

CHILDREN'S LITERATURE: *The Bed Book*, 1976.

BIBLIOGRAPHY

Alvarez, A. *The Savage God: A Study of Suicide.* New York: Random House, 1972. Probes the connections between Plath's thematic preoccupation with suicide and the inner traumas that led her to take her own life. Uses the life and work of Plath as a focal point for a broadly based discussion of the theme of self-destruction and annihilation present in the work of many artists.

Bundtzen, Lynda K. *Plath's Incarnations: Woman and the Creative Process.* Ann Arbor: University of Michigan Press, 1983. A collection of critical essays exploring various issues in Plath's poetry and fiction, particularly those related to feminine identity. Contains an exceptionally perceptive analysis of *The Bell Jar* and Plath's related, "autobiographical" fiction.

Butscher, Edward. *Sylvia Plath: Method and Madness.* New York: Seabury Press, 1976. The first major critical biography of Plath; a highly accessible account of the forces that shaped her distinctive poetic and fictive voices.

_____, ed. *Sylvia Plath: The Woman and the Work.* New York: Dodd, Mead, 1977. A collection of critical essays on the life and work of Plath compiled by her principal biographer. Opens with a biographical essay by the editor, followed by critical essays on Plath's work by a number of prominent writers and critics, including Joyce Carol Oates, Irving Howe, and Marjorie Perloff. Devotes two chapters directly to the discussion of Plath's fiction.

Hall, Caroline King Barnard. *Sylvia Plath, Revised.* Boston: Twayne, 1998. As the title implies, a pointedly revisionist view of Plath's work. Noting that much of the significant criticism of Plath's poetry and fiction appeared in the 1970's, this collection attempts to reinterpret Plath's poetry and fiction in a more contemporary context. Features one of the most detailed discussions of her short fiction to date.

Hughes, Ted. *Birthday Letters.* New York: Farrar, Straus & Giroux, 1998. A collection of poems written by Hughes on the subject of his heavily mythologized relationship with Plath. At times joyous, at others painfully self-revealing, the book offers valuable insights into both the professional and personal relationship shared by these two literary icons.

Stevenson, Anne. *Bitter Fame: A Life of Sylvia Plath.* Boston: Houghton Mifflin, 1989. More personal in nature than Butscher's biography, this book focuses more closely on the pathology of Plath's struggle with depression. Draws heavily on insights gained from close friends and acquaintances of Plath's, making it as much a depiction of Plath the person as Plath the writer.

Gregory D. Horn

WILLIAM PLOMER

Born: Pietersberg, Transvaal (now South Africa), December 10, 1903

Died: Hassocks, Sussex, England, September 21, 1973

PRINCIPAL SHORT FICTION

I Speak of Africa, 1927

Paper Houses, 1929

The Child of Queen Victoria and Other Stories, 1933

Four Countries, 1949

OTHER LITERARY FORMS

Electric Delights, William Plomer's posthumously published 1978 collection of "scattered pieces," reveals the breadth of the author's interests. During his long career he published many volumes of poetry and many novels, as well as biographies and autobiographies. He also wrote librettos for operas and cantatas composed by the prominent British composer Benjamin Britten.

ACHIEVEMENTS

William Plomer received the Queen's Gold Medal for Poetry in 1963 and was made a Commander of the Order of the British Empire in 1968. He was corecipient with Alan Aldridge of the Whitbread Literary Award for best children's book (*The Butterfly Ball and the Grasshopper's Feast*) in 1973.

BIOGRAPHY

William Charles Franklyn Plomer was born of English parents in Transvaal (now South Africa) on December 10, 1903. He was educated at Rugby in England and St. John's College in Johannesburg. In South Africa he worked on farms and later operated a trading store with his father in Zululand. He became sensitized both to the beauty of the country and the injustice of white colonialism. He left South Africa when outrage on the part of his fellow white colonists forced the closure of his antiracist journal *Voorslag*

(whiplash). He had already scandalized the white elite minority with his first novel, Turbott Wolfe (1925), because of its condoning of intermarriage between whites and blacks and criticism of the multiple ways in which blacks were exploited and in some instances brutalized by whites. He traveled extensively—notably in Japan, Greece, and Italy—before finally settling in England in 1932, where he eventually became a prominent British man of letters. During World War II he served in British Naval Intelligence. He was noted for his wide range of literary interests, which included short stories, poems, novels, memoirs, essays, travel sketches, translations, musical librettos, and a children's book. He knew many of the most important writers of his time. For more than thirty years he was senior editor at the London publishing firm of Jonathan Cape. He died in East Sussex, England, on September 21, 1973.

ANALYSIS

Most of William Plomer's short stories were written in his twenties. His best stories deal with Africa, where he was born and spent much of his early life. His major claim to fame is that he was one of the first white colonists to sympathize with the exploited natives and to foresee the time—which has since arrived—when they would demand democracy and equality.

Plomer was a poet as well as a polished fiction and nonfiction writer. His poetic sensibility is evident in his remarkably mature powers of description. He has the ability to make the reader see, smell, hear, and feel—so that the reader is drawn into a three-dimensional setting.

Plomer was a world traveler for many years, like other famous British writers such as Joseph Conrad, Rudyard Kipling, W. Somerset Maugham, and Graham Greene. The two short-story writers who influenced him most strongly were Guy de Maupassant and Ivan Bunin. Plomer's remarkable sensitivity made him an accurate recorder of the differences and similarities of humans everywhere—a gift indispensable to a fiction writer. It also made him aware of the social unrest that would lead to such dramatic social and political changes after World War II.

Plomer's stories are characterized by polished prose, poetic sensitivity to impressions, modesty, sincerity, and freedom from prejudice. In the preface to *Four Countries*, a collection of stories set in South Africa, Japan, Greece, and England, Plomer wrote: "In their way I think most of my stories reflect the age by isolating some crisis caused by a change of environment or by the sudden and sometimes startling confrontation of different races and classes."

"ULA MASONDA"

Ula Masonda is the name of a young South African native who, like many of his contemporaries, leaves his village to go to Johannesburg to work in the mines. Torn from family, friends, and native soil, Ula Masonda undergoes a character change. He becomes more and more like the dissolute, proletarianized natives who arrived before him. Evil companions lure him into committing robberies in order to support their corrupt lifestyle. He falls in love with a black prostitute. His dangerous occupation leads to his being injured in a rock fall. He is sent back home wearing European clothing which makes him look ridiculous. He no longer feels a sense of belonging and even rejects his own mother as a "heathen." He is a man without a country, despised by the whites, a stranger among his own people.

This story displays Plomer's creative imagination as well as his social and political awareness. "Ula Masonda" is unique because it incorporates a long poem prophesying revolution and liberation, presented as part of the hero's delirium while lying under the rubble. J. R. Doyle, the best explicator of Plomer's stories, writes: "Clearly Ula Masondo is a symbol, and William Plomer is here concerned not with one human being but with millions."

"THE CHILD OF QUEEN VICTORIA"

"The Child of Queen Victoria" is one of Plomer's best and best-known short stories. Like all of Plomer's South African fiction, it draws heavily on his personal experience. It was written when he was quite young and reflects a young man's libido. The viewpoint character, Frant, a young Englishman with a good education and genteel manners, goes to South Africa to "find himself," as so many young Englishmen did in the days when the British Empire girdled the globe. He is employed by an ignorant, materialistic, and racist couple named MacGavin, who operate a trading station in Lembuland selling cheap manufactured goods to the natives. Unlike his employers, Frant finds himself in sympathy with the natives and recognizes them as individuals rather than "niggers" who have to be kept in their place.

Frant feels lonely. He has nothing in common with the MacGavins and is unable to make friends among the natives. As a member of the white ruling class, he has to maintain a certain distance, and the natives regard him as a strange alien whom they call "the child of Queen Victoria." Then Frant falls in love with a beautiful young native woman named Seraphina, who also seems attracted to him. He is torn with desire but cannot establish an intimate relationship. Marriage is out of the question, even illegal. She would not consider anything less—although sexual relations between white men and black women are hardly unknown in the region. Ultimately, Frant's dilemma is resolved when Seraphina and her family are wiped out in a flash flood.

"The Child of Queen Victoria" resembles Joseph Conrad's famous long story *Heart of Darkness* (1899, serial; 1902) in its ability to evoke the sights, sounds, and atmosphere of Africa. Plomer makes the reader feel he is actually in South Africa and even right inside the crowded, noisy trading station. His story also resembles Conrad's in dealing with the impact of environment on human character. Frant, like Conrad's Kurtz, is gradually and irrevocably changed and—as MacGavin repeatedly warns him—is in danger of "going native." The story's only flaw is its *deux-ex-machina* ending. Frant's internal conflict is unresolved, and perhaps unresolvable; Plomer is forced to end his story by arbitrarily killing the object of his hero's obsession.

"WHEN THE SARDINES CAME"

This story is told through the viewpoint of a minor character, but the dramatic events concern his hostess Mrs. Reymond and her husband. Charles Edwards, a young medical student, is staying at their home near the coast. They promise a thrilling spectacle when the annual sardine run takes place in June. Life is uneventful until the huge shoals of sardines appear, pursued by bigger fish and diving gulls and gannets. This creates a sort of mass hysteria among the human population. People of all races and all social classes rush to gather beached sardines and catch the bigger fish pursuing them. One young man named Boris is badly injured while trying to haul his five-foot-long catch ashore. Mrs. Reymond, excited by the blood sport and Boris's animal magnetism, has him carried to her bedroom, where she nurses him back to health. They become lovers. After Boris recuperates, Mr. Reymond confides to Edwards that he was aware of what was going on and felt jealous but did nothing. He saw this affair for what it was: a middle-aged woman's last taste of romance before accepting the boredom and sexlessness of old age.

This ostensibly simple story, like "Black Peril," is fraught with implications. It reflects Plomer's belief in the supremacy of the life force, the hypocrisy of middle-class values, his antipathy for the repression of women everywhere, and the indelible influence of environment on human character.

"BLACK PERIL"

This is another story of adultery but was even more daring for its time than "When the Sardines Came" because it involves a white woman and a black native African. Vera Corneliussen is a sensual woman married to a man who takes her for granted and is preoccupied with his own affairs, like George Tessman in Henrik Ibsen's play *Hedda Gabler* (1890) or Leonce Pontellier in Kate Chopin's novel *The Awakening* (1899). Vera takes advantage of her husband's extended absence to seduce Charlie, a young black house servant who exudes sexuality and "the lure of the forbidden." This avant-garde, impressionistic story is told mostly through the rambling thoughts and memories of Vera while in a delirium. Eventually she dies—but Plomer leaves the cause of her death unclear. At any rate, Charlie is automatically considered a rapist and murderer because of his race. He will inevitably be captured and lynched by white colonials.

OTHER MAJOR WORKS

LONG FICTION: *Turbott Wolfe*, 1925; *Sado*, 1931 (also pb. as *They Never Came Back*, 1932); *The Case Is Altered*, 1932; *Cecil Rhodes*, 1933; *The Invaders*, 1934; *Ali the Lion: Ali of Tebeleni, Pasha of Jannina, 1741-1822*, 1936.

PLAYS: *Gloriana*, pr., pb. 1953 (libretto); *Curlew River: A Parable for Church Performance*, pb. 1964 (libretto); *The Burning Fiery Furnace: Second Parable for Church Performance*, pb. 1966 (libretto); *The Prodigal Son: Third Parable for Church Performance*, pb. 1968 (libretto).

POETRY: *The Family Tree*, 1929; *The Fivefold Screen*, 1932; *Visiting the Caves*, 1936; *Selected Poems*, 1940; *The Dorking Thigh and Other Satires*, 1945; *Borderline Ballads*, 1955 (pb. in England as *A Shot in the Park*, 1955); Collected Poems, 1960 (enlarged edition, 1973); *Taste and Remember*, 1966; *Celebrations*, 1972.

NONFICTION: *Notes for Poems*, 1927; *Double Lives: An Autobiography*, 1943 (revised, 1956); *Museum Pieces*, 1952; *At Home: Memoirs*, 1958; *The Autobiography of William Plomer*, 1975.

CHILDREN'S LITERATURE: *The Butterfly Ball and the Grasshopper's Feast*, 1973.

EDITED TEXTS: Haruko Ichikawa, *Japanese Lady in Europe*, 1937; Robert Francis Kilvert, *Kilvert's Diary, 1870-1879* (1938-1940; 3 volumes; revised, 1961); Herman Melville, *Selected Poems*, 1943; William D'Arfey, *Curious Relations*, 1945, 1947; Richard Rumbold, *A Message in Code: The Diary of Richard Rumbold, 1932-1961*, 1964.

MISCELLANEOUS: *Electric Delights*, 1978 (essays, poems, stories, and travel sketches).

BIBLIOGRAPHY

Allen, Walter. *The Modern Novel in Britain and the United States*. New York: E. P. Dutton, 1964. Professor Allen includes Plomer in this discussion of the most important modern fiction writers, hailing him as the ancestor of South African fiction. Allen states that Plomer's theme "has always been that of the Displaced Person in the larger and literal sense of the phrase."

Doyle, John Robert, Jr. *William Plomer*. New York:

Twayne, 1969. Part of the distinguished Twayne World Authors Series, this is one of the best studies of William Plomer available. Doyle, an authority on Plomer's writings, taught at many South African universities and published essays in a number of South African periodicals. Chapter 2 describes and analyzes Plomer's short stories in depth. Contains a chronology, copious reference notes, a bibliography, and an index.

Spender, Stephen. "A Singular Man." *New Statesman* 86 (November 9, 1973): 690. Spender, a leading English poet and influential literary figure, published this tribute shortly after his friend Plomer's death. Spender writes: "All his qualities were wind-blown, sun-saturated, sparkling, and in his writing the language shines and curls like waves animated by a strong breeze on a clear day."

Tucker, Martin. *Africa in Modern Literature: A Survey of Contemporary Writing in English*. New York: Frederick Ungar, 1967. This interesting and authoritative discussion of all modern literature about the African continent contains many pages about Plomer in various contexts. Tucker hails him as the first white South African writer to treat miscegenation and interracial fraternization from the viewpoint of social and political protest rather than as something forbidden and shameful.

Bill Delaney

EDGAR ALLAN POE

Born: Boston, Massachusetts; January 19, 1809
Died: Baltimore, Maryland; October 7, 1849

PRINCIPAL SHORT FICTION

Tales of the Grotesque and Arabesque, 1840
The Prose Romances of Edgar Allan Poe, 1843
Tales, 1845
The Short Fiction of Edgar Allan Poe, 1976 (Stuart and Susan Levine, editors)

OTHER LITERARY FORMS

During his short literary career, Edgar Allan Poe produced a large quantity of writing, most of which was not collected in book form during his lifetime. He published one novel, *The Narrative of Arthur Gordon Pym* (1838), and several volumes of poetry, the most famous of which is *The Raven and Other Poems* (1845). Poe earned his living mainly as a writer and as an editor of magazines. For magazines, he wrote reviews, occasional essays, meditations, literary criticism, and a variety of different kinds of journalism, as well as poetry and short fiction.

ACHIEVEMENTS

During his life, Edgar Allan Poe was a figure of controversy and so became reasonably well known in literary circles. Two of his works were recognized with prizes: "Manuscript Found in a Bottle" and "The Gold-Bug." "The Raven," his most famous poem, created a sensation when it was published and became something of a best-seller. After his death, Poe's reputation grew steadily—though in the United States opinion remained divided—until by the middle of the twentieth century he had clear status as an author of worldwide importance. Poe's achievements may be measured in terms of what he has contributed to literature and of how his work influenced later culture.

Poe was accomplished in fiction, poetry, and criticism, setting standards in all three that distinguish him from most of his American contemporaries. In fiction, he is credited with inventing the conventions of the classical detective story, beginning the modern genre of science fiction, and turning the conventions of gothic fiction to the uses of high art in stories such as "The Fall of the House of Usher." He was also an accomplished humorist and satirist. In poetry, he produced a body of work that is respected throughout the world and a few poems that have endured as classics, notably "The Raven," as well as several poems that, in part because of their sheer verbal beauty, have persistently appealed to the popular imagination, such as "The Bells" and "Annabel Lee." In criticism, Poe is among the first to advocate and demonstrate methods of textual criticism that came into their own in the twentieth century, notably in his essay "The Philosophy of Composition," in which he analyzed with remarkable objectivity the process by which "The Raven" was built in order to produce a specified effect in its readers.

Poe's influence on later culture was pervasive. Nearly every important American writer after Poe shows signs of influence, especially when working in the gothic mode or with grotesque humor. The French, Italians, and writers in Spanish and Portuguese in the Americas acknowledge and demonstrate their debts to Poe in technique and vision. Only to begin to explore Poe's influence on twentieth century music and film would be a major undertaking. In terms of his world reputation, Poe stands with William Faulkner and perhaps T. S. Eliot as one of the most influential authors of the United States.

Edgar Allen Poe (Library of Congress)

BIOGRAPHY

Edgar Allan Poe was born in Boston on January 19, 1809. His parents, David and Elizabeth Arnold Poe, were actors at a time when the profession was not widely respected in the United States. David was making a success in acting when alcohol addiction brought an end to his career. He deserted his family a year after Edgar's birth; Elizabeth died a year later in 1811, leaving Edgar an orphan in Richmond, Virginia. There, he was taken in by John Allan, who educated him well in England and the United States. Poe was a sensitive and precocious child; during his teens, his relations with his foster father declined. Stormy relations continued until Allan's first wife died and his second wife had children. Once it became unlikely that he would inherit anything significant from the wealthy Allan, Poe, at the age of

twenty-one, having already published a volume of poetry, began a literary career.

From 1831 to 1835, more or less dependent on his Poe relatives, he worked in Baltimore, writing stories and poems, a few of which were published. In 1835, he secretly married his cousin, Virginia Clemm, when she was thirteen. From 1835 to 1837, he was assistant editor of *The Southern Literary Messenger*, living on a meager salary, tending to drink enough to disappoint the editor, publishing his fiction, and making a national reputation as a reviewer of books. When he was fired, he moved with his wife (by then the marriage was publicly acknowledged) and her mother to New York City, where he lived in poverty, selling his writing for the next two years. Though he published *The Narrative of Arthur Gordon Pym* in 1838, it brought him no income. He moved to Philadelphia that same year and for several months continued to live on only a small income from stories and other magazine pieces. In 1839, he became coeditor of *Burton's Gentleman's Magazine*. Before drinking led to his losing this job, he wrote and published some of his best fiction, such as "The Fall of the House of Usher." He took another editing position with *Graham's Magazine* that lasted about a year. He then lived by writing and working at occasional jobs. In 1844, he went with his family back to New York City. His wife, Virginia, had been seriously ill, and her health was declining. In New York, he wrote for newspapers. In 1845, he published "The Raven" and *Tales*, both of which were well received ("The Raven" was a popular success), though again his income from them was small. In the early nineteenth century, an author could not easily earn a satisfactory income from writing alone, in part because of the lack of international copyright laws. He was able to purchase a new weekly, *The Broadway Journal*, but it failed in 1846.

After 1845, Poe was famous, and his income, though unstable, was a little more dependable. His life, however, did not go smoothly. He was to some extent lionized in literary circles, but his combination of desperation for financial support with alcoholism and a combative temper kept him from dealing well with being a "star." Virginia died in 1847, and Poe was seriously ill for much of the next year. In 1849, he found himself in Richmond, and for a few months he seemed quite well. His Richmond relatives received and cared for him kindly, and he stopped drinking. In October, however, while on a trip, he paused in Baltimore, became drunk, was found unconscious, and was carried to a local hospital, where he died on October 7, 1849.

ANALYSIS

The variety of Edgar Allan Poe's short fiction cannot be conveyed fully in a short introduction. Though he is best known for his classics of gothic horror such as "The Fall of the House of Usher" and his portraits of madmen and grotesques such as "The Tell-Tale Heart" and "The Cask of Amontillado," he is also the author of detective stories, "The Purloined Letter"; science fiction, *The Narrative of Arthur Gordon Pym*; parodies, "The Premature Burial"; satires, "The Man That Was Used Up"; social and political fiction, "The

System of Dr. Tarr and Prof. Fether"; and a variety of kinds of humor, "Diddling Considered as One of the Exact Sciences" and "Hop-Frog."

Three stories that illustrate some of this variety while offering insight into Poe's characteristic themes are "A Descent into the Maelström," "The Purloined Letter," and "The Fall of the House of Usher." Among Poe's central themes is an emphasis on the mysteries of the self, of others, of nature, and of the universe. His stories usually function in part to undercut the kinds of easy optimism and certainty that were characteristic of popular thought in his time.

"A DESCENT INTO THE MAELSTRÖM"

"A Descent into the Maelström," which first appeared in *Graham's Magazine* in May, 1841, and was collected in *Tales*, opens with a declaration of mystery: "The ways of God in Nature, as in Providence, are not as our ways; nor are the models that we frame any way commensurate to the vastness, profundity, and unsearchableness of His works, which have a depth in them greater than the well of Democritus." In using this epigraph, slightly altered from the seventeenth century English essayist Joseph Glanvill, Poe announces several motifs for the story that follows. One of these is the mystery of how God acts and, therefore, may be revealed in nature. Another is inadequacy of humanly devised models for explaining nature or God's presence in nature. Yet another is the idea of the multiple senses of depth, not merely the physical depth of a well or a maelstrom, but also the metaphorical depths of a mystery, of God, of nature, of God's manifestation in nature.

The story is relatively simple in its outline, though interestingly complicated by its frame. In the frame, the narrator visits a remote region of Norway to look upon the famous maelstrom, an actual phenomenon described in contemporary reference books that were Poe's sources. There, he encounters an apparently retired fisherman, who guides him to a view of the whirlpool and who then tells the story of how he survived being caught in it. In the main body of the story, the guide explains how a sudden hurricane and a stopped watch caused him and his two brothers to be caught by the maelstrom as they attempted to return from a routine, if risky, fishing trip. He explains what the experience was like and how he managed to survive even though his boat and his brothers were lost. Poe carefully arranges the frame and the fisherman's narration to emphasize his themes.

The frame narrator is a somewhat comic character. The guide leads him to what he calls a little cliff and calmly leans over its edge to point out the sights, but the narrator is terrified by the cliff itself: "In truth so deeply was I excited by the perilous position of my companion, that I fell at full length upon the ground, clung to the shrubs around me, and dared not even glance upward at the sky—while I struggled in vain to divest myself of the idea that the very foundations of the mountain were in danger from the fury of the winds." On one level this is high comedy. The narrator professes to be worried about his companion's safety but cannot help revealing that he is personally terrified, and his resulting posture contrasts humorously with the equanimity of his guide. On another level, however, Poe is also suggesting at least two serious ideas. The narrator's description of the cliff, with its sheer drop of sixteen hundred feet, should remind most readers that in a strong wind, they would feel and behave much the same as the narrator. This realization makes the next idea even more significant: The pose the narrator has adopted is pointedly a pose of worship drawn from the Old Testament of the Bible. The narrator abases himself full-length, not daring to look up while clinging to the earth. He behaves as if he is in the presence of God, and this is before the tide turns and the maelstrom forms. The tame scene evokes in the narrator the awe of a mortal in a god's presence; when he sees the maelstrom, he feels he is looking into the heart of awesome, divine mystery.

When the maelstrom forms, when the earth really trembles and the sea boils and the heavens shout and the guide asks him what he sees and hears, he replies, "this *can* be nothing else than the great whirlpool of the Maelström." The narrator continues to see it as a more than natural phenomenon. Unable to accept the naturalistic account of it offered by the *Encyclopædia Britannica*, he is drawn instead by the power that it exerts over his imagination to see it as a manifesta-

tion of occult powers, an eruption of supernatural power into the natural world. This view forms the context within which the guide tells his tale.

An important feature of the guide's story is the contrast between his sense of chaotic threat and his repeated perceptions that suggest an ordered purpose within this chaos. It almost seems at times as if the episode were designed to teach the fisherman a lesson that he would then pass on through the narrator to the reader, though conveying a simple moral seems not to be the fisherman's purpose. For the fisherman, it was good fortune, assisted perhaps by a kind Providence, that allowed him to find a means of escape once his fishing boat had been sucked into the gigantic whirlpool and had begun its gradual descent toward the rushing foam at the bottom of the funnel of water. The main sign of design in these events is that just as the boat is blown into the whirlpool by the sudden and violent hurricane, a circle opens in the black clouds, revealing a bright moon that illuminates the scene of terror. This event makes the weather into a symmetrical picture: An inverted funnel of clouds ascending to an opening where the moon appears, over a funnel of whirling seawater descending into an obscured opening where a rainbow appears, "like that narrow and tottering bridge which Musselmen say is the only pathway between Time and Eternity." This view of a tremendous overarching cosmic order composing a scene of mortal chaos produces other kinds of order that help to save the fisherman.

Bewitched by the beauty that he sees in this scene, the fisherman, like the narrator on the cliff-top, gains control of himself, loses his fear, and begins to look around, merely for the sake of enjoying it: "I began to reflect how magnificent a thing it was to die in such a manner . . . in view of so wonderful a manifestation of God's power." Studying the beauty, he regains his self-possession, and in possession of his faculties, no longer terrified, he begins to understand how the whirlpool works, and he learns that different shapes and sizes of objects descend its sides at different rates. Attaching himself to a cylindrical barrel, he slows his descent enough that instead of going to the bottom and so across the mystical bridge he envisions there, he is borne up until the maelstrom stops and he finds himself again in comparatively calm water.

For the fisherman, his narrow escape is a tale of wonder, luck, and divine mercy. For the reader, however, carefully prepared by the narrator and supported by elements in the fisherman's story upon which he does not comment, the story also illustrates the inscrutability of the God that may be visible in nature. This is not a God who operates nature solely for human benefit, though He has given humanity reason, aesthetic sense, and the power of faith that can allow people to survive in, and even enjoy, the terrors of nature. The fisherman's brother, who survives the onslaught of the storm to experience the maelstrom with him, is never able to move by means of faith or the appreciation of beauty beyond his terror; this makes his despair at impending death insuperable, so he cannot discover a way of escape or even attempt the one offered by the fisherman.

Though not necessarily unique in this respect, the United States has throughout its history been a nation where large groups of people tended to assume that they had discovered the one truth that explained the universe and history and where it seemed easy to believe that a benevolent God had designed a manifest destiny for the nation and, perhaps, for humankind as a whole if led by American thought. Poe was among those who distrusted such thinking deeply. "A Descent into the Maelström" is one of many Poe stories in which part of the effect is to undercut such assumptions in his readers by emphasizing the mysteries of nature and the inadequacy of human ideas to encompass them, much less encompass the divinity of which nature might be a manifestation.

"THE PURLOINED LETTER"

While "A Descent into the Maelström" emphasizes the inadequacy of human intelligence to comprehend God's purposes in the universe, it also emphasizes the crucial importance of people using what intelligence they have to find truth and beauty in nature and experience. "The Purloined Letter," one of Poe's best detective stories, places a greater emphasis on the nature and importance of intelligence, while still pointing at mysteries of human character. This story first appeared in two magazine versions in 1844: a shorter version in *Chamber's Edinburgh Journal* and what has become the final version in *The Gift*. It was then collected in *Tales*.

The narrator and his friend C. Auguste Dupin are smoking and meditating in Dupin's darkened library, when they are interrupted by the comical Monsieur G—, the prefect of the Paris police. The prefect tries to pretend that he is merely paying a friendly call, but he cannot help making it clear that he has come to Dupin with a troubling problem. He eventually explains that the Minister D—has managed, in the presence of an important lady, presumably the queen, to steal from her a compromising letter with which he might damage her severely by showing it to her husband. He has since been using the threat of revealing the letter to coerce the queen's cooperation in influencing policy. As the prefect repeats, to Dupin's delight, getting the letter back without publicity ought to be simple for an expert policeman. One merely finds where it is hidden and takes it back. The letter must be within easy reach of the minister to be useful, and so by minute searching of his home and by having a pretended thief waylay him, the letter should surely be found. All these things have been done with great care, and the letter has not been found. The prefect is stumped. Dupin's advice is to search again. A few weeks later, the prefect returns, still without success. Dupin then manipulates the prefect into declaring what he would pay to regain the letter, instructs him to write Dupin a check for that amount, and gives him the letter. The prefect is so astonished and gratified that he runs from the house, not even bothering to ask how Dupin has managed this feat.

The second half of the story consists of Dupin's explanation to the narrator, with a joke or two at the prefect's expense, of how he found and obtained the letter. As in Dupin's other cases, notably the famous "The Murders in the Rue Morgue," the solution involves a rigorous and seemingly miraculous application of rationality to the problem. Although in these stories Poe was establishing conventions for detection and stories about it that would flower richly in Sir Arthur Conan Doyle's tales of Sherlock Holmes, the principles upon which Dupin works are slightly but significantly different from Holmes's principles.

One key difference is the importance of poetic

imagination to the process. Most of Dupin's explanation of his procedure has to do with how one goes about estimating the character and ability of one's opponent, for understanding what the criminal may do is ultimately more important to a solution than successful deduction. It requires a kind of poet to penetrate the criminal's mind, a "mere" mathematician can make competent deductions from given ideas, as the prefect has done. It takes a combination of poet and mathematician—in short, Dupin—to solve such a crime dependably. The prefect has greatly underestimated the minister because he is known to be a poet and the prefect believes poets are fools. Dupin says that the police often fail because they assume that the criminal's intelligence mirrors their own, and therefore over- or underestimate the criminal's ability. Having established that the minister is a very cunning opponent who will successfully imagine the police response to his theft, Dupin is able to deduce quite precisely how the minister will hide the letter, by placing it very conspicuously, so as not to appear hidden at all, and by disguising it. Dupin's deduction proves exactly right, and by some careful plotting, he is able to locate and regain it.

The two main portions of the story, presenting the problem and the solution, illustrate the nature and powers of human reason. The end of the story emphasizes mystery by raising questions about morality. While reason is a powerful instrument for solving problems and bringing about actions in the world, and solving problems is a satisfying kind of activity that makes Dupin feel proud and virtuous, his detecting occurs in a morally ambiguous world. The end of the story calls attention repeatedly to the relationship between Dupin and the Minister D——, a final quotation from a play even hinting that they could be brothers, though there is no other evidence that this is the case. Dupin claims intimate acquaintance and frequent association with the minister; indeed, these are the foundation of his inferences about the man's character and ability. They disagree, however, politically. The nature of this disagreement is not explained, but the story takes place in nineteenth century Paris, and Dupin's actions seem to support the royal family against a rebellious politician. Dupin, in leaving a

disguised substitute for the regained letter, has arranged for the minister's fall from power and may even have endangered his life.

By providing this kind of information at the end, Poe raises moral and political questions, encouraging the reader to wonder whether Dupin's brilliant detection serves values of which the reader might approve. To those questions, the story offers no answers. In this way, Dupin's demonstration of a magnificent human intellect is placed in the context of moral mystery, quite unlike the tales of Sherlock Holmes and related classical detectives. On a moral level, who are Dupin and the minister, and what are the meanings of their actions with regard to the well-being of French citizens? While Poe invented what became major conventions in detective fiction—the rational detective, his less able associate, the somewhat ridiculous police force, the solution scene—his detective stories show greater moral complexity than those of his best-known followers.

"THE FALL OF THE HOUSE OF USHER"

"The Fall of the House of Usher" has everything a Poe story is supposed to have according to the popular view of him: a gothic house, a terrified narrator, live burial, madness, and horrific catastrophe. One of his most popular and most discussed stories, this one has been variously interpreted by critics, provoking controversy about how to read it that remains unsettled. This story was first published in 1839, and it appeared in both of Poe's fiction collections.

The narrator journeys to the home of his boyhood chum, Roderick Usher, a man of artistic talent and generous reputation. Usher has been seriously ill and wishes the cheerful companionship of his old friend. The narrator arrives at the grimly oppressive house in its equally grim and oppressive setting, determined to be cheerful and helpful, but finds himself overmatched. The house and its environs radiate gloom, and though Usher alternates between a kind of creative mania and the blackest depression, he tends also on the whole to radiate gloom. Usher confides that he is upset in part because his twin sister, Madeline, is mortally ill. It develops, however, that the main reason Usher is depressed is that he has become in some way hypersensitive, and this sensitivity has revealed to him that his house is a living organism that is driving him toward madness. The narrator does not want to believe this, but the longer he stays in the house with Usher, the more powerfully Usher's point of view dominates him. Madeline dies and, to discourage grave robbers, Usher and the narrator temporarily place her in a coffin in a vault beneath the house. Once Madeline is dead, Usher's alternation of mood ceases, and he remains always deeply gloomy.

On his last evening at Usher, the narrator witnesses several events that seem to confirm Usher's view that the house is driving him mad. Furthermore, these confirmations seem to suggest that the house is just one in a nest of Chinese boxes, in a series of closed, walled-in enclosures that make up the physical and spiritual universe. This oft-repeated image is represented most vividly in one of Usher's paintings, what appears to be a burial vault unnaturally lit from within. This image conveys the idea of the flame of human consciousness imprisoned, as if buried alive in an imprisoning universe. The terrifying conviction of this view is one of the causes of Usher's growing madness. On the last evening, a storm seems to enclose the house as if it were inside a box of wind and cloud, on which the house itself casts an unnatural light. The narrator tries to comfort both himself and Usher by reading a story, but the sound effects described in the story are echoed in reality in the house. Usher, as his reason crumbles, interprets these sounds as Madeline, not really dead, breaking through various walls behind which she has been placed—her coffin and the vault—until finally, Usher claims, she is standing outside the door of the room where they are reading. The door opens, perhaps supernaturally, and there she stands. The narrator watches the twins fall against each other and collapse; he rushes outside only to see the house itself collapse into its reflection in the pool that stands before it, this last event taking place under the unnatural light of a blood-red moon.

Such a summary helps to reveal one of the main sources of conflicting interpretation. How could such events really occur? Is not this a case of an unreliable narrator, driven toward a horrific vision by some internal conflicts that might be inferred from the content of the vision? This viewpoint has tended to dom-

inate critical discussion of the story, provoking continuous opposition from more traditionally minded readers who argue that "The Fall of the House of Usher" is a supernatural tale involving occult forces of some kind. Both modes of interpretation have their problems, and so neither has been able to establish itself as superior to the other.

One of the main difficulties encountered by both sides is accounting for the way that the narrator tells his story. He seems involved in the same sort of problem that the community of literary critics experiences. He is represented as telling the story of this experience some time after the events took place. He insists that there are no supernatural elements in his story, that everything that happened at the House of Usher can be accounted for in a naturalistic way. In this respect, he is like the narrator of "A Descent into the Maelström." He "knows" that the natural world operates according to regular "natural" laws, but when he actually sees the whirlpool, his imagination responds involuntarily with the conviction that this is something supernatural. Likewise, the narrator of "The Fall of the House of Usher" is convinced that the world can be understood in terms of natural law and, therefore, that what has happened to him at Usher either could not have happened or must have a natural explanation. Like the narrator of "The Black Cat," another of Poe's most famous stories, this narrator hopes that by telling the story, perhaps again, he will arrive at an acceptable explanation or that his listener will confirm his view of the events.

Perhaps "The Fall of the House of Usher" is a kind of trap, set to enmesh readers in the same sort of difficulty in which the narrator finds himself. If this is the case, then the story functions in a way consistent with Poe's theme of the inadequacy of models constructed by human intelligence to map the great mysteries of life and the universe. The narrator says he has had an experience that he cannot explain and that points toward an inscrutable universe, one that might be conceived as designed to drive humans mad if they find themselves compelled to comprehend it. Likewise, in reading the story, the reader has an experience that finally cannot be explained, that seems designed to drive a reader mad if he or she insists upon achieving a final view of its wholeness. The story itself may provide an experience that demonstrates the ultimate inadequacy of human reason to understand the mysteries of creation.

Although Poe wrote a variety of stories, he is best remembered for his tales of terror and madness. His popular literary reputation is probably a distorted view of Poe, both as person and as artist. While he was tragically addicted to alcohol and while he did experience considerable difficulty in a milieu that was not particularly supportive, he was nevertheless an accomplished artist whose work, especially when viewed as a whole, is by no means the mere outpouring of a half-mad, anguished soul. To look closely at any of his best work is to see ample evidence of a writer in full artistic control of his materials, calculating his effects with a keen eye. Furthermore, to examine the range and quantity of his writing, to attend to the quantity of his humor—of which there are interesting examples even in "The Fall of the House of Usher"—to notice the beauty of his poetry, to study the learned intelligence of his best criticism—in short, to see Poe whole—must lead to the recognition that his accomplishments far exceed the narrow view implied by his popular reputation.

OTHER MAJOR WORKS

LONG FICTION: *The Narrative of Arthur Gordon Pym*, 1838.

PLAY: *Politician*, pb. 1835-1836.

POETRY: *Tamerlane and Other Poems*, 1827; *Al Aaraaf, Tamerlane, and Minor Poems*, 1829; *Poems*, 1831; *The Raven and Other Poems*, 1845; *Eureka: A Prose Poem*, 1848; *Poe: Complete Poems*, 1959; *Poems*, 1969 (volume 1 of *Collected Works*).

NONFICTION: *The Letters of Edgar Allan Poe*, 1948; *Literary Criticism of Edgar Allan Poe*, 1965; *Essays and Reviews*, 1984.

MISCELLANEOUS: *The Complete Works of Edgar Allan Poe*, 1902 (17 volumes); *Collected Works of Edgar Allan Poe*, 1969, 1978 (3 volumes).

BIBLIOGRAPHY

Bittner, William. *Poe: A Biography*. Boston: Little, Brown, 1962. This volume is a reliable study of Poe's life and is suitable for general readers.

Brown, Arthur A. "Literature and the Impossibility of Death: Poe's 'Berenice.'" *Nineteenth-Century Literature* 50 (March, 1996): 448-463. Argues that Poe's stories of the dead coming back to life and of premature burial dramatize the horror of the impossibility of dying. In "Berenice," our attention to the details of the tale reproduces the narrator's obsession with that which speaks of death and does not die and thus implicates us in his violation of the still-living Berenice in her tomb.

Buranelli, Vincent. *Edgar Allan Poe*. 2d ed. Boston: Twayne, 1977. This study of Poe's life and works offers an excellent introduction. The book includes a chronology of his life and an annotated, select bibliography.

Burluck, Michael L. *Grim Phantasms: Fear in Poe's Short Fiction*. New York: Garland, 1993. Considers the question of why Poe focused primarily on portraying weird events in his stories. Discusses the gothic conventions Poe used to achieve his effects. Argues that neither drugs nor insanity are responsible for Poe's gothic tales, but rather they were a carefully thought out literary tactic meant to appeal to current public taste and the general human reaction to fear.

Carlson, Eric, ed. *Critical Essays on Edgar Allan Poe*. Boston: G. K. Hall, 1987. This supplement to Carlson's 1966 volume (below) offers a cross section of writing about Poe from the 1830's to the 1980's. Many of the essays deal with short stories, illustrating a variety of interpretive strategies.

_____, ed. *The Recognition of Edgar Allan Poe*. Ann Arbor: University of Michigan Press, 1966. This selection of critical essays from 1829 to 1963 is intended to illustrate the development of Poe's literary reputation. It includes a number of the most important earlier essays on Poe, including Constance Rourke's discussion of Poe as a humorist. Also includes several essays by French and British critics.

Crisman, William. "Poe's Dupin as Professional, the Dupin Stories as Serial Text." *Studies in American Fiction* 23 (Autumn, 1995): 215-229. Part of a special section on Poe. Argues that the Dupin stories bear out his mesmeric revelation that mind forms one continuum with inert substance. Poe's emphatic insistence on the role of the material and the materialistic in his detective tales makes them important psychological statements.

Frank, Lawrence. "'The Murders in the Rue Morgue': Edgar Allan Poe's Evolutionary Reverie." *Nineteenth-Century Literature* 50 (September, 1995): 168-188. Claims that Poe's story explores the implications of the nebular hypothesis and did not reinforce the prevailing orthodoxy; rather it may have been in the service of an emerging Darwinian perspective.

Howarth, William L. *Twentieth Century Interpretations of Poe's Tales*. Englewood Cliffs, N.J.: Prentice-Hall, 1971. This volume contains fifteen essays on Poe's stories, several offering general points of view on his fiction but most offering specific interpretations of tales such as "The Fall of the House of Usher," "Ligeia," "William Wilson," "The Black Cat," and "The Tell-Tale Heart." Includes a chronology of Poe's life, a bibliography, and a helpful index to the stories discussed.

Hyneman, Esther K. *Edgar Allan Poe: An Annotated Bibliography of Books and Articles in English, 1827-1973*. Boston: G. K. Hall, 1974. The quantity and variety of writings on Poe make it exceedingly difficult to compile complete lists. This volume, supplemented by *American Literary Scholarship: An Annual* for coverage of subsequent years, will provide an ample resource for most readers.

Irwin, John T. *The Mystery to a Solution: Poe, Borges, and the Analytical Detective Story*. Baltimore: The Johns Hopkins University Press, 1994. An analytical/theoretical discussion of Poe and Borges's contribution to the detective story. Argues that Borges doubles Poe's three most famous detective stories—"The Murders in the Rue Morgue," "The Purloined Letter," and "The Mystery of Marie Roget"—in three of his own stories.

Martin, Terry J. *Rhetorical Deception in the Short Fiction of Hawthorne, Poe and Melville*. Lewiston, N.Y.: Edwin Mellen Press, 1998. An original reading of "The Murders in the Rue Morgue." Martin seeks to identify this story and those by Hawthorne and Melville as "a significant subgenre of the modern short story."

May, Charles E. *Edgar Allan Poe: A Study of the Short Fiction*. Boston: Twayne, 1991. An introduction to Poe's short stories that attempts to place them with the nineteenth century short narrative tradition and within the context of Poe's aesthetic theory. Suggests Poe's contributions to the short story in terms of his development of detective fiction, fantasy, satire, and self-reflexivity. Includes passages from Poe's narrative theory and three essays by other critics illustrating a variety of critical approaches.

Pillai, Johann. "Death and Its Moments: The End of the Reader in History." *MLN* 112 (December, 1997): 836-875. Argues that Poe's "The Tell-Tale Heart" establishes its modernity by both affirming and denying its status as a narrative of historical events; contends the story declares its fictive nature in its relation to history, which it purports to transcend or slide past; concludes it is the hermeneutical relation of the narrative voice of the tale to the narrative voice of criticism that determines the story's paradoxical temporality.

Quinn, Arthur Hobson. *Edgar Allan Poe: A Critical Biography*. Baltimore: The John Hopkins University Press, 1998. A comprehensive biography of Poe, with a new introduction by Shawn Rosenheim, is devoted to fact and describes how Poe's life and legend were misconstrued by other biographers.

Thoms, Peter. *Detection and Its Designs: Narrative and Power in Nineteenth-Century Detective Fiction*. Athens: Ohio University Press, 1998. A study of early detective fiction from readings of Poe's Dupin stories to Arthur Conan Doyle's *The Hound of the Baskervilles*.

Whalen, Terence. *Edgar Allan Poe and the Masses: The Political Economy of Literature in Antebellum America*. Princeton, N.J.: Princeton University Press, 1999. A brilliant study of Poe that provides an inventive understanding of his works and his standing in American literature.

Terry Heller

KATHERINE ANNE PORTER

Born: Indian Creek, Texas; May 15, 1890
Died: Silver Spring, Maryland; September 18, 1980

PRINCIPAL SHORT FICTION

Flowering Judas and Other Stories, 1930
Hacienda, 1934
Noon Wine, 1937
Pale Horse, Pale Rider: Three Short Novels, 1939
The Leaning Tower and Other Stories, 1944
The Old Order, 1944
The Collected Stories of Katherine Anne Porter, 1965

OTHER LITERARY FORMS

Katherine Anne Porter wrote, in addition to short stories, one novel, *Ship of Fools* (1962), parts of which were published separately from 1947 to 1959, in such magazines and journals as *The Sewanee Review, Harper's*, and *Mademoiselle*. She wrote essays of various kinds, some of which she published under the title of one of them, *The Days Before* (1952); these included critical analyses of Thomas Hardy's fiction and biographical studies of Ford Madox Ford and Gertrude Stein. Porter was a reporter with unsigned journalism for the Fort Worth weekly newspaper *The Critic* in 1917 and the Denver *Rocky Mountain News* in 1918-1919. Early in her career, she worked on a critical biography of Cotton Mather, which she never finished; she did, however, publish parts in 1934, 1940, 1942, and 1946. Her few poems and most of her nonfictional prose have been collected in *The Collected Essays and Occasional Writings* (1970) under the following headings: "Critical," "Personal and Particular," "Biographical," "Cotton Mather," "Mexican," "On Writing," and "Poems." In 1967, she composed *A Christmas Story*, a personal reminiscence of her niece, who had died in 1919. Her memoir of the Sacco and Vanzetti trial, *The Never-Ending Wrong*, was published in 1977 on the fiftieth anniversary of their deaths. She was a prodigious writer of personal letters; many have been published, first, by her friend Glenway Wescott, as *The Selected Letters of Katherine Anne Porter* (1970), and later by another friend, Isabel Bayley, as *Letters of Katherine Anne Porter* (1990).

ACHIEVEMENTS

Katherine Anne Porter is distinguished by her small literary production of exquisitely composed and highly praised short fiction. Although she lived to be ninety years old, she produced and published only some twenty-five short stories and one long novel. Nevertheless, her work was praised early and often from the start of her career; some of her stories, such as "Flowering Judas," "Pale Horse, Pale Rider," and "Old Mortality," have been hailed as masterpieces. Sponsored by Edmund Wilson, Allen Tate, Kenneth Burke, and Elizabeth Madox Roberts, Porter won a Guggenheim Fellowship in 1931 and went to Berlin and Paris to live while she wrote such stories as "The Cracked Looking-Glass" and "Noon Wine," for which she won a Book-of-the-Month Club award in 1937. After publication of the collection *Pale Horse, Pale Rider: Three Short Novels* in 1939, she received a gold medal for literature from the Society of Libraries of New York University, in 1940. Elected a member of the National Institute of Arts and Letters in 1943, Porter was also appointed as writer-in-residence at Stanford University in 1949, and, in the same year, she received an honorary degree, doctor of letters, from the University of North Carolina. Such awards and honors continued, with writer-in-residence appointments at the University of Michigan in 1954 and the University of Virginia in 1958, honorary degrees at the University of Michigan, Smith College, and La Salle College. In 1959, she received a Ford Foundation grant, in 1962 the Emerson-Thoreau gold medal from the American Academy of Arts and Sciences, and in 1966-1967, the National Book Award for Fiction, the Pulitzer Prize in fiction, and the Gold Medal for fiction, National Institute of Arts and Letters.

BIOGRAPHY

There are conflicting reports of dates from Katherine Anne Porter's life, partly because Porter herself was not consistent about her biography. Nevertheless, the main events are fairly clear. Her mother, Mary Alice, died less than two years after Katherine Anne's birth. Subsequently, her grandmother, Catherine Anne Porter, was the most important adult woman in her life, and after the death of her grandmother in 1901, Katherine Anne was sent away by her father to an Ursuline convent in New Orleans, then in 1904 to the Thomas School for Girls in San Antonio. She ran away from her school in 1906 to marry John Henry Kroontz, the twenty-year-old son of a Texas rancher. She remained with him seven years (some reports say her marriage lasted only three years), and in 1911 she went to Chicago to earn her own way as a reporter for a weekly newspaper and as a bit player for a film company. From 1914 to 1916, she traveled through Texas, earning her way as a ballad singer. Then she returned to journalism, joining the staff of the Denver *Rocky Mountain News* in 1918. At about this time, Porter was gravely ill, and she thought she was going to die. Her illness was a turning point in the development of her character, and it was the basis for her story "Pale Horse, Pale Rider," which she finished twenty years later.

After she recovered her health, Porter lived briefly in New York and then Mexico, where she studied art while observing the Obregón revolution in 1920. Her experiences in Mexico provided material for Porter's earliest published stories, "María Concepción" and "The Martyr" in 1922 and 1923. She married and promptly divorced Ernest Stock, a young English art student in New York, in 1925. Soon after, she participated in protests against the trial of Nicola Sacco and Bartolomeo Vanzetti, and then, in 1928, she began work on her biography of Mather, which was never completed. Porter traveled often during these years, but she wrote some of her greatest stories at the same time, including "He," "The Jilting of Granny Weatherall," "Theft," and "Flowering Judas."

After publication of her collection *Flowering Judas and Other Stories* in 1930, Porter was awarded a Guggenheim Fellowship to support her while living

Katherine Anne Porter (Washington Star Collection, D.C. Public Library)

in Berlin and Paris, from 1931 to 1937. While in Europe, she composed "The Leaning Tower" and "The Cracked Looking-Glass," and she wrote an early draft of "Noon Wine." In 1933, she married Eugene Pressly, whom she divorced to marry Albert Erskine in 1938, when she returned to the United States to live with her new husband in Baton Rouge, Louisiana. At that time, she became a friend of Tate and his family.

In 1941, Porter appeared on television with Mark Van Doren and Bertrand Russell; in 1944, she worked on films in Hollywood; and in 1947, she undertook a lecture tour of several southern universities. The novel that she began as a story, "Promised Land," in 1936, was finally published in 1962 as *Ship of Fools* to mixed reviews. Apart from her work on this long fiction, Porter wrote little except for occasional essays and reviews, some of which she published as *The Days Before* in 1952. Porter spent most of her life after 1950 lecturing, traveling, buying and selling property, and slowly composing her novel along with her biography of Mather. In October, 1976, she read her essay "St. Augustine and the Bullfight" at the Poetry Center in New York City, and in 1977, she published a memoir of Sacco and Vanzetti, whose trials of injustice had haunted her for fifty years. When she died, in 1980, in Silver Spring, Maryland, she left behind a small canon of fiction and a great achievement of literary art.

ANALYSIS

Katherine Anne Porter's short fiction is noted for its sophisticated use of symbolism, complex exploitation of point of view, challenging variations of ambiguously ironic tones, and profound analyses of psychological and social themes. Her career can be divided into three main (overlapping) periods of work, marked by publications of her three collections: The first period, from 1922 to 1935, saw the publication of *Flowering Judas and Other Stories*; the second, from 1930 to 1939, ended with the publication of *Pale Horse, Pale Rider: Three Short Novels*; and the third, from 1935 to 1942, shaped many of her characters that later appear in the collection *The Leaning Tower and Other Stories*. Her one novel and two stories "The Fig Tree" and "Holiday" were published long after the last collection of short stories, in 1962 and 1960, respectively. These constitute a coda to the body of her work in fiction.

From 1922 to 1935, Porter's fiction is concerned with the attempts of women to accommodate themselves to, or to break the bounds of, socially approved sexual roles. They usually fail to achieve the identities that they seek; instead, they ironically become victims of their own or others' ideas of what they ought to be. Violeta of "Virgin Violeta" fantasizes about her relationship with her cousin Carlos, trying to understand it according to the idealistic notions that she has learned from church and family; when Carlos responds to her sensual reality, she is shocked and disillusioned. The ironies of Violeta's situation are exploited more fully, and more artfully, in "María Concepción," "Magic," and "He."

In the first, María manages, through violence, to assert her identity through the social roles that she is expected to play in her primitive society; she kills her sensual rival, María Rosa, seizes the baby of her victim, and retrieves her wandering husband. Social norms are also triumphant over poor Ninette, the brutalized prostitute of "Magic," in which the narrator is implicated by her own ironic practice of distance from her story and her employer, Madame Blanchard. The mother of "He," however, cannot maintain her distance from the image that she has projected of her retarded son; she is willing to sacrifice him, as she had the suckling pig, to preserve the social image she values of herself toward others. In the end, however, Mrs. Whipple embraces, helplessly and hopelessly, the victim of her self-delusion: She holds her son in tragic recognition of her failures toward him, or she holds him out of ironic disregard for his essential need of her understanding. "He" does not resolve easily into reconciliation of tone and theme.

Images of symbolic importance organize the ironies of such stories as "Rope," "Flowering Judas," "Theft," and "The Cracked Looking-Glass." In the first story, a husband and wife are brought to the edge of emotional chaos by a piece of rope that the husband brought home instead of coffee wanted by his wife. As a symbol, the rope ties them together, keeps them apart, and threatens to hang them both. "Flowering Judas," one of Porter's most famous stories, develops the alienated character of Laura from her resistance to the revolutionary hero Braggioni, to her refusal of the boy who sang to her from her garden, to her complicity in the death of Eugenio in prison. At the center of the story, in her garden and in her dream, Laura is linked with a Judas tree in powerfully mysterious ways: as a betrayer, as a rebellious and independent spirit. Readers will be divided on the meaning of the tree, as they will be on the virtue of Laura's character.

"THE CRACKED LOOKING-GLASS"

The same ambivalence results from examining the symbolic function of a cracked mirror in the life of Rosaleen, the point-of-view character in "The Cracked Looking-Glass." This middle-aged Irish beauty sees herself as a monster in her mirror, but she cannot replace the mirror with a new one any more than she can reconcile her sexual frustration with her maternal affection for her aged husband, Dennis.

This story twists the May-December stereotype into a reverse fairy tale of beauty betrayed, self deceived, and love dissipated. Rosaleen treats young men as the sons she never had to rear, and she represses her youthful instincts to nurse her impotent husband in his old age. She does not like what she sees when she looks honestly at herself in the mirror, but she will not replace the mirror of reality, cracked as she sees it must be.

"THEFT"

More honest and more independent is the heroine of "Theft," an artist who chooses her independence at the cost of sexual fulfillment and social gratification; she allows her possessions, material and emotional, to be taken from her, but she retains an integrity of honesty and spiritual independence that are unavailable to most of the other characters in these early stories. A similar strength of character underlies the dying monologue of Granny Weatherall, but her strength has purchased her very little certainty about meaning. When she confronts death as a second jilting, Granny condemns death's cheat as a final insult to life; she seems ironically to make meaningful in her death the emptiness that she has struggled to deny in her life.

"OLD MORTALITY"

In the middle period of her short fiction, Porter's characters confront powerful threats of illusion to shatter their tenuous holds on reality. Romantic ideals and family myths combine to shape the formative circumstances for Miranda in "Old Mortality." Divided into three parts, this story follows the growth of the young heroine from 1885, when she is eight, to 1912, when she is recently married against her father's wishes. Miranda and her older sister, Maria, are fascinated by tales of their legendary Aunt Amy, their father's sister whose honor he had risked his life to defend in a duel, and who died soon after she married their Uncle Gabriel. The first part of the story narrates the family's anecdotes about Aunt Amy and contrasts her with her cousin Eva, a plain woman who participated in movements for women's rights. Part 2 of the story focuses on Miranda's disillusionment with Uncle Gabriel, whom she meets at a racetrack while she is immured in a church school in New

Orleans; he is impoverished, fat, and alcoholic, remarried to a bitter woman who hates his family, and he is insensitive to the suffering of his winning race horse.

Part 3 describes Miranda's encounter with cousin Eva on a train carrying them to the funeral of Uncle Gabriel. Here, Miranda's romantic image of Aunt Amy is challenged by Eva's skeptical memory, but Miranda refuses to yield her vision entirely to Eva's scornful one. Miranda hopes that her father will embrace her when she returns home, but he remains detached and disapproving of her elopement. She realizes that from now on she must live alone, separate, and alienated from her family. She vows to herself that she will know the truth about herself, even if she can never know the truth about her family's history. The story ends, however, on a note of critical skepticism about her vow, suggesting its hopefulness is based upon her ignorance.

"NOON WINE"

Self-delusion and selfish pride assault Mr. Thompson in "Noon Wine" until he can no longer accept their terms of compromise with his life. A lazy man who lets his south Texas farm go to ruin, he is suddenly lifted to prosperity by the energetic, methodical work of a strangely quiet Swede, Mr. Helton. This man appears one day in 1896 to ask Mr. Thompson for work, and he remains there, keeping to himself and occasionally playing the tune of "Noon Wine" on his harmonica. The turn into failure and tragedy is more sudden than the turn to prosperity had been. Mr. Hatch, an obnoxious person, comes to Mr. Thompson looking for Helton, wanted for the killing of Helton's brother in North Dakota. Thompson angrily attacks and kills Hatch, and Helton flees. Helton, however, is captured, beaten, and thrown in jail, where he dies. Thompson is acquitted of murder at his trial.

Thompson, however, cannot accept his acquittal. He believes that his neighbors think that he is really guilty. His wife is uncertain about his guilt, and his two sons not only are troubled by his part in the deaths but also accuse him of mistreating their mother. Burdened by pains of conscience, Thompson spends his days after the trial visiting neighbors and retelling the story of Hatch's visit. Thompson believes he saw Hatch knife Helton, but no one else saw it, and Helton had no knife wound. The problem for Thompson is that he cannot reconcile what he saw and what was real. All of his life has been spent in a state of delusion, and this crisis of conscience threatens to destroy his capacity to accept life on his own visionary terms. The irony of the story is that Thompson must kill himself to vindicate his innocence, but when he does so, he paradoxically accepts the consequences of his delusions even as he asserts his right to shape reality to fit his view of it.

"PALE HORSE, PALE RIDER"

Love and death mix forces to press Miranda through a crisis of vision in "Pale Horse, Pale Rider." This highly experimental story mixes dreams with waking consciousness, present with past, and illness with health. Set during World War I, it analyzes social consequences of a military milieu, and it uses that setting to suggest a symbolic projection of the pressures that build on the imagination and identity of the central character. Miranda is a writer of drama reviews for a newspaper; her small salary is barely enough to support herself, and so when she balks at buying Liberty Bonds, she has her patriotism questioned. This worry preoccupies her thoughts and slips into her dreaming experience. In fact, the opening of the story seems to be an experience of a sleeper who is slowly coming awake from a dream of childhood in which the adult's anxieties about money are mixed. Uncertainty about the mental state of Miranda grows as she mixes her memories of past with present, allowing past feelings to affect present judgments.

Miranda meets a young soldier, Adam, who will soon be sent to battle. They both know that his fate is sealed, since they are both aware of the survival statistics for soldiers who make assaults from trenches. Miranda becomes gravely ill just before Adam leaves for the war front, and he nurses her through the earliest days of her sickness. Her delirium merges her doctor with Adam, with the German enemy, and with figures of her dreams. By this process, Miranda works through her attractions to Adam, to all men, and survives to assert her independence as a professional artist. The climax of her dream, echoing certain features of Granny Weatherall's, is her refusal to follow the pale rider, who is Death. This feature of her dream is present at the beginning of the story, to anticipate that Miranda will have to contend with this, resolve her inner battle, even before the illness that constitutes her physical struggle with death. The men of her waking life enter her dreams as Death, and so when Adam actually dies in battle, Miranda is symbolically assisted in winning her battle for life. The story makes it seem that her dreaming is the reality of the men, that their lives are figments of her imagination. Her recovery of health is a triumph, therefore, of her creative energies as well as an assertion of her independent feminine identity.

In the final, sustained period of her work in short fiction, from 1935 to 1942, Porter subjects memories to the shaping power of creative imagination, as she searches out the episodes that connect to make the character of Miranda, from "The Source" to "The Grave," and she traces the distorting effects of social pressures on children, wives, and artists in the remaining stories of the third collection. The crucial, shaping episodes of Miranda's childhood constitute the core elements of several stories in the collection called *The Leaning Tower and Other Stories*. Beginning with a sequence under the title "The Old Order," Miranda's growth is shaped by her changing perceptions of life around her. Helping her to interpret events are her grandmother, Sophia Jane, and her grandmother's former black slave and lifetime companion, Aunt Nannie; in addition, Great-Aunt Eliza plays an important role in Miranda's life in the story that was later added to the sequence, "The Fig Tree." Two of the stories of this collection, "The Circus" and "The Grave," are examples of remarkable compression and, particularly in "The Grave," complex artistry.

"THE CIRCUS"

Miranda cries when she sees a clown perform high-wire acrobatics in "The Circus." Her fear is a child's protest against the clown's courtship with death. There is nothing pleasurable about it for Miranda. In fact, she seems to see through the act to recognize the threat of death itself, in the white, skull-like makeup of the clown's face. The adults enjoy the spectacle, perhaps insensitive to its essential message or, on the other hand, capable of appreciating the artist's defiance of death. In any event, young Miranda is such a problem that her father sends her home with one of the servants, Dicey. The point of poignancy is in Miranda's discovery of Dicey's warm regard for her despite the fact that Dicey had keenly wanted to stay at the circus. When Miranda screams in her sleep, Dicey lies beside her to comfort her, to protect her even from the dark forces of her nightmares. This sacrifice is not understood by the child Miranda, although it should be apparent to the adult who recalls it.

"THE GRAVE"

"The Grave" is more clear about the function of time in the process of understanding. Miranda and her brother Paul explore open graves of their family while hunting. They find and exchange a coffin screw and a ring, then skin a rabbit that Paul killed, only to find that the rabbit is pregnant with several young that are "born" dead. The experience of mixing birth with death, sexual awareness with marriage and death, is suddenly illuminated for Miranda years later when she recalls her brother on that day while she stands over a candy stand in faraway Mexico.

"THE DOWNWARD PATH TO WISDOM"

Other stories of *The Leaning Tower and Other Stories* collection have disappointed readers, but they have virtues of art nevertheless. The strangely powerful story of little Stephen in "The Downward Path to Wisdom" has painful insights that may remind one of some of the stories by Flannery O'Connor, a friend of Porter. The little boy who is the object of concern to the family in this story grows to hate his father, mother, grandmother, and uncle; in fact, he sings of his hate for everyone at the end of the tale. His hatred is understandable, since no one genuinely reaches out to love him and help him with his very real problems of adjustment. His mother hears his song, but she shows no alarm; she may think that he does not "mean" what he sings, or she may not really "hear" what he is trying to say through his "art." A similar theme of hatred and emotional violence is treated in the heartless marital problems of Mr. and Mrs. Halloran of "A Day's Work." Here, however, the vio-

lence is borne by physical as well as emotional events, as the story ends with a deadly battle between the aging husband and wife. First one, and then the other, believes the other one is dead. The reader is not sure if either is right.

"THE LEANING TOWER"

Charles Upton, the artist hero of "The Leaning Tower," encounters emotional and physical violence during his sojourn in Berlin in 1931. When he accidentally knocks down and breaks a replica of the Leaning Tower, Charles expresses in a symbolic way his objection to values that he finds in this alien city. He must endure challenges by various other people, with their lifestyles and their foreign values, to discover an underlying humanity that he shares with them. Although he is irritated when he finds that his landlady, Rosa, has repaired the Leaning Tower, he cannot say exactly why he should be so. German nationalism and decadent art have combined to shake Charles's integrity, but he searches for inner resources to survive. The story concludes with a typically ambiguous gesture of Porter's art: Charles falls into his bed, telling himself he needs to weep, but he cannot. The world is invulnerable to sorrow and pity.

"THE FIG TREE"

The coda of her work in short fiction, "The Fig Tree" and "Holiday," are revisits to earlier stories, as Porter reexamines old themes and old subjects with new emphases: "The Fig Tree" relocates Miranda in the matriarchal setting of her childhood, and "Holiday" reviews ironies of misunderstanding alien visions. In "The Fig Tree," young Miranda buries a dead baby chicken beneath a fig tree, and then thinks she hears it chirping from beneath the earth. Frantic with anxiety, she is unable to rescue it because her grandmother forces her to leave with the family for the country. Later, Miranda's Great-Aunt Eliza, who constantly studies nature through telescopes and microscopes, explains to Miranda that she hears tree frogs when Miranda thinks she is hearing the weeping of the dead chicken. Her guilt is relieved by this, and since Miranda has emotionally mixed her burial of the chicken with burials of family members, resolution of guilt for one functions as resolution of guilt for the other.

"HOLIDAY"

The story of "Holiday" is much different in subject and setting, but its emotional profile is similar to "The Fig Tree." The narrator spends a long holiday with German immigrants in the backlands of Texas. The hardworking Müllers challenge, by their lifestyle, the values of the narrator, who only gradually comes to understand them and their ways. The most difficult experience to understand, however, is the family's attitude toward one of the daughters, Ottilie; at first, this girl seems to be only a crippled servant of the family. Gradually, however, the narrator understands that Ottilie is in fact a member of the family. She is mentally retarded and unable to communicate except in very primitive ways. Just when the narrator believes she can appreciate the seemingly heartless ways Ottilie is treated by her family, a great storm occurs and the mother dies. Most of the family follow their mother's corpse to be buried, but Ottilie is left behind. The narrator thinks Ottilie is desperate to join the funeral train with her family, and so she helps Ottilie on board a wagon and desperately drives to catch up with the family. Suddenly, however, the narrator realizes that Ottilie simply wants to be in the sunshine and has no awareness of the death of her mother. The narrator accepts the radical difference that separates her from Ottilie, from all other human beings, and resigns herself, in freedom, to the universal condition of alienation.

The critical mystery of Katherine Anne Porter's work in short fiction is in the brevity of her canon. Readers who enjoy her writing must deplore the failure of the artist to produce more than she did, but they will nevertheless celebrate the achievements of her remarkable talent in the small number of stories that she published. Whatever line of analysis one pursues in reading her stories, Porter's finest ones will repay repeated investments of reading them. They please with their subtleties of technique, from point of view to patterned images of symbolism; they inform with their syntheses of present feeling and past sensation; and they raise imaginative energy with their ambiguous presentations of alien vision. Porter's stories educate the patiently naïve reader into paths of radical maturity.

OTHER MAJOR WORKS

LONG FICTION: *Ship of Fools*, 1962.

NONFICTION: *My Chinese Marriage*, 1921; *Outline of Mexican Popular Arts and Crafts*, 1922; *What Price Marriage*, 1927; *The Days Before*, 1952; *A Defence of Circe*, 1954; *A Christmas Story*, 1967; *The Collected Essays and Occasional Writings*, 1970; *The Selected Letters of Katherine Anne Porter*, 1970; *The Never-Ending Wrong*, 1977; *Letters of Katherine Anne Porter*, 1990.

BIBLIOGRAPHY

Bloom, Harold, ed. *Katherine Anne Porter: Modern Critical Views*. New York: Chelsea House, 1986. Bloom introduces twelve classic essays, by Robert Penn Warren, Robert B. Heilman, Eudora Welty, and others. The symbolism of "Flowering Judas," the ambiguities of "He," and the dreams in "Pale Horse, Pale Rider" are focuses of attention. Porter is compared with Flannery O'Connor. Includes a chronology, a bibliography, and an index.

Brinkmeyer, Robert H., Jr. *Katherine Anne Porter's Artistic Development: Primitivism, Traditionalism, and Totalitarianism*. Baton Rouge: Louisiana State University Press, 1993. Applying Mikhail Bakhtin's theory of the dialogic and monologic to Porter's fiction, Brinkmeyer argues that when she created a memory-based dialogue with her southern past, she achieved her height as an artist, producing such important stories as "The Jilting of Granny Weatherall" and "Noon Wine."

Fornataro-Neil, M. K. "Constructed Narratives and Writing Identity in the Fiction of Katherine Anne Porter." *Twentieth Century Literature* 44 (Fall, 1998): 349-361. Discusses "Old Mortality," "He," "Noon Wine," and "Holiday" in terms of Porter's fascination with characters who cannot or do not speak; claims that her silent characters are alienated because they communicate by a sign system that others cannot understand.

Graham, Don. "Katherine Anne Porter's Journey from Texas to the World." *Southwest Review* 84 (1998): 140-153. Argues that because the dominant figure in Texas literary mythology was the heroic cowboy, Porter, who had nothing to say about cowboys in her writing, chose instead to identify herself as southerner.

Hartley, Lodwick, and George Core, eds. *Katherine Anne Porter: A Critical Symposium.* Athens: University of Georgia Press, 1969. A collection of seminal essays, this book includes an interview with Porter in 1963, as well as a personal assessment by Porter's friend Glenway Wescott. A group of five essays provide general surveys, and another five focus on particular stories, including "The Grave" and "Holiday." Select bibliography, index.

Hendrick, George. *Katherine Anne Porter.* New York: Twayne, 1965. A biographical sketch precedes studies grouped according to settings from Porter's life: the first group from Mexico, the second from Texas, and the third from New York and Europe. After a chapter on *Ship of Fools*, the book surveys Porter's essays and summarizes major themes. Notes, annotated bibliography, index, and chronology.

Liberman, M. M. *Katherine Anne Porter's Fiction.* Detroit: Wayne State University Press, 1971. In this study of Porter's methods and intentions, seven chapters concentrate analyses on *Ship of Fools*, "Old Mortality," "Noon Wine," "María Concepción," "Flowering Judas," and "The Leaning Tower." Chapter 6 examines "people who cannot speak for themselves," the central characters of "Holiday," "He," and "Noon Wine." Includes notes and an index.

Nance, William L. *Katherine Anne Porter and the Art of Rejection.* Chapel Hill: University of North Carolina Press, 1964. An emerging thematic pattern of rejection is found in the early stories, up to "Hacienda." Variations are illustrated by the middle stories. The Miranda stories are presented as fictional autobiography, and *Ship of Fools* is closely analyzed as a failure to make a novel out of character sketches. Complemented by a bibliography and index.

Spencer, Virginia, ed. *"Flowering Judas": Katherine Anne Porter.* New Brunswick, N.J.: Rutgers University Press, 1993. A volume in the Women Writers: Texts and Contexts series, this collection of critical discussions of Porter's most famous story features background material and important essays, from Ray B. West's influential 1947 discussion of the story to debates about the character of Eugenio as Christ figure.

Stout, Janis. *Katherine Anne Porter: A Sense of the Times.* Charlottesville: University Press of Virginia, 1995. Chapters on Porter's background in Texas, her view of politics and art in the 1920's, her writing and life between the two world wars, and her relationship with the southern agrarians. Also addresses the issue of gender, the problem of genre in *Ship of Fools*, and the quality of Porter's "free, intransigent, dissenting mind." Includes notes and bibliography.

Walsh, Thomas F. *Katherine Anne Porter and Mexico.* Austin: University of Texas Press, 1992. Chapters on Porter and Mexican politics, her different periods of residence in Mexico, and *Ship of Fools*. Includes notes and bibliography.

Warren, Robert Penn. "Irony with a Center: Katherine Anne Porter." In *Selected Essays.* New York: Random House, 1951. In this important early essay on Porter's stories, Warren asserts Porter's fiction is characterized by rich surface detail apparently casually scattered and a close structure that makes such detail meaningful.

Richard D. McGhee

J. F. POWERS

Born: Jacksonville, Illinois; July 8, 1917
Died: Collegeville, Minnesota; June 12, 1999

PRINCIPAL SHORT FICTION

Prince of Darkness and Other Stories, 1947
The Presence of Grace, 1956
Lions, Harts, Leaping Does, and Other Stories,
   1963
Look How the Fish Live, 1975
The Old Bird: A Love Story, 1991 (limited special
   edition)
The Stories of J. F. Powers, 2000

OTHER LITERARY FORMS

J. F. Powers is the author of two novels: *Morte
d'Urban*, which received the National Book Award
for fiction in 1962, and *Wheat That Springeth Green*
(1988), a National Book Award nominee. In addition,
he has published essays and reviews.

ACHIEVEMENTS

Like Flannery O'Connor, a Catholic writer with
whom he is often compared, J. F. Powers is widely
recognized as a distinctive figure in the modern
American short story despite having produced only a
small body of work. A master of comedy whose
range encompasses cutting satire, broad farce, and
gentle humor, Powers explores fundamental moral
and theological issues as they are worked out in the
most mundane situations. While he is best known for
stories centering on priests and parish life, Powers, in
several early stories of the 1940's, was among the
first to portray the circumstances of black people who
had migrated from the South to Chicago and other urban centers.

BIOGRAPHY

John Farl Powers was born into a Catholic family
in a town in which the "best" people were Protestant,
a fact which he said "to some extent made a philosopher out of me." He attended Quincy Academy,
taught by Franciscan Fathers, and many of his closest

friends there later went into the priesthood. Powers
himself was not attracted to clerical life, principally
because of the social responsibilities, although he has
said the praying would have attracted him. After
graduation he worked in Marshall Field and Co., sold
insurance, became a chauffeur, and clerked in
Brentano's bookshop. During World War II, Powers
was a conscientious objector; as a result, he spent
more than a year in a federal prison. His first story
was published in 1943. In 1946, he married Elizabeth
Wahl, also a writer. They were to have five children;
at the time of her death, in 1988, they had been married for forty-two years.

After the war, Powers and his family lived in Ireland as well as in the United States. He supplemented
income from writing by teaching at various colleges
and universities; in addition, he received a Guggenheim Fellowship and two fellowships from the
Rockefeller Foundation. In 1976, Powers settled in
Collegeville, Minnesota, where he became Regents
Professor of English at St. John's University.

ANALYSIS

The most frequently reprinted of J. F. Powers's
short stories and therefore the best known are not the
title stories of his two collections—"Prince of Darkness" and "The Presence of Grace"—but rather
"Lions, Harts, Leaping Does," "The Valiant Woman,"
and "The Forks"—stories that are firmly rooted in social observation and realistic detail but have at their
center specifically moral and theological issues.
Powers is a Catholic writer, not a writer who happens
to be a Catholic or one who proselytizes for the
Church, but rather (as Evelyn Waugh has said) one
whose "art is everywhere infused and directed by his
Faith."

For Powers the central issue is how in the midst of
a fallen world to live up to the high ideals of the
Church. Since that issue is most sharply seen in the
lives of those who have chosen the religious life as
their vocation, parish priests, curates, friars, nuns,
and archbishops dominate Powers's stories. As might

J. F. Powers (Hugh Powers)

be expected of a religious writer who admires, as Powers does, the art of James Joyce and who learned the satiric mode from Sinclair Lewis and Evelyn Waugh, Powers's stories are frequently ironic and often satiric portraits of clerics who fail to measure up to the ideals of their priestly vocation. Many are straightforward satires.

"Prince of Darkness"

"Prince of Darkness," for example, is the fictional portrait of a priest, Father Burner, who in his gluttony, his ambition for material rewards and professional success, and his lack of charity toward sinners in the confessional, reveals himself to be a modern incarnation of the devil himself. In opposition to Father Burner is the Archbishop, an elderly cleric in worn-out slippers who in the proper spirit of moral firmness and Christian compassion reassigns Father Burner not to the pastorate he covets but to another parish assistant's role where, presumably, his power of darkness will be held in check.

"The Devil Was the Joker"

"The Devil Was the Joker" from Powers's second collection resembles "Prince of Darkness" in theme and conception, except here the satanic figure is a layman who has been hired by a religious order to sell its publication in Catholic parishes. Mac, the salesman—"Fat and fifty or so, with a candy-pink face, sparse orange hair, and popeyes"—hires a young former seminarian to travel about with him as his companion-driver. Myles Flynn, the former seminarian, also becomes the drinking companion and confidant of Mac, who gradually reveals himself to be totally cynical about the religious wares he is peddling, and who is, moreover, neither religious nor Catholic. Mac exploits the priests he encounters on his travels and attempts to use Myles to further his financial interests. As a way of making a sale, for example, he will frequently "take the pledge," that is, promise to refrain from alcohol. In return, he usually manages to extract from the priest to whom he made the pledge a large order for his wares. One day, after drunkenly confessing to Myles that he is not Catholic, he tries to repair the damage he imagines has been done to his position by trying to get Myles to baptize him, alleging that Myles has been responsible for his sudden conversion. It is through Myles's response that Powers provides the perspective for understanding and judging Mac. Myles perceives that Mac "was the serpent, the nice old serpent with Glen-plaid markings, who wasn't very poisonous." In conclusion, Myles not only refuses to baptize Mac but also leaves him and attempts once more to get back into the seminary.

"Prince of Darkness" and "The Devil Was the Joker" are both loosely constructed revelations of character rather than stories of conflict and action. Powers's two best-known pieces are also among the best things he has done, including those in *Look How the Fish Live*. Both are told from the point of view of a priest caught in a moral dilemma.

"The Forks"

In "The Forks," a young curate, Father Eudex, assistant to a Monsignor in a middle-class parish, is presented with a check from a manufacturing company that has been having labor trouble. Father Eudex, born on a farm, a reader of the *Catholic Worker*, and a sympathizer with the strikers, regards the check as hush money and therefore finds it unacceptable. His superior, the Monsignor, who drives a long black car like a politician's and is friendly with bankers and businessmen, suggests that Father Eudex use the check as down payment on a good car. The Monsignor is a man of impeccable manners, concerned with the appearance of things, with laying out a walled garden, with the perfection of his salad, and disturbed by the fact that Father Eudex strips off his shirt and helps the laborer spade up the garden, and that he uses the wrong fork at dinner. Quite clearly the Monsignor represents to Powers a modern version of the secularized church, Father Eudex, the traditional and, in this story, powerless Christian virtues. At the end of the story, Father Eudex, who has considered sending the check back to the company or giving it to the strikers' fund, merely tears it up and flushes it down the toilet, aware that every other priest in town will find some "good" use for it. True goodness in Powers's stories tends to be helpless in the face of such worldliness.

"THE VALIANT WOMAN"

In "The Valiant Woman" the same issue is raised in the conflict between a priest and his housekeeper. The occasion in this story is the priest's fifty-ninth birthday celebration, a dinner from which his one remaining friend and fellow priest is driven by the insistent and boorish presence of the housekeeper. The theological and moral issue is dramatized by the priest's dilemma: according to church law he can rid himself of the housekeeper but he can only do so by violating the spirit of Christian charity. The housekeeper, being totally unconscious of the moral implications of her acts, naturally has the advantage. Like the wily mosquito who bites the priest, her acts are of the flesh only, while his, being conscious and intellectual, are of the will. The priest cannot bring himself to fire her and so in a helpless rage at being bitten by a mosquito (after having been, in effect, stung by the housekeeper), he wildly swings a rolled up newspaper at the mosquito and knocks over and breaks a bust of Saint Joseph.

When summarized, Powers's stories sound forbidding, when, in fact, they are—despite the underlying seriousness—delightfully humorous. About the housekeeper in "The Valiant Woman," for instance, Powers has the priest think:

[She] was clean. And though she cooked poorly, could not play the organ, would not take up the collection in an emergency and went to card parties, and told all— even so, she was clean. She washed everything. Sometimes her underwear hung down beneath her dress like a paratrooper's pants, but it and everything she touched was clean. She washed constantly. She was clean.

Not all of Powers's stories have been about priests. Four of those in his first collection deal with racial and religious prejudice; three are about blacks ("The Trouble," about a race riot, "He Don't Plant Cotton," in which black entertainers in a Northern nightclub are badgered by a visitor from Mississippi and quit their jobs, and "The Eye," about a lynching of an innocent black), and one about anti-Semitism ("Renner"). Two stories from *The Presence of Grace* are also not explicitly religious: "The Poor Thing" and "Blue Island." Even these apparently secular stories arise out of the same moral concern that may be seen more clearly in the overtly religious ones.

"THE POOR THING"

In "The Poor Thing" a crippled woman, Dolly, who goes through the motions of being religious, is revealed as a pious hypocrite when she slyly exploits an elderly spinster, forcing her to serve for little pay as her constant companion. The elderly woman had been talked into accepting the position in the first place and then when she tried to leave, was falsely accused by Dolly of having stolen from her. The woman then has the choice of either returning to Dolly or having her reputation at the employment office ruined.

"BLUE ISLAND"

In "Blue Island" the oppressor is a woman who sells pots and pans by arranging "coffees" in other women's houses and then arriving to "demonstrate" her wares. Under the guise of neighborly concern for a young woman who has recently moved into the neighborhood and is unsure of herself (and ashamed of her origins), she persuades the young woman to have a coffee to which all of the important neighbor women are invited; then the saleswoman arrives with her wares and the young woman, the victim, stricken by the deception practiced on her and on the neighbors she has tried to cultivate, rushes to her bedroom and weeps, while downstairs the neighbor women file out, leaving her alone with her oppressor. In both "The Poor Thing" and "Blue Island," Powers also shows that the victims participate in their victimization, the spinster through her pride and the young woman in "Blue Island" by denying her past and attempting to be something she is not.

"LIONS, HARTS, LEAPING DOES"

Powers's best stories are undoubtedly those that bring the moral and religious issue directly into the main action. The story still most widely admired is the one written when Powers was twenty-five that established his early reputation as a master of the short story: "Lions, Harts, Leaping Does." The popularity of this story may result not only from the high level of its art but also from the way it deals so gently with the issues and creates in Father Didymus and in the simple Friar Titus two appealing characters. Indeed, one of Powers's major achievements is his ability in many of his stories to create characters with the vividness and complexity one expects only from the longer novel. For this reason, if for no other, the stories of J. F. Powers will continue to engage the attention of discriminating readers.

OTHER MAJOR WORKS

LONG FICTION: *Morte d'Urban*, 1962; *Wheat That Springeth Green*, 1988.

BIBLIOGRAPHY

Evans, Fallon, ed. *J. F. Powers*. St. Louis: Herder, 1968. A collection of essays and appreciations emphasizing the Catholic context of Powers's fiction. Among the contributors are Hayden Carruth, W. H. Gass (whose essay "Bingo Game at the Foot of the Cross" is a classic), Thomas Merton, and John Sisk. Also includes an interview with Powers and a bibliography.

Gussow, Mel. "J. F. Powers, 81, Dies." *The New York Times*, June 17, 1999, p. C23. In this tribute to Powers, Gussow traces his literary career, commenting on his first important story, "Lions, Harts, Leaping Does," and his best-known collection, *Prince of Darkness and Other Stories*, noting his frequent focus on priests.

Hagopian, John V. *J. F. Powers*. New York: Twayne, 1968. The first book-length study of Powers, this overview comprises a biographical sketch and a survey of Powers's work through *Morte d'Urban*. Gives extensive attention to Powers's stories. Includes a useful bibliography.

McCarthy, Colman. "The Craft of J. F. Powers." *The Washington Post*, June 12, 1993, p. A21. A brief tribute to Powers, commenting on his teaching and fiction, and recounting an interview, in which Powers laments the fact that college students do not read any more.

Meyers, Jeffrey. "J. F. Powers: Uncollected Stories, Essays and Interviews, 1943-1979." *Bulletin of Bibliography* 44 (March, 1987): 38-39. Because Powers has published relatively little in his long career, it is particularly useful to have a list of his uncollected stories. The essays and interviews listed here provide valuable background.

Powers, J. F. "The Alphabet God Uses." Interview by Anthony Schmitz. *Minnesota Monthly* 22 (December, 1988): 34-39. At the time of this interview, occasioned by the publication of Powers's novel *Wheat That Springeth Green*, Schmitz himself had just published his first novel, which also deals with the Catholic clergy. He makes an ideal interviewer, and his conversation with Powers provides an excellent introduction to the man and his works.

Powers, Katherine A. "Reflections of J. F. Powers: Author, Father, Clear-Eyed Observer." *The Boston Globe*, July 18, 1999, p. K4. A reminiscence of Powers by his daughter; discusses the writers that most influenced Powers, particularly his admiration for Evelyn Waugh, and comments on his writing and reading habits.

Preston, Thomas R. "Christian Folly in the Fiction of J. F. Powers." *Critique: Studies in Modern Fiction* 16, no. 2 (1974): 91-107. The theme of the "fool for Christ," whose actions confound the wisdom of this world, has a long tradition. Focusing on the stories "Lions, Harts, Leaping Does" and "The Forks" and the novel *Morte d'Urban*, Preston explores Powers's handling of this theme, showing how Powers uses priests as protagonists, not to dwell on concerns peculiar to the priesthood but rather to illumine the nature of the Christian life. See also *Critique: Studies in Modern Fiction* 2 (Fall, 1958), a special issue devoted to Powers and Flannery O'Connor.

Votteler, Thomas, ed. *Short Story Criticism: Excerpts from Criticism of the Works of Short Fiction Writers*. Vol. 4. Detroit: Gale Research, 1990. Contains a chapter on Powers with a good selection of criticism on his short fiction.

W. J. Stuckey

REYNOLDS PRICE

Born: Macon, North Carolina; February 1, 1933

PRINCIPAL SHORT FICTION
The Names and Faces of Heroes, 1963
Permanent Errors, 1970
The Foreseeable Future, 1991
The Collected Stories, 1993

OTHER LITERARY FORMS

In addition to short stories, Reynolds Price's works include plays, teleplays, award-winning poetry, and the novels for which he is best known, which include *The Honest Account of a Memorable Life: An Apocryphal Gospel* (1994) and *The Promise of Rest* (1995). Price's essays and articles have been collected in several volumes, and he has also published translations from the Bible, a memoir, *Clear Pictures: First Loves, First Guides* (1989), and *Learning a Trade: A Craftsman's Notebooks, 1955-1997* (1998).

ACHIEVEMENTS

A Rhodes scholar at Oxford University, Reynolds Price has held John Simon Guggenheim Memorial Foundation and National Endowment for the Arts fellowships. His numerous honors also include a National Association of Independent Schools award, a National Institute of Arts and Letters award, a North Carolina Award, a Bellamann Foundation award, the Roanoke-Chowan Poetry Award, the Elmer H. Bobst

Award, a Fund for New American Plays grant, and an R. Hunt Parker Award, as well as honorary doctorates from St. Andrew's Presbyterian College, Wake Forest University, Washington and Lee University, and Davidson College. His *A Long and Happy Life* (1962) won both the William Faulkner Foundation First Novel Award and the Sir Walter Raleigh Award. *The Surface of Earth* (1975) won the Lillian Smith Award in 1976, and *Kate Vaiden* (1986), a best-seller, received the National Book Critics Circle Award for Fiction. *The Collected Stories* was a finalist for the Pulitzer Prize in Fiction. Price's books have been translated into sixteen languages.

BIOGRAPHY

The first child of William Solomon Price and Elizabeth Rodwell Price, Edward Reynolds Price was born February 1, 1933, at the Rodwell family homestead in Macon, North Carolina. When the doctor told Will that neither his wife nor his child was likely to survive, Will made a pledge to God: If their lives were spared, he would never drink again. He kept this difficult promise, which marked the beginning of a deep bond between Reynolds and his parents. Young Reynolds heard this story many times—as he heard the other oral memories of his large extended family—and has said that these tales were his introduction to the power of narrative.

During the Depression, Will Price worked as an appliance salesman, moving his family through a succession of small North Carolina towns. Although a brother was born when Reynolds was eight, he was still essentially a solitary child, spending most of his free time reading, drawing, or playing alone in the woods. The family moved to Warrenton in 1944, where Reynolds met the farm children who served as prototypes for his early fiction. In 1947, Reynolds entered high school in Raleigh, where, during what he has called a miserable adolescence, he decided that writing would be his vocation.

In 1951, Price entered Duke University as an Angier Duke Scholar and studied English literature and history. Although he wrote relatively little fiction as an undergraduate, his story "Michael Egerton" was praised by visiting author Eudora Welty, and he was also encouraged by his professors. After graduation in 1955, Price spent three years at Merton College, Oxford, as a Rhodes scholar. While there, in addition to writing his thesis on John Milton's *Samson Agonistes* (1671), Price wrote poetry and short stories and traveled widely in Europe. In 1958, he received a B.Litt. degree and returned to Duke University to join the English faculty. Price continued to teach at Duke, interrupted only by visiting professorships and a few trips abroad.

Price's first two novels and collection of short stories, published between 1962 and 1966, were unanimously acclaimed. Some readers and critics were disturbed, however, by what they perceived as darker tone and harsher style in his third novel, *Love and Work* (1968), and his second short-story collection, *Permanent Errors*. Price continued to publish steadily in a variety of forms: a collection of essays in 1972; another award-winning novel, *The Surface of Earth*, in 1975; his first play in 1977; and a volume of contemporary translations of biblical stories in 1978. In 1981, he published *The Source of Light* (1981), a sequel to *The Surface of Earth*, which, like its predecessor, was praised but also criticized for its cumbersome plot.

In 1984, following surgery for spinal cancer, Price became paraplegic, but his literary output after that time has, if anything, only increased. For more than thirty years, Price's home has been outside Durham, North Carolina. Situated on forty acres of land, with a

Reynolds Price (Margaret Sartor)

pond and pine trees, it is filled with what Price calls an aging boy's museum: objects as diverse as arrowheads, old 78 rpm records, myriad photographs of family and friends, and a personal letter from Dwight D. Eisenhower dated 1943. In 1977, Price became a James B. Duke Professor of English at Duke University, where he continued to teach and write.

ANALYSIS

Reynolds Price is one of the United States' most respected contemporary men of letters. After publication of his first novel in 1962, Price was instantly acclaimed as a regional writer and compared to William Faulkner. He resists, however, being called a southern writer because the label, he believes, encourages people to focus on the surface similarities among works rather than look at their deeper truths. Price writes out of his vision of the spirituality of all existence, particularly as expressed through the myriad interactions of family. He is known as a serious writer of rich, dense prose that is simultaneously but not incongruously infused with comic moments and homespun wisdom.

Critics have observed that it is hard to separate Reynolds Price's work and literary persona from Price himself. Although events and characters in his stories and novels often bear strong resemblance to his personal circumstances, Price denies that his writing is autobiographical, saying,

> Only very occasionally and fragmentarily do I write autobiographically. My ideas come from all sorts of places, generally an exterior fact or object will precipitate an interior crystallization.

Interior crystallization is the heart of Price's fiction, which he has described as an attempt to seize territory from chaos. Price seeks to uncover the natural order that he perceives underlies the seemingly chaotic surface of daily happenings, investigating it as it manifests itself in different layers of life. Although religion has a definite presence in Price's work, it is this absolute value of existence that is paramount.

THE NAMES AND FACES OF HEROES

Price published his first volume of short fiction, *The Names and Faces of Heroes*, in 1963. Like his award-winning first novel of the year before, it was enthusiastically acclaimed. Set in Warren, North Carolina, like much of Price's work, these seven stories focus on a characteristic theme: love and its responsibilities, love that grows naturally—although sometimes crookedly—from within the nature of family, related by blood or by community. The first story, "A Chain of Love," is representative of Price's early fiction in that it presents an unsophisticated, rural, adolescent protagonist trying to make sense of the world—often through memories, often in hospitals or churches, and always moving toward a kind of healing that, without contrivance, love can bring.

"A Chain of Love" introduces Price's abiding sense of honor, almost reverence, for the power of family. It contains images and events that figure prominently in later works, including focus on duty, the giving of gifts, the power of the name, images of light and dark, death, and the parent/child relationship—most commonly father and son. This story (published individually in 1958) is also Price's introduction of the Mustian family, who reappear in three of his novels. Rosacoke Mustian is staying in the Raleigh hospital with her Papa, who is suffering from a "tired heart." From Papa's room, Rosa can see a statue of Jesus Christ outside, and this symbol reappears in her memory of the Phelps boy, who drowned and then returned from the dead. "Papa is my duty," she says, and tries to do more for him than his nurse does.

Rosa is also aware of the pain of others in the ward. She considers how to help—perhaps by bringing them ice water—but realizes that they "probably wouldn't want that anyhow" and that her attempts to relieve such great suffering would be "like trying to fill up No-Bottom Pond." Still, Rosa thinks, there ought to be "something you could say even in the dark that would make them know why you were standing there looking." Rosa's compassion finds a focus through a case of mistaken identity. She thinks that she sees Wesley—the boy back home—sitting in the hospital corridor and approaches him playfully, only to find that it is the boy whose father is dying of lung cancer across the hall. Embarrassed by her intrusion into his sorrow "like some big hussy," Rosacoke determines to get to know the Ledwell family (though she does not know their individual names) and be kind to them, but she decides to do so in secret.

The narrative dances with images of light and dark, and Rosa is first associated with the dark. As she steps toward the Ledwell boy, "bleached light" strikes her, and she drops back

> the way one of those rain snails does that is feeling its path . . . till you touch its gentle horn, and it draws itself back . . . into a tight piece you would never guess could think or move or feel, even.

After much inner debate, however, Rosa decides to leave a bouquet for Mr. Ledwell, "flowers that would say better than she could how much she felt." Quietly opening Mr. Ledwell's door to deliver the anonymous gift, Rosa sees a priest administering the last rites and intends to back out unobserved. She is instead drawn in, however, by the Ledwell boy, who turns and sees her "through all that dark." Rosa decides to leave because they might switch on the light and see her "looking on at this dying which was the most private thing in the world." After placing the flowers on a chair, where "in the [later] light somebody might see them and be glad that whoever it was stepped over to bring them, stepped over without saying a word," Rosa returns to Papa's room. There, in a slow voice that "cut through all the dark," she is finally able to speak her grief and acknowledge her wish that the Ledwells might have known that it was she, "that Rosacoke Mustian was sorry to see it happen."

PERMANENT ERRORS

Price's second volume of short fiction, *Permanent Errors*, was published in 1970. His introduction says that it is

> an attempt to isolate in a number of lives the central error of act, will, understanding which, once made, has been permanent, incurable, but whose diagnosis and palliation are the hopes of continuance.

The protagonists in these stories are no longer rural adolescents but rather intense, often literary individuals. Like the novel that preceded it, *Permanent Errors* sparked controversy among critics and readers, some of whom objected to what they saw as a darker perspective and new compactness, even severity, in Price's style. Price has agreed that these stories were a break with, or advance on, past work, but he also explains that people who thought his first three books were "joyous, rambunctious, yea-saying . . . found themselves abandoned in the middle of the road . . . not having seen, of course, that they'd misread the first three books."

The four pieces that form the first section, "Fool's Education," can be read independently but also form a larger wholeness when read consecutively. The first, "The Happiness of Others," introduces Charles Tamplin, a young American writer living in England who views life from a protective distance. He is referred to by his full name, but the reader knows only the first name of Sara, the woman with whom he has had a long-term relationship. Charles Tamplin and Sara are spending their last day together before they

part permanently. Tamplin wants dutifully to "kill" the day "as painlessly as possible," believing that without Sara, it will be easier for him to create, to write, to get his work done. Sara, however, is still able to view the day as a sort of gift, "like a baby dumped on their doorstep, gorgeous but unwanted, condemning as an angel." Visiting a church near Oxford, they choose and recite epitaphs to each other, which reflect these differing views. Tamplin's inscription talks of love as necessarily temporary, while Sara's envisions the possibility of continuity even beyond death. Although Tamplin is not influenced by Sara's interpretation, he does realize that the ending of their relationship is not mutual, as he had supposed, and that she is accusing him of refusing to engage himself in life's changes, preferring instead to learn what he learns by watching the involvement of others.

Later, as they drive along, Tamplin feels some relief from "their airless symbiosis," thinking about how he will turn the day into a story. When their car almost collides with a flock of sheep crossing the road, Tamplin muses on the setting, which "might as easily be Galilee as Oxfordshire, before Christ." He also wonders, however, why the sheep are bothering to cross the road at all since the "grass seemed no greener there than where they had left, browner in fact." Their shepherd, "a credible David," appears almost magically, rubbing his eyes to wake himself up and apologizing for the delay soundlessly—and directly to Sara—through the windshield. She smiles at the shepherd, pardoning him, and Tamplin realizes that life's artistry, like the shepherd with "grace as natural as breath," flows simply and intimately to Sara but not to himself. He sees "a door blown fiercely open on a world, older, simpler, deeper than he'd known." Tamplin will not recover like Sara, who will grow to embrace love again. Rather, it will be his duty to write about the happiness of others, "to describe, celebrate, adore at a distance." Tamplin's error—letting Sara go, separating what he sees as art from life—is the inevitable consequence of his character up to that point.

In the second story of the section, Tamplin returns home "alone but not lonely" and agrees to witness the death of his landlady's dog. Again, he avoids intimacy and is most concerned with the ritualized rules of behavior that he creates for himself, "no word, no touch." In the third story, taking place three weeks later, Tamplin feels himself "leaned on only by the afternoon sun, the light a quiet unneedful companion." Through interactions with his landlady and her friend Mary, which evoke memories of both Sara and Tamplin's mother, it is clear that Tamplin is not really at ease. Although he is disgusted by the disorder he perceives in others' lives, thinking that "the name of all [their] stories was Scars not Seeds," Tamplin nevertheless comes to worship "their wasteful courage, ruinous choices, contingency," realizing that the name of his own story is Flight.

Written directly to Sara, the fourth story focuses on an earlier trip the couple took, but it really deals with the extent to which Tamplin has completed his fool's education. He concludes by asking Sara to come back, and some critics have suggested that Price seems to give Tamplin the benefit of the doubt here. The real question Price asks, however, is left hanging in the air: Is there sufficient space in Tamplin's life for Sara to be able to survive and grow? One may also hear its echo: Is there even space in Tamplin's life for himself? Price's work was seen by some—especially those who were disturbed by its changes after the 1962-1966 "Mustian Years"—to present the struggle between human companionship and solitude. Price, however, gave a better understanding in an interview in 1978, when he stated that he writes "books about human freedom—the limits thereof, the possibilities thereof, the impossibilities thereof." He also elaborated in a later interview that the main lens through which he has looked at human freedom has been love.

THE FORESEEABLE FUTURE

The Foreseeable Future, Price's third collection of short fiction, continues to develop this vision of love, which Price sees "as the greatest reward of human life and also one of the greatest terrors and dangers." The stories investigate moments of liberation from boundaries, moments that expand to include what Price considers "forms of reality quite beyond those forms which we encounter in our daily routines," mo-

ments that can be used as reference points in order to navigate back into greater harmony with the inherent balance and order of life. Each of these three substantial pieces is set in North Carolina and focuses on a male protagonist who is at a spiritual crossroads. Each deals with the threat of death and includes a perceptive child who helps the protagonist make his way home.

"Fare to the Moon" takes place toward the end of World War II. Kayes is spending his last night with Leah, the "one real woman . . . who had finally cared so deep and steady as to all but fill the gully cut in him," before he joins the army. As the story unfolds, the reader learns quietly that Leah is black, though "born nearly white and stayed that way when most children shade on off, tan or dark," and Kayes is white. One also learns that six months ago, Kayes left his wife—who still "watched him like the first angel landed"—and son for Leah, thereby alienating both of them from their communities. Driving with his brother Riley to the induction center, Kayes asks Riley to look after Leah but also admits his readiness to "leave now awhile." Riley responds that now Leah will have to leave town, too. Kayes realizes that this is true and asks, more to himself than to his brother, "How much have I broke?"

As the two men travel toward the induction center, the boy Curtis goes to help his mother retrieve Kayes's car from Leah's place. While there, he speaks with Leah briefly. Bitter about her before, Curtis now sees that Leah speaks the "clean deadlevel eye-to-eye truth" and later says to a friend, wildly and fiercely, "I flatout liked her. I saw the damned point." Curtis is thus tentatively uncovering the possibility of pardon. After passing his army physical, Kayes telephones Riley to say good-bye, telling him "I plan to live," and then tries to reach Curtis. Curtis is out, however, so Kayes speaks to Daphne, amazing himself by asking her how much she still cares. Kayes also thinks of Leah, but the "sight in his mind of Leah alone hurt too bad to watch," so he shuts his eyes and, "for the first time, asked to know how he could heal some part of the lives he'd crushed—his wife and son and Leah Birch." When no answer comes, "no word, no clue," Kayes decides to unearth his wedding ring from his shaving kit, knowing that it would be "wrong to all concerned" to wear it now but still thinking that "this empty circle might hold inside it his only chance of coming back whole . . . and starting over in decency."

Kayes wonders who on earth will ever risk Kayes Paschel again. The response comes from Curtis, who for the second time holds out the possibility of healing. Curtis dreams that night that he is with a friend but "deep gone in the dark, and losing blood." He tries to call his friend's name but finds he has forgotten it, and so he calls out his own name, "more than once," instead. Then, something pulls his hands up toward "a new light," and Curtis sees that someone "is flying there in a kind of fire that he seems to throw as he moves." Curtis sees that his friend is "moving now like a kite, and I've got the string." He reels the friend back in, until he is on the ground within reach, but "once he moves though, he's dark again," and Curtis says, "I feel the line draw tight once more." He guesses it is Kayes, "without even knowing his face or voice," and says, "I try to bet he's taking me home." Even as he dreams, Curtis realizes that he has "watched Kayes soar and wished him luck" and finds that this sight of "a useful father" will be enough to let him sleep through the night. Thus, Price concludes the story.

Such an appreciation of reality as composed of many layers—manifest and unmanifest, perceptible through the senses or in other ways—runs throughout Price's fiction. Through Price's graceful, elaborate prose, which sounds more like poetry, one is thrust into moments of truth and restoration that touch universal chords. The characters speak of love that they feel—or do not feel—for others in this collection. It is clear, however, that Price is exploring the ultimate power of love to bind one back, more securely, to oneself. This is true freedom and, ironically, the foundation for both meaningful solitude and real companionship. Characters tell of their pasts in order to know their own struggles, to heal them, and to build on them, and Price holds out the promise of the future, complete with successes and failures, based on the possibilities for freedom within each present moment. Thus, his stories are not contrived aesthetic

structures separate from life (as Charles Tamplin's were), but rather they are the stuff of life itself. Because people live, Price seems to say, they automatically have stories to tell. Because of the stories that Price tells, his readers will find themselves able to participate more fully, and with greater compassion, in the stories of their own lives.

THE COLLECTED STORIES

In 1993 Price published *The Collected Stories*, a complete anthology of his short fiction. Half of the fifty stories in the collection were newly published, while the remainder were culled from previous collections. Many of the stories are set in North Carolina and involve adult male characters reflecting on incidents from their past that often were shaped by "the floods of puberty." In "Deeds of Light" a fatherless young boy, starving for the presence of an adult male in his life, befriends a soldier stationed near his home, who quickly becomes "the thorough man to learn and copy in every trait and skill I lacked." In retrospect, he views the arrival of the soldier as coming at a critical stage in his youth, when hopes for a successful transition to adulthood were withering. Friends, he learns in later life, "can show you sights like nothing your kin, your lovers, God or Nature herself will ever show."

The "Enormous Door," the story of a young boy's emerging sexual awareness, reveals how the insecurities of youth often trigger imaginative reactions to inexplicable human experiences. In this case the youth, through a voyeuristic whim, observes two of his teachers engaging in sexual acts. As the scene unfolds, a rush of carnal images produce at once a sense of confusion and capabilities in the mind of the boy. His inability to fully comprehend the event sets him off on a flight of fancy intended to fill the void left in his understanding. What appears to be an "angel," cloaked in the form of a human body, intervenes to instill a sense of the sacred in a most unusual scene.

With "The Company of the Dead" and "Golden Child," Price again utilizes the device of an adult male ruminating on a chance incident in his youth. In the former, an adolescent boy and his friend take jobs as "setters" whose task is to sit all night by coffins of deceased family members to keep them company. It is the reactions of the living to the dead, some of them bordering on the bizarre, that provide the boy insight into the relationships of loved ones. The ultimate lesson he learns is that love "will freeze one life and char the next; no way to predict who lives or dies." Death also becomes a reality in "Golden Child" when a young boy is subjected to unwanted comparisons with a cousin who died at a young age. At first resentful, the boy soon realizes his best hope of overcoming his own fear of death is to take up his cousin's memory and by preserving it, share in her glory.

Price's fascination with the consequences of past actions is played out in dark progression in "Truth and Lies" when a woman decides to confront her husband's young mistress, a former student of the wife. The teacher-student relationship is portrayed in ironic detail by the author, as the woman attempts to lecture her unrepentant former charge on the error of her ways but in so doing comes to the realization that the truth cannot be fixed nor the past erased. They are two lessons from which Price never strays far in his rich body of stories.

OTHER MAJOR WORKS

LONG FICTION: *A Long and Happy Life*, 1962; *A Generous Man*, 1966; *Love and Work*, 1968; *The Surface of Earth*, 1975; *The Source of Light*, 1981; *Mustian: Two Novels and a Story, Complete and Unabridged*, 1983; *Kate Vaiden*, 1986; *Good Hearts*, 1988; *The Tongues of Angels*, 1990; *Blue Calhoun*, 1992; *The Honest Account of a Memorable Life: An Apocryphal Gospel*, 1994; *The Promise of Rest*, 1995; *Roxanna Slade*, 1998.

PLAYS: *Early Dark*, pb. 1977; *Private Contentment*, pb. 1984; *New Music: A Trilogy*, pr. 1989; *Full Moon and Other Plays*, pb. 1993.

TELEPLAY: *House Snake*, 1986.

POETRY: *Late Warning: Four Poems*, 1968; *Lessons Learned: Seven Poems*, 1977; *Nine Mysteries (Four Joyful, Four Sorrowful, One Glorious)*, 1979; *Vital Provisions*, 1982; *The Laws of Ice*, 1986; *The Use of Fire*, 1990.

NONFICTION: *Things Themselves: Essays and Scenes*, 1972; *A Common Room: Essays 1954-1987*, 1987; *Clear Pictures: First Loves, First Guides*, 1989; *A Whole New Life*, 1994; *Three Gospels*, 1996; *Learning a Trade: A Craftsman's Notebooks, 1955-1997*, 1998; *Feasting the Heart: Fifty-two Essays for the Air*, 2000.

TRANSLATIONS: *Presence and Absence: Versions from the Bible*, 1973; *Oracles: Six Versions from the Bible*, 1977; *A Palpable God: Thirty Stories Translated from the Bible with an Essay on the Origins and Life of Narrative*, 1978.

BIBLIOGRAPHY

Black, James T. "A Conversation with Reynolds Price." *Southern Living* 27 (September, 1992): 38. A brief biographical sketch of Price's life; discusses the ways in which families deal with crisis in his fiction.

Fodor, Sarah J. "Outlaw Christian: An Interview with Reynolds Price." *The Christian Century* 112 (November 22-29, 1995): 1128-1131. Price discusses eroticism in literature, the role of children in his fiction, the women in his novels, the importance of solitude in his life, his views on religion and the author Flannery O'Connor.

Henry, William A. "The Mind Roams Free." *Time* 143 (May 23, 1994): 66-68. A brief biographical account, focusing on Price's struggle with spinal cancer and the significant amount of work he has written since being told a decade ago he would not survive it.

Humphries, Jefferson, ed. *Conversations with Reynolds Price*. Jackson: University Press of Mississippi, 1991. In these fifteen interviews, which originally appeared between 1966 and 1989 in literary quarterlies, student literary journals, newspapers, and magazines, Price speaks articulately and frankly. The collection is indexed and includes a chronology and an informative introduction.

Price, Reynolds. Interview by Wendy Smith. *Publishers Weekly* 241 (May 9, 1994): 51-52. Price discusses his sense of malevolent fate, his troubled family history, his discovery of himself as a writer, his previous works, and the process of writing about his ordeal with cancer.

Rooke, Constance. *Reynolds Price*. Twayne's United States Authors series. Boston: Twayne, 1983. Focuses on Price's consistency of vision. After a brief biography and discussion of Price within a literary and geographical context, this study analyzes each of his first seven volumes of fiction—including his first two short-story collections—in detail. Includes a chronology and a select bibliography.

Sadler, Lynn Veach. "Reynolds Price and Religion: The 'Almost Blindlingly Lucid' Palpable World." *Southern Quarterly* 26 (Winter, 1988): 1-11. This article examines religious underpinnings, especially the influence of biblical narrative, in Price's fiction, and also investigates Price's perceptions of the deeper reality of life underlying what is commonly visible.

Schiff, James A., ed. *Critical Essays on Reynolds Price*. New York: G. K. Hall, 1998. A good first stop for the student of Price. Includes a bibliography and an index.

_____. *Understanding Reynolds Price*. Columbia: University of South Carolina Press, 1996. A general introduction to Price's work, focusing primarily on the novels, but also commenting on the relationship of Price's short stories to his longer fiction and memoirs.

Stevenson, John W. "The Faces of Reynolds Price's Short Fiction." *Studies in Short Fiction* 3 (1966): 300-306. Although this article deals only with the stories in Price's first collection, its perceptive insights provide a thoughtful foundation from which to approach the evolution of Price's work.

Jean C. Fulton, updated by
William Hoffman

V. S. PRITCHETT

Born: Ipswich, England; December 16, 1900
Died: London, England; March 20, 1997

PRINCIPAL SHORT FICTION

The Spanish Virgin and Other Stories, 1930
You Make Your Own Life and Other Stories, 1938
It May Never Happen and Other Stories, 1945
Collected Stories, 1956
The Sailor, the Sense of Humour, and Other Stories, 1956
When My Girl Comes Home, 1961
The Key to My Heart, 1963
The Saint and Other Stories, 1966
Blind Love and Other Stories, 1969
The Camberwell Beauty and Other Stories, 1974
Selected Stories, 1978
The Fly in the Ointment, 1978
On the Edge of the Cliff, 1979
Collected Stories, 1982
More Collected Stories, 1983
A Careless Widow and Other Stories, 1989
Complete Collected Stories, 1990

OTHER LITERARY FORMS

V. S. Pritchett's sixty-year career as a writer, apart from his many short stories, produced several novels (not well received), two autobiographies (*A Cab at the Door*, 1968, and *Midnight Oil*, 1972), several travel books (the noteworthy ones including *The Spanish Temper*, 1954, and *The Offensive Traveller*, 1964), volumes of literary criticism, literary biographies (*George Meredith and English Comedy*, 1970; *Balzac*, 1973; *The Gentle Barbarian: The Life and Work of Turgenev*, 1977), essays (among them *New York Proclaimed*, 1965, and *The Working Novelist*, 1965), and journalistic pieces from France, Spain, Ireland, and the United States that remain in the literary canon, so well are they written.

ACHIEVEMENTS

In his long and distinguished career, V. S. Pritchett, who prefers the abbreviation V. S. P., produced an impressive number of books in all genres—from novels and short stories, on which rests his fame, to literary criticism, travel books, and journalistic pieces written for *The Christian Science Monitor* when he covered Ireland, Spain, and France. His most successful genre was the short story, which resulted from his razor-sharp characterizations of all classes, both in England and on the Continent, his focus on the moment of epiphany, his graceful writing, and his ironic, bittersweet wit. Pritchett has the uncanny ability to select a commonplace moment and through imagery, wit, and irony lift it to a transfiguration. He focuses on the foibles of all people without malice, anger, or sentimentality but rather with humor, gentleness, and understanding. In his preface to *Collected Stories*, Pritchett states that although some people believe that the short story has lost some of its popularity, he does not think so: "[T]his is not my experience; thousands of addicts still delight in it because it is above all memorable and is not simply read, but re-read again and again. It is the glancing form of fiction that seems to be right for the nervousness and restlessness of contemporary life."

BIOGRAPHY

Victor Sawden Pritchett was born in Ipswich, Suffolk, England, of middle-class parents. His father, Walter, a Yorkshireman, espoused a strict Congregationalism. He married Beatrice of London, whom he had met when both worked in a draper's shop. Enthralled by wild business schemes, Walter often left his family for months as he pursued dreams that shattered and left the family destitute, forcing it into innumerable moves and frequent sharing of flats with relatives. Often a traveling salesman, Pritchett's father, despite his long absences, caused the family unmitigated misery when he returned. Pritchett's dictatorial father is reflected in many of his stories and novels, and Pritchett is completely frank in his autobiography about his father's brutality.

Most remarkable, Pritchett received only the barest of formal training at Alleyn's Grammar School, which he left when he was only sixteen to enter the leather trade. Clever with languages, he soon showed proficiency in French. He read omnivorously. In his stories, he reflects a cerebral ability, perceptiveness, and imagism. Despite his lack of formal training in literature, he is, in the twentieth century, considered to be one of the best writers of the short story in England. In 1975, he was knighted as Sir Victor for his contributions to literature.

After working in the leather trade for several years as a tanner, he left for a two-year interlude in Paris. Those years as a tanner were fruitful, he has declared, for he encountered all classes of people in England, a factor noted in his short stories, depicting the monied aristocrats and the working classes, together with the middle classes that he fixes in amber. In Paris, he worked in a photography shop as clerk and letter writer but soon wearied of the routines and determined to become a writer. His connection with *The Christian Science Monitor* became the key transitional phase, for he wrote and published for this newspaper a series of articles. When there was no longer a need for these articles written in Paris, *The Christian Science Monitor* sent him to Ireland, where

V. S. Pritchett (Nancy Crampton)

the civil war raged. Pritchett soaked up experiences from his wide travels as he journeyed from Dublin to Cork, Limerick, and Enniskillen. A year later the newspaper editors informed him that they needed him in Spain, and he left for Iberia with Evelyn Maude Vigors, whom he married at the beginning of 1924. There are virtually no details about his first wife, except that she was an actress. Their marriage, however, turned out not to be a happy one; the couple was divorced in 1936, and during that same year, Pritchett married Dorothy Roberts. His wife continued to assist him in his literary work, and he has invariably dedicated his work to her, one inscription reading "For Dorothy—always."

The years in Spain were productive, with Pritchett writing novels, short stories, travel books, and journalistic pieces. While there, he learned Spanish easily and immersed himself in its literature, especially being influenced by Miguel de Unamuno y Jugo, whose philosophic themes often concern the intensity of living near the jaws of death, and by Pío Baroja, whose books often focus on atheism and pessimism. Pritchett especially was influenced by Baroja's empathy for character. After two years in Spain, Pritchett visited Morocco, Algeria, Tunisia, the United States, and Canada, travels that further shaped his contours of place and people. In the 1930's, his writing approached the luminous. In the second volume of his autobiography, *Midnight Oil*, Pritchett wrote to this point:

> If I began to write better it was for two reasons: in my thirties I had found my contemporaries and had fallen happily and deeply in love. There is, I am sure, a direct connection between passionate love and the firing of the creative power of the mind.

Critics agree that Pritchett reached a high level of achievement in the short story in the 1930's. He continued writing on a high level until all was interrupted, as it was for many other writers, by the onset of World War II, during which he served in the Ministry of Information.

Pritchett became literary editor of *New Statesman* in 1945, resigning this position in 1949 to become its director from 1951 to 1978. Along the way, he had

been given lectureships at Princeton University (1953, Christian Gauss Lecturer) and the University of California, Berkeley (1962, Beckman Professor), and he was appointed as writer-in-residence at Smith College in 1966. Brandeis University, Columbia University, and the University of Cambridge also invited him to teach.

Honors poured on Pritchett. He was elected Fellow by the Royal Society of Literature, receiving a C.B.E. in 1969. Two years later he was elected president of the British PEN and was made Honorary Member of the American Academy of Arts and Letters. In 1974, he was installed as international president of PEN for two years. One of his greatest honors came from Queen Elizabeth as she received him into knighthood in 1975 for his services to literature. Also, Pritchett through the years received academic honors from several universities in the Western world, including honorary D.Litt. degrees from Leeds (1972) and Columbia University (1978).

Pritchett continued to contribute to journals both in the United States and Europe and England. Not wishing to rest on his innumerable laurels, this grand master of the short story continued to write and to select stories for his collections. By many, he is thought to be a writer's writer. He died on March 20, 1997, at the age of ninety-six, in London, England.

ANALYSIS

V. S. Pritchett writes in *Midnight Oil*,

> I have rarely been interested in what are called "characters," i.e., eccentrics; reviewers are mistaken in saying I am. They misread me. I am interested in the revelations of nature and (rather in Ibsen's fashion) of exposing the illusions or received ideas by which they live or protect their dignity.

An approach to the short stories reveals that Pritchett is projecting comic incongruities. He captures the moment of revelation when his men and women recognize an awareness of their plight. His panoply of people ranges from sailors, divers, clerks, blind men, and shop girls to piano accompanists, wastrels, and the penurious wealthy. Pritchett concentrates on selected details with tart wit and irony in dialogue that characterizes those who people his short stories. Two highly discrete characters often interrelate to their despair or to their joy. With such irony, the reader may conclude that in reading a Pritchett story, nothing is but what is not.

One of the earliest collections of short stories by Pritchett, *You Make Your Own Life and Other Stories*, already reflects the mature touch of the writer. Although showing some slight inconsistency, the tales attest variety in narrative, theme, tone, and style. Some stories are stark and Kafkaesque, especially "The Two Brothers," in which a nightmarish suicide is the central concern. The longest story in this group is "Handsome Is as Handsome Does," set on the French Mediterranean.

"Handsome Is as Handsome Does"

The focus is on Mr. and Mrs. Coram, an English couple, both of whom are unusually ugly. Their ugliness is their only similarity. He is rude, inarticulate, and slow-witted, and he quarrels with everyone. He is especially rude to M. Pierre, the proprietor of the hotel, insulting him in English which he does not understand. Mrs. Coram is left to play the role of diplomat and apologist. Soon after the English couple's arrival, Alex, whose forebears are flung throughout Europe, also vacations at the inn. He is young and handsome and delights in swimming. Childless, Mrs. Coram views Alex as the son she might have had. Yet one day, she attempts to seduce him while he watches unfeelingly, and she, scorned, feels ridiculous. One day, the Corams, Alex, and M. Pierre go to a deserted beach that is known for its dangerous undertow. M. Pierre dives in and before long, it is apparent to all that he is drowning. Alex rescues him while Mr. Coram looks on, never even thinking of saving the innkeeper. His wife is silently furious at him. Later, as M. Pierre brags at the hotel about his narrow escape, Mrs. Coram blandly tells some recent English arrivals that her husband saved M. Pierre's life.

Clearly, the Corams are loathsome people, but through Pritchett's portrayal of them as wounded, frustrated, and vindictive, even grotesque, they emerge as human beings, capable of eliciting the reader's empathy. Alex, protected by his "oily" youth, remains the catalyst, rather neutral and asex-

ual. The aging couple, in Pritchett's lightly satirical portraiture, in the end claim the reader's sympathy.

"Sense of Humour"

Another well-known and often-quoted story in this collection is "Sense of Humour." Arthur Humphrey, a traveling salesman, is the narrator. On one of his trips, he meets Muriel MacFarlane, who is dating a local boy, Colin Mitchell, who always rides a motorcycle. Colin is obsessively in love with Muriel. Arthur courts Muriel, who stops dating Colin. Nevertheless, the motorcyclist compulsively follows the couple wherever they go. Muriel says that she is Irish, and she has a sense of humor. Yet she never exhibits this so-called Irish trait. When Colin, who is also an auto mechanic, announces that he cannot repair Humphrey's car and thereby hopes to ruin the couple's plan, they take the train to Humphrey's parents' house. Shortly after their arrival, Muriel receives a call from the police: Colin has been killed in a motorcycle crash nearby. That night, Muriel is overwhelmed with grief for Colin; Arthur begins to comfort her, and they eventually, for the first time, have sex. All the while, Muriel is crying out Colin's name. To save Colin's family the expense, Colin's body is returned to his family in a hearse belonging to Arthur's father. Both Muriel and the obtuse Arthur feel like royalty when the passing drivers and pedestrians doff their hats in respect. Arthur says, "I was proud of her, I was proud of Colin, and I was proud of myself and after what happened, I mean on the last two nights, it was like a wedding." Colin is following them for the last time. When Arthur asks Muriel why she stopped seeing Colin, she answers that he never had a sense of humor.

Critics believe that Pritchett in this story exerts complete control in keeping the reader on tenterhooks between crying and guffawing. The narrator, like the reader, never concludes whether Muriel is marrying Arthur for his money or for love or whether she loves Colin or Arthur, in the final analysis. The story underscores one of Pritchett's favorite techniques: peeling away at the character with grim irony and even then not providing enough details to see the character's inner self. As Pritchett declared, however, his interest is in the "happening," not in overt characterization. Yet, in death, Colin after all does seem to win his love. Still, in the conclusion, it appears that all three people have been deluded. Some of the grim gallows humor in this story reminds the reader of Thomas Hardy, whom Pritchett acknowledged as an important influence.

"WHEN MY GIRL COMES HOME"

More than a decade after the end of World War II, *When My Girl Comes Home* was published. The mature style of Pritchett is readily discernible in this collection. The stories become somewhat more complex and difficult in morality, in situations, and in the greater number of characters. The moral ambiguities are many. The title story, "When My Girl Comes Home," is Pritchett's favorite short story.

Although World War II is over, the bankruptcy of the war ricochets on many levels. The "girl" coming home is Hilda Johnson, for whom her mother has been working and scrimping to save money. Residents of Hincham Street, where Mrs. Johnson lives, had for two years implored the bureaucracies of the world to obtain news about the whereabouts and the condition of Hilda, who was believed to be wasting away in a Japanese concentration camp. Now Hilda has come home, not pale and wan but sleek and relaxed. Only gradually does the story emerge, but never completely. In fact, because Hilda's second husband was a Japanese officer, she survived the war comfortably. She does not need the money that her mother saved from years of sewing. En route home, Hilda met two men, one of whom, Gloster, a writer, wished to write Hilda's story. The narrator observes, when he first sees her, that

> her face was vacant and plain. It was as vacant as a stone that has been smoothed for centuries in the sand of some hot country. It was the face of someone to whom nothing had happened; or, perhaps, so much had happened to her that each event wiped out what had happened before. I was disturbed by something in her—the lack of history, I think. We were worm-eaten by it.

Hilda sleeps with her mother in a tiny bedroom while she waits for help from Gloster, who never appears. She seems to become involved with a real prisoner of the Japanese, Bill Williams, who survived through the war, as he terms it, with "a bit of trade." Some of the neighbors begin to understand that Hilda, too, survived by trading as well. At one point in the tale, Hilda begs her friends to save her from Bill Williams, and she stays away from her apartment that night. When she returns to her flat, she discovers that Bill Williams has robbed her flat completely and has disappeared. Soon after, Hilda leaves London and surfaces only in a photograph with her two boyfriends, Gloster and someone else. Gloster does publish a book, not about Hilda's war experiences but about the people on Hincham Street.

The story's subtext may suggest that it might have been better for Hincham Street had the "girl" not come home, for then they would have retained their illusions about her. The illusion versus reality theme is one often used by Pritchett. Mrs. Johnson, now dead, seemed to have kept the street together in a kind of moral order, now destroyed on Hincham Street. After her death, Hilda and Bill were involved in seamy happenings. In the Hincham Street pubs, the war is discussed but only fitfully and inconclusively because "sooner or later, it came to a closed door in everybody's conscience." Hilda and Bill, surviving the Japanese camps through moral bankruptcy, form a mirror image of those Englishman who became black marketers, malingerers, ration thieves, and hoodlums. Moral codes were shattered by Englishmen—whether at home or abroad. Pritchett is deliberately murky in theme and relationships, but the story suggests that just as the Japanese disturbed the civil and moral order thousands of miles away, the disruption caused a moral decay at home at the same time that the war was fought to reestablish the world order. Perhaps Pritchett is suggesting that England during the war and after was a microcosm. Despite the disillusionment that touches the entire street and the gravity of the theme, Pritchett never fails to use the restorative of humor and subtle satire, watchwords of the writer.

At the end of the 1960's, *Blind Love and Other Stories* appeared. This collection reflects Pritchett's admiration of Anton Chekhov and Ivan Turgenev, whose bittersweet irony enfolds the characters as they experience, at the end, self-revelation. In his later years, Pritchett continued to grow as an artist in many ways. The story lines are compelling, and no matter what the theme, Pritchett's wit provides humor and pathos. The transition between time present and time past is accomplished with laser-beam precision.

"THE SKELETON"

"The Skeleton," concerning George Clark, fleshes out a skinny man who has never loved. Cantankerous, selfish, perfectionistic, and thoroughly narcissistic, George is painted to perfection with satirical brushes. His encounter with Gloria Archer, whom George accuses of corrupting his favorite painter, transforms him. The comic becomes almost caricature and is flawless. Pritchett shows him guarding his whiskey bottle like a Holy Grail, but his valet finds it mistakenly left on the table, drinks a bit, and then dilutes the bottle with water. Dean R. Baldwin, who wrote the excellent Twayne biography of Pritchett, wrote, "George is the skeleton, until Gloria puts a bit of meat on his emotional bare bones."

"BLIND LOVE"

Like many of Pritchett's best stories used as title stories, "Blind Love" is a masterful portrait of two people who are scarred by nature but who succumb to pride before their fall. Mr. Armitage, a wealthy lawyer living in the country and blind for twenty years, has been divorced because of his affliction. He interviews Mrs. Johnson by feeling her face and hands, and he hires her as a secretary/housekeeper. As Thomas Gray would say, nothing disturbed the even tenor of their ways for a few years. One day, Armitage, walking in his garden, loses his balance when a dog chases a rabbit, and he falls into his pool. Mrs. Johnson sees the fall but before she can rush out to help him, he is rescued. When Mrs. Johnson tries to help him change his clothes in his room, she breaks the cardinal rule of never changing the physical order of things because Armitage has memorized the place for every item. He screams at her to get out and leave him alone. This verbal attack stimulates a flashback that reveals that Mrs. Johnson had heard "almost exactly those words, before. Her husband had said them. A week after the wedding." She recalls that he was shocked and disgusted at

a great spreading ragged liver-coloured island of skin which spread under the tape of her slip and crossed her breast and seemed to end in a curdle of skin below it. She was stamped with an ineradicable bloody insult.

After Armitage's rudeness, Mrs. Johnson decides to leave, for, in addition to those scorching words, she disliked the country. Armitage apologizes and begs her to stay. Soon thereafter, he gropes toward her and kisses her, and they make love. Mrs. Johnson, initially motivated by the pleasure of revenge against her husband, begins in time to enjoy Armitage's lovemaking. Religion is woven into the story when Armitage mocks Mrs. Johnson for going to church, and at one time, he insists that she use spittle and dirt on his eyes to mock a miracle of Christ: "Do as I tell you. It's what your Jesus Christ did when he cured the blind man."

Armitage then goes to Mr. Smith, an expensive faith healer, actually a charlatan-*manqué*, to regain his sight. Once, Mrs. Johnson accompanies him. As she leaves, Armitage hears her telling Smith that she loves Armitage as he is. Earlier, Smith appeared when Mrs. Johnson had been sunbathing nude at the pool. After wondering whether he saw her, Mrs. Johnson concludes that he did not. When Armitage later asks her whether Smith had seen her at the pool, Mrs. Johnson explodes and says that Smith saw everything. Unzipping her dress, she cries, "You can't see it, you silly fool. The whole bloody Hebrides, the whole plate of liver."

Later, when Mrs. Johnson for some strange reason is found lying face down in the pool, she, like Armitage earlier, is rescued. Both have had their "fall." This parallel happening seems to be a moment of epiphany, and the story ends with the couple living in Italy, where Mrs. Johnson describes churches and gallery pictures to her "perhaps" husband. In the last paragraph, Mrs. Johnson proclaims her love for her husband as she eyes the lovely Italian square below. She says that she feels "gaudy," leaving the reader wrestling over her selection of the word. Long after the reading, the poignancy of the story resonates.

This title story, an intensely poignant one, forthright and absorbing, shows the handicaps bringing people together and almost tearing them apart. They are both anointed by their "fall" from pride, and in their moment of epiphany, they see their need of each other and the love accompanying the need. Through each other and by self-analysis, they transcend their limitations and experience the joy of seeing themselves anew. Again, this revelatory process is a mainstay of Pritchett.

"THE DIVER"

Five years later, Pritchett continued his consistent stream of productivity by publishing *The Camberwell Beauty and Other Stories*. This volume particularly focuses on the eccentric foibles of the middle class. "The Diver," set in Paris, is an enjoyable tale of a diver who is a metaphor for sexual encounters. This diver is sent to retrieve bundles of leather goods that a Dutch ship accidentally spews into the Seine. A young clerk for the leather tannery is assigned to count the sodden bales. Quite by chance, he himself falls into the Seine and is fished out by the onlookers. His boss takes him across the street to a bar and expects the lad to pay for his own brandy. Mme Chamson, feeling sorry for the youth, takes him to her shop for a change of clothing. As he disrobes, she notices his inflamed member and becomes furious at his disrespect. A few minutes later, she calls him into her bedroom, where he finds her nude, and she initiates a sexual encounter. The youth, yearning to become a writer, feels inarticulate. This encounter with Mme Chamson, his first sexual experience, has released his creative wellsprings. A simple tale, "The Diver" is rib-tickling in its theme of innocence lost and creativity gained. Pritchett elsewhere has written of the link between sexuality and creativity.

"THE CAMBERWELL BEAUTY"

Again, the long title story, "The Camberwell Beauty," is one of the most arresting. The ambience is that of the antique dealers of London, a cosmos of its own. Each antique dealer has his own specialty, and "within that specialty there is one object he broods on from one year to the next, most of his life; the thing a man would commit murder to get his hands on if he had the nerve."

The narrator is a former antique dealer. A current art dealer, Pliny, an elderly man, has married a beauti-

ful woman, and the narrator is determined to get hold of the Camberwell beauty, who is essentially a work of art. Once more, Pritchett writes of illusion, this time using the art world and the gulf between the greed of the dealers and the loveliness of the art and the artifacts. Isabel, the Camberwell beauty, is exploited by being held captive, like any *object d'art*. The narrator fails in his attempt at seduction, which might have replicated another sexual exploitation. Isabel insists that Pliny is a good lover, but Pritchett strongly suggests that there is no intimacy between them. She, like William Blake's Thel, seems not to descend into generation (or sexuality). Remaining under the illusion that she is safe and protected in her innocence, and content to be in stasis and in asexuality, she never does reach a moment of self-awareness. She might just as well have been framed and hung on a wall.

"THE ACCOMPANIST"

The last collection of original stories, *On the Edge of the Cliff*, was published in 1979, and it contains stories wrought with a heightened sensibility and subtlety. The humor and technical brilliance are very much in evidence. Marital infidelity is the theme of several tales, especially in "The Fig Tree" and "A Family Man." A well-carved cameo, "The Accompanist" also portrays an unfaithful mate. William, the narrator, on leave from his Singapore job, is having an affair with Joyce, a piano accompanist, married to Bertie, impotent but particularly likable by a circle of friends who gather for dinner in his flat. The furniture, Victorian monstrosity, obsesses Bertie, since it is a link to the past. For undisclosed reasons, the furniture may almost affirm his asexuality. Critics invariably remark on a Henry James-like subtlety of sensitivity and particularity of detail. This texture surfaces when Bertie, accompanied by his wife, sings a French bawdy song about a bride who was murdered on her wedding night. Despite Bertie's problems with sex, he seems not to be aware of the irony in singing this song and in being anchored in the protected illusion of bygone Victorian days. His wife, Joyce, may emerge from the decadence of her marriage if, as the narrator says at the end, she will hear her tune: "And if she heard it, the bones in her legs, arms, her fingers, would wake up and she would be out of breath at my door without knowing it." William is saying that *if* she arrives out of a sexual impulse, there will be hope for her liberation from Bertie and from the historical frost symbolized by the Victorian furnishings.

"ON THE EDGE OF THE CLIFF"

The centerpiece story, "On the Edge of the Cliff," unravels the tale of a May-December liaison. Harry, a botanist in his seventies, and Rowena, an artist and twenty-five, have a happy affair in his house on the edge of a cliff. Driving down to a nearby village fair, they engage in role playing. The omniscient narrator declares, "There are rules for old men who are in love with young girls, all the stricter when the young girls are in love with them. It has to be played as a game." The game stimulates the love affair. At the fair, Harry meets Daisy Pyke, who was a former mistress and who has a young man in tow, mistakenly thought by Harry and Rowena to be her son but actually her lover. Daisy subsequently visits Harry, not to resume any romance but to beg Harry to keep the two young people apart so that her own love life will not be jeopardized. She cries, "I mean it, Harry. I know what would happen and so do you and I don't want to *see* it happen."

Ironically, both Harry and Rowena rarely venture into society. When Harry denies that Rowena is being kept prisoner, Daisy shrewdly insists, "You mean *you* are the prisoner. That is it! So am I!" Harry replies, "Love is always like that. I live only for her." In this tale, as in many of Pritchett's stories, there are contrasting sets of people who are often foils for each other. Both Daisy and Rowena are jealous of their lovers and want their May-December relationships to continue. Pritchett is undoubtedly concerned with the aging process and the capacity to sustain love. Both Daisy and Harry find their capacity to love undiminished with age. Yet, although their love affairs are viable, Pritchett's metaphor of the house on the cliff may suggest that the lovers are aware of inherent dangers because of the differences in ages. At the same time, Pritchett may be implying that even with no age differences between lovers, there is an element of risk. Illusion in this and many other of Pritchett's

tales plays an important role. As Harry and Daisy discuss their younger lovers, illusion is implicit. Yet, in their confronting the reality of age differences, they become intensely aware of their predicament, and it is at this moment that they experience a Pritchett epiphany. This realization will help them to savor the time spent on the edge of the cliff.

In his short fiction, Pritchett fashions a host of unique characters, uses witty and humorous dialogue, employs a variety of "happenings," and leaves readers with the sense that they themselves have been mocked not with bitterness or caustic wit but with gentleness and love.

OTHER MAJOR WORKS

LONG FICTION: *Claire Drummer*, 1929; *Shirley Sanz*, 1932 (also known as *Elopement into Exile*); *Nothing Like Leather*, 1935; *Dead Man Leading*, 1937; *Mr. Beluncle*, 1951.

NONFICTION: *Marching Spain*, 1928; *In My Good Books*, 1942; *The Living Novel and Later Appreciations*, 1946; *Why Do I Write? An Exchange of Views Between Elizabeth Bowen, Graham Greene, and V. S. Pritchett*, 1948; *Books in General*, 1953; *The Spanish Temper*, 1954; *London Perceived*, 1962; *The Offensive Traveller*, 1964 (also known as *Foreign Faces*); *New York Proclaimed*, 1965; *The Working Novelist*, 1965; *Shakespeare: The Comprehensive Soul*, 1965; *Dublin: A Portrait*, 1967; *A Cab at the Door*, 1968; *George Meredith and English Comedy*, 1970; *Midnight Oil*, 1972; *Balzac: A Biography*, 1973; *The Gentle Barbarian: The Life and Work of Turgenev*, 1977; *The Myth Makers: Literary Essays*, 1979; *The Tale Bearers: Literary Essays*, 1980; *The Other Side of the Frontier: A V. S. Pritchett Reader*, 1984; *A Man of Letters*, 1985; *Chekhov: A Spirit Set Free*, 1988; *Lasting Impressions*, 1990; *The Complete Essays*, 1991; *Balzac*, 1992.

BIBLIOGRAPHY

Angell, Roger. "Marching Life." *The New Yorker* 73 (December 22-29, 1997): 126-134. In this biographical sketch, Angell contends that although Pritchett was called First Man of Letters, the title never fit properly because he was neither literary nor a stylist, and he liked to say he was a hack long before he was a critic.

Baldwin, Dean. *V. S. Pritchett*. Boston: Twayne, 1987. This slim book of 133 pages contains a superb short biography of Pritchett, followed by a clear-cut analysis of his novels, short stories, and nonfiction. One caution is to be noted: Baldwin says there is no article analyzing any of Pritchett's short stories, yet the *Journal of the Short Story in English*, an excellent journal published in Angers, France, devoted an entire volume as a special Pritchett issue. It may be that Baldwin's book was already in the process of publication when the journal issue was completed.

Johnson, Anne Janette. "V(ictor) S(awdon) Pritchett." In *Contemporary Authors, New Revision Series*, edited by James G. Lesniak. Vol. 31. Detroit: Gale Research, 1990. This article includes general material on Pritchett's life and work, with a wide range of critical comments by magazines and literary journals such as *The Times Literary Supplement, The New York Times*, and *The New Republic*. Contains a listing of Pritchett's writings divided into genres and biographical and critical sources, especially those articles that appeared in newspapers, magazines, and literary journals. Geared for the general reader, with the variety of quotes appealing to a specialist.

Oumhani, Cecile. "Water in V. S. Pritchett's Art of Revealing." *Journal of the Short Story in English* 6 (1986): 75-91. Oumhani probes the immersion motif in the pattern of water imagery in Pritchett's short stories, especially in "On the Edge of a Cliff," "The Diver," "The Saint," and "Handsome Is as Handsome Does." Oumhani believes that Pritchett's views about sensuality can be intuited from the stories she analyzes. The article will appeal to the introductory reader of Freud.

Pritchett, V. S. "An Interview with V. S. Pritchett." Interview by Ben Forkner and Philippe Sejourne. *Journal of the Short Story in English* 6 (1986): 11-38. Pritchett in this interview reveals a number of salient details about writing in general and the influences of people like H. G. Wells and Arnold Bennett. He talks at length about the Irish predilection for storytelling and the Irish ideas about morality and the art of concealment. Pritchett reveals his penchant for the ironic and pays homage to Anton Chekhov, one of his models. He believes that the comic is really a facet of the poetic. The interview is written in a question-answer style and is a straightforward record of Pritchett's views.

Stinson, John J. *V. S. Pritchett: A Study of the Short Fiction*. New York: Twayne, 1992. An introduction to Pritchett's short fiction. Suggests that Pritchett's stories have been largely ignored by critics because they do not have the symbolic image pattern favored by formalist critics. Provides interpretations of a number of Pritchett's stories. Includes Pritchett's own comments on writers who have influenced him, as well as essays on his short fiction by Eudora Welty and William Trevor.

Theroux, Paul. "V. S. Pritchett." *The New York Times Book Review* 102 (May 25, 1997): 27. A biographical tribute, claiming that Pritchett was probably the last man who could be called a man of letters; notes that Pritchett worked slowly and with confidence.

Julia B. Boken

FRANCINE PROSE

Born: Brooklyn, New York; April 1, 1947

PRINCIPAL SHORT FICTION

Women and Children First and Other Stories, 1988
The Peaceable Kingdom, 1993
Guided Tours of Hell, 1997

OTHER LITERARY FORMS

Francine Prose's first three novels, *Judah the Pious* (1973), *The Glorious Ones* (1974), and *Marie Laveau* (1977), are historical fictions, which combine the rational and the mythic, dreaming and waking, legend and reality. The novels *Household Saints* (1981) and *Hungry Hearts* (1983) have twentieth century settings, but still focus on spiritual matters and create seemingly legendary worlds. In addition to her novels, which include *Primitive People* (1992) and *Hunters and Gatherers* (1995), and her short stories, Prose has published nonfiction articles and essays on various subjects in a wide range of popular periodicals, such as *Redbook*, *Glamour*, *The Atlantic*, *Mademoiselle*, and *Harper's Bazaar*. She has also written the children's book *The Angel's Mistake: Stories of Chelm* (1997).

ACHIEVEMENTS

Francine Prose won the Jewish Book Council Award in 1973 for her novel *Judah the Pious*. She won the MLLE Award from *Mademoiselle* magazine in 1975 and the Edgar Lewis Wallant Memorial Award from the Hartford Jewish Community Center in 1984 for her novel *Hungry Hearts*.

BIOGRAPHY

Francine Prose was born on April 1, 1947, in Brooklyn, New York, the daughter of two doctors. She received her B.A. degree in English from Radcliffe College in 1968 and an M.A. degree in English from Harvard University in 1969. She taught creative writing at the University of Arizona in 1971-1972. She has been a visiting lecturer in fiction and a faculty member in M.F.A. programs at schools such

as Warren Wilson College and Sarah Lawrence College, and was an instructor at the Breadloaf Writers Conference in 1984. She married artist Howard Michels in 1976.

Prose is a professional journalist as well as a fiction writer. She has written articles and reviews for many American magazines and newspapers, including *The New York Times*, *Harper's*, *Redbook*, and *The Atlantic*. She is currently an editor at *Doubletake* magazine. She has two sons and lives in New York City and upstate New York.

ANALYSIS

Francine Prose is, above all, a professional writer—competent, skilled, intelligent, and knowledgeable about the various conventions of the prose fictions and articles she writes. However, her stories, for all their surface flash and verbal cleverness, are often highly formal exercises that seldom, to quote her own character Landau in "Guided Tours of Hell," "achieve that transcendental state" that lifts writer and reader above the realm of the ordinary world.

Prose is frequently admired for her domestic whimsy, her adroitness at satire, her offbeat and acerbic humor, and her gifts of irony and observation. However, her fictions are usually formal, well-made stories, self-consciously literary, and thus highly predictable and pat. Her use of the analogies to writer Franz Kafka in "Guided Tours of Hell," for example, are so carefully woven throughout the story that they get in the way of any genuine anguish that might be experienced by her characters. Just as Landau, the competent but dispassionate and disengaged writer of this story knows he is not Kafka, Francine Prose is always Landau, for her stories are mostly professional products, rather than passionate explorations.

"EVERYDAY DISORDERS"

Although simple, everyday disorders form the background of this story, the single disruption of the everyday on which it focuses is uncommon and threatening. The story centers on the fears of Gilda, a housewife and mother of four, when her husband Na-

Francine Prose (©Miriam Berkley)

than, a photographer and professor, brings home a glamorous and adventuresome female war photographer named Phoebe Morrow. The contrast between Gilda's own prosy home life and Phoebe's exciting life on the road and on the battlefield establishes the story's central conflict and interest. Prose is her usual clever self in the story, establishing Gilda's domesticity and fears by having her try to imagine that Phoebe probably looks like aviator Amelia Earhart but instead thinking of her as the cartoon character Snoopy, the Red Baron. Gilda's response is complicated by her knowledge that her husband, who has made his own reputation as a photographer of "everyday disorder," envies Phoebe.

While Phoebe has gone on commando raids with Sandinista guerillas, Gilda's main claim to fame seems to be the homemade mushroom soup she has prepared for dinner. The evening comes to a comic/pathetic climax when Gilda overhears Phoebe telling a group of admiring students a story about being wounded in a plane crash. She tells them she was cared for by a beautiful Israeli nurse who looked like Rita Hayworth and who made her homemade mushroom soup. Phoebe says she became a kind of junkie

for the soup and that the nurse brought her her favorite food, linguine with steamed mussels. This is a revelation Gilda is not sure how to handle, as earlier she had told Phoebe that she became a kind of junkie for being pregnant and that her favorite food is linguine with steamed mussels. The story ends with Gilda's realization that Phoebe is not someone to be envied, for there is some essential component of selfhood missing in her, which she tries to patch "with borrowed scraps from other people's lives." At the end, Gilda wants to tell Nathan there is a kind of heroism in facing everyday messes.

THE PEACEABLE KINGDOM

Francine Prose's second collection of short stories contains highly polished presentations of contemporary characters whose peaceable lives are disrupted by challenge and change. The stories in this collection are clever, well-written, highly formal fictions, complete with the conventional, vaguely dissatisfying sense of closure contemporary readers have come to expect in the well-made short story. On the surface, the characters seem ordinary enough: a young woman on her honeymoon who already questions her commitment to her husband, a reserved librarian whose fascination with a man is based on the books she reads, a teenage girl who is followed to Paris by a boy she thought she loved.

Beneath the peaceable surface of everyday life, however, Prose unearths and exposes those moments of awareness when the smooth flow of things becomes jagged and undependable. In many of these stories, characters have made what they think are reasonable choices, only to experience an unpredicted and inexplicable disruption of that formerly comfortable decision. As in many modern short stories, things are simply not what they seem in the world of Francine Prose; the reader is always in tension with the strange and enigmatic. Even the titles of many of the stories suggest this combination of the mundane and the mysterious: "Talking Dogs," "Cauliflower Heads," "Rubber Life," "Amateur Voodoo," "Potato World," and "Dog Stories." Prose's stories in this collection are a pleasure to read, but it is a somewhat bloodless, formalist pleasure. One comes to the end of these stories full of admiration for a job well done but not always full of awe for the complex mystery of what it means to be human.

"GUIDED TOURS OF HELL"

Prose tackles a delicate subject in the title story of her collection *Guided Tours of Hell*—a comic, satiric treatment of the Jewish Holocaust. The way she manages this task is to focus on two characters—Jiri Krakauer, a poet whose only claim to fame is that he survived two years in a death camp where he had an affair with Kafka's sister, Ottla, and Landau, a second-rate writer who has written a play entitled *To Kafka from Felice*. The story takes place in the present time at a Kafka conference in Germany where Landau reads his play and Krakauer reads his poetry.

The central event of the story is a tour that the two men make with the attendees of the conference to the death camp where Krakauer was imprisoned. Landau is filled with jealousy at Krakauer's star status and angry that he has been largely ignored. Thinking there is something obscene about a guided tour of hell, unless you are the poet Dante, Landau suffers throughout the story, convinced that Krakauer never really suffered at all during his incarceration at the hands of the Nazis. The fact that Krakauer has profited from the Holocaust is more than Landau can bear.

Landau's problem, says the ironic narrator, is his falseness, his lack of depth, "the reason why, he secretly fears, his play is basically garbage, idiotic, hysterical." Throughout the story, Landau shifts back and forth between justifying and castigating himself, between thinking that the world needs writers like Krakauer for he has experienced the real thing and thinking that Krakauer is a fake, posturing for praise and toadying for applause. The basic irony of the story is that Landau envies Krakauer his experience in the death camp—a fact that Krakauer understands, as he says near the end of the story: "The dirty truth is, you envy us, you wish it had happened to you. You wish you'd gotten the chance to survive Auschwitz or the Gulag."

However, this realization does not does not exonerate Krakauer; Landau is right about him—he is making the Holocaust into a party piece, he revels in his survival, and he lies about his experience, plagia-

rizing the works of other writers to create those lies. In her usual formally structured way, Prose has Landau realize at the end that they are living a Kafka story, specifically "The Judgment," reenacting the classic Kafka confrontation between father and son.

OTHER MAJOR WORKS

LONG FICTION: *Judah the Pious*, 1973; *The Glorious Ones*, 1974; *Marie Laveau*, 1977; *Animal Magnetism*, 1978; *Household Saints*, 1981; *Hungry Hearts*, 1983; *Primitive People*, 1992; *Hunters and Gatherers*, 1995; *Blue Angel*, 2000.

CHILDREN'S LITERATURE: *Dybbuk: A Story Made in Heaven*, 1996; *You Never Know: A Legend of the Lamedvavniks*, 1988; *The Angel's Mistake: Stories of Chelm*, 1997; *The Demon's Mistake: A Story from Chelm*, 2000.

BIBLIOGRAPHY

Baker, Alison. "The Bearable Lightness of Being." A review of *The Peaceable Kingdom*, by Francine Prose. *Los Angeles Times Book Review*, October 10, 1993, p. 3. A positive review, which describes the stories as tales of lost innocence and high hopes exposed for the common things they are. Argues that although the characters occasionally seem shallow, Prose's language lifts them out of the ordinary and allows them to redeem themselves by what they have learned.

Brown, Rosellen. "Where Love Touches Death." Review of *Guided Tours of Hell*, by Francine Prose. *New Leader* 79 (December 16, 1997): 24-27. Extended discussion of the title story and "Three Pigs in Five Days." Argues that "Guided Tours of Hell" is motivated by the paradoxes of late twentieth century "consumer-friendly horror-gazing." Compares the central character, Landau, with Fyodor Dostoevski's Underground Man. Claims that "Three Pigs in Five Days" is diffuse and confusing and too contrived to be compelling.

Caldwell, Gail. "Inferno of Irony." *The Boston Globe*, January 19, 1997, p. N17. A review of *Guided Tours of Hell* that focuses on Prose's ironic sensibility. Suggests that her characters are hapless romantics who revel in the despair of self-analysis.

Describes the two stories in *Guided Tours of Hell* as descents into the maelstrom that are irreverent and funny; both deal with travel abroad where misgivings that could be minor at home have the potential to color reality.

Lodge, David. "Excess Baggage." *The New York Times*, January 12, 1997, p. 7. Lodge praises the collection of two stories in *Guided Tours of Hell*; places them in the tradition of the adventures of Americans in Europe, and argues that the characters' problems in the two stories come to a head more urgently than they would have at home and are purged in tragic and farcical epiphanies.

Prose, Francine. Interview by John Baker. *Publishers Weekly* 239 (April 13, 1992): 38-39. Prose discusses her writing career, her marriage to Howard Michels, and her nonfiction contributions to newspapers and magazines. Baker argues that in her novel *Primitive People* Prose writes more darkly than in her past fantastical novels and stories.

Reynolds, Susan Salter. "A Tour Through the Heart's Twists, the Mind's Turns." Review of *Guided Tours of Hell*, by Francine Prose. *Los Angeles Times*, January 10, 1997, p. E8. Reynolds discusses how Prose's characters combine humor and wisdom; argues that in the stories shallow characters have giant revelations, feeble characters rise to historic occasions, and strong characters crumble; history, however, she suggests, triumphs in the end in these two stories.

Yardley, Jonathan. "Fictions About Women Writers." *The Washington Post*, June 8, 1998. p. D2. A commentary on Prose's controversial article in *Harper's*, pointing out how rarely stories by women appear in the major magazines that publish fiction, how rarely fiction by women is reviewed in serious literary journals, and how rarely work by women dominates short lists and year-end "best" lists.

Charles E. May

E. ANNIE PROULX

Born: Norwich, Connecticut; August 22, 1935

PRINCIPAL SHORT FICTION

Heart Songs and Other Stories, 1988
Close Range: Wyoming Stories, 1999

OTHER LITERARY FORMS

Early in her career, E. Annie Proulx was a free-lance journalist, writing cookbooks, how-to manuals, and magazine articles on everything from making cider to building fences. Her first novel, *Postcards* (1992), received good reviews. However, it was the enthusiastic reception of her second novel, *The Shipping News* (1993), that brought her international fame and popular success. Her novel *Accordion Crimes* (1996) did not enjoy the same acclaim as her Pulitzer Prize-winning *The Shipping News*.

ACHIEVEMENTS

For her *Postcards*, E. Annie Proulx was the first woman to win the PEN/Faulkner Award for fiction. In 1993, *The Shipping News* won many awards, including the *Chicago Tribune* Heartland Prize, *The Irish Times* International Fiction Prize, the National Book Award, and the Pulitzer Prize. Four stories from her collection *Close Range: Wyoming Stories* were selected for the 1998 and 1999 editions of *The Best American Short Stories* and *Prize Stories: The O. Henry Awards*. "The Half-Skinned Deer" was selected for *The Best American Short Stories of the Century*.

BIOGRAPHY

Edna Annie Proulx was born in Norwich, Connecticut, in 1935, the oldest of five daughters. Her father worked his way up in the textile mills to the position of vice president; her mother painted landscapes in watercolors. Because her father was frequently transferred, the family moved several times when she was young. She entered Colby College in the 1950's but dropped out to, as she says, "experience two terrible marriages, New York City, the Far East, and single-mother-with-two-children poverty." She returned to school in 1963, graduating Phi Beta Kappa. She entered the graduate program at Sir George Williams University (now Concordia University), in Montreal, specializing in Renaissance economic history, and finished all the work for the Ph.D. degree except the dissertation.

By this time Proulx had been married and divorced three times and was the mother of three sons. She worked as a freelance journalist from 1975 to 1988, writing books and articles on a wide range of subjects. In the mid-1990's, Proulx moved from Vermont to Centennial, Wyoming (population 100), where she lives and writes in relative isolation. She travels part of the year to Australia and Ireland and across the United States.

ANALYSIS

Although E. Annie Proulx's first collection, *Heart Songs and Other Stories*, was relatively conventional in structure and language, her interest in what one of her characters calls the "rural downtrodden" is much in evidence here. The stories, featuring such quaintly named characters as Albro, Eno, and Snipe, take place in rural Vermont and New Hampshire. Without condescension, Proulx describes trailer-dwelling men and women who drink, smoke, feud, and fornicate without much introspection or analysis.

CLOSE RANGE: WYOMING STORIES

In *Close Range: Wyoming Stories*, Proulx shifts her milieu to the rural west, where her characters are similarly ragged and rugged, but where, either because of her increased confidence as a writer or because she was inspired by the landscape and the fiercely independent populace, her characters are more compellingly caught in a world that is grittily real and magically mythical at once. Claiming that her stories gainsay the romantic myth of the West, Proulx admires the independence and self-reliance

she has found there, noting that the people "fix things and get along without them if they can't be fixed. They don't whine."

Place is as important as the people who populate it in *Close Range*, for the Wyoming landscape is harsh yet beautiful, real yet magical, deadly yet sustaining. In such a world, social props are worthless and folks are thrown back on their most basic instincts, whether they be sexual, survival, or sacred. In such a world, as one character says in "Brokeback Mountain," "It's easier than you think to yield up to the dark impulse." E. Annie Proulx's Wyoming is a heart of darkness both in place and personality.

"BROKEBACK MOUNTAIN"

The most remarkable thing about "Brokeback Mountain" is that although it is about a sexual relationship between two men, it cannot be categorized as a homosexual story; it is rather a tragic love story that simply happens to involve two males. The fact that the men are Wyoming cowboys rather than San Francisco urbanites makes Proulx's success in creating such a convincing and emotionally affecting story all the more wonderful.

Jack Twist and Ennis del Mar are "high-school drop-out country boys with no prospects" who, while working alone at a sheep-herding operation on Brokeback Mountain, abruptly and silently engage in a sexual encounter, after which both immediately insist, "I'm not no queer." Although the two get married to women and do not see each other for four years, when they meet again, they grab each other and hug in a gruff masculine way, and then, "as easily as the right key turns the lock tumblers, their mouths came together."

Neither has sex with other men, and both know the danger of their relationship. Twenty years pass, and their infrequent encounters are a combination of sexual passion and personal concern. The story comes to a climax when Jack, who unsuccessfully tries to convince Ennis they can make a life together, is mysteriously killed on the roadside. Although officially it was an accident, Ennis sorrowfully suspects that Jack has been murdered after approaching another man. Although "Brokeback Mountain" ends with Jack a victim of social homophobia, this is not a story about the social plight of the homosexual. The issues Proulx explores here are more basic and primal than that. Told in a straightforward, matter-of-fact style, the story elicits a genuine sympathy for a love that is utterly convincing.

"THE HALF-SKINNED STEER"

Chosen by writer John Updike for *The Best American Short Stories of the Century*, this brief piece creates a hallucinatory world of shimmering significance out of common materials. The simple event on which the story is based is a cross-country drive made by Mero, a man in his eighties, to Wyoming for the funeral of his brother. The story alternates between the old man's encounters on the road, including an accident, and his memories of his father and brother. The central metaphor of the piece is introduced in a story Mero recalls about a man who, while skinning a steer, stops for dinner, leaving the beast half skinned. When he returns, he sees the steer stumbling stiffly away, its head and shoulders raw meat, its staring eyes filled with hate. The man knows that he and his family are doomed.

The story ends with Mero getting stuck in a snow storm a few miles away from his destination and trying to walk back to the main highway. As he struggles through the wind and the drifts, he notices that one of the herd of cattle in the field next to the road has been keeping pace with him, and he realizes that the "half-skinned steer's red eye had been watching for him all this time." In its combination of stark realism and folktale myth, "The Half-Skinned Steer" is reminiscent of stories by Eudora Welty and Flannery O'Connor, for Mero's journey is an archetypal one toward the inevitable destiny of death.

"THE MUD BELOW"

E. Annie Proulx has said that this is her favorite story in *Close Range*, for "on-the-edge situations" and the rodeo interest her. The title refers to the mud of the rodeo arena, and the main character is twenty-three-year-old Diamond Felts, who, at five foot three has always been called "Shorty," "Kid," "Tiny," and "Little Guy." His father left when he was a child, telling him, "You ain't no kid of mine." His mother taunts him about his size more than anyone else, always calling him Shorty and telling him he is stu-

pid for wanting to be a bull rider in the rodeo.

The force of the story comes from Diamond's identification with the bulls. The first time he rides one he gets such a feeling of power that he feels as though he were the bull and not the rider; even the fright seems to fulfill a "greedy physical hunger" in him. When one man tells him that the bull is not supposed to be his role model, Diamond says the bull is his partner. The story comes to a climax when Diamond is thrown and suffers a dislocated shoulder. Tormented by the pain, he calls his mother and demands to know who his father is. Getting no answer, Diamond drives away thinking that all of life is a "hard, fast ride that ended in the mud," but he also feels the euphoric heat of the bull ride, or at least the memory of it, and realizes that if that is all there is, it must be enough.

"THE BUNCHGRASS EDGE OF THE WORLD"

Like most of the stories in *Close Range*, "The Bunchgrass Edge of the World" is about surviving. As Old Red, a ninety-six-year-old grandfather, says at the end, "The main thing in life was staying power. That was it: stand around long enough, you'd get to sit down." Picked by Amy Tan to be included in *The Best American Short Stories 1999*, it is one of the most comic fictions in the collection. A story about a young woman named Ottaline, with a "physique approaching the size of a propane tank," being wooed by a broken-down John Deere 4030 tractor could hardly be anything else.

Ottaline's only chance for a husband seems to be the semiliterate hired man, Hal Bloom, with whom she has silent sex, that is, until she is first approached by the talking tractor, who calls her "sweetheart, lady-girl." Tired of the loneliness of listening to cellular phone conversations on a scanner, Ottaline spends more and more time with the tractor, gaining confidence until, when made to take on the responsibility of cattle trading by her ill father, she meets Flyby Amendinger, whom she soon marries. The story ends with Ottaline's father getting killed in a small plane he is flying. The ninety-six-year-old grandfather, who sees how things had to go, has the powerfully uncomplicated final word—that the main thing in life is staying power.

OTHER MAJOR WORKS

LONG FICTION: *Postcards*, 1992; *The Shipping News*, 1993; *Accordion Crimes*, 1996.

BIBLIOGRAPHY

Elder, Richard. "Don't Fence Me In." *The New York Times*, May 23, 1999, p. 8. An extended review of *Close Range: Wyoming Stories*. Says the strength of the collection is Proulx's feeling for place and how it affects her characters. Claims Proulx's extraordinary knowledge of male behavior is most remarkable in "Brokeback Mountain." Argues that the best story in the collection is "The Mud Below."

Hustak, Alan. "An Uneasy Guest of Honor." *The Montreal Gazette*, June 10, 1999, p. D10. An interview-story on the occasion of Proulx's receiving an honorary degree from her alma mater, Concordia University. Provides biographical information about her education and her literary career. Proulx discusses her years as a freelance journalist, the film production based on *Shipping News*, and the relationship of character to place in her fiction.

Liss, Barbara. "Wild, Wearying Wyoming." Review of *Close Range: Wyoming Stories*, by E. Annie Proulx. *The Houston Chronicle*, June 20, 1999, p. Z23. Praises the book's magical realism, but suggests that its "downbeat weirdness" will not be to everyone's taste. Says that "Brokeback Mountain" is the best story, with Proulx pouring a great deal of sympathy on the two young men and their passionate relationship.

See, Carolyn. "Proulx's Wild West." *The Washington Post*, July 2, 1999, p. C2. See says she is in awe of *Close Range*, claiming that Proulx has the most amazing combination of things working for her: an exquisite sense of place, a dead-on accurate sense of working class, hard-luck Americans, and a prose style that is the best in English today.

Singleton, Janet. "Proulx's Keen Insights Focus on Life, not Awards." *The Denver Post*, June 6, 1999, p. F3. In this interview-based story, Proulx talks about her research, her nomadic lifestyle, and the stories in *Close Range: Wyoming Stories*; says she writes stories that question the romantic myth of the West. Singleton claims Proulx's characters may live in God's country, but they seem godforsaken.

Steinbach, Alice. "E. Annie Proulx's Novel Journey to Literary Celebrity Status." *The Baltimore Sun*, May 15, 1994, p. 1K. An interview-based story that reveals Proulx's lighter side. Provides biographical information about her education, marriages, divorces, and rise to fame. Proulx discusses her love of writing, her male characters, and feminism.

Streitfeld, David. "The Stuff of a Writer." *The Washington Post*, November 16, 1993, p. B1. A long, interview-based story on Proulx on the occasion of *Shipping News* being nominated for the National Book Award. Provides much insight into Proulx's life in rural Vermont, her preference for "the rough side of things" and her rugged independence.

Thompson, David. "The Lone Ranger." *The Independent*, May 30, 1999, pp. 4-5. An interview-story that describes Proulx's life in her Wyoming home. Thompson draws out the cantankerous Proulx better than most other interviewers. He provides some context for Proulx's life and gets her to talk about what she thinks is important.

Charles E. May

PU SONGLING

Born: Zichuan, Shandong, China; June 5, 1640
Died: Shandong, China; February 25, 1715

PRINCIPAL SHORT FICTION

Liaozhai zhiyi, 1766 (also known as *Liao-chai chih-i*; *Strange Stories from a Chinese Studio*, 1880)
Liaozhai zhiyi weikan gao, 1936
Chinese Ghost and Love Stories: A Selection from the Liaozhai Stories by Pu songling, 1946

OTHER LITERARY FORMS

Although Pu Songling's literary fame rests solely on his collection of short fiction, *Strange Stories from a Chinese Studio* (composed of 431 stories), he was a versatile writer in both classical and colloquial Chinese. He was the author of various works, including a remarkable novel written in the vernacular titled *Xingshi yinyuan zhuan* (1870; the story of a marriage to rouse the world). Written under the pseudonym Xizhoushang (Scholar of the Western Chou Period), this novel's author remained anonymous for two centuries, until Dr. Hu Shih, in the course of his important studies in the history of Chinese vernacular literature, revealed that the real name of the author was Pu Songling. The earliest known printed edition is dated 1870, but in 1933 a punctuated edition was published to which were added some discussions of the authorship problem by various authors who were in agreement with Hu Shih's finding. Pu Songling's literary efforts were by no means confined to the writing of fiction, whether short or long. A man of parts, he wrote several kinds of poems: *Shi* poems in regular meter; folk musical narratives; drum songs; and folk songs. He wrote plays and numerous essays. He indulged in miscellaneous writings (*tongchu*); a lexicon of colloquial expressions in daily use in the Zichuan district; a treatise on agriculture and sericulture; a treatise on grass and trees; a manual on truancy; a satire on the examination of the self; books on dealing with hungry ghosts; correspondence; and desultory and neglected pieces. Apart from the

Liaozhai zhiyi and the novel mentioned above, all the works subsequently attributed to Pu Songling are included in the two-volume collection, *Liaozhai Quanzhi* (1933; complete works from the Chinese studio).

ACHIEVEMENTS

The Ch'ing, or Manchu, Dynasty, between its establishment in 1644 and the Opium War of 1840-1842, gave birth to at least four great literary masterpieces in drama and fiction. Drama produced Hongshang's *chuan qi* style opera, *Zhangshang dian* (c. 1688; *The Palace of Eternal Youth*, 1955). Long fiction produced two great novels: Cao Xueqin's romance, *Hungloumeng* (1792; *Dream of the Red Chamber*, 1929) and Wu Ching-tzu's satire, *Ju-lin wai-shih* (1768-1779; *The Scholars*, 1957). Pu Songling's *Strange Stories from a Chinese Studio* is the great masterpiece of short fiction of the Ch'ing era. The American scholar Allan Barr concluded that no really precise progression in sequence of characterization, theme, and structure corresponds to the chronological sequence. Hence he proposed that readers regard the *Liaozhai zhiyi* as "falling into three phases": early (c. 1675-1683), middle (c. 1683-1705), and late (c. 1690-1705). Despite the great variety of the narrative aspects throughout the whole work, there is, according to Barr, a perceivable sense of "creative growth and technical development" from first to last of the volumes that can be appreciated by a close reader.

After the printing of 1766, *Strange Stories from a Chinese Studio* attracted such widespread attention that the author's fame was assured. Educated readers with some literary training recognized that his work represented the perfected culmination of a long tradition of the use of classical Chinese for fictional narrative from the *shan ji* ("records of marvels") of the Wei and Tsin dynasties to the *chuan qi* ("strange transmissions")—the short prose romances of the T'ang Dynasty, whose range of subject matter is practically identical with that of Pu's stories. His superb handling of the *guwan* style, his ability to revivify old plots that had become hackneyed and flimsy through a new "magic realism" that made the improbable and the impossible probable and supernatural creatures, such as flower or fox spirits, seem human, went far beyond what had been accomplished in the past.

His stories appealed to an unprecedented number of readers from many walks of life, not simply educated people with some literary training. Consequently, his fictions revived the *chuan qi* tradition for nearly a century. Pu's tales are admired for their masterly style, which combines terse expression with abundant literary allusions and succeeds in maintaining a contrasting yet harmonious balance between the fantastic and the realistic elements of his fiction.

BIOGRAPHY

Pu Songling was born on June 5, 1640, in Zichuan, Shandong, China. Possibly of Mongol ancestry, he was the son of Pu Pan, a merchant, who was also a man of action as well as of some learning. In this old but impoverished family of gentry there were scholars and officials such as Pu's granduncle, Pu shangwan, who held the *jinshi* ("entered scholar"), the highest, or "doctor's," degree, and was the magistrate of Youtian, in Zhili. In addition to his family name of Pu and his personal name of Songling, Pu Songling had two "courtesy names," taken at age twenty, by which he was known among his friends: Liu Xian (last of the immortals) and Jian Chan (knight-errant). He further had two "artistic names," adopted on occasion as names for his library or studio, by which he was popularly known after he became famous: Luo Chuan (willow spring) and Liao Zhai (casual studio).

In 1658, at age eighteen, Pu qualified for the lowest, or "bachelor's," degree, which required him to pass three successive sets of examinations by writing eight or ten essays on themes assigned from the "Four Books and Five Classics," as well as five poems on prescribed patterns. Yet, although he regularly took the provincial examinations for the next highest degree, he consistently failed. Not until 1711, at age seventy-one, did he succeed in being made a senior licentiate. Apparently his diverse interests pre-

vented him from pursuing the traditional program of study rigorously enough.

As a result, Pu Songling spent his life in a variety of activities. In 1670 he was employed as a secretary to the magistrate at Baoying, Jiangsu. In 1672 he became secretary to a wealthy friend, Bi Jiyou, sometime department magistrate of Tongzhou, Kiangsu, a position which Pu held for nearly twenty years. The rest of his activities consisted of his employment as a licentiate to the district school from 1685 onward, private tutoring in the homes of local gentry, the management of his family affairs (he was happily married to an amiable wife by whom he had four sons, three of whom became licentiates), and the writing of short stories, poems, songs, and miscellaneous essays.

His writing of short stories apparently began as early as 1660 and extended to, and possibly beyond, 1679, when he wrote a preface to *Strange Stories from a Chinese Studio*. Although in his day his literary genius was little known beyond the circle of his friends and acquaintances, eventually his fame was to spread over China and even to foreign lands. By 1848, his stories had been translated into Manchu, and by 1880, into English. In the twentieth century they have been translated into French, Japanese, German, and Russian.

Pu Songling's preface to *Strange Stories from a Chinese Studio* reveals decided connections between his short stories and his personal life and sentiments. He begins, through references to clothes, by ridiculing the official classes and suggesting that they hold posts for which, from a literary standpoint, they are unfit. Furthermore, in his view, political intrigue in official circles is all too common. The evil machinations of bad and false men often destroy good and true men.

Evidently a man much attached to the Buddhist faith, Pu provides a Buddhist interpretation of his existence in the preface. In sum, taking the attitudes and sentiments appearing in Pu Songling's preface and the circumstances of his biography and comparing these things with the short stories—their characterizations, themes, satire, and social criticism—leads to the definite conclusion that they embrace Pu's personal philosophy: his dreams, faith, and worldview.

In his last years Pu Songling's family fortunes are said to have slightly improved. In 1713, his wife (née Liu) died. He and she had apparently led a happy but uneventful life together. His fondness for her is shown by the sketch of her life he wrote following her death and the several poems he composed dedicated to her memory. In three more years he himself died, on February 25, 1715, at his home in Zichuan.

Analysis

In his *Strange Stories from a Chinese Studio*, Pu Songling mostly presents encounters between human beings and supernatural or fantastic creatures. The human beings may be students, scholars, officials, peasants, Daoist or Buddhist priests, fortune-tellers, magicians, maidens, wives, concubines, and so on. Some of these human beings, especially the Daoist or Buddhist priests and the magicians, may possess supernatural powers or illusionary skills of various kinds. The supernatural or fantastic creatures may be animals, birds, flowers, fairies, devils, or ghosts who have assumed human shape, or they may retain their natural forms but have the human powers of speech and understanding. Although when portraying supernatural or fantastic creatures Pu is highly imaginative, in dealing with ordinary mortals he controls his imagination to the degree that they are not exaggerated or unnatural. He appears to seek to make the extraordinary plausible and the ordinary interesting and to press home the point that the ordinary world is endowed always with extraordinary possibilities.

His favorite themes seem to be changeableness, in which animals or devils are changed into human form or vice versa; reincarnation; living humans becoming immortals; the dead being brought back to life; male students falling in love with beautiful women; exposure of corrupt or incompetent officials; and criticism of the civil service examination system and of pedantic scholarship. Although Pu imitated the classical short tales of the T'ang Dynasty, he introduced original elements in terms of his personal views and he included criminal and detective stories in his collection. Some of his stories seem to have been written from motives of pure entertainment, but the majority of them state or imply some moral lesson. The stories demonstrate Pu's sincere or facetious conviction that in this world evildoers are eventually punished and the kindhearted are in the long run rewarded for their good deeds.

"The Tiger of Zhaochang"

"Zhaochang hu" ("The Tiger of Zhaochang") is the story of a tiger who eats the son of an elderly widow who has no relations besides her son and depends entirely on him for her support. Thus left to starve to death, the mother indignantly journeys to town, where she levels a charge against the tiger with the magistrate. Eventually, the tiger confesses to the crime of having eaten the young son. The magistrate informs the tiger that it must forfeit its own life unless it can act as the old woman's son and support her in the same manner that he did, in which case the magistrate will allow it to go free. The tiger declares that it can fulfill this obligation and does. In conclusion, the narrator warns the reader not to take the story as true; on the other hand, he says, it is not to be considered a joke. Indeed, it is a moral exemplum. Although the tiger is of the brute, it displayed human feelings. Hence it is quite unlike some human beings of the present day, who follow the practice of oppressing orphans and widows and are far from being equal to a member of the brute creation.

"The Pupils of the Eyes That Talked"

In "Tongran yu" ("The Pupils of the Eyes That Talked"), a young scholar, Fang Lian, a married man, has a character weakness: He likes to look at pretty women and girls other than his wife. On one occasion his ogling results in a handful of dirt thrown in his face, which blinds him. Although a variety of medical remedies are tried over a good period of time, he remains a blind man. Now very worried, he repents of his past sins. He obtains a copy of the Buddhist sutra known as the *Guangming jing* and begins to recite it daily. Although its recitation at first is boring, he eventually experiences a quietude of mind that he has never known before. He starts to hear a voice in each eye. These voices turn out to be two tiny men, who exit through Fang Lien's nose to see what is transpiring outside.

Eventually, Fang Lien hears a small voice in his left eye say, "It's not convenient for us to go and come by way of these nostrils. We had each better open a door for ourselves." The small voice in the right eye, however, declares that his wall is too thick to break through. They therefore break through the wall of the left eye. Immediately the light flows into Fang Lien's darkened orb. To his great delight, he can see again. Although he always remains blind in his right eye, he never ventures to fix his good eye on any woman other than his own wife.

In an annotation to this story, the translator implies that its plot is based partly on a folk belief widely held throughout China—namely, that each of a person's eyes contains a tiny human figure. He thinks this myth originated from one experiencing the reflection of oneself when looking into another person's eyes, or into one's own when viewing oneself in a mirror.

"THE PICTURE HORSE"

The story "Huama" ("The Picture Horse") concerns a Mr. Cui, who finds a strange horse—black marked with white and with a scrubby tail—lying in the grass inside his premises. Although he repeatedly drives it away, it persists in returning to the same spot. Mr. Ts'ui decides to borrow the horse and ride it to see a friend, some distance away.

Mr. Ts'ui finds that the horse travels at an astonishingly rapid rate, and it needs no food and little rest. It is not long before Mr. Ts'ui reaches his destination. When the local prince hears of the speed and endurance of this remarkable horse, he purchases it after a long wait for its owner to appear.

After a time, the prince has business near Mr. Ts'ui and rides there on the remarkable horse. Upon his arrival, he leaves it in the custody of one of his officers. The horse breaks away from its custodian and escapes. The officer gives chase to the home of Mr. Ts'ui's neighbor, a Mr. Tsâng, wherein it disappears. The officer accosts Mr. Tsâng and demands the return of the prince's horse, but Mr. Tsâng denies knowing anything about any horse, whereupon the officer bursts into Mr. Tsâng's private quarters. To his dismay, he finds no horse, but upon one wall he observes a picture of a horse exactly like the one he seeks. It becomes clear to him and to Mr. Ts'ui that the prince's horse is a supernatural horse. Since the offi-

cer is afraid to return to the prince without the horse, Mr. Ts'ui intervenes and refunds the purchase price willingly. Naturally, Mr. Tsâng greatly appreciates his neighbor's generosity, since he never knew that the horse had been sold in the first place.

According to Pu, the picture of the horse in Mr. Tsâng's apartment was painted by the early T'ang poet and painter Chan Tzuang, who, although apparently specializing in the painting of horses, was even better known as a writer. In China a close bond existed between painting and scholarship. The object of the painting was to capture the *qi*, or the life-spirit and the vitality of a thing, and writing was regarded as "mind painting." In this case the painted thing has such powerful vitality that it leaves the picture plane and take up an existence in the real world. Such stories as Pu's "The Picture Horse" remind one of the American writer Edgar Allan Poe's tapestry horse that comes alive in his story "Metzengerstein" (1832), as well as his "The Oval Portrait" (1842), in which an artist has extracted the life-spirit from his female model and put it into her portrait, thus leaving the former living model dead.

"THE PAINTED SKIN"

In Pu's story "Huapi" ("The Painted Skin"), a Mr. Wang meets a pretty girl who claims that she was sold as a concubine, cruelly abused, and has run away. Mr. Wang invites her to his home. She gratefully accepts his offer. He lets her stay in the library, and she requests him not to tell anyone where she is staying. Although he agrees to keep her secret, he tells his wife of the girl's presence as soon as he sees her.

When Wang is out walking again, he encounters a Daoist priest, who asks him if he has met any stranger recently. Wang denies that he has. Walking away from him, the priest calls him a fool and remarks that some people never know when they are in danger of dying. Although Wang thinks that the Daoist is simply trying to land a client, upon returning home he peeks in the library window. Inside he sees a hideous-looking devil with a green face and sawtooth teeth. The devil has spread out a human skin on a table and is painting it with a brush. Having completed the design it is putting on the skin, the devil picks up the skin, shakes it out like a coat, and throws it over its shoulders. To Wang's amazement, he sees that the devil is now the pretty concubine!

Terrified out of his wits, Wang finds the Daoist priest, who presents Wang with a fly-brush and prescribes that he hang it on the door of the premises occupied by the devil. Wang complies. When the devil appears, it responds to the fly-brush by gnashing its teeth and cursing. It grabs the fly-brush and tears it to pieces, then, rushing into the room occupied by Wang and his wife, the devil grabs Wang and tears out his heart. Still raging, the devil departs. Wang is dead.

Wang's wife sends his brother to report the tragedy to the Daoist priest. The priest inquires of him whether any stranger has just come to Wang's house. The brother replying that an old woman has just been hired as a maid, the priest informs him that the person must be the devil in disguise. Taking up his wooden sword, the Daoist accosts the presumed maid face-to-face, exposing her as the devil. Calling her a "base-born fiend," he demands the return of the fly-brush. His demand not met, he raises his sword and strikes her. As she falls to the ground, the human skin separates from her body to reveal her devilish hideousness. Then he cuts off the devil's head. As for the sheet of human skin, complete with eyebrows, eyes, hands, and feet, the priest rolls it up into a scroll. He is about to depart when Wang's wife tearfully pleads with him to restore her dead husband to life. He replies that he does not possess such power, she must apply to the town maniac. Mrs. Wang finds the maniac raving by the roadside. She approaches the man on her knees and entreats him to restore her husband to life. He laughs at her. Then he gives her a thrashing with his staff. She endures this harsh treatment without a murmur. Then he hands her a distasteful-looking pill and orders her to swallow it. She does so with great difficulty.

Returning home, Wang's wife mourns bitterly over her dead husband, greatly regretting the action she has taken. She undertakes to prepare the corpse herself. As she does so, she feels a great lump rising in her throat which soon pops out of her mouth straight into the open wound of the dead man. She sees that it is a human heart. Excitedly, she closes the

wound over it, holding the sides together with her hands. Rubbing the corpse vigorously for a time, she then covers it over with clothes. During the night she inspects the dead man and discovers breath coming from his nostrils. By morning Wang is alive again.

Except for a number of very short stories, the stories discussed above represent a fair cross section of those in Pu Songling's collection in terms of treatment and plot structure. Apart from the sketches which are mere anecdotes, they range from very simple plots, such as that found in "The Tiger of Zhaochang," to rather complicated ones, such as that of "The Painted Skin." Other tales of special interest might be added to this list: "Dou xishi" ("The Fighting Cricket"), "Laoshan daozi" ("The Daoist Priest of Laoshan"), "Zhi qingxu" ("The Wonderful Stone"), "Niaoyu" ("The Talking of the Birds"), "Zhanban" ("Planchette"), "Toutao" ("Theft of the Peach"), "Jiannuo" ("Miss Jiannuo"), and "Hua quzi" ("The Flower-nymphs"). All these stories are included in Herbert A. Giles's collection of 164 of Pu's stories, *Strange Stories from a Chinese Studio*, which was reprinted in 1969, under the English titles given above. Rose Qong's collection, *Chinese Ghost and Love Stories: A Selection from the Liao-chai Stories by Pu Songling*, contains forty tales. Translations of one or several tales are scattered in various anthologies and periodicals.

Pu Songling weaves together the natural and the supernatural in a more realistic manner than the T'ang authors of *chuan qi*. In his criticism of Confucian officialdom, he introduces new moral principles. Yet his treatment of Daoism and Buddhism hardly departs from theirs. He ignores philosophical Daoism to emphasize the superstition, magic, and exorcism of the popular religion of that name. This sort of Daoism concerned itself with the alchemical promise of the prolongation of life by discovering the elixir of immortality; with communication with *xian*, or immortals; with magic pills; and with defeating devils.

In like manner, Pu favors Buddhism over Daoism, giving the Buddhist clergy more integrity, dignity, and respect than he does the Daoist priesthood or Confucian officials. He mainly ignores the intellectual, meditative Buddhist Chan sect in favor of the popular Qing Tu, or Pure Land School, which concerns itself with the worship of Buddha Amitabha, who saves into his Pure Land all those who call upon his name in faith. Adhering to the doctrine of Karma and reincarnation, the followers of Qing Tu Buddhism believe in a whole pantheon of Buddhas and bodhisattvas and in a variety of celestial and terrestrial realms, including heavens and hells. It emphasizes right living and the value of the recitation of favored Buddhist *sutras*.

In sum, Pu Songling treated the natural and the supernatural in terms of Chinese popular religion, according to which men sought communication with gods and spirits primarily to obtain benefits and avoid calamities.

OTHER MAJOR WORKS

LONG FICTION: *Xingshi yinyuan zhuan*, 1870.

MISCELLANEOUS: *Liaozhai Quanzhi*, 1936 (also known as *Liao-chai ch'üan-chi*)

BIBLIOGRAPHY

Barr, Allan. "A Comparative Study of Early and Late Tales in *Liaozhai zhiyi*." *Harvard Journal of Asiatic Studies* 45 (1985): 157-202. Since a comparison of the text's narrative development with its chronological progression shows no precise relationship between them, Barr believes it best to consider the text as having progressed through early, middle, and late periods.

_____. "Disarming Intruders: Alien Women in *Liaozhai zhiyi*." *Harvard Journal of Asiatic Studies* 49 (1989): 501-517. Barr offers a new interpretation of Pu's "alien women," or women of supernatural character—ghosts, fox spirits, flower nymphs, predatory femme fatale demons—analyzing their relationships with their lovers and other humans and classifying them as residents, transients, and wicked predators.

_____. "The Textual Transmission of *Liaozhai zhiyi*." *Harvard Journal of Asiatic Studies* 44 (1984): 515-562. A comparison of the arrangement of the extant text with the individual stories that can be dated provides a means of tracking its chronological development.

Chang, Chun-shu, and Shelley Hsueh-lun Chang. *Redefining History: Ghosts, Spirits, and Human Society in P'u Sungling's World, 1640-1715*. Ann Arbor: University of Michigan Press, 1998. An examination of the characters, human and nonhuman, in Pu's fiction.

Li, Wai-yee. "Rhetoric of Fantasy and Rhetoric of Irony: Studies in Liao-chai chih-i and Hung-lou mâng." In *Dissertation Abstracts International* 49 (August, 1988): 249A. A fine study of truth, fiction, irony, and illusion in a collection of classical short stories and a vernacular novel, with analysis of the play and limitations of the structure of desire—embracing freedom, justice, and the ideal—and the structure of order—embracing morality, individual discipline, love, and the real.

Prusek, Jaroslav. "*Liao-chai chih-i* by Pu Songling." In *Chinese History and Literature: Collection of Studies*. Dordrecht, Netherlands: Reidel, 1970. (Article originally published in 1959). A sensitive discussion of Pu's life when employed as a tutor in various rich families and while engaged in the writing of *Liao-chai chih-i*, especially while residing with the Pi family. Prusek links certain aspects of Pu's life during this period with certain of his poems to advantage and corrects an important misinterpretation that alters those facts as given in the American collection *Eminent Chinese of the Ch'ing Period* (1976).

_____. "Pu Songling and His Work." In *Chinese History and Literature: Collection of Studies*. Dordrecht, Netherlands: Reidel, 1970. (Article orginally published in 1962). A fine general discussion of the circumstances of Pu's unfulfilled life of poverty; his personality, family life, and political philosophy; his literary achievements, especially the realism of his fantasies; and his literary importance both in respect to the history of Chinese literature and as a world figure. This piece was originally a foreword to Prusek's volume of selections under the title *Zkazky o sestery cest osudu* (1955; tales of six different paths of destiny).

_____. "Two Documents Relating to the Life of P'u Sung-ling." In *Chinese History and Literature: Collection of Studies*. Dordrecht, Netherlands: Reidel, 1970. (Article originally published in 1959-1960). Two documents concerning Pu's life are presented which heretofore have never been translated into any European language: one written by Pu himself at the age of seventy-four; the other an inscription on the stela erected on Pu's grave.

Yang, Rui. "Oedipal Fantasy in Disguise: A Psychoanalytic Interpretation of Liaozhai Zhiyi." *Tamkang Review* 25 (Winter, 1994): 67-93. Using the psychoanalytic theories developed by Norman Holland in *The Dynamics of Literary Response*, this essay discusses Pu Songling's treatment of the Oedipal conflict.

Zeitlin, Judith T. *Historian of the Strange: Pu Songling and the Chinese Classical Tale*. Stanford, Calif.: Stanford University Press, 1993. A good study of Pu's fiction and its place in modern short-fiction canon.

Zhou, Jianming. "A Literary Rendition of Animal Figures: A Comparison Between Kafka's Tales and P'u Songling's Stories," translated by Jerry Krauel and Dariusz Rybicki. In *Kafka and China*, edited by Adrian Hsia. Bern, Switzerland: Peter Lang, 1996. Discusses Kafka and Pu Songling's treatment of animals in their fiction.

Richard P. Benton

JAMES PURDY

Born: Near Fremont, Ohio; July 14, 1923

PRINCIPAL SHORT FICTION

Don't Call Me by My Right Name and Other Stories, 1956

Sixty-three: Dream Palace, 1956

Color of Darkness: Eleven Stories and a Novella, 1957 (contains *Don't Call Me by My Right Name and Other Stories* and *Sixty-three: Dream Palace*)

Children Is All, 1961

The Candles of Your Eyes, 1985

The Candles of Your Eyes, and Thirteen Other Stories, 1987

Sixty-three: Dream Palace, Selected Stories, 1956-1987, 1991

OTHER LITERARY FORMS

James Purdy, in more than four decades of literary work, beginning in the 1950's, has written—besides his short fiction—a number of novels (including *Malcolm*, published in 1959, and *In a Shallow Grave*, published in 1976) several collections of poetry, and

numerous plays, some of which have been staged in the United States as well as abroad.

ACHIEVEMENTS

James Purdy has received a National Institute of Arts and Letters grant in literature (1958), John Simon Guggenheim Memorial Foundation Fellowships (1958, 1962), and a Ford Foundation grant (1961). *On Glory's Course* was a finalist for the PEN/Faulkner Award (1985). He also received a Rockefeller Foundation grant, a Morton Dauwen Zabel Fiction award from the American Academy of Arts and Letters (1993), and an Oscar Williams and Gene Derwood award for poetry and art (1995).

BIOGRAPHY

James Otis Purdy was born near Fremont, Ohio, on July 14, 1923, the son of William and Vera Purdy, and he has told many interviewers that the exact location of his birthplace is now unknown, since the community no longer exists. Purdy's parents were divorced when he was quite young. He lived, as he once said, with his father for a time in various locations and at other times with his mother and an aunt who had a farm, an experience which he has recalled favorably.

Purdy has explained that his ethnic background was that of a very long line of Scotch-Irish Presbyterians, but that most of his family is now deceased, as are many of his oldest friends. Purdy's formal education began with his attendance at the University of Chicago, where he was to drop out during World War II to serve with the U.S. Air Corps. He has indicated that he was not the best of soldiers but that his military service gave him the necessary background for his later novel *Eustace Chisholm and the Works* (1967).

Purdy also attended for a time the University of Puebla, Mexico, and enrolled in graduate school at the University of Chicago. He taught from 1949 to 1953 at Lawrence College in Appleton, Wisconsin, and later worked as an interpreter in Latin America, France, and Spain. In 1953, however, he gave up other work to pursue a full-time career as a writer.

Although he has been a prolific writer throughout his career, Purdy's fiction, while enjoying considerable critical success, has not been commercially successful, a fact that Purdy often attributes to a conspiratorial elite in New York that foists more commercial, but less substantive, literature on the American public.

Purdy's early work was rejected by most major American publishing houses, and his first fiction was published privately by friends in the United States and later through the help of writers such as Carl Van Vechten and, in Great Britain, Edith Sitwell. Both Purdy's volumes *Sixty-three: Dream Palace* and *Don't Call Me by My Right Name and Other Stories* were printed privately in 1956, and in 1957, the novella *Sixty-three: Dream Palace* appeared with additional stories under the title *Color of Darkness*, published by Gollancz in London. These early works gained for Purdy a small, devoted following, and his allegorical novel *Malcolm* followed in 1959. In that work, Malcolm, a beautiful young man, is led by older persons through a wide range of experiences, until he finally dies of alcoholism and sexual hyperesthesia. In a way, Malcolm is a forerunner of

James Purdy (Library of Congress)

many Purdy characters, whose driven states of being take them ultimately to disaster. (*Malcolm* was later adapted to play form by Edward Albee, an admirer of Purdy's work. The 1966 New York production, however, was not successful.)

Two Purdy novels of the 1960's expanded the author's literary audience: *The Nephew* (1960) explores small-town life in the American Midwest and centers on the attempt of an aunt to learn more about her nephew (killed in the Korean War) than she had known about him in his lifetime, and *Cabot Wright Begins* (1964) is a satirical attack on the totally materialistic American culture of consumers and competitors, where all love is either suppressed or commercialized. Cabot Wright Begins relates the comic adventures of a Wall Street broker-rapist who manages to seduce 366 women. The novel was sold to motion-picture firms, but the film version was never made.

The inability of people to deal with their inner desires—a major theme of Purdy's fiction—and the resultant violence provoked by that inability characterize Purdy's next novel, *Eustace Chisholm and the Works*. Another recurring Purdy theme is that of the self-destructive, cannibalistic American family, in which parents refuse to let go of their children and give them an independent life of their own. That self-destructive family theme and his earlier motif—the search for meaning in an unknown past—mark his trilogy of novels *Sleepers in Moon-Crowned Valleys*, the first volume of which, *Jeremy's Version*, appeared in 1970 to considerable critical acclaim. The second and third volumes of the trio of novels, however, *The House of the Solitary Maggot* (1974) and *Mourners Below* (1981), received little critical notice. Purdy once said that parts of the trilogy had come from stories that his grandmother had related to him as a child at a time when he was living with her.

Perhaps the most bizarre of Purdy's novels, *I Am Elijah Thrush*, was published in 1972. Set in New York, the novel deals with an aged male dancer (once a student of Isadora Duncan and known as "the most beautiful man in the world") who becomes obsessed with a mysterious blond, angelic child known as Bird of Heaven, a mute who communicates by making peculiar kissing sounds.

Purdy's later works reinforce these themes of lost identity and obsessive but often suppressed loves: *In a Shallow Grave* concerns a disfigured Vietnam veteran who has lost that most personal form of identity, his face; *Narrow Rooms* (1977) details the complex sexual relationships of four West Virginia boys who cannot cope with their emotional feelings for one another and who direct their feelings into garish violence. That novel, Purdy said, was partially derived from fact; Purdy said that he frequently ran into hillbilly types in New York who told him such terrible stories of their lives.

Purdy's later works include *On Glory's Course* (1984), *In the Hollow of His Hand* (1986), and the 1989 novel dealing with acquired immunodeficiency syndrome (AIDS), *Garments the Living Wear*. Purdy, who remained unmarried, continued to live and write in Brooklyn, New York. His novel *In a Shallow Grave* was made into a motion picture in 1988.

ANALYSIS

James Purdy is one of the more independent, unusual, and stylistically unique of American writers, since his fiction—novels, plays, and short stories—maintains a dark vision of American life while stating that vision in a literary voice unlike any other American writer. In more than a dozen novels, several collections of short fiction, and volumes of poetry and plays, Purdy has created an unrelentingly tragic view of human existence, in which people invariably are unable to face their true natures and thus violate—mentally and physically—those around them. In an interview in 1978, Purdy said:

> I think that is the universal human tragedy. We never become what we could be. I believe life is tragic. It's my view that nothing ever solves anything. Oh yes, life is full of many joys . . . but it's essentially tragic because man is imperfect. He can't find solutions by his very nature.

As a result of his tragic view of humankind, Purdy's fiction often contains unpleasant, violent, even repellent actions by his characters.

The short fiction of James Purdy is marked—as are many of his novels—by the recurrence of several themes, among them the conflict in the American family unit caused by the parental inability to relinquish control over children and allow them to live their own lives, a control to which Purdy has often referred as the "cannibalization" present in the family. A second theme frequently found in Purdy's short fiction is that of obsessive love that cannot be expressed, both heterosexual and homosexual. This inability of individuals to express their emotional yearning and longing often is turned into an expression of violence against those around them. The homoerotic element in Purdy's fiction only accentuates this propensity to violence, since Purdy often sees the societal repression of the homosexual emotion of love as one of the more brutal forms of self-denial imposed on an individual. Thus, many of his stories deal with such a latent—and tension-strained—homoeroticism. These two themes are conjoined occasionally in many of his novels and short stories to produce the unspeakable sense of loss: the loss of self-identity, of a loved one, or of a wasted past.

"COLOR OF DARKNESS"

In "Color of Darkness," the title story of the collection by the same name, a husband can no longer recall the color of the eyes of his wife, who has left him. As his young son struggles with the memory of his lost mother, he begins to suck regularly on the symbol of his parents' union, their wedding ring. In a confrontation with his father—who is concerned for the boy's safety because of the metal object in his mouth—the youngster suddenly kicks his father in the groin and reduces him to a suffering, writhing object at whom the boy hurls a crude epithet.

This kind of terrible family situation, embodying as it does loss, alienation from both a mate and a parent, and violence, is typical of the kind of intense anguish that Purdy's short stories often portray. In the world of Purdy, the American family involves a selfish, possessive, and obsessive struggle, which, over time, often becomes totally self-destructive, as individuals lash out at one another for hurts that they can no longer endure but that they cannot explain.

"DON'T CALL ME BY MY RIGHT NAME"

Elsewhere in the collection *Color of Darkness*, "Don't Call Me by My Right Name" portrays a wife who has begun using her maiden name, Lois McBane, because after six months of marriage she finds that she has grown to hate her new name, Mrs. Klein. Her loss of name is, like many such minor events in Purdy's fiction, simply a symbol for a larger loss, that of her self-identity, a theme that Purdy frequently invokes in his novels (as in his later novel *In a Shallow Grave*). The wife's refusal to accept her husband's name as her new label leads to a violent physical fight between them following a party which they both attend.

"WHY CAN'T THEY TELL YOU WHY?"

This potential for violence underlying the domestic surface of the American family is seen again in one of the author's most terrifying early stories, "Why Can't They Tell You Why?" A small child, Paul, who has never known his father, finds a box of photographs. These photographs become for the boy a substitute for the absent parent, but his mother, Ethel, who appears to hate her late soldier-husband's memory, is determined to break the boy's fascination

with his lost father. In a final scene of real horror, she forces the child to watch as she burns the box of photographs in the furnace, an act that drives the boy into, first, a frenzy of despair and then into a state of physical and emotional breakdown, as she tries to force the child to care for her and not for his dead father. Again, Purdy has captured the awful hatreds that lie within a simple family unit and the extreme malice to which they can lead.

"SLEEP TIGHT"

A similar tale of near-gothic horror affecting children is found in Purdy's story "Sleep Tight," which appears in his 1985 collection, *The Candles of Your Eyes*. In it, a fatally wounded burglar enters the bedroom of a young child who has been taught to believe in the Sandman. The child, believing the man to be the Sandman whom his sister, Nelle, and his mother have told him about, does not report the presence of the bleeding man, who takes refuge in the child's closet. After the police have come and gone, the child enters the closet where the now-dead man has bled profusely. He believes the blood to be watercolors and begins painting with the burglar's blood, and he comes to believe that he has killed the Sandman with his gun.

"CUTTING EDGE"

Domestic violence within the family unit is but one of Purdy's terrible insights into family life in America. Subdued family tensions—beneath the surface of outright and tragic violence—appear in "Cutting Edge," in which a domineering mother, her weak-willed husband, and their son (an artist home from New York wearing a beard) form a triangle of domestic hatred. The mother is determined that her son must shave off his beard while visiting, so as to emasculate her son symbolically, the way she has emasculated his father. The son is aware of his father's reduced status at his mother's hands and even suggests, at one point, that his father use physical violence against the woman to gain back some control over her unpleasant and demanding, dictatorial manner. Purdy directly states in the story that the three are truly prisoners of one another, seeking release but unable to find it. Purdy thus invokes once again the entrapment theme that he sees typical of American families. The father, in insisting on his son's acquiescence to the mother's demand for the removal of the beard, has lost all credibility with his son. (The father had told the son that if the offending beard was not shaved off, then the mother would mentally torture her husband for six months after their son had returned to New York.)

The story's resolution—when the son shaves off the beard and mutilates his face in the process as a rebuke to his parents—is both an act of defiance and an almost literal cutting of the umbilical cord with his family, since he tells his parents that he will not see them at Christmas and that they cannot see him in New York, since he will again have his beard. This story also introduces another theme upon which Purdy frequently touches: the contempt for artistic pursuit by the narrow and materialistic American middle class. The parents, for example, see art as causing their son's defiance of their restrictive lives.

"DAWN"

A similar mood is found in the story "Dawn," from the collection *The Candles of Your Eyes*. Here, a father, outraged because his son has posed for an underwear advertisement, comes to New York, invades the apartment where his son Timmy lives with another actor, Freddy, and announces that he is taking Timmy home to the small town where the father still lives. The father, Mr. Jaqua, resents his son's attempt to become an actor. He has urged the boy into a more respectable profession: the law. The story turns on Timmy's inability to resist his father's demands and his ultimate acquiescence to them. After Timmy has packed and left the apartment, Freddy is left alone, still loving Timmy but aware that he will never see him again.

This inability of American middle-class culture to accept or deal logically with homosexual love as a valid expression in men's emotional makeup is also found in Purdy's novels and elsewhere in his short fiction. The theme occurs in *Eustace Chisholm and the Works* as well as in *The Nephew, In a Shallow Grave, Malcolm,* and *Narrow Rooms,* and this denial of one's homosexual nature often leads Purdy's characters to violent acts.

"EVERYTHING UNDER THE SUN"

A slightly suppressed homoeroticism is also found in "Everything Under the Sun," in Purdy's collection *Children Is All*. Two young men, Jesse and Cade, two of those flat-spoken country (or hillbilly) types who often appear in Purdy's fiction, are living together in an apartment on the south end of State Street (Chicago possibly). Their basic conflict is whether Cade will work or not, which Jesse desires, but which Cade is unwilling to do. Cade ultimately remains in full control of the tense erotic relationship by threatening to leave permanently if Jesse does not let him have his own way. While there is talk of liquor and women, the real sexual tension is between the two men, who, when they bare their chests, have identical tattoos of black panthers. Although neither would acknowledge their true relationship, their sexual attraction is seen through their ungrammatically accurate speech patterns and the subtle erotic undertones to their pairing.

"SOME OF THESE DAYS"

The stories in *The Candles of Your Eyes* exhibit a homoerotic yearning as part of their plot. In "Some of These Days," a young man (the first-person narrator of the story) is engaged in a pathetic search for the man to whom he refers as his "landlord." His quest for the elusive "landlord" (who comes to be known merely as "my lord") takes him through a series of sexual encounters in pornographic motion-picture theaters as he tries desperately to find the man whose name has been obliterated from his memory.

"SUMMER TIDINGS"

"Summer Tidings," in the same collection, portrays a Jamaican working as a gardener on an estate, where he becomes obsessed with the young blond boy whose parents own the estate. In a subtle ending, the Jamaican fancies the ecstasy of the perfume of the blond boy's shampooed hair.

"RAPTURE"

In "Rapture," an army officer visits his sister, who is fatally ill, and she introduces the man to her young son, Brice. The soldier develops a fetish for the boy's golden hair, which he regularly removes from the boy's comb. After the boy's mother dies and her funeral is held, the uncle and his nephew are united in a wild love scene, a scene that the mother had foreseen when she thought of leaving her son to someone who would appreciate him as she had been appreciated and cared for by her bridegroom.

"LILY'S PARTY"

"Lily's Party," in the same collection, is even more explicit in its homosexual statement. In this story, Hobart, a man obsessed with his brother's wife, follows the woman to her rendezvous with a new lover, a young preacher. Hobart then watches as the woman, Lily, and the preacher make love. Then, the two men alternately make love with Lily and take occasional breaks to eat pies that Lily had cooked for a church social. Finally, the two men smear each other with pies and begin—much to Lily's consternation—to nibble at each other. As their encounter becomes more explicitly sexual, Lily is left alone, weeping in the kitchen, eating the remains of her pies, and being ignored by the two men.

Purdy's fiction has a manic—almost surreal—quality, both in the short works and in the novels. In his emphasis on very ordinary individuals plunging headlong into their private hells and their nightmarish lives, Purdy achieves the same kind of juxtaposition of the commonplace, seen through warped configuration of the psyche, that one finds in surrealist art.

SIXTY-THREE: DREAM PALACE

Nowhere is that quality as clearly to be found as in Purdy's most famous piece of short fiction, his early novella *Sixty-three: Dream Palace*, a work that, by its title, conveys the grotesque vision of shattered illusion and the desperation of its characters. Not only does *Sixty-three: Dream Palace* have the surreal quality of nightmare surrounding its action, but also it contains the latent homoeroticism of many of Purdy's other works and the distinctive speech rhythms, this time in the conversation of its principal character, the West Virginia boy Fenton Riddleway.

Fenton Riddleway, together with his sick younger brother Claire, has come from his native West Virginia to live in an abandoned house, on what he calls "sixty-three street," in a large city. In a public park, Fenton encounters a wealthy, largely unproductive "writer" named Parkhearst Cratty. Parkhearst seeks to introduce the young man to a wealthy woman named

Grainger (but who is referred to as "the great woman"). Ostensibly, both Parkhearst and Grainger are attracted to the youth, and it is suggested that he will be cared for if he will come and live in Grainger's mansion. Fenton also likes to spend time in a film theater (somewhat like Purdy's main character in "Some of These Days"). At one point in the story, Fenton is picked up by a handsome homosexual named Bruno Korsawski, who takes the boy to a production of William Shakespeare's *Othello*, starring an actor named Hayden Banks. A violent scene with Bruno serves to let readers realize Fenton's capability for violence, a potentiality that is revealed later when readers are told that he has killed his younger brother, who would not leave the abandoned house to go and live in the Grainger mansion. Faced with his younger brother's reluctance, his own desire to escape from both his derelict life, and the burden of the child Claire, Fenton killed the child, and the story's final scene has Fenton first trying to revive the dead child and then placing the child's body in a chest in the abandoned house.

Desperation, violence, an inability to deal with sexual longing, and the capacity to do harm even to ones who are loved are found in *Sixty-three: Dream Palace*, and it may be the most representative of Purdy's short fiction in its use of these thematic elements, strands of which mark so many of his various short stories. The tragic vision of life that Purdy sees as the human condition thus haunts all of his short fiction, as it does his most famous story.

In 1981 Purdy published *Sixty-three: Dream Palace, Selected Stories, 1956-1987*, a collection of reprints of twenty-six stories and one novella from the author's earlier works, including *Color of Darkness*, *Children is All*, and *The Candles of Your Eyes*. The collection provides readers the opportunity to reappraise the unconventional literary style and trademark blend of quirky characters and bizarre settings Purdy uses to confront racial and sexual stereotypes in American culture.

"YOU MAY SAFELY GAZE"

In "You May Safely Gaze," one of his less successful efforts, two narcissistic male exhibitionists put on an open display of affection at a beach, while a male colleague, obsessed with their behavior, complains to his disinterested female companion. Not only does the female companion appear detached, but also the author, who in an attempt to infuse a superficiality to the entire scene, never appears to rise above the surface level himself in constructing a meaningful framework that would help establish the motivations behind his characters' actions.

"EVENTIDE"

Emotional voids, another favorite Purdy theme, is explored with more piercing insight in "Eventide," the tale of two African American sisters grieving over lost young sons, one of whom simply disappeared, the other having died. Faced with a life without their offspring, the sisters seek their solace in the darkness that surrounds them, as if life beyond it is a threat to the memory of their sons, which represents the only security they have left.

"MAN AND WIFE"

Husbands and wives fare badly in Purdy's America when faced with personal crises. In "Man and Wife," a mentally disabled husband is fired from his job for an alleged sexual deviancy, prompting his wife to accuse him of having no character because "he had never found a character to have" and the husband to bemoan a marriage invaded by "something awful and permanent that comes to everybody." Only the sense of hopelessness that pervades the marriage is left to bind them in the end. In "Sound of Talking," the reality of a marriage turned sour becomes starkly evident when a wife's patience in catering to the demands of a wheelchair-bound husband runs dry. In both stories Purdy's characters are only able to raise their voices in plaintive cries, unable to explain to their spouses or themselves the source of their discomfort and disdain for each other. Attempts at escape often appear feeble, as in the wife's recommendation in "Sound of Talking" that she and her husband purchase a pet as a remedy for their trouble.

If the promise of marriage seems a distant memory in "Man and Wife" and "Sound of Talking," it becomes a cruel reality in the author's "Ruthanna Elder" when a young man learns his prospective bride has been sexually violated by her uncle, causing the groom-to-be to suddenly take his own life. It is a

tragic tale, simply told, yet one that illustrates perhaps Purdy's most enduring theme, that of the human heart's great potential for great good or great evil.

OTHER MAJOR WORKS

LONG FICTION: *Malcolm*, 1959; *The Nephew*, 1960; *Cabot Wright Begins*, 1964; *Eustace Chisholm and the Works*, 1967; *Jeremy's Version*, 1970; *I Am Elijah Thrush*, 1972; *The House of the Solitary Maggot*, 1974; *In a Shallow Grave*, 1976; *Narrow Rooms*, 1977; *Mourners Below*, 1981; *On Glory's Course*, 1984; *In the Hollow of His Hand*, 1986; *Garments the Living Wear*, 1989; *Out with the Stars*, 1992; *Gertrude of Stony Island Avenue*, 1997.

PLAYS: *Mr. Cough Syrup and the Phantom Sex*, pb. 1960; *Wedding Finger*, pb. 1974; *Two Plays* (includes *A Day After the Fair* and *True*), pb. 1979; *Proud Flesh: Four Short Plays*, pb. 1980; *Scrap of Paper, and the Berry-Picker*, pb. 1981

POETRY: *The Running Sun*, 1971; *Sunshine Is an Only Child*, 1973; *She Came out of the Mists of Morning*, 1975; *Lessons and Complaints*, 1978; *The Brooklyn Branding Parlors*, 1986.

MISCELLANEOUS: *An Oyster Is a Wealthy Beast*, 1967 (story and poems); *My Evening: A Story and Nine Poems*, 1968; *On the Rebound: A Story and Nine Poems*, 1970; *A Day After the Fair: A Collection of Plays and Stories*, 1977.

BIBLIOGRAPHY

Adams, Stephen D. *James Purdy*. New York: Barnes & Noble Books, 1976. Adams's study covers Purdy's major work from the early stories and *Malcolm* up through *In a Shallow Grave*. Of particular interest is his discussion of the first two novels in Purdy's trilogy *Sleepers in Moon-Crowned Valleys*.

Chudpack, Henry. *James Purdy*. Boston: Twayne, 1975. Chudpack's book is notable for students of Purdy's short fiction in that he devotes an entire chapter to the early stories of the author. He also offers an interesting introductory chapter on what he terms the "Purdian trauma."

Ladd, Jay L. *James Purdy: A Bibliography*. Columbus: Ohio State University Libraries, 1999. An annotated bibliography of works by and about James Purdy.

Lane, Christopher. "Out with James Purdy: An Interview." *Critique* 40 (Fall, 1998): 71-89. Purdy discusses racial stereotypes, sexual fantasy, political correctness, religious fundamentalism, gay relationships, and the reasons he has been neglected by the literary establishment.

Peden, William. *The American Short Story: Front Line in the National Defense of Literature*. Boston: Houghton Mifflin, 1964. Peden discusses Purdy in comparison with some of the "southern gothic" writers, such as Truman Capote and Carson McCullers, and in relation to Purdy's probing of themes about the strange and perverse in American life.

Renner, Stanley. "'Why Can't They Tell You Why?' A Clarifying Echo of *The Turn of the Screw*." *Studies in American Fiction* 14 (1986): 205-213. Compares the story with Henry James's famous tale; argues that both are about a female suppressing a male's sexual identity.

Schwarzchild, Bettina. *The Not-Right House: Essays on James Purdy*. Columbia: University of Missouri Press, 1968. Although the primary focus of these essays is on Purdy's novels, there is some comparative discussion of such early works as *Sixty-three: Dream Palace* and "Don't Call Me by My Right Name."

Skaggs, Calvin. "The Sexual Nightmare of 'Why Can't They Tell You Why?'" In *The Process of Fiction*, edited by Barbara McKenzie. New York: Harcourt, Brace and World, 1969. Argues that the mother tries to destroy the boy's masculine identification because of her own ambiguous sexual identity. Claims that in the final scene a strong female emasculates a weak male.

Tanner, Tony. Introduction to *Color of Darkness* and *Malcolm*. New York: Doubleday, 1974. Tanner's introductory essay discusses Purdy's novel *Malcolm* and *Sixty-three: Dream Palace*. It also compares Purdy's effects with those achieved by the Russian realist Anton Chekhov.

Jere Real, updated by William Hoffman

ALEXANDER PUSHKIN

Born: Moscow, Russia; June 6, 1799
Died: St. Petersburg, Russia; February 10, 1837

PRINCIPAL SHORT FICTION

Povesti Belkina, 1831 (*Russian Romance*, 1875; better known as *The Tales of Belkin*, 1947)
Pikovaya dama, 1834 (*The Queen of Spades*, 1858)

OTHER LITERARY FORMS

Generally considered the greatest poet in the Russian language, Alexander Pushkin is known not only for his lyrical and narrative poems but also for his brilliant verse novel *Evgeny Onegin* (1825-1832, 1833; *Eugene Onegin*, 1881), as well as his play *Boris Godunov* (1831; English translation, 1918), which was the inspiration for the opera by Modest Mussorgsky.

ACHIEVEMENTS

Often termed the father of Russian literature, Alexander Pushkin occupies a unique position in Russian literary history. During his age, the language of the Russian aristocracy was French, not Russian, and Pushkin's literary sensibility was largely formed by French writers, particularly writers of the eighteenth century. He combined their classical approach with the Romantic elements of the English poet George Gordon, Lord Byron and native Russian materials such as folktales in a transformation that produced a number of masterpieces, primarily in poetry. Yet Pushkin's general influence on nineteenth century Russian prose writers is immeasurable because his primary contribution was neither to character type nor to technique but to the very language of fiction itself. Precision and brevity, he believed, are the most important qualities of prose—elements which the eighteenth century French essayists also held in high regard—and his tales are characterized by a concise, plain language which set the standard for Russian prose writers who followed. Although character analysis was not Pushkin's primary achievement, his insight into the protagonist in *The Queen of Spades* is considered a precursor to the development of the psychological analysis of character which was the hallmark of the great Russian novelists of the nineteenth century. Ivan Turgenev, Leo Tolstoy, and Fyodor Dostoevski all acknowledged the influence of various aspects of his work. Russian critics have long expected Pushkin's reputation to become more firmly established in other countries, but since Pushkin's primary achievement is in poetry, and his particular, precise language is so difficult to translate, his reputation outside Russia has remained limited.

BIOGRAPHY

Alexander Sergeyevich Pushkin was born into the Russian aristocracy and lived the relatively privileged life of a member of the nobility. One element which set him apart from other aristocrats who gathered around the czar was his heritage on his mother's side: His great grandfather was the black slave Hannibal, whom Peter the Great bought in Turkey and brought back to Russia. At an early age, Pushkin's poetic talents were recognized, but the subject of some of his poetry was the desire for liberty, and for political reasons the czar banished him from Moscow to his mother's estate when he was twenty years old. Although Pushkin eventually was called back to Moscow by the czar, for the remainder of his life he was subject to the czar's direct censorship. At the height of his literary powers, Pushkin died a tragic death. He married a woman who was in favor with many members of the czar's court because of her beauty; she was not an intellectual, however, and did not appreciate Pushkin's writing. When Pushkin discovered that she was secretly meeting a member of the court in a liaison, he challenged the man to a duel in which Pushkin was wounded in the stomach. He died two days later.

Alexander Pushkin (Library of Congress)

ANALYSIS

Alexander Pushkin's short fiction exhibits the classic characteristics of the Romantic tale. The focus is on event, on plot, with character portrayal subordinated to dramatic action. These cleverly plotted, entertaining stories have much in common with such early masters of the modern short story as Sir Walter Scott, Washington Irving, Edgar Allan Poe, and Honoré de Balzac. As Romantic tales, Pushkin's stories have been termed perfect. Yet his reputation as one of the developers of the modern short story rests on a remarkably small body of work: the five tales which make up the collection *The Tales of Belkin* and the masterpiece *The Queen of Spades*. In addition to these completed stories, a number of fragments were published after his death which illustrate Pushkin's struggle in writing fiction. In contrast to his early achievements in poetry, his technical mastery of fiction required a long, difficult period of apprenticeship.

One of Pushkin's most challenging technical problems was the appropriate management of point of view, and in *The Tales of Belkin* he finally solved that problem. He framed the tales with an opening device, as Scott had done in a series of novels titled "Tales of My Landlord" (1816-1819) and as Irving had done in his *Tales of a Traveller* (1824)—works popular in Russia at the time that Pushkin began writing fiction. Pushkin's tales are presented as stories told by various people to one Ivan Petrovich Belkin, who wrote them down; upon his death, they were passed on to a publisher. The opening section of the collection is not a story but an address to the reader by this fictitious publisher, who comments on the background of the tales in a short paragraph and then presents a letter by a friend of Belkin which describes Belkin's life. This elaborate device does function to place the tales together in a coherent arrangement wherein Pushkin's voice carries consistently from one tale to the next.

"THE SHOT"

The opening tale of the collection is "Vystrel" ("The Shot"), one of the most widely anthologized tales in short fiction. Within that single story, Pushkin exhibits a master's manipulation of point of view, with a central narrator who, in turn, relates narration by two other characters. The central narrator is a young army officer, Lieutenant I. L. P., who describes the conditions of his regiment in a small, isolated town. The young officers spend their evenings gambling at the house of a thirty-five-year-old civilian named Silvio, who is a Byronic figure—a Romantic hero, detached and proud, somewhat ironic and cynical, with an obsessive personality. When Silvio is insulted by a newcomer, everyone expects Silvio to kill the brash young newcomer in a duel, for Silvio is a renowned shot who practices daily. Silvio passes up the opportunity, however, and the incident is forgotten by everyone but the lieutenant/narrator, who secretly cannot forgive Silvio for what he considers his cowardice.

Later, however, when Silvio learns that he must leave town, he calls the lieutenant aside and explains his reason for passing up the duel by relating a series of previous events, thus becoming a second narrator

in the story. Six years previously, as a hussar himself, Silvio had a duel with another young officer, a brilliant count of great social position and wealth. From the details which Silvio relates, it is obvious that subconsciously he was jealous of the man. The conditions of the duel were such that the two men drew lots for the first shot; Silvio's opponent won, but his shot missed, passing through Silvio's cap. As Silvio prepared for his shot, the young count possessed such aplomb that he ate cherries, calmly spitting out the seeds, as he waited. Angered by this show of superiority, Silvio made the strange request that he be allowed to take his shot at some future date, at any time he should choose to do so; the young count, with his great poise, agreed without any sign of apprehension. Now, Silvio has learned that the count is to be married, and Silvio is leaving to take his revenge. Because of this previous commitment to his honor, Silvio was forced to allow the recent insult to go unchallenged; consequently, the lieutenant learns that Silvio is not a coward after all. After Silvio relates these events, however, the lieutenant has strange, contradictory feelings about him: What kind of a man would do such a thing? An antihero in the Byronic tradition, Silvio is an elevated figure who believes that he is beyond the common sensibilities of society; the response of the narrator illustrates his ambivalence toward that Byronic role, an ambivalence which reflects Pushkin's own attitude.

The first section of the story ends with Silvio's departure, and the second begins four or five years later, when the lieutenant has left the army to return to his country estate. His neighbor, a Countess B., has been absent from her estate, but when she returns with her husband, the narrator visits them to relieve his boredom. In a short while, the narrator discovers that the husband is the same man whom Silvio left to kill, the brilliant young count, and he becomes the third narrator as he relates the events that followed Silvio's departure at the end of the first section of the story. Silvio indeed did appear at the estate, finding the count enjoying his honeymoon, but when Silvio claimed his shot, the count agreed. Silvio, however, in the spirit of the duelist, determined that they should draw lots once more. Once more, the count wins the first shot, but once more he misses, his stray shot striking a painting on the wall. Yet as Silvio readies himself to fire the deciding shot, the countess rushes in and, seeing her husband in danger, throws her arms around his neck. This action is too much for the count, and he angrily demands that Silvio shoot. Silvio, now satisfied that he has broken the count's poise, fires his shot off to one side, into the same painting that the count struck. The story ends with the comment by the central narrator that Silvio was killed some years later in a military battle. The portrayal of Silvio that emerges from the separate narrators of this highly crafted tale is that of a principled, intriguing figure. There is a new twist to this tale, however, which deviates from the literary type of the day: The Byronic antihero has been bested by a straightforward, decent man. Although Pushkin actually began this story as a parody on the Byronic figure, his technical proficiency enabled him to explore the larger meanings of that figure, and "The Shot" became a masterpiece.

"THE BLIZZARD"

The two stories which follow "The Shot" in the collection, "Metel" ("The Blizzard") and "Grobovshchik" ("The Undertaker"), are not as complex. "The Blizzard" revolves around a case of mistaken identity, which was a popular subject for Romantic tales at the time. A young heroine, Maria Gavrilovna, who has been brought up reading French novels, falls in love and sneaks off to marry her lover at night. Without her knowledge, a blizzard causes her lover to lose his way while going to the church, and she marries a man who, unknown to her, is not her lover. She returns to her parents' home and four years later learns that her lover—whom she believes is her husband—was killed in the War of 1812. Afterward, she meets a Colonel Burmin, a veteran of the same war, and falls in love with him. He responds to her love but declares that one night on a whim he married an unknown woman who mistakenly thought he was someone else, and thus he cannot marry. The situation recalls that of Irving's "The Spectre Bridegroom," not only in its mistaken identities in marriage but also in its tone; as in Irving's story, all ends happily as the events eventually reveal the true identities: The hero-

ine is, indeed, the unknown woman whom Colonel Burmin married that night. The events in Pushkin's story move much more quickly than those in Irving's, for they are presented without Irving's relaxed digressions; the influence of the occasional essayist was much stronger in Irving's work, and his tales, in general, do not have the quickly paced dramatic action of Pushkin, in whose stories one seldom finds superfluous material or inessential detail.

"THE UNDERTAKER"

"The Undertaker" is a humorous tale about an undertaker who is visited one night by the corpses he has buried, in response to an invitation he impulsively made at a party the previous night. The descriptions of the corpses are the highlight of this supernatural story, which ends with the undertaker waking from what proves to have been a dream. The tone and events of this story, particularly the corpses who come back to haunt the living, were to influence Nikolai Gogol—Pushkin's younger contemporary, another major prose writer of the period—in his famous "Chinel" ("The Overcoat"). Gogol had read Pushkin's collection and thought highly of it. One specific aspect of Pushkin's "Stantsionnyi smotritel" ("The Station Master") influenced Gogol: the character of the "little man." The story, narrated by government official "Titular Counsellor A. G. N.," is about a poor post-office station master of low rank, Samson Vyrin, a "little man," who has a beautiful daughter, Dunya. When the narrator was traveling one day, he happened to stop at Samson's station for horses; there he noticed a series of pictures on the wall depicting the story of the Prodigal Son. He also first saw the girl Dunya, who was fourteen at the time. Her beauty deeply impressed him, and one day some years later, when he happens to be in the same district, he remembers her and stops at the same station. He asks about her, and the station master, now a broken man, relates her story, thus becoming a second narrator.

Three years previously, the station master tells the traveler, a hussar named Captain Minsky stopped at the station and, seeing the beautiful Dunya, pretended to be too ill to continue his journey. The hussar remained at the station several days, with Dunya nursing him, and then, one day when the station master was away, fled with her. The station master followed, until it became obvious that Dunya had willingly run off with Minsky. Later, the station master takes a two-month leave and, on foot, traces the pair to St. Petersburg. There he discovers the pair living in a fancy hotel, and he confronts Minsky alone, demanding the return of his daughter before she is ruined. Yet Minsky declares that he is in love with Dunya and that neither she nor the station master could ever be happy with each other because of what has happened. The station master leaves, but he returns to find his daughter, and he discovers her enjoying her elegant surroundings as she tenderly winds her fingers in Minsky's hair. When she sees her father, she faints, and Minsky drives the father away.

The station master's narration at this point in the story is ended, and the original narrator, the government official, tells how the station master has now taken to drink. In the closing scene of the story, some years later, the official returns once more to the station house and discovers that the station master has, indeed, died from drink. In asking directions to the grave, he learns that a wealthy lady recently visited the area with her children in a coach-and-six and also asked for the station master. On learning of his death, she began weeping and then visited the grave herself; the woman was the daughter Dunya.

The twist of the young daughter returning not lost and ruined but happy and in good spirits creates the dramatic irony in these events. On one level, the story is thus an attack on the sentimental tales of the day about the young daughter gone to ruin. Once again, Pushkin elevated a story begun in parody to a masterpiece—many critics consider it the finest in the collection. The foolishness of the station master in drinking himself to death for his lost daughter becomes the object lesson of the events as it completely reverses the story of the Prodigal Son.

"THE SQUIRE'S DAUGHTER"

The last story in the collection, "Barishnya krestyanka" ("The Squire's Daughter"), is a light-hearted and delightful tale, related to Belkin by "Miss K. I. T.," the same source as for "The Blizzard." As in "The Blizzard," events revolve around a case of mistaken identity. Two landowners are at odds; one has a

seventeen-year-old daughter, Liza, and the other a young son, Alexey, home from the university, where he has picked up the Byronic posturing so common to the age. Here, Pushkin gently satirizes that behavior, in contrast to his probing of it in "The Shot." Liza seeks to meet the young man, and learning that he likes peasant girls, she dresses up one morning as such a girl and goes to a forest through which she knows he will be passing. He sees her, is attracted by her, and they begin to meet regularly at the same place in the forest, she continuing with her disguise. Meanwhile, the two landowners reconcile their differences, and Alexey's father demands that he marry the other landowner's daughter. Alexey refuses because of his love for the "peasant" girl, but at the crucial moment, Liza's true identity as the landowner's daughter is revealed, and all ends happily in light comedy.

THE QUEEN OF SPADES

The Queen of Spades, written after *The Tales of Belkin* was published, remains one of the most widely known stories in the history of short fiction. In this complex story, Pushkin uses an omniscient point of view, moving from one character to another as the situation demands; the narrative is divided into six sections and a conclusion. The story opens after an all-night game of cards with a young officer named Hermann, a Russified German, who learns that the grandmother of a fellow officer, an old countess, supposedly has special knowledge of the three cards that will appear in faro—a gambling game in which only someone with supernatural powers can predict the cards and their sequence before they appear. Hermann himself cannot play cards; he can only watch, for his financial circumstances would not allow him to lose. At heart, however, he is a gambler who feverishly longs to play, and the countess' supernatural ability fires his imagination. He begins to hang around the street where the countess lives, his imagination dwelling on her secret. Then, one night after a compelling dream about winning at cards, he wakes and wanders the streets until he finds himself mysteriously before the house of the old countess. He sees in the window the face of a fresh, young woman, Lizaveta, and that moment seals his fate. She is the ward of the countess, and she is receptive to Hermann's advances. He uses her to gain entrance one night to the countess' bedchamber, where he surprises the countess as she is going to bed. He pleads with the countess to tell him the secret, but she insists that the story is only a joke, that there is no secret. Hermann becomes agitated, convinced that she is lying, and when she refuses to talk to him, he draws a pistol to scare her into answering. This threat is too much for her, and she suddenly collapses in death.

Hermann confesses the situation to Lizaveta, and they conceal the real events of the countess' death. At the funeral, Hermann hallucinates that the old countess is winking at him from the coffin. That night, her corpse, or "ghost," visits him, and, in exchange for the promise that he will marry Lizaveta, tells him the winning sequence: three, seven, ace. The device of the returning corpse, or ghost, has been popular in literature from William Shakespeare's *Hamlet* (c. 1600-1601) to Charles Dickens's *A Christmas Carol* (1843), and, as in both of those works, the returning ghost indicates an unnatural situation and a disturbed personality. In this Pushkin story, the reader is to assume that the ghost is not "real" but rather an indication of Hermann's disturbed mind. It is this aspect of the tale that was to influence the psychological analysis of character that became the hallmark of the great Russian novels, especially Dostoevski's *Prestupleniye i nakazaniye* (1866; *Crime and Punishment*, 1866). The three cards are perpetually in Hermann's mind and on his lips, and one night he takes all the money he has in the world to a famous gambling house, where he bets on the three; he wins and returns the following night to stake everything on the seven; again he wins, and the third night he returns to bet on the ace. A large crowd gathers, having heard of his previous success. This night, however, instead of the ace appearing, the queen of spades is the chosen card, and Hermann sees the face of the old countess in the figure on the card, smiling up at him. The short paragraph of the conclusion relates that Hermann is now at a mental hospital, where he simply repeats, over and over, "Three, seven, queen! Three, seven, queen!" Lizaveta, however, has married a very pleas-

ant young man and is happy. In the opera by Pyotr Tchaikovsky, based on this story, the events differ somewhat. In the opera, Hermann and Lizaveta become lovers, and when he leaves her to gamble, she throws herself into the river; after the appearance of the queen, Hermann stabs himself. During the remainder of his life, Pushkin was never to equal the dramatic intensity of this story. It remains a classic, one of those tales that helped shape the direction of modern short fiction.

OTHER MAJOR WORKS

LONG FICTION: *Evgeny Onegin*, 1825-1832, 1833 (*Eugene Onegin*, 1881); *Arap Petra velikogo*, 1828-1841 (*Peter the Great's Negro*, 1896); *Kirdzhali*, 1834 (English translation, 1896); *Kapitanskaya dochka*, 1836 (*The Captain's Daughter*, 1846); *Dubrovsky*, 1841 (English translation, 1892); *Yegipetskiye nochi*, 1841 (*Egyptian Nights*, 1896); *Istoriya sela Goryukhina*, 1857 (*History of the Village of Goryukhino*, 1966).

PLAYS: *Boris Godunov*, wr. 1824-1825, pb. 1831 (English translation, 1918); *Skupoy rytsar*, wr. 1830, pr., pb. 1852 (*The Covetous Knight*, 1925); *Kamyenniy gost*, wr. 1830, pb. 1839 (*The Stone Guest*, 1936); *Motsart i Salyeri*, pr., pb. 1832 (*Mozart and Salieri*, 1920); *Pir vo vremya chumy*, pb. 1833 (*Feast in Time of the Plague*, 1925); *Stseny iz rytsarskikh vryemen*, wr. 1835, pr., pb. 1937; *Rusalka*, pb. 1837 (*The Water Nymph*, 1924); *Little Tragedies*, pb. 1946 (includes *The Covetous Knight, The Stone Guest, Mozart and Salieri*, and *Feast in Time of the Plague*).

POETRY: *Ruslan i Lyudmila*, 1820 (*Ruslan and Liudmila*, 1936); *Gavriiliada*, 1822 (*Gabriel: A Poem*, 1926); *Kavkazskiy plennik*, 1822 (*The Prisoner of the Caucasus*, 1895); *Bratya razboyniki*, 1824; *Bakhchisarayskiy fontan*, 1827 (*The Fountain of Bakhchisarai*, 1849); *Graf Nulin*, 1827 (*Count Nulin*, 1967); *Tsygany*, 1827 (*The Gypsies*, 1957); *Poltava*, 1829 (English translation, 1936); *Domik v Kolomne*, 1833 (*The Little House of Kolomna*, 1977); *Skazka o mertvoy tsarevne*, 1833 (*The Tale of the Dead Princess*, 1924); *Skazka o rybake ir rybke*, 1833 (*The Tale of the Fisherman and the Fish*, 1926); *Skazka o tsare Saltane*, 1833 (*The Tale of Tsar*

Saltan, 1950); *Skazka o zolotom petushke*, 1834 (*The Tale of the Golden Cockerel*, 1918); *Medniy vsadnik*, 1841 (*The Bronze Horseman*, 1936); *Collected Narrative and Lyrical Poetry*, 1984; *Epigrams and Satirical Verse*, 1984.

NONFICTION: *Istoriya Pugacheva*, 1834 (*The Pugachev Rebellion*, 1966); *Puteshestviye v Arzrum*, 1836 (*A Journey to Arzrum*, 1974); *Dnevnik, 1833-1835*, 1923; *Pisma*, 1926-1935 (3 volumes); *The Letters of Alexander Pushkin*, 1963 (3 volumes); *Pisma poslednikh let 1834-1837*, 1969.

MISCELLANEOUS: *The Captain's Daughter and Other Tales*, 1933; *The Works of Alexander Pushkin*, 1936; *The Poems, Prose, and Plays of Pushkin*, 1936; *Polnoyne sobraniye sochineniy*, 1937-1959 (17 volumes); *The Complete Prose Tales of Alexander Pushkin*, 1966; *Pushkin Threefold*, 1972; *A. S. Pushkin bez tsenzury*, 1972; *Polnoye sobraniye sochineniy*, 1977-1979 (10 volumes); *Alexander Pushkin: Complete Prose Fiction*, 1983.

BIBLIOGRAPHY

Bayley, John. *Pushkin: A Comparative Commentary.* Cambridge, England: Cambridge University Press, 1971. Offers erudite commentaries on Pushkin's works. Chapter 7 deals with his prose and its relationship to his entire canon.

Bethea, David, and Sergei Davidov. "Pushkin's Saturnine Cupid: The Poetics of Parody of *The Tales of Belkin*." *Publication of Modern Language Association of America* 96 (1971): 748-761. This article is basically an answer to the essay by Richard Gregg. The authors emphasize, among other things, the parody of *The Tales of Belkin* as their most pronounced facet.

Debreczeny, Paul. *The Other Pushkin: A Study of Alexander Pushkin's Prose Fiction.* Berkeley: University of California Press, 1983. In his encompassing study, Debreczeny discusses all Pushkin's prose works, drawing upon the extensive scholarship on the subject. Pushkin's stories are also discussed at length, with interesting results.

_____. *Social Functions of Literature: Alexander Pushkin and Russian Culture.* Stanford, Calif.: Stanford Univ. Press, 1997. Debreczeny divides his study into three parts: the first is devoted to selected readers' responses to Pushkin; the second explores the extent to which individual aesthetic responses are conditioned by their environment; and the third concerns the mythic aura that developed around Pushkin's public persona.

Emerson, Caryl. "'The Queen of Spades' and the Open End." In *Pushkin Today*, edited by David M. Bethea. Bloomington: Indiana University Press, 1993. Summarizes briefly the socioliterary, psychoanalytical, linguistic, and numerological studies of the story, and argues that what is parodied in the story is the reader's search for a system or a key; contends that Pushkin teases his readers with fragments of codes, partial keys that do not add up.

Feinstein, Elaine. *Pushkin: A Biography.* Hopewell, N.J.: Ecco Press, 1999. An excellent, updated biography of Pushkin.

Gregg, Richard. "A Scapegoat for All Seasons: The Unity and the Shape of *The Tales of Belkin*." *Slavic Review* 30 (1971): 748-761. Gregg discusses *The Tales of Belkin* as a unified cycle within Pushkin's total output.

_____. "Pushkin's Novelistic Prose: A Dead End?" *Slavic Review* 57 (Spring, 1998): 1-27. Argues that Pushkin systematized, perfected, and pushed to its furthest limit a kind of prose that had never been practiced before with such consistency, elegance, and taste. Contends that in terms of the novel, however, which was the preeminent fictional genre by the 1840's, prose of this kind was not possible.

Kropf, David. *Authorship as Alchemy: Subversive Writing in Pushkin, Scott, Hoffmann.* Stanford, Calif.: Stanford University Press, 1994. A discussion of the social institution of authorship. Focuses on Pushkin's creation of an invented persona, Belkin; addresses Pushkin's author as a textual or semiotic entity; discusses the story "The History of the Village of Foriukhino."

Lezhnev, Abram. *Pushkin's Prose.* Ann Arbor, Mich.: Ardis, 1974. In one of the rare examples of Russian scholarship translated into English, Lezhnev presents views of a native scholar on Pushkin's prose as seen in the thought and criticism of Pushkin's contemporaries.

O'Toole, Michael L. "'The Post-Stage Master.'" "'The Pistol Shot.'" In *Structure, Style, and Interpretation in the Russian Short Story*. New Haven, Conn.: Yale University Press, 1982. A structuralist discussion of "The Post-Stage Master" in terms of a fable (fabula), and of "The Pistol Shot" in terms of plot. O'Toole bases his approach on the analytical model of Russian Formalists and on their belief that serious discussion of literature must start with the "text" itself. The result is a lively analysis of the two stories.

Rosenshield, Gary. "Choosing the Right Card: Madness, Gambling, and the Imagination in Pushkin's 'The Queen of Spades.'" *PMLA* 109 (October, 1994): 995-1008. A discussion of madness in the story; argues that Hermann's vulgar imagination devalorizes madness; claims that in taking the queen of spades instead of the ace, Hermann chooses the right card, for it constitutes for him a victory of the imagination and thus of life over death.

Terras, Victor. "Pushkin's Prose Fiction in an Historical Context." In *Pushkin Today*, edited by David M. Bethea. Bloomington: Indiana University Press, 1993. Discusses Pushkin's importance in the ascendancy of prose fiction in Russia in the nineteenth century. Comments on the basic characteristics of Pushkin's prose style.

_____. "The Russian Short Story, 1830-1850." In *The Russian Short Story: A Critical History*, edited by Charles A. Moser. Boston: Twayne, 1986. Contends that Pushkin's tales are parodies of early nineteenth century prose fiction. Argues that parodic deconstruction, like that in Pushkin's tales, was a common feature of the Romantic tale.

Troyat, Henry. *Pushkin*. New York: Pantheon Books, 1950. This standard biography of Pushkin by the French author Troyat reads like a novel. Literary works are mentioned without extended discussion. Unfortunately, the critical discussion, as well as the extensive bibliography, have been omitted from the original.

Ronald L. Johnson, updated by
Vasa D. Mihailovich

THOMAS PYNCHON

Born: Glen Cove, New York; May 8, 1937

PRINCIPAL SHORT FICTION

"Mortality and Mercy in Vienna," 1959
"The Small Rain," 1959
"Entropy," 1960
"Low-Lands," 1960
"Under the Rose," 1961
"The Secret Integration," 1964
Slow Learner: Early Stories, 1984

OTHER LITERARY FORMS

In addition to his short stories, Thomas Pynchon has published one piece of reportage, "A Journey into the Mind of Watts," in *The New York Times Magazine*, June 12, 1966. He is best known, however, as a novelist. His novels include *The Crying of Lot 49* (1966) and *Gravity's Rainbow* (1973). After the publication of *Gravity's Rainbow*, Pynchon published nothing for seventeen years, with the exception of a few articles in *The New York Times Book Review*. In 1989, he published the novel *Vineland*, which received mixed reviews from the popular press and almost immediately was the subject of a large number of scholarly articles and papers. This dynamic was repeated in 1997 with the publication of the long-awaited opus, *Mason and Dixon*.

ACHIEVEMENTS

Thomas Pynchon is one of the greatest prose stylists of the twentieth century, a master of the novel, short story, and expository essay. His works have received literary acclaim and their fair share of controversy, as well as generating a remarkable amount of literary scholarship. There is even a scholarly journal entitled *Pynchon Notes* that is dedicated exclusively to the author. Pynchon has received almost every major American literary award, including the National Book Award for *Gravity's Rainbow* (shared with Isaac Bashevis Singer), the Pulitzer Prize (which was later withdrawn), the William Faulkner Foundation Award for his first novel, *V.* (1963), the Richard and Hinda Rosenthal Foundation Award for Fiction from the National Institute of Arts and Letters for *The Crying of Lot 49*, and the Howells Medal, which Pynchon refused to accept.

BIOGRAPHY

Thomas Ruggles Pynchon, Jr., is one of the most intensely private writers who has ever lived, even outdoing J. D. Salinger in his quest for seclusion and privacy. Only his close friends are even sure of what he looks like—the last available photograph of him is from high school. What is known of Pynchon is available only from public records. He was graduated from high school in 1953 and entered Cornell University that year as a physics student, but in 1955 he left college and entered the U.S. Navy. He returned to Cornell in 1957, changing his major to English and was graduated in 1959. He lived in New York for a short time while working on *V.*, then moved to Seattle, where he worked for the Boeing Company assisting in the writing of technical documents from 1960 to 1962. For several years after that, his whereabouts were uncertain, although he seems to have spent much time in California and Mexico. In the late 1980's and early 1990's, the ever-reclusive Pynchon was reported to have established residence in Northern California, the site of his novel *Vineland*. Confirmed sightings of Pynchon in New York City abounded in the late 1990's.

ANALYSIS

Not counting two excerpts from his second novel, which were printed in popular magazines, Thomas

Pynchon has published a number of short stories, one of them, "The Small Rain," in a college literary magazine, as well as the collection *Slow Learner: Early Stories*. Nevertheless, the stories are important in themselves and as aids to understanding Pynchon's novels. Most of the stories were written before the publication of Pynchon's first novel, *V.*, and share the thematic concerns of that novel. The characters of these stories live in a modern wasteland devoid of meaningful life, which they seek either to escape or to redeem. Often they feel that the world itself is about to end, either in a final cataclysm or by winding down to a state lacking energy and motion, characterized by the physical state known as entropy: the eventual "heat death" of the universe when all temperature will be the same and all molecules will be chaotically arranged, without motion or potential energy. Although the actions of the characters in the first stories vary widely, they all indicate a similar degree of hopelessness.

"THE SMALL RAIN"

Pynchon's first known short story, "The Small Rain," gives the reader insight into the author's early attempts at explicating these ideas. The story focuses on a two-day period in the life of Nathan "Lardass" Levine, a U.S. Army communications specialist from the Bronx stationed at Fort Roach, Louisiana, during the summer of 1957. After receiving a college degree from the City College of New York, Levine has refused entry into middle-class life, becoming a career enlisted soldier instead. Levine's nickname is apropos, as his Army career has consisted of attempt after attempt to avoid any and all work duties, to simply be alive but unthinking in modern life.

Levine is offered the possibility to reconsider these choices when a hurricane destroys the Louisiana village of Creole, and he is one of those assigned to reconstruct communications with the region and to find corpses in the disaster area. Basing their camp at the nearby McNeese State College, Levine is given another chance to see what he has refused—the life of upward mobility he left behind for his stagnating military existence. Rather than realizing that he may have made the wrong decisions thus far in his life, Levine blithely participates in his duties. Returning from Creole to McNeese, Levine simply gets drunk in a local campus bar and has casual sex with a female college student, "little Buttercup." The story concludes with Levine's complaints about the weather—he hates the ever-present rain—and his refusal to consider anything but his upcoming leave in New Orleans.

Like many of the characters in *V.*, Levine accepts the idea of doing nothing. While capable of changing his chosen way of life, he is unwilling to make any effort. It is far easier for him to receive his three meals a day and his occasional leaves from duty than it is to participate in life. As Pierce, his lieutenant, suggests at one point, Levine seems content to keep extending the width of his rear-end. Although limited in overall scope, this story is important to understanding a number of issues raised throughout Pynchon's texts. Like his first novel, *V.*, this first of Pynchon's stories forces readers to make their own conjunctions, to make the connections between ideas and events that Levine himself is incapable of doing. As "The Small Rain" shows, from the outset of his writing career, Pynchon was concerned with lives filled with boredom, modern life's lack of meaning, and the choices people do not make.

"MORTALITY AND MERCY IN VIENNA"

Pynchon's first nationally published short story, "Mortality and Mercy in Vienna," also illustrates many of these themes. The protagonist, a career diplomat named Cleanth Siegel, arrives at a party in Washington, D.C., only to find that the host, a lookalike named David Lupescu, is abandoning the apartment and appointing Siegel to take his place. In the course of the party, Siegel finds himself listening to the confusing details of his guests' convoluted and pointless sexual and social lives. Although he takes on the role of a father-confessor and although he wants to be a healer—"a prophet actually"—he has no cure for these people's problems. He does find a cure of sorts, however, in Irving Loon, an Ojibwa Indian who has been brought to the party. Siegel recalls that the Ojibwa are prone to a psychic disorder in which the Indian, driven by a cosmic paranoia, comes to identify with a legendary flesh-eating monster, the Windigo, and goes on a rampage of destruction, kill-

ing and eating his friends and family. Siegel speaks the word "Windigo" to Loon and watches as the Indian takes a rifle from the wall. As Loon begins shooting the members of the party, Siegel himself escapes. Like Mr. Kurtz in Joseph Conrad's *Heart of Darkness* (1902), with whom he explicitly compares himself, Siegel finds the only possible salvation to be extermination.

The presentation of the modern world as a spiritual wasteland and the theme of paranoia continue throughout these early short stories, as well as *V.*, but none of Pynchon's other characters is able to act as forcefully as Siegel, even though his action is a negative one. The later stories, however, also demonstrate Pynchon's greater ability and growth as a writer. "Mortality and Mercy in Vienna," relying as it does on references to Conrad and T. S. Eliot and on a narrative voice which generally tells rather than shows, presents itself too self-consciously as a story even as it strives for verisimilitude. Pynchon's next story, "Low-Lands," demonstrates his growth in a short period of time.

"LOW-LANDS"

Dennis Flange, a former sailor now unhappily married, is thrown out of the house by his wife because of a surprise visit by his old Navy friend, Pig Bodine (who also later appears in *V.* and *Gravity's Rainbow*). He takes refuge with Pig in a shack in the local garbage dump, which is presided over by a black caretaker. This caretaker has barricaded his shack against gypsies who are living in the dump, but that night when Flange hears someone call him he goes outside. There he meets a young woman named Nerissa who leads him to her room in a tunnel beneath the dump. At the story's end, Flange seems prepared to stay with her.

The title of "Low-lands" comes from an old sea chantey which causes Flange to think of the sea as "a gray or glaucous desert, a wasteland which stretches away to the horizon, . . . an assurance of perfect, passionless uniformity." This "perfect, passionless uniformity" might be an apt description of Pynchon's view of modern life, his great fear of the ultimate end to surprise and adventure. Cleanth Siegel's response to this same fear is to obliterate the problem; Dennis

Flange's response is to hide from it. Flange fears the uniformity suggested by his "low-lands," but he also desires it, wishing not to be exposed and lonely on that wasteland surface, "so that he would be left sticking out like a projected radius, unsheltered and reeling across the empty lunes of his tiny sphere."

In order not to be left "sticking out," Flange has taken refuge in his marriage and his house but finds that they can no longer shelter him. He finds his surrogate for a hiding place in the gypsy girl, Nerissa. Within Nerissa's underground room, he knows he can find at least a temporary sanctuary. Like the underground refuge of Ralph Ellison's Invisible Man, this room suggests a place of recuperation and preparation to reemerge into life. In Nerissa herself, the image of the sea is restored to life: "Whitecaps danced across her eyes; sea creatures, he knew, would be cruising about in the submarine green of her heart." This ending, with its gypsies and secret tunnels, suggests the possible existence of alternatives to the wasteland of modern society, a possibility to which Pynchon was to return in *The Crying of Lot Forty-nine*; at the time, this ending made "Low-lands" one of the most positive of Pynchon's short stories.

"ENTROPY"

A tone of hope, although somewhat more muted, can also be found in "Entropy," the best-known and perhaps most successful of Pynchon's short stories. Here Pynchon returns to the scene of "Mortality and Mercy in Vienna"—a party taking place in Washington, D.C.—but theme, characters, and plot are now handled with much more sophistication. The party itself is a lease-breaking party being hosted by one Meatball Mulligan, whose guests arrive and depart, engage in various kinds of strange behavior, and pass out at random. Upstairs, a man named Callisto lives in another apartment which he has converted into a hermetically sealed hothouse with the aid of a French-Annamese woman named Aubade. The story shifts back and forth between the two apartments although Meatball and Callisto are connected only by the fact of living in the same building and by the theme of entropy which concerns them both.

Although there is in "Low-lands" a brief reference to the Heisenberg principle of nuclear physics (that

an event is affected by the fact of being observed), "Entropy" is the first of Pynchon's works to make sustained use of information and metaphors drawn from science and mathematics—a use which has become one of his hallmarks as a writer. Entropy manifests itself in the story in two different forms: as *physical* entropy—the tendency toward randomness and disorder within a closed system—and as *communications* entropy—a measure of the lack of information within a message or signal. In both cases, the tendency is toward stasis and confusion—lack of motion or lack of information; in either case and in human terms, the result is death.

Physical entropy is especially frightening to Callisto, which is why he has barricaded himself within his apartment. Since he fears that the "heat death" of the universe is imminent, he has built a private enclave where he can control the environment and remain safe. The concept of physical entropy can also be applied to Meatball's party as the behavior of the individual party guests becomes more and more random and disordered. Ironically, Meatball manages (at least temporarily) to avoid chaos and to reverse entropy, while Callisto fails. Realizing that he can either hide in a closet and add to the chaos and mad individualism of his party or work "to calm everybody down, one by one," Meatball chooses the latter. Callisto, on the other hand, fails to stop entropy within his own apartment. An ailing bird which he had been holding, trying to warm, dies in his hands after all; he wonders, "Has the transfer of heat ceased to work? Is there no more. . . ."

Part of the reason for Callisto's failure has to do with communications entropy. Order in communication is essential for the maintenance of order in Callisto's hothouse. Aubade brings "artistic harmony" to the apartment through a process by which all sensations "came to her reduced inevitable to the terms of sound: of music which emerged at intervals from a howling darkness of discordancy." Noise from Meatball's party threatens to plunge that music back into discord, and with the death of Callisto's bird, Aubade can no longer continue her effort. She smashes the window of the apartment with her fists and with Callisto awaits the triumph of physical entropy "and the final absence of all motion."

The fact that Meatball can bring order to his party suggests that order must be consciously created, not merely maintained as Callisto has sought to do. Even with Meatball's effort, his resolution of discord is not permanent and the final image of the party trembling "on the threshold of its third day" is not reassuring. Pynchon's message seems to be that of the physicists: Entropy is an inevitable condition although it can be reversed for a while in some places. "Entropy" is notable for its organization and style as well as for its subject matter. The characters and the alternation of story lines are models for Pynchon's first novel, *V.*, but the story succeeds on its own as well. This "contrapuntal" structure combined with a number of references to music makes it evident that the story is structured like a musical fugue.

"UNDER THE ROSE"

"Under the Rose," Pynchon's last short story before *V.*, is also especially interesting for its style and structure. Set in Cairo at the end of the nineteenth century during the Fashoda crisis—when Britain and France nearly came to war over the colonization of the Sudan—the story is Pynchon's first re-creation of a historical setting and his first successful use of a narrative limited to the point of view of a single character. With very little authorial intrusion, Pynchon skillfully describes the activities of two spies, Porpentine and Goodfellow, in seeking to prevent the assassination of the British ambassador and the international war which would inevitably follow. The story was later reworked by Pynchon, broken up into eight vignettes seen through the eyes of outside spectators, and installed as chapter 3 of *V.*

These early stories are generally characterized by a pessimism concerning the possibilities of human action and change. They are also marked by a sense of social isolation; with the exception of "Under the Rose," there is little or no suggestion of the political, economic, and social pressures that shape life, and even in that story, these pressures are subordinated to a suggested nameless, hostile, possibly nonhuman intelligence at work in history. Following the publication of *V.*, however, Pynchon has steadily moved back into the world, combining his imaginative perception

of the condition of modern life with a recognition of the forces which can play a part in shaping that condition. That recognition is first manifested in Pynchon's "The Secret Integration."

"THE SECRET INTEGRATION"

"The Secret Integration" centers on a group of children living in the Berkshire town of Mingeborough, Massachusetts, who act in league to subvert adult institutions and encourage anarchistic liberty. The adults are seen as constantly seeking to make the children conform to their way of life: for example, Grover Snodd, "a boy genius with flaws," is certain that adults are planting Tom Swift books for him to read in order to foster a sense of competition and avarice as well as to promote racism.

Racism is, in fact, the key theme of the story. Carl Barrington, a central member of the children's gang, is himself black, his parents having recently moved into Northumberland Estates, a new development in Mingeborough. These newcomers are resented by the white adults of the town, and the children are aware of the presence of racism in their families, even though they do not quite understand it. There is also a flashback to the night the children—one of them a nine-year-old reformed alcoholic—go to the town hotel to sit with a black jazz musician because the adults in Alcoholics Anonymous are unwilling to help a black. After a night-long vigil, the boys see the musician hauled away by the police and never learn what really happens to him. In retaliation and as an affirmation of color, the boys stage a raid on the local train at night wearing green-colored masks and costumes to scare the passengers.

Color is a threat to Mingeborough and to a white way of life which thrives on the competition, separateness, and blandness exemplified by Tom Swift. The Barringtons are a special annoyance because they live in Northumberland Estates, which seems to have been built purposely to suppress differences and encourage uniformity. This development is like the "low-lands" of Dennis Flange, but with an important difference: Rather than an abstract psychological condition, it is a real, physical place with more than enough correlatives in the nonfictional world to make it all too recognizable.

The children, however, are able to overcome this prejudice; even though Grover only understands the word "integration" as a mathematical term, they accept Carl as an equal. Yet in the end, the group capitulates. They find garbage dumped on the Barringtons' front lawn and recognize it as having come from their own houses. Unable to cut themselves off from their parents and repudiated by the Barringtons themselves, they say good-bye to Carl, who, it turns out, is imaginary, "put together out of phrases, images, possibilities that grownups had somehow turned away from, repudiated, left out at the edges of town. . . ." The children return to the safety and love of their parents "and dreams that could never again be entirely safe."

"The Secret Integration" is concerned once again with the quest for possibilities and alternatives, which is the theme of *The Crying of Lot Forty-nine*, and with the prevalence of racism, which is one of the many concerns of *Gravity's Rainbow*. Although the children admit defeat, one still feels the hope that life will be somewhat better once they have grown up, that they will retain some of the lessons they have learned.

SLOW LEARNER

Pynchon's own estimation of his short stories is ambivalent and has been the subject of much scholarly discussion, especially since the publication in 1984 of *Slow Learner*, an anthology of the author's short stories. In the introduction to this book, Pynchon disparages his short stories to such an extent that it is remarkable that he permitted their republication in the first place. The first-person Thomas Pynchon of the 1984 introduction discussing the third-person Thomas Pynchon of the 1960's, however, may be no more than a fictional creation of the present Thomas Pynchon, with the introduction to *Slow Learner* being no more than another of the author's highly equivocal and extraordinarily convoluted short stories.

It is impossible to say whether Pynchon will ever return to the short-story form for its own sake, and certainly his stories are less important than his novels. Nevertheless, these works are helpful introductions to this writer's sometimes complex and baffling fictional world, and some of them—especially "En-

tropy" and perhaps "The Secret Integration"—will stand on their own as minor classics.

OTHER MAJOR WORKS

LONG FICTION: *V.*, 1963; *The Crying of Lot 49*, 1966; *Gravity's Rainbow*, 1973; *Vineland*, 1989; *Mason and Dixon*, 1997.

NONFICTION: *Deadly Sins*, 1993.

BIBLIOGRAPHY

Birkerts, Sven. "Mapping the New Reality." *The Wilson Quarterly* 16 (Spring, 1992): 102-110. Claims that the American novel has ceased to provide the reader with an encompassing, relevant, challenging picture of life as it is really experienced; suggests the reason is that the texture of contemporary life does not lend itself well to realism; discusses those fiction writers who have adopted strategies for galvanizing the chaos around us, such as Robert Stone, Thomas Pynchon, Don DeLillo, and Norman Mailer.

Bloom, Harold, ed. *Thomas Pynchon*. New York: Chelsea House, 1986. An extremely useful collection of essays on all aspects of Pynchon's literary works. Contains essays of an introductory nature for first-time readers of Pynchon's prose.

Chambers, Judith. *Thomas Pynchon*. New York: Twayne, 1992. A critical and interpretive examination of Pynchon's work. Includes bibliographical references and an index.

Cowart, David. *Thomas Pynchon: The Art of Allusion*. Carbondale: Southern Illinois University Press, 1980. This book is one of the best volumes on Pynchon's prodigious use of allusions in his prose. Useful chapters are included on the allusive functioning of music and cinema in Pynchon's novels and short stories.

Diamond, Jamie. "The Mystery of Thomas Pynchon Leads Fans and Scholars on a Quest as Bizarre as His Plots." *People Weekly* 33 (January 29, 1990): 64-66. A brief biographical sketch and discussion of Pynchon's dropping out of sight in the 1960's.

Dickson, David. *The Utterance of America: Emersonian Newness in Dos Passos' "U.S.A." and Pynchon's "Vineland."* Göteborg, Sweden: Acta Universitatis

Gothoburgensis, 1998. This comparison study includes a bibliography and an index.

Dugdale, John. *Thomas Pynchon: Allusive Parables of Power*. New York: St. Martin's Press, 1990. Dugdale provides a critical review and interpretation of Pynchon's work. He includes thorough bibliographical references and an index.

Gussow, Mel. "Pynchon's Letters Nudge His Mask." *The New York Times*, March 4, 1998, p. E1. Discusses the insights into Pynchon's creative process and emotions in more than 120 letters that he sent to his agent, Candida Donadio.

Hawthorne, Mark D. "Pynchon's Early Labyrinths." *College Literature* 25 (Spring, 1998): 78-93. Discusses Pynchon's use of labyrinths in his early stories in the 1960's; argues that while first using the labyrinth to describe escape from a confining middle-class marriage, Pynchon slowly turned it into a metaphor for the quest for self-awareness.

Hume, Kathryn. *Pynchon's Mythography: An Approach to "Gravity's Rainbow."* Carbondale: Southern Illinois University Press, 1987. This excellent book examines in detail Pynchon's use of myths and legends in *Gravity's Rainbow*. The comments are also applicable to the rest of his prose works. The range of Pynchon's mythography extends from the grail and Faust legends to non-Western myths.

Levine, George, and David Leverenz, eds. *Mindful Pleasures: Essays on Thomas Pynchon*. Boston: Little, Brown, 1976. A useful selection of essays on Pynchon's prose. The essays on Pynchon's use of scientific theories and terminology are particularly valuable in understanding the novel *Gravity's Rainbow* and the short story "Entropy."

McHoul, Alec, and David Wills. *Writing Pynchon: Strategies in Fictional Analysis*. Urbana: University of Illinois Press, 1990. Although the authors rely heavily on deconstructive critical methods, the book includes an interesting discussion (pages 131 to 160) of Pynchon's introduction to his collection of short stories *Slow Learner*.

Sales, Nancy Jo. "Meet Your Neighbor, Thomas Pynchon." *New York* 29 (November 11, 1996): 60-64. Discusses Pynchon's almost mythical status; comments on his popularity in the 1970's and his subsequent reclusiveness.

Weisenburger, S. C. *A "Gravity's Rainbow" Companion: Sources and Contexts for Pynchon's Novel*. Athens: University of Georgia Press, 1988. This volume is an extraordinarily detailed encyclopedia of the sources for the allusions used in Pynchon's novel. Since several of the characters from Pynchon's short stories reappear in *Gravity's Rainbow*, this book is useful in order to trace the influence that Pynchon's short stories have had on his novels.

Donald F. Larsson, updated by
William E. Grim and Joshua Stein

Q

ELLERY QUEEN

Manfred Bennington Lee
(Manfred Lepofsky)

Born: Brooklyn, New York: January 11, 1905
Died: Near Waterbury, Connecticut; April 3, 1971

Frederic Dannay
(Daniel Nathan)

Born: Brooklyn, New York: October 20, 1905
Died: White Plains, New York; September 3, 1982

PRINCIPAL SHORT FICTION

The Adventures of Ellery Queen: Problems in Deduction, 1934
The New Adventures of Ellery Queen, 1940
The Case Book of Ellery Queen, 1945
Calendar of Crime, 1952
QBI: Queen's Bureau of Investigation, 1954
Queens Full, 1965
QED: Queen's Experiments in Detection, 1968

OTHER LITERARY FORMS

Manfred B. Lee and Frederic Dannay's career as mystery writer Ellery Queen began in 1929 with the publication of *The Roman Hat Mystery*. They went on to write more than forty other mystery novels, including four under the pseudonym Barnaby Ross, as well as their numerous short stories. During the 1940's, the pair produced weekly scripts for the long-running radio series *The Adventures of Ellery Queen*, and they worked briefly for Paramount Pictures, Columbia Pictures Entertainment, and Metro-Goldwyn-Mayer, writing screenplays featuring their namesake detective. Several of the mysteries that appeared in *Ellery Queen's Mystery Magazine* are written in play form. Dannay and Lee also produced several works of criticism on the detective story, the most important of which is perhaps *Queen's Quorum: A History of the Detective-Crime Short Story as Revealed by the 106 Most Important Books Published in This Field Since 1845* (1951).

ACHIEVEMENTS

Ellery Queen is often thought to be one of the most influential figures in the development of detective fiction, both as a writer and as an editor. "His" work was recognized several times by the Mystery Writers of America (which Dannay and Lee founded) in its annual Edgar Allan Poe Awards, and in 1960, Queen won the association's Grand Master Award. Like his contemporaries of the "golden age" of mystery and detective fiction—Agatha Christie, Rex Stout, John Dickson Carr, and others—Queen works in the puzzle tradition of Arthur Conan Doyle's Sherlock Holmes, in which mysteries are solved by using a process of logical thought.

Queen's work as editor of *Ellery Queen's Mystery Magazine* has been credited with "rescuing American detective fiction from the pulps and restoring its reputation as high quality literature." From its inception in 1941, the magazine tried to publish the best in mystery fiction of all types, and it introduced new writers alongside established authors and such mainstream figures as Arthur Miller and Sinclair Lewis.

BIOGRAPHY

In 1928, two first cousins adopted the pseudonym Ellery Queen and entered a contest sponsored by *McClure's Magazine* for the best mystery story. The first prize was seventy-five hundred dollars. The cousins won but never received the money, as the magazine ceased publication before the prize was distributed. Publisher Frederick A. Stokes, who had

On left, Frederic Dannay (Library of Congress)

ran his own orchestra. Lee went on to become an advertising copywriter for a New York film company, while Dannay began working in an advertising agency as a copywriter and art director.

Their collaboration as Ellery Queen was highly successful. Dannay and Lee apparently alternated devising plots and doing the writing; in a 1969 interview with *The New York Times*, Dannay commented that their "clash of personalities is good for the ultimate product. . . . We're not so much collaborators as competitors. It's produced a sharper edge."

The first ten years of the collaboration were very prolific, and the novels were tightly plotted, ingenious puzzles that emphasized the logic of deduction. Indeed, twelve of the first fourteen novels are subtitled *A Problem in Deduction*. The years between the publication of *Calamity Town* (1942) and *The Finishing Stroke* (1958) are generally considered to be Queen's best. By then the logical puzzles were still tightly constructed, but Queen began giving more emphasis to elements of characterization, setting, mood, and theme. Though the plot of *The Finishing Stroke* implied an end to the Ellery Queen series, nine more Ellery Queen novels were written after its publication.

In the 1930's, Lee and Dannay also wrote screenplays featuring Ellery Queen, and in 1939, they began writing a script per week for the radio series *The Adventures of Ellery Queen*, which lasted until 1948. In 1941, Dannay suggested to magazine publisher Lawrence Spivak that he start a magazine devoted to mystery stories. Dannay and Lee had edited *Mystery League Magazine* in 1933 and 1934, but Dannay became the sole editor of *Ellery Queen's Mystery Magazine*, which was a worldwide success. The magazine is frequently credited with raising the standard of the mystery story, and along with publishing well-established writers, it introduced numerous newcomers, many of whom went on to become successful authors. Dannay also edited scores of anthologies consisting of stories drawn from the magazine and from his and Lee's collection of detective fiction.

Lee, who was married twice and had eight children—four boys and four girls—died in 1971 of a heart attack soon after Queen's last novel, *A Fine and*

been associated with the contest, offered to publish their entry as a novel, and *The Roman Hat Mystery* was successful enough that the cousins quit their jobs and turned to writing full-time as Ellery Queen. For approximately ten years, the cousins managed to keep the public from knowing that Ellery Queen was a pseudonym. In fact, they adopted a second pseudonym, Barnaby Ross, for four mystery novels and once staged a masked debate as Ross and Queen. After 1938, it became known that Ellery Queen was in reality Frederic Dannay and Manfred B. Lee.

Born Manfred Lepofsky, Lee was the elder of the cousins by nine months. He and Dannay, who changed his name from Daniel Nathan by adopting Frédéric Chopin's first name and creating a surname from the first syllables of his original name, went to Boys' High School in Brooklyn. Lee continued his education at New York University, where his main interest was music; he played the violin and for a time

Private Place (1971), was published. Dannay, who married three times and had three sons, wrote no more Ellery Queen novels after Lee's death, though he continued his work as editor of *Ellery Queen's Mystery Magazine* until his own death in 1982.

ANALYSIS

Ellery Queen's mystery stories often are a sort of animated crossword puzzle: As the puzzle solver fills in the grid according to the clues, the answers to the clues that he or she does not understand become clear through the answers to the clues that are interpreted correctly. Other stories are like riddles: The clues to the mystery must be interpreted and added together to find a logical answer. Still others are like jigsaw puzzles, where one has to fill in what is missing to get a true picture. Francis M. Nevins, Jr., in *Twentieth-Century Crime and Mystery Writers* (1980), wrote that Queen follows several motifs in most of his stories, those of "the negative clue, the dying message, the murderer as Iagoesque manipulator, the patterned series of clues deliberately left at scenes of crimes, the false answer followed by the true and devastating solution." All these techniques work well to keep the reader in suspense, yet Queen is scrupulously fair in making sure that all the clues are available to the reader as well as to Ellery Queen, the detective in all of his stories. In fact, many of Queen's stories have a formal "Challenge to the Reader" after all the clues have been presented and before Ellery solves the crime. Even the stories without this challenge, however, are structured in such a way that the reader can attempt to solve the problem before the solution is presented. Queen is not above throwing in a red herring or two, but Ellery must deal with these as must the reader. Occasionally, solutions are farfetched, but the stories never admit of more than one solution.

Queen's stories are puzzles, and as such they sometimes lack any emotional punch. While police officers, doctors, and the like often do become somewhat hardened to violent death, it is nevertheless slightly shocking to the reader's sensibilities to have Ellery calmly, almost absentmindedly, stepping over bodies as he examines potential clues. When some-

one does react, the tone of the account often becomes rather amused: In "The Adventure of the Three R's," after Nikki Porter, Ellery's secretary, discovers that she is virtually sitting on a skeleton, she screams and draws over Ellery and two professors; the story notes that

> the top of the skull revealed a deep and ragged chasm, the result of what could only have been a tremendous blow.
> Whereupon the old pedagogue and the young took flight, joining Miss Porter, who was quietly being ill on the other side of the cabin.

Few of Queen's stories display any horror over an act of murder; instead, the tone seems to be one of faint disapproval.

Through the years, Queen gave Ellery several different foils, whose main purpose is to bring Ellery to the scene of a crime. The first and most important is his father, Inspector Richard Queen, who seems to call Ellery in on all of his difficult cases. Inspector Queen deals with the police routine, while Ellery takes the pieces that his father digs up and puts them together. Detective-Sergeant Thomas Velie is Inspector Queen's usual accompaniment, and he appears to have little intelligence but large bulk for dangerous situations. Another foil is Ellery's pretty young secretary, Nikki Porter, who can be counted on to come to the wrong conclusion. Nikki can also be depended upon to take Ellery to a party or visiting to places where something nasty is likely to happen. Ellery must have been a most uncomfortable houseguest, as something disturbing seems likely to occur when he visits. Early in his career, Ellery was also involved with Hollywood gossip columnist Paula Paris, who supplied a mild love interest and tickets to various events where disagreeable things took place. Djuna, the Queens' houseboy, appears in several stories as well. While these characters do not appear in every Queen story, the role of a foil to Ellery's intelligence is common. There is usually someone to whom the solution must be explained.

Queen's first stories were not collected until 1934, after more than half a dozen novels featuring his detective had been published. Thus, the character of Ellery Queen was already well known and popular, so Queen wastes little time in his short stories establishing characters: The reader is plunged straight into the plot. In "The African Traveller," the first story in *The Adventures of Ellery Queen*, Ellery has agreed to teach a class in applied criminology to several university students. Conveniently, Inspector Queen has just been called to the scene of a murder on the first day of the class, and he will allow Ellery and his students to examine the case and come to their own conclusions. All the clues are presented during the students' exploration of the room, and Ellery sends them off to consider the case and develop a solution. The students in this case are Ellery's foils, and though they blanch when they are first faced with the dead man, they are soon happily poking around the body. Each student later presents a coherent theory as to the killer; all are wrong. The story thus follows Nevins's pattern of the false answer followed by the true solution: Ellery tells the students where they went wrong—each ignored some clue—and lays out the logical solution, which takes into account *every* clue presented. The story is similar to a crossword puzzle: Not until all the answers to the clues have been filled in is the solution complete.

"THE BEARDED LADY"

In "The Bearded Lady," the most important clue is a painting done by the victim. The murdered man is a doctor and amateur painter who has just been willed one thousand dollars, which is to be divided between his benefactor's stepchildren upon his death. Dr. Arlen is killed in his studio and near one of his paintings, on which he has painted a beard onto a woman's face. Ellery concludes that the bearded woman is a clue to the identity of the killer: "With his murderer present, he *couldn't* paint the name; the murderer would have noticed it and destroyed it. Arlen was forced, then, to adopt a subtle means: leave a clue that would escape his killer's attention." This story, then, falls into Nevin's category of the "dying message": Ellery must interpret this message correctly in order to solve the crime. The clue is a kind of riddle: To whom does the bearded lady refer? If it is the beard that is important, then the clue points to the

stepson, who has a beard. The clue, however, could also point to the stepdaughter, whose eight-year-old son had just been punished the day before for chalking a beard onto one of Arlen's paintings. When all the other clues are taken into account as well, however, Ellery realizes that the killer is Mrs. Royce, a man who has dressed up as a woman in order to claim the inheritance of his sister, who was to receive from the same benefactor as Dr. Arlen two hundred thousand dollars. Dr. Arlen, the family physician, had been scheduled to examine Mrs. Royce the day after he was killed, whereupon Royce's ruse would have been discovered.

"DEAD RINGER"

The story "Dead Ringer" takes the motif of the dying message to absurdity, though the clues still hold together and the solution is logical given the clues presented. The "dead ringer" is a security agent who had been placed in a tobacconist's shop, which was suspected of being a drop for enemy agents, because he resembles the man who runs the shop. Hours after he telephoned his office to say that, in examining the shop's customer ledger, he had discovered the identities of the foreign agents, he is found dead, clutching an empty can of tobacco labeled "MIX C." Ellery deduces that, since the security agent "made his extraordinary dying effort to call your attention to the otherwise empty can," there must be something about the label that is a clue to the identities of the foreign agents. "*Every letter in* MIX C *is also a Roman numeral*," so the foreign agents must be numbers 1,009 and 100 in the customer ledger. While within the terms of the story this is the logical answer, it still strikes the reader as absurd. That someone would make that kind of intellectual connection while dying a painful death and still be able to get to the can at all stretches the reader's credulity too far. Queen recognizes that the story type of the dying message has its limitations; in "E = Murder" he writes,

we're confronted with a dying message in the classic tradition. . . . Why couldn't he have just written the name? The classic objection. The classic reply to which is that he was afraid his killer might come back, notice it, and destroy it. . . . which I'll admit has never really satisfied me.

Nevertheless, Queen has written dozens of stories of the dying message type.

"THE INVISIBLE LOVER"

Another frequent pattern that Queen employs is what Nevins calls the "negative clue": the clue that is important because it is not there when it should be. The story "The Invisible Lover" fits this pattern, as well as embodying Nevins's category of "the murderer as Iagoesque manipulator." One of Iris Scott's suitors has been murdered, and her childhood friend and beau, Roger Bowen, has been arrested for the deed. The most damning evidence against Bowen is that the coroner has had examined the bore marks on the bullet found in the dead man's body, and they match Bowen's gun. Ellery, puzzled by the rearrangement of furniture in the dead man's room, looks behind the highboy and finds a dent in the plaster that looks to have been made by a bullet. If it were made by a bullet, a loose bullet should have been found in the room, and since Bowen's bullet was found in the body, two shots should have been fired to account for the mark. No bullet was found, and two shots were not heard. Ellery thus deduces the solution to the crime because what he expected to find was not there: There was no bullet to account for the mark on the wall, and if there was no bullet, the bullet that killed the victim *must* have passed through his body and the chair on which he was sitting to make the indentation on the wall and then must have been picked up by the murderer. Ellery discovers a chair with a hole in it in the coroner's room, and when he has the body exhumed, he finds an exit wound. Therefore, the coroner must have lied about Bowen's bullet being found in the body, and the only reason for him to lie is because he is the murderer. All the pieces of the jigsaw have been put into place, and the true picture is revealed.

"PAYOFF" AND "THE PRESIDENT REGRETS"

Two stories that fit loosely into Nevins's category of a "patterned series of clues" are "Payoff" and "The President Regrets." "Payoff" also employs the device of the dying message: A dying man gasps out that the four men who head the racketeering organization he did the books for use as code names the names of four cities. He dies, however, before he can tell the authorities which code name belongs to the top man. Inspector Queen and Ellery know the names of the four men involved, and Ellery discovers who the boss is by matching the code names with the real names of the criminals: *Hous*ton with Hughes, *Phil*adelphia with Filippo, *Berke*ley with Burke, and *Bos*ton with the boss—who must thus be the fourth man, Ewing. "The President Regrets" is a similar puzzle, in which a screen star named Valetta Van Buren writes a letter to Ellery telling him that one of her four lovers has threatened to kill her. Without telling him the name of her potential killer, she writes that "she had something in common with three of the four, and that the fourth was the one who had threatened her." The point in common is a presidential name: Three of her lovers were called Taylor, Wilson, and Harrison, while the fourth was named Price. The patterned clues in these stories are fairly simplistic; in his novels, however, Queen used more complex ones.

Queen's stories, as well as his novels, belong to the style of the "golden age" of the formal detective story, though many of them were actually written outside that time period of the 1920's to 1940's. They are, for the most part, well written, and they are often amusing. Ellery, despite his arrogant erudition, is a likable character, but his main function is to serve the plot. The plot is king in Queen's stories: The puzzle is all. Ingenuity is the key word to the puzzle, and while some of the puzzles are so ingenious as to border on fantasy, most of them are reasonably plausible and intriguing. The stories endure because they can still involve and challenge the reader.

OTHER MAJOR WORKS

LONG FICTION: *The Roman Hat Mystery: A Problem in Deduction*, 1929; *The French Powder Mystery: A Problem in Deduction*, 1930; *The Dutch Shoe Mystery: A Problem in Deduction*, 1931; *The Greek Coffin Mystery: A Problem in Deduction*, 1932; *The Tragedy of X*, 1932 (as Barnaby Ross); *The Tragedy of Y*, 1932 (as Barnaby Ross); *The Egyptian Cross Mystery: A Problem in Deduction*, 1932; *The Ameri-*

can Gun Mystery: A Problem in Deduction, 1933 (also published as *Death at the Rodeo*, 1951); *The Tragedy of Z*, 1933 (as Barnaby Ross); *Drury Lane's Last Case*, 1933 (as Barnaby Ross); *The Siamese Twin Mystery: A Problem in Deduction*, 1933; *The Chinese Orange Mystery: A Problem in Deduction*, 1934; *The Spanish Cape Mystery: A Problem in Deduction*, 1935; *Halfway House*, 1936; *The Door Between: A Problem in Deduction*, 1937; *The Devil to Pay*, 1938; *The Four of Hearts: A Problem in Deduction*, 1938; *The Dragon's Teeth: A Problem in Deduction*, 1939 (also published as *The Virgin Heiresses*, 1954); *Ellery Queen, Master Detective*, 1941 (also as *The Vanishing Corpse*); *The Penthouse Mystery*, 1941; *The Perfect Crime*, 1942; *Calamity Town*, 1942; *There Was an Old Woman*, 1943 (also published as *The Quick and the Dead*, 1956); *The Murderer Is a Fox*, 1945; *Ten Days' Wonder*, 1948; *Cat of Many Tails*, 1949; *Double, Double*, 1950 (also published as *The Case of the Seven Murders*, 1958); *The Origin of Evil*, 1951; *The King Is Dead*, 1952; *The Scarlet Letters*, 1953; *The Golden Summer*, 1953 (by Frederic Dannay writing as Daniel Nathan); *The Glass Village*, 1954; *Inspector Queen's Own Case*, 1956; *The Finishing Stroke*, 1958; *The Player on the Other Side*, 1963; *And on the Eighth Day*, 1964; *The Fourth Side of the Triangle*, 1965; *A Study in Terror*, 1966 (British title, *Sherlock Holmes vs. Jack the Ripper*, 1967); *Face to Face*, 1967; *The House of Brass*, 1968; *Cop Out*, 1969; *The Last Woman in His Life*, 1970; *A Fine and Private Place*, 1971.

RADIO PLAY: *The Adventures of Ellery Queen*, 1939-1948.

NONFICTION: *The Detective Short Story: A Bibliography*, 1942; *Queen's Quorum: A History of the Detective-Crime Short Story as Revealed by the 106 Most Important Books Published in This Field Since 1845*, 1951, revised 1969; *In the Queen's Parlor, and Other Leaves from the Editors' Notebook*, 1957; *Ellery Queen's International Case Book*, 1964; *The Woman in the Case*, 1966 (in Great Britain as *Deadlier than the Male*, 1967).

CHILDREN'S LITERATURE: (as Ellery Queen, Jr.): *The Black Dog Mystery*, 1941; *The Green Turtle Mystery*, 1941; *The Golden Eagle Mystery*, 1942; *The Red Chipmunk Mystery*, 1946; *The Brown Fox Mystery*, 1948; *The White Elephant Mystery*, 1950; *The Yellow Cat Mystery*, 1952; *The Blue Herring Mystery*, 1954; *The Mystery of the Merry Magician*, 1961; *The Mystery of the Vanished Victim*, 1962; *The Purple Bird Mystery*, 1965.

BIBLIOGRAPHY

Grella, George. "The Formal Detective Novel." In *Detective Fiction: A Collection of Critical Essays*, edited by Robin W. Winks. Englewood Cliffs, N.J.: Prentice-Hall, 1980. Though Grella's essay is on the detective novel and only briefly mentions the work of Ellery Queen, the essay does discuss the characteristics of the formal detective story of the "golden age" and is thus very useful in considering Queen's stories.

Grossberger, Lewis. "Ellery Queen: A Man of Mystery and He Likes It That Way." *The Washington Post*, March 16, 1978, p. D1. A brief biographical sketch, discussing how Frederic Dannay developed the Ellery Queen persona and the *Ellery Queen Mystery Magazine*; also discusses his popularity in Japan and his editing work, as well as his shyness and stage fright.

Keating, H. R. F., ed. *Whodunit? A Guide to Crime, Suspense, and Spy Fiction*, London: Windward, 1982. Keating's short entry on Ellery Queen contains some useful biographical information but has little in the way of literary criticism.

Nevins, Francis M., Jr. "Ellery Queen." In *Twentieth-Century Crime and Mystery Writers*, edited by John M. Reilly. 2d ed. New York: St. Martin's Press, 1985. Nevins's article on Queen is perceptive and critically useful. His discussion focuses on Queen's novels, but his delineation of story motifs applies well to the short stories. Includes a complete bibliography.

Routley, Erik. *The Puritan Pleasures of the Detective Story: A Personal Monograph*. London: Victor Gollancz, 1972. Routley's book is a highly personal survey of detective fiction, but it includes several pages on the work of Ellery Queen that are fairly perceptive about Queen's characters of the novels.

Symons, Julian. *Bloody Murder: From the Detective Story to the Crime Novel, a History*. London: Faber & Faber, 1972. Symons's history of the detective story includes several pages on Ellery Queen in the chapter entitled "The Golden Age:

The Thirties." His focus is on Queen's novels, but his observations apply equally well to the short stories.

Karen M. Cleveland Marwick

HORACIO QUIROGA

Born: El Salto, Uruguay; December 31, 1878
Died: Buenos Aires, Argentina; February 19, 1937

PRINCIPAL SHORT FICTION
Los arrecifes de coral, 1901
El crimen del otro, 1904
Cuentos de amor, de locura y de muerte, 1917
Cuentos de la selva para los niños, 1918 (*South American Jungle Tales*, 1923)
El salvaje, 1920
Anaconda, 1921
El desierto, 1924
La gallina degollada, 1925 (*The Decapitated Chicken and Other Stories*, 1976)
Los desterrados, 1926 (*The Exiles and Other Stories*, 1987)
Más allá, 1925

OTHER LITERARY FORMS

Though famous to readers of Spanish American literature exclusively for his short fiction, Horacio Quiroga wrote, to a limited degree and with equally limited success, in other forms as well. He published two novels, *Historia de un amor turbio* (1908; story of a turbulent love) and *Pasado amor* (1929; past love), as well as one theatrical work. He also included poems in his first book, *Los arrecifes de coral* (coral reefs), a work written in the *fin de siècle* tradition of Spanish American modernism and completely anti-Quiroga in both style and content. He also wrote literary criticism and theory. His most famous (at least among experts in Spanish American fiction) foray

into this particular area was a handful of articles that he wrote for the magazine *El Hogar* (the hearth), in which he discussed the theory and practice of writing short stories.

ACHIEVEMENTS

Horacio Quiroga holds much the same position in Spanish American literature as does Edgar Allan Poe in North American letters. Like Poe, whom Quiroga admired and who influenced the Uruguayan writer's work significantly, Quiroga dedicated his literary efforts almost entirely to the short-story genre, and in the process he not only penned some of the most famous and most anthologized stories to be found in Spanish American literature but also wrote about the genre, even offering a decalogue of suggestions to other writers on how they should approach writing the short story. These suggestions appeared in his essay "Manual del perfecto cuentista" (manual for the perfect short-story writer), published in *El Hogar* on April 10, 1925.

Quiroga is without a doubt one of the most highly regarded and most widely read short-story writers in the history of Spanish American literature and is considered by most to be the foremost Spanish American short-story writer prior to the arrival of Jorge Luis Borges, Julio Cortázar, and other writers of the so-called new narrative on the Spanish American literary scene. While critical interest in Quiroga diminished during the Borges and post-Borges eras, the Uruguayan writer's popularity among readers did not—all of which, perhaps, is just as well, for Quiroga's stories, with rare exception the highly polished gems of a consummate short-story writer, lend themselves far more to reader enjoyment than to literary criticism.

BIOGRAPHY

Two elements play significant roles in Horacio Quiroga's life and also frequently find their way into some of the writer's most famous stories. These two elements are tragic violence and the Uruguayan author's fascination with the jungle-filled Misiones region of northern Argentina. The first of these elements, tragic violence, punctuates Quiroga's life—so much so, in fact, that were his biography offered as fiction, it would almost certainly be roundly criticized for being unbelievable, for no one's life, in the real world, could be so tragically violent, especially when a good portion of said violence comes through accident. The author's fascination with the harsh jungles of Misiones cost him at least one wife and possibly a second in real life, while this unforgiving environment provided him at the same time with the setting and thematic point of departure for many of his most famous stories.

Horacio Silvestre Quiroga y Forteza was born on December 31, 1878, in El Salto, Uruguay, the youngest of four children born to Prudencio Quiroga and Pastora Forteza. Three months after Horacio's birth, don Prudencio was killed when his hunting rifle went off accidentally as he was stepping from a boat. Quiroga's mother, doña Pastora, ashore with infant son Horacio in her arms, witnessed the tragic event and fainted, dropping her son to the ground. Later the same year, doña Pastora moved the family to the Argentine city of Córdoba. She remarried in 1891, taking Ascencio Barcos as her second husband, and the family moved to Montevideo, Uruguay. On a September afternoon in 1896, don Ascencio, having suffered a cerebral hemorrhage earlier, took his own life with a shotgun. Seventeen-year-old Horacio was the first to arrive on the scene.

Personal tragedy followed Quiroga in 1901 with the death of both his brother Prudencio and his sister Pastora. Then in 1902, the budding writer, who had published his first book, the above-mentioned *Los arrecifes de coral* (coral reefs), the previous year, accidentally shot and killed one of his closest friends and literary companions, Federico Ferrando. After teaching off and on for several years in Buenos Aires, in September of 1909 Quiroga married Ana María Cirés and moved with her to San Ignacio, in the Misiones section of Argentina. Quiroga had first visited this jungle hinterland in 1903, with friend and Argentine writer Leopoldo Lugones. Enamored of the region, he bought land there in 1906 and divided his time between Misiones and Buenos Aires for the rest of his life. In 1915, unable to cope with the hardships of living in the jungle, Ana María poisoned herself, leaving Quiroga a widower with the couple's two children. The following year, the writer returned to Buenos Aires, and over the next ten years he saw the publication of his most famous collections of stories, the above-mentioned *Cuentos de amor, de locura y de muerte* (stories of love, madness, and death), *South American Jungle Tales*, *Anaconda*, and *The Exiles and Other Stories*, all the while moving periodically between the backlands and the Argentine capital. He remarried in 1927, taking a nineteen-year-old friend of his daughter as his second wife (he was forty-nine). Quiroga and his new wife moved to Misiones in 1931, but she returned to Buenos Aires with their infant daughter the following year. Quiroga's health deteriorated significantly in 1934. He returned to Buenos Aires in 1936, where he was diagnosed with cancer in 1937. He took a lethal dose of cyanide to end his life in February of the same year.

ANALYSIS

Horacio Quiroga published approximately two hundred short stories, many of which are considered classics within the Spanish American literary canon. Most of the author's stories, classics or not, fall within one (or more) of the following three general categories: Poesque stories of horror, often punctuated by madness and/or genetic defect; stories of human beings against a savage and thoroughly unromanticized nature; and Kiplingesque animal stories that frequently contain an underlying moral message. The vast majority of Quiroga's stories are dramatic, intense, even memorable tales that captivate the reader and in general reveal a true master of the genre at work.

Some of Quiroga's most popular stories come from the first of the three categories listed above, that of Poesque stories of horror, often featuring madness and/or genetic defect. Two widely read and exemplary stories from this category are "El almohadón de plumas" ("The Feather Pillow"), first published in 1907, and "La gallina degollada" ("The Decapitated Chicken"), first published in 1909.

"THE FEATHER PILLOW"

"The Feather Pillow" is the more purely Poesque of these two stories. In it, a newlywed woman falls mysteriously ill and quickly progresses toward death. Her husband and doctor are at a complete loss as to what ails her as well as what to do to help her. Finally, she dies. Shortly thereafter, a servant finds what appears to be two small punctures in her feather pillow. Further examination reveals that the pillow is inordinately heavy. The husband cuts the pillow open and in it finds a swollen creature (later identified as a bird parasite), which had been sucking the blood out of its victim for some time, literally draining the life out of her.

This story is both classic Poe and classic Quiroga. It is classic Poe in large part because of the horrific nature of its content. It is classic Quiroga for numerous elements, almost all of which have to do with the manner in which the writer presents the content. The story runs only three to five pages (depending on the print of the edition), yet in this short span the narrator takes the reader from an introduction of the characters to the conflict itself to the horrifying ending. As in most of Quiroga's stories, not a single word is wasted, as each contributes not only to the tale being told but to the overall effect of the story as well. This story is also a classic Quiroga story because of the inclusion of a seemingly insignificant detail, which, at the time it is mentioned, is almost overlooked by the reader (the narrator mentions rather offhandedly after several paragraphs about the couple's relationship that the woman had taken ill), the dramatic and surprise ending (featuring the blood-laden anthropoid), and the foreshadowing of said ending (the narrator states that the woman had seen an "anthropoid" staring at her from the carpet, but the reader is told that this is a hallucination), even though the first-time reader is not aware that said foreshadowing is indeed foreshadowing at the time that he or she encounters it. Also typical of Quiroga in this story is the writer's ability to turn a tale that deals with specific characters and apply its situation to the world of the reader. Quiroga accomplishes this in "The Feather Pillow" by adding a paragraph after the action of the story itself had ended, a paragraph in which the narrator states, matter-of-factly, that such creatures, bird parasites are frequently found in feather pillows. In this way, the narrator makes the previously distanced and protected reader a potential victim of the same fate as the woman in the story. As a result, certainly more than a few readers of "The Feather Pillow" have checked their own pillows before sleeping on the night they read this particular story, an effect on the reader that would please both Quiroga and his chief influence for this story, Poe, to no small degree.

"THE DECAPITATED CHICKEN"

"The Decapitated Chicken" is less purely Poesque and more in the naturalist tradition, but it is no less horrifying in content. The story opens with a couple's four "idiot" (the word used by Quiroga) sons seated on a bench on a patio, their tongues sticking out, their eyes staring off into space. The narrator recounts how, with the birth of each son, the couple had hoped for a "normal" child and how each had blamed the other for the defective genes (a naturalist element) that produced the "idiot" sons. Finally, the couple's fifth child, a daughter, is "normal." She receives all the couple's attention, while the sons are relegated to the less than loving care of a servant. One day, the four sons wander into the kitchen as the servant is cutting the head off of a chicken to prepare it for lunch. Later, by accident, both the sons and the daughter are left unattended. The daughter attempts to climb the garden wall on the patio, where her "idiot" brothers sit, her neck resting on the top as she works to pull herself up the wall. Captivated by the sight, the four sons grab the daughter, drag her into the kitchen, and behead her just as the servant had beheaded the chicken.

This story features several classic Quiroga traits that are on display in "The Feather Pillow" as well. Chief among them are the early and rather offhand mention of something that will be of tantamount importance later in the story (the decapitation of the chicken) and the presence of subtle foreshadowing (the narrator mentions that though believed incapable of true learning, the four sons do possess at least a limited ability to imitate things that they see—again the decapitation of the chicken), though once again said foreshadowing is almost certainly missed by the first-time reader. This story also demonstrates Quiroga's penchant for surprise and horrifying endings, endings that place Quiroga among the best writers of this type of tale.

MAN VS. NATURE

Some of the most famous stories from the second of the fore-mentioned categories, that concerning man against savage and thoroughly unromanticized nature, share many of the characteristics found in the stories referred to above: dramatic, detailed narration, the inclusion of an often seemingly insignificant detail or event that will eventually cause a character's demise, subtle though undeniably present foreshadowing, death and/or surprise in the end, and no small amount of irony, particularly as it pertains to fate (an element that, though present in "The Decapitated Chicken," is even more prominent in stories in this category). If Quiroga's stories, particularly those of this second category, are any indication of his philosophy, then he saw human beings as anything but the masters of their own destiny, particularly in the harsh and unforgiving environment of the author's beloved Misiones, where even the most careful person (and particularly the least careful) was at the mercy of the jungle. The slightest misstep or false move could spell disaster, and, in fact, it almost always did, if not in real life then at least in Quiroga's stories. In this environment, Quiroga's stories demonstrate, there is little or no room for error, and accidents befall even the most diligent of individuals. This is fairly vividly illustrated in some of the author's most famous stories, such as "A la deriva" ("Drifting"), "La miel silvestre" (wild honey), "El hombre muerto" ("The Dead Man"), and "El hijo" ("The Son").

"DRIFTING"

The first of these stories, "Drifting," tells of a man who, by accident (and in the very first sentence of the story), steps on a snake and is bitten. A few pages later, after considerable (and detailed) effort to make his way, by canoe, down river for help, he is dead. Near the end of the story, briefly, it appears as though the protagonist's condition is improving, but his apparent improvement is but the illusion of a dying man, for a few sentences later he dies, another victim of the unforgiving environment in which he has lived. The protagonist of "La miel silvestre" (wild honey), an accountant, sets out to conquer the jungle, a world totally foreign to him. At one point, he stops to sample some wild honey. Within seconds, he is paralyzed, a result of the particular type of honey that he has eaten. Almost immediately thereafter, an army of carnivorous ants (skillfully foreshadowed by Quiroga earlier in the story) begins making its way toward him. His skeleton is found a few days later. The protagonist of "The Dead Man" is nearing the end of his work for the morning, clearing his banana grove with his machete and self-satisfied in his work, when suddenly, and quite by accident, he falls. He falls well, he believes, except, he soon discovers, for one significant detail: He has fallen on his machete. For the rest of the story, he watches as the rest of the world, from which he is suddenly and unexpectedly separated, goes on as usual around him, as he, helpless and unable to seek help, slowly dies, ironically, within sight of the roof of his own house.

"THE SON"

In "The Son," a father sees his son off as the latter heads into the jungle to hunt alone. While he is gone, the father thinks of his son and even imagines what he is doing at every moment. The reader is told that the father suffers from hallucinations (an important piece of information later in the story) and has often even envisioned the violent death of his son. When the father hears two shots in the distance, he believes that his son has killed two doves. Later, when his son does not return home on time, he sets off looking for him. While searching, the father imagines finding his son dead. The narrator suggests, however, that the father has found the son safe and sound. A final paragraph, though, separated from the rest of the text, reveals that this has been a hallucination and that the son, in fact, has died, much as his father had earlier envisioned, accidentally, by his own hand, his dead body entangled in a wire fence.

While Quiroga's stories of horror seem to be intended principally for the entertainment of the reader, these stories of human beings versus the jungle unmistakably communicate the dual themes that human beings are indeed no match for nature and that life, ironically, can be whisked away not only suddenly but also by the slightest of accidents. This latter aspect of the writer's thematic intent is nowhere more apparent than in "The Dead Man," in which one moment the protagonist is working happily on his land and the next he lies dying, his life suddenly coming to an end, with neither pomp nor circumstance, as a result of a simple fall.

ANIMAL STORIES

The third and final category in which one may easily classify Quiroga's stories, that of Kiplingesque animal stories that frequently contain an underlying moral message, features, from a technical standpoint, probably some of the weakest of the Uruguayan author's most famous stories. These stories are generally far less tightly structured, narratively less compact than the stories found in the first two categories, and in part, as a result, do not possess the dramatic intensity present in these other stories. Even the narrative voice is frequently different from that found in most of Quiroga's other stories. While "The Feather Pillow," for example, or "The Dead Man" features a distanced, omniscient narrator, these stories often read more like fairy tales, with the narrator's voice more like that of an old storyteller. Their technical differences from Quiroga's other stories aside, however, many, and in fact some of the author's most widely read works, fit into this category and display, even more so than his other stories, the vivid imagination of their author.

"ANACONDA" AND "JUAN DARIÉN"

Two of the most famous stories from this category are "Anaconda," the story (almost novella in length) of a group of snakes that band together in an attempt to kill the team of scientists who have invaded their

territory and whose work to develop an antivenom serum threatens the snakes' very existence, and "Juan Darién" (English translation), the story of a tiger cub that, through love, turns into a boy, a human, only to turn into a tiger once again and return to the animal world when he is rejected by humans for being different. The first of these two stories, "Anaconda," is interesting, if nothing else, for its imaginative description of the snake world, complete with interspecies prejudice and a congress for debating issues of concern to the group. The second story, "Juan Darién," with its Christ-figure protagonist, sends an obvious moral message concerning human intolerance and cruelty and with its magical reality in some ways serves as a precursor for the works of "new narrativists" such as Borges and Cortázar.

Quiroga is one of the most widely acclaimed and most popular short-story writers in the history of Spanish American literature. He is known, for the most part, for intense, even dramatic narration, the offhand inclusion of a pivotal detail or event, skillful foreshadowing, and surprising and frequently horrific endings. If Quiroga has one significant defect, it may be that his stories are a bit too predictable. A veteran reader of Quiroga can often identify the seemingly insignificant detail and the foreshadowing and immediately thereafter discern exactly where the story is going. This potential defect, however, is hardly a defect at all since even if one can predict the story's direction, even its outcome, the story is still entertaining and interesting, because of how Quiroga gets the reader to the outcome. In other words, much like an old joke for which one already knows the punch line but which one never tires of hearing, Quiroga's stories, even his most predictable ones, are true pleasures to read. While literary fashion, particularly among critics, may come and go, Quiroga's stories, given both their content and their skillful presentation, will always, it seems, have a wide audience. They are, after all, plainly and simply, good stories, and as such they will probably never lose their appeal to readers.

OTHER MAJOR WORKS

LONG FICTION: *Historia de un amor turbio*, 1908; *Pasado amor*, 1929.

BIBLIOGRAPHY

Brushwood, John S. "The Spanish American Short Story from Quiroga to Borges." *The Latin American Short Story: A Critical History*, edited by Margaret Sayers Peden. Boston: Twayne, 1983. Brushwood dedicates most of the first four pages of this twenty-six-page chapter to Quiroga. The critic comments on Quiroga's place in the Spanish American short story, discusses the Uruguayan writer's decalogue for the perfect short-story writer, and considers various aspects of the stories "The Decapitated Chicken," "Juan Darién," and "The Dead Man." Contains interesting although brief commentary.

Englekirk, John. "Horacio Quiroga." In *Edgar Allan Poe in Hispanic Literature*. New York: Instituto de las Españas, 1934. In a lengthy study of Edgar Allan Poe's influence on numerous Spanish and Spanish American writers, Englekirk dedicates his longest chapter (twenty-nine pages) to Poe's influence on Quiroga. The critic discusses Poe's influence in some of the most obviously Poesque stories in Quiroga's repertoire but finds Poe's influence in many other stories as well, stories not usually thought of as influenced by Poe. An interesting read.

Peden, William. "Some Notes on Quiroga's Stories." *Review* 19 (Winter, 1976): 41-43. Peden reviews the chief characteristics of Quiroga's stories and briefly refers to a number of stories that contain these characteristics. Succinct and on target, though perhaps equally if not more useful for its presentation in English translation of Quiroga's decalogue of the "Perfect Short Story Writer." Published as part of a twenty-page "Focus" section on Quiroga.

Pupo-Walker, Enrique. "The Brief Narrative in Spanish America: 1835-1915." In *The Cambridge History of Latin American Literature*. Vol. 1, edited by Robert González Echevarria and Enrique Pupo-Walker. Cambridge: Cambridge University Press, 1996. Provides a valuable historical and cultural context for Quiroga by charting the development of short narrative in Spanish America in the nineteenth century, from the early sketches of customs and manners and the influence of Edgar Allan Poe through the early part of the twentieth century.

San Roman, Gustavo. "Amor Turbio, Paranoia, and the Vicissitudes of Manliness in Horacio Quiroga." *The Modern Language Review* 90 (October, 1995): 919-934. Discusses the theme of love in Quiroga's fiction, focusing on the novella *Historia de un amor turbio*; comments on the links between the story and paranoia; argues that Quiroga's texts are more of a victim than of a self-controlled author.

Schade, George D. "Horacio Quiroga." In *Latin American Literature in the Twentieth Century: A Guide*, edited by Leonard S. Klein. New York: Ungar, 1986. Largely a three-page version of Schade's introduction to Margaret Sayers Peden's *The Decapitated Chicken and Other Stories*, listed below. Provides concise discussion of the writer's life, career, and chief characteristics and limited consideration of specific stories. Includes a list of "Further Works" (most in Spanish) by Quiroga and a brief bibliography (most in Spanish).

_____. Introduction to *The Decapitated Chicken and Other Stories*. Edited and translated by Margaret Sayers Peden. Austin: University of Texas Press, 1976. In this ten-page introduction to Peden's English-language collection of twelve of Quiroga's most famous stories, Schade provides an introduction to Quiroga for the uninitiated reader, discussing the writer's life and career as well as the chief characteristics of his works. In the process, he comments briefly on the stories included in the collection, among them "The Feather Pillow," "The Decapitated Chicken," "Drifting," "Juan Darién," "The Dead Man," "Anaconda," and "The Son."

Keith H. Brower

R

VALENTIN RASPUTIN

Born: Ust'-Uda, Russia; March 15, 1937

OTHER LITERARY FORMS

Valentin Rasputin has written sparingly outside the short fiction genre. To be sure, some of his stories belong to what is called in Russian literature *povest'*, and there is a legitimate question whether they are long stories or short novels. They are considered abroad to be both. Because of Rasputin's strong allegiance to short fiction, they are treated here as short stories.

ACHIEVEMENTS

Valentin Rasputin belongs to the generation of Soviet writers that appeared in the mid-1960's, after Soviet literature had awakened from the nightmare of Socialist Realism. Along with Vasilit Belov, Fyodor Abramov, and others, Rasputin has written almost exclusively about village life. He has raised the village prose to a higher artistic level. He is also one of few to write about Siberia. Above all, his ability to present seemingly mundane events in a high artistic fashion and to create fine characters has made him a prominent writer in contemporary Russian literature.

BIOGRAPHY

Valentin Rasputin was born on March 15, 1937, in central Siberia, in Ust'-Uda, a small village on the Angara River, halfway between Irkutsk and Bratsk. His parents were peasants. During much of his childhood, most of which fell during and shortly after World War II, his father was away at war. After finishing elementary and high school, Rasputin enrolled at Irkutsk University to be a teacher. Before he was graduated in 1959, he started working as a journalist for the local newspaper and continued to work in that capacity after moving to Krasnoyarsk.

Rasputin published his first story, "Ia zabyl sprosit' u Lioshki" ("I Forgot to Ask Lyoshka"), in 1961, and his first novella, *Krai vozle samogo neba* (the land next to the very sky), in 1966. Between those two years, he traveled as a newspaper correspondent, covering a wide area and meeting many interesting people. These experiences served him well as sources for his stories. In 1968, he published another book as well as his first longer story, *Money for Maria*, venturing into the novella—a genre that would become his main mode of expression. The same year he was admitted to the Union of Soviet Writers, usually a sign that a writer "has arrived." Three more novellas followed in the next ten years–*Borrowed Time, Live and Remember*, and *Farewell to Matyora*—along with a number of short stories. In 1977, he received the State Prize for Literature in recognition of his contribution to Russian literature.

A serious accident in 1980 sidelined him for a while. He was mugged on a street in Irkutsk by four men demanding his jeans, and he underwent two operations in Moscow, having suffered a temporary loss of memory. After recuperation, he continued to publish, but at a slower pace. An introspective story, "Chto peredat' vorone?" ("What Shall I Tell the Crow?"), along with several other stories and a book, *You Live and Love, and Other Stories*, were published in the early 1980's. A later novella, *Pozhar*, was published in 1985.

Rasputin is a private man, reluctant to speak about himself. For that reason, not much is known about his private life. The best sources for his biography are his stories, especially those about his childhood. He continues to live in Irkutsk, spending his summers in his *dacha* on Lake Baikal.

Valentin Rasputin (AP/Wide World Photos)

ANALYSIS

All Valentin Rasputin's stories take place in the area around Irkutsk and Lake Baikal in south-central Siberia. All of them are about village life or life in a small town. Most of his characters are peasants or people who have just moved into towns from villages. Almost all the events depicted are of post-World War II vintage, with sporadic flashbacks to the prewar time.

Rasputin's creativity can be divided into two distinct periods: the first period, from the mid-1960's to the mid-1970's, and the second one beginning with the 1980's. The pause in his writing was caused by the serious injury to his head that he suffered in March of 1980. Apparently, the period of recuperation gave him time to take stock of his career up to that point; as a result, the stories that followed are somewhat different from those written before.

Rasputin's first stories show characteristics typical of a novice: unassuming subject matter; no stand on issues; somewhat two-dimensional characters, without psychological probing; and a straightforward realistic, almost journalistic, style. As his writing ability progressed, his stories gained in significance.

In the first noteworthy story, "Vasilii i Vasilisa" ("Vasily and Vasilisa"), Rasputin is already more interested in the psychological makeup of his characters, while the depiction of village life is used primarily as a frame. Vasily and Vasilisa, husband and wife, at first pass for common villagers coping with daily life and beset with postwar woes and shortages. When Vasily takes another woman for a wife because Vasilisa has refused to live with him, she displays typical signs of jealousy and resentment, and she fights the intruder. Yet when the new woman reveals to Vasilisa her own problems and heartaches, Vasilisa shows remarkable understanding and even willingness to help. Thus, a simple woman seemingly incapable of rising above the common meanness does exactly the opposite. She is the first of a number of remarkable women characters Rasputin has created.

"FRENCH LESSONS"

Another early story, "Uroki francuzskogo" ("French Lessons"), shows Rasputin's further progress as a writer. On the surface, it is a charming autobiographical story about Rasputin's difficult childhood and school days, when he had to play games for money to buy food and avert starvation. His young French teacher attempts to help him by inviting him to eat with her, but he refuses out of dignity. She then makes him play games with her for money and pretends to lose, losing her job in the process. Instead of a simple childhood story, "French Lessons" becomes a story of coming of age and of learning—in inconspicuous fashion—the value of human kindness.

MONEY FOR MARIA

Rasputin achieved great success with his first novella, *Money for Maria*. Not only does the plot reveal his growing preoccupation with social problems besetting the Russian peasants, but also his characters are fully credible human beings, not puppets. When Maria—another remarkable female character—faces a deficit in the shop that she manages and is forced either to repay a thousand rubles or to go to jail, the calamity gives her husband, Kuzma, a chance to show his true character. It also gives the villagers a chance to reveal what they are made of. Kuzma goes around asking for loans with varied success but eventually collects the money. What is important here is the characters' adherence to family life and the sense of solidarity among the villagers, which make up for the state's shortcomings or fate's cruel indifference. As one of the helpers says, "A person's got to have a conscience. We've got to help each other without thinking of ourselves. . . . Another time you'd do as much for me. A person's got to be decent to his neighbors if he wants to win their esteem." This statement, though potentially maudlin, rings true, coming from Rasputin's skillfully executed characters. Criticism of the state's allowing such sorry situations is muted because the characters regard the state as an unimportant agent, emphasizing their own interrelationships.

BORROWED TIME *and* LIVE AND REMEMBER

The second novella, *Borrowed Time*, features another strong female character, Anna, in her last hours. Before she dies, she witnesses the meanness of her children, who have been summoned to her deathbed. Instead of comforting her, they argue about who has done more for her, until Anna realizes that she and her children belong to different worlds and that her world is that of the past and will never return.

Rasputin shows his growth by tackling some of the most difficult problems of Russian society—or of any society, for that matter. He bemoans the loss of family values and the tearing up of society's fabric, as illustrated by the conflict not only between the past (Anna) and the present (children) but also among the children themselves. He also dwells on the different roles of men and women—a recurrent theme in his stories. Rasputin considers *Borrowed Time* to be his best story, out of which many others emanate. Undoubtedly, the changes in the social and moral life of his people have become his prime concern by now.

Rasputin is also interested in his characters' reaction to various difficult situations. In *Live and Remember*, he makes the plight of his simple villagers universal, as a loving wife, Nastena, is compelled to hide her husband, who had deserted the army in the last days of war. When she becomes pregnant, she is faced with the dilemma of whether to reveal her husband's whereabouts or to admit publicly her infidelity to him; either way, she will suffer indignities. She drowns herself rather than face the grim reality. Rasputin posits here a host of moral questions, each one worthy of a Greek tragedy. Once again, he sidesteps the criticism of the society (after all, the husband's desertion had mitigating circumstances) for the sake of concentrating on fundamental human problems.

FAREWELL TO MATYORA

Farewell to Matyora turns to more mundane matters, although human concern is still the focus of Rasputin's attention. Matyora is a village, located on a river island; the village is slated for destruction so that a dam can be built. Daria, the protagonist, leads a number of her villagers opposed to the destruction, without understanding the need and rationale for it. The conflict between the past and the future, played out in the present, becomes the focal point of the story. Rasputin seems to side with Daria in describing the callous burning of the village by outsiders before the flooding, symbolizing the intrusion of outside forces that do not understand the bond with nature that the villagers have enjoyed all of their lives. At the end, Daria and her supporters are defeated; they stay behind until the last moment, and, because a thick fog descends upon the island, it is not clear whether they got out or drowned. This is Rasputin's favorite device—not providing the story with a clear ending, leaving it up to readers to draw their own conclusions. Another ambiguity lies in the fact that the end of Matyora signifies the end of the life that Daria and people like her used to live, while for the younger generation, it is the beginning of a new, seemingly better life. The author does not intrude upon the reader's judgment, although his sympathies lie clearly with those who want to preserve their values and their bond with nature.

The second period in Rasputin's creativity, which began in the early 1980's, has yielded fewer stories. After his head injury, he became more introspective, as evidenced in several stories that he published in 1981. "Chto peredat' vorone" ("What Shall I Tell the Crow?"), "Natasha," and "Vek zhivi—vek liubi" ("You Live and Love") all show visible changes in Rasputin's approach to literature. He began mixing reality and the dream world with abandon. While he has always used dreams as a device, this time it is more of an experience of "losing oneself in oneself" and "non-being in oneself," for which processes dreams are a suitable vehicle. Earlier features can still be found, as Teresa Polowy rightly states: the altered states of consciousness and unconsciousness, the communion between human beings and nature, guilt and responsibility, and the preservation of values that are in danger of extinction. In the new stories, Rasputin stresses individuals, their emotional and mental processes, and their moral responsibilities that extend to their society. "Natasha," in particular, signals the change in Rasputin toward the inner world of his characters (all of these stories are told in the first person) as he describes the protagonist's stay in the hospital, drifting from consciousness into a dream world.

Rasputin's later novella, *Pozhar*, goes back to his previous preoccupation with social issues. The novella resembles *Farewell to Matyora* in that it depicts the same clash between the old and the new, between nature and progress, and between the individual and society. New factors here include a stronger, almost strident voice of the author, protesting the blind advance of technological progress at the expense of everything else, and a male character who carries the struggle for the preservation of old values, instead of a woman, as in many of his previous stories. The message and the commitment, however, are the same.

OTHER MAJOR WORKS

NONFICTION: *Zemlia rodiny*, 1984; *Essays*, 1988; *Sibir, Sibir*, 1991 (*Siberia, Siberia*, 1996).

MISCELLANEOUS: *Sobranie sochinenii v trekh tomakh*, 1994 (3 volumes).

BIBLIOGRAPHY

Bagby, Lewis. "A Concurrence of Psychological and Narrative Structures: Anamnesis in Valentin Rasputin's 'Upstream, Downstream.'" *Canadian Slavonic Papers* 22 (1980): 388-399. Through the analysis of *Borrowed Time, Money for Maria* and "Upstream, Downstream," Bagby discusses Rasputin's fascination with death, his retrospective themes and anamnestic personality, and his adherence to memory as a constructive principle.

Brown, Deming. "Valentin Rasputin: A General View." In *Russian Literature and Criticism*. Berkeley, Calif.: Berkeley Slavic Specialties, 1982. In his general essay, Brown concentrates on the settings and the treatment of nature in Rasputin's stories.

Gillespie, David C. "Childhood and the Adult World in the Writing of Valentin Rasputin." *The Modern Language Review* 80 (1985): 387-395. Gillespie treats Rasputin's depiction of children and their relationship to the adult world as one of the basic themes in his works.

_____. *Valentin Rasputin and Soviet Russian Village Prose*. London: Modern Humanities Research Association, 1986. In this relatively brief study, Gillespie focuses on Rasputin's treatment of rural life and how it relates to Soviet society in general.

Mikkelson, Gerald. "Religious Symbolism in Valentin Rasputin's Tale *Live and Remember*." In *Studies in Honor of Xenia Gasiorowska*, edited by L. G. Leighton. Columbus, Ohio: Slavica, 1983.

An attempt to understand the situations, events, and characters in *Live and Remember* through the novella's symbolic structure as a modern-day Christian parable and Nastena as a suffering saint and martyr.

Porter, R. C. *Four Contemporary Russian Writers*. New York: St. Martin's Press, 1989. Examines the works of Rasputin, Chingiz Aitmatov, Vladimir Voinovich, and Georgii Vladimov.

Polowy, Teresa. *The Novellas of Valentin Rasputin: Genre, Language, and Style*. New York: Peter Lang, 1989. The most serious treatment of the works of Rasputin. Polowy covers, in a scholarly fashion, his themes, characterization, and the formal aspects, such as plot and structure. The matters of language and style are discussed at length. A select bibliography is appended. An excellent introduction to Rasputin.

Rich, Elizabeth. "Fate?" *Soviet Literature*, no. 3 (1987): 149-168. Rich examines Rasputin's treatment of women characters, their attitude toward self-sacrifice, and Rasputin's views on this moral question.

Vasa D. Mihailovich

ELWOOD REID

Born: Cleveland, Ohio; 1966 or 1967

PRINCIPAL SHORT FICTION
What Salmon Know, 1999

OTHER LITERARY FORMS

Elwood Reid's 1998 first novel, *If I Don't Six*, won critical acclaim with its roughly autobiographical tale of a university football player's ultimate rejection of the culture of violence and abuse surrounding the game. His second novel, *Midnight Sun*, was published in 2000.

ACHIEVEMENTS

Elwood Reid has been hailed as a major new voice, telling stories of the world of blue-collar men. Delighted critics have compared his short stories to those of Raymond Carver.

BIOGRAPHY

Brian Elwood Reid grew up in suburban Cleveland, Ohio. His father Thomas Reid was a teacher and coach in Willoughby, Ohio, where his mother, Charlotte Reid, née Ellwood, worked as a principal's secretary. The oldest of three children, Reid earned a full four-year athletic scholarship to play football at the University of Michigan after he graduated from high school in the mid-1980's.

After two years as an offensive lineman on the team, during which he never played in a varsity game, Reid ruptured several discs in his spine, ending his athletic career. For the next ten years, Reid, who dropped his first name Brian in favor of his middle name Elwood, to signal a shift in character, stayed generally around the campus at Ann Arbor, Michigan. Continuing his education while working a variety of odd jobs, including stints as a bouncer, a carpenter, and a writing instructor, Reid earned a bachelor of arts degree in general studies and then a master of fine arts from the University of Michigan.

In 1996, he submitted a first version of his short story "What Salmon Know" to the annual fiction contest of *Gentleman's Quarterly* magazine. He did not win but placed among the final five, and *Gentleman's Quarterly* published his story in its February, 1997, issue. Contacts with an agent led Reid to write and publish his first, semi-autobiographical novel *If I Don't Six*. After marriage to fellow writer Nina Reid and the birth of their daughter Sophia, Reid moved to Obernburg, New York, in 1997.

Elwood Reid (©Miriam Berkley)

ANALYSIS

Elwood Reid's first collection of short stories seeks to give a literary voice to characters who generally would not be expected to write about their experiences themselves. They are almost all blue-collar men who battle the hardships imposed by physically demanding yet financially unsatisfactory jobs, precarious love lives, and varying degrees of alcohol abuse. Many of the narratives read like the stories one would expect to hear talking to one of these men in a bar or beside a fish-rich river.

Critics have compared Reid to Raymond Carver and detected emotional and stylistic similarities between Carver's and Reid's protagonists. Like Carver, Reid strives hard to create for his characters genuine voices and to make them react realistically to experiences and circumstances that could be those of a frustrated working-class man.

Pain and suffering, whether emotional or physical, abound in Reid's fictional universe. Most of his narrators, and their friends and enemies, have been hit hard by life. There are also adult men who have become mentally disabled as a result of car accidents, and their fate could be read as a symbolic reminder of the harshness with which contemporary society treats working-class men.

As an author, Reid has worked hard to establish his blue-collar credentials. His characters exemplify some of the roughness existing in working-class life, yet the reader may be reminded of Jack Nicholson's character Bobby Dupea in Bob Rafaelson's movie, *Five Easy Pieces* (1970). Bobby tried hard to eradicate his past as a concert pianist by becoming an oil-rig worker, yet he never lost the sense of being an outside observer of his new world. Occasionally, the reader may feel that such a slight but real distance exists between Elwood Reid and some of his most successfully drawn characters.

"WHAT SALMON KNOW"

The tale of two rough, drunken carpenters fishing salmon in Alaska is Reid's first published story and a powerful reflection on humanity's relationship with nature. In "What Salmon Know," Craig and Marley, coworkers in the cold wilderness of Alaska, face a crisis in their friendship when Craig, the narrator, ponders an offer to work on "a new fruit-juice plant in Hawaii." The hardened Marley scoffs at Craig for even considering a "soft" life. The choice between Alaska and Hawaii, however, becomes almost too simplistic a dramatic device to illustrate two extremes.

Marley is a character who perceives of life as a series of self-set challenges and appears to be a vulgarized version of an Ernest Hemingway character. When he and Craig start fishing, he loses expensive equipment to the harsh river and yet is satisfied to land fish after fish, demonstrating that money itself has no value to him. Yet Marley and Craig experience a certain fall from grace when, in their haste to make it back to the beer and the warmth of a nearby bar, they fail to kill the salmon. Instead, they carry the live fish on a string over their back as they walk to the bar.

In a typically graphic scene, the dying salmon spawn sperm and eggs onto the backs of the men. Astonished, they react with humor but Craig realizes that they have somehow violated an unwritten code of conduct.

Cleaning the fish outside the bar, they are approached by two soldiers. One soldier, who has caught a large salmon, cuts two fillets out of the live fish before releasing it to die in the water. This callous conduct enrages Marley to the point that he assaults the uncomprehending soldiers. As Craig says, the salmon will not die until they have spawned, and even the mortally wounded, mutilated, and profusely bleeding fish attempts to do exactly this. The salmon's single-minded purposefulness, to swim, spawn, and die, is what Craig admires in them. The salmon live and act like Craig and Marley would want to, guided by an absolute knowledge of their purpose in life.

"OVERTIME"

A well constructed story with a clear moral message, "Overtime" focuses on the ethical choices made by its protagonist Drew, literally a man in the middle. After graduating from college, Drew accepts a job as a production manager who must ensure a steady output of product for the factory owner, Big Joe. While Big Joe enjoys his life in Puerto Rico, Drew must ask unwilling workers to work overtime operating the plant's metal presses. Somewhat of a moral coward, Drew picks the easiest target, Frank Cooper, whose "good blue-collar work ethic" makes him unable to say no to a request which puts the needs of the factory above those of his family. As Drew learns the next day, Frank's daughter has been murdered because Frank was working and unable to pick her up after her volleyball game. It is this pivotal plot detail that tells the reader of the high price Drew has paid by accepting this job. The workers blame Drew, and he accepts their verdict, even though his wife tells him the murder was just a coincidence. Out of guilt, Drew stops enforcing production quotas, gets fired, starts drinking, and is left by his upset wife. The story ends with Drew in a bar, punishing himself for his moral shortcomings.

"LAURA BOREALIS"

If many of Reid's short stories are tightly constructed and offer their readers a moral, "Laura Borealis" falls into a second category of stories which end like a snapshot taken at a moment of hilarious surprise. Jim, the narrator and protagonist, is an underemployed carpenter in Alaska. One afternoon at a lo-

cal bar, he meets the beautiful Linda, who seems to appear out of nowhere. When his friend Sammy Landewski tells him of a rich Texan looking to remodel a decrepit lodge and Linda fails to return from the bathroom, Jim leaves for the lodge to try to secure employment. James Jaspers, the new owner, is a buffoonish rich man, somewhat typical of the wealthy characters in Reid's stories. Recently divorced, Jaspers wants to enjoy himself and install an outside hot tub. The fact that he shares a first name with the narrator is a storytelling detail which highlights the idea that it is only money, not morals, that distinguishes rich James from poor Jim. Together with his fellow carpenter and rival Marv Stacks, Jim begins work and is asked to come back the next day.

Indicative of the subtlety with which Reid constructs clues for his plot, there is a fictional newspaper report of Japanese tourists, who "considered it good luck to consummate a marriage under the northern lights," sitting in a Jacuzzi in Alaska. When Jaspers hires some exotic dancers for a pool party, Linda reappears under the stage name Laura Borealis, "aurora borealis" being the Latin name for the northern lights. While Jaspers passes out from drink, Jim and Linda/Laura hit it off in the tub. This lasts until Marv's smelly dog jumps in, whereupon the bouncer accompanying the women points a gun at Jim, telling Jaspers, "It's your move." Rather than being terrified, Jim feels happy in that absurd situation with Linda, and the story suddenly ends. Reid's keen eye for the occasional absurdity of life is caught nicely here, and the story provides a comical counterpart to his more graphic fiction.

"BUFFALO"

"Buffalo" features many familiar elements of Reid's short fiction. Dan, the narrator, is a carpenter fighting alcoholism and relishing his friendship with his fishing buddy Murphy. Murphy has been left by his former wife Katrina and works in a factory demanding so much overtime of him that Murphy has to ask Dan to take his adult son Jeff to the town's "Frontier Days" to see the buffalo. Like a character in another story in *What Salmon Know*, Jeff has been mentally disabled ever since he got drunk, hit a patch of black ice on the road, and skidded his car into a telephone pole. At the fair, Dan becomes distracted while drinking beer with a friendly woman, and Jeff enters the buffalo pen. As Jeff is burying his face in the smelly fur of a buffalo, Dan wonders whether Jeff's disability has saved him from a worse life. For Reid, working-class life is hard on the men who live it, and their moments of happiness or satisfaction appear to be few and far between. What distinguishes the best of his short fiction is an often tightly constructed view of a harsh life of danger and violence, in which the wealthy do not show any concern for those less fortunate.

OTHER MAJOR WORKS

LONG FICTION: *If I Don't Six*, 1998; *Midnight Sun*, 2000.

BIBLIOGRAPHY

Reid, Elwood. "My Body, My Weapon, My Shame." *Gentleman's Quarterly* 67 (September, 1997): 360-367. Reid tells of the brutality he encountered as college football player for the University of Michigan and how his injury forced him to rethink his life. Written for the magazine that in February, 1997, published his first short story "What Salmon Knew" and for which Reid has continued to write short stories and nonfiction articles, this piece offers a valuable background on the life of the author. The reader realizes that Reid has worked in many of the same jobs as his characters. Reid adds that his manual labor was motivated by his desire to extinguish the image of himself as a failed athlete and that he considered himself an oddity of a football player because he loved to read literature.

Rubin, Neal. "Harsh Portrait of Schembechler Is Latest Move in Former U-M Lineman's Literary Career." *Detroit Free Press* (September 26, 1999). Extensive biographical portrait of Reid by a reporter on the occasion of Reid's negative article about his former coach in the September, 1997, issue of *Gentleman's Quarterly*. Talks about Reid's life, his sports career, and his emergence as a writer of short fiction and novels. Informative background on the author; shows how closely Reid is to the subject matter of his stories and how much emphasis he places on rewriting his work until it satisfies him.

Rungren, Lawrence. "*What Salmon Know*." Review of *What Salmon Know*, by Elwood Reid. *Library Journal* 124 (July, 1999): 139. Brief review of Reid's first short-story collection, generally positive in tone. Provides one-sentence summaries of some of the stories and likens Reid to authors Raymond Carver and Thom Jones. Recommends his fiction to public libraries for acquisition.

Smothers, Bonnie. "What Salmon Know." Review of *What Salmon Know*, by Elwood Reid. *Booklist* 95 (July, 1999): p. 1924. Very brief positive review of Reid's short fiction which focuses on its male-oriented themes and Reid's good description of the plight of working-class males. Discusses the collection's title story as representative of Reid's powerful and graphic writing style.

R. C. Lutz

JEAN RHYS

Ella Gwendolen Rees Williams

Born: Roseau, Dominica Island, West Indies; August
  24, 1894
Died: Exeter, England; May 14, 1979

PRINCIPAL SHORT FICTION

The Left Bank and Other Stories, 1927
Tigers Are Better-Looking, 1968
Sleep It Off, Lady, 1976
The Collected Short Stories, 1987

OTHER LITERARY FORMS

Jean Rhys wrote five novels: *Postures* (1928),
which was published in the United States in 1929 under the title *Quartet; After Leaving Mr. Mackenzie*
(1929); *Voyage in the Dark* (1934); *Good Morning,
Midnight* (1939), which was dramatized for radio by
the British Broadcasting Corporation (BBC) in 1958;
and *Wide Sargasso Sea* (1966), which many consider
to be her masterpiece. She also wrote *Smile Please:
An Unfinished Autobiography* (1979). Her letters
were published in 1984.

ACHIEVEMENTS

During the first decade of her writing career, Jean
Rhys achieved only limited success. Although her
books were well received by critics, they attracted
only a small readership. After years of neglect, however, interest in her work increased dramatically following the publication of *Wide Sargasso Sea*. She
was elected a Fellow of the Royal Society of Literature; her novel won the W. H. Smith literary award
and the Award for Writers from the Arts Council of
Great Britain. Throughout the 1970's, her reputation
grew, and she holds a secure place in the first rank of
twentieth century novelists. Her work is notable for
its unsparing exploration of a particular character
type: the dispossessed, dependent, exploited single
woman, struggling to survive in a society in which
she has no roots, no money, no power, and often, no
hope.

BIOGRAPHY

Jean Rhys was born Ella Gwendolen Rees Williams on August 24, 1894, in Roseau, Dominica Island, in the West Indies. Her father was a Welsh doctor, and her mother a white Creole (a native West
Indian of European ancestry). In 1910, she was sent
to England to live with an aunt in Cambridge, and she
later studied acting at the Royal Academy of Dramatic Art. When her father died, she was forced to
make her living as a chorus girl in touring musical
companies. In 1919, she married a French-Dutch poet
and journalist and went to live on the Continent,
where the couple led a bohemian life. The marriage
ended in divorce in 1927. In 1938, she married again
and settled in Cornwall, England. Following her second husband's death in 1945, she married for the
third time in 1946. Her literary career flourished
moderately in the late 1920's and 1930's, but she disappeared entirely from the literary scene during
World War II and did not reappear until 1958, when
the BBC adapted *Good Morning, Midnight* for radio.
Encouraged by the new interest in her work, she began writing again, and her reputation was still growing at her death in 1979, at the age of eighty-four.

ANALYSIS

The range of Jean Rhys's stories, as of her novels,
is narrow. She focuses on the world of the lonely, the
outcast, the vulnerable. Her central characters are all
women who live in a world they cannot control,
which regards them with indifference and cruelty.
Communication is often found to be impossible, and
the protagonists' fragmented, tormented world is perpetually on the verge of falling apart. The dominant
note is of isolation, dependency, and loss, with more
than a smattering of self-pity.

THE LEFT BANK AND OTHER STORIES

Rhys's first collection, *The Left Bank and Other
Stories*, consists of twenty-two stories, most of them
short sketches, of life on the Parisian Left Bank. A
few stories, "In the Rue de l'Arrivée," "A Night," and

"Learning to Be a Mother," end on an optimistic note, as does "Mannequin," in which a young girl, at the end of her first day as a mannequin, feels a surge of happiness as she steps into the street and merges into the vibrant life of the city. She is one of the few heroines in Rhys's fiction who discover a sense of belonging. The dominant mood of the collection, however, is one of helplessness and troubled uncertainty, and as such it sets the tone for Rhys's later work. The stories focus on characters who inhabit the fringes of society: artists, exiles, misfits, deprived women. "Hunger," for example, is a despairing, first-person monologue of an English woman who is down and out in Paris. She takes the reader, day by day, through her experience of five days without food.

"LA GROSSE FIFI"

"La Grosse Fifi" is a more ambitious story, one of a group at the end of the collection which is set outside Paris—in this case, on the French Riviera. Fifi is a huge, vulgar woman who keeps a gigolo half her age in a sleazy hotel. The other main character is a young woman named Roseau. The name, she explains, means reed, and her motto in life is "a reed shaken by the wind" (a motto which might adequately describe virtually all Rhys's helpless and vulnerable heroines). Roseau can survive, she says, only as long as she does not think. Unhappy and lonely, without home, friends, or money, she is comforted one night by Fifi, who reveals herself to be infinitely kind and understanding. Fifi knows the foolishness of her own situation, yet she genuinely loves her man, however irregular and unhappy the relationship appears. When her lover abruptly leaves her, she faces the hostile world with dignity, still attracting men and still cheerfully defying the darker elements in her life. Roseau feels protected by her presence, which is so full of life that she cannot help but feel gladdened by it. The story reaches a climax when Roseau learns that Fifi has been stabbed to death in a quarrel with her lover.

Fifi's almost tragic grandeur serves as a measure of Roseau's inadequacy. She knows that she can never love with such full abandon or live so wholeheartedly. She decides to leave the hotel, and the story ends with her packing (a typical activity for the rootless Rhys heroine) while the yellow sunshine—yellow always carries negative connotations for Rhys—streams through the window.

"THE LOTUS"

Rhys wrote no more short stories until the early 1960's, and then eight of them were published in *Tigers Are Better-Looking*. These stories are longer, more complex, and the characters more fully realized than those in *The Left Bank and Other Stories*, but Rhys's vision has become even more bleak and despairing. "The Lotus," told with a taut economy and a ruthless fidelity to what Rhys saw as reality, is one of the bleakest. Lotus Heath is an eccentric middle-aged poet and novelist. Ronnie Miles invites her for drinks one evening, since they live in the same apartment building. His wife Christine dislikes Lotus, however, and her frequent cruel insults sabotage Ronnie's attempts to be polite and sociable. When Ronnie helps Lotus down to her own small, ill-smelling apartment, her cheerful guise suddenly drops and she reveals her own despair and frustration. Later, Ronnie sees Lotus running naked and drunk (she is one of many Rhys heroines who drink too much) down the street, soon to be escorted away by two policemen. When one of the policemen inquires at the Miles's apartment about Lotus, Ronnie denies that he knows much about her, and no one else in the building will admit to knowing her either. An ambulance takes her to the hospital. Christine, who found her own insults highly amusing, ignores the whole affair, lying in bed smiling, as if Lotus's eclipse has somehow made her own star rise. The story ends when Ronnie, his kindness revealed as shallow and ineffectual, begins to make love to Christine—cruelty has its reward, and compassion is snuffed out without a trace. Nor can there be any escape or consolation through art, which is represented, however inadequately, by Lotus and mocked by Christine. In this story, the only arts which flourish are popular songs preserved on secondhand gramophone records.

"TILL SEPTEMBER PETRONELLA"

The best-known story in the collection is probably "Till September Petronella." It opens with the heroine and narrator, Petronella Grey, performing a typical action—packing. She dislikes London, with its gray days, and heartless people, a recurring theme in Rhys's fiction. Typically also, Petronella has no money and has cut herself off from her family. She admits to herself that she has never lived in a place that she liked, and the story chronicles the directionless drift of her life. She visits her boyfriend Marston in the country, and his guests Frankie and her lover Julian. During a lunch loosened by drink, they fall to pointless quarreling. Petronella decides to return to London, and Marston says that he will see her in September. The date of their parting is significant: July 28, 1914.

In London, she is befriended by an eager young man, Melville, and during their evening together she recalls that her career as a chorus girl failed because she could not remember the only line she had to speak. The incident keeps coming back to her; it is a parable of her life. She has lost her connections, the threads which bind her to the rest of life and society. She cannot fit smoothly into the flow of life. When Melville tells her that he, too, is going away until September, their lighthearted farewell does not disguise for the reader the dangerous period of loneliness which Petronella is about to enter. Not only does the story emphasize her dependence on men, who provide her with distractions but not fulfillment, but also it makes it clear that Petronella enters her private wasteland just as Europe begins to tear itself apart in World War I. Her aimlessness is somehow linked to a wider spread of chaos. There will be no September reunions.

Much of the story's power comes through Rhys's gift for subtle suggestion rather than overt statement. The reader is forced to penetrate beyond the apparently trivial nature of the dialogue, which makes up nine-tenths of the story, to the darkness which lies behind it and threatens to engulf it. When the story ends with Petronella sitting quietly, waiting for the city clock to strike, the moment has acquired an ominous quality, as if the striking clock will inaugurate some dreadful Day of Judgment which she, waiting passively, can do nothing to avert.

SLEEP IT OFF, LADY

Sleep It Off, Lady consists of sixteen stories. They are predominantly tales of regret and loss and fall into a rough chronological sequence which resembles the chronology of Rhys's own life. The first five take place in the West Indies at the beginning of the twentieth century. Two of these ("Pioneers, Oh, Pioneers," and "Fishy Waters") deal with the difficulties of white settlers in the West Indies, isolated in the land they were responsible for colonizing. A strongly autobiographical middle group centers on a young female protagonist who goes to school in Cambridge, England, trains as an actress, and becomes a member of the chorus in a touring company. Three stories toward the end of the collection ("Rapunzel, Rapunzel," "Who Knows What's Up in the Attic?" and "Sleep It Off, Lady") feature elderly female protagonists.

"SLEEP IT OFF, LADY"

There is probably no more quietly horrifying story in English literature than "Sleep It Off, Lady." Told with an unsentimental, almost clinical precision, it centers on an elderly heroine, Miss Verney, a spinster who lives in one of the poorer parts of the village, where she does not really belong. The central action consists of her attempts to rid herself of a dilapidated old shed which stands next to her cottage, but she cannot persuade any of the local tradesmen to pull it down. She feels increasingly helpless, and the shed begins to acquire a sinister power over her. She dreams of it as a coffin.

One day, she sees a rat in the shed, and the powerful rat poison which Tom, her neighbor, puts down seems to have no effect. The rat walks unhurriedly across the shed, as if he is in charge of everything (while she feels herself to be in charge of nothing). Tom suggests that the rat must be a pink one, the product of her excessive drinking. She feels trapped and misunderstood and retreats into a closed world of her own. She stops going for walks outside. Letters remain unanswered, and she rejects the good-neighborliness of Tom.

What makes the story so poignantly effective is that just before her inevitable demise she undergoes a form of rebirth. On her birthday, she awakes feeling refreshed, happy, and young again. It is a windless day, with a blue sky overhead. Poised between one year and the next, she feels ageless, and she makes plans to reach out to other people once more when her new telephone is installed. Yet her optimism is misplaced. Later in the day, as she struggles to move a garbage container back to the shed, she falls and loses consciousness. When she awakes it is nearly dark, and she is surrounded by the contents of the trash can, including broken egg shells (symbolizing the failure of her rebirth). When she calls to some passing women for help, the wind drowns out her cries. Even nature has turned against her. A local child named Deena finds her but refuses to help and makes it clear that Miss Verney is despised in her own neighborhood. The next morning, Miss Verney is discovered by the postman, who is carrying a parcel of books for her. The parcel—like the telephone, a symbol of communication with the outside world—comes too late. She dies that evening. Her individual will to live proves useless in the face of the hostility and indifference of her neighbors. Regarded as trash, she dies surrounded by trash. Her feeling of renewal was only the last and the cruellest trick that life was to play upon her.

"I USED TO LIVE HERE ONCE"

The last story in the collection, only one-and-a-half pages, serves as an appropriate epitaph for all of Rhys's stories. "I Used to Live Here Once" features an unnamed protagonist who in later life returns to her childhood home in the West Indies. She crosses a stream, using the stepping stones she still remembers well, and approaches her old house. In the garden, she sees a young boy and a girl under a mango tree and calls to them twice, but they do not answer. When she says hello for the third time, she reaches out, longing to touch them. The boy turns to her, looks her directly in the eye, and remarks how cold it has suddenly become, and he and the girl run back across the grass into the house. The story ends with the pregnant sentence "That was the first time she knew."

She knows that she cannot return to the freshness and vitality of her youth. She also knows that the coldness emanates from her, and therefore she must have frozen into a kind of living death. Yet beyond this, it is as if she knows everything that Rhys's stories have depicted, time after time: the pain of final separation, the loneliness of exile, the failure of people to connect with one another, the horrible realization of what life can become. Several critics have seen the woman as posthumously returning to the scenes of her childhood and achieving no emotional accommodation or reconciliation even after death. Jean Rhys's stories do not elevate the spirit but rather reveal the gradual strangulation of the life force. They do not make easy or comfortable reading. Rhys's merit lies in her quiet but devastating presentation of the hopeless and the forgotten. She looks on despair and futility with an unblinking eye; she does not flinch or sentimentalize, and she does not deceive.

OTHER MAJOR WORKS

LONG FICTION: *Postures*, 1928 (published in the United States as *Quartet*, 1929); *After Leaving Mr. Mackenzie*, 1930; *Voyage in the Dark*, 1934; *Good Morning, Midnight*, 1939; *Wide Sargasso Sea*, 1966.

NONFICTION: *Smile Please: An Unfinished Autobiography*, 1979; *The Letters of Jean Rhys*, 1984 (also known as *Jean Rhys: Letters, 1931-1966*).

BIBLIOGRAPHY

Angier, Carole. *Jean Rhys*. New York: Viking, 1985. A biography of Rhys that treats her fiction as essentially autobiographical. Far from being seen as a feminist, Rhys is presented as an intensely lonely individualist and solipsist without a program or external loyalties. Her lifelong attempt to understand herself was governed by a tragic and pessimistic view of human nature and the world.

_____. *Jean Rhys: Life and Work*. Boston: Little, Brown, 1990. This monumental work of Rhys scholarship combines detailed biographical study with sections devoted to interpretations of the fiction. Unfortunately, chapters specifically examining the short stories were deleted due to length considerations. The book contains voluminous notes and an extensive bibliography.

Davidson, Arnold E. *Jean Rhys*. New York: Frederick Ungar, 1985. Drawing heavily on a number of critical sources, Davidson supports a feminist interpretation of the texts and provides a useful approach to the major works, including the stories.

Emery, Mary Lou. "Refiguring the Postcolonial Imagination: Tropes of Visuality in Writing by

Rhys, Kincaid, and Cliff." *Tulsa Studies in Women's Literature* 16 (Fall, 1997): 259-280. Emery uses one of Rhys's novels to illustrate a dialectical relationship of the European means of visualization and image-making in postcolonial literatures. Discusses Rhys's use of the rhetorical device of ekphrasis, the use of language to create a spatial image.

James, Louis. *Jean Rhys*. London: Longman, 1978. Although concentrating on *Wide Sargasso Sea*, James provides a good short introduction to Rhys's life and work.

Kineke, Sheila. "'Like a Hook Fits an Eye': Jean Rhys, Ford Maddox Ford, and the Imperial Operations of Modernist Mentoring." *Tulsa Studies in Women's Literature* 16 (Fall, 1997): 281-301. Discusses how fatalism, submission, and masochism of Rhys's main female characters are a side effect of the female condition in white Western culture and specifically of the operation of male mentorship by Ford Madox Ford.

Lonsdale, Thorunn. "Literary Allusion in the Fiction of Jean Rhys." In *Caribbean Women Writers*, edited by Mary Condé and Thorunn Lonsdale. New York: St. Martin's Press, 1999. Discusses the many critically neglected, intertextual references to nineteenth and twentieth century European and American literature in her novels and short stories. Discusses such stories as "Again the Antilles" and "Let Them Call It Jazz."

Malcolm, Cheryl Alexander, and David Malcolm. *Jean Rhys: A Study of the Short Fiction*. New York: Twayne, 1996. This book makes up for what Angier's biography—and most critical assessments of Rhys—lacks. After a section devoted to their assessment of Rhys's short fiction, the Malcolms provide a chapter on Rhys's own views of herself—conveyed in excerpts from her letters and an interview—and conclude with a section that reprints a wide range of critical opinion about Rhys's fiction.

Morrell, A. C. "The World of Jean Rhys's Short Stories." *World Literature Written in English* 18 (1979): 235-244. Rhys's stories are seen as having a unity of vision achieved through the expression of a consistent center of consciousness and sensibility no matter what the narrative point of view. Critical analysis is provided and demonstrates that Rhys's stories can be categorized as either episodes or completed experiences.

Wolfe, Peter. *Jean Rhys*. Boston: Twayne, 1980. This book, part of a widely available critical series, contains errors in chronology, questionable judgments, and some oddly off-center writing. Rhys is viewed as a meliorist out to civilize and improve relations between the sexes. The long chapter on the short stories should, as with much of the rest of this book, be approached with caution.

Bryan Aubrey, updated by Douglas Rollins

MORDECAI RICHLER

Born: Montreal, Canada; January 27, 1931

PRINCIPAL SHORT FICTION

The Street: Stories, 1969

OTHER LITERARY FORMS

Although primarily a novelist, Mordecai Richler has written in many forms, including essays, articles, screenplays, journalism, television plays, and children's literature. Two of his novels, *Cocksure: A Novel* (1968) and *St. Urbain's Horseman* (1971), have won Canada's foremost literary prize, the Governor-General's Award. In 1997, he published the novel *Barney's Version*.

ACHIEVEMENTS

Mordecai Richler's achievements over the course of his writing career are considerable. He has been awarded both a John Simon Guggenheim Memorial Foundation Fellowship in creative writing and a Canada Council Senior Arts Fellowship. His literary awards include the President's Medal for Nonfiction from the University of Western Ontario (1959), a humor prize from the *Paris Review* (1967), two Governor-General's Awards for Fiction (1969 and 1972), the *London Jewish Chronicle* literature award (1972), a Book of the Year for Children Award from the Canadian Library Association and a Ruth Schwartz Children's Book Award (both 1976), an H. H. Wingate award for fiction from the *London Jewish Chronicle* (1981), a Commonwealth Writers Prize (1990), the Giller Prize (1997), a Hugh MacLanna Prize, and the Stephen Leacock Prize (both 1998). The screenplay based on his novel *The Apprenticeship of Duddy Kravitz* (1959) earned him a Screenwriters Guild of America Award in 1974; the film itself garnered a Golden Bear Award at the Berlin Film Festival in 1974.

After his return to Canada in 1972, after twenty years in England and continental Europe, his journalistic writing on Canada, widely published both in Canada and in the United States, has chronicled his crotchety love and growing sadness for the fate of Canada, his home and native land. His subjective, often savagely funny and derisive depictions of Canadian political and cultural life have made Americans in particular aware of a Canada they had never known or contemplated: his adroit skewering of Canadian pretensions has both entertained and enraged his Canadian readers. His later essays, which appear regularly in major American and Canadian periodicals, have concentrated with increasing vitriol on Quebec's nationalist aspirations.

Perhaps his major achievement has been the group of fictional works that explores so thoroughly and captures so vividly the lives and fractious spirit of Jewish-Canadian immigrants in a Montreal community now largely dispersed. As Richler has said, "That was my time and my place, and I have elected myself to get it exactly right."

BIOGRAPHY

Mordecai Richler was born on January 27, 1931, in the Jewish ghetto of east Montreal. His parents Moses and Lily made sure their son received a solid Jewish education first at United Talmud Torah and then at Baron Byng High School in Montreal. He attended Sir George Williams University from 1949 to 1951 but left school to work as a writer in London, England, and later worked briefly as a news editor for the Canadian Broadcasting Company. For almost twenty years he resided in London, publishing much of his work there. In 1972, Richler returned to Montreal, where he settled with his wife and children. For ten years Richler was a member of the editorial board of the Book-of-the-Month Club. After his return to Canada, he published works whose spiritual center is still Montreal, though their scope is broader. Otherwise, his writing has been devoted to essays, articles, and reviews; many of these—funny, biting, and wearily resigned—have been collected in his book *Broadsides* (1990). He and his wife Florence settled in a house on Lake Memphramagog, outside Montreal.

ANALYSIS

George Woodcock says of Mordecai Richler, "The worlds he creates are not autonomous entities remade each time. Rather, they belong to a fictional continuum that perpetually overlaps the world in which Richler himself lives and feels, thinks and writes." The reader receives a distinct impression of the primacy of memory over imagination in Richler's work. Most of his stories and novels deal with the characters and situations of the Montreal ghetto of his early years; the stories in his collection *The Street* and the scenes of many of the novels examine with compassion and realism the lives of Canadian and immigrant Jews in this restricted and variegated environment. Most of the author's work functions within this frame of reference, with only an occasional change of focus. A peripheral character in one story comes under more thorough scrutiny in another. Often a new character will be introduced to interact with the established ones. The reader is given a continuity of the values and traditions of the old world as they evolve in the setting of their new Canadian world. There seems to be, then, no clear distinction between the fictional and the autobiographical elements of Richler's narrative. In fact, *The Street*, his only episodic collection that can be considered to comprise stories, has been more accurately described as "a lightly fictionalized memoir."

The importance of Richler's work, consequently, is the analysis of age-old human problems found in familiar situations. He sees things with little sentimentality; life is filled with illusions, poverty, despair, and selfishness. Richler reacts positively in spite of these negative aspects, despite showing how limiting they are. This view is emphasized by a keen sense of the ridiculous which sharpens our perceptions and evaluations. Absurd as his characters sometimes are, however, Richler still has a tender attitude toward them. Despite their moral and social blindness, they are human beings, desperately trying to control their own lives, and the author wants the reader to understand them rather than love them. Although their environment is a Jewish neighborhood with its own laws, legends, and language, these characters speak to all readers; in fact, they become even

Mordecai Richler (Christopher Morris)

more authentic by belonging to a particular social setting. The external circumstances only show more clearly that their reactions are human and universal.

"THE SUMMER MY GRANDMOTHER WAS SUPPOSED TO DIE"

The story "The Summer My Grandmother Was Supposed to Die" is perhaps Richler's best. Here the author forces the reader to confront lingering death and its implications for a family. The story is graphically realistic. Since life must go on, even in tragedy, the reader is shown the absurd black comedy of ordinary existence. As are all the stories in *The Street*, this one is in the format of a recollection by old Malka's grandson, Jake Hersh. Dr. Katzman discovers that Malka has gangrene, and he says she will not last a month; he says the same thing the second, third, and fourth months. She remains bedridden for seven years; hers is a common story of the courageous person with an incredible will to live. The grotesque nature of the situation is dramatized very quickly when Jake says, "When we sat down to eat we could smell her." While Mr. and Mrs. Hersh wait for her to die, saying it will be for the best, the neighborhood children wait to peek up the nurse's dress. The grotesque and the ridiculous are simply integral parts of life—and death.

Malka, the widow of Zaddik, one of the Righteous, is described as beautiful, patient, shrewd, and resourceful. When she was married to Zaddik, these qualities were necessary since he often gave his money away to rabbinical students, immigrants, and widows. As Jake says, this "made him as unreliable a provider as a drinker." Their sons are prominent men, a rabbi, a lawyer, and an actor, but it is left to Jake's mother to take care of Malka. No one, it seems, wants the old woman despite all that she has done for them; she becomes an inconvenience, "a condition in the house, something beyond hope or reproach, like a leaky ice-box." Jake can no longer kiss her without a feeling of revulsion, and he wonders if she knows that he covets her room. The shock of the tragic illness over a period of time gives way to resignation. Malka becomes only a presence, no longer recognizable as a human being. Instead of love being engendered by the grandmother's plight, there is resentment.

After the fourth year of her illness the strain begins to show. Mrs. Hersh is openly scornful of her husband and finds fault with her two children; she also takes to falling asleep directly after supper. Hersh seeks escape more often to Tansky's Cigar & Soda, and people tell him that he might as well be a bachelor. Malka's children finally take her, against her will, to the Jewish Old People's Home. With the reminder of death gone from the home, family relationships improve. Mrs. Hersh no longer needs the comfort of her bed, her cheeks glow with health, and she even jokes with her children. Mr. Hersh begins to come home early, no longer finding it necessary to go to Tansky's. Malka is seldom mentioned.

When Jake asks if he can move back to his room, however, his mother's caring instinct returns, and she decides to bring Malka home. The cycle of despair starts again, and the family returns to their habits of escape. Mr. Hersh says, "I knew it, I was born with all the luck." For two more years there is no change in Malka's condition; she seems to gain her strength at the expense of the family. The tension is almost unbearable for the Hershes. The fatigue and morbidity are most noticeable in Mrs. Hersh, but they are also evident in each member of the household.

Finally, in the seventh summer, Malka dies. When Jake returns home from a baseball game, he is not allowed to see her; he is only told what he and his sister will receive from their grandmother's belongings. When Jake's sister Rifka tells him that he can now have Malka's room, he changes his mind, saying "I couldn't sleep in there now." Rifka, sensing his discomfort, approaches his bed with a sheet over her head to frighten him. When all the family members gather together, cousin Jerry is skeptical of their reactions, claiming that now everyone will be sickeningly sentimental. Mr. and Mrs. Hersh, however, are openly scornful of these relatives, especially the rabbi, who did very little to comfort Malka during her illness. Ironically, Dr. Katzman tries to console this religious man. The rabbi can be pensive, but he does not feel the emotions of being involved. The comfort and simple decency of being allowed to die at home gave Malka the courage and strength to live, but the demands of caring for her have sapped the strength of the family.

"SOME GRIST FOR MERVYN'S MILL"

Richler also examines the problem of involvement when an outsider, Mervyn Kaplansky, moves to the St. Urbain area. Within the borders of his Montreal ghetto, peopled with established families and the Jewish immigrants, there is an exaggerated emphasis on getting ahead, most forcefully presented by Richler in his novel *The Apprenticeship of Duddy Kravitz*. Any display of talent is treated with admiration, especially if that talent is recognized in the United States. There is a considerable amount of difference between the pressure to succeed and actual success, and expectations are often greater than achievement itself. "Some Grist for Mervyn's Mill" illustrates this point and its consequences. Mervyn, a short, fat man from Toronto about twenty-three years of age, rents a room in the Hersh household. When he says that he is a writer, Mrs. Hersh is enraptured. Mervyn even carries with him a check for $14.50 which he received from the *Family Herald & Weekly Star*. This small check has given Mervyn a great ego; he says, "I try not to read too much now that I'm a wordsmith myself. I'm afraid of being influenced, you see."

Mervyn is now writing a novel entitled *The Dirty Jews* "about the struggles of our people in a hostile society"; he spends much time discussing this book and other literary matters with Mrs. Hersh. Again, Mr. Hersh is alienated from the family and goes to Tansky's to play cards. In order to finish the novel, Mervyn rarely leaves his room. Thinking that this is bad for him, Mrs. Hersh arranges a date for him with Molly Rosen, the "best looker" on St. Urbain Street. The match is unsuccessful, but Mervyn writes to her anyway. All the letters, however, come back unopened. Mervyn's love-life seems to parallel his unattained success as a writer.

Ironically, roles begin to reverse when Mr. Hersh sees a story, "A Doll for the Deacon," supposedly published under Mervyn's pseudonym. For Mr. Hersh this is proof that Mervyn is a writer, and he overlooks his faults as well as his overdue rent, now treating the budding wordsmith as an author in full flower. He clips out material from papers for him, takes him to meet the boys at Tansky's, and talks more tenderly to him than he does to his own children. Mervyn soon becomes more important to Molly, even though she knows that a publisher has rejected his novel. Winning the praise of Mr. Hersh and the fancy of Molly puts a great deal of pressure on Mervyn. He knows that he has gained recognition on false pretenses, although he never doubts his talent as a writer.

To prove something to the locals, Mervyn concocts a lie about receiving an advance from a United States publisher. Unfortunately, Mr. Hersh proclaims a celebration including the men from Tansky's and the Rosens, and at the party Molly announces their engagement. Mervyn can only drink heavily and suffer the pain caused by his deceit. Later he tells Jake that Molly only wanted his fame; before the rumors of his success, he was an object of ridicule, but with established fame, everyone feels possessive. Mervyn is now accepted for what they think is his achievement, and to save face, Mervyn perpetuates the illusion by showing Mr. Hersh a telegram with an offer from Hollywood. He leaves immediately, saying that he must check out the offer. A few days later the

Hershes receive a bill for the telegram, and no one sees Mervyn again. The boys at Tansky's are scandalized, and Molly is disgraced. After a month Mr. Hersh starts to receive money from Toronto for the unpaid rent, but Mervyn never answers any of his letters.

Richler is at his best satirizing the subtle human relationships that make up the social fabric. The consequences of almost insignificant and innocent efforts have a kind of ripple effect until a number of people become involved; the microcosm around St. Urban Street is only a focus for broader social problems. Personal human contact creates deception, pain, family alienation, and only very rarely a sense of joy. Individuals struggle in a social context with only a hope that things will get better. Richler's characters, then, are survivors who exist not as victims of a cruel, impersonal fate but as victims of their own actions. There is no significant harm done when Mervyn is exposed as a fraud. Life resumes at Tansky's, and Mr. Hersh has merely to take a severe ribbing from his friends. For most of Richler's people, this is what life is all about—a comedy of bearable suffering in which only minor victories, at best, are won.

"PLAYING BALL ON HAMPSTEAD HEATH"

Perhaps Richler's his best known short story is "Playing Ball on Hampstead Heath," which was first published in the August, 1966, issue of *Gentleman's Quarterly*, a men's fashion magazine which contains advertisements for expensive men's clothing. These advertisements express the subliminal message that men who wear such clothing will succeed in business and appear attractive to women. At first glance, it may seem odd that a serious writer like Richler would publish in such a vain and superficial magazine, but the characters in this short story would be at ease in the fantasy world of *Gentleman's Quarterly*.

The characters in this short story are middle-aged Americans and Canadians who work in the entertainment industry in London. Some are actors but most are producers of financially successful but superficial movies. They have not adapted at all to English culture, and their popular summer activity is to play baseball on Hampstead Heath, a park in London. As their game begins, the players have difficulty concentrating because their eyes wander. Some players ogle attractive young women and for this reason they commit several errors. Most of the players are divorced and both their present and former wives are watching this game. Perspectives keep changing. Sometimes the men look at their new and young wives, who married them for their money, and at other times, they look at their old wives, who are on the opposite side of the field. The men refer to their former wives as the "Alimony Gallery." Their former wives are understandably still very bitter. They sacrificed and worked at menial jobs while their husbands were struggling to succeed. Richler tells his readers that these women have not changed, whereas their former husbands have. An extraordinarily selfish man named Ziggy Alter justifies his divorce from his first wife and his marriage to a much younger woman by saying that he wanted to grow old with a younger woman whom he "can now afford" and not with a woman his own age.

These men are not just insensitive and selfish, they are also racist. In a clear effort to improve the quality of his mediocre team, Lou Caplan persuades an African American actor named Tom Hunt to join. Readers soon realize that if Hunt had refused this request to join Caplan's team, he would not have been hired for future movies. Hunt is very polite, but the other male characters refer to him as "a surly Negro actor" because he is not subservient. "Playing Ball on Hampstead Heath" is a witty short story that satirizes the vanity and mental cruelty of these superficial men.

OTHER MAJOR WORKS

LONG FICTION: *The Acrobats*, 1954; *Son of a Smaller Hero*, 1955; *A Choice of Enemies*, 1957; *The Apprenticeship of Duddy Kravitz*, 1959; *The Incomparable Atuk*, 1963; *Cocksure: A Novel*, 1968; *St. Urbain's Horseman*, 1971; *Joshua Then and Now*, 1980; *Solomon Gursky Was Here*, 1989; *Barney's Version*, 1997.

SCREENPLAYS: *The Apprenticeship of Duddy Kravitz*, 1959; *No Love for Johnnie*, 1961; *Young and Willing*, 1964 (with Phipps); *Life at the Top*, 1965.

NONFICTION: *Hunting Tigers Under Glass: Essays and Reports*, 1968; *Shovelling Trouble*, 1972; *Notes on an Endangered Species and Others*, 1974; *The Great Comic Book Heroes and Other Essays*, 1978; *Home Sweet Home*, 1984; *Broadsides: Reviews and Opinions*, 1990; *Oh Canada! Oh Quebec!: Requiem for a Divided Country*, 1992; *This Year in Jerusalem*, 1994.

CHILDREN'S LITERATURE: *Jacob Two-Two Meets the Hooded Fang*, 1975; *Jacob Two-Two and the Dinosaur*, 1987; *Jacob Two-Two's First Spy Case*, 1997.

EDITED TEXT: *Canadian Writing Today*, 1970; *Writers on World War II: An Anthology*, 1991.

BIBLIOGRAPHY

Arsenault, Michel. "Mordecai Richler Was Here." *World Press Review* 37 (June, 1990): 74-75. A brief biographical sketch, noting how Richler satirized the experiences of the French, the Canadians, Jews, and women; contends that although Richler is often accused of presenting an extremely critical view of Canada, he believes it his right to do so.

Brenner, Rachel Feldhay. *Assimilation and Assertion: The Response to the Holocaust in Mordecai Richler's Writings*. New York: P. Lang, 1989. Examines the role of Jewishness in Richler's writing and his portrayal of the Holocaust. Includes a bibliography and an index.

Came, Barry. "A Magical Craftsman." *Maclean's* 103 (December 31, 1990): 18-19. Discusses the universal appeal of Richler's fiction; provides a biographical sketch, emphasizing his most famous works.

Craniford, Ada. *Fiction and Fact in Mordecai Richler's Novels*. Lewiston, N.Y.: E. Mellen, 1992. A good study of Richler's Jewishness and his identity as a Canadian. Includes a bibliography and an index.

Darling, Michael, ed. *Perspectives on Mordecai Richler*. Toronto: ECW Press, 1986. In eight richly footnoted articles by eight different writers, the reader encounters different analyses of Richler's craft and the especially moral vision expressed in his fiction. Some of the articles provide an illuminating overview of Richler's themes; others, particularly those concentrating on his style, may be too specialized for the student reader.

Iannone, Carol. "The Adventures of Mordecai Richler." *Commentary* 89 (June, 1990): 51-53. Notes that Richler is among those Jewish writers who take an interest in the shadier side of Jewish experience, challenging the stereotype of the "good Jewish boy."

McSweeney, Kerry. "Mordecai Richler." In *Canadian Writers and Their Works*, edited by Robert Lecker, Jack David, and Ellen Quigley. Vol. 6. Toronto: ECW Press, 1985. McSweeney provides an orderly, lucid, and insightful analysis of Richler's fiction through *Joshua Then and Now*. The notes and the select bibliography document a wealth of reference material.

Ramraj, Victor J. *Mordecai Richler*. Boston: Twayne, 1983. This six-chapter study of Richler's fiction to *Joshua Then and Now* is enriched by a preface, a useful chronology of Richler's writing life, and a thorough select bibliography. *The Street*, the only one of Richler's fictional works that can be considered a work of short fiction, is examined in the context of Richler's vision and stance toward the Jewish community that he depicts so vividly in all of his fiction.

Richler, Mordecai. Interview by Sybil S. Steinberg. *Publishers Weekly* 237 (April 27, 1990): 45-46. Richler discusses the difficulty of writing the novel *Solomon Gursky*, partly because it was the first time he had to rely on research to authenticate his story and partly because of the complexity of the time sequences.

Sheps, G. David, ed. *Mordecai Richler*. Toronto: McGraw-Hill Ryerson, 1971. The seventeen articles and essays in this book treat Richler's fictional works both specifically and in more general contexts such as their place in Jewish fiction in English. The authors of the pieces are amongst the preeminent names in Canadian literary criticism. Includes a thoughtful introduction by Sheps.

Woodcock, George. *Mordecai Richler*. Toronto: McClelland and Stewart, 1970. Woodcock has a talent for presenting analyses in a down-to-earth prose style accessible to student readers. In this early work on Richler's fiction, the concluding seventh chapter includes a short assessment of *The Street*.

James MacDonald, updated by Jill Rollins and
Edmund J. Campion

TOMÁS RIVERA

Born: Crystal City, Texas; December 22, 1935
Died: Fontana, California; May 16, 1984

PRINCIPAL SHORT FICTION

. . . y no se lo tragó la tierra/. . . and the earth did not part, 1977 (also pb. as *This Migrant Earth*, 1985; *. . . and the earth did not devour him*, 1987)
The Harvest: Short Stories, 1989
Tomás Rivera: The Complete Works, 1991

OTHER LITERARY FORMS

Tomás Rivera has authored numerous essays, including "Into the Labyrinth: The Chicano in Literature." *The Searchers*, a collection of Rivera's poetry, was published in 1990, and *Always and Other Poems* in 1973. He has had numerous other essays on education and short stories appear in anthologies, magazines, and textbooks. A collection of Rivera's work, *Tomás Rivera: The Complete Works*, was published in 1991.

ACHIEVEMENTS

. . . And the earth did not part won the Premo Quinto Sol National Chicano Award in 1970. As Chancellor of the University of California, Riverside, Tomás Rivera is credited with bringing Chicano Studies to the academic forefront. He was a founding member of

the Tomás Rivera Policy Institute in Claremont, California. The Institute, which is affiliated with the Claremont Graduate School and the Department of Government at the University of Texas at Austin, holds a reputation as the nation's premier Latino think tank.

BIOGRAPHY

Tomás Rivera was born in Crystal City, Texas, on December 22, 1935, the son of Mexican migrant workers who were part of the influx of Mexican laborers into the United States in the 1930's and 1940's. Much of Rivera's boyhood was spent alongside his parents as they worked in the fields. Even through his junior college days, Rivera worked as a farm laborer in Texas, a fact that played a key role in his writing and, later, his work as an educational advocate on behalf of the Chicano worker.

He was graduated from Texas State University in San Marcos with a B.A. in English, and he earned a master's degree in English and administration at Southwest Texas State University. In 1969, Rivera received a doctorate in Spanish literature at the University of Oklahoma. He served as vice president of administration at the University of Texas at San Antonio and executive vice president at the University of Texas at El Paso. In 1979, Rivera became the first Chicano to earn the distinction of appointment to a chancellor's post in the University of California system—a particular honor for one of such humble beginnings and a testament to the perseverance of his individualistic spirit.

ANALYSIS

Although his writing career was comparatively brief, Tomás Rivera developed a singular voice that spoke for a whole group of displaced people. It was his dual passions, academic advocacy and literature, which fueled his desire to have the Chicano experience regarded seriously by the greater academic community. In regard to his style, critic Juan Bruce-Novoa, commenting on . . . *and the earth did not part*, states that Rivera "achieves . . . the evocation of an environment with a minimum of words." Rivera admires Sherwood Anderson and William Faulkner, and Mexican writer Juan Rulfo.

In the novella . . . *and the earth did not part* and in such stories as "The Zoo Island," Rivera conveys his characters' thoughts seemingly without editing or judgment. He even resists inclusion of how a line of dialogue is delivered, leaving the interpretation open to the reader. His style has a documentary feel to it, bearing witness to the years of migrant work Rivera did that undoubtedly honed his ear for dialogue. He admired the field worker's spiritual strength, but he did not sentimentalize his subjects, recognizing, perhaps, the potential people have to be cruel or indifferent to even their "own kind." The idea of searching provided a compelling metaphor for Rivera, who saw in it the origin of American identity. His characters are often adolescent boys, and as such, the ones who most yearn for inclusion while fiercely protecting their turf. The young boys of his short stories struggle to remain loyal to their mothers' wishes but gravitate toward the forbidden world of sex under cover of darkness. The women are often lost, unable to pull their spouses, fathers, or sons from the wreckage of a migrant worker's transitory lifestyle. There is some indication Rivera had written another novel, "La casa grande," but no such manuscript was found among his papers after he died of a heart attack in 1984.

. . . AND THE EARTH DID NOT PART

Although he wrote essays and short fiction, . . . *and the earth did not part*, a novella set in the 1970's in southern Texas, is the centerpiece of Rivera's literary career. It comes closest to what one would imagine the lives of field workers to be: gritty, dismal, and rife with daily challenges to survival. Narrators in the twelve thematically connected pieces vary from an omniscient third person in "His Hand in His Pocket," concerning a boy's perilous association with a murderous Mexican couple, to a dialogue between two young Mexican students in "It Is Painful." In the latter story, one of the Mexican boys is attacked by white boys in the bathroom, but only he faces expulsion. In the title story, a boy has seen several relatives die of tuberculosis. He then grapples with an unjust God who also strikes down his father with sunstroke as he labors in the fields. After his kid brother also succumbs to the heat, the boy curses God and is later amazed when the earth does not swallow him, as he had been told would happen. While contemporary critics regard . . . *and the earth did not part* primarily as a novel narrated by one central character, it can also be viewed as a mosaic of short stories from a variety of perspectives. Regardless how one might interpret the work, there is an overwhelming sense of loss throughout; however, Rivera also celebrates the indomitable spiritual power of the Mexican field-worker.

"ZOO ISLAND"

From *The Harvest: Short Stories* collection, "Zoo Island" is a reference to Monkey Island at Brackenridge Park Zoo. The story concerns a fifteen-year-old Mexican boy, Juan, who spontaneously decides to start a census of all the migrant workers on an Iowa farm where he lives with his family. Juan discusses tactics of census gathering with his father as they journey to a field filled with thistles they have been hired to clear. His father proudly comments that he does not use gloves, a fact he believes proves his stamina to the white bosses. Juan decides that he will post the results of the census and give the farm a name, like a real town. He counts the families who live in converted chicken coops easily, but he has a hard time getting Don Simon, an old man, to cooperate. After responding to questions about his origins rather elusively, Don Simon tells the boy that, "by counting yourself, you begin everything." Juan names the farm Zoo Island, feeling triumphant now that he has accounted for each and every one of his people, including a newborn child. The notion of the accountability of people, Rivera suggests, is what helps to give greater significance to otherwise overlooked lives. Along the way, one also understands that these human beings live in chicken coops, not houses as they should. Like chickens, they are valued only for their productivity, and not, like the human beings they are, for their spirit or character.

"THE SALAMANDERS"

"The Salamanders" is a first-person narrative from the perspective of a child migrant worker trapped penniless with his family in a small town, Crystal Lake, in northern Iowa. As the rain enters a fourth week, they are forced out of Minnesota for lack of work, arriving in yet another place with no prospects.

He, his parents, and siblings drive from farm to farm in search of work. Most farmers will only say no from inside the safety of their houses. The constant rejections cause the boy to feel separated from his mother and father. When the car's wiring shorts while going through the rain, they are forced to sleep in the car by the side of a road. Seeing his sleeping family, the boy experiences further isolation. After days of no work, they finally find a farmer who tells them they can start harvesting beets from a flooded field as soon as the water level goes down. That night, sick of sleeping together in the car, the family pitches a tent at the end of the field. What most profoundly affects the boy is waking during the night to find that salamanders have infested the tent. They begin killing the salamanders, and the boy notes his strange satisfaction in squeezing the life out of them. Finally, he catches one and, looking deeply into its eyes, feels the "very pure" sensation of "original death." Like many of Rivera's stories, "The Salamanders" refrains from judging the characters, thus allowing the horror and desperation of the situation to speak for itself. The powerful emotional impact of the story lies in its minimalist approach.

"FIRST COMMUNION"

In "First Communion," Rivera tells a story imbued with an understanding of the conflict between spiritual purity and desires of the flesh. After the male adolescent in . . . *and the earth did not part* has done battle with the Devil and challenged God, he describes what happens prior to his passage from boyhood into the life of an adult Catholic. The priest talks to the gathered children about "venial sins," impelling them to confess all their sins or suffer the damnation of Hell. The boy dresses excitedly the following morning for his Communion. On his way to church, he secretly watches a man and woman making love in a tailor's shop. Disturbed and stimulated by what he has witnessed, he cannot bring himself to tell the priest. Later at home, he feels different, as though it had been he who committed the "sin of the flesh." He recalls a missionary discussing "the grace of God," and the boy finds that he now wants to know more about everything. Rivera shifts between direct, present-tense dialogue and a first-person recollection of the event, re-creating accurately how human memory works—it brings details up without warning. For a boy on the cusp of a momentous rite of passage, the sex act in particular is fraught with both allure and danger, searing itself forever into his memory.

OTHER MAJOR WORKS

POETRY: *Always and Other Poems*, 1973; *The Searchers: Collected Poetry*, 1990.

MISCELLANEOUS: *Tomás Rivera: The Complete Works*, 1991.

BIBLIOGRAPHY

Castañeda-Shular, Antonia, Tomás Ybarra-Frautos, and Joseph Sommers, eds. *Chicano Literature: Text and Context*. Englewood Cliffs, N.J.: Prentice-Hall, 1972. A rich source of information on Mexican American life, history, criticism, and literature, with Rivera's place in the Chicano literary canon clearly delineated.

Grajeda, Ralph F. "Tomás Rivera's Appropriation of the Chicano Past." In *Modern Chicano Writers: A Collection of Critical Essays*. Edited by Joseph Sommers and Tomás Ibarra-Frausto. Englewood Cliffs, N.J.: Prentice-Hall, 1979. Grajeda thoroughly examines and analyzes Rivera's . . . *and the earth did not part*, putting it into a historical context.

Kanellos, Nicolás, ed. *Short Fiction by Hispanic Writers Of the United States*. Houston, Tex.: Arte Público Press: 1993. Calling Rivera "one of the most beloved figures in Chicano literature," Kanellos offers an overview of Rivera's academic career, and an introduction to . . . *and the earth did not part*. "First Communion," from this book, focuses on the teenager's passage into adulthood. The anthology also includes "The Salamanders."

_____. "Tomás Rivera." *The Hispanic Literary Companion*. Detroit: Visible Ink, 1996. Includes quotes from other criticism of . . . *and the earth did not part*, a biography, and Rivera's short stories, "Zoo Island" and "The Salamanders" from *The Harvest: Short Stories*. There is also a listing of his writings. Kanellos further discusses Rivera's deep devotion to Chicano education and belief in the ability of literature to enlighten and inform.

Saldívar, Ramón. "Tomas Rivera." In *Heath Anthology of American Literature*. Vol. 1. Lexington, Mass.: D.C. Heath, 1994. 2752-2753. A compact biography covering Rivera's life and work, and his literary influences. This inclusion in a two-volume, lengthy anthology divided according to broad literary periods in America contains an excerpt from . . . *and the earth did not part*. There is a useful long essay, balancing between historical and literary details, which provides a broad background from 1945 through the 1980's.

Stavans, Ilan. *Art and Anger: Essays on Politics and the Imagination*. New Mexico: University of New Mexico Press, 1996. Nineteen far-ranging essays with a focus on the difficulties of translating Latin American literature and the Spanish language while retaining their integrity. A Jew living in Mexico, Stavans takes on Octavio Paz, Magical Realism, and Peruvian history, among other topics. These essays provide a broad context, thus helping to see Rivera's position as a Chicano who bridges the gap between the North American and the Latino.

Tatum, Charles M. "Contemporary Chicano Novel." *Chicano Literature*, Boston: New Mexico State University. Twayne Publishers, 1982. 102-137. Beginning with Jose Antonio Villareal's *Pocho* (1959), this chapter places Rivera's . . . *and the earth did not part* at the forefront of modern Chicano literature.

Nika Hoffman

ALAIN ROBBE-GRILLET

Born: Brest, France; August 18, 1922

PRINCIPAL SHORT FICTION

Instantanés, 1962 (*Snapshots*, 1965)

OTHER LITERARY FORMS

Alain Robbe-Grillet is the author of numerous novels and is known principally for them. The best known are *Les Gommes* (1953; *The Erasers*, 1963), *Le Voyeur* (1955; *The Voyeur*, 1958), *La Jalousie* (1957; *Jealousy*, 1959), *Dans le Labyrinthe* (1959; *In the Labyrinth*, 1960), *Topologie d'une cité fantôme* (1976; *Topology of a Phantom City*, 1977), *Angelique: Ou, L'Enchantement* (1987), and *Les Derniers jours de Corinthe* (1994). He also published a collection of critical essays: *Pour un nouveau roman* (1963; *For a New Novel: Essays on Fiction*, 1965) as well as several movie scenarios and feature-length screenplays.

ACHIEVEMENTS

Alain Robbe-Grillet won several French literary prizes, including the Prix Fénéon (1954), the Prix des Critiques (1955), and a production of *L'Année dernière à Marienbad* (1961; *Last Year at Marienbad*, 1962), for which he wrote the screenplay, won the Prix du Lion d'Or at the Venice Film Festival and the Melies Prize in France.

BIOGRAPHY

Alain Robbe-Grillet was born near Brest, France, in 1922, where he attended the local school and then the Lycée Buffon in Paris. He received a first bachelor's degree in mathematics from Lycée Saint-Louis in Paris and a second one from the Lycée de Brest. From 1941 to 1942, during the German occupation in World War II, he attended the French National Institute of Agronomy in Paris. Robbe-Grillet started writing in 1949 and worked for the French colonial administration in the French West Indies; the period of his greatest literary production started in 1953 with *Les Gommes*. He became a literary consultant for the publisher Éditions de Minuit in 1955.

In 1959, he began working in cinema as well as continuing to write fiction; his collaboration in 1960-1961 on *Last Year at Marienbad* was successful. He published *Snapshots*, a collection of short fiction, in 1962. He began to appear on French television and to tour American universities in the 1960's. Collaborations with French and American artists produced *Topologie d'une cité fantôme* (1976; *Topology of a Phantom City*, 1977) and *Construction d'un temple en ruines à la Déesse Vanadé* (1975). He was also inducted into the French Legion of Honor. He published *Les Derniers jours de Corinthe* in 1994.

ANALYSIS

In the 1950's and 1960's Alain Robbe-Grillet was the spokesperson for a group known as the New Novelists, writers who were reacting against traditional French literature. Even such novelists as André Malraux and André Gide were rejected by the New Novelists, particularly Robbe-Grillet, in their explorations of the inner movements of the mind and the outer, objective realities of the world.

In the style of the New Novel, Robbe-Grillet's collection of short stories, *Instantanés*, is a kind of "objective literature," to borrow a phrase from Roland Barthes, one of the critics who championed the New Novelists. At the same time the collection rejects traditional realism. Characters, for example, are stick figures and have no development; the stories are about pure, precise, and repetitive description, and there is no plot. Themes are simple and include a coffeepot on a table with a dressmaker's dummy nearby, a walk on an island about to be engulfed by the rising tide, and an escalator in the Paris subway. The descriptions of these scenes or objects are repetitive and at the same time minimalist, and at no time does the reader enter into the private thoughts of the characters. Robbe-Grillet has a horror of sentiment, and his stories are clearly objective and meant to show an expressionless world.

Only one story, "La chambre secrète" ("The Secret Room"), breaks somewhat with the others. It has the element of a pornographic mystery: a nude body, murder, violence, and a mysterious caped man, all of this in a darkened, dungeonlike room.

"THE DRESSMAKER'S DUMMY"

One of the most famous lines in New Novel fiction begins the first story of the collection *Instantanés:* "The coffeepot is on the table." The story is typical of Robbe-Grillet in this collection; in fact, "story" is a misnomer for most of his short pieces of fiction, as there is no plot. Robbe-Grillet starts by describing the coffeepot on the table, the square ceramic tile beneath it, then moves to the reflection of the window in the mirror. The whole effect is of a room, silent, waiting for something to begin.

The story is like the panning of a camera through the field of vision of an anonymous viewer. The eye of the omniscient narrator moves from coffeepot to mirrored reflection to dressmaker's dummy, of which there is at first one, then three. There are no human figures in this setting, no human presence, except perhaps toward the end of the extended description, when the narrator mentions the smell of freshly brewed coffee, thus implying a character who brewed it. In sum, this short piece of fiction, which cannot really be called a story, summarizes and epitomizes Robbe-Grillet's style: no plot, little human figuration, no character development, pure description.

"THE WAY BACK"

This story adds several elements to the pure description of the first story: first-person narration, characters, dialogue, and tension. There is still no plot, but there are the stirrings of one: Three men, Legrand, Franz, and the narrator, are stuck on an island, entrapped by the rising tide. In fact, nearly the only lines of dialogue are "We won't be able to get back" and "It's not rising so fast." The story starts with a description of the mainland as seen from the island. Numerous elements of this first description are repeated, notably the mossy algae on the stones and the swirling dust in the eddies of water that move through the rocks as the tide rises. Other repeated elements in the scene include the roadway parallel to the shore, the parapet, and the water rising in eddies to cover the roadway.

Alain Robbe-Grillet in 1962 (AP/Wide World Photos)

The element of tension comes from the three men's realization that they may not be able to get back to the shore of the mainland. At the end of the story, they come upon a boatman who offers to take them across. Here again, Robbe-Grillet chooses to focus on repetition and sameness as the boatman appears to be rowing always in the same place. Everything in the description contributes to the sense of tension, which is underplayed by the repeated motifs of eddies of dust and other elements of the landscape, which change only slightly as they are repeated. "Le chemin du retour" ("The Way Back") is more like a short story than other short selections in that it does have characters and dialogue, as well as description. The story clearly has no resolution, no conclusion—at the end, the three men in the boat are being rowed to shore but the boatman appears to be making no progress against the current. The reader will see the same lack of resolution in other stories.

"THE SHORE"

This story is written with mathematical precision. More than in the other stories, in "La plage" ("The Shore") the reader sees the careful, symmetrical addition of descriptive elements. The description is of three children, blond, tan, and with serious expressions, walking abreast on a sandy beach. To their left a cliff rises high; to their right, there is the ocean, where a small wave unfurls in a milky foam. The three children progress along the beach in an unbroken line, their steps unvarying and their feet making parallel tracks behind them.

In this story, Robbe-Grillet uses a third-person narrator, and the only elements of the description that are not visual are the sounds of the little wave, the brief dialogue of the children, the sound of a distant bell, and the flapping of wings, as a flock of gulls, which the children startle as they approach, takes flight.

Compared to "The Way Back" or "The Secret Room," this brief piece displays none of the tension that is sometimes present in other stories. The scene is absolutely calm; the weather is beautiful, and there is only the steady progress of the children, the wave, and the birds. Robbe-Grillet has developed in this story a cinematic technique, mathematical and precise, for creating a movement in space-time of complete peacefulness.

"THE SECRET ROOM"

This short story is often anthologized, chosen for its craft and careful technique. The last word of the story gives a clue to what the reader is seeing: a kind of canvas that becomes animated as the reader watches it. "The Secret Room" has all the elements of a pornographic, sadistic murder mystery. There is a dead female nude (whose murder is seen in flashback or retrospect), a dark and cavernous room ("a dungeon, a sunken room, or a cathedral"), a mysterious male figure wrapped in a cloak, who commits the murder or sacrificial act, and the presence of dark colors—purple, black, and blood red.

At the beginning of the story the reader sees a red stain in close-up on a pearly white globe, which, as the viewer moves back, proves to be the wounded or stabbed breast of the sacrificial victim, a beautiful black-haired woman lying on her back. The man is on the top stair, poised to leave, but as this story progresses the reader realizes that he or she is being drawn into the events of the action about five minutes too late, that the murder or sacrifice has just taken

place. The whole scene begins to unfurl in reverse. The murder takes place before the reader's eyes, as the reader moves backward in time; the victim hurls herself from side to side, chained by the limbs to columns. The cape-wearing killer flees up the stairs.

The key element of the story is suspense. Who is the victim? Who is the killer? Where are they? Even the title of the story leads the reader to believe that he or she is witnessing some kind of sadistic, secret ritual. Robbe-Grillet's technique reaches its highest point in this story, which stands as the best example of the experiments of the New Novelists.

OTHER MAJOR WORKS

LONG FICTION: *Les Gommes*, 1953 (*The Erasers*, 1964); *Le Voyeur*, 1955 (*The Voyeur*, 1958); *La Jalousie*, 1957 (*Jealousy*, 1959); *Dans le labyrinthe*, 1959 (*In the Labyrinth*, 1960); *La Maison de rendez-vous*, 1965 (English translation, 1966); *Projet pour une révolution à New York*, 1970 (*Project for a Revolution in New York*, 1972); *La Belle Captive*, 1975 (René Magritte, illustrator; English translation, 1995); *Topologie d'une cité fantôme*, 1976 (*Topology of a Phantom City*, 1972); *Un Régicide*, 1978; *Souvenirs du traingle d'or*, 1978 (*Recollections of the Golden Triangle*, 1984); *Djinn*, 1981 (English translation, 1982); *Le Miroir qui revient*, 1984 (*Ghosts in the Mirror*, 1988); *Angelique: Ou, L'Enchantement*, 1987; *Les Derniers jours de Corinthe*, 1994.

SCREENPLAYS: *L'Année dernière à Marienbad*, 1961 (*Last Year at Marienbad*, 1962); *L'Immortelle*, 1963 (*The Immortal One*, 1971); *Trans-Europ Express*, 1967; *L'Homme qui ment*, 1968; *L'Éden et après*, 1970; *Glissements progressifs du plaisir*, 1974; *Le Jeu avec le feu*, 1975; *La Belle Captive*, 1983.

NONFICTION: *Pour un nouveau roman*, 1963 (criticism; *For a New Novel: Essays on Fiction*, 1965); *Rêves de jeunes filles*, 1971 (photographs by David Hamilton; *Dreams of a Young Girl*, 1971); *Les Demoiselles d'Hamilton*, 1972 (photographs by Hamilton; *Sisters*, 1973); *Construction d'un temple en ruines à la Déesse Vanadé*, 1975 (etchings by Paul Delvaux); *Le Rendez-vous*, 1981.

BIBLIOGRAPHY

Fletcher, John. *Alain Robbe-Grillet*. New York: Methuen, 1983. This short study is by one of the best critics of French twentieth century fiction, who takes a thematic approach. Fletcher concludes that Robbe-Grillet has hastened the demise of modernism even though Robbe-Grillet felt that he had championed it.

Hellerstein, Marjorie H. *Inventing the Real World: The Art of Alain Robbe-Grillet*. Selinsgrove, Pa.: Susquehanna University Press, 1998. A study of Robbe-Grillet's work in film includes discussions of his fiction, a good bibliography, and an index.

Jefferson, Ann. *The Nouveau Roman and the Poetics of Fiction*. Cambridge: Cambridge University Press, 1980. A survey of the French New Novel that covers Robbe-Grillet in several chapters, including two on *The Erasers* and *Jealousy.* Jefferson describes his narratives as "unnatural." This study, although it covers novelists other than Robbe-Grillet, is useful for setting his writing into perspective and seeing Robbe-Grillet as a part of a French literary movement of the 1950's and 1960's.

Leki, Ilona. *Alain Robbe-Grillet*. Boston: Twayne, 1983. Leki takes each of Robbe-Grillet's major novels and discusses it in turn, finishing with *Un Regicide*. She concludes that after the debate on subjectivity and objectivity diminished, the discussions focused on Robbe-Grillet's use of narrative strategies. Excellent study for general survey of this work. Includes a good bibliography.

Morrisette, Bruce. *The Novels of Robbe-Grillet*. Ithaca: Cornell University Press, 1975. A translation of a French-language work by an American expert on Robbe-Grillet. Morrisette is, along with Fletcher, the dean of criticism on Robbe-Grillet, and in this study takes the reader through the major novels by examining such themes as the maze, the narrator and his doubles, and the cinematic novels.

Nelson, Roy Jay. "Mental-Representation Fiction," in *Causality and Narrative in French Fiction from Zola to Robbe-Grillet*. Columbus: Ohio State University Press, 1990. Nelson approaches Robbe-Grillet by discussing the narrative, which he calls a description of mental representation.

Ramsay, Ralene L. *Robbe-Grillet and Modernity: Science, Sexuality, and Subversion*. Gainesville: University Press of Florida, 1992. Ramsay discusses modernity, complementarity, myth, and sado-eroticism, all elements of Robbe-Grillet's narrative. The study also includes interviews with Robbe-Grillet, which shed light on the creative process. Excellent survey. Contains a bibliography.

Stoltzfus, Ben. *Alain Robbe-Grillet: The Body of the Text*. London: Associated University Presses, 1985. Stoltzfus contends that Robbe-Grillet exaggerates images of sex and violence in his novels in order to expose and undermine them.

Margaret Wade Krausse

ELIZABETH MADOX ROBERTS

Born: Perryville, Kentucky; October 30, 1881
Died: Orlando, Florida; March 13, 1941

PRINCIPAL SHORT FICTION
The Haunted Mirror, 1932
Not by Strange Gods, 1941

OTHER LITERARY FORMS

Elizabeth Madox Roberts is best known for her novels, particularly her first, *The Time of Man* (1926), a story of Kentucky hill people, and *The Great Meadow* (1930), her epic story of American pioneers in Kentucky in the 1770's. Her other five novels were less well received and are not well known. Of her three collections of poetry, only *Under the Tree* (1922) had much success.

ACHIEVEMENTS

While still in undergraduate school, Elizabeth Madox Roberts won the Fiske Prize for a group of poems highly praised by critics. She later won the John Reed Memorial Prize in 1928 and the Poetry Society of South Carolina Prize in 1931 for her poetry. Her first novel, *The Time of Man* (1926), earned her an international reputation when it was translated into several languages. Her story "The Sacrifice of the Maidens" won second prize in the O. Henry Memorial Award contest in 1932. In 1936 and 1937, she was awarded Doctor of Letters degrees by Centre College, Danville, Kentucky, and by the University of Louisville. She was elected to the National Institute of Arts and Letters in 1940.

BIOGRAPHY

Elizabeth Madox Roberts was born in Perryville, Kentucky, on October 30, 1881, the second of eight children. Her family moved to Springfield, Kentucky, in 1894, where she spent most of her life. She was educated at Covington Institute, a private school in Springfield, and later attended high school in the city of Covington. After graduation, from 1900 to 1910, she taught classes both pri-

vately and in public high schools in the area.

Roberts did not enter college until she was thirty-six, when, at the urging of a family friend, she enrolled in the University of Chicago. Influenced and encouraged by the poet Harriet Monroe, Roberts concentrated on poetry, publishing *Under the Tree* in 1922. After graduation, she returned to Kentucky to devote herself full time to writing; her first novel, *The Time of Man*, brought her several years of critical recognition, culminating in her second great success, *The Great Meadow*, in 1930.

From 1935 until her death, Roberts suffered from skin infections, nervous disorders, chronic anemia, and Hodgkins disease. In spite of failing health, she continued to work on various projects, one of which was an epic account of Daniel Boone. She died on March 13, 1941, in Orlando, Florida, and was buried in Springfield, Kentucky. Her second collection of short stories, *Not by Strange Gods*, appeared just after her death.

ANALYSIS

Although Elizabeth Madox Roberts once wrote, "I do not think that the 'short story' is a satisfactory form or that anything very good can be done with it," at least half a dozen of the stories in her two collections are haunting poetic transformations of the older regional tale into the modern lyrical short story—a genre more popularly mastered by Eudora Welty and Katherine Anne Porter. Unlike local colorists, with whom she is often compared, Roberts does not focus on rural life to celebrate the exotic quaintness of its inhabitants, but rather, in such stories as "On the Mountainside" and "The Haunted Palace," to explore the most basic human conflicts resulting from rural life.

Moreover, her poetic style is not merely a decorative device to sentimentalize the rural world, but rather a means by which she can transform the stuff of that world into embodiments of the inner life of her characters. Although the general critical consensus is that Roberts is a competent but not a brilliant

Elizabeth Madox Roberts (National Archives)

writer of short stories, this view may be the result of an unexamined bias for the novel, as well as the failure of many critics to appreciate how she uses poetic language to create stories that, while grounded in rural reality, are haunted by the lyrical longing of their characters.

"The Haunted Palace"

Roberts's most famous story, "The Haunted Palace," whose title is derived from the poem in Poe's "Fall of the House of Usher," focuses on an old antebellum mansion that sharecropper Hubert and his wife Jess plan to buy—a house so possessed by all those who have lived in it that it becomes a hallucinatory embodiment to Jess of her own inner conflicts. The most compelling scene in the story occurs when the couple bring over thirty sheep into grand rooms of the old house to give birth; surrounded by the bloody and bleating beginnings of life, Jess confronts a ghostly apparition and beats at it with her club while it beats her with identical blows: "Herself and the creature then were one. . . . She and the creature had beaten at the mirror from opposite sides." Then she

knows she has been flailing at her own reflection and has broken the great mirror. The shattering of the mirror is like the breaking of a spell, and the story ends with the quiet contentment of the sheep nursing their lambs. The story thus ends in the triumph of the couple's prosaic present reality over the past romance of the old nobility.

"On the Mountainside"

Set in the Kentucky mountains, "On the Mountainside" is Roberts's poetic treatment of the classic conflict of highlands people—whether to stay in their ancestral home or to leave the hills for the cities below. The central character, Newt Reddix, having been introduced to the mysteries of book learning, feels he has received a report from the outside world and is compelled to leave to attend a school down in the settlements.

After traveling on foot through the woods for days, Newt spends the night at a house where he meets an old man on his way back to the mountains after having lived in the settlement for years. Calling himself a traitor to his God when he left the mountains, the old man describes a spring from his childhood. When Newt, "eager to enter the drama of the world," says he got a drink from that same spring a week before, the old man is astonished, cautioning Newt that the places he knew as a boy will never go out of his head. Although this prophetic warning puts terror into Newt's thoughts, making him "bereft, divided, emptied of his every wish," he watches the young wife of the house spread quilts before the fire for him and takes delight in seeing her strong body and the strange room; thus an "amorous pulse" is laid on his determination to go to the settlements to get the learning he cherishes.

"The Sacrifice of the Maidens"

The single scene at the heart of this story is a religious service in which several young girls take their vows to become nuns in the small chapel of a rural convent. The scene is described from the perspective of an adolescent boy, Felix Barbour, whose sister Anne is one of the postulants. The story moves back and forth between poetic descriptions of the ritual as a process of death and regeneration and Felix's half-dream reveries about his past realization of the loveliness of girls, their "soft round flesh and the shy, veiled laughter that hid under their boldness."

Over the priest's repeated intonations of "Hail Mary, full of grace, Blessed art thou among women," Felix recalls Anne and other girls as they were before taking the vows, "soft to touch . . . given to laughter, easy to come to tears, easy with pity, easy with anger" who easily became women. Fascinated by one of the girls, who enter the chapel dressed as brides, Felix longs to know her name, and wishes to "say it in his mind, to name his sense of her loveliness with a word." Ironically, this desire is fulfilled at precisely the moment when the girl becomes inaccessible to Felix's fantasies—the moment when the priest utters the name she was known by in the world, "Aurelia," and pronounces the name she will be known by henceforth—Sister Mary Dolores."

"THE SCARECROW"

Joan, the central figure of this, one of Roberts's most haunting stories, can "scarcely endure to let any other flesh touch her own." One of her chores is to keep the crows out of her father's corn field, a task she performs with the aid of a scarecrow she has made from some of her own clothes. The central scene in the story occurs when she falls asleep in the field and dreams about Tony Wright, a young man who wishes to marry her, stroking her body, bending her this way and that.

When her family arranges her marriage to Tony, he takes her to his home, where she sees into the future and rejects the place as never being her own. To protect herself from Tony's touch, much as the scarecrow has protected the corn from the crows, she hides a knife in the bosom of her dress. However, because he has seen her do it, he stays away from her until she leaves on foot and goes back to her father's house. For Joan the marriage, a mere incident, has come to an end. The story concludes with the mother crying that Joan is Mrs. Tony Wright and must return, but the father insists, "Joan, Joan! She won't marry where she's not of a mind."

OTHER MAJOR WORKS

LONG FICTION: *The Time of Man*, 1926; *My Heart and My Flesh*, 1927; *Jingling in the Wind*, 1928; *The*

Great Meadow, 1930; *A Buried Treasure*, 1931; *He Sent Forth a Raven*, 1935; *Black Is My True Love's Hair*, 1938.

POETRY: *In the Great Steep's Garden*, 1915; *Under the Tree*, 1922, 1930; *Song in the Meadow*, 1940.

BIBLIOGRAPHY

Campbell, Harry Modean, and Ruel E. Foster. *Elizabeth Madox Roberts: American Novelist*. Norman: University of Oklahoma Press, 1956. This biographical/critical study includes a chapter on the short stories that focuses on the symbolism in several of her stories, particularly "The Scarecrow," "The Sacrifice of the Maidens," and "The Haunted Palace." Also discusses analogies to music in Roberts's stories, particularly her use of musical devices in "The Shepherd's Interval."

Hall, Wade. "Place in the Short Fiction of Elizabeth Madox Roberts." *The Kentucky Review* 6 (Fall/Winter, 1986): 3-16. Discusses the ways that place affects Roberts's short fiction: in the speech of her characters, in the creative relationship between character and place, and as the landscape of one's life. Argues that in Roberts's short fiction place has a bearing on who characters are, how they behave, what happens in the stories, and how they are structured and written.

McDowell, Frederick P. W. *Elizabeth Madox Roberts*. New York: Twayne Publishers, 1963. In this basic introduction to Roberts's life and work, McDowell argues that her best short stories are the earliest ones, which resemble the novels in their expression of significant moments in the psychological life of their characters. Provides brief discussions of such stories as "On the Mountainside," "The Sacrifice of the Maidens," and "The Betrothed."

Rovit, Earl H. *Herald to Chaos: The Novels of Elizabeth Madox Roberts*. Lexington: University of Kentucky Press, 1960. Rovit discusses Roberts's presentation of heroic characters engaged in epic struggles against the forces of nature; discusses her critical neglect and her role in American literature and provides a thorough analysis of her style.

Simpson, Lewis P. "The Sexuality of History." *The Southern Review* 20 (October, 1984): 785-802. In this special issue of memoirs, reminiscences, and essays on Roberts, Simpson discusses her as a particularly modern writer whose struggle to repudiate the philosophy of idealism is the major thematic motive of her work; compares her to William Faulkner in their awareness of the inwardness of history.

Spivey, Herman E. "The Mind and Creative Habits of Elizabeth Madox Roberts." In *All These To Teach*, edited by Robert A. Bryan, Alton C. Morris, A. A. Murphree, and Aubrey L. Williams. Gainesville: University of Florida Press, 1965. 237-248. Argues that although Roberts's achievements were greater than realized by her contemporaries, her handicaps as an artist were more than she was able to overcome. Claims that Roberts is too much concerned with man in general and too little with individual man, that there is too little external action in her work, and that her unmastered technical experiments prevent reader understanding.

Tate, Linda. "Elizabeth Madox Roberts: A Bibliographical Essay." *Resources for American Literary Study* 18 (1992): 22-43. A summary and critique of previous criticism of Roberts's work. Concludes that she lacks a definitive biography; argues that her role in the Southern Renaissance has not been sufficiently explored; claims that the highest untapped appeal of her work is feminist criticism.

Charles E. May

MARY ROBISON

Born: Washington, D.C.; January 14, 1949

PRINCIPAL SHORT FICTION

Days, 1979
An Amateur's Guide to the Night, 1983
Believe Them, 1988

OTHER LITERARY FORMS

Mary Robison's first novel, *Oh!,* was published in 1981 by Alfred A. Knopf. The novel deals satirically with the problem of American family life. *Oh!* was followed ten years later by another novel, *Subtraction* (1991, also published by Knopf), which describes the difficulties that can arise when writers become teachers.

ACHIEVEMENTS

Mary Robison's short fiction has often been compared to that of older, more established contemporary writers such as Raymond Carver, Ann Beattie, and Frederick Barthelme because of its spare, laconic humor and its presentation of empty lives in a hopelessly materialistic society. Her story "Yours" was anthologized in *Discovering Literature* (2000), along with the work of Raymond Carver and Sandra Cisneros. She did receive high critical praise for her earliest stories, which appeared in *The New Yorker,* and her first collection of short fiction, *Days,* garnered outstanding notices from many literary critics and fellow writers, even though she was only thirty years old when it was published. Though her stories embody the cool precision that has become characteristic of *The New Yorker,* her style is anything but derivative. She possesses an authentically original voice and a writing style that captures, simultaneously, the stark banality and the comic irony of the late stages of the American Dream in the last quarter of the twentieth century.

She has received fellowships from the Yaddo Writers and Artists Colony (1978) and the Breadloaf Writers Conference (1979). She has been honored with awards by the Authors Guild (1979) and PEN (1979) and received a grant from the John Simon Guggenheim Memorial Foundation.

BIOGRAPHY

Mary Robison was born in Washington, D.C., in 1949. Her father, Anthony Cennomo, was an attorney, and her mother, F. Elizabeth Reiss, a psychologist and the mother of eight children. She married James Robison, a writer. She spent most of her youth in the Midwest, but she received her M.A. at The Johns Hopkins University in Baltimore. She was visiting lecturer (1979-1980) at Ohio University, writer-in-residence at the University of Southern Mississippi, and has taught at the University of North Carolina at Greensboro, College of William and Mary, Bennington College, Oberlin College, and in 1981 became the Briggs-Copeland assistant professor of English in the Department of Creative Writing at Harvard University. She has stated that her finest teacher at The Johns Hopkins University was the renowned novelist John Barth. She claims that she would not have taken her fiction writing seriously had it not been for The Johns Hopkins University's Writing Program and Barth's ability to inspire her to use her talent and publish her stories. As she put it: "John Barth charged a dead battery in me." Robison has also judged national fiction competitions such as the one sponsored by the *Mississippi Review.*

Mary Robison (©Miriam Berkley)

ANALYSIS

Mary Robison's early stories deal with the recurrent theme of the spiritual torpor at the center of a materialistic American society that is shallow, banal, boring, and bored. Her stories can be read as variations on the theme of stasis and, as such, resemble James Joyce's *Dubliners* (1914) as much as the work of Carver or Beattie. Novelist David Leavitt accurately analyzes the common dilemmas of many of her characters as their inability to move "because they're terrified of what will happen to them if they try to change." Waiting and fear of change characterize a number of her early stories, but the waiting and fear eventually create a prevailing sense of lassitude and ennui, the desperation of a Sunday afternoon in November.

Barth describes her style as "hard-edged, fine-tooled, enigmatic super-realism," phrases that could as well describe the early Joyce. Robison, however, differs from early Joyce principally because much of her work, in spite of presenting bleak lives, is extremely comical, a quality that some overly serious critics usually miss. She is a comic writer even in the dark world of her first collection, *Days*, a pun that immediately establishes the malady of the quotidian as a major theme but also describes the "dazed" condition that many of her characters inhabit.

The gnomic titles of many of her stories are quite humorous, and when they are not ironic, they mix humor with sadness. They are, however, unerring objective correlatives, which permit plot, character, theme, and tone to coalesce comfortably. Her stories are extremely difficult to analyze with the usual literary methods because she rarely begins them at the beginning; she opens *in medias res*—that is, in the middle of things. Indeed, her stories are not stories in a narrative sense but rather parables of emptiness or scenes resembling the kind that the composer Robert

Schumann evokes in his heartrending *Kinderszenen* (1838). In spite of the sorrow depicted in much of her work, however, Robison consistently creates stories whose titles and proper nouns can evoke comic responses: Bluey and Greer Wellman of "The Wellman Twins," Dieter and Boffo of "For Real," Sherry, Harry, and Daphne Noonan of "Coach," Ohio congressman Mel Physell, who writes poems on prosecutorial immunity, and a Great Dane named Lola from "Apostasy."

"KITE AND PAINT"

The opening of the first story in *Days*, entitled "Kite and Paint," illustrates clearly the theme of waiting, which recurs frequently throughout Robison's fiction: "It was the last day of August in Ocean City, and everybody was waiting for Hurricane Carla." Two men in their sixties, Charlie and Don, have been living together for some time. Don is not in good health but continues to care for his rose garden. He is a painter but seems to have lost interest in his craft; Charlie chides him for his unwillingness to paint anything. It is not clear whether they are lovers, though Don's former wife, Holly, has come to warn them that Hurricane Carla is imminent. The hurricane has temporarily given both men first a focus, then a purpose for action since neither seems frightened of it. It is as though they have been waiting for a disaster such as this all their lives.

The stasis in the story has been broken, and the artist, Don, spent the previous night drawing geometric figures on six kites and naming them with titles such as "Comet," "Whale," "My Beauty," and "Reddish Egret." The hurricane has mysteriously revived Don's imagination after a long hiatus and, more importantly, he decides to fly the kites as the hurricane arrives. "It'd be fun to waste them in the blow," Don declares. Robison fuses the joy of reawakened creativity with a vague death wish as the couple decides to confront "Carla," which is the feminine form of the proper name "Charles," the name itself meaning "man." By matching two important proper names, "Carla" and "Charlie," Robison also invites a humorous Freudian interpretation to the possible final hours of a nearly dried-up painter and a retired junior high school shop teacher.

"PRETTY ICE"

Most of the characters in Robison's fiction live their lives unaware of their deepest motivations and remain ignorant of the power of the unconscious. One of the sources of the sardonic tone in much of Robison's fiction is observing so many characters blind to their self-destructive impulses; they literally do not know what they are doing. The perennial graduate student in plant taxonomy, Will, in the story "Pretty Ice," is a case in point of someone whose scientific mind-set has cut him off from the potential joys of impulse and prevents him from viewing the aesthetic side of an ice storm in Columbus, Ohio. His fiancé, Belle, who holds a Ph.D. in musicology, decides at the story's conclusion that she cannot marry someone who is unable to share her and her mother's view that "an ice storm is a beautiful thing. Let's enjoy it. . . . It's twinkling like a stage set." The literal-minded taxonomist, Will, responds: "It'll make a bad-looking spring. A lot of shrubs get damaged and turn brown, and trees don't blossom right." His inability to permit his imagination to make something "pretty" becomes the final blow to a seven-year relationship that was over some time before. His icy response puts his fiancé in touch, finally, with her real unconscious feelings.

"BUD PARROT"

The long story "Bud Parrot" illustrates, if the reader observes closely, an unspoken sexual subtext upon which the narrative rests. The occasion is a wedding in Ohio, of Bud Parrot's closest friend and longtime roommate, Dean Blaines, to Gail Redding. Both men are in their middle thirties, and Bud Parrot is there to try, somehow, to win Dean back. They have probably been lovers. The tension rises as Bud, accompanied by Gail's sister, Evaline, whose constant knowing wink alerts the reader to the "real" story, impulsively surprises the newlyweds in their honeymoon suite at the Columbus Hilton. Evaline and Bud have just come from a visit to the Columbus Zoo. They find little evidence that anything sexual has occurred between husband and wife, but Dean assures Bud and Evaline that the "real" honeymoon will take place in Madrid. The tense scene ends with Bud Parrot excoriating Spain, chomping on an apple, and acting as a tempter as Dean rubs Gail's back while she glares knowingly at the handsome Bud Parrot. Once again, Robison, who trusts her reader completely, does not need to explain that some of the wedding guests probably know about the true nature of the lengthy relationship between Bud and Dean; she invites the reader to compare the "zoo" in the Honeymoon Suite at the Columbus Hilton to life in the actual Columbus zoo.

"MAY QUEEN"

Mary Robison can move from the sexual desperation and commercial surrealism of expensive Ohio weddings to, in "May Queen," an unconscious re-enactment of human sacrifice in Indianapolis with consummate ease and assurance. Mickey and Denise observe with horror as their May queen daughter, Riva, catches fire from holy candles in St. Rose of Lima church on a glorious spring day. The choice of the name of the parish, St. Rose of Lima, adds to the irony of the story since Saint Rose was renowned for the severity of the penitential sufferings that she inflicted upon herself. The story ends with Riva's father trying to relieve his daughter's pain with promises of vacations on the shores of Lake Erie, "where we can lie around and bake in the sun all day . . . and you'll be eighteen then. You'll be able to drink, if you want to."

"HEART"

Not all Robison's stories document lives of quiet desperation so blatantly. "Heart" records the life of a lonely, aging man, Roy, who lives his life vicariously by starting conversations with teenagers at the local roller skating rink and with the friendly paperboy, whose line "Pretty soon, a new guy will be collecting" records another loss for a solitary person such as Roy. The story is an American version of British writer Katherine Mansfield's classic "Miss Brill," but without its sentimental ending. "Heart" concludes with Roy exhorting a local dog to "Wake up and live. . . . Count the Fords that pass" and telling Mrs. Kenny, who lives on the other side of Roy's duplex, that Mickey Rooney was in town with major advice: "He says you've got to have your heart in it. Every minute. . . . The dog knows." Robison's sharp ear picks up the pathetic locker-room Boosterisms that many Americans exchange on empty Sunday afternoons. Mrs. Kenny notices that Roy's hands are trembling, and when she asks him why, he says he cannot

sleep. She blames him for listening to the radio all night and for not trying hard enough to sleep. "Oh," he says, "that's probably it. I don't try."

Few writers capture the cruelty of the Protestant work ethic as it systematically justifies everything bad that happens to people as really being their own fault. Roy, like many lonely people, takes refuge in late-night radio to comfort him in his solitude. That sad attempt turns into proof that he does not possess the "heart" that Mickey Rooney promotes. His inability to sleep, then, becomes proof that he has not tried hard enough. Few writers are able to delineate the Calvinist circle of self-blame with the subtle but savage accuracy of Robison.

"THE NATURE OF ALMOST EVERYTHING"

The stories in Robison's next collection, *An Amateur's Guide to the Night*, are less bitter and dark principally because the humor focuses more on the absurdities of a specifically American system of values, or lack thereof. There is also a growing ability of some characters to laugh at themselves in a healthier way; the humor has become less self-deprecatory. The opening line of one of the finest stories in the book, "The Nature of Almost Everything," establishes the tone of the collection: "Tell you, at thirty-six, my goals are to stay sober and pay off my MasterCard bill." Crises are labeled clearly and dealt with directly. People have become more honest with themselves and can live vivid lives even when they must watch loved ones around them falling apart.

"AN AMATEUR'S GUIDE TO THE NIGHT"

The story "An Amateur's Guide to the Night" shows how a teenage girl, Lindy, in Terre Haute, Indiana, has worked out successful fictive defenses to help her cope with a mother who refuses to grow up and who takes refuge in pills, horror movies, and pretensions that she and Lindy are really sisters. They double-date and call each other "Sis." Lindy's real spiritual center lies in her devotion to the stars and their celestial movements, which she views through her telescope at night.

"COACH"

The story "Coach" shows a good-natured midwestern football coach, Harry Noonan, enjoying early success in his first college job. His artist wife,

Sherry, has carved out a life of her own with her printmaking, private studio, and a five-year plan to learn French. Their daughter, Daphne, a sexily attractive high school girl, flirts with as many football hunks as possible. The coach's unbounded optimism centers the story in an atmosphere reminiscent of a stereotypical 1950's America. All situations and problems are analyzed and solved in the most cliché-ridden banalities. The emptiness in this story is palpable but oddly comic.

"IN JEWEL"

The story "In Jewel" is about another female artist, an art teacher educated at the Rhode Island School of Design, who has returned to teach at her old high school in Jewel, West Virginia. Though she is engaged, she takes great consolation in her gifted students and lets them get close to her. She is torn, though, between wanting to leave her hometown and her inability to do so. As she aptly puts it: "So, I like feeling at home. I just wish I didn't feel it here." Brad Foley, a student whom she helped through a family crisis and who will probably never escape Jewel, sends her a note congratulating her on her engagement and urging her to move. The final scene records in dismal detail that all she really has is what she sees before her on her desk in her room. Again, stasis wins and the fear of the unknown paralyzes even the ones who previously had an opportunity to escape.

"YOURS"

The short-short story "Yours" also deals with art but as a project that a dying, thirty-five-year-old woman named Allison and her seventy-eight-year-old husband, Clark, are pursuing. It is Halloween, and they are carving jack-o'-lanterns ostensibly for the neighborhood children. Robison delicately examines the way the imagination can create what Wallace Stevens called "the violence within that protects us from the violence without"—that is, individuals create images that sum up their lives in somewhat the same way that Don in "Kite and Paint" vivified his final years. The image at the conclusion of this story is one of great iconographic mystery. Clark stares at the eight illuminated faces sitting in the darkness: "He was speaking into the phone now. He watched the jack-o'-lanterns. The jack-o'-lanterns watched him."

"I AM TWENTY-ONE"

Reassuring images that comfort and enable people to find small satisfactions are also the subject of "I Am Twenty-one." A grieving college student, whose parents had been killed in a car accident two years earlier, is trying desperately to earn good grades on her test for a course called "The Transition from Romanesque to Gothic," a phrase that could apply as well to the direction that her life seems to be taking as her isolation deepens. Though she has attempted to create a life of monastic severity and simplicity in her small room, she permits herself one picture that "wasn't of a Blessed Virgin or a detail from Amiens of the King of Judah holding a rod of the tree of Jesse. Instead, it was an eight-by-ten glossy of Rudy and Leslie, my folks." Her desire and grief have caused her to create an icon of her own genealogical tree of Jesse (the Blessed Virgin Mary's family tree): "I kept the picture around because, oddly, putting away the *idea* of my folks would have been worse than losing the real them." She has enacted the exact process by which a mere image takes on the numinous quality of an icon and so has unconsciously learned an important lesson in both her academic course and her life.

BELIEVE THEM

Robison's third collection of short fiction is entitled *Believe Them*, and the mood in these stories is definitely more upbeat than in her previous two. They also generally run longer than her earlier stories. A stronger controlling voice narrates even though the pain of living has changed little within the stories themselves. The humor in the stories is less sardonic and bitter; the characters in some of them are actually enjoying themselves.

"SEIZING CONTROL"

The title of the volume comes from the mouth of the oldest of six children, Hazel, who is retarded and cannot read, but she has memorized the important facts that she needs to know for an orderly life. The first story, "Seizing Control," records what happens when five children stay up all night while their mother is having her sixth child. Hazel does not tell her parents, when asked later, any of the negative parts of the all-night party but rather lists for them everything she knows that her parents had taught her, from "Don't pet strange animals" to "Put baking soda on your bee stings" to "Whatever Mother and Father tell you, believe them."

"FOR REAL"

"For Real" is one of Robison's strongest stories. It mixes humor and pathos in the life of Boffo, the girl clown who hosts Channel 22's "Mid-day Matinee," and her handsome German boyfriend, Dieter, who works at the same television station and is several years her junior. Dieter has been trying to get Boffo to marry him so that he can remain in the United States, but she has resisted his proposals for some time. The story develops when the reader and Boffo realize that Dieter has been to his lawyer and is obviously making other plans to secure citizenship papers. Boffo realizes that she has actually enjoyed his company more than she thought, but the issue of control quickly becomes the focus of the story. As he takes charge of his life and becomes less dependent on Boffo, she sees herself not only as a television clown but also possibly as a clown "For Real." She also sees clearly, and for the first time, that her clown routine, for better or worse, is her life. Her three-year preoccupation with Dieter has distracted her from becoming the "best" clown she can be, and the story concludes with her realization that if she is a clown, it is worth doing right: "Excuse me, viewers? Ladies and germs? You've been being cheated, in all truth. You've been seeing a lazy job of Boffo. But stay watching. We're about to press the pedal to the floor. We're about to do it right." Her announcement is to herself as she fully understands the true nature of her life. What may seem like failure has become for her an occasion of genuine illumination, recognized and acknowledged by her fellow workers' laughter on the set.

"TRYING"

The story "Trying" is also about a clown, the class clown, Bridie O'Donnell, who has become the resident 1960's liberal at the Virginia Benedictine Convent School near Washington, D.C. Her lawyer parents are aging radicals who practice poverty law in a Washington, D.C., storefront office. Bridie spends much of her time and energy in iconoclastic wisecracking, particularly in Sister Elspeth's history class. Sister Elspeth is a six-foot, eight-inch-tall nun who suffers from giantism. Robison balances Bridie's stubborn efforts to convince her conservative classmates and teachers of the wisdom of liberal thinking against Sister Elspeth's conservative proposal of starting a "civics club." Neither character ever stops trying, though they emerge from opposite political traditions. The moment of revelation comes, however, when they recognize their mutual isolation from the rest of the community; they are grotesques, and they know it and understand each other's plight with perfect clarity.

"ADORE HER"

One of Robison's bitterest attacks on Yuppies is "Adore Her," though she has dealt with them before in "Bud Parrot," "Falling Away," and "Mirror." In a story of classic narcissism, Steve spends most of his time fawning over his girlfriend, Chloe, and polishing his Saab in the late afternoon shade. "Adore Her" is one of Robison's finest parables of emptiness, especially when Chloe explains to Steve the secret of her success: "Appearance is all." Steve is so bored with his job as a claims investigator for an insurance company that he openly tempts his very serious boss to fire him. A major issue in the story is control, as Steve begins to see himself as a slave to his job, his Yuppie materialism, and to Chloe. He becomes obsessed with finding the owner of a wallet containing many photographs of different women and spends considerable energy trying to track him down. His brief time away from attending to the beautiful but empty Chloe has taught him that he is controlled totally by her. After seducing her into drinking a beer with him even though she has a hangover, he decides to leave her: "He would run from the unalterables: from Chloe, the apartment building, his job at Tidewater Assurance. He'd run from everything he couldn't change about what he had been calling his life." Steve is one of the few characters in Robison's fiction who sees his life paralyzed in the stasis of debilitating boredom yet seems willing to take radical and courageous steps to change the things that he can.

Mary Robison is one of the United States' most perceptive delineators of the acedia and sterility at the center of American materialism. With flawless lucidity her highly attuned ear can expose it in the voices of the old, the bored, the desperate, and the hopeless. Her stories do not preach and never moralize. Like her teacher John Barth, she presents as accurately as she can. What saves most of her characters, at least those willing to change, is their sense of humor, their lack of self-pity, and their ability to laugh at themselves.

OTHER MAJOR WORKS

LONG FICTION: *Oh!*, 1981; *Subtraction*, 1991.

BIBLIOGRAPHY

Angell, Roger, ed. *Nothing But You: Love Stories from "The New Yorker."* New York: Random House, 1997. An interesting collection of items from The New Yorker, with an introduction by Angell.

Bell, Madison Smartt. "Less Is Less: The Dwindling American Short Story." *Harper's* 272 (April, 1986): 64-69. Argues that writers influenced by Robison, Ann Beattie, and Raymond Carver should resist their penchant for commercialism, homogeneity, and nihilism; critiques the "minimal" style, as characterized by obsession with surface detail, a tendency to slight distinctions, and a deterministic and even nihilistic worldview.

Birkerts, Sven. "The School of Lish." *The New Republic* 195 (October 13, 1986): 28. Discusses the young writers, including Robison, nurtured by Knopf editor Gordon Lish; argues they represent a crisis in American literature, for they lack a vision of larger social connection; claims writers such as Robison falsify experience.

Flower, Dean. "An Amateur's Guide to the Night." *The Hudson Review* 37 (Summer, 1984): 307-308. Critic Flower finds the stories in *An Amateur's Guide to the Night* narrow and turned in upon themselves, mere glimpses of domestic life. Most of them, however, are successful close-ups of middle-class young people undergoing the pangs of growing up. He praises Robison for her fine ear that accurately records the queer metaphors of everyday speech.

Guth, Hans P., and Gabriele L. Rico. *Discovering Literature*. Upper Saddle River, N.J.: Prentice-Hall, 2000. An anthology collection of works by various writers, including Robison. Includes a bibliography and an index.

Hallett, Cynthia Whitney. *Minimalism and the Short Story: Raymond Carver, Amy Hempel, and Mary Robison*. Lewiston, N.J.: Edwin Mellen Press, 1999. Compares the minimalist styles of these three writers. Includes a bibliography and an index.

Inness-Brown, Elizabeth. "Mary Robison, *Days*." *Fiction International* 12 (1980): 281-283. Inness-Brown praises Robison's ability to "show" readers everything they need to know about the characters and refuse to "tell" them anything. Inness-Brown characterizes Robison's stories as "bolts of lightning revealing ravages of a storm" and points out her strongest quality as a "beautiful precision."

Leavitt, David. "An Amateur's Guide to the Night." *The Village Voice* 29 (January 10, 1984): 44. Given that Robison consistently describes bleak landscapes, the vigor and enthusiasm of this collection brighten the darkness. Leavitt finds the stories in *Days* flawless because of Robison's "perfect eye for detail and ear for dialogue." He states that no short-story writer speaks to modern times "more urgently or fondly," and that her work demands critical attention.

_____. "New Voices and Old Values." *The New York Times Book Review* 90 (May 12, 1985): 1. Discusses the new generation of writers, born in the 1950's and early 1960's, who write from a world in which people marry to separate, families dissolve, and loneliness and disillusionment, as their parents show them, are life's only prizes; discusses the influence of Raymond Carver, Ann Beattie, and Mary Robison.

Pollitt, Katha. "Family and Friends." *The New York Times Book Review*, August 23, 1981, 14, 29. Pollitt credits Robison's work with embodying the "unconscious surrealism of commercial America." She also finds Robison's offbeat cheerfulness and buoyancy refreshing.

Stokes, Geoffrey. "Uh Oh!" *The Village Voice* 26 (August 5, 1981): 32. Stokes calls Robison's *Days* the "Darwin of helplessness" and points out that most of her works are variations on the theme of stasis. He also indicates that her novel *Oh!*, contains a picaresque plot with some fine "truly batty humor." He sees her fiction closer to British mod-

els such as P. G. Wodehouse than to American literary antecedents.

Patrick Meanor, updated by
Nika Hoffman

PHILIP ROTH

Born: Newark, New Jersey; March 19, 1933

PRINCIPAL SHORT FICTION

Goodbye, Columbus and Five Short Stories, 1959
"Novotny's Pain," 1962, revised 1980
"The Psychoanalytic Special," 1963
"On the Air," 1970
"'I Always Wanted You to Admire My Fasting':
    Or, Looking at Kafka," 1973

OTHER LITERARY FORMS

Philip Roth has published a number of novels, many of which were excerpted as self-contained short stories in various magazines. He has written essays of literary criticism and social commentary, dramatic works for stage and screen, and book-length works of autobiography. He also served as general editor of the Penguin series "Writers from the Other Europe" (1975-1989).

ACHIEVEMENTS

Philip Roth is first and foremost a consummate storyteller. Whether the genre is short fiction, novel, or autobiography, and whether the subject matter is serious, comic, or somewhere in between, Roth's great narrative power entertains readers. This ability to spellbind his audience stems from Roth's seemingly effortless command of the English language and his remarkable agility of mind as he maintains a rapid pace of invention, action, and ideas. These talents have been recognized by numerous critics. In addition to his 1959 National Book Award for *Goodbye, Columbus and Five Short Stories*, Roth has won the *Paris Review*'s Aga Khan Award (1958) for "Ep-

stein," a National Institute of Arts and Letters grant (1959), a John Simon Guggenheim Memorial Foundation Fellowship (1959), the Daroff Award, offered by the Jewish Book Council of America (1960; also for *Goodbye, Columbus and Five Other Stories*), and an O. Henry second-prize award (1960) for "Defender of the Faith." He was elected to the National Institute of Arts and Letters in 1969. Both *The Counterlife* (1986) and *Patrimony: A True Story* (1991) won the National Book Critics Circle Award (1987 and 1992, respectively), and in 1991 Roth was awarded the National Arts Club Medal of Honor for Literature. *Operation Shylock: A Confession* (1993) won the PEN/Faulkner Award, *Sabbath's Theater* (1995) won the National Book Award, and *American Pastoral* (1997) won the Pulitzer Prize in 1998. He has been awarded honorary doctorates by Dartmouth College, Brandeis University, Columbia University, Rutgers University, and other universities.

Roth has also been heavily criticized over the years. Critics accuse him of wasting his talent on a limited, self-absorbed vision of the world, having a sexist attitude toward women, portraying Jews in an unflattering light, and being needlessly pessimistic. While these charges may or may not have validity, no one doubts Roth's skills as a wordsmith. Moreover, the continuing appeal of Roth's work indicates that his apparent aimlessness and moral anguish reflect deeply felt trends in contemporary life.

BIOGRAPHY

Philip Milton Roth was reared in Newark, New Jersey, where he was influenced by the rising urban Jewish culture that dominated the intellectual and

Philip Roth (Nancy Crampton)

cultural life of part of that city. After graduating from Weequahic High School, he attended Newark College of Rutgers University from 1950 to 1951, finished his B.A. at Bucknell University in 1954, and earned an M.A. at the University of Chicago in 1955. After a stint in the United States Army, he returned to the University of Chicago, where he completed most of his work toward a Ph.D. and taught literature from 1956 to 1958. Roth's stormy personal relationships and health problems have figured in much of his writing. In 1959 he was married to Margaret Martinson Williams, from whom he obtained a legal separation in 1963. She died in 1968. In 1990, Roth married his long-term companion, the actress Claire Bloom, and they divorced in 1995. Roth suffered serious appendicitis and peritonitis in 1967, drug-induced depression following knee surgery in 1987, and quintuple-bypass surgery in 1989; he also spent time in a psychiatric hospital during his marriage to Bloom.

ANALYSIS

Philip Roth's most important collection of stories is the 1959 volume *Goodbye, Columbus*. Roth has produced other individual stories, however, which have been printed in such magazines as *The New Yorker, Esquire, Harper's Magazine*, and *The Atlantic Monthly*. Additionally, portions of several of his novels were first released as short stories. The shorter fiction serves to introduce the reader both to Roth's typical range of styles and to his complex themes. The author's Newark-Jewish background lends a prominent urban-ethnic flavor to his early fiction, but read in the context of his later work, which sometimes deals less directly with "Jewish" matters, it becomes clear that the Jewish elements in his work are used to exemplify larger concerns endemic to American society as a whole.

Technically, Roth's fiction runs the gamut from broad satire to somber realism to Kafkaesque surrealism. Beneath the wide range of styles, however, is the strain of social realism, which attempts to depict, often without overt judgment, the pressures brought to bear on the modern individual searching for (or trying to recover) moral, ethical, and cultural roots in a society that prides itself on the erasure of such differences in its attempt to achieve homogeneity. Implicit in many of the stories is the problem of the leveling down into a normalcy of behavior which, although perhaps a socially acceptable way of "getting along," nevertheless mitigates against the retention of cultural eccentricities or personal individuality. While Roth's Jewish milieu provided ample opportunity to observe this phenomenon, some of his later fiction explores these matters in non-Jewish settings.

"ELI, THE FANATIC"

"Eli, the Fanatic" embodies many of Roth's themes and techniques. Taking place in suburban America, the tale concerns a young, "secularized" Jewish lawyer, Eli Peck, who is retained to convince a European Jew, who operates a resident Jewish academy in the town (aptly and symbolically named Woodenton), to close his establishment. The town is embarrassed by the presence of the yeshiva, since it calls the largely gentile residents' attention to the Jewishness of some of the inhabitants who wish to blend in peacefully with the rest of the population. Significantly, it is the Jews who hire Eli, and not the gentiles, Jews who believe all too literally in the "melting pot" theory of assimilation. Of particular annoyance is one resident of the yeshiva—a Hasidic Jew who wears the traditional long black coat and wide-brimmed hat and walks about the town shopping for supplies for the school.

When Eli confronts the headmaster, he is touched by the old man's integrity and his fierce but philosophically stoical attachment to his cultural and religious roots—an attachment, however, which Eli cannot share. Eli realizes that the old man will never abandon his school and has no "respect" for the zoning laws which prohibit such establishments. Eli attempts a compromise. After soliciting reluctant approval from his clients, he tries to persuade the old man to insist that his Hasidic employee wear modern garb, in the hope that the visible manifestation of the enclave will be removed, thus mollifying the community. Eli is informed by the headmaster that, after the man's escape from the Holocaust, the clothes he wears are "all he's got." Eli realizes that the remark is symbolic as well as literal—that the clothes are a symbol of the identity not even the Nazis could take away from the man. Nevertheless, Eli brings to the yeshiva two of his own suits in the hope that the man will adopt the inoffensive dress.

Although he does so, much to the temporary relief of Eli and the modern Jewish community, he also leaves his old clothes on Eli's doorstep and parades about the town in Eli's ill-fitting clothes as a kind of silent reproach to a town which would rob him of his identity. Only Eli senses the meaning of the man's act. In what can only be termed a mystical transformation, Eli feels compelled to put on the Hasidic garb, and he begins to walk through the village, achieving a "conversion" to the values and sense of belonging that the man had represented. Moreover, as he literally "walks in the man's shoes," he defies the leveling and dehumanizing impetus represented by his role in enforcing the town's desires. He finally visits the hospital where his wife has recently given birth to their first son and is berated by her and several of the town's citizens and accused of having another of what has apparently been a series of nervous breakdowns. Eli realizes that this time he is totally sane and lucid; but at the close of the story he feels the prick of a hypodermic needle, and the reader knows that he will be tranquilized and psychoanalyzed back to "normalcy."

The story illustrates the major concerns in Roth's fiction. Eli is a normally nonaggressive hero who nevertheless is prodded to assert his individuality actively and thus assuage his own guilt. The pressures of society exert a counter force which annihilates this thrust toward individuality. The story is not really about conversion to an obscure form of Judaism so much as it is about the desire to resist the loss of cultural identity and personal individuality. In a world of diminished passions, the Rothian hero attempts to assert himself in the midst of the society which inhibits him. Unlike the "activist" heroes of much of American fiction who "light out for the territory," or who "make a separate peace," Roth's activists stand their ground and attempt to triumph over, or at least to survive within, the society—often without success.

"EPSTEIN"

Not all of Roth's heroes are activists—many become *passive* victims to these societal forces. "Epstein," an early story which appeared in the *Paris Review* and was incorporated into *Goodbye, Columbus*, illustrates this second pattern. The central character, Lou Epstein, is a financially and socially successful owner of a paper-bag company. An immigrant to America as a child, he has achieved apparent success by subscribing to the essentially Protestant work ethic of his adopted country.

Epstein's life, however, has not been happy. A son died at age eleven, and he broods about his company falling into the hands of a stranger. His wife, Goldie, a compulsive housekeeper, is aging rapidly and unattractively, and while Epstein is not young, he feels youthful sexual drives which do not tally with his wife's rejection of him or her diminished appeal. His only daughter has become fat, and her fiancé is a "chinless, lazy smart aleck." Epstein is, in short, going through a midlife crisis, surrounded by signs of unfulfilled goals and waning capacities and opportunities.

Jealous of the "zipping and unzipping" which accompany midnight teenage assignations in his living room, thus heightening the frustrations of his airless marriage, he begins an affair with the recently widowed mother of his brother's son's girlfriend. The woman represents all that his life lacks and all that his wife is not—sensuousness, lust, adventure. The "Calvinist" gods are not mocked, however, because Epstein contracts a suspicious rash that his wife discovers to her horror, resulting in a hilarious but apocalyptic battle waged by the naked pair over the bed sheets, which Goldie seeks to burn. The next day, Epstein, seeking to confront his amour, collapses in the street with a heart attack; at the close of the story, his wife, riding in the ambulance with Epstein, assures him that he will be all right. "All he's got to do," the doctor tells her, "is live a normal life, normal for sixty." Goldie pleads, "Lou, you'll live normal, won't you? *Won't you?*"

Normal means a return to the external success and internal misery of his life before the liberating affair. The issue is not the morality of the situation but the desperate attempt to control one's life consciously and seize experience. Epstein laments,

> When they start taking things away from you, you reach out, you *grab*—maybe like a pig even, but you grab. And right, wrong, who knows! With tears in your eyes, who can even see the difference!

Epstein is returned unwillingly to the world of "normalcy." He is trapped—even biologically trapped—by a society which has adopted essentially Protestant-Calvinist values that distrust appetites, roots, and eccentric behavior, and which inculcates a sense of moral guilt, which is essentially the same as so-called Jewish guilt.

"DEFENDER OF THE FAITH"

Sergeant Nathan Marx, the Jewish protagonist of "Defender of the Faith," another story collected in *Goodbye, Columbus*, has achieved assimilated normalcy by serving honorably in World War II. After the war's end in Europe, he finds himself in charge of new soldiers in Camp Crowder, Missouri. One of his charges, Sheldon Grossbart, tries to use their shared Jewishness to gain special privileges. While his interactions with Grossbart cause Marx to rediscover his Jewish identity, Marx also increasingly refuses to do Grossbart favors. The story's crisis occurs as Gross-

bart manages to have himself assigned to service in New Jersey rather than in the Pacific, where the war still rages. When Marx breaks the rules to see that Grossbart is reassigned to the Pacific, Marx considers himself a defender of American values, military values, and Jewish values, but Marx also knows that his vindictive violation of his own principles leaves him cut off from all the communities of which he longs to be a member. The story's ending leaves Marx in a richly paradoxical situation of a very Rothian sort. The story's various discussions of how lies relate to truth also raise issues of how a professional writer, as a professional teller of lies, can be a good American or a good Jew.

"NOVOTNY'S PAIN"

In another early story (with no Jewish characters) entitled "Novotny's Pain," the title character, conscripted into the army as a willing, if frightened, recruit, suffers unspecified and clearly psychosomatic lower back pain which Novotny endures in the hope that it will eventually go away. He clearly is not a "gold-bricker." He is engaged to be married, and when out on pass, he and his girlfriend enjoy a rich and acrobatic sex life despite occasional back pain.

Novotny, in desperate discomfort and moral unease, seeks medical help, but tests reveal nothing pathologically wrong. The young man admits that he fears going into battle but also sincerely asserts that if the root of the pain can be removed he will be more than willing to do his duty. The army authorities regard him, however, as a mental case, or worse, and eventually he is given a dishonorable discharge. Novotny wonders if he is being punished for all the ecstatic sex and happiness he has had with his fiancé, which his back has not prevented him from experiencing; even after he marries her, although threats that the discharge will destroy his civilian prospects turn out to be groundless, Novotny still suffers twinges of pain that correspond to his twinges of guilt. At the end, Novotny asks himself a central question: "What good was it, being good?" All of Roth's heroes try to deal with the concept of "goodness" but are impaled on the varying definitions of the term: goodness arising out of socially acceptable conformity or goodness coming from an existential attempt to define one's self satisfactorily in terms of needs, roots, and desires.

"'I ALWAYS WANTED YOU TO ADMIRE MY FASTING'"

In a later story, "'I Always Wanted You to Admire My Fasting': Or, Looking at Kafka," Roth first relates and then rewrites the last part of the life of one of Roth's favorite writers in order to examine what creates "goodness" in a writer. In Roth's biographical analysis, Franz Kafka died of tuberculosis at the happiest point of his life, and Roth notes signs in Kafka's late story "The Burrow" that Kafka was achieving progress toward love and toward understanding and accepting himself. Yet Kafka's greatness as a writer might have never been known if Kafka had lived and been able to decide for himself whether to publish the works for which he became famous. As if to prove that advantages for others can be disadvantages for writers, the final section fancifully reimagines Kafka's life, allows him to survive until age seventy and even escape to America. Kafka becomes the nine-year-old Roth's teacher in Hebrew school in New Jersey, suffers through a romance with Roth's Aunt Rhoda—a romance that fails despite the absence of several impediments Kafka faced in real life—and finally dies unpublished. Roth concludes that one must maintain a high level of discomfort in one's society and in one's family, and one must be very lucky, to become known as a good writer.

The acerbity of Roth's vision, his honesty in portraying the deficiencies in American culture and values, and his refusal to prescribe overt solutions have led to critical charges of anti-Semitism and defeatism. His characters' valiant, if often thwarted, attempts to achieve some identity and sense of placement, however, belie the latter charge, and the honest, if not always affectionate, portrayal of both Jewish and non-Jewish characters in similar situations negates the former accusation.

OTHER MAJOR WORKS

LONG FICTION: *Letting Go*, 1962; *When She Was Good*, 1967; *Portnoy's Complaint*, 1969; *Our Gang*, 1971; *The Breast*, 1972, revised 1980; *The Great American Novel*, 1973; *My Life as a Man*, 1974; *The Professor of Desire*, 1977; *The Ghost Writer*, 1979; *Zuckerman Unbound*, 1981; *The Anatomy Lesson*, 1983; *Zuckerman Bound*, 1985 (includes *The Ghost Writer, Zuckerman Unbound, The Anatomy Lesson*, and *Epilogue: The Prague Orgy*); *The Counterlife*, 1986; *Deception*, 1990; *Operation Shylock: A Confession*, 1993; *Sabbath's Theater*, 1995; *American Pastoral*, 1997; *I Married a Communist*, 1998; *The Human Stain*, 2000.

NONFICTION: *Reading Myself and Others*, 1975, expanded 1985; *The Facts: A Novelist's Autobiography*, 1988; *Patrimony: A True Story*, 1991.

BIBLIOGRAPHY

Baumgarten, Murray, and Barbara Gottfried. *Understanding Philip Roth*. Columbia: University of South Carolina Press, 1990. Interpretation and discussion of Roth's fiction. Includes a bibliography and index.

Bloom, Harold, ed. *Philip Roth*. New York: Chelsea House, 1986. A good study of Roth's fiction. Includes a bibliography and index.

Cooper, Alan. *Philip Roth and the Jews*. Albany: State University of New York Press, 1996. A carefully researched examination and consideration of Roth's work, his biography, and Roth's political views which are evident in his writing.

Guttmann, Allen. *The Jewish Writer in America: Assimilation and the Crisis of Identity*. New York: Oxford University Press, 1971. This book provides a broader context for interpreting Roth's work, one that a number of critics believe to be essential, particularly for some of the early short stories.

Halio, Jay L. *Philip Roth Revisited*. New York: Twayne, 1992. Discusses the critical response to Roth's fiction. Includes a bibliography and index.

Meeter, Glenn. *Philip Roth and Bernard Malamud: A Critical Essay*. Grand Rapids, Mich.: Wm. B. Eerdmans, 1968. An interesting comparison of Roth and Malamud, authors with compelling similarities as well as important differences.

Milbauer, Asher Z., and Donald G. Watson, eds. *Reading Philip Roth*. New York: St. Martin's Press, 1988. This collection of essays is consistently insightful, examining Roth as a social critic and an exemplar of Jewish alienation. Also compares him to some prominent American novelists, as well as to Franz Kafka.

Pinsker, Sanford. *The Comedy That "Hoits": An Essay on the Fiction of Philip Roth*. Columbia: University of Missouri Press, 1975. Pinsker knows Roth inside out. In this relatively early work he does a good job of analyzing the precise relation of Roth's humor to the more serious issues addressed in his work.

_____, ed. *Critical Essays on Philip Roth*. Boston: G. K. Hall, 1982. Composed of fourteen reviews of various Roth works, including his short story "The Conversion of the Jews" and an equal number of critical essays. Several of the essays deal with Roth's treatment of the Jewish American experience, and one essay compares Roth to Kafka. Pinsker provides a helpful introduction.

Rand, Naomi R. *Silko, Morrison, and Roth: Studies in Survival*. New York: Peter Lang, 1999. A study of how Silko, Morrison, and Roth each use a "survival narrative motif" as a way of defining their ethnic stance.

Rodgers, Bernard F., Jr. *Philip Roth*. Boston: Twayne, 1978. This book examines a variety of Roth's work, including several of his short stories, arguing that Roth's experimentation with different literary forms should not disguise his overriding commitment to "realism" as socio-moral therapy.

Roth, Philip. *Conversations with Philip Roth*. Edited by George J. Searles. Jackson: University Press of Mississippi, 1992. Roth talks about his life and the influences on his fiction. Includes a bibliography and index.

Wade, Stephen. *The Imagination in Transit: The Fiction of Philip Roth*. Sheffield: Sheffield Academic Press, 1996. Wade details Roth's growth as a novelist through a study of his fiction, relates the connection of Roth's work to American Jewish literary style, and lists influences on Roth's work.

David Sadkin, updated by Ira Smolensky and Marshall Bruce Gentry

---

JUAN RULFO

Born: Barranca de Apulco, Jalisco, Mexico; May 16, 1918
Died: Mexico City, Mexico; January 7, 1986

PRINCIPAL SHORT FICTION

El llano en llamas, 1953 (*The Burning Plain and Other Stories*, 1967, revised 1970 and 1980)

OTHER LITERARY FORMS

Juan Rulfo is known for two major works, his novel *Pedro Páramo* (1955, rev. 1959, 1964, 1980; English translations 1959, 1994) and his collection of short stories. Rulfo also wrote a novelette, screenplays, and essays of literary criticism. In 1994, the posthumous *Los cuadernos de Juan Rulfo* was published.

ACHIEVEMENTS

Juan Rulfo's two major works have been translated into more than ten languages. His novel *Pedro Páramo* is widely credited with changing the course of Mexican literature. Rulfo received two fellowships to the Center for Mexican Writers (1952-1954) and was awarded Mexico's National Literature Prize in 1970. He was elected to membership in the Mexican Academy of Letters in 1980 and received the Príncipe de Asturias Prize from Spain in 1983. He was honored after death by the creation of the Juan Rulfo Latin American and Caribbean Literature Award.

BIOGRAPHY

Juan Rulfo was born in Barranca de Apulco, in Jalisco, Mexico, on May 16, 1918, but his family

Juan Rulfo (©Layle Silbert)

soon moved to San Gabriel, in the same state of Jalisco, where the young Rulfo suffered the assassination of his father in 1925 and the death of his mother by heart attack two years later. In 1928 Rulfo enrolled in an orphanage in Guadalajara run by Josephine nuns, where he remained until 1932, when he entered the seminary to become a priest. He left the seminary upon the death of his grandmother, preferring to study business and law. A strike at the University of Guadalajara forestalled his higher education, and in 1935 he moved to Mexico City, where he immediately began working in the Office of the Ministry of Migration. He left the Ministry in 1946 to become a traveling salesman for Goodrich Tires. He married Clara Aparicio in 1948 and had four children. He worked in public relations for Goodrich, then in publishing and television before joining the Instituto Indigenista in 1962.

Rulfo published his first stories in periodicals as early as 1945. In 1952 a fellowship at the Center for Mexican Writers made it possible for him to complete and collect his stories for his first book, *The Burning Plain and Other Stories*. A second year of fellowship allowed him to complete his novel *Pedro*

Páramo. Though he continued to write, Rulfo did not continue to publish, publishing only a novelette, screenplays, and occasional essays of literary criticism until his death on January 7, 1986, from lung cancer.

ANALYSIS

Juan Rulfo's international reputation rests on only two slender volumes published in his thirties. In contrast to the novel of the Mexican Revolution, with its descriptive realism and nationalism, Rulfo introduced the new Mexican narrative that would lead to what has been called the boom in Latin American literature, an outpouring of innovative fiction. Colombian novelist and Nobel Prize winner Gabriel García Márquez claimed Rulfo as one of his greatest influences. The Mexican poet and Nobel winner Octavio Paz praised Rulfo as "the only Mexican novelist to have provided us with an image—rather than a mere description—of our physical surroundings."

The isolation and desolation of the rural Mexican desert landscape of his stories provide a setting where human characters have as little hope or possibility as the landscape has fertility. Just as the sterility of the desert is broken only by the implied violence of snakes and buzzards, so too are Rulfo's stories studded with vengeance and violence, death and despair. Several critics have suggested that Rulfo's preoccupation with violence stems from the violent death of his father when he was only seven and the violent condition of a Mexico still in turmoil after a revolution that ended in 1920.

The journey, which is often a physical journey combined with a symbolic quest (inevitably doomed to failure), is the dominant theme and organizing principle in many of Rulfo's stories. The relationship between father and son, or the absence of a father, is a recurring motif. Other recurring themes include poverty and power, such as the poor versus the government, or the poor versus the local *cacique*, or landowner-boss.

"WE'RE VERY POOR"

Like all of Rulfo's stories, "Es que somos muy pobres" ("We're Very Poor") reveals much about the lives of Mexico's poor *campesinos*, or rural people. A first-person narrator, the boy in a poor family, tells his story in the present tense to an unnamed listener, which creates a sense of immediacy, as if events are unfolding along with the narrative. A series of disasters has affected this family: Aunt Jacinta just died and was buried; the rains came unexpectedly, without giving the family time to salvage any of their rye harvest, which was stacked outside to dry in the sun; and now the cow his father gave his sister Tacha for her twelfth birthday has been swept away by the newly overflowing river. Tacha is the last of three sisters. The other two "went bad" and became prostitutes. Tacha's cow was her only hope for a better life; without her cow she has nothing to attract a man to marry her. Tacha's dowry and the only bank account she will ever have has washed away in the floodwaters of the river. As the boy observes his sister crying, he notes that her "two little breasts bounce up and down . . . as if suddenly they were beginning to swell, to start now on the road to ruin." Tacha is devastated by the loss of her cow, but she does not yet understand the depth of her loss nor what seem to be the inescapable consequences of that loss. These people, like so many of Rulfo's characters, are helpless victims of poverty and all it entails.

"TALPA"

"Talpa" combines some of Rulfo's common themes, using the physical journey as the means to a frustrated quest. Natalia and the anonymous first-person narrator agree to take Natalia's husband Tanilo to the religious center of Talpa so he can pray to the Virgin there for a cure for the weeping wounds on his arms and legs. Tanilo's quest is for a miracle—the miracle of renewed health. The narrator and Natalia agree to take him because they hope he will die en route.

It is a long journey on foot. Every night along the way Natalia and the narrator, who is Tanilo's brother, steal off to make passionate love. Tanilo's condition worsens, and he asks to go home, but the lovers push him onward, not wanting an end to their freedom from societal restrictions. They arrive at Talpa with Tanilo in serious condition. After rallying briefly to dance to the Virgin with other pilgrims, he dies, his quest for new health unsatisfied. Even though

Tanilo's death is the desired object of his brother's quest, his brother regrets Tanilo's passing. After burying Tanilo, Natalia and the narrator-brother make the long trip home in silence. Upon arriving home and seeing her mother, the hitherto stoic Natalia breaks down in inconsolable sobbing. The love and passion between the narrator and Natalia are forever quenched by guilt. In death Tanilo exercises more power than in life.

"TELL THEM NOT TO KILL ME"

Rulfo considered "Diles que no me maten!" ("Tell Them Not to Kill Me") his best story. Unlike most of Rulfo's stories, an anonymous first-person narrator does not relate "Tell Them Not to Kill Me." Rather, dialogue between Juvencio Nava, the sixty-year-old protagonist, and his son Justino opens the story, followed by third-person narration from Juvencio's point of view, followed by dialogue between Juvencio and the Coronel who orders his death, and closing with a brief dialogue between Justino and the corpse of his father.

Thirty-five years ago Juvencio Nava killed Don Lupe Terreros in a dispute over livestock. Lupe refused to let Juvencio use his pastures. Juvencio cut a hole in Lupe's fence, Lupe killed one of Juvencio's yearlings, and Juvencio killed Lupe in a particularly violent manner, hacking him with a machete. As a result of his rash act, Juvencio loses everything: The cows he killed to save go to pay a corrupt judge; his wife leaves him; and he lives a hidden life with his son. The unnamed Coronel who captures Juvencio is Lupe's son and determines to avenge his father's death. Juvencio pleads for his life, saying he has already paid many times over. In an act of mercy, the Coronel instructs his men to give Juvencio plenty to drink "so the shots won't hurt him." Violence begets violence.

"LUVINA"

"Luvina" is set in two locations and two times: in the present time of the inn where an anonymous storyteller is talking to an unknown listener and in the past Luvina of the narrator's memory. The narrator is a teacher who went to San Juan Luvina many years ago. He explains his experience to his listener, who intends to go there. As he describes it, Luvina is a ghost town of ghostly inhabitants. There is no restaurant, no inn, and no school. It is a town full of women dressed in black, who move among the shadows like otherworldly shades. Occasionally husbands return with the winds, remaining long enough to beget another child, then disappearing again. The children leave as soon as they are able. When the teacher suggests to Luvina's inhabitants that they move somewhere else with the help of the government, they laugh. The government only remembers Luvina when it kills one of its sons, they say, and besides, our dead "live here and we can't leave them alone." The narrator keeps drinking and telling his tale, saying, "I left my life there—I went to that place full of illusions and returned old and worn out." He describes Luvina as if it were a dream, an illusion rather than a reality, but a frightful illusion, a nightmare rather than a dream. The phantasmagoric landscape takes on near-human characteristics and, along with the listener, the reader seems to be transported to purgatory.

OTHER MAJOR WORKS

LONG FICTION: *Pedro Páramo*, 1955, rev. 1959, 1964, 1980 (English translations 1959, 1994).

SCREENPLAYS: *El gallo de oro y otros textos para cine*, 1980 (partial translation "The Golden Cock," 1992).

NONFICTION: *Juan Rulfo: Autobiografía armada*, 1973 (compiled by Reina Roffé); *Inframundo: El México de Juan Rulfo*, 1980 (*Inframundo: The Mexico of Juan Rulfo*, 1983).

MISCELLANEOUS: *Toda la obra* (critical edition), 1992; *Los cuadernos de Juan Rulfo*, 1994.

BIBLIOGRAPHY

Burton, Julianne. "A Drop of Rain in the Desert: Something and Nothingness in Juan Rulfo's 'Nos han dado la tierra' ['They've Given Us the Land']." *Latin American Literary Review* 2, no. 3 (Fall/Winter, 1973): 55-62. Analysis of Rulfo's use of absences ("nothingness") such as barrenness, poverty, isolation, in combination with the presence ("something") of elements like the buzzards that symbolize death and magnify the sterility of the locale and the people's lives.

Ekstrom, Margaret V. "Frustrated Quest in the Narratives of Juan Rulfo." *The American Hispanist* 2, no. 12 (November, 1976): 13-16. Discusses "No Dogs Bark," "Talpa," "The Burning Plain," and "Macario" in relation to the actual journeys and symbolic quests undertaken by Rulfo's characters, who are "unsuccessful" heroes on frustrated quests.

Janney, Frank, ed. and trans. *Inframundo: The Mexico of Juan Rulfo*. New York: Ediciones del Norte, 1983. Collection of critical articles by major Latin American authors like the Nobel-prize-winning Gabriel García Márquez, along with Rulfo's story "Luvina" and nearly a hundred of his stunning black and white photographs illustrating the Mexico described in his works.

Jordan, Michael S. "Noise and Communication in Juan Rulfo." *Latin American Literary Review* 24, no. 27 (January-June, 1996): 115-130. Excellent analysis of several short stories and *Pedro Páramo*, investigating the presence of noise and abundance of "speech acts" in a narrative universe in which real communication is ultimately impossible.

Leal, Luis. *Juan Rulfo*. Boston: Twayne, 1983. The first full-length study in English of Rulfo's work. Relates Rulfo's first unpublished novel, *The Son of Affliction*, to Rulfo's difficult childhood. Divides Rulfo's writing into the first prose work, the early stories, and the later stories, then focuses on the novel, *Pedro Páramo*, by examining "Context and Genesis" and "Structure and Imagery." Also a brief chapter on Rulfo's screenplays and the films made from them, as well as his public lectures. Excellent bibliography.

Lyon, Ted. "Ontological Motifs in the Short Stories of Juan Rulfo." *Journal of Spanish Studies: Twentieth Century* 3 (Winter, 1973): 161-168. Examines all fifteen stories of *The Burning Plain and Other Stories* according to four motifs: walking, memory, futility of effort, and vision impeded by darkness.

Ramírez, Arthur. "Juan Rulfo: Dialectics and the Despairing Optimist." *Hispania* 65 (December, 1982): 580-585. Claims that despite the tensions between the dualities of life and death, love and hate, hope and despair, heaven and hell, reality and unreality in Rulfo's fiction, the overall effect is cohesiveness rather than polarities. Further finds that Rulfo's pessimism contains a kind of affirmation: a preoccupation with death underscores the importance of life and love.

Reinhardt-Childers, Ilva. "Sensuality, Brutality, and Violence in Two of Rulfo's Stories: An Analytical Study." *Hispanic Journal* 12, no.1 (Spring 1991): 69-73. Discusses "At Daybreak" and "The Burning Plain" from the perspective of extreme and unpredictable violence they contain, perhaps because Rulfo witnessed violence while growing up during the aftermath of the Mexican Revolution.

Linda Ledford-Miller

SALMAN RUSHDIE

Born: Bombay, India; June 19, 1947

PRINCIPAL SHORT FICTION

East, West: Stories, 1994
"The Firebird's Nest," 1997
"Vina Divina," 1999

OTHER LITERARY FORMS

Best known for *The Satanic Verses* (1988), Salman Rushdie's other novels include *Grimus* (1975), *Midnight's Children* (1981), *Shame* (1983), *The Moor's Last Sigh* (1995), and *The Ground Beneath Her Feet* (1999). Additionally, he has written a children's fable, *Haroun and the Sea of Stories* (1990); a monograph on cinema, *The Wizard of Oz: A Short Text About Magic* (1992), and two books of essays: *The Jaguar Smile: A Nicaraguan Journey* (1987) and *Imaginary Homelands: Essays and Criticism, 1981–1991* (1991).

ACHIEVEMENTS

Salman Rushdie received the James Tait Black Memorial Prize in 1982 and was made a Fellow of the Royal Society of Literature in 1983. *Shame* won the Prix du Meilleur Livre Étranger in 1984; *The Satanic Verses* and *The Moor's Last Sigh* won Whitbread Literary Awards in 1988 and 1995, respectively. His *Midnight's Children* won a Booker McConnell Prize while *Shame* and *The Satanic Verses* were finalists for that award.

BIOGRAPHY

After early education at Bombay's Cathedral School (1954 to 1961), Salman Rushdie was sent by his nominally Moslem but Anglophile parents to England for an even more British training: Rugby (1961 to 1964) and King's College, Cambridge (1965 to 1968). After traveling to Pakistan, he was forced to return to England because his production of Edward Albee's *The Zoo Story* (pr., pb. 1959) mentioned "pork," thereby inciting Moslem protests. He tried acting, worked as an advertising copywriter, and composed the poorly received *Grimus* (1975). Not until his success with *Midnight's Children* in 1981 could he earn a living from his fiction.

In 1988, his life changed radically with the publication of *The Satanic Verses*. Even though its references to Muhammad are part of a dream sequence, conservative Moslems were outraged. Protests against it included one in Islamabad, Pakistan, where five rioters were killed and more than one hundred injured. In Iran, Ayatollah Ruhollah Khomeini issued a *fatwa* (religious decree) condemning Rushdie and his publishers to death for blasphemy. Rushdie himself has had to live under police protection and in hiding. Casualties of the *fatwa* include the assassination of the Japanese translator and the serious injury of the Norwegian publisher. The *fatwa* may have contributed to the collapse of Rushdie's year-long marriage (1988-1989) to the novelist Marianne Wiggins. Despite the threats, Rushdie continued to publish nonfiction, short stories, and novels. In 1998, the Iranian government declared that it would not continue to enforce the *fatwa*.

ANALYSIS

Because of their shared love of puns and allusions, Salman Rushdie often compares himself to James Joyce, a predecessor Rushdie also resembles in the fate of his reputation. Their humorous, vertiginous, multicultural mixture of erudition and popular culture might never have reached large audiences if they had not had works condemned for blasphemy and pornography, respectively. Rushdie's texts are more erotic than Joyce's and Joyce's more blasphemous than Rushdie's, so their public images are largely a misunderstanding. Both are best seen as postcolonial authors, Joyce condemning the web of British oppression that stagnated Ireland while Rushdie has satirized vestiges of it in India, Pakistan, and émigré communities.

A significant difference, however, divides the importance short stories have played in the careers of each. Joyce learned his craft through writing his collection of stories, *Dubliners* (1914), which marked a major advance for the genre; the interconnecting stories focus on a single locale. Rushdie's works of short fiction (the casual fruits of the middle period of his career), although skillful in their dazzling ironic twists and word play, signal only a refinement, not a major change in the genre. Instead, each functions largely within some past tradition (such as those of Tom Stoppard or Donald Barthelme). With the exception of "Vina Divina" (an extension of one of his novels), they do not have an original voice that would give them the importance of his larger works. The latter, however, have a rambling, episodic movement that makes them sometimes resemble short-story collections (such as *Harmoun and the Sea of Stories*); thus, in a sense, he has followed the lead of *Dubliners* by eroding further the distinction between short-story collection and novel.

"GOOD ADVICE IS RARER THAN RUBIES"

The title conflates Middle Eastern sayings about the preciousness of wisdom, which the biblical book Proverbs likens to a woman as desirable as rubies.

Salman Rushdie (©Jerry Bauer)

Consequently, this title seems to predict a story about useful information or feminine beauty. It concerns both, but in an ironic manner, it is meant to make a political statement. Its protagonist is an advice *wallah* (specialist), cheating "Tuesday" women who come nervously on that day for visas from India to Britain, as if their salvation depended on escaping their homeland. Because of one woman's beauty, however, instead of giving his usually perfidious counsel, the *wallah* offers a forged passport. She refuses lest she confirm the British in their assumption that all Indians are liars (a dishonesty forced on them by English oppression). When he sees her smile upon exiting the embassy, he assumes that her beauty has also triumphed over the "*Sahibs*"—what he calls the British because they are still to him the lords and masters of the land. Nonetheless, she has received no visa; therefore, she will avoid marrying a man old enough to be her father. Without disobeying her parents (who arranged the match), she avoids being pulled into their and the *wallah*'s folly. A slave to the colonial past, he deludes both others and himself with such obsolete notions as the desirability of immigrating to racist Britain, because he has found nothing in modern India to love. Miss Rehana, though, enjoys being the governess of three children. Of virtue and wisdom like hers, Proverbs contends, "her price *is* far above rubies."

"THE PROPHET'S HAIR"

Another of the narratives from the Asian third of *East, West*, this tale is the kind of satire that has caused Rushdie so much trouble—his subjecting Moslem influence in India to a critique almost as severe as he addresses against the British. "The Prophet's Hair" is based on a real incident: A relic is stolen from a Kashmir mosque and then recovered. Rushdie, however, imagines the circuitous path of its return as it works a series of miracles, all of them disastrous. Held illegally by a moneylender (a profession condemned by Islam), the hair, nonetheless, makes him hypocritical enough to force Moslem rigors upon his family, beating them and wishing to cut off the hand of one of his debtors. To escape this religiosity, his son tries to restore the hair to the mosque, but it miraculously returns to the moneylender. Then, risking their lives, the son and daughter hire a violent thief, who like the moneylender has previously led a tolerable life because it was free from religion. The supernatural power of the hair, however, cures his children (whom the thief kindly crippled), and they will thus starve because their income from begging is thereby cut by 75 percent. Death or madness destroys practically everyone else who comes anywhere near the hair. Ironically, the story concludes that Kashmir is closer to Paradise than any other spot on earth—a depressing revelation in a story of widespread horror. D. C. R. A. Goonetilleke compares the story to Robert Louis Stevenson's *The New Arabian Nights* (1882) in their borrowing rapid action from the Oriental folktale but reversing its characteristic optimism. One might also read "The Prophet's Hair" as a parable of the misfortune of recovering faith, based on Rushdie's own experience—his publicly returning to Islam in 1990 only to renounce it again in 1992.

"AT THE AUCTION OF THE RUBY SLIPPERS"

Author of a monograph-length study of the film *The Wizard of Oz* (1939), Rushdie employs the Barthelme-like Magical Realism of this story to evoke what that film means to a culture looking to cinematic fantasies as its past and auctioning even these away. The bidders are expected to go insane. One of them schizophrenically interweaves the auction and his love affair with his cousin Gale, whose name is linked through a pun to the film's tornado. The "Ruby Slippers," preserved behind bulletproof glass, are the ones that Dorothy used to return home. In Rushdie's erotic subplot, however, "home" is given obscene meaning, and that subplot is acknowledged to be itself at least partly hallucination, so there seems to be no real, untainted home in a world of migrants and delusion—one with which Rushdie is very familiar. Significantly, fundamentalists threaten to purchase the slippers in order to burn them, since they insist on having a complete monopoly on hope.

"THE COURTER"

In a 1994 interview, Rushdie revealed that this tale was partly autobiographical. Demonstrating skill at depicting a cross-cultural world that Rushdie knows so well, this nostalgic reminiscence of the narrator's teen years in London portrays his family's elderly *ayah* and her romance with Mecir, a porter. The porter, whose title the *ayah* mispronounces as "courter," courts her by teaching her chess, a game of which he is a grand master (a status in obvious contrast to the humble occupation forced on him as an émigré from Eastern Europe). Violent racism leaves the *ayah* torn between East and West and marks the end of the narrator's innocence. Telling the tale many years later, he realizes that his youthful impertinence in nicknaming Mecir as "Mixed Up" was itself racist, foreshadowing the forces that bring the romance to tragedy. The story concludes the intercultural third of *East, West* (whose middle portion was Occidental, including "At the Auction of the Ruby Slippers").

"VINA DIVINA"

Released a month before Rushdie's six-hundred-page novel *The Ground Beneath Her Feet*, this *New Yorker* story is the novel's first chapter retitled and reworked just enough so that it constitutes a relatively self-contained unit. Both fictions take place in an alternative world where the greatest rock celebrities are Ormus Cama and Vina Apsara, modeled on the mythical Orpheus and Eurydice. An alternative version of the novel's introductory section, this tale is an instance of how Rushdie's short fiction has been engulfed by epic projects (undertaken to distract him from the *fatwa*). As in that novel, the tale is told by Rushdie's persona, the photographer Rai, who engages in long diatribes against religious fanaticism and is worried about being assassinated by terrorists. He is famous for his photograph of Vina's descent into the earth: "The Lady Vanishes." That title echoes not only Rushdie's disappearance but also "The One Who Vanished," Franz Kafka's title for a work of fiction that, like "Vina Divina," evokes a dreamlike version of the United States.

OTHER MAJOR WORKS

LONG FICTION: *Grimus*, 1975; *Midnight's Children*, 1981; *Shame*, 1983; *The Satanic Verses*, 1988; *Harmoun and the Sea of Stories*, 1990; *The Moor's Last Sigh*, 1995; *The Ground Beneath Her Feet*, 1999.

NONFICTION: *The Jaguar Smile: A Nicaraguan Journey*, 1987; *Imaginary Homelands: Essays and Criticism, 1981–1991*, 1991; *The Wizard of Oz: A Short Text About Magic*, 1992; *Conversations with Salman Rushdie*, 2000.

BIBLIOGRAPHY

Ahsan, A. R. *Sacrilege Versus Civility: Muslim Perspectives on "The Satanic Verses" Affair*. Markfield, Leicester: Islamic Foundation, 1993. Among the more than seventy books that have been written about the *fatwa*, this is one of many that are largely critical of Rushdie.

Brennan, Timothy. *Salman Rushdie and the Third World: Myths of the Nation*. London: Macmillan, 1989. This sociopolitical study was the first book-length analysis of Rushdie's art.

Cundy, Catherine. *Salman Rushdie: Contemporary World Writers*. Manchester: Manchester University Press, 1996. Although it gives very little attention to *East, West*, this is a readable overview of his work.

Fletcher, M. D., ed. *Reading Rushdie: Perspectives on the Fiction of Salman Rushdie*. Amsterdam: Cross/Cultures, 1994. This is a convenient collection of essays, most previously published.

Goonetilleke, D. C. R. A. *Salman Rushdie*. Modern Novelists. New York: St. Martin's Press, 1998. Its fine chapter on *East, West* is virtually the only extensive treatment of Rushdie's short fiction.

Harrison, James. *Salman Rushdie*. English Author Series. New York: Twayne, 1992. It notes Rushdie's difficulties (as one of the British-educated elite) in representing what Brennan somewhat apologetically calls the "Third World."

MacDonogh, Steve, ed. *The Rushdie Letters: Freedom to Speak, Freedom to Write*. Kerry, Ireland: Brandon Book Publishers, 1993. It is a collection of letters from such notables as Gunter Grass, Paul Theroux, and Nadine Gordimer, supporting Rushdie.

Parameswarn, U. *The Perforated Sheet: Essays on Salman Rushdie's Art*. New Delhi: Affiliated East-West, 1988. Despite some heterogeneity to the essays, it offers insight into Rushdie's Indian context.

James Whitlark

S

SAKI
Hector Hugh Munro

Born: Akyab, Burma (now Myanmar); December 18, 1870

Died: Beaumont Hamel, France; November 14, 1916

PRINCIPAL SHORT FICTION

Reginald, 1904
Reginald in Russia, 1910
The Chronicles of Clovis, 1911
Beasts and Super-Beasts, 1914
The Toys of Peace, 1919
The Square Egg, 1924
The Short Stories of Saki (H. H. Munro) Complete, 1930

OTHER LITERARY FORMS

Saki's fame rests on his short stories, but he also wrote novels, plays, political satires, a history of imperial Russia, and journalistic sketches.

ACHIEVEMENTS

The brilliant satirist of the mind and manners of an upper-crust Great Britain that World War I would obliterate, Saki operates within a rich national tradition that stretches from the towering figure of Jonathan Swift well into the present, in which fresh wits such as Douglas Adams have obtained a certain stature. An intelligent, perceptive, and uncannily unsentimental observer, Saki focuses many of his deeply sarcastic pieces, which fill six volumes, on the criminal impulses of a privileged humanity. In his tightly wrought stories, for which surprise endings, ironic reversals, and practical jokes are de rigueur, Saki's mischievous protagonists thus arrive on the scene to wreak havoc on victims who have invited their tormentors out of folly or a streak of viciousness of their own. The frequent inclusion of intelligent, indepen-dent, and improbable animal characters further betrays Saki's fondness for the supernatural as a powerful satirical device.

BIOGRAPHY

Born in colonial Burma (now Myanmar) to a family that had for generations helped to rule the British Empire, Hector Hugh Munro grew up in a Devonshire country house where, reared along with his brother and sister by two formidable aunts, he had the secluded and strictly supervised sort of childhood typical of the Victorian rural gentry. This upbringing decisively shaped—or perhaps warped, as some sources suggest—his character. After finishing public school at Bedford, Munro spent several years studying in Devonshire and traveling on the Continent with his father and sister. In 1983, he went to Burma to accept a police post obtained through his father's influence. Much weakened by recurrent malaria, he returned to Devonshire to convalesce and write. In the first years of the twentieth century he turned to journalism, wrote political satires, and served as a foreign correspondent in Eastern Europe and Paris. At this time he adopted the pseudonym "Saki," which may refer to the cupbearer in *The Rubáiyát of Omar Khayyám* (1859) or may contract "Sakya Muni," one of the epithets of the Buddha. After 1908, Saki lived and wrote in London. Despite being over-age and far from robust, he volunteered for active duty at the outbreak of World War I. Refusing to accept a commission, to which his social position entitled him, or a safe job in military intelligence, for which his education and experience equipped him, Munro fought as an enlisted man in the trenches of France. He died in action.

ANALYSIS

Saki is a writer whose great strength and great weakness lie in the limits he set for himself. Firmly rooted in the British ruling class that enjoyed "dominion over palm and pine," Saki wrote about the prosperous Edwardians among whom he moved. His stories, comedies of manners, emphasize the social side of the human animal as they survey the amusements, plots, and skirmishes that staved off boredom for the overripe leisure class whose leisure ended in August, 1914, with the onset of World War I.

Just as Saki wrote about a particular class, so he aimed his stories at a comparatively small and select readership. Although he was indifferent to wealth, Saki subsisted by his pen; he was, therefore, obliged to write stories that would sell. From the first, he succeeded in producing the "well-made" story savored by literate but not necessarily literary readers of such respected journals as the liberal *Westminster Gazette* and the conservative *Morning Post*. His debonair, carefully plotted stories full of dramatic reversals, ingenious endings, and quotable phrases do not experiment with new literary techniques but perfect existing conventions. Without seeming to strain for effect, they make of Hyde Park an enchanted forest or treat the forays of a werewolf as an ordinary country occurrence. Like the Paris gowns his fictional duchesses wear, Saki's stories are frivolous, intricate, impeccable, and, to some eyes, obsolete.

If Saki's background, subjects, and techniques were conventional, however, his values and sympathies certainly were not. As a satirist, he mocked the people he entertained. His careful portraits of a complacent ruling class are by no means flattering: They reveal all the malice, pettiness, mediocrity, and self-interest of people intent on getting to the top or staying there. His heroes—Reginald, Clovis, Bertie, and the like—are aristocratic iconoclasts who share their creator's distaste for "dreadful little everyday acts of pretended importance" and delight in tripping the fools and hypocrites who think themselves exceptional but walk the well-worn path upward. "Cousin Theresa," a variation on the theme of the Prodigal Son, chronicles the frustration of one such self-deluder.

Saki

"COUSIN THERESA"

In Saki's version of the parable, the wandering brother—as might be expected in an age of far-flung Empire—is the virtuous one. Bassett Harrowcluff, a young and successful bearer of the "white man's burden," returns from the colonies after having cheaply and efficiently "quieted a province, kept open a trade route, enforced the tradition of respect which is worth the ransom of many kings in out of the way regions." These efforts, his proud father hopes, might earn Bassett a knighthood as well as a rest.

The elder brother Lucas, however, a ne'er-do-well London bachelor, claims to have his own scheme for certain success—a refrain that, appended to a song and embodied in a musical revue, should catch the ear of all London: "Cousin Theresa takes out Caesar,/ Fido, Jock, and the big borzoi." Fate bears out Lucas's prophecy. Theresa and her canine quartet enthrall the city. Orchestras acquire the four-legged accessories necessary for proper rendition of the much-demanded melody's special effects. The double thump commemorating the borzoi rings throughout London: Diners pound tables, drunks reeling home pound doors, messenger boys pound smaller messenger boys. Preachers and lecturers discourse on the song's "inner meaning." In Society, the perennial mystifications of politics and polo give way to discussions of "Cousin Theresa." When Colonel Harrowcluff's son is knighted, the honor goes to Lucas.

Saki's parable offers two lessons: an obvious one for the "eminent," a subtler one for the enlightened. If the reader takes the story as an indictment of a foolish society that venerates gimmicks and ignores achievements, that rewards notoriety rather than merit, he classes himself among the Bassett Harrowcluffs. For the same delicate irony colors Saki's accounts of both brothers' successes: Whether this treatment whimsically elevates the impresario or deftly undercuts the pillar of empire is problematic. As Saki sees it, administering the colonies and entertaining the populace are equally trivial occupations. To reward Lucas, the less self-righteous of two triflers, seems just after all.

Saki, then, does not profess the creed of the society he describes; both the solid virtues and the fashionable attitudes of the adult world come off badly in his stories. In contrast to other adults, Saki's dandy-heroes and debutante-heroines live in the spirit of the nursery romp; and when children and animals appear (as they often do) he invariably sides with them. "Laura," a fantasy in which a mischievous lady dies young but returns to life first as an otter and then as a Nubian boy to continue teasing a pompous fool, is one of many stories demonstrating Saki's allegiance to *Beasts and Super-Beasts* at the expense of men and supermen.

Saki's favorites are never sweetly pretty or coyly innocent. The children, as we see in "The Lumber-Room," "The Penance," and "Morlvera," are cruel, implacable, the best of haters. The beasts, almost as fierce as the children, tend to be independent or predatory: wolves and guard dogs, cats great and small, elk, bulls, and boars figure in Saki's menagerie. Em-

bodied forces of nature, these animals right human wrongs or counterpoise by their example the mediocrity of man throughout Saki's works, but nowhere more memorably than in the chilling tale of "Sredni Vashtar."

"SREDNI VASHTAR"

In "Sredni Vashtar," Conradin, a rather sickly ten-year-old, suffers under the restrictive coddling of his cousin and guardian, Mrs. De Ropp, a pious hypocrite who "would never, in her honestest moments, have confessed to herself that she disliked Conradin, though she might have been dimly aware that thwarting him 'for his good' was a duty which she did not find completely irksome." Conradin's one escape from her dull, spirit-sapping regime is the toolshed where he secretly cherishes Sredni Vashtar, the great ferret around whom he has fashioned a private religious cult. Offering gifts of red flowers, scarlet berries, and nutmeg that "had to be stolen," Conradin prays that the god Sredni Vashtar, who embodies the rude animal vitality the boy lacks, will smite their common enemy the Woman. When Mrs. De Ropp, suspecting that the toolshed harbors something unsuitable for invalids, goes to investigate, Conradin fears that Sredni Vashtar will dwindle to a simple ferret and that he, deprived of his god, will grow ever weaker under the Woman's tyranny.

Eventually, however, Conradin sees Sredni Vashtar the Terrible, throat and jaws wet with a dark stain, stalk out of the shed to drink at the garden brook and slip away. Mrs. De Ropp does not return from the encounter, and Conradin, freed from his guardian angel, helps himself to the forbidden fruit of his paradise—a piece of toast, "usually banned on the ground that it was bad for him; also because the making of it 'gave trouble,' a deadly offense in the middle-class feminine eye."

"THE OPEN WINDOW"

The brutal vengeance of "Sredni Vashtar" demonstrates that Saki's preference is not founded on the moral superiority of children and animals. "The Open Window," probably Saki's most popular story, makes the point in a more plausible situation, where a "self-possessed young lady of fifteen" spins from the most ordinary circumstances a tale of terror that drives her visitor, the nervous and hypochondriacal Mr. Frampton Nuttel, to distraction. In the Saki world the charm and talent of the liar makes up for the cruelty of her lie; the reader, cut adrift from his ordinary values, admires the unfeeling understatement of Saki's summing up: "Romance at short notice was her specialty." The reader joins in applauding at the story's end not injustice—the whimpering Nuttel gets no worse than he deserves—but justice undiluted by mercy, a drink too strong for most adults most of the time.

What Saki admires about the people and animals he portrays is their fidelity to absolutes. They follow their natures single-mindedly and unapologetically; they neither moralize nor compromise. Discussing the preferences of a character in his novel *When William Came* (1913), Saki indirectly explains his own austere code: "Animals . . . accepted the world as it was and made the best of it, and children, at least nice children, uncontaminated by grown-up influences, lived in worlds of their own making." In this judgment the satirist becomes misanthrope. Saki endorses nature and art but rejects society.

It is this moral narrowness, this refusal to accept compromise, that makes Saki, despite the brilliance of his artistry, an unsatisfying writer to read in large doses. His dated description of a vanished world is really no flow, for he does not endorse the dying regime but clearly shows why it ought to die. His lack of sentiment is refreshing; his lack of emotion (only in such rare stories as "The Sheep," "The Philanthropist and the Happy Cat," and "The Penance" does Saki credibly present deep or complex feelings) does not offend present-day readers long inured to black comedy. Saki's defect is sterility. He refuses to be generous or make allowances as he considers society, that creation of adults, and he sends readers back empty-handed to the world of compromise where they must live.

OTHER MAJOR WORKS

LONG FICTION: *The Unbearable Bassington*, 1912; *When William Came*, 1913.

PLAYS: *The Death-Trap*, pb. 1924; *Karl-Ludwig's Window*, pb. 1924; *The Watched Pot*, pr., pb. 1924 (with Cyril Maude); *The Square Egg and Other Sketches, with Three Plays*, pb. 1924.

NONFICTION: *The Rise of the Russian Empire*, 1900; *The Westminster Alice*, 1902.

BIBLIOGRAPHY

Birden, Lorene M. "Saki's 'A Matter of Sentiment.'" *Explicator* 5 (Summer, 1998): 201-204. Discusses the Anglo-German relations in the story "A Matter of Sentiment" and argues that the story reflects a shift in Saki's image of Germans.

Gillen, Charles H. *H. H. Munro (Saki)*. New York: Twayne, 1969. A comprehensive presentation of the life and work of Saki, with a critical discussion of his literary output in all of its forms. Balanced and readable, Gillen's work also contains an annotated bibliography, which naturally does not include studies since then.

Lambert, J. W. Introduction to *The Bodley Head Saki*. London: Bodley Head, 1963. A perceptive, concise, and persuasive review of Saki's work. Written by a biographer who enjoyed a special and productive working relationship with Saki's estate.

Langguth, A. J. *Saki*. New York: Simon & Schuster, 1981. Probably the best biography, enriching an informed, analytical presentation of its subject with a fine understanding of Saki's artistic achievement. Eight pages of photos help bring Saki and his world to life.

Munro, Ethel M. "Biography of Saki." In *The Square Egg and Other Sketches, with Three Plays*. New York: Viking, 1929. A warm account of the author by his beloved sister, who shows herself deeply appreciative of his work. Valuable for its glimpses of the inner workings of Saki's world and as a basis for late twentieth century evaluations.

Salemi, Joseph S. "An Asp Lurking in an Apple-Charlotte: Animal Violence in Saki's *The Chronicles of Clovis*." *Studies in Short Fiction* 26 (Fall, 1989): 423-430. Discusses the animal imagery in the collection, suggesting reasons for Saki's obsessive interest in animals and analyzing the role animals play in a number of Saki's major stories.

Spears, George J. *The Satire of Saki*. New York: Exposition Press, 1963. An interesting, in-depth study of Saki's wit, which combines careful textual analysis with a clear interest in modern psychoanalysis. The appendix includes four letters by

Ethel M. Munro to the author, and the bibliography lists many works that help to place Saki in the context of the satirical tradition.

Peter W. Graham, updated by R. C. Lutz

J. D. SALINGER

Born: New York, New York; January 1, 1919

PRINCIPAL SHORT FICTION
Nine Stories, 1953
Franny and Zooey, 1961
Raise High the Roof Beam, Carpenters, and Seymour: An Introduction, 1963

OTHER LITERARY FORMS

The most famous work of J. D. Salinger, besides his short stories, is the novel *The Catcher in the Rye* (1951), which influenced a generation of readers and is still considered a classic.

ACHIEVEMENTS

The precise and powerful creation of J. D. Salinger's characters, especially Holden Caulfield and the Glass family, has led them to become part of American folklore. Salinger's ironic fiction and enigmatic personality captured the imagination of post-World War II critics and students. His authorized books were published over the course of twelve years, from 1951 to 1963, yet his works still remain steadily in print in many languages throughout the world.

Salinger received a number of awards in his career. "This Sandwich Has No Mayonnaise" was selected as one of the distinguished short stories published in American magazines for 1945 and was later included in *The Best Short Stories 1946*. "Just Before the War with the Eskimos" was reprinted in *Prize Stories of 1949*. "A Girl I Know" was selected for *The Best American Short Stories 1949*. "For Esmé—with Love and Squalor" was selected as one of the distinguished short stories published in American magazines in 1950 and is included in *Prize Stories of 1950*.

The novel *The Catcher in the Rye* was a Book-of-the-Month Club selection for 1951.

Martin Green remarked that Salinger is not so much a writer who depicts life as one who celebrates it, an accurate characterization of the humor and love in his work. Ultimately, the most serious charge against him is that his output is too small.

BIOGRAPHY

Jerome David Salinger is the second child—his sister, Doris, was born eight years before him—and only son of Sol and Miriam Jillich Salinger, a Jewish father and a Christian mother. His father was a successful importer of hams and cheeses. Salinger was a serious child who kept mostly to himself. His IQ test score was above average, and his grades, at public schools in the upper West Side of Manhattan, were in the "B" range. Socially, his experiences at summer camp were more successful than in the Manhattan public schools. At Camp Wigwam, in Harrison, Maine, he was voted at age eleven "the most popular actor of 1930."

In 1934, Salinger entered Valley Forge Military Academy, in Pennsylvania, a school resembling Pencey Prep in *The Catcher in the Rye*. Salinger, however, was more successful at Valley Forge than Holden had been at Pencey, and in June, 1936, Valley Forge gave him his only diploma. He was literary editor of the Academy yearbook and wrote a poem that was set to music and sung at the school.

In 1937, he enrolled in summer school at New York University but left for Austria and Poland to try working in his father's meat import business. In 1938, after returning to the United States, he briefly attended Ursinus College in Collegeville, Pennsylvania. There, he wrote a column, "Skipped Diploma," which featured film reviews for the college newspaper. In 1939, he signed up for a short-story course at Columbia University, given by Whit Burnett, editor of *Story* magazine. In 1940, his first short story, "The Young Folks," was published in the March/April issue of *Story* magazine, and he was paid twenty-five dollars for it.

The story "Go See Eddie" was published in the December issue of the University of Kansas City *Review*. In 1941, "The Hang of It" appeared in *Collier's* and "The Heart of a Broken Story" in *Esquire*. Salinger sold his first story about Holden Caulfield to *The New Yorker*, but publication was delayed until 1946 because of the United States' entry into World War II.

In 1942, Salinger was drafted. He used his weekend passes to hide in a hotel room and write. He attended Officers, First Sergeants, and Instructors School of the Signal Corps. He engaged in a brief romantic correspondence with Oona O'Neill, daughter of the playwright Eugene O'Neill and later to be the wife of Charles Chaplin. In 1943, he was stationed in Nashville, Tennessee, with the rank of staff sergeant and transferred to the Army Counter-Intelligence Corps. "The Varioni Brothers" was his first story in *The Saturday Evening Post*. He received counter-intelligence training in Devonshire, England. During the war, he landed on Utah Beach in Normandy as part of the D-Day invasion force and participated in five campaigns. It was during this period that he met war correspondent Ernest Hemingway.

In 1945, Salinger was discharged from the Army. He continued to publish stories, including two stories with material later to be used in *The Catcher in the Rye*. In 1948, he began a long, exclusive association with *The New Yorker* with "A Perfect Day for Bananafish," the first story about Seymour Glass. Early in 1950, Salinger began studying Advaita Vedanta, Eastern religious philosophy, in New York City. In 1951, *The Catcher in the Rye* was published, and in 1953, he moved to Cornish, New Hampshire.

In the following years, several of his stories were published in *The New Yorker*, including "Franny," "Raise High the Roof Beam, Carpenters," "Zooey," "Seymour: An Introduction," and "Hapworth 16,

J. D. Salinger (National Archives)

1924." Salinger married Claire Douglas on February 17, 1955. A daughter, Margaret Ann, was born in 1955, and a son, Matthew, in 1960. Salinger was divorced from his wife in 1967. In 1987, Matthew Salinger starred in a made-for-television film. In the mid-1980's, Salinger, known to be a reclusive person, became the center of public attention when he protested the publication of an unauthorized biography by Ian Hamilton. The suit led to the rewriting of Hamilton's biography, which was published in 1988.

ANALYSIS

The main characters of J. D. Salinger, neurotic and sensitive people, search unsuccessfully for love in a metropolitan setting. They see the phoniness, egotism, and hypocrisy around them. There is a failure of communication between people: between husbands and wives, between soldiers in wartime, between roommates in schools. A sense of loss, especially the loss of a sibling, recurs frequently. Many of his stories have wartime settings and involve characters who have served in World War II. Some of these characters cannot adjust to the military, some have unhappy marital relationships, and others are unsuccessful in both areas. The love for children occurs frequently in his stories—for example, the love for Esmé, Phoebe, and Sybil. Like William Wordsworth, Salinger appreciates childhood innocence. Children have a wisdom and a spontaneity that is lost in the distractions and temptations of adult life.

Salinger's early stories contain elements foreshadowing his later work. Many of these stories are concerned with adolescents. In "The Young Folks," however, the adolescents resemble the insensitive schoolmates of Holden Caulfield more than they resemble Holden himself. Salinger demonstrates his admirable ear for teenage dialogue in these stories.

The reader sees how often members of the Glass family are present in the stories or novelettes. Looking back at Salinger's early works, one sees how these selections can be related to events in the actual life of Salinger as well as how they contain characters who are part of the Glass family saga.

"For Esmé—with Love and Squalor"

An early example is the character of Sergeant X in "For Esmé—with Love and Squalor," from the collection *Nine Stories*. The time and setting of this story tie it into the experiences of Salinger abroad during World War II. At the same time, Sergeant X is Seymour Glass. The reader is shown the egotism of the wife and mother-in-law of Sergeant X, who write selfish civilian letters to the American soldier about to be landed in France, requesting German knitting wool and complaining about the service at Shrafft's restaurant in Manhattan.

This behavior is the same as that of the insensitive wife of "A Perfect Day for Bananafish" and that of the wife and mother-in-law of "Raise High the Roof Beam, Carpenters." The only person who offers love to Sergeant X is the brave British orphan Esmé, who sings with a voice like a bird and offers him the wristwatch of her deceased father. Esmé is too proper a British noblewoman to kiss Sergeant X, but she drags her five-year-old brother, Charles, back into the tearoom to kiss the soldier good-bye and even invites him to her wedding, five years later. Esmé's love restores Sergeant X from the breakdown that he suffered from the war. The gestures of love from Esmé lead to Sergeant X finally being able to go to sleep, a sign of recovery in the Glass family.

The love of Esmé is contrasted to the squalor of the other people around Seymour. His wife, "a breathtakingly levelheaded girl," discourages Sergeant X from attending the wedding of Esmé because his mother-in-law will be visiting at the same time (another selfish reason). The "squalor" that is contrasted to the pure, noble love of Esmé is also exemplified in the letter of the older brother of Sergeant X, who requests "a couple of bayonets or swastikas" as souvenirs for his children. Sergeant X tears up his brother's letter and throws the pieces into a wastebasket into which he later vomits. He cannot so easily escape the squalor of the "photogenic" Corporal Z, from whom readers learn that Sergeant X had been released from a hospital after a nervous breakdown. Corporal Clay, the jeep-mate of Sergeant X, personifies even more the squalor that Sergeant X is "getting better acquainted with," in one form or another. Clay has been "brutal," "cruel," and "dirty" by unnecessarily shooting a cat and constantly dwelling upon the incident.

Clay has a name that represents earth and dirt. He is obtuse and insensitive. He is contrasted to the spirituality, sensitivity, and love expressed by Esmé. Clay brings news of the officious character Bulling, who forces underlings to travel at inconvenient hours to impress them with his authority, and of Clay's girlfriend Loretta, a psychology major who blames the breakdown of Sergeant X not on wartime experiences but on lifelong instability, yet excuses Clay's sadistic killing of the cat as "temporary insanity." The killing of the cat is similar to Hemingway's killing a chicken in the presence of Salinger when the two men met overseas. The love of Esmé redeems and rejuvenates Sergeant X from his private hell in this well-written and moving story.

"Uncle Wiggily in Connecticut"

References to other members of the Glass family

tie other stories to the saga of the Glass children. Eloise, the Connecticut housewife in "Uncle Wiggily in Connecticut" had been in love with a soldier named "Walt." Walt was one of the twin brothers in the Glass family. He had been killed during the war not in battle but in a senseless accident. The central characters in the story are Eloise, a frustrated housewife, living trapped in a wealthy Connecticut home with a man she does not love and her memories of the soldier Walt whom she had loved dearly; and Ramona, her young daughter. Salinger himself was living in Connecticut at the time when he wrote this story.

Ramona may lack the nobility and capacity to show affection that Esmé had, yet she is an imaginative child, with abilities that her mother does not understand or appreciate. Ramona compensates for her loneliness by creating imaginary friends, such as "Jimmy Jimmereeno." This imaginative spontaneity in Ramona is in danger of being stifled by Eloise. Once when drunk, Eloise frightens her daughter by waking her up during the night after seeing her sleeping on one side of the bed to leave space for her new playmate, "Mickey Mickeranno." Eloise herself was comforted by memories of her old beloved Walt but did not permit Ramona also to have an imaginary companion. The suburban mother suddenly realizes what has happened to her and begins to cry, as does her frightened daughter. All Eloise has left is the small comfort of her memories of Walt. She now realizes that she had been trying to force Ramona to give up her fantasies about imaginary boyfriends too. In this Salinger story, again there is a contrast between the "nice" world of love that Eloise remembers she once had and the rude, "squalid" Connecticut world in which she is currently living.

THE GLASS FAMILY CYCLE

The writings of Salinger can be best discussed by dividing them into three sections: his early writings, his great classic works, and the Glass family cycle. The later works of Salinger are more concerned with religion than the earlier ones. Most of these later works deal with members of the Glass family, characters who have elements in common with Salinger himself. They are sensitive and introspective, they

hate phoniness, and they have great verbal skill. They are also interested in mystical religion. "Glass" is an appropriate name for the family. Glass is a clear substance through which a person can see to acquire further knowledge and enlightenment, yet glass is also extremely fragile and breakable and therefore could apply to the nervous breakdowns or near breakdowns of members of the family. The Glass family also attempts to reach enlightenment through the methods of Zen Buddhism. Professor Daisetz Suzuki of Columbia University, whose work is said to have influenced Salinger, commented that "the basic idea of Zen is to come in touch with the inner workings of our being, and to do this in the most direct way possible, without resorting to anything external or superadded. . . . Zen is the ultimate fact of all philosophy and religion."

What Seymour, Zooey, and Franny Glass want to do is to come in touch with the inner workings of their being in order to achieve nonintellectual enlightenment. With all religions at their fingertips, the Glass siblings utilize anything Zen-like, and it is their comparative success or failure in this enterprise that forms the basic conflict in their stories. In "Raise High the Roof Beam, Carpenters," the point made is that Seymour, who has achieved the satori, or Zen enlightenment, is considered abnormal by the world and loved and admired only by his siblings. He is despised by other people who cannot comprehend his behavior. The maid of honor at the wedding that Seymour failed to attend describes him as a schizoid and latent homosexual. His brother Buddy, the only Glass family member attending the wedding, is forced to defend his brother by himself. After enduring all the misinformed verbal attacks on his brother, Buddy replies: "I said that not one God-damn person, of all the patronizing, fourth-rate critics and column writers, had ever seen him for what he really was. A poet, for God's sake. And I mean a *poet*."

The central figure around whom all the stories of the Glass family revolve is Seymour, Seymour alive, Seymour quoted by Zooey, and the memory of Seymour when he is no longer physically alive. Once the Zen experience is understood by the reader, the meaning of earlier stories about the Glass siblings becomes more intelligible as contributing to Salinger's goal in his later stories. Zen is a process of reduction and emptying of all the opinions and values that one has learned and has been conditioned to that interfere with one's perceptions.

"A PERFECT DAY FOR BANANAFISH"

The first Glass story, "A Perfect Day for Bananafish," is a kind of Koan, one whose meaning the Glass children will be mediating upon for years to come. Seymour is the Bananafish. He has taken in so much from outside himself, knowledge and sensations, and he is so stuffed that he cannot free himself and climb out of the banana hole.

Seymour, in this first story, is married to Muriel and is in a world of martinis and phony conversations in Miami Beach. He discovers that Muriel looks like Charlotte, the girl at whom he threw a stone in his earlier life because her physical loveliness was distracting him from his spiritual quest. He cannot communicate with his wife either. Muriel Fedder was aptly named because her presence serves as a "fetter" to Seymour. The only one with whom he *can* communicate is Sybil, the young child who is still so uncorrupted by the opinions and values of the world that her clear perceptions give her the status of the mythological Sybil.

Seymour has found, unfortunately, that Muriel Fedder Glass will not serve, teach, or strengthen him, as Seymour's diary entry before his marriage had indicated: "Marriage partners are to serve each other. Elevate, help, teach, strengthen each other, but above all, serve." Boo Boo Glass wrote a more admiring tribute to Seymour on the bathroom mirror than one senses from Muriel. Muriel is found reading a *Reader's Digest* article, "Sex Is Fun—or Hell." Marriage to Muriel has turned out not to be a spiritually enlightening experience. The only move that Seymour can make in his spiritual quest is to empty himself totally of all the opinions, values, and drives, of all sensations that distract and hinder him in achieving his spiritual goal. He is best able to move forward in his search by committing suicide and becoming pure spirit. Warren French wrote, "When Muriel then subsequently fails to live up to his expectations of a spouse, he realizes the futility of continuing a life that

promises no further spiritual development."

The critic Ann Marple noted that "Salinger's first full-length novel, *The Catcher in the Rye*, emerged after scattered fragments concerning his characters appeared over a seven-year span. For some time now it has been evident that Salinger's second novel may be developing in the same way." Salinger wrote of *Franny and Zooey*: "Both stories are early, critical entries in a narrative series I am doing about a family of settlers in 20th Century New York, the Glasses." The remaining stories deal with Zen Buddhism and the effort to achieve a Zen-inspired awakening. They continue to deal with Seymour Glass and his influence on his siblings. In addition, the work of Salinger becomes increasingly experimental as he continues to write.

"FRANNY" AND "ZOOEY"

When "Franny" was first published in the January 29, 1955, issue of *The New Yorker*, no mention was made that Franny was a member of the Glass family. All the reader knows is that Franny is visiting her boyfriend Lane for a football weekend at an Ivy League college. Lane is an insensitive pseudointellectual who brags about his successful term paper on Gustave Flaubert as he consumes frogs' legs. Lane is not interested in the religious book *The Way of the Pilgrim* that Franny describes to him or in hearing about the Jesus prayer that has a tremendous mystical effect on the whole outlook of the person who is praying. The luncheon continues, with Lane finishing the snails and frogs' legs that he had ordered. The contrast has deepened between the mystical spirituality of Franny and Lane's interest in satisfying his physical appetites. The reader is shocked at the part of the story when Franny faints. She is apparently suffering from morning sickness. The implication is that Lane is the father of her unborn child.

Almost two and a half years pass before the title character is identified as Franny Glass. "Zooey" was published in the May 4, 1957, issue of *The New Yorker*. It continued the story of Franny Glass, the youngest of the siblings of Seymour Glass. It is made clear in this story that Franny was not pregnant in the earlier story but was suffering from a nervous breakdown as a result of her unsuccessful attempt to achieve spiritual enlightenment. In "Zooey," her brother identifies the book that Franny is carrying to their mother as *The Pilgrim Continues His Way*, a sequel to the other book, both of which she had gotten from the old room of Seymour. Zooey cannot console his sister at first. Franny is crying uncontrollably. Zooey finally goes into the room that had been occupied previously by Seymour and Buddy. Zooey attempts to impersonate Buddy when he calls Franny on the telephone, but Franny eventually recognizes the voice of the caller. Zooey is finally able to convince his sister that the mystical experience she should strive for is not of seeing Christ directly but that of seeing Christ through ordinary people. "There isn't anyone anywhere who isn't Seymour's Fat Lady," who is really "Christ himself, buddy." Reassured by the words of her brother, Franny can finally fall asleep.

In "Franny," as in many other Salinger short stories, character is revealed through a series of actions under stress, and the purpose of the story is reached at the moment of epiphany, an artistic technique formulated by James Joyce, in which a character achieves a sudden perception of truth. In "Franny," Salinger uses the theatrical tricks of a telephone in an empty room and of one person impersonating another. He often uses the bathroom of the Glass apartment as a place where important messages are left, important discussions are conducted, important documents are read. It is on the bathroom cabinet mirror that Boo Boo Glass leaves the epithalamium prayer for her brother on his wedding day, from which the title of the story "Raise High the Roof Beams, Carpenters" is taken. The Glass bathroom is almost a sacred temple. Bessie Glass, in the "Zooey" portion of *Franny and Zooey*, goes in there to discuss with Zooey how to deal with Franny's nervous breakdown. Buddy closes the bathroom door of the apartment he had shared with Seymour to read the diary of Seymour on his wedding day. He reads that Seymour is so happy that he cannot attend his wedding on that date (although he subsequently elopes with Muriel Fedder). The reader sees in *Franny and Zooey* the role Seymour played in the lives of his youngest brother and sister, the influence he had over them and

their religious education. The reader sees in "Franny" a spiritual crisis in her efforts to retain her spiritual integrity, to live a spiritual life in an egotistical, materialistic society, a society personified by Lane Coutell.

"Franny" can be considered as a prologue to "Zooey," which carries the reader deeply into the history of the Glass family. The last five pieces that Salinger published in *The New Yorker* could constitute some form of a larger whole. The narrative possibly could constitute parts of two uncompleted chronicles. One order in which the stories could be read is with Buddy as the narrator, the order in which they were published (this is the order in which Buddy claims to have written them); the other order is the one suggested by the chronology of events in the stories. Arranged one way, the stories focus on Buddy and his struggle to understand Seymour by writing about him; arranged the other way, the stories focus on the quest of Seymour for God. J. D. Salinger has for some years been a devoted student of Advaita Vedanta Hinduism, and the teachings of Seymour Glass reflect this study.

If one focuses on Seymour Glass, his spiritual quest, and how this quest is reflected in the behavior and beliefs of his siblings, one sees as a result an unfinished history of the Glass family. Salinger announced, in one of his rare statements about his intentions, on the dust jacket of a later book, that he had "several new Glass family stories coming along," but, by the close of the century, only "Hapworth 16, 1924" had appeared, in 1965. Readers see in this story the presence of Seymour, a presence that is evident in the four stories published after that time.

These four stories became more experimental in literary technique and are also involved with the Eastern mystical religious beliefs studied by Salinger and promoted by his character Seymour Glass. One interpretation of the stories that deal with Seymour (that of Eberhard Alsen) is that together these selections constitute a modernist hagiography, the account of the life and martyrdom of a churchless saint. "Raise High the Roof Beam, Carpenters" is the first story to be published after "Franny" and the first to introduce all the members of the Glass family. "Zooey" continues the account of specific events introduced in "Franny," and the reader learns that the behavior of Franny is influenced by two books of Eastern religion that she found in the old room of Seymour. In "Zooey" the name of Seymour is evoked when Franny wants to talk to him. In "Raise High the Roof Beam, Carpenters," the reader learns what Seymour has written in his diary, although Seymour is not physically present. In "Seymour: An Introduction," the reader is offered a much wider range of what he said and wrote, conveyed by his brother Buddy. In "Hapworth 16, 1924," which appeared in *The New Yorker* on June 19, 1965, Buddy, now at age forty-six, tries to trace the origins of the saintliness of his older brother in a letter that Seymour wrote home from Camp Simon Hapworth in Maine when he was seven. In giving the reader the exact letter, Buddy provides one with a full example of how things are seen from the point of view of Seymour and introduces the reader to the sensitivity and psychic powers that foreshadow his spirituality. The reader sees the incredibly precocious mind of Seymour, who reflects on the nature of pain and asks his parents to send him some books by Leo Tolstoy, Swami Vivekananda of India, Charles Dickens, George Eliot, William Makepeace Thackeray, Jane Austen, and Frederick Porter Smith.

"Seymour: An Introduction" and "Hapworth 16, 1924"

In these last two works, "Seymour: An Introduction" and "Hapworth 16, 1924," the reader sees Seymour Glass more closely than anywhere before. The reader sees the brilliance of Seymour, his spirituality, his poetic ability, and his capacity for love. With the character of Seymour, Salinger is trying to create a modern-day saint.

Salinger's last works received mixed critical reception. Some critics believe that Salinger has lost the artistic ability he had showed during his classic period. His characters write, and others subsequently read, long, tedious letters filled with phrases in parentheses and attempts at wit. Buddy describes "Zooey" as "a sort of prose home movie." Some critics criticize these last works, calling "Zooey" the longest and dullest short story ever to appear in *The New Yorker*, but others recognize that Salinger is no longer trying to please conventional readers but, influenced by his many years of study of Eastern religious philosophy, is ridding himself of conventional forms and methods accepted by Western society. In his later years, Salinger has continued to become increasingly innovative and experimental in his writing techniques.

Other major works

LONG FICTION: *The Catcher in the Rye*, 1951.
SCREENPLAY: *My Foolish Heart*, 1950.

Bibliography

Alexander, Paul. *Salinger: A Biography*. Los Angeles: Renaissance Books, 1999. An excellent, updated look at the life and times of Salinger.

Bloom, Harold, ed. *J. D. Salinger: Modern Critical Views:* New York: Chelsea House, 1987. A collection of criticism by respected critics who deal with topics ranging from Salinger and Zen Buddhism to Salinger's heroes and love ethic. Includes an introduction, chronology, and bibliography.

French, Warren. *J. D. Salinger, Revisited*. Boston: Twayne, 1988. One of the most helpful and informative books on Salinger. French, who has written an earlier book on Salinger, explains here how he changed his perspective on some of Salinger's works. In addition to offering a useful chronology and bibliography, French discusses the New Hampshire area, where Salinger and French have lived. French also makes enlightening comparisons of the stories to films. Notes, references, index.

Gardner, James. "J. D. Salinger, Fashion Victim." *National Review* 49 (April 7, 1997): 51-52. Contends Salinger is intensely different from what American culture has become since he was last heard from; the adolescent challenge to the falsity of one's elders that inspired *The Catcher in the Rye* has become the most established kind of conformity; analyzes the reasons for the outdatedness of Salinger's last story, "Hapworth 16, 1924."

Grunwald, Henry Anatole. *Salinger: A Critical and Personal Portrait*. New York: Harper & Row, 1962. This first collection of articles about Salinger contains a biographical sketch by Jack

Skow from *Time* (September 15, 1961). Also includes a long introduction by Grunwald, who became senior editor of *Time*, and articles by such well-known Salinger critics as Ihab Hassan and Joseph Blotner. The Postscripts contain a select catalog of the early stories and a discussion of the language of *The Catcher in the Rye*.

Laser, Marvin, and Norman Furman, eds. *Studies in J. D. Salinger: Reviews, Essays, and Critiques of "The Catcher in the Rye" and Other Fiction*. New York: Odyssey Press, 1963. This volume, in addition to discussing the publishing history and early reviews of *The Catcher in the Rye*, also provides a collection of some of the most important criticism of the shorter fiction. A bibliographical apparatus has been supplied for the convenience of teachers and students, as well as suggested topics for writing.

Maynard, Joyce. *At Home in the World: A Memoir*. New York: Picador USA, 1998. This memoir reveals many details of Salinger's private life, which he struggled to suppress. Best source for biographical information.

Pinsker, Sanford. *"The Catcher in the Rye": Innocence Under Pressure*. New York: Twayne, 1993. Argues that *The Catcher in the Rye* has affinities with several great American novels told by a retrospective first-person narrator and that it is perhaps the best portrait of a sixteen-year-old American boy ever written.

Purcell, William F. "Narrative Voice in J. D. Salinger's 'Both Parties Concerned' and 'I'm Crazy.'" *Studies in Short Fiction* 33 (Spring, 1996): 278-280. Argues that "I'm Crazy" lacks the essential characteristic of *skaz* narrative that communicates the illusion of spontaneous speech.

Salinger, Margaret A. *Dream Catcher: A Memoir*. Washington Square Press, 2000. Salinger's daughter describes her experience growing up in the shadow of her famous yet reclusive father.

Silverberg, Mark. "A Bouquet of Empty Brackets: Author-Function and the Search for J. D. Salinger." *Dalhousie Review* 75 (Summer/Fall, 1995): 222-246. Examines the consequences of J. D. Salinger's "disappearance" from the literary scene and looks at the obsessive desire to find him; explores how Salinger's characters and name have been freed from his person and re-created in various fictional and nonfictional contexts, concluding that while Salinger may have disappeared, his name and creations remain.

Linda S. Gordon

WILLIAM SANSOM

Born: London, England; January 18, 1912
Died: London, England; April 20, 1976

PRINCIPAL SHORT FICTION

Fireman Flower, 1944
Three, 1946
Something Terrible, Something Lovely, 1948
South, 1948
The Passionate North, 1950
A Touch of the Sun, 1952
Lord Love Us, 1954
A Contest of Ladies, 1956
Among the Dahlias, 1957
The Stories of William Sansom, 1963
The Ulcerated Milkman, 1966
The Marmalade Bird, 1973

OTHER LITERARY FORMS

William Sansom's writings include literary criticism, biography, especially *Proust and His World* (1973), essays such as *The Birth of a Story* (1972), travel articles, and literary commentaries such as *The Icicle and the Sun* (1958) and *Blue Skies, Brown Studies* (1961). He has also written three children's books, with illustrations, and nine novels, with the three outstanding ones being *The Body* (1949), *The Loving Eye* (1956), and *The Cautious Heart* (1958).

ACHIEVEMENTS

Known by many critics as the quintessential short-fiction stylist, William Sansom evoked high praise from Elizabeth Bowen, who called him a "short-storyist *par excellence*; the short-storyist by birth, addiction and destiny." His stories display a keen interest not only in surrealism and grotesque horror but also in fantasy, comedy, and downright playfulness. Influenced by music and art and by his work in film, Sansom wrote cameo portrayals of all social classes, both English and continental. His two collections of short stories, *South* and *The Passionate North*, are innovations in travel stories, a blending of the travel article and fiction. Rather than following the traditional pattern of character and plot, Sansom favored the aesthetic of places, objects, and people, not the emphasis on conflicts and feelings. Sansom said this of his literary ethos:

> A writer lives best, in a state of astonishment. Beneath any feeling he has of the good or evil of the world lies a deeper one of wonder at it all. To transmit that feeling, he writes.

He received the Society of Authors Award in 1946 and 1947. The Royal Society of Literature elected him as Fellow in 1951.

BIOGRAPHY

William Sansom was born in London, the only child of Ernest Brooks, a naval architect, and Mabel Clark. His father encouraged him to enter the banking profession and, with this career in mind, Sansom, after preparatory school, lived in Bonn, Germany, for three years, learned German and other foreign languages, and traveled throughout Europe. On his return to London, he trained and later worked in the Anglo-German Bank for five years. From the ages of seventeen to twenty-three, he was stricken with an odd vocal problem in not being able to control his modulation, speaking only in whispers or shouts. This nightmarish experience eventually resonated in a number of the short stories.

Following a stint in banking, Sansom became an advertising copywriter; while working at the advertising agency, he met a fellow worker, Norman Cameron, a poet and a translator, who strongly influenced Sansom's life. These kindred spirits discussed literature, politics, and art. A visit to a surrealist exhibition became a turning point in Sansom's life. He said, "I was immediately addicted forever." Indeed, there are countless reverberations of surrealism in his short stories and novels. Cameron encouraged Sansom to read Arthur Rimbaud, Rainer Maria Rilke, and Ernest Hemingway, all of them impinging in theme and style on Sansom's writing. Along with his work in advertising, Sansom composed jazz at night, played the piano at a nightclub, and also participated in running this same nightclub. Unfit for military service during World War II, Sansom joined the National Fire Brigade and continued to serve until the end of the war. This fortuitous experience became a rich mine for future stories and novels. Many of the National Fire Brigade fire fighters lost their lives or limbs and became the unsung heroes of the war. This terrifying and dangerous work provided Sansom with Kafkaesque situations, which he used in *Fireman Flower*, a collection of short stories that received instant critical acclaim and catapulted Sansom to literary fame.

Following his advertising career, Sansom joined a film company to write scripts. Shortly thereafter, he assumed the risk of writing fiction full-time and did so until the end of his life. Sansom published travel articles in various magazines and eventually developed a unique genre—a combination of travel and short stories—particularly exemplified in such well-known books as *South* and *The Passionate North*.

At forty-two, Sansom married for the first time. His wife, Ruth Grundy, an actress and a literary agent, brought with her two sons from a previous marriage. The family settled in St. John's Wood, a suburb of London; Sansom lived there for the rest of his life. This environment provided him with much material for his writing. A frequent pub patron, Sansom met there many workers and other people from the vicinity; these relationships were woven into his fiction. He particularly absorbed the dialects and the rhythms of his neighbors and fellow pub patrons.

Sansom's early allegorical fiction gave way to romance and eventually to comedy. *Lord Love Us*, one of his favorite collections of short stories, reflects fancy run riot, and its joyous mélange is portrayed in a virtual arabesque of magical language, according to many critics and general readers. It is noteworthy that the publication date of *Lord Love Us* and his work on *The Loving Eye*, one of his most comic and irresistible novels, together with *A Contest of Ladies*, published the same year as *The Loving Eye*, coincided with the first years of his happy marriage.

Sansom particularly read and reread the work of the Russian writer Ivan Bunin, the stories of Edgar Allan Poe, and the work of Marcel Proust. In 1976,

the year of his death, Sansom was involved in writing an introduction to the short stories of Bunin. Always an experimentalist in his approach to the short story, Sansom often explored the Blakeian contrarieties. His approach is neither social nor political nor even psychological, but in the final analysis, it is aesthetic. His language, often akin to a kind of Joycean brio, is elegant and musical. The themes in his stories are often the search for an essence and a meaning of life, a reconciliation of opposites, or a balance and harmony in existence. His vision, although at times reflecting the surrealism of Franz Kafka and the morbidity of Poe, remains strangely something at the same time terrifying and beautiful, these last words almost a literary axiom in the writings of the short stories of Sansom.

ANALYSIS

William Sansom is distinct in the writing of short stories in England from the 1940's onward, since he does not focus necessarily on plot or character but is rather interested in setting and situation or a moment of revelation, a rendering of the visual. His concern is primarily aesthetic, and he emphasizes the very process of writing. Most significant, his short fiction presents a Seeing Eye that renders the visual as an ideal. He often speaks of a canvas, and, like the artist/writer, he concentrates on process as development. Often, Sansom focuses on a moment of Joycean epiphany, a significant opportunity lost, or an awareness too late for reconciliation.

"THE WALL"

The course of Sansom's short fiction began with the Fireman stories (*Fireman Flower*), which are often characterized by a Kafkaesque stream of consciousness. Many of these stories seem to be reportage blended with art, since they stem from Sansom's actual experiences as a firefighter in London during the nightmare of the German buzz bombs and heavy blitzing of London. The first collection of short stories about firefighters contains "The Wall," the first story Sansom wrote about the tireless men who extinguished the London blazes. This story, a hallucinatory and apocalyptic fantasy of a wall that collapses on the firefighters, stuns the reader. It begins with, "It was our third job that night. . . . I suppose we were worn down and shivering." Suddenly, a five-story wall started collapsing on the firefighters. The narrator says, "I was thinking of nothing at all and then I was thinking of everything in the world." Time stopped as the narrator waited for the wall to smash into the four men. He was hypnotized, arrested in time and space. One man was killed and three survived with severely burned faces because the three crouching men had been framed by a window space. The action lasts for a few seconds, but the frozen moment in time keeps resonating. Sansom achieves this effect in four pages.

These Fireman stories are often allegories. The men search for the source of fire as if for the Holy Grail. The fire, smoke, and steam symbolize obstacles. In the title story, Fireman Flower remarks that he has at last "come face to face with the essence of things." The firefighters encounter odd and strange businesses—coffee warehouses, clothing stores, even candy storages. Awestruck at the convulsion of man and nature, the workers are struck dumb.

"THE WITNESS"

One of the most harrowing of the tales is "The Witness," set in a coffee bean warehouse in flames. The steam of the water used to fight the fire creates an eeriness when the air is filled with the pungency of roasting boiling coffee beans. The men see a fireman poised on the wall far above; he is panic-stricken because he has had an earlier argument with the hose operator. Believing that he sees the operator smile (and it could have been only a grimace), "a yellow snarl of delight," he jumps into the boiling furnace of beans and perishes. The story, horrifying in its mere telling, reflects the untrustworthiness of sense perceptions. The men who witness the horror cannot verify that the hose operator really would or did increase the water pressure. The steam obscured their vision. Bombed London becomes a microcosm of the world. The men who extinguish fires or search through debris for bodies, living or dead, become crusaders and knights of the Apocalypse.

"SOMETHING TERRIBLE, SOMETHING LOVELY"

Published in 1948, *Something Terrible, Something Lovely* is a kaleidoscope of twenty-one memorable stories, narratives and sketches depicting not only traditional realism but also surreal landscapes, pathological personalities, satirical comedy, and weird tales. Sansom displays himself as a magus of landscape and a facile raconteur. The title story, "Something Terrible, Something Lovely," leads the reader along the garden path as Nita, who is nine, and her younger cousin talk about the boys. "It was a boy done it . . . we'll do it back on the boys." The reader is led to believe that some catastrophe has occurred and that the girls will exact an awful revenge. The secret is revealed only at the end of the story. The boys had written on a hospital wall in spidery, capital letters, "NITA HOBBS LOVES STAN CHUTER." The charming and naïve girls exact their pound of flesh sweetly and humorously. They cross out the five-word message and write their seven words, "THE PERSON WHO WROTE THIS IS DAFT." The charming artlessness reminds the reader of Jane Austen's heroine Catherine Morland in *Northanger Abbey* (1818) when she looked for gothic mystery and found only a laundry list. Sansom succeeds in his theme of revenge, a favorite one, in future stories that will entail neither children nor unadulterated charm (such as "A Contest of Ladies").

"THE VERTICAL LADDER"

In this same collection, *Something Terrible, Something Lovely*, are two Sansom cameos. One is the harrowing tale "The Vertical Ladder," portraying Flegg, a young boy, who is dared by his friends to climb a vertical ladder on an ancient gasometer. A young girl, perhaps showing sexual awareness, particularly urges him to mount the ladder. As he climbs upward with growing vertigo, he loses a sense of familiarity and feels endangered and defenseless. He begins to descend but discovers that his friends, who have left, removed the ladder below. As he climbs back upward toward the platform, he finds that the top rungs are missing. Flegg is arrested in space, unable to climb to safety either above or below. The tale ends as "Flegg stared dumbly, circling his head like a lost animal . . . then he jammed his legs in the lower rungs and his arms past the elbows to the armpits in through the top rungs and there he hung shivering and past knowing what more he could ever do." The story does not probe character but delineates simply what happened. Readers can conclude what they will—a moral, pride, sexual awakening, exploration into the unknown, desertion of friends, risk-taking or, as a final possibility, the terrible aloneness of the individual.

"DIFFICULTY WITH A BOUQUET"

"Difficulty with a Bouquet," a two-page story, is one of Sansom's best-known anthologized pieces. The protagonist, Seal, has picked in his garden a bouquet of flowers that he wishes to give to a Miss D., a neighbor, but after a few moments he is aware that the gift might be considered an affectation. Miss D. watches the discarding of the flowers from an adjacent window (Sansom was preoccupied with windows, especially in the novel *The Loving Eye*, depicting an almost compulsive voyeurism). Miss D. wishes that Seal had given her the flowers, but at the same time, she is glad that he did not. "I should have been most embarrassed. It's not as if he wanted me. It would have been just too maudlin for words." Anthologists dearly favor this short-short story because in a neat nutshell, Sansom, on a deeper level, is articulating the difficulty of two persons' interrelating on a simple level—any gift given unsolicited and a simple explanation of appreciation in return. The marvel of the story is its simplicity. "Difficulty with a Bouquet" is an ironic vignette of quiet tone and is painted with a few deft brush strokes.

"TUTTI-FRUTTI"

In the next few years, Sansom's creativity flowered. *South* and *The Passionate North* both introduced a unique genre that formed a transition from the early Poesque and Kafkaesque stories. This new genre combines a distinct sense of place with that of a short-story form. *South* includes a bittersweet story "Tutti-Frutti," set in Nice, a concept of place as important as Egdon Heath in Thomas Hardy's *The Return of the Native* (1878). These two places are as important as the characters. The main character, Ohlsson, a Swede and a romantic, is overpowered by the unexpected attention of a woman and is equally overpowered by the beauty of this Mediterranean port. Spending the entire day with this mystery woman, Ohlsson, having the prospect of seeing her again, goes onto the balcony to smoke a cigarette, which he drops, and in attempting to retrieve it, reaches out too far and falls several stories below. He is seriously injured and will never walk again. He remains in Nice to become a writer. Romance fatalistically turns to a tragedy manqué, and Ohlsson, losing the woman, whom he does not tell of his accident and who probably would have gone off with another man, becomes the writer that he would not have become if the accident had not occurred. Yet, it is the account at Nice that the readers remember and that interacts with Ohlsson. Sansom blends the tale with the city, a new genre that succeeds with the reader.

"THREE DOGS OF SIENA"

In *South*, also, appears another memorable story, "Three Dogs of Siena." The tale again features a place: Siena, with all of its history, *palios*, and *Sbandierata* (a flagwaving ceremony). The story unfolds from the standpoint of three dogs from Naples, Genoa, and Venice. As the animals run around the city searching for new experiences (a favorite theme of Sansom—risk-taking is life-affirming), the animals are cruelly mistreated. Since the Italians love their dogs as they love life, this attitude appears strange, but the people also love ceremony. Sansom writes, "in all ceremony there is the touch of death." The pomp and circumstance become more important than the dogs, who after being kicked and beaten, slink back into the shadows. Just as important as the dogs is Siena, whose observances of history and religion are rich and traditional. The reader sees the subtext: The Italians, who ignore the mistreatment of dogs, are contrasted to the English, who observe and are horrified at the mistreatment. The story appeals to the reader for many reasons, but the interest is maintained from the story's projection of animals as the perceivers.

"THE GIRL ON THE BUS"

Many stories from *The Passionate North*, also combining the travel and short-story technique, are concerned with love or its absence. Elizabeth Bowen calls this craving or the absence of love the resignation-reconciliation theme. In this collection, the story element becomes a shade more significant than place. The "place" obviously is the North. In "The Girl on the Bus," Sansom writes, "Since to love is better than to be loved, unrequited love may be the finest love of all." The protagonist, Harry, sees a beautiful woman skiing by; he is breathless at her loveliness, but he feels that he will never see her again. Yet she sets a standard that will never be met by another woman. Lamenting over his chance meeting at Haga Park, he curses himself for having gone there. In Denmark, he boards a train that will eventually take him to England. There, he encounters the woman but lacks the courage to speak to her—an opportunity lost. Yet, happily for him, the woman eventually talks to him, and they are finally married. Harry was resigned to his loss, yet the "reconciliation" eventually occurs. Critics generally agree that there is a better integration of story and locale in this collection.

Sansom's oeuvre strikes out in another direction with *A Touch of the Sun*. Although again Sansom blends his travel experiences with the short story, these tales reflect the protagonist's encounter with nightmare. These stories show the influence of Ivan Bunin, who is known for comic portrayals and whom Sansom greatly admired. "Episode at Gastein" is set in a German spa where Ludwig De Broda, forty but distinctly older in demeanor, aristocratic and wealthy, meets Fräulein Laure, distinctly inferior in education and social advantage. Both have marriage in mind. De Broda is immersed in the history of Gastein and its geography; Laure is interested in the cinema. De Broda intends to be Pygmalion to her Galatea, and it all backfires. Because Laure initiates a kiss in a *Weinstube*, De Broda feels that his proposal might be attributed to the excitement of the evening, and his rationality is the obstacle that ruins the possibility of marriage with Laure, who finds a younger, more physical Swiss and becomes immediately engaged to him. This story, almost forty pages, is almost a novella. The theme is a frequent one: Action delayed is action defeated. The pace is leisurely, and the nightmare is sudden. De Broda attempts suicide. His sense of failure is overpowering and Sansom depicts him in a bathtub contemplating suicide with a razor blade in each hand.

"LIFE, DEATH"

There is a shift in the collection *Lord Love Us*, especially since the year it was published was the year

of Sansom's marriage. The technique is experimental—the tones ranging from the seriocomic to even the frivolous, charming, amusing, and yet tragic and sorrowful. Sansom claimed that this collection was his favorite. A particularly appealing story is "Life, Death." In this tale, a fishmonger is a veritable artist as he sculpts the display of fish. Eventually, he meets a damsel whom he courts with free fish, and they marry. This delightful tale ends in tragedy when his wife and child die. No explanation is given: They simply die, and the fishmonger laments at the end, "Why, if *you* can tell me, such happy days? Why with happy days such shade?" At the end, even the slab that was his canvas no longer attracts him. His slide into sorrow is reminiscent of Samuel Taylor Coleridge's Ancient Mariner, who must keep repeating his tale. The meaning is implicit: Fate rules, bestowing bliss and sorrow. The story ends with questions but no answers.

A CONTEST OF LADIES

A Contest of Ladies gathers stories written over a period of years, and the terrain ranges from the ludicrous to the grotesque, from the melodramatic to the humorous. The title story, almost a novella, presents a retired actor who has designed his house like a hotel. Six international beauty contestants search for a hotel, and the local pranksters direct these lovelies to Morley's house. Morley entertains them and soon tells them that his home is not an inn. Most attracted to the Danish Miss Great-Belt, Morley becomes angry with her because she stands him up one evening, and he convinces his fellow jurors not to vote for her. She loses, but she wins Morley. Some critics called this tale a morality play, comically rendered.

"AMONG THE DAHLIAS"

Among the Dahlias is not a memorable collection except for the title story, wryly amusing and somewhat farcical. Mr. Doole loves animals and often visits the zoo. One day, he encounters a full-maned lion in a path, and he is frozen in terror. They stare at each other, and Doole almost begs the lion to let him live. When the lion obliges by walking away, the protagonist spends a good part of his life wondering why the lion turned away. The absurdity of Doole's narcissistic concern with his physique underscores theme, technique, and tone. Clara, in "Various Temptations," another tale in this collection, becomes the victim of an insane murderer, who falls in love with his victim until she preens herself to become more attractive, the very trait that the strangler seeks out, since he finds beauty akin to prostitution. Both Doole and Clara are rejected—one survives and the other perishes.

"THE MARMALADE BIRD"

Sansom's final collection, *The Marmalade Bird*, contains less comedy and more ironic humor. Especially absorbing is the title story, set in Marrakech. Sansom echoes disenchantment in this final volume. "The Marmalade Bird" focuses on a married couple who, though content, find that they must have conflict. A bird enjoys their marmalade pot and visits them daily. One day, they believe that the bird is gone, and they put some facial tissue over the pot. When the bird returns and dives into the pot, his beak is stuck in the tissue. The tragedy of the bird brings the couple together. Sansom delighted in this story, aware that marriage means strife but that reconciliation follows, and this becomes the human condition, the bittersweetness of life.

These last stories in *The Marmalade Bird* vividly contrast with Sansom's early Fireman stories, when the characters survive through illusion. His final short fiction reflects a disillusionment and a disenchantment with fantasy. Especially in his stories of marriage in this final volume, Sansom confronts the challenges and the bare realities of life to be lived now, not in some never-never land of an enchanted forest. Yet this final vision is not a dour one: Human beings facing the struggle to survive in an industrialized world will prevail and find their own identity.

OTHER MAJOR WORKS

LONG FICTION: *The Body*, 1949; *The Face of Innocence*, 1951; *A Bed of Roses*, 1954; *The Loving Eye*, 1956; *The Cautious Heart*, 1958; *The Last Hours of Sandra Lee*, 1961; *Goodbye*, 1966; *Hans Feet in Love*, 1971; *A Young Wife's Tale*, 1974.

NONFICTION: *Pleasures Strange and Simple*, 1953; *The Icicle and the Sun*, 1958; *Blue Skies, Brown Studies*, 1961; *Away to It All*, 1964; *Grand*

Tour Today, 1968, *The Birth of a Story*, 1972; *Proust and His World*, 1973.

CHILDREN'S LITERATURE: *The Light That Went Out*, 1953; *It Was Really Charlie's Castle*, 1953; *Skimpy*, 1974.

BIBLIOGRAPHY

Allen, Walter. *The Short Story in English*. New York: Oxford University Press, 1981. Discusses Sansom's "Old Man Alone," "The Wall," and "How Claeys Dies"; argues that Sansom transmits a Poe-Bierce horror in a Defoesque way.

Beachcroft, T. O. *The Modest Art: A Survey of the Short Story in English*. New York: Oxford University Press, 1968. A brief discussion of Sansom's prose style; claims he is a master of sensuous and atmospheric effects; comments on his being influenced by Kafka and the similarity of his comic stories to those of V. S. Pritchett.

Bernard, Jeffrey. "Low Life: Very Much in Love." *The Spectator* 274 (June, 1995): 54. In this tribute, Bernard remembers meeting Sansom.

Chalpin, Lila. *William Sansom*. Boston: Twayne, 1980. This short volume is a clear approach to Sansom's life and work, particularly tracing the development of his fictional techniques. Contains a comprehensive treatment of the early fiction, the novels, and travel books, and the later short stories. Chalpin stresses the influence of Edgar Allan Poe rather than Franz Kafka. Chalpin, like many other commentators, laments the critical neglect of a first-class short-story writer. Includes a chronology of his life and work and a bibliography.

Hanson, Clare. *Short Stories and Short Fictions, 1880-1980*. New York: St. Martin's Press, 1985. Discusses "Fireman Flower" and "The Wall" as stories that are concerned with the relationship between illusion and reality, chance and design.

Mason, Ronald. "William Sansom." In *Modern British Writing*, edited by Denys Val Baker. New York: Vanguard Press, 1947. A provocative commentary on Sansom's symbolism and realism used in the early fiction. Mason traces the writer's development from the Fireman stories and evaluates his growth from a miniaturist to a seasoned artist.

Michel-Michot, Paulette. *William Sansom: A Critical Assessment*. Paris: Société d'Édition, 1971. This doctoral dissertation was published as a thorough analysis and examination of all Sansom's work, excepting the last five years of his productivity. It is an exhaustive account of his short fiction, novels, and essays. Michel-Michot, like most critics of Sansom, believes that his penchant is for the short story, not the novel. The author interviewed Sansom and provides in-depth material concerning theme, symbolism, technique, and criticism.

Peden, William H. "The Short Stories of William Sansom: A Retrospective." *Studies in Short Fiction*, no. 4 (1988): 421-431. Since there is little contemporary criticism on Sansom, this article, although brief, is a high-density approach to his short fiction. Peden's conclusion is that all Sansom's fiction is enjoyable to read and reread. He particularly commends Sansom's short stories as "alive with excitement" and considers his fictional world unforgettable.

Vickery, John B. "William Sansom and Logical Empiricism." *Thought* 36 (Summer, 1961): 231-245. Sansom's early fiction is discussed in terms of his surrealistic phase. Although Sansom is not a university graduate of Cambridge or Oxford, Vickery believes that these centers exerted an influence on Sansom philosophically instead of the continental influence of rationalism or of the later existentialism.

Julia B. Boken

WILLIAM SAROYAN

Born: Fresno, California; August 31, 1908
Died: Fresno, California; May 18, 1981

PRINCIPAL SHORT FICTION

The Daring Young Man on the Flying Trapeze and Other Stories, 1934
Inhale and Exhale, 1936
Three Times Three, 1936
The Gay and Melancholy Flux: Short Stories, 1937
Little Children, 1937
Love, Here Is My Hat and Other Short Romances, 1938
The Trouble with Tigers, 1938
Three Fragments and a Story, 1939
Peace, It's Wonderful, 1939
My Name Is Aram, 1940
Saroyan's Fables, 1941
The Insurance Salesman and Other Stories, 1941
Forty-eight Saroyan Stories, 1942
Some Day I'll Be a Millionaire: Thirty-four More Great Stories, 1944
Dear Baby, 1944
The Saroyan Special: Selected Stories, 1948
The Fiscal Hoboes, 1949
The Assyrian and Other Stories, 1950
The Whole Voyald and Other Stories, 1956
William Saroyan Reader, 1958
Love, 1959
After Thirty Years: The Daring Young Man on the Flying Trapeze, 1964
Best Stories of William Saroyan, 1964
The Tooth and My Father, 1974

OTHER LITERARY FORMS

William Saroyan published almost fifty books, including novels, plays, and several autobiographical memoirs. Among his most famous plays are *My Heart's in the Highlands* (pr., pb. 1939) and *The Time of Your Life* (pr., pb. 1939). The latter was awarded the Pulitzer Prize in 1939, but Saroyan rejected it because he "did not believe in official patronage of art." His screenplay, *The Human Comedy* (1943), was one of the most popular wartime films and was later revised into a successful novel. Saroyan's talents also extended to songwriting, his most famous song being "Come Ona My House." His last work, *My Name Is Saroyan*, a potpourri of stories, verse, play fragments, and memoirs, was published posthumously in 1983.

ACHIEVEMENTS

William Saroyan's reputation rests mainly on his pre-World War II plays and fictional sketches that embraced an upbeat, optimistic, and happy view of people during a period of deep economic depression and increasing political upheaval. His immense popularity and critical acclaim in the United States declined after the war, though in Europe, notably France and Italy, his reputation has remained high. His plays and fiction have been translated into several languages.

Although highly diversified in technique, Saroyan's best works all bear an irrepressible faith in the goodness of the human spirit. His unique, multifaceted style has been emulated by other writers who lack his sanguine outlook and control of craft. Occasional flashes of brilliance partially restored Saroyan's reputation after World War II, and his memoir, *Obituaries* (1979), was nominated for the American Book Award. Saroyan's greatest and most influential works, however, belong to his early, experimental period.

BIOGRAPHY

William Saroyan was born in Fresno, California, in 1908. His father, who died when William was two, was a minister turned grape farmer; upon his death, young Saroyan spent seven years in an orphanage, after which his family was reunited. He worked at many odd jobs, including a stint as a telegraph operator, spending most of his time in Fresno and San Francisco. His first short stories began to appear in 1934 and found instant success. In his first year as a writer his work appeared in the O'Brien volume of *The Best Short Stories*, and he published what is still his best-received volume of short stories, *The Daring Young Man on the Flying Trapeze*. Thereafter he produced an amazingly prolific stream of short stories, plays, novels, and memoirs. Saroyan was twice married to Carol Marcus, with whom he had two children. In 1959, after his second divorce, he declared

William Saroyan (D. C. Public Library)

himself a tax exile and went to live in Europe. He returned in 1961 to teach at Purdue University and later returned to live in Fresno. He was actively writing right up to his death from cancer in 1981.

ANALYSIS

While William Saroyan cultivated his prose to evoke the effect of a "tradition of carelessness," of effortless and sometimes apparently formless ruminations and evocations, he was in reality an accomplished and conscious stylist whose influences are varied and whose total effect is far more subtle than the seemingly "breezy" surface might at first suggest. His concern for the lonely and poor—ethnic outsiders, barflies, working girls, children—and their need for love and connectedness in the face of real privation recalls Sherwood Anderson. All of Saroyan's best work was drawn from his own life (although the central character must be regarded as a persona, no matter how apparently connected to the author). In this aspect, and in his powerful and economical capacity to evoke locale and mood, Saroyan is in the tradition of Thomas Wolfe. The empathetic controlling consciousness and adventurous experiments with "formless form" also place Saroyan in the tradition that includes Walt Whitman and Gertrude Stein. It might also be noted that Saroyan's work shows the influence of Anton Chekhov in his use of seemingly "plotless" situations which nevertheless reveal some essential moment in the characters' lives and philosophical insight into the human condition.

Certainly, while the tone of Saroyan's stories evolves from the richly comic to the stoical to the sadly elegiac mood of his later work, his ethos stands counter to the naturalists and the ideologically programmatic writers of the 1930's, the period during which he produced some of his best work. Often his stories portray the world from the perspective of children, whose instinctual embrace of life echoes the author's philosophy. Saroyan wrote, "If you will remember that living people are as good as dead, you will be able to perceive much that is very funny in their conduct that you might never have thought of perceiving if you did not believe that they were as good as dead." Both the tone and outlook of that statement are paradigmatic.

"THE DARING YOUNG MAN ON THE FLYING TRAPEZE"

The title story of his first and most enduring collection, "The Daring Young Man on the Flying Trapeze," is still one of the most ambitious stylistic exercises of the Saroyan canon and an embodiment of the first phase of his career. The impressionistic style uses a welter of literary allusions in a stream-of-consciousness technique to portray the inner mind of an educated but destitute writer during the Depression who is literally starving to death as his mind remains lucid and aggressively inquiring. The poignant contrast between the failing body and the illuminated mind might evoke pity and compassion on the part of the reader, but somehow Saroyan invokes respect and acceptance as well.

The story begins with the random associated thoughts of the half-dreaming writer which reveal both the chaos of the present era—". . . hush the queen, the king, Karl Franz, black Titanic, Mr. Chaplin weeping, Stalin, Hitler, a multitude of Jews . . ."— and the young protagonist's literary erudition: ". . . Flaubert and Guy de Maupassant, a wordless rhyme of early meaning, Finlandia, mathematics highly polished and slick as green onions to the teeth, Jerusalem, the path to paradox."

Upon awakening, the writer plunges into "the trivial truth of reality." He is starving, and there is no work. He ironically contemplates starvation as he combines the food in a restaurant into a mental still life; yet without a shred of self-pity, and with great dignity in spite of a clerk's philistine and patronizing attitude, he attempts to obtain a job at an employment agency where the only skill which the writer can offer to a pragmatic world is the ability to type. He is relieved when there is no work because he can now devote his remaining energies to writing a literary last will and testament, an "Apology for Permission to Live."

He drinks copious amounts of water to fill his empty belly, steals some writing paper from the Y.M.C.A., and repairs to his empty apartment to compose his manifesto. Before beginning to write, he polishes his last remaining coin—a penny (he has sold his books for food, an act of which he feels ashamed)— and savors the "absurd act." As he contemplates the words on the coin which boast of unity, trust in God, and liberty, he becomes drowsy, and he takes final leave of the world with an inner act of grace and dignity reminiscent of the daring young man of the title. His last conscious act of thought is the notion that he ought to have given the coin to a child.

> A child could buy any number of things with a penny.
> Then swiftly, neatly, with the grace of the young man
> on the trapeze he was gone from his body. . . . The city
> burned. The herded crowd rioted. The earth circled
> away, and knowing that he did so, he turned his lost
> face to the empty sky and became dreamless, unalive,
> perfect.

The story embodies Saroyan's control of his materials and the sensitive and ironic understatement for which he is famous. While the stories written during the Depression express bitterness about the situation,

Saroyan eschews political solutions of any particular stripe and emphasizes the dignity of the individual and his tenacious connection to the forces of life and survival with grace and good humor.

MY NAME IS ARAM

A second collection which gained worldwide fame is the series of interconnected stories which form the book *My Name is Aram*. Told through the eyes of the title character, a young boy in the milieu of Armenian Fresno, the collection reveals the characteristics of the stories of the middle part of Saroyan's career and foreshadows the direction taken in his later work. The reader sees childlike adults and children imbued with the burdens of adulthood. Throughout, the collection explores the often contradictory claims of emotional, poetic, and instinctive needs and the claims of reality. The author's vision is dualistic. Some of the stories show a happy symbiosis between the poetic and the rational needs of his characters; others portray the conflicting demands unresolved. Even in the latter case, however, his characters cheerfully accept their fate, not with a stoicism so much as with a recognition that such a condition is a necessity to life and does not preclude savoring the moments of beauty which occur even in the midst of squalor or hardship.

"THE SUMMER OF THE BEAUTIFUL WHITE HORSE"

The first aspect of the mature and late phase of Saroyan's writing is aptly illustrated by the story "The Summer of the Beautiful White Horse." Typical of Saroyan's boyhood reminiscences, this tale concerns the seven-year-old Aram Garoghlanian and his slightly older cousin Mourad, who "borrow" a horse from their neighbor's barn and keep him for months at an abandoned farm, enjoying clandestine early morning rides. The owner of the horse, John Byro, complains to the boys' uncle Khosrove, a Saroyan eccentric who responds, "It's no harm. What is the loss of a horse? Haven't we all lost the homeland? What is this crying over a horse?" When the owner complains that he must walk, the uncle reminds him that he has two legs. When Byro laments that the horse had cost him sixty dollars, the uncle retorts, "I spit on money." Byro's loss of an agent to pull his surrey brings a roar of "Pay no attention to it!"

Uncle Khosrove's attitude is typical of the charming impracticality of many of Saroyan's characters. When the boys at last secretly return the animal, the farmer is merely thankful that it has been returned and makes no attempt to find out who had stolen it. He marvels that the horse is in better condition than when it had been stolen. The story charmingly resolves the conflicting demands of the poetic and the practical (in favor of the poetic).

"POMEGRANATE TREES"

"Pomegranate Trees" illustrates the darker and more elegiac side of the later Saroyan canon. Uncle Melik purchases some arid desert land which he intends to farm. The land is obviously impossible to render productive; yet the uncle persists in tilling the soil, planting his crops, and beating back the encroaching cactus while holding little dialogues with Aram and the prairie dogs. He decides against all reason to produce pomegranate trees, since he associates the fruit with his Assyrian past, but the trees are stunted, and the fruit yield is merely enough to fill a few boxes. When the meager harvest fails to bring a high enough price to suit Melik, he has the fruit sent back to him at still more expense. For the uncle, the enterprise has nothing to do with agriculture. "It was all pure aesthetics. . . . My uncle just liked the idea of planting trees and watching them grow."

The real world of unpaid bills intrudes, however, and the man loses the land. Three years later Aram and his uncle revisit the land which had given Melik such quixotic pleasure. The trees have died and the desert has reclaimed the land. "The place was exactly the way it had been all the years of the world." Aram and his uncle walk around the dead orchard and drive back to town. "We didn't say anything because there was such an awful lot to say, and no language to say it in."

There is nominal defeat, yet the still wistfully remembered joy in attempting the impossible for its own sake is a counterweight to the sadness of the finality of the experience. Such a resonance is at the heart of Saroyan's ethos, expressed in countless stories which have made him a popular favorite, and which are beginning to elicit a high critical acclaim as well.

OTHER MAJOR WORKS

LONG FICTION: *The Human Comedy*, 1943; *The Adventures of Wesley Jackson*, 1946; *Rock Wagram*, 1951; *Tracy's Tiger*, 1951; *The Laughing Matter*, 1953 (reprinted as *The Secret Story*, 1954); *Mama I Love You*, 1956; *Papa You're Crazy*, 1957; *Boys and Girls Together*, 1963; *One Day in the Afternoon of the World*, 1964.

PLAYS: *The Hungerers: A Short Play*, pb. 1939; *My Heart's in the Highlands*, pr., pb. 1939; *The Time of Your Life*, pr., pb. 1939 (also includes essays); *Love's Old Sweet Song*, pr., pb. 1940; *Three Plays: My Heart's in the Highlands, The Time of Your Life, Love's Old Sweet Song*, pb. 1940; *A Special Announcement*, pb. 1940; *Subway Circus*, pb. 1940; *The Ping-Pong Game*, pb. 1940 (one act); *The Beautiful People*, pr. 1940; *The Great American Goof*, pr. 1940; *Across the Board on Tomorrow Morning*, pr., pb. 1941; *Jim Dandy*, 1941; *Three Plays: The Beautiful People, Sweeney in the Trees, Across the Board on Tomorrow Morning*, pb. 1941; *Razzle-Dazzle*, pb. 1942 (collection); *Talking to You*, pr., pb. 1942; *Get Away Old Man*, pr. 1943; *Sam Ego's House*, pr. 1947; *A Decent Birth, a Happy Funeral*, pb. 1949; *Don't Go Away Mad*, pr., pb. 1949; *The Slaughter of the Innocents*, pb. 1952; *The Cave Dwellers*, pr. 1957; *Once Around the Block*, pb. 1959; *Sam the Highest Jumper of Them All: Or, The London Comedy*, pr. 1960; *Settled Out of Court*, pr. 1960 (adaptation with Henry Cecil); *The Dogs: Or, The Paris Comedy and Two Other Plays*, pb. 1969.

SCREENPLAYS: *The Human Comedy*, 1943.

NONFICTION: *The Time of Your Life*, 1939; *Harlem as Seen By Hirschfield*, 1941; *Hilltop Russians in San Francisco*, 1941; *Why Abstract?*, 1945 (with Henry Miller and Hilaire Hiler); *The Twin Adventures: The Adventures of William Saroyan*, 1950; *The Bicycle Rider in Beverly Hills*, 1952; *Here Comes, There Goes, You Know Who*, 1961; *A Note on Hilaire Hiler*, 1962; *Not Dying*, 1963; *Short Drive, Sweet Chariot*, 1966; *Look at Us: Let's See: Here We Are*, 1967; *I Used to Believe I Had Forever: Now I'm Not So Sure*, 1968; *Letters from 74 Rue Taitbout*, 1969; *Days of Life and Death and Escape to the Moon*, 1970; *Places Where I've Done Time*, 1972; *Sons Come and Go, Mothers Hang in Forever*, 1976; *Chance Meetings*, 1978; *Obituaries*, 1979; *Births*, 1983.

CHILDREN'S LITERATURE: *Me*, 1963; *Horsey Gorsey and the Frog*, 1968.

MISCELLANEOUS: *My Name Is Saroyan*, 1983 (stories, verse, play fragments, and memoirs).

BIBLIOGRAPHY

Balakian, Nona. *The World of William Saroyan.* Lewisburg, Ohio: Bucknell University Press, 1998. Balakian, formerly a staff writer for *The New York Times Book Review*, knew Saroyan personally in his last years, and her observations of him color her assessment of his later works. She viewed it as her mission to resurrect his reputation and restore him to his place among the finest of twentieth century American writers. Traces his evolution from ethnic writer to master of the short story, to playwright, and finally to existentialist.

Dyer, Brenda. "Stories About Stories: Teaching Narrative Using William Saroyan's 'My Grandmother Lucy Tells a Story Without a Beginning, a Middle, or an End.'" In *Short Stories in the Classroom*, edited by Carole L. Hamilton and Peter Kratzke. Urbana, Ill.: National Council of Teachers of English, 1999. Offers some suggestions for teaching Saroyan's story as a story about storytelling; argues that the story provides tools that empower and enrich when taught this way.

Floan, Howard R. *William Saroyan.* New York: Twayne, 1966. Floan's study remains one of the best extensive critical monographs on Saroyan's work. It focuses on Saroyan's early literature, glossing over the post-World War II period as less productive and durable. Contains a valuable annotated bibliography through 1964.

Foster, Edward Halsey. *William Saroyan.* Boise, Idaho: Boise State University Press, 1984. A condensed but helpful survey stressing Saroyan's unique voice. This work draws parallels between his work and that of the Beat generation.

_____. *William Saroyan: A Study of the Short Fiction.* New York: Twayne, 1991. An introduction to Saroyan's short stories that discusses his use of the oral tradition, his Armenian heritage, and his usual themes and experimental techniques. Includes Saroyan's own comments on his fiction as well as previously published essays by other critics.

Haslam, Gerald W. "William Saroyan." In *A Literary History of the American West*, edited by Thomas J. Lyon et al. Fort Worth: Texas Christian University, 1987. A good introductory essay. Haslam focuses on Saroyan's post-World War II decline in popularity and its cause. Includes a select bibliography.

_____. "William Saroyan and San Francisco: Emergence of a Genius (Self-Proclaimed)." In *San Francisco in Fiction: Essays in a Regional Literature*, edited by David Fine and Paul Skenazy. Albuquerque: University of New Mexico Press, 1995. Discusses the influence of San Francisco in a number of Saroyan's stories. Suggests that his stylistic triumph in "The Daring Young Man on the Flying Trapeze" is to force the readers to become co-creators in the story.

Keyishian, Harry, ed. *Critical Essays on William Saroyan*. New York: G. K. Hall, 1995. A collection of essays on Saroyan, from early reviews to critical articles. Helpful essays to a study of Saroyan's short stories are Edward Halsey Foster's discussion of Saroyan's relationship to Gertrude Stein and Walter Shear's essay on Saroyan's ethnicity.

Kherdian, David. *A Bibliography of William Saroyan, 1934-1964*. San Francisco: R. Beachman, 1965. Although in need of updating, this volume is a thorough and indispensable bibliographical guide to both primary and secondary works.

Lee, Lawrence, and Barry Gifford. *Saroyan: A Biography*. New York: Harper & Row, 1984. Lee and Gifford's study is rich with anecdotes and segments of interviews with Saroyan's family, friends, and associates. Supplemented by a chronology and a bibliography.

David Sadkin, updated by John W. Fiero

JEAN-PAUL SARTRE

Born: Paris, France; June 21, 1905
Died: Paris, France; April 15, 1980

PRINCIPAL SHORT FICTION

Le Mur, 1939; (*The Wall and Other Stories*, 1948)

OTHER LITERARY FORMS

Trained as a philosopher, Jean-Paul Sartre emerged during and after World War II as a major intellectual force in France and around the world, thanks mainly to his developing doctrine of existentialism. Unlike the rank and file of philosophers, Sartre soon proved to have a vivid literary and dramatic imagination, using the medium of creative writing to illustrate his major precepts. He is best known as a dramatist and the author of such plays as *Les Mouches, Huis clos* (pr. 1944; *In Camera*, 1946,

better known as *No Exit*, 1947), and *Les Mains sales* (pr., pb. 1948; *Dirty Hands*, 1949). Sartre is remembered also for the experimental novel *La Nausée* (1938; *Nausea*, 1949). *Les Chemins de la liberté* (1945-1949; *The Roads to Freedom*, 1947-1950), a projected tetralogy of which only three volumes were ever completed, represents Sartre's only other venture into long fiction. Thereafter, apart from his plays, Sartre wrote mainly essays, both literary and political, collected in *Situations* (1947-1976; partial translation, 1965-1977); he is known also for psychobiographical studies of eminent French authors, including *Baudelaire* (1947; English translation, 1950) and *L'Idiot de la famille* (1971-1972; partial translations, *The Family Idiot*, 1981, 1987), a study of the youth and maturity of Gustave Flaubert before the publication of *Madame Bovary* in 1857.

Published in France in the early 1970's, *The Family Idiot* did not appear in English translation until after Sartre's death.

ACHIEVEMENTS

Ironically, Jean-Paul Sartre's continuing reputation as a writer of short fiction rests on a single volume published at the start of his career and more specifically on the title story in the collection. "Le Mur" ("The Wall"), for all of its flaws, remains among the more arresting and memorable short stories of the twentieth century, defying imitation even as it invites increasingly "revisionist" criticism. The "other stories" included with "The Wall" are decidedly uneven in quality, of interest primarily to those interested in tracing Sartre's development as a writer and thinker. Meanwhile, "The Wall" itself remains standing, still viable because of its analysis of human nature as well as its documentation of a regrettable moment in history. Shortly after publication of Sartre's autobiographical essay *Les Mots* (*The Words*, 1964), Sartre was awarded the Nobel Prize in Literature but saw fit to decline the honor, ostensibly on political grounds.

BIOGRAPHY

A much younger first cousin, on his mother's side, of the physician, humanitarian, and musician Albert Schweitzer, Jean-Paul Sartre was born June 21, 1905, in Paris, losing his father to disease not long thereafter. Reared in a household filled with female relatives as well as with books, Sartre soon turned to reading and eventually to writing in order to assert his masculinity. Somewhat frail of health, with increasingly impaired vision, Sartre distinguished himself as a student; upon graduation from the prestigious Lycée Henri IV in Paris, he easily won admission to the even more elitist École Normale Supérieure, where he continued to work at creative writing in his spare time. In retrospect, he may have found too much time to spare, for he failed in his first attempt, in 1929, at the competitive examination for the *agrégation*, or teaching credential; the novel produced during those years was soon destroyed, for want of a publisher. In the meantime, Sartre had made the acquaintance of Simone de Beauvoir, a classmate and budding writer

Jean-Paul Sartre (Library of Congress)

who would remain his friend and frequent consort for life, even as both disdained to endure the "bourgeois" institution of marriage.

During the 1930's, his consciousness increasingly raised toward the political Left, Sartre pursued his career as a teacher of philosophy at the secondary level in various French cities, including Le Havre, soon immortalized in his writing as the Bouville, or "Mudville," of *Nausea*. As in the case of Antoine Roquentin, the narrator-protagonist of *Nausea*, Sartre was soon able to write and travel on the proceeds of a small inheritance, which helped to produce his earliest publications.

Briefly held captive as a prisoner of war after the fall of France to the Nazis in 1940, Sartre continued writing both before and after his release, initially producing the massive philosophical treatise *L'Être et le néant* (1943; *Being and Nothingness*, 1956). While in prison, however, Sartre had written a play to entertain his fellow captives, and before long, the ideas of *Being and Nothingness* began to find their way into such plays as *The Files* and *No Exit*, reaching a much wider audience than the treatise ever would, or could. Thus encouraged, Sartre tried to express his ideas through the medium of long fiction as well but met with considerably less success than he did on the stage. The projected tetralogy *The Roads to Freedom* would remain unfinished, though still in print as a trilogy during the years following Sartre's death. As founder, editor, and guiding spirit of the Left-leaning periodical *Les Temps modernes* (modern times), which was named by Sartre and Beauvoir in honor of their favorite Charles Chaplin film, Sartre would retain, and remain, an active voice in liberal French politics, visibly committed to Marxism but refusing to compromise his independence by ever joining the Communist Party. Already ailing, infirm, and almost totally blind, Sartre was hailed as an inspiration and a hero by student rebels during the far-reaching social upheavals in Paris during 1968, succumbing some twelve years later to a variety of ailments.

ANALYSIS

Like many writers and thinkers drawn to the political Left, Jean-Paul Sartre tended to see most existing literature, especially that of the nineteenth century, as part of a capitalist plot to maintain and perpetuate the prevailing social order. In terms that he would soon define as he proceeded to elaborate his philosophy of existentialism, most literature was "inauthentic," offering a false portrayal of life based on lies, or at least on false assumptions. No author, he claimed, could possibly presume to "understand" his characters or to attribute motivation to behavior portrayed. "The Wall," written during—and about—the Spanish Civil War of 1936-1939, was conceived at least in part as an illustration of Sartre's developing theories, showing behavior "in situation," recounted in the first person by a far from "omniscient" narrator who is himself a major participant in the action portrayed.

"THE WALL"

Pablo Ibbieta, arrested by General Franco's Nazi-supported Falangist forces, tells only what he sees and feels, little mindful of cause and effect. Although no doubt an educated man, an informed political activist on the Republican side, Pablo has plausibly been reduced by his recent experiences to a kind of automaton, responding quickly and unreflectively to such external stimuli as light and darkness, heat and cold. His narrative begins with the start of his captivity, when he is pushed into a makeshift holding cell with two other prisoners. After cursory interrogation, the three are sentenced to death at sunrise, with a Belgian physician assigned to watch over them during their final hours. The stage is thus set—and it is useful here to remember that Sartre would soon hit his true stride as a playwright—for a conflict of wills and aspirations that is truly dramatic in structure and tone. Pablo, a stereotypical if quite plausible Hispanic male in whom the "macho" ideal is ingrained, determined to be a "tough guy" to the bitter end, will observe and judge both captors and fellow captives in accordance with that standard and will predictably find them wanting.

Imprisoned along with Pablo are Tom Steinbock (oddly identified as Irish within the text despite his Germanic surname) and Juan Mirbal, an effeminate youngster who repeatedly asserts his innocence, claiming that he has been mistaken for an anarchist brother. Tom, perhaps in fact an American or Canadian attracted to the Republican cause, tends to talk too much, at least to Pablo's way of thinking, which also judges Juan Mirbal as a whiner. Pablo's evident attitude is that, when death is inevitable, one must face it with whatever dignity remains.

The Belgian doctor, who is soon identified by Pablo with the enemy, is sent in to record with scientific precision—as did the Nazis—the behavior and reactions of men getting ready to die. He serves within the story as an object-lesson among the "living," those not condemned to death who can still feel cold, heat, pain and, in short, "think about tomorrow." The doomed men, by contrast, soon lose touch with their surroundings as well as with their bodies and bodily functions; Pablo, who considers himself, perhaps not without reason, as the most lucid of the trio, looks on with mounting indignation, bordering upon disgust, as his fellow prisoners unconsciously succumb to the fear of death while he, Pablo, strains his resources to the limit in order to remain "tough." Quickly revisiting his life and loves as a potential suicide might see his past flash before him as he jumps from a bridge, Pablo Ibbieta concludes that only the illusion of immortality could lend meaning to life and that human aspirations add up to a "damned lie." Even Pablo's latest girlfriend, Concha, falls victim to the nihilism that invades his person as he faces death; he is now sure that he would find Concha's flesh quite as repulsive as he now finds his own and that their eyes could never meet again.

At dawn, as his cellmates are led off to death by firing squad within plain earshot, Pablo himself is detained for further questioning concerning the whereabouts of the agitator Ramon Gris, whom he allegedly harbored under his own roof before being arrested. Having sensed the absurdity of the entire situation, Pablo Ibbieta indulges himself in a final joke, sending his pompous, beribboned captors off to the local cemetery, where he claims Gris might well be hiding. Nothing, as Pablo well knows, could be further from the truth, nor does he still harbor any loyalty toward Gris or even to "the cause," all of which died in him at the same time as his feelings toward Concha. All he cares about now is the ridiculous parade of the self-absorbed officers through the deserted graveyard, imagining the look on their faces when they figure out that they have been "had."

The officers have been gone no longer than a half-hour when Pablo is suddenly and unexpectedly turned loose among newly arrested prisoners still awaiting sentence. It is one of the latter, the apolitical baker Garcia, who explains to Pablo what has happened: Ramon Gris, unable to seek refuge with Pablo after Pablo's arrest, had in fact been hiding out in the cemetery, in the grave diggers' shack, and was killed by return fire after shooting at the Falangists sent—by Pablo—to look for him. As the truth begins to sink in, Pablo sinks to the ground in a fit of helpless laughter.

The image of the wall, literally the wall against which prisoners stand when shot by a firing squad, serves to represent the boundary separating life from death. The tone of Pablo's narrative indicates that he has been quite as good as dead from the moment that he grasped the fact of his own mortality. He has, so to speak, passed through the wall to the nothingness beyond it, quite unable to pick up where he left off, and although he has somehow survived to tell the tale, his life might as well have ended. Arguably, readers of a later generation, aware of Sartre's sustained interest in psychology, might well see in Pablo's disorientation an early literary example of post-traumatic stress syndrome, but the author's intentions here reach well beyond the topical and clinical toward the timeless and universal, evoking humankind's inability to accept the finality of death, especially violent death resulting from war.

Like many of Sartre's later characters, especially in the plays that would follow, and complete, the philosophical statement set forth in *Being and Nothingness*, Pablo has learned, or believes himself to have learned, that aspirations count for nothing and that life is nothing more than the total of acts completed at the time of death, leaving little for posterity.

Limited to—and by—the consciousness of Pablo as narrator, told in a colloquial, even "earthy" style with certain words no doubt appearing in print for the first time, "The Wall" breaks sharply with the omniscient, "bourgeois" literary tradition that Sartre had come to distrust and detest. Except for Pablo's random recollections as his life passes before him, the characters are shown entirely "in situation," revealed only by their actions; what is more, the setting and atmosphere of Pablo's incarceration are evoked entirely through sensory perceptions often graphically rendered. The story's "surprise" ending, though no doubt as contrived as any to be found in Guy de Maupassant's or O. Henry's works, is nevertheless so well prepared by the preceding action as to underscore the author's conviction that life, in its contingency and unpredictability, is frequently stranger than fiction.

"EROSTRATUS"

Of the "other stories" collected with "The Wall," only two appear to have withstood the test of time; drawn perhaps too close to Freudian stereotype to appear fully credible, "Erostrate" and "Enfance d'un chef" ("Childhood of a Boss") still contain valuable insights into human behavior that may well appear prophetic to readers of later generations. "Erostratus," also told in the first person, presents the threats and rantings of a would-be psychopathic killer, a social and sexual misfit who has come to detest his shared humanity. Resigning his job in order to plan a symbolic mass murder, Paul Hilbert then mails identical poison-pen letters to a hundred prominent writers, each of whom is guilty, in Hilbert's eyes, of having professed love for his fellow mortals. Outlining his projected crime, Hilbert warns his addressees to watch for his name in the papers. In his own mind, Hilbert likens his gesture to that of Erostratus, of whom he has only recently heard, whose destructive act in burning down the temple at Ephesus has caused his name to be remembered while that of the temple's architect is long since forgotten. Eerily prophesying certain mass murders and assassinations of the middle to late twentieth century, Sartre's portrayal of Hilbert shows a warped conscience attempting to emerge from anonymity through an act of violence; Hilbert, however, will manage to botch his plans as he has botched his life. Instead of killing five pedestrians with his revolver, saving the last bullet for himself in the peace and quiet of his own room, Hilbert panics and fires the first three rounds into one victim, then fires two more to disperse the crowd when he finds that he is running away from his lodgings. Seeking refuge in the washroom of a nearby café, Hilbert in the end will lack even the resolve to shoot himself, meekly opening the door to his pursuers; presumably, he has written the story while in prison—or in a madhouse—although the exact venue is not specified.

"Childhood of a Boss"

"Childhood of a Boss," at nearly one hundred pages, is the longest narrative collected in "The Wall." It combines psychology with politics in a memorable, if stereotypical, portrait of a capitalist with carefully cultivated Fascist leanings. Told in the third person, "Childhood of a Boss" traces the negative evolution, from around age three through adolescence to young manhood, of Lucien Fleurier, who in time will inherit his father's lucrative enterprise. Like "Erostrate," Lucien's biography often seems like a

Freudian case history, or indeed a parody of one. In the opening scene, little Lucien is shown dressed as a hermaphroditic angel, embarrassed when mistaken for a girl; not long thereafter, the boy is disturbed by the dimly understood event of his parents' lovemaking and imagines himself to be an orphan. Uncomfortable before "the eyes of God" in church, Lucien feels great pride when his father takes him on a tour of the Fleurier enterprise, dimly sensing that the place and its deferential workers will one day be his own to boss around.

At school, Lucien, as earlier in his angel suit, uneasily feels the eye of the "Other" upon him; no sooner has he described a classmate as a bug than he finds himself described as an asparagus or a bean pole, because of his gangly height. Constantly unsure of who or what he is, the definition changing daily depending upon how he is perceived—or sees himself to be perceived—by others, Lucien Fleurier is soon well on his way to a life lived in what Sartre would later define in *Being and Nothingness* as "bad faith," outer-directed inauthenticity as opposed to inner-directed integrity. Like the characters in *No Exit*, the growing Lucien will continue to use his fellow mortals as a mirror in search of self-definition. Following the trends of the time (he is roughly the same age as Sartre, born soon after the turn of the twentieth century), Lucien will dabble in surrealism and psychoanalysis, both presented under a skeptically satirical light. With joy and relief, for example, Lucien will diagnose himself with the Oedipus complex, only to leave himself open to an unpleasant and unanticipated episode of homosexual seduction in which he unwillingly yet "logically" allows the "Other" to define him, however briefly. Soon thereafter, he will try to deny—to himself—the entire situation, plunging into heterosexual and sexually exploitative behavior with a zeal befitting his stature as a "born boss," meanwhile gravitating toward a particular group of male acquaintances because they seem firm in their convictions, thus uncommonly mature for their age; Lucien, it seems, would like nothing better than to share their self-confidence, having given up on psychoanalysis after his encounter with homosexuality.

Typically, perhaps stereotypically, it turns out that Lucien's new "friends" are strongly anti-Semitic, highly sympathetic to Adolf Hitler and his cause. Lucien, who has yet to form any conviction about Jews one way or the other, still feels drawn to Lemordant and his crowd by the apparent force and inflexibility of their political "faith," a faith that reaches well beyond politics to prescribe an entire lifestyle. As he approaches age thirty, having drifted hither and yon in search of "himself," Lucien Fleurier at last feels "at home." Like the bigots profiled in *Réflections sur la question juive* (1946; *Anti-Semite and Jew*, 1948), written during 1943, Lucien cannot accept the contingency of his own being, the constant need to make intelligent choices, opting instead for the security of "belonging" to a faceless throng in which choices are neither necessary nor desired. Typically, however, Lucien will not commit himself to the "Young Royalists" until after he has performed an apparent act of murder in their service; roaming Paris with Lemordant and his confederates, Lucien delivers a fatal blow to a Jewish pedestrian after the others have begun the beating. During the weeks to follow, Lucien will take as his mistress a certain Maud, herself inclined toward leftist causes yet, like Lucien himself, sufficiently malleable to seek her identity in the gaze of others. At first, Maud is as reluctant to return Lucien's affections as was Lucien with the homosexual artist Bergère; in time, however, Maud will yield to the authority and gravity of Lucien's newly acquired confidence. Lucien, however, decides that the conquest of Maud has been too easy, that she is in fact a whore (which may well be true), and above all, that he has failed to possess the "otherness" about Maud that made her attractive to him in the first place. Turning his sights instead toward someone "like" Pierrette, the younger sister of his friend Guigard who had introduced him to Maud, Lucien begins to imagine the "proper wife" for someone of his station in life.

At Pierrette's birthday party not long thereafter, Lucien further "defines" himself by stuffing his hands in his pockets and refusing to shake hands with another guest, and friend of Guigard, who happens to be Jewish. Still shaky in his convictions, Lucien leaves the gathering in a hurry, fully expecting Guigard to upbraid him for his churlish behavior. Instead, it is Guigard who apologizes, having been admonished by his parents to be more understanding and "tolerant" of Lucien's "convictions." In the story's final scene, Lucien, sure of himself at last, goes alone to a café, where, oblivious to his surroundings, he can savor both his food and his newfound sense of security. After all, he reasons, he was born to be a boss, with a virginal wife and eventually many children. Such a woman will, in fact, be his possession, and Lucien idly wonders just how long he will have to wait before his father dies, leaving him the business. Glancing into a mirror on his way out of the café, he decides to grow a mustache after deciding that his face is still a bit too callow and youthful to go with his "responsibilities and rights."

Although nearly a caricature of the Right as seen from the Left, "Childhood of a Boss" nevertheless goes a long way toward explaining the possible causes and origins of certain political and social attitudes that contributed to World War II and that would continue to haunt both national and international politics for decades to come. In *Anti-Semite and Jew*, first published approximately five years later, Sartre would recast in thoughtful essay form many of the poses, dodges, and self-doubts here projected onto Lucien, showing the typical bigot to be afraid of his own being, in desperate search of a scapegoat to blame for the fact that both he and the world are ill-made. "If the Jew did not exist," concludes Sartre, "the anti-Semite would have to invent him." Like Lucien, the bigot seeks above all to be a "rock," a force of nature, in short, anything but a human being who, like Sartre's prototypical existentialist, must constantly seek his own being—existence, not essence—through continual acts of choice.

More than fifty years after its publication, Sartre's short fiction—although it constitutes only a small portion of his total output and he soon abandoned the form altogether—continues to strike a responsive chord in many potential readers thanks to Sartre's keen insights into human nature and behavior. With the passage of time, the stories—at least the three here discussed—have additionally acquired a strong documentary value, helping the reader to discover, and in large measure to understand, the historical period of their composition. "The Wall," in particular, re-creates the singular horrors of the Spanish Civil War quite as effectively as Ernest Hemingway's *For Whom the Bell Tolls* (1940), with considerably greater economy of style and space.

OTHER MAJOR WORKS

LONG FICTION: *La Nausée*, 1938 (*Nausea*, 1949); *Les Chemins de la liberté*, 1945-1949 (*The Roads to Freedom*, 1947-1950; includes *L'Âge de raison*, 1945 [*The Age of Reason*, 1947], *Le Sursis*, 1945 [*The Reprieve*, 1947], *La Mort dans l'âme*, 1947 [*Troubled Sleep*, 1950; also as *Iron in the Soul*, 1950]).

PLAYS: *Les Mouches*, pr., pb. 1943 (*The Flies*, 1946); *Huis clos*, pr. 1944 (*In Camera*, 1946; better known as *No Exit*, 1947); *Morts sans sépulture*, pr., pb. 1946 (*The Victors*, 1948); *La Putain respectueuse*, pr., pb. 1946 (*The Respectful Prostitute*, 1947); *Les Jeux sont faits*, pr., pb. 1947 (*The Chips Are Down*, 1948); *Les Mains sales*, pr., pb. 1948 (*Dirty Hands*, 1948); *Le Diable et le bon Dieu*, pr. 1951 (*The Devil and the Good Lord*, 1953); *Kean: Ou, Désordre et génie*, pb. 1952 (adaptation of Alexandre Dumas, *père*'s play, *Kean: Or, Disorder and Genius*, 1954); *Nekrassov*, pr. 1955 (English translation, 1956); *Les Séquestrés d'Altona*, pr. 1959 (*The Condemned of Altona*, 1960); *Les Troyennes*, pr. 1965 (adaptation of Euripides' play, *The Trojan Women*, 1967).

NONFICTION: *L'Imagination*, 1936 (*Imagination: A Psychological Critique*, 1962); *Esquisse d'une théorie des émotions*, 1939 (*The Emotions: Outline of a Theory*, 1948); *L'Imaginaire: Psychologie phénoménologique de l'imagination*, 1940 (*The Psychology of Imagination*, 1948); *L'Être et le néant*, 1943 (*Being and Nothingness*, 1956); *L'Existentialisme est un humanisme*, 1946 (*Existentialism*, 1947; also as *Existentialism and Humanism*, 1948); *Réflexions sur la question juive*, 1946 (*Anti-Semite and Jew*, 1948); *Baudelaire*, 1947 (English translation, 1950); *Qu'est-ce que la littérature?*, 1947

(*What Is Literature?*, 1949); *Situations*, 1947-1976 (10 volumes; partial translation, 1965-1977); *Saint-Genet: Comédien et martyr*, 1952 (*Saint Genet: Actor and Martyr*, 1963); *Critique de la raison dialectique, précéde de question de méthode*, 1960 (*Search for a Method*, 1963); *Critique de la raison dialectique, I: Théorie des ensembles pratiques*, 1960 (*Critique of Dialectical Reason I: Theory of Practical Ensembles*, 1976); *Les Mots*, 1964 (*The Words*, 1964); *L'Idiot de la famille: Gustave Flaubert, 1821-1857*, 1971-1972 (3 volumes; *The Family Idiot: Gustave Flaubert, 1821-1857*, partial translations, 1981, 1987); *Un Théâtre de situations*, 1973 (*Sartre on Theater*, 1976).

BIBLIOGRAPHY

Aronson, Ronald, and Adrian van den Hoven. *Sartre Alive*. Detroit: Wayne State University Press, 1991. Sections on Sartre's continuing political relevance, rethinking his political and philosophical thought, his fiction and biography, his relationship with de Beauvoir and other writers, and concluding assessments of his career. Aronson and van den Hoven provide a judicious and well-informed introduction.

Barnes, Hazel E. *The Literature of Possibility: Studies in Humanistic Existentialism*. Lincoln: University of Nebraska Press, 1959. Among the earliest expositions of existentialist thought, this first of several books by Barnes (also a frequent translator of Sartre) that deal with postwar French thought and writing is still noteworthy for its analysis of the short stories, a genre often overlooked by Sartre's other critics. Using the short fiction as a point of entry into Sartre's developing thought, Barnes is especially authoritative in her reading of "Childhood of a Boss."

Brosman, Catherine Savage. *Jean-Paul Sartre*. Boston: Twayne, 1983. An introduction to Sartre's life and thought; includes chapters on Sartre's life, philosophy, fiction, and drama. A brief discussion of the five stories in *The Wall* appears in the chapter on the early fiction.

Cranston, Maurice. *Jean-Paul Sartre*. New York: Grove Press, 1962. A short introductory volume with chapters on Sartre's life, drama, fiction, and critical theories. Contends "The Wall," although it along with *Nausea* made Sartre's name in France, is one of his least characteristic works of fiction; in fact, with its neat plot and ironical final twist, it belongs to a tradition of fiction typical of Guy de Maupassant which Sartre repudiated.

Hayman, Ronald. *Sartre: A Life*. New York: Simon & Schuster, 1987. Well written, Hayman's life of Sartre shows the biographical and historical context of the various works, suggesting how and why Sartre explored various literary genres in search of the most accessible vehicle for his ideas.

Hill, Charles G. *Jean-Paul Sartre: Freedom and Commitment*. New York: Peter Lang, 1992. Discusses Sartre's quest for freedom and authentic actions as well as his recognition of the ambiguities of commitment. See especially chapter 2, on *Nausea*. Includes chronology, notes, and bibliography.

Peyre, Hanri. *French Novelists of Today*. New York: Oxford University Press, 1967. This volume is a revision of *The Contemporary French Novel*, originally published in 1955. Peyre's exhaustive survey of then-recent French fiction devotes an entire chapter to Sartre's narrative prose, including the short stories. Unlike many of Sartre's commentators both before and since, Peyre sees Sartre's fiction as forming a significant portion of his total literary statement.

_____. *Jean-Paul Sartre*. New York: Columbia University Press, 1968. A brief monograph in the Columbia Essays on Modern Writers series. Peyre asserts there may not be another volume of short stories in French literature of the last hundred years as remarkable as *The Wall*. He argues that because they are early works, they are not marred by philosophy or obtrusive symbolism, but rather are as concrete as the stories of Ernest Hemingway.

Plank, William. *Sartre and Surrealism*. Ann Arbor, Mich.: UMI Press, 1981. One of the few studies of Sartre to discuss the short fiction at length in detail, Plank's monograph situates the stories with regard to intellectual as well as political history.

David B. Parsell

JOHN SAYLES

Born: Schenectady, New York; September 28, 1950

PRINCIPAL SHORT FICTION
The Anarchists' Convention, 1979

OTHER LITERARY FORMS

John Sayles has written three novels: *The Pride of the Bimbos* (1975); *Union Dues* (1977), which was nominated for both the National Book Award and the National Book Critics Circle Award; and *Los Gusanos* (the worms, 1991). With Gavin Smith, he published *Sayles on Sayles* (1998), in which he discusses his career and his films. In addition, his *Thinking in Pictures: The Making of the Movie "Matewan,"* which concerns his shooting of the mining film, was published in 1987. He has written many screenplays, a television series, and even one-act plays.

ACHIEVEMENTS

John Sayles's "I-80 Nebraska, m.490-m.205" (1975) and his "Breed" (1977) won O. Henry Awards. He has made twelve feature films and in 1983 received a John D. and Catherine T. MacArthur Foundation ("genius") Award: a grant of thirty thousand dollars per year for five years, tax-free.

BIOGRAPHY

John Thomas Sayles was born in Schenectady, New York, on September 28, 1950, and attended Mount Pleasant High School in Schenectady, earning letters in basketball, baseball, track, and football. After being turned down by the U.S. Army, in 1968 Sayles enrolled at Williams College, where he took creative writing classes and acted in dramatic productions. Following his graduation in 1962, he worked in a variety of jobs, including one in a meatpacking plant, and hitchhiked thousands of miles. In 1975 he published his first novel, *The Pride of the Bimbos*, and won an O. Henry Award for "I-80 Nebraska, m.490-m.205." In 1977 he published his second novel, *Union Dues*, and began writing for Roger Corman's New World Pictures. *The Return of the Secaucus Seven* (1979), his first feature film, was a critical and financial success; and in the same year he published his collection of short stories, *The Anarchists' Convention*. Aside from writing and staging his one-act plays in 1981, the rest of his career has primarily been devoted to working in films as an actor, screenplay writer, editor, and director. Two of his screenplays (*Alligator*, 1980; *Wild Thing*, 1987) are based on his short stories. In 1991 he published his third novel, *Los Gusanos*, but Sayles has become primarily a filmmaker rather than a writer of fiction.

ANALYSIS

John Sayles's fiction is in the realist tradition of Theodore Dreiser and James Farrell in its economic determinism, but as in the fiction of Stephen Crane, that determinism is tempered by occasional passages of sentimentality and romanticism. Though his blue-collar workers are often depicted as victims of their environment, they are resilient and resourceful ones. Like Crane, Sayles, especially in the Brian McNeil stories, focuses on the initiation of a young man on a quest for identity and manhood. In that quest Sayles's characters encounter a variety of misfits, people on the margins of society. Sayles's narratives are relatively straightforward, with the exception of "Tan," which uses flashbacks to juxtapose present and past, and "Schiffman's Ape," which uses flashbacks and provides parallels between scientific observations and the scientists' lives.

These narratives, with the exception of the somewhat surreal "I-80 Nebraska, m.790-m.205," which uses a cinematic sound montage of short CB mes-

John Sayles (AP/Wide World Photos)

sages to heighten tension, are recounted in an efficient, plain style without rhetorical flourishes. Sayles has a fetish for technical details, especially when the subject is something he has experienced, and the wealth of details engages the reader. Much of the fiction, especially the Brian McNeil stories, seems closely tied to Sayles's own life. Partly because of the somewhat "autobiographical" nature of the content, Sayles is compassionate about his characters, even when they are seriously flawed.

"AT THE ANARCHISTS' CONVENTION"

"At the Anarchists' Convention" is an ironic title, for anarchy is antithetical to organization, especially as manifested in a meeting with name tags, place cards, and committees. Leo, the elderly narrator, recounts the events that culminate in a confrontation with hotel management, which has also booked a Rotary Club, full of "gin and boosterism," into the Elizabethan Room, an ironic venue for anarchists. Leo, in love with Sophie and jealous of Brickman's relationship with her some forty years ago, reminisces with old left-wing colleagues about past political battles and even manages a eulogy about Brickman, now deceased. When the hotel manager informs the aging leftists that they must vacate the room, they barricade the doors, link arms, and sing "We Shall Not Be Moved." In his exhilaration, Leo holds Sophie's hand and thinks that if Brinkman, his old rival, were here, "we'd show this bastard the Wrath of the People."

"Schiffman's Ape"

In "Schiffman's Ape" Warden, an associate professor, and Lisa, his graduate assistant and wife, study Esau, a rare Schiffman ape in the ape's natural habitat. In the course of the story Sayles neatly parallels Warden's recorded observations of Esau's sexual activity with the fading relationship between the two academics. The parallel is comically reinforced by a native legend, fabricated by Sayles, about the creator separating twin brothers into men and apes. Warden, whose name suggests his tendency to imprison others, is a patriarchal, macho, control-oriented person who magnanimously "forgives" Lisa for saving Esau, when he himself was ready to intervene. He also has a double standard for sexual infidelity, condemning hers while dismissing his own as trivial. As Lisa becomes increasingly disenchanted with Warden, Esau experiences difficulty having sex with female Schiffman apes, all of this recorded by Warden. Warden observes Esau giving up his pursuit of a female and resorting to masturbation just before Lisa and he observe Esau drown without either intervening. Esau's death is the death of their relationship.

"Tan"

Sayles's story begins with Con Tinh Tan sitting in a waiting room and quickly flashes back to Tan as a thirteen-year-old girl in 1963 Vietnam. Her first experience with Americans is ostensibly positive because the American dentist fixes her teeth and improves her appearance, but she believes that the "American had taken her face." The rest of the story details the other things that are taken from her as a result of American interference in Southeast Asia. Soon after her father's imprisonment and death, she sees a monk set himself on fire and die, and when she moves to her uncle's house, he rapes her during the Tet offensive. After the Communists take her uncle away, she is on the streets. At age twenty, she is "befriended" by Sergeant Plunkett, who gives her food for sex and gets her pregnant. Dr. Yin, who performs the abortion, also implants opium in her breasts; and Plunkett sends her to America, where he promises to meet her. When Plunkett does not appear, she decides to have the implants removed. She is surprised to find out that the surgeon who is to do the surgery is Dr. Yin, who has been "expecting" her. When Tan loses her identity through two operations designed to "improve her" and is sexually exploited, she becomes both the real and the symbolic victim of Western exploitation.

"I-80 Nebraska, m. 490-m. 205"

On a section of Interstate 80 a rebel trucker named Ryder P. Moses leads his pursuers, fellow truckers obsessed with finding him, on a chase that ends with his deliberately driving his tractor-trailer into the concrete support of an overpass. Moses, whose name ironically suggests he is a leader of the people, becomes a phantom driver, a legend on westbound 80, which Sayles describes as "an insomniac world of lights passing lights to the music of the Citizens Band." While the narrator occasionally comments on the action, the narrative is primarily a series of Citizens Band conversations by truckers and Moses, who is "breaking every trucker commandment." The gossip about him is as erroneous and widespread as are the suppositions about the identity of the Great Gatsby. Moses, who identifies himself as the Paul Bunyan of Interstate 80, scares and thrills the other truckers with monologues induced by drugs and devoted to condemning American culture. Just before he crashes, Moses says, "Going west. Good night and happy motoring," a bitter echo of a 1960's ad for Esso gasoline and an ironic farewell to a world gone bad.

The Anarchists' Convention

The six stories that comprise the second part of Sayles's collection of short stories are linked by Brian McNeil, a high school basketball player who drops out of school and hitchhikes across the United States. The stories, which may have been intended as episodes in a picaresque novel, take Brian from high school sexual initiation ("Bad Dogs") and basketball success ("Hoop") to California, where he sees his future ("Golden State"). Brian's story, which closely resembles Sayles's early life, includes a short farewell to his mother ("Buffalo") before he leaves. In "Fission" Brian encounters an obese drug-dealing woman whose family farm has been lost to agribusiness and a mad recluse whose fear of missiles has led him to build an underground bomb shelter for his promiscuous daughter and himself. Farther west in Wyoming, Brian meets Cody Sprague, whose futile entrepreneurial efforts cast some doubt on the American Dream, and a group of Native Americans, whose plight reflects their treatment by white America ("Breed"). Finally in "Golden State," Sayles ironically uses the familiar term for California to suggest that what Brian finds on the Pacific beach is not golden at all. When Brian, whose alcoholic father had praised the Pacific, gets to the city by the sea, he sees coins in a pool. Almost destitute, he dives into the pool only to discover that the pool is too deep and the illusory money is beyond his reach. The theme of illusion resurfaces when he meets two alcoholics at the beach: Cervantes (an allusion to Don Quixote's failed idealistic quester) and Daniel Boone (an allusion to the idealistic pioneer whose quest ended at the Alamo). When Brian leaves them and returns to the pool, he finds Stuffy, another alcoholic attracted to illusory money, dead by drowning. In a sense, Brian sees himself in the pool.

OTHER MAJOR WORKS

LONG FICTION: *The Pride of the Bimbos*, 1975; *Union Dues* 1977; *Los Gusanos*, 1991.

NONFICTION: *Thinking in Pictures: The Making of the Movie "Matewan,"* 1981.

BIBLIOGRAPHY

Bourjaily, Vance. "A Revivalism of Realism." *The New York Times Book Review* (April 1, 1979): 15, 33. Lengthy review of *The Anarchists' Convention*, stressing Sayles's links to the realism of Theodore Dreiser and James Farrell, tempered by a limited amount of optimism. He also points out Sayles's fascination with the technical details of particular kinds of work, usually jobs Sayles has had at one point in his life.

Butscher, Edward. "Books in Brief: *The Anarchists' Convention*." *Saturday Review* 6 (April 28, 1979): 46. Butscher suggests that Sayles's tendency toward sentimentality, caused by his sympathy for his lower-class characters, occasionally interferes with his ability to translate "acute psychological insights into viable fiction."

Epps, Garrett. "Tales of the Working Class." *Book World—The Washington Post*, April 29, 1979, p. M5. Epps focuses on the blue-collar workers in Sayles's fiction and praises his "unerring ear for American speech." According to Epps, Sayles presents keen observations about America in the 1970's and succeeds in depicting characters without caricature or sentiment.

Carson, Diane, ed. *John Sayles: Interviews*. Jackson: University Press of Mississippi, 1999. Carson's questions are primarily about Sayles's films, but there are scattered references to the stories through the book. The book contains an invaluable four-page chronology of Sayles's life and career.

Smith, Gavin, ed. *Sayles on Sayles*. London: Faber and Faber, 1998. An extended interview by Smith, who tends to focus on Sayles's films, but who also elicits some comments by Sayles about *The Anarchists' Convention* and the two stories ("Breed" and "Hoop," in which he compares basketball to jazz) that were adapted to film. Sayles compares the stories in *The Anarchists' Convention* to an album, with each picture or story having its own "emotion and rhythm."

Thomas L. Erskine

BRUNO SCHULZ

Born: Drohobycz, Poland; July 12, 1892
Died: Drohobycz, Poland; November 19, 1942

PRINCIPAL SHORT FICTION

Sklepy cynamonowe, 1934 (British edition, *Cinnamon Shops and Other Stories*, 1963; U.S. edition, *The Street of Crocodiles*, 1963)
Sanatorium pod klepsydra, 1937 (*Sanatorium Under the Sign of the Hourglass*, 1978)
The Complete Fiction of Bruno Schulz, 1989

OTHER LITERARY FORMS

Two collections of stories were the only literary works Bruno Schulz published during his lifetime. Since 1964, all of his extant works have been published in Poland; these have included prose sketches, essays and critical reviews of other literary works, and letters. The main collections in Polish are *Proza* (1964; prose) and *Księga listów* (1975; collected letters, edited by Jerzy Ficowski). All of his papers, and sketches for a work titled "Mesjasz" (the messiah), were destroyed during World War II.

Before he became known as a writer, Bruno Schulz was active as an engraver, sketch artist, and painter. Two collections of his artistic production are available in English: *Letters and Drawings of Bruno Schulz* (1988) and *The Drawings of Bruno Schulz* (1990). Schulz's drawings, variously erotic and grotesque, call to mind George Grosz, Ernst Ludwig Kirchner, and Marc Chagall. Schulz often depicts sadomasochistic themes, showing men groveling at the feet of women. Among his drawings are illustrations for a number of his stories, including "Sanatorium Under the Sign of the Hourglass," "Spring," and a few others.

ACHIEVEMENTS

Bruno Schulz created a prose style and a mode of narration like those of no other writer of the twentieth century. He was unquestionably one of the finest Polish prose writers of the period between the two world wars. *Cinnamon Shops*, his first book (translated in the United States as *The Street of Crocodiles*), was immediately recognized by Polish literary critics and honored by the Polish Academy of Literature. Since World War II, Schulz's works have been translated into more than a dozen languages. His influence on contemporary writers has been very strong, and he has been compared to the greatest of twentieth century authors. Isaac Bashevis Singer, winner of the Nobel Prize for Literature in 1978, wrote:

> Schulz cannot be easily classified. He can be called a surrealist, a symbolist, an expressionist, a modernist. . . . He wrote sometimes like Kafka, sometimes like Proust, and at times succeeded in reaching depths that neither of them reached.

Schulz's impact on writers of longer fiction and novelists has been as great as his influence on short-story writers. One example, among many, is Cynthia Ozick's novel *The Messiah of Stockholm* (1987), partly based on Schulz's life and writings. It is difficult to define the exact genre of his prose. In *Cinnamon Shops* each of the fifteen parts has a title, and Schulz occasionally refers to them as "tales" (in Polish, *opowiadania*). Yet the term is loose. Three of the parts are an extended "Traktat o manekinach" ("Treatise on Tailors' Dummies"), and the whole has unity of character, place, time, and tone. In the book, Schulz broke decisively with the traditional forms of both the short story and the novel.

In a letter to the Polish playwright and novelist Stanisław Ignacy Witkiewicz, in 1935, Schulz wrote:

> To what genre does *Cinnamon Shops* belong? How should it be classified? I consider it an autobiographical novel, not merely because it is written in the first person and one can recognize in it certain events and experiences from the author's own childhood. It is an autobiography—or rather, a genealogy—of the spirit . . . since it reveals the spirit's pedigree back to those depths where it merges with mythology.

Schulz created a new genre of prose that belongs to him alone.

BIOGRAPHY

When Bruno Schulz was born, in 1892, Drohobycz was a small Polish town in Galicia, then a province of the Austro-Hungarian Empire. Poland had lost its independence and was partitioned; it became independent in 1918, when Schulz was twenty-six years old. Drohobycz had a population of about thirty thousand, largely Jewish and Polish.

Schulz's family was Jewish and spoke Polish. His father, Jakub, was the owner and bookkeeper of the textile fabrics shop described in his son's stories. Bruno was the youngest of three children; he was educated at home and in a school named for Emperor Franz Joseph. The merchant profession to which his parents belonged separated them from the Hasidim, and Schulz never learned Yiddish; although he knew German he wrote in Polish, the language of his immediate family. After completing high school, he studied architecture in Lwów for three years, until the outbreak of World War I. He taught himself to draw and produced graphics, hoping to make art his career. Instead, he obtained the post of teacher of drawing and handicrafts at the state high school, or *gimnazjum*, named for King Władysław Jagiełło, in Drohobycz. He was to teach in the school for seventeen years, until his death in 1942.

In the 1920's it was only drawing and painting that Schulz practiced openly, in full view of his friends; he kept his literary works to himself, sharing them with few people in Drohobycz. It was through correspondence with friends in distant cities that Schulz began his literary career. *Cinnamon Shops* began in the letters he sent to Deborah Vogel, a poet and doctor of philosophy who lived in Lwów. Fragment by fragment, episode by episode, the book progressed, embedded in Schulz's letters; she urged him to continue, until the book took its final form. Schulz gained the support of the eminent novelist Zofia Nałkowska, who helped him in the publication of the book. Stanisław Witkiewicz in Kraków became an early enthusiast of Schulz's work, and a correspondent; other admirers and correspondents came to include the novelist Witold Gombrowicz, the poet Julian Tuwim, and the German writer Thomas Mann.

After his literary success, Schulz continued to live in Drohobycz. Because of his prize from the Polish Academy of Letters, a "golden laurel," his school gave him the title of "professor" but no raise in salary. His brother died in an accident in 1936, and Schulz's financial responsibilities grew; he became the sole supporter of his widowed sister, her son, and an aged cousin. Schulz became engaged, but his fiancé was Catholic, there were religious complications, and their relationship eventually ended. With the help of friends in Poland and France, Schulz managed to travel to Paris in the summer of 1938, and he stayed there for three weeks—it was his first trip abroad.

War broke out in Poland in September, 1939. According to the Molotov-Ribbentrop secret pact, Germany attacked western Poland on September 1, and its ally, the Soviet Union, had agreed to attack eastern Poland simultaneously. Drohobycz was in eastern Poland, and the Red Army with the People's Commissariat of Internal Affairs invaded it on September 17. For the next twenty months, they occupied the town. Schulz continued to teach drawing in his high school; he had stopped writing. In the summer of 1941, the Germans attacked their Soviet allies, occupying Drohobycz in turn. Together with other Jews, Schulz was confined to the ghetto. One day in November, 1942, he ventured with a special pass to the "Aryan" quarter; he was bringing home a loaf of bread when he was recognized by a Gestapo officer, who shot him dead on the street. That night, a friend recovered his body and buried it in the nearby Jewish cemetery.

That cemetery no longer exists. In addition, the manuscripts of Schulz's unpublished works, given to a friend for safekeeping, have been lost—they disappeared along with their custodian. Schulz's major work was to have been the novel titled "Mesjasz." No trace of this work remains either.

ANALYSIS

Very high claims have been made for Bruno Schulz's work ever since Stanisław Witkiewicz wrote enthusiastically about *Cinnamon Shops*; Schulz's reputation as a twentieth century Polish writer has been consistently high. Czesław Miłosz, in his *History of Polish Literature* (1983), stressed Schulz's humor, intuition, and the metaphorical richness of his language, confirming that "today, Schulz is regarded as one of the most important prose writers between the two wars." Isaac Bashevis Singer has called him "one of the most remarkable writers who ever lived," and Cynthia Ozick has written that Schulz had "one of the most original imaginations in modern Europe." The Yugoslav writer Danilo Kiš has said, "Schulz is my god." These are very high evaluations. On what are they based?

The twentieth century has witnessed a number of literary movements that have claimed to have a special relation to reality, or a hold upon it: surrealism and hyperrealism, ultraism, expressionism. In theory or in practice, the movements attempted to combine the individual and the world around him in a new synthesis, to combine in a single outlook both subject and object in all their breadth. In practice, and with a minimum of theory or dubious abstraction, Schulz seemed to achieve that synthesis. It is true that Schulz developed a theory of the mythical transformation of the everyday world that he described in his correspondence and in his essay "Mityzacja rzeczywistości" (mythization of reality), but of infinitely greater importance was the artistic synthesis itself, displayed above all in his book *Cinnamon Shops*.

CINNAMON SHOPS

The basic cast of characters is simple. The narrator is a boy—and the man he came to be—describing events using the first-person pronoun. His father Jacob is perhaps the most important character, owner of the dry-goods shop which is the major source of torment as well as the basis for the livelihood of the family. The mother is of far lesser importance; Adela, a practical, sensuous servant, dominates the family. In addition there are shop assistants, diverse relatives, the huge, amorphous presence of the house with its many rooms, and the town. Although the father is an unusual character, the basic situation is ordinary. Even boredom is taken into account, taking up the time that becomes a major ingredient of the book.

One of Schulz's major innovations is his use of a child narrator and adult narrator merged into a single viewpoint. Ever since the nineteenth century, a traditional device of European and American fiction has been an observing narrator through whose consciousness and senses the events of the novel were filtered. This consciousness was different from that of the author; the narrative consciousness was aware of some things the author might know but unaware of others. Usually the narration did not completely coincide with this consciousness, because if it did it would be too chaotic and disorderly, private and undirected. Instead, this consciousness—what might be called a fictional construct—was located just outside the point of view of the narrative consciousness, in the middle distance. In *Cinnamon Shops*, the young boy provides this narrative consciousness, but only partly. It is difficult to pinpoint the boy's age, which might be anywhere between five and twelve. This ambiguity builds on the important presence of the house and rooms, which have accumulated the associations stored up over many years. More important, the childhood consciousness is overlaid by that of an adult and artist. The book was written by an author already approaching forty. The narration is a highly synthetic—and successful—mix of different developmental stages. The density of the sense of reality is thicker, more solid and opaque, than that available to most observers confined to a single moment in space and time. Because of the book's subtle artistry, this often goes unrecognized by the reader. Yet the resurrection of the shop, and the reconstruction of childhood with all its emotional riches, took place only after the father and the business had long disappeared.

For Schulz, this is not linear. Whether time is "really" linear is for the individual reader to judge. It might be that time's linearity is a tradition which our culture has found convenient, that it is a fictional construct that is difficult to judge objectively. Certainly Schulz's synthetic time provides the reader with a shock of recognition; it is strikingly real, or realistic.

"PAN"

In "Pan," Schulz evokes intense, midsummer heat before presenting the young narrator's encounter with a vagabond:

It was there that I saw him first and for the only time in my life, at a noon-hour crazy with heat. It was at a moment when time, demented and wild, breaks away from the treadmill of events and like an escaping vaga-bond, runs shouting across the fields. Then the summer grows out of control, spreads at all points all over space with a wild impetus, doubling and trebling itself into an unknown, lunatic dimension.

"THE NIGHT OF THE GREAT SEASON"

In the title story, the reader is told,

Amidst sleepy talk, time passed unnoticed. It ran by unevenly, as if making knots in the passage of hours, swallowing somewhere whole empty periods. Without transition, our whole gang found ourselves on the way home long after midnight. . . .

Schulz constantly calls calendar time into question. The story "Noc wielkiego sezonu" ("The Night of the Great Season") begins, "in a run of normal uneventful years that great eccentric, Time, begets sometimes other years, different, prodigal years which—like a sixth, smallest toe—grow a thirteenth freak month."

These are not merely verbal effects. They underlie a uniquely solid and sensuous concept of reality and psychology. Schulz's descriptions of interiors, of rooms, closets, and walls, are among the finest and most evocative that exist in literature. Like the Dutch painter Jan Vermeer, he renders simple concrete details with superb suggestiveness:

His eyes, like minuscule mirrors, reflected all the shin-ing objects: the white light of the sun in the cracks of the window, the golden rectangle of the curtains, and enclosed, like a drop of water, all the room with the stillness of its carpets and its empty chairs (from "Pan Karol," "Mr. Charles").

Schulz is particularly good at describing the blurred transitions between different psychological states; here his aptitude is similar to that of Marcel Proust. His descriptions of boredom and the revolt against boredom ring with truth—and of waking, going to sleep, or the sheer softness of a bed and bedclothes, a sleeper who "still hung on to the verge of night, gasp-ing for breath, while the bedding grew around him, swelled and fermented—and again engulfed him in a mountain of heavy, whitish dough." His use of meta-phor is always evocative, rendering the associations memory imparts to physical objects. In describing the

bolts of cloth in his father's shop, Schulz writes of "the powerful formations of that cosmogony of cloth, under its mountain ranges that rose in imposing mas-sifs. Wide valleys opened up between the slopes . . . the interior of the shop formed itself into the pan-orama of an autumn landscape, full of lakes and dis-tance." The blend of subject and object becomes almost seamless. The density of psychological asso-ciation—or investment—and palpable concrete ob-jects comes together in some of the most sensuous descriptions in literature.

Probably the key to these passages is memory. For Schulz, memory is like an onion, providing layer af-ter layer of physical growth. Objects and memory of objects become interchangeable. It is the father who explains that in old apartments there are rooms which are sometimes forgotten, and, unvisited for months on end,

they wilt neglected between the old walls and it hap-pens that they close in on themselves, become over-grown with bricks, and, lost once and for all to our memory, forfeit their only claim to existence . . . they merge with the wall, grow into it, and all trace of them is obliterated in a complicated design of lines and cracks (in the "Treatise on Tailors' Dummies: Conclu-sion").

For Schulz, "Reality is as thin as a paper and betrays with all its cracks its imitative character." Reality is always fluid, it is dense, shifting, frequently "half-baked and undecided," constantly threatened by pos-sibilities that approach fulfillment and then retreat again, on the verge of realization. Reality is in a con-stant fermentation, participating in the psychology of multiple observers with their preoccupations, mem-ory, and fantasy. The narrator's father speaks of the "make-believe of matter which had created a sem-blance of life," and physical objects have as much solid palpability—as much feeling—as people have. He asks, "How much ancient suffering is there in the varnished grain, in the veins and knots of our old fa-miliar wardrobes? Who would recognize in them the old features, smiles, and glances, almost planed and polished out of all recognition?" As the father asks this question his own wrinkled face appears to be an old plank, full of knots and veins, from which all memories had been planed away.

Was Schulz influenced by Sigmund Freud and by psychoanalysis? Probably only to a limited extent. After World War I, the movement enjoyed a period en vogue; Bruno Bettelheim has described how, for many, it became an all-encompassing way of life that occupied all the free time of its enthusiasts. Schulz was interested in psychoanalysis, but his verdict was largely negative; the description of the psychoanalysis of his Uncle Edward is a savage parody that concludes *Cinnamon Shops*, ending with the uncle's complete loss of personality, reduction to the state of an automaton responding only to the ringing of a bell, and, ultimately, death. Schulz was responding to some of the same historical currents that produced psychoanalysis and the later movement of Surrealism, but his attitudes toward the subconscious, as revealed in *Cinnamon Shops*, were entirely his own. What he stressed above all was the synthetic, cumulative function of memory and growth. Linear cause and effect and the somewhat rigid, theoretical mechanisms of Freud have little place in Schulz's world. On the other hand, he subjected the inner world of the psyche to one of the most sustained, probing explorations of his time.

SANATORIUM UNDER THE SIGN OF THE HOURGLASS

Schulz's second collection of stories, *Sanatorium Under the Sign of the Hourglass*, did not provoke the same excitement that met the first collection. It is a virtuoso performance, especially the title story, but differs in important ways from *Cinnamon Shops*. First, its mode of composition was different. *Cinnamon Shops* was elaborated in correspondence with Deborah Vogel, and Schulz was oblivious to the presence of any other reader or larger audience. The intensity of the attention riveted upon his experience is unhindered, uninterrupted. The author of the stories in *Sanatorium Under the Sign of the Hourglass* was famous, and he became intimidated by what he felt was a spotlight shining on him, intruding on his act of writing. Now he was writing for a public, and it made him uncomfortable. Also, as with other mature writers, he was subjected to powerful literary influences

from the past. He read widely—Rainer Maria Rilke, Thomas Mann, and Franz Kafka, among others—and borrowed what he found useful for his own stories. The story "Sanatorium Under the Sign of the Hourglass" incorporates successfully ideas from Mann's *Der Zauberberg* (1924; *The Magic Mountain*, 1927); in some ways Schulz even goes beyond Mann in his evocation of atmosphere and in his concept of human transformation. In "Ostatnia ucleczka ojca" ("Father's Last Escape"), the metamorphosis of the father into a kind of crustacean or crab shows an obvious debt to Kafka's *Die Verwandlung* (1915; *The Metamorphosis*, 1936). Schulz's own translation of Kafka's *Der Prozess* (1925; *The Trial*, 1937) appeared in 1936. Schulz's stories in his second collection are on a consistently high plane, yet they do not represent an advance. Schulz was now a writer of fiction. He was branching out; his focus was less exclusively on his own childhood. His Ovidian transformations occur with a certain ease, as when the irritated father turns into a buzzing fly, or when Simon, the old age pensioner, is subject to an assumption and rises into the sky. Many of the effects are allegorical; they are partly willed by the intellect, yet the transformations do not engage the author's sense of an all-encompassing reality. The allegory is more abstract and brittle than it was in *Cinnamon Shops*. Some stories are frankly experimental, as when Schulz uses an obtuse first-person narrator and an arch, *faux naïf* speaking voice in "Emeryt" ("The Old Age Pensioner") and "Samotnóśc" ("Loneliness"). The stories "Dodo" and "Edzio" ("Eddie"), on the other hand, are extremely realistic, almost naturalistic. No doubt it is good that he was experimenting in new directions; his new undertakings were certain to lead to new forms of synthesis in the future.

In the late 1930's, however, his creative work began to slacken. More and more frequently he fell into barren and agonizing states of depression. His isolation and solitude in Drohobycz had advantages but also great disadvantages. Still, he continued to work on his project for "Mesjasz." Two parts originally destined for it—"Księga" (the book) and "Genialna epoka" (the age of genius)—found their way into the collection *Sanatorium Under the Sign of the Hour-*

glass. During the war, he read aloud to his friends sections of "Mesjasz"; in this work, the myth of the coming of the Messiah was to symbolize a return to the happy perfection that existed at the beginning—the return to childhood.

One cannot know what artistic form this return would have taken. Friends of Schulz returned to Drohobycz in 1944 and 1945 to search for his papers. They had no success. All of Schulz's manuscripts, records, letters, and papers were lost, with a single exception: One drawing was found.

OTHER MAJOR WORKS

NONFICTION: *Proza,* 1964; *Księga listów,* 1975 (edited by Jerzy Ficowski); *Letters and Drawings of Bruno Schulz,* 1988; *The Drawings of Bruno Schulz,* 1990.

BIBLIOGRAPHY

Brown, Russell E. "Bruno Schulz and World Literature." *Slavic and East European Journal* 34 (Summer, 1990): 224-246. An excellent article placing Schulz not in his native Polish tradition but in the context of writers such as Franz Kafka, Marcel Proust, Thomas Mann, Louis Aragon, and Robert Walser. Brown also traces the lineage of Schultz in contemporary writers such as the Czech, Bohumil Hrabal; the Yugoslav, Danilo Kiš; the American, Cynthia Ozick; and the Israeli, David Grossman.

_____. "Metamorphosis in Bruno Schulz." *The Polish Review* 30 (1985): 373-380. Brown explores patterns of metamorphosis in Schulz's fiction and considers their allegorical meanings. He distinguishes between the ways Schulz and Franz Kafka use metamorphosis, noting that Kafka transforms the boy while Schulz always transforms the father figure.

Budurowycz, Bohdan. "Galicia in the Work of Bruno Schulz." *Canadian Slavonic Papers: An Inter-Disciplinary Quarterly* 28 (December, 1986): 359-368. Budurowycz points to the significance of Galicia, "a region suffering from an acute identity crisis and divided against itself," as a significant formative influence on Schulz's fiction. To this real world can be tied the bizarre, imaginary world of Schulz's fiction.

Kuprel, Diana. "Errant Events on the Branch Tracks of Time: Bruno Schulz and Mythical Consciousness." *Slavic and East European Journal* 40 (Spring, 1996): 100-117. Discusses mythologizing in Schulz's fiction, using Ernst Cassirer's *The Philosophy of Symbolic Forms*; argues that Schulz's fictions are expressions of Cassirer's "mythical consciousness."

Nelson, Victoria. "An Exile on Crocodile Street: Bruno Schulz in America." *Salmagundi,* nos. 101/102 (Winter/Spring, 1994): 212-225. Discusses Schulz's influence on American writers and readers, particularly John Updike and Cynthia Ozick; concludes that the terms under which Schulz's work gained approval from American literary culture highlight the often arbitrary and superficial ways in which authors are transplanted successfully into another language and culture.

Newton, Adam Zachary. "'Nothing but Face'—'To Hell with Philosophy'? Witold Gombrowicz, Bruno Schulz, and the Scandal of Human Countenance." *Style* 32 (Summer, 1998): 243-260. Argues that Schulz discovers a deep pathos in human faces but, unlike Gombrowicz, links it to the pathos of metaphor and figuration generally: a fundamental principle of transmigrated form.

Prokopczyk, Czesław Z, ed. *Bruno Schulz: New Documents and Interpretations.* New York: Peter Lang, 1999. A contemporary look at Schulz's works.

Rachwal, Tadeusz, and Andrew Lakritz. "Bruno Schulz: An Introduction." *Chicago Review* 40 (1994): 62-65. An introduction to a symposium on Schulz in which scholars and artists discuss Schulz's work, particularly "territorialization," or the imaginative movement beyond and across social, political, cultural, and religious borders.

Schonle, Andreas. "Of Sublimity, Shrinkage, and Selfhood in the Works of Bruno Schulz." *Slavic and East European Journal* 42 (Fall, 1998): 467-482. Discusses the work of Schulz in relation to continental theories of the self and the sublime, from Immanuel Kant to Jean-François Lyotard;

examines Schulz's exposure of reason's potential irrelevance in a world devoid of stability and unity. Claims that Schulz's modernism answers the same need as Kant's aesthetics, but it betrays the increasing fragility and depersonalization of the self.

Schulz, Bruno. "An Interview with Bruno Schulz." Interview by Lou Weiss. Translated by Tom Mc-Donald. *Pequod: A Journal of Contemporary Literature and Literary Criticism* 16-17 (1984): 144-148. In this rare, short interview, Schulz talks about the motif of the hackney-coach in his work, his early childhood memories, his drawings and his prose, his debt to Thomas Mann, his notions of "reality," and destructive tendencies critics have noted in his work.

Stala, Krzysztof. *On the Margins of Reality: The Paradoxes of Representation in Bruno Schulz's Fiction.* Stockholm, Sweden: Almqvist & Wiksell International, 1993. A good look at Schulz's fiction. Includes bibliographical references and an index.

Updike, John. Introduction to *Sanatorium Under the Sign of the Hourglass.* Translated by Celina Wieniewska. New York: Penguin Books, 1979. Reprinted in *Hugging the Shores.* New York: Alfred A. Knopf, 1983. Updike considers Schulz a real find. His appreciation stems from the sheer inventiveness of the writer; the Jewish, Eastern European flavor of his work; and his innovative prose style.

John Carpenter, updated by
Allen Hibbard

DELMORE SCHWARTZ

Born: Brooklyn, New York; December 8, 1913
Died: New York, New York; July 11, 1966

PRINCIPAL SHORT FICTION

In Dreams Begin Responsibilities, 1938
The World Is a Wedding, 1948
Successful Love, and Other Stories, 1961

OTHER LITERARY FORMS

Besides being an author of short fiction, Delmore Schwartz was a poet, playwright, critic, editor, and prolific letter writer.

ACHIEVEMENTS

Delmore Schwartz's merit as both poet and short-story writer has been widely recognized. Along with his contemporaries John Berryman, Robert Lowell, and Randall Jarrell, Schwartz can be seen as a representative literary figure who poignantly lived and wrote about his personal struggles, which were also the struggles of a generation of American writers.

Schwartz's stories deal, above all, with the problems associated with creating a Jewish identity in the United States. Schwartz obsessively depicts the son's relation to his parents and a pre-American past. In the face of the twin burdens of an active intellect and a Jewish past, the son/hero is overwhelmed by a profound sense of alienation.

Doubtless these qualities, which made Schwartz a legend, were what attracted Saul Bellow sufficiently to create a fictionalized version of Schwartz in *Humboldt's Gift* (1975). Ultimately, Schwartz's life might be seen in the wider context of American literature. His negotiation of, and escape from, the trappings of mainstream American society are akin to those of Huckleberry Finn and Nick Adams.

BIOGRAPHY

From earliest youth, Delmore Schwartz's entire identity was shaped by his expectation that he would become a great American writer. Tied in with this grandiose fantasy was the anticipation of inheriting great wealth. Although his father had been a millionaire, the crash of the stock market in 1929 eroded much of his fortune, and a dishonest executor dissipated the remaining funds. Schwartz, however, continued to hope for his legacy until as late as 1946. His childhood was much damaged by his parents' arguments. When Delmore was nine, in 1923, his father left, but his mother resisted a divorce until 1927.

Schwartz attended the University of Wisconsin and then transferred to New York University, where he received his B.A. in 1935. That same year he finally received a few thousand dollars from his father's estate and enrolled in Harvard graduate school in philosophy, having to leave school in March, 1937, however, because of debts. From 1940 to 1947 Schwartz taught at Harvard as a Briggs-Copeland Fellow. Schwartz's first marriage—to Gertrude Buckman on June 14, 1938—ended in divorce. On June 10, 1949, he married Elizabeth Pollet. Schwartz was a frequent contributor to *Partisan Review*, of which he was an editor from 1946 to 1955. Later, from 1962 to 1966, he taught at Princeton and Syracuse Universities. He died at fifty-two without having fulfilled his great early promise. A paranoid failure, he was destroyed by drugs, drink, and many shock treatments.

ANALYSIS

Delmore Schwartz's place in American literature is unique and problematic. His life, as well as his modest literary production, which includes thirty-five poems, a verse play, short stories, and other works, has continued to fascinate a select group of critics and writers. The rezpublication of Schwartz's stories, *In Dreams Begin Responsibilities*, by New Directions in 1978, and the appearance of Schwartz's letters and journals, have helped solidify Schwartz's position and shed light on his career. Critics have dwelt on the importance of Schwartz's Jewish heritage and have tried as well to stress how American are his concerns.

"IN DREAMS BEGIN RESPONSIBILITIES"

The character of Schwartz's work can be felt in "In Dreams Begin Responsibilities." Published when the writer was twenty-five, the story, like practically everything else he wrote, is distinctly autobiographical. The story is divided into six parts. It opens on a Sunday afternoon, June 12, 1909, in Brooklyn, as his

father is courting his mother. They take the streetcar to Coney Island to inhale the sea air from the boardwalk and to watch the strollers promenade in their Sunday clothes. They ride the merry-go-round and snatch at the brass ring. Later they eat dinner, while his father boasts of all the money he will make, and then proposes. His mother begins to cry because this is what she has wanted him to say ever since she met him. They have their picture taken, but the photographer corrects their pose so many times that his father becomes impatient; his smile becomes a grimace, hers "bright and false." Then they argue about having their fortune told, and in terrible anger, he strides out of the booth. The story of his parents' courtship is narrated by their child, who watches it as if it were a movie, reacts to the scenes being portrayed on the screen, and is threatened with expulsion from the theater by the rest of the audience who object to his interruptions. Finally the usher reprimands him, seizing his arm and dragging him away. He awakens on the morning of his twenty-first birthday, a bleak, snowy, wintry day.

The undisguised autobiographical elements of this story are the use of Schwartz's actual birthday, December 8, which took place four years after this mismatched couple was married; the use of his real mother's name, Rose; the grouping of his real relatives around the dinner table; and the depiction of his father's financial ambitions. To a certain extent, the cinematic presentation could also be considered autobiographical since Schwartz was a lifelong movie addict. Saul Bellow, in his fictionalized version of Schwartz's life, shows him as an aficionado of old films and portrays him as acting out scenes from the movies he doted on, quoting from them, and even scripting one collaboratively and composing a scenario for another.

The psychological implications of this perspective are frightening. The author on his birthday night five times tries to interrupt the film which will end in his conception. Once he freezes a frame into a still shot. Three times he actually leaves his seat because he cannot endure what is coming, but he returns in horrified fascination to watch it being relentlessly played out to the end, except that he is forcibly expelled from the theater for having created such commotion with his outcries. He awakens in the cold present of his own manhood to the recognition that this has been an anxiety dream. To have wished his parents not to marry is to have wished his own extinction. To suffer such fears of dissolution, as Schwartz did nightly, is to suffer from insomnia, a condition for which Schwartz was famous. He dreaded sleep because it meant losing control. Much of his erudition resulted from the thousands of books he read at night to fend off his terrors, taking fistfuls of Benzedrine tablets to stay awake.

The Brechtian alienation effect of interrupting the narrative flow in each of the sections of the story is an authorial strategy which makes the experience of the reader conform to the experience of the author, who is also the narrator. It is a perfect narcissistic mirroring technique: The content reflects the form, which reflects the theme; the home movie being replayed on the dream screen reflects a past in which he could not have participated in any other guise because he had not yet been born. The youth must reconstruct the images of his parents' youth, as well as images of their parents, from faded images in old-fashioned clothes on family photos.

The story opens in the subjunctive mood, "I feel as if I were in a motion picture theater," then shifts into the indicative. The author's use of the present tense throughout to describe things in the distant past has a curious effect; if all the verbs were changed to their past-tense forms, this story would become a simple retrospective narrative. Their obtrusive presentness makes the artificiality more conspicuous. This is not a story intended to entertain, but a series of obsessive images which relentlessly thrust themselves upon the dream screen and which can no more be stopped than the paralyzed dreamer can obliterate the visions that insist upon playing themselves out in his consciousness.

The first interruption is posed as a break in the film. Just at the point when his mother's father is indicating his doubts about the contemplated engagement, "something happens to the film." The audience protests by clapping vigorously until it is fixed. Instead of going on, however, it replays the same scene

again, and once more, the grandfather critically watches the prospective husband of his eldest daughter, worried about his character. This is both effective literary technique and valid psychology. The reiterated episode foreshadows the imminent disaster. To the narrator, the recurrent scene is a way of coping with his own sense of foreboding. The father is awkward and uneasy. The narrator, totally identified with him, "stirs uneasily also, slouched in the hard chair of the theater," and at the end of this second section, he begins to weep.

The third section is based on a contrast of perceptions, and it ends like an incremental repetition with another gush of tears while the old lady sitting next to him pats him consolingly on the shoulder and says, "There, there, all of this is only a movie, young man, only a movie." Because he knows that it is not, however, he stumbles out over the feet in his row to hide his uncontrollable grief in the men's room. The double irony of the movie's being real, while the old lady seeking to assure him of its unreality is herself unreal, augments the solipsism which the story so terrifyingly expresses. The narrator's parents feel no "danger"; they are "unaware"; they stare at the ocean "absently." Overhead the sun's lighting strikes and strikes, but neither of them is at all aware of it. The unborn son, watching their "indifference" to the ocean's force, harshness, and fierceness, is shocked. "I stare at the terrible sun which breaks up sight, and the fatal, merciless, passionate ocean . . . and finally shocked by the indifference of my father and mother, I burst out weeping once more." He is as divorced from them, in the intensity of his perceptions, as they are from each other and from the miracles of nature. Their reactions are stereotyped and superficial; they look at the bathing suits and buy peanuts. He sees the "terrifying sun and the terrifying ocean."

The fourth part begins: "When I return, feeling as if I had awakened in the morning sick for lack of sleep, several hours have apparently passed and my parents are riding on the merry-go-round." Their mechanical revolution in endless cycles is an appropriate metaphor for the meaningless rounds of their lives. When his father proposes in the restaurant, the son stands up and screams: "Don't do it. It's not too late to change your minds, both of you. Nothing good will come of it, only remorse, hatred, scandal, and two children whose characters are monstrous." The entire audience glares at him, the usher approaches brandishing his flashlight, and the old lady tries to tug him back down into his seat; because he cannot bear to see what is happening, he shuts his eyes. The irony of his behavior is that shutting his eyes cannot obliterate the pictures because he is already dreaming them with his eyes shut. No amount of protest can stop the film that is unreeling in the theater of his mind, and there is nowhere that he can go to escape it.

The fifth episode is a tour de force. The photographer who wants to fix a beautiful image of his parents and cannot find a way of posing them so that the picture will be "right" is the artistic son. He wants to "fix" them forever in his word picture as the shapers and reflectors of his identity, but he is frustrated by their inadequacies from defining them permanently. The print that emerges from the photographer's dedicated efforts is patently false. The writer that emerges from their doomed conjunction is condemned to uncertain and fluctuating ego boundaries.

In the sixth part, a terrible quarrel arises in the fortune-teller's booth. Enraged, the father stalks out yanking at the mother's arm, but she stubbornly refuses to budge, so he strides away. The son, in terrible fear, screams "What are they doing?" The ensuing passage mirrors both the actions and the words of the preceding one. "The usher has seized my arm and is dragging me away, and as he does so, he says: 'What are *you* doing? Don't you know that you can't do whatever you want to do? Why should a young man like you, with your whole life before you, get hysterical like this?'" As the usher drags him through the lobby of the theater into the cold light, he awakens into the bleak winter morning of his twenty-first birthday. His fortune has been foretold; it is a cold and bleak one with which he enters chronological maturity, aware that he will never attain the emotional maturity which this day should mark.

"AMERICA! AMERICA!"

The protagonist of another story, "America! America!," is Shenandoah Fish. This name is one of a number of self-mocking ones that Schwartz invented for his personae. He felt sharply the incongruity of his Latinate first name and his Hebraic surname, so all his fictional surrogates have equally incongruous names. His alter egos are Shenandoah Fish, Marquis Fane, Richmond Rose, Berthold Cannon, Maximilian Rinehart, Cornelius Schmidt, and Hershey Green. In "America! America!" an author, unable to write, listens to his mother's monologue about the Bauman family. He is troubled by his loss of fluency, feeling it as "a loss, or a lapse of identity." Because he feels real only when he is working, he asks anxiously, "Who am I?" As he listens to the story about the insurance agent and his family whom his mother had known for thirty years, he wonders whether "its cruelty lay in his mother's tongue or in his own mind. And his own thoughts which had to do with his own life, and seemed to have nothing to do with these human beings, began to trouble him." As his mother drones on about the sons, Sydney and Dick, who were never able to make a living even in a land where everyone who is willing to work hard enough can get rich, he listens with irony and contempt. His mother interrupts her ironing to tell him that it is late afternoon and time he got dressed. As he changes from his pajamas, he stares in the mirror, thinking that no one truly sees himself as he is. "I do not see myself. I do not know myself. I cannot look at myself truly."

His mother's representation of the Baumans becomes a metaphor for the writer's handling of his subject. Her summation of the theme of the story she has just told is that the Bauman sons were spoiled by having had too pleasant a family life. They were so indulged that they became indolent and lost the will and the aggressiveness necessary for success. He feels that her judgment is external, merely gossip, and that the story would be very different if seen from the inside. As he stares at the mirror, he realizes that she has stirred up his self-contempt with her tale of waste and failure. He becomes aware that he is defending his own rationalizations; her story with its abstractions, its outlines, has exhausted him. While he had listened to it at such a distance, it remained a caricature, but as he enters into it, it becomes a self-criticism. The Baumans, who had seemed so remote from his concerns, now merge with his own ruined life, and the scorn with which he had fended them off stares back at him from the mirror. The accusation reflected there is that his own indolence and lassitude are equal to those of the Baumans', whose story has only aggravated his anxiety about lacking the volition to work, and this last scene answers the question he had asked in the first. In this story about telling a story, the cruelty is not in his mother's tongue but rather is engendered in his own mind.

OTHER MAJOR WORKS

PLAY: *Shenandoah*, pb. 1941.

POETRY: *In Dreams Begin Responsibilities*, 1938 (includes poetry and prose); *Genesis, Book I*, 1943; *Vaudeville for a Princess, and Other Poems*, 1950; *Summer Knowledge*, 1959; *Last and Lost Poems of Delmore Schwartz*, 1979 (edited by Robert Phillips).

NONFICTION: *Selected Essays of Delmore Schwartz*, 1970; *Letters of Delmore Schwartz*, 1984; *Portrait of Delmore: Journals and Notes of Delmore Schwartz, 1939-1959*, 1986; *The Ego Is Always at the Wheel: Bagatelles*, 1986.

CHILDREN'S LITERATURE: *"I Am Cherry Alive,"* the Little Girls Sang, 1958.

BIBLIOGRAPHY

Ashbery, John. *The Heavy Bear: Delmore Schwartz's Life Versus His Poetry—A Lecture Delivered at the Sixty-seventh General Meeting of the English Literary Society of Japan on 21st May 1995*. Tokyo: English Literary Society of Japan, 1996. This printing of a lecture on Schwartz compares and contrasts his life and his work.

Atlas, James. *Delmore Schwartz: The Life of an American Poet*. New York: Farrar, Straus & Giroux, 1977. Atlas's biography, the first one devoted entirely to Schwartz, places the author's literary production in the context of his life.

Bawer, Bruce. *The Middle Generation: The Lives and Poetry of Delmore Schwartz, Randall Jarrell, John Berryman, Robert Lowell*. Hamden, Conn.: Archon Books, 1986. Bawer persuasively argues that these poets "shared an affliction." His particu-

larly useful study, integrating biographical detail with literary analysis, teases out the important thematic threads connecting these late modern writers: rocky childhoods, quests for love and faith, and disillusionment in maturity.

Goldman, Mark. "Reflections in a Mirror: On Two Stories by Delmore Schwartz." *Studies in American Jewish Literature* 2 (1982): 86-97. In his discussion of two stories, "America! America!" and "The Child Is the Meaning of Life," Goldman draws the reader's attention to Schwartz's obsession with personal history and identity, relations between children and parents, and determinism.

Howe, Irving. Foreword to *In Dreams Begin Responsibilities*. New York: New Directions, 1978. Howe's introduction, appreciative and sensitive, is a good place to start with Schwartz. Very concisely he guides the reader through the development of Schwartz's work, noting salient elements of stories and placing them historically.

McDougall, Richard. *Delmore Schwartz*. New York: Twayne, 1974. Provides an overview of Schwartz's writing career, placing emphasis on the theme of alienation and relating it to Schwartz's status as poet and Jew in modern times.

Malin, Irving. *Jews and Americans*. Carbondale: Southern Illinois University Press, 1965. Malin discusses the writings of Schwartz along with those of Karl Shapiro, Isaac Rosenfeld, Leslie Fiedler, Saul Bellow, Bernard Malamud, and Philip Roth. His object is to try to identify and discuss the "Jewishness" that these writers' works share.

New, Elisa. "Reconsidering Delmore Schwartz." *Prooftexts: A Journal of Jewish Literary History* 5, no. 3 (September, 1985): 245-262. In this fine essay, New suggests that the Jewish American heroes in Schwartz's stories "map out danger zones of intergenerational paralysis where we languish in the throes of a cultural adolescence that will not let us stop selling ourselves as Americans, hawking our goods, both material and intellectual."

Schwartz, Delmore. *Delmore Schwartz and James Laughlin: Selected Letters*. Edited by Robert Phillips. New York: W. W. Norton, 1993. This collection of letters reveals insight into Schwartz's character.

Waldhorn, Arthur, and Hilda K. Waldhorn, eds. *The Rite of Becoming: Stories and Studies of Adolescence*. Cleveland, Ohio: World Publishing, 1977. An extended analysis of "In Dreams Begin Re-

sponsibilities," focusing on how the story embodies Sigmund Freud's idea that dreams are wish-fulfillments.

Ruth Rosenberg, updated by
Allen Hibbard

LYNNE SHARON SCHWARTZ

Born: Brooklyn, New York; March 19, 1939

PRINCIPAL SHORT FICTION

Acquainted with the Night, and Other Stories, 1984
The Melting Pot and Other Subversive Stories,
    1987

OTHER LITERARY FORMS

Lynne Sharon Schwartz has published several novels, including *Rough Strife* (1980), *Balancing Acts* (1981), *Disturbances in the Field* (1983), *Leaving Brooklyn* (1989), *The Fatigue Artist: A Novel* (1995), and *In the Family Way: An Urban Comedy* (1999). She has also written much poetry and nonfiction. Other publications include a children's book, *The Four Questions* (1989), and a memoir, *Ruined by Reading: A Life in Books* (1996).

ACHIEVEMENTS

Lynne Sharon Schwartz's awards for her short fiction include the James Henle Award (1974) and the Lamport Foundation Award (1977). Her work has been included in *The Best American Short Stories 1978*; *The Best American Short Stories 1979*; *Prize Stories: The O. Henry Awards*, 1979, and *Imagining America*, 1992.

BIOGRAPHY

Lynne Sharon Schwartz was born in Brooklyn, New York, on March 19, 1939. She married Harry Schwartz (a city planner) on December 22, 1957;

they would have two children, Rachel Eve and Miranda Ruth. She attended Barnard College, earning a B.A. in 1959, and Bryn Mawr College, where she earned the M.A. in 1961, followed by further graduate study at New York University, 1967-1972. She left the program without completing her dissertation, deciding instead to devote her time to her writing. She worked from 1961 to 1963 as an associate editor for *Writer Magazine* and as a writer for a civil rights-fair housing organization, Operation Open City (1965-1967). From 1970-1975 she lectured at Hunter College of the City University of New York and taught fiction workshops at the University of Iowa (1982-1983), Columbia University (1983-1985), Boston University (1984-1985), Rice University (1987), University of California at Irvine (1991), and University of Hawaii at Manoa (1994).

Schwartz's stories, poems, articles, translations, and reviews have appeared in literary journals and popular magazines, including *The North American Review*, *Salmagundi*, *Michigan Quarterly Review*, *Prairie Schooner*, *The Sewanee Review*, *The Hudson Review*, *The Ontario Review*, *Harper's*, *The New York Times Book Review*, *The Washington Post Book World*, *Ploughshares*, *Redbook*, and *The Chicago Review*.

ANALYSIS

Lynne Sharon Schwartz's short stories and novels often focus on fear, especially the fear of loss: of love, of spouse, of children, of looks and physical capacities, of mind and personhood. Most but not all of her principal characters are females who strive mightily to avoid loss of one sort or another and then, often, to survive its inevitability. In the short story "Do Something About It," for instance (published in May/June, 1995, in *The North American Review*), her central figure struggles to come to terms with the senseless death of her husband, a reporter who has been killed in a police raid in the Bronx. An earlier story, "What I Did for Love," develops the similar theme of a woman's trying to survive the unimaginable death of her husband; in this story she is also trying to protect her daughter from the realities of death, first of guinea pigs, then of Carl, husband and father. One cannot change the world very much, especially in overcoming the fundamental reality of death and loss.

Many of her works of fiction appear to have close connections to events within her own life. "The Last Frontier," for example, utilizes as its inciting event the fire that took place in her own New York City apartment building (owned by Columbia University) and that engendered her first nonfiction work, *We Are Talking About Homes: A Great University Against Its Neighbors.* "Two Portraits of Rembrandt" is in some measure a tribute to her father, as she writes in *Ruined by Reading.* "The Wrath-Bearing Tree," in *Acquainted with the Night, and Other Stories*, would appear to stem in part from the death of her father, a lawyer, in a hospital. Certainly her fictional pieces develop from the close observation of ordinary life around her, its pains and its pleasures, its obsessive and irrational fears, and its very real losses. As she argues in her discussion in *Ruined by Reading* of Henry James's *The Awkward Age* (1897-1899), his characters "simply didn't care enough about ordinary human fulfillments—love, sex, work—to be credible." Schwartz's characters care very much about "ordinary human fulfillments" and that is the compelling charm of her fiction.

ACQUAINTED WITH THE NIGHT, AND OTHER STORIES

In this 1984 collection of sixteen stories, all of which were previously published elsewhere, Schwartz explores in a variety of voices a number of painful issues: the death of a parent; the nature of marriage; the effects of the mental illness of a child on a relationship; the difficulties of breaking the social barriers between races of the same class; the strategies one employs to deal with loss, whether of identity or of a life partner; the births and deaths of relationships; the adaptations of immigrants. The more satisfying of the stories offer technically clever and effective beginnings and endings, as well as a strongly realized narrative voice, whatever the technical narrative point of view.

"The Age of Analysis" takes a sharply satiric look at the vogue for psychoanalytical "talk therapy." In the story, a happily married professional couple, both of whom are therapists, find themselves incapable of dealing with their son, Paul, who is, from an early age, prone to temper tantrums and destructive fits. Thus, they engage first a child psychiatrist and then, in the natural course of things, a specialist in adolescent psychology to treat him. The regular long talk sessions, however, do little to instill in Paul maturity, wisdom, control, understanding, or limits. Thus, when Paul's father makes an apparently sudden decision to leave his wife and son for a young client because he "needs to find his space," Paul is outraged, especially because his father takes the Steinway piano, and "acts out" even more violently than before, finally attempting suicide by slicing one wrist in front of his parents, brought together to talk about the father's wishes for a new life. Paul's dramatic gesture breaks through their psychobabble and results in his being rushed to the hospital by his guilt-stricken parents, who promise to do anything and everything for poor Paul.

"The Middle Classes" focuses on the consequences of the social changes in a middle-class Brooklyn neighborhood during the 1950's and 1960's, when growing numbers of African Americans moved into the middle class and hence changed what had been a Jewish middle-class neighborhood into a black middle-class neighborhood. The story explores retrospectively the narrator's deepening understanding of the nature of race relations by focusing on a time in her life when her family employed a talented black pianist to provide her advanced piano lessons. She grows attached to Mr. Simmons, an excellent teacher, who is willing to pronounce "awful" as "beautiful," and they consequently enjoy a "mutually appreciative" relationship. She is somehow offended that her parents go out of their way to develop a middle-class relationship with Mr. Simmons, perhaps because friendship with a black man is for them a new and strange phenomenon, one that erodes the prejudices of ignorance.

THE MELTING POT AND OTHER SUBVERSIVE STORIES

A growing control over tone and material characterizes the eleven stories in *The Melting Pot and Other Subversive Stories*. The title story examines a deliciously complex relationship between Rita and Sanjay. The daughter of a Jewish man and a Mexican immigrant, Rita has been reared by her very conservative Jewish grandparents in New York City because her mother killed her father and is serving time in prison. Rita is involved in a relationship with Sanjay, a recently widowed Hindu twice her age, who wants to marry her. The complexities of love, marriage, and relationships in this new land play out wonderfully in this deftly constructed story.

"So You're Going to Have a New Body" appeared first in *Mother Jones* magazine. Its wryly ironic tone and feminist attack on the facile (and arrogant) attitudes of many male gynecologists are tempered by Schwartz's humor in this first-person account of a woman who undergoes a hysterectomy and removal of ovaries or so-called female castration. Urged to ask her doctor all about it because he can help, the protagonist feels betrayed by the condescending attitude and behavior of both her doctor and his staff, resolving during her exit exam never again to permit any male doctor to treat her.

"The Last Frontier" first appeared in the publication *Witness*. In it, George Madison, his wife Louise, and their three children, immigrants from Saint Thomas, struggle to find a home in New York City after a fire in their first apartment building has left them homeless. Despite being employed, George and Louise are unable to find an apartment because of the lack of affordable public housing and a stubborn prejudice against blacks, but George is resourceful and determined "to take care of his family." The family "homesteads" in a building that wholesales household furnishings and maintains display rooms that look like "a regular house" without, however, the third wall. George's initiative and buoyant attitude sustain the family on this urban frontier in direct contrast to the generally hostile attitude of New Yorkers and the necessity of packing up before the store's employees arrive—and being careful to leave no trace. The story makes a powerful argument about human resourcefulness and homelessness.

"What I Did for Love" chronicles the efforts of Chris to cope with the changes brought to her life and her relationship with Carl, her husband. Former political radicals of the 1960's, they have changed: Their youthful ambitions to change the "power structure and [make] the world a better place" have been altered by the birth of their daughter, Martine. Carl drives a cab; Chris works as an X-ray technician. As their daughter grows up, they turn their attention to making her life the best they can, in a familiar switch from lofty enterprises to rearing one's child. Schwartz cleverly structures the story around four guinea pigs, sequential pets of Martine, despite Chris's aversion to such animals. The unexpected death of Carl, alone in his cab, causes Chris to redouble her efforts to protect Martine, which include sending her to camp again and making every possible effort to care for Rusty, "a one-eyed guinea pig who is going to live out his four-to-six-year life span no matter what it takes, in the middle of the journey of my life. . . ."

OTHER MAJOR WORKS

LONG FICTION: *Rough Strife*, 1980; *Balancing Acts*, 1981; *Disturbances in the Field*, 1983; *Leaving Brooklyn*, 1989; *The Fatigue Artist*, 1995; *In the Family Way: An Urban Comedy*, 1999.

NONFICTION: *We Are Talking About Homes: A Great University Against Its Neighbors*, 1985; *Ruined by Reading: A Life in Books*, 1996; *Face to Face: A Reader in the World*, 2000.

CHILDREN'S LITERATURE: *The Four Questions*, 1989.

TRANSLATION: *Smoke Over Birkenau*, 1991.

MISCELLANEOUS: *A Lynne Sharon Schwartz Reader: Selected Prose and Poetry*, 1992.

Bibliography

Burke, Kathleen. Review of *Ruined by Reading*, by Lynne Sharon Schwartz. *Smithsonian* 27 (December, 1996): 137. Summarizes the book as a celebration of reading.

Hulbert, Ann. *Acquainted with the Night, and Other Stories*, by Lynne Sharon Schwartz. *The New York Times Book Review* 89 (August 26, 1984): 9. Only the title story sustains the "wry tone and . . . spiritual struggle" that mark her best novels.

Klass, Perri. Review of *The Melting Pot and Other Subversive Stories*, by Lynne Sharon Schwartz. *New York Times Book Review* 92 (October 11, 1987): 15-16. Focuses on "What I Did for Love," "The Sound of Velcro," "Killing the Bees," and "The Melting Pot."

Mano, D. Keith. Review of *Acquainted with the Night, and Other Stories*, by Lynne Sharon Schwartz. *National Review* 37 (February 22, 1985): 48-49. Argues that Schwartz's stories are often perceptive, smooth, careful but reflect exactly the state of short fiction today, which Mano finds generally "elitist, condescending, narrow, 'caring,' and relatively unimaginative."

Mellard, James M. "Resisting the Melting Pot: The Jewish Back-Story in the Fiction of Lynne Sharon Schwartz." In *Daughters of Valor: Contemporary Jewish American Women Writers*, edited by Jay Halio and Ben Siegel. Newark, Del.: University of Delaware Press, 1997. Argues that although Schwartz seeks to capture the "value and power of the American 'melting pot'" in her fiction, an ethnic "back story" about origins underlies it and is implicit in the details if absent from the surfaces of both her novels and the short stories. Analyzes in detail "Opiate of the People" and "The Melting Pot."

Schwartz, Lynne Sharon. Interview by Wendy Smith. *Publishers Weekly* 226 (August 3, 1984): 68-69. In an interview occasioned by the publication of *Acquainted with the Night, and Other Stories* Schwartz reveals some relationships between her three earlier novels and her short fiction.

Theodore C. Humphrey

SIR WALTER SCOTT

Born: Edinburgh, Scotland; August 15, 1771
Died: Abbotsford, Scotland; September 21, 1832

Principal short fiction

"Wandering Willie's Tale," 1824
Chronicles of the Canongate, 1827
"Death of the Laird's Jock," 1828
"My Aunt Margaret's Mirror," 1828
"The Tapestried Chamber," 1828

Other literary forms

A giant of European Romanticism, Sir Walter Scott made important contributions to many literary forms. He wrote the Waverley novels (1814-1831), a series that virtually created the historical novel. Particularly admired are the Scottish novels, including *Waverley: Or, 'Tis Sixty Years Since* (1814), *Old Mortality* (1816), *Rob Roy* (1817), *The Heart of Midlothian* (1818), *The Bride of Lammermoor* (1819), and *Redgauntlet* (1824). Scott also wrote extremely popular poetry, including *The Lay of the Last Minstrel* (1805), *Marmion: A Tale of Flodden Field* (1808), and *The Lady of the Lake* (1810). He also collected ballads in the three-volume *Minstrelsy of the Scottish Border* (1802-1803), published critical editions of the works of John Dryden (1808) and Jonathan Swift (1814), and wrote histories, essays, reviews, criticism, and plays.

ACHIEVEMENTS

Sir Walter Scott's life was a series of remarkable achievements. In literature, he was a pioneer whose works still stand on their own merits. He collected ballads for the *Minstrelsy of the Scottish Border*, a milestone in the study of Scottish antiquities. From 1805 to 1810, Scott wrote the most popular poetry in Great Britain, setting unprecedented sales records. In 1813, he was offered the poet laureateship, which he refused. His greatest achievement came in the field of fiction. The Waverley novels virtually created a new genre, the historical novel, and made Scott one of the two most popular novelists of the century. He was knighted in 1819. Scott was also an accomplished writer of short fiction, and three of his six stories are generally acknowledged to be among the best in the genre. Finally, Scott wrote a series of literary prefaces, criticisms, and reviews that made him an important literary theorist.

Sir Walter Scott (Library of Congress)

BIOGRAPHY

Walter Scott was born in Edinburgh, Scotland, on August 15, 1771, and attended Edinburgh Royal High School and Edinburgh College. In 1786, he signed indentures to become a Writer to the Signet and, in 1792, he became a Scottish Advocate. In 1797, he married Charlotte Carpenter, with whom he had four children. He became Sheriff-Deputy of Selkirkshire in 1799 and Clerk to the Scottish Court of Session in 1806. From 1805 to 1810, he published best-selling poetry. In 1812, he bought Abbotsford, his home for life. Two years later, Scott published *Waverley*, the first in the series of remarkably successful and influential Waverley novels. He became a baronet in 1819, and later, in 1822, he arranged and managed the visit to Scotland of King George IV. Four years following this peak in his social career, Scott's wife died and he suffered bankruptcy, which he struggled to overcome during the remainder of his life. In 1827, he acknowledged publicly his authorship of the Waverley novels, and, in 1829, he began publication of the "Magnum Opus," a forty-eight-volume edition of the Waverley novels. He died at Abbotsford on September 21, 1832.

ANALYSIS

Sir Walter Scott is known primarily as a novelist and secondarily as a poet. He wrote only six short stories. Nevertheless, he remains an important figure in that genre, too. In *The Short Story in English* (1981), the distinguished critic Walter Allen begins his survey of the genre with Scott's story "The Two Drovers," which he calls "the first modern short story in English." In addition, three of his stories (as mentioned above) are generally acknowledged to be among the masterpieces of the form.

Scott uses the same methods and explores the same subjects in his stories as in his novels. He places his characters in concrete historical situations; they are social beings rooted in a particular time and place. Conflicts between individuals symbolize larger issues—the conflict between past and present, the conflict between national traditions and temperaments, the tragedy of cultural incomprehension. Scott presents these themes more starkly, however, in his stories. The demanding form of the short story forced him into a directness and concision often lacking in his novels. Thus, to many readers, Scott's short stories may be the most satisfactory works he ever wrote.

"WANDERING WILLIE'S TALE"

Scott's first short story, "Wandering Willie's Tale," appeared in the novel *Redgauntlet*. Although it attains its full significance only in the context of that larger work, this universally admired tale stands on its own merits. It presents a comic version of serious Scott themes. Steenie Steenson, the grandfather of the narrator, goes on a strange odyssey. When he brings his rent to his landlord, Sir Robert Redgauntlet, the old persecutor dies in burning agony just before giving Steenie a receipt. The silver disappears. Sir John Redgauntlet, the son and successor, threatens to evict Steenie from his hereditary home unless he can produce either rent or receipt. Poor Steenie, tossing off a mutchkin of brandy, makes two toasts: the first to "the memory of Sir Robert Redgauntlet, and might he never lie quiet in his grave till he had righted his poor bond-tenant"; the second, "a health to Man's Enemy, if he would but get him back the pock of siller." Immediately afterward, riding through the dark wood of Pitmurkie, Steenie is accosted by a strange gentleman who takes him to Redgauntlet Castle, where dead Sir Robert is reveling with a set of ghastly persecutors. Avoiding various temptations, Steenie demands and obtains his receipt. When Sir Robert insists that he return every year to pay homage, Steenie cries, "I refer myself to God's pleasure, and not to yours." Losing consciousness, he awakens in this world. He brings the receipt to Sir John and, acting upon a hint from Sir Robert, unlocks the mystery of the missing silver.

This comic tale of demonism has a serious side. The portrayal of Sir Robert and his cohorts from "the killing times" is a grim reminder of Scotland's bloody past. Like other Scott heroes, Steenie cannot evade the past but must come to terms with it. When the past demands his unconditional loyalty, however, he struggles to retain his freedom. Nor is the present time idealized. Sir John, the advocate, can be just as tyrannical as his father. As wartime Scotland evolves into civil peace, physical coercion gives way to legal. Scott balances the evils of the past against those of the present. In like manner, he balances the natural

against the supernatural. He suggests the possibility of a rational explanation for the extraordinary events; perhaps Steenie was having a drunken dream. Where did the receipt come from, though, and how did Steenie know where to recover the silver? As usual, Scott suggests something at work beyond the rational.

"Wandering Willie's Tale" is a gem of formal art. The onward rush of events is played off against the balanced structure. For example, Steenie's first meeting with Sir Robert is contrasted with his first meeting with Sir John. Scott highlights the contrast by focusing on the account book in each scene. The second meeting with Sir Robert also necessitates a second meeting with Sir John. The short-story form allows Scott to achieve a superb structure that is lacking in his novels. Finally, it is generally acknowledged that Scott writes his freest, raciest, most humorous prose when he is writing in Scots dialect. His only story related wholly in the vernacular, "Wandering Willie's Tale" is his one sustained masterpiece of prose.

"THE HIGHLAND WIDOW"

"The Highland Widow" first appeared in *Chronicles of the Canongate* (which also includes "The Two Drovers"). It is the tragedy of Elspat MacTavish, who must live with the guilt of having caused the death of her only son. She is compared to Orestes and Oedipus, and the inevitability and starkness of her drama are indeed Sophoclean. Yet the method is unmistakably Scott's. The tragedy arises out of particular historical circumstances.

Scott's narrator declares that his object is "to throw some light on the manners of Scotland as they were, and to contrast them, occasionally, with those of the present day." Elspat MacTavish grew to womanhood in the years before the rebellion of 1745, when the Highlands was a law unto itself. She became the wife and faithful companion of the famous MacTavish Mhor, who did not hesitate to take anything, lawfully or not, that he desired to have. The morality of husband and wife is that of the old Highland, one of "faithful friends and fierce enemies." In Scott, however, the old order changes, yielding place to new. MacTavish Mhor is killed by soldiers, the rebellion of 1745 is foiled, the Highlands are pacified, and military violence is replaced by civil order. Only Elspat MacTavish, dwelling in the wildest recesses of the Highlands, remains unconscious of the great change. Even her son, Hamish Bean, mingling more with people in this world, understands that his father's trade of cateran is now dangerous and dishonorable. To provide for his mother and himself, he enlists in a new Scottish regiment. Living in the past, Elspat finds Hamish's actions incomprehensible—to be a soldier, to fight under a Campbell, their hereditary enemies, and to support the government of Hanover. Conditioned by her historical environment, acting by her own best lights, she determines to save Hamish from dishonor.

The tragic climax comes inexorably. Elspat drugs Hamish's parting drink, preventing him from returning to his regiment in time. She knows that her son retains enough of the old Highland traditions to consider the promised scourging for lateness as appropriate only for dogs. Caught between his duty to his new masters and his old Highland dread of dishonor, and urged on by his mother, Hamish kills the sergeant sent to secure him. He himself is speedily apprehended, found guilty, and executed. Hamish's fate is sad, but that of Elspat is tragic. She continues to live with the knowledge that she has killed her only child. The parallels with Orestes and Oedipus suggest not only the mental torment that results from such epic crimes but also the deep love between mother and son.

Once again, the strict demands of the short-story form compelled Scott into a concentration of effort and intensity of effect that are absent from his novels. Everything is directed toward the tragic end. The opening description of old Elspat and her crime eliminates all suspense about what happened but stimulates wonder as to how it happened. It also gives the following story of long ago a sense of inevitability. In like manner, although there are occasional references to Fate, the action develops inevitably out of the characters of the two major figures, who are themselves products of their historical environments. Finally, Scott raises the language of Elspat to the heroic level, partly to suggest her Gaelic speech but mostly to give her the tragic tone.

"THE TWO DROVERS"

"The Two Drovers" also appeared in *Chronicles of the Canongate*. Whereas "The Highland Widow" is based on a conflict between different times, "The Two Drovers" is based on a conflict between different places. Robin Oig M'Combich is a Highlander, Harry Wakefield a Yorkshireman. The two are best of friends but, because neither understands the national traditions or temperament of the other, tragedy results.

The story begins with an ominous instance of second sight. Robin's aunt warns him not to undertake the cattle drive because she sees Saxon blood on his dirk. Robin's reply, "All men have their blood from Adam," indicates that he is unaware of the great national differences between men. He gives his weapon to Hugh Morrison, but the sense of doom hangs over him.

The story modulates into the realistic mode. Scott quickly establishes the genuine friendship between the two drovers. When Robin unintentionally gains possession of the very field that Harry had been seeking for his own cattle, however, the simple Yorkshireman suspects the canny Scot of duplicity. Even when Robin offers to share the field, Harry's hurt pride makes him refuse. His anger is increased by his drinking, the wretchedness of the pasturage he finally obtains, and the taunts of his English cronies "from the ancient grudge against the Scots." Consequently, when Robin arrives at the inn, Harry challenges him in characteristic English fashion, "a tussle for love on the sod . . . and we shall be better friends than ever." To a Highlander, however, to be beaten with fists stains a man with irremovable dishonor. When Robin tries to leave, Harry knocks him down.

The story hastens to its inevitable climax. Despite the sense of doom, the tragedy can be understood entirely in terms of the actors and their backgrounds. Robin walks ten miles to obtain his dirk from Hugh Morrison, tells Harry, "I show you now how the Highland dunnièwassel fights," and plunges his dagger into Harry's heart. Throwing the fatal weapon into the turf-fire, he exclaims, "take me who likes—and let fire cleanse blood if it can." His aunt's vision was accurate: The imagery of blood, prominent from the start, ends here. Before leaving, though, Robin looks "with a mournful but steady eye on the lifeless visage" of his friend and remarks, "He was a pretty man!" Scott's capacity for expressing the most intense dramatic emotions in the simplest language, his realistic eloquence, justifies his title of the most Shakespearean of prose writers.

The story ends with the trial judge's lengthy summation, which reflects Scott's own view of historical tragedy. No villains are involved. The crime arose from an "error of the understanding . . . men acting in ignorance of each other's national prejudices." The judge also points out that, if Robin had had his dirk and killed Harry immediately, he would have been guilty of manslaughter. Ironically, his aunt's second sight caused him to commit murder. Robin acknowledges the justice of the death sentence, and the story closes on his simple but resonant monosyllables: "I give a life for the life I took, and what can I do more?"

Scott's last three short stories were published in *The Keepsake* (a Christmas gift book published annually) of 1828. "My Aunt Margaret's Mirror" and "The Tapestried Chamber" are ghost stories; "Death of the Laird's Jock" is a sketch of "a subject for the pencil" of an artist. None is significant literature.

In contrast, Scott's first three stories set the highest standards for the newly emerging genre. "Wandering Willie's Tale," a marvelous comic tale, was regarded by Dante Gabriel Rossetti and Andrew Lang as the finest short story in English. "The Highland Widow" and "The Two Drovers" triumph on a nobler plane, reaching the heights of tragedy. All three stories exemplify Scott's major contribution to British fiction: the portrayal of man as a social and historical being.

OTHER MAJOR WORKS

LONG FICTION: *Waverley: Or, 'Tis Sixty Years Since*, 1814; *Guy Mannering*, 1815; *The Antiquary*, 1816; *The Black Dwarf*, 1816; *Old Mortality*, 1816; *Rob Roy*, 1817; *The Heart of Midlothian*, 1818; *The Bride of Lammermoor*, 1819; *A Legend of Montrose*, 1819; *Ivanhoe*, 1819; *The Monastery*, 1820; *The Abbot*, 1820; *Kenilworth*, 1821; *The Pirate*, 1821; *The Fortunes of Nigel*, 1822; *Peveril of the Peak*, 1823; *Quentin Durward*, 1823; *St. Ronan's Well*, 1823; *Redgauntlet*, 1824; *The Betrothed*, 1825; *The Talisman*, 1825; *Woodstock*, 1826; *The Highland Widow*, 1827; *The Two Drovers*, 1827; *The Surgeon's Daughter*, 1827; *The Fair Maid of Perth*, 1828; *Anne of Geierstein*, 1829; *Count Robert of Paris*, 1831; *Castle Dangerous*, 1831; *The Siege of Malta*, 1976.

PLAYS: *Halidon Hill*, pb. 1822; *Macduff's Cross*, pb. 1823; *The House of Aspen*, pb. 1829; *The Doom of Devorgoil*, pb. 1830; *Auchindrane: Or, The Ayrshire Tragedy*, pr., pb. 1830.

POETRY: *The Eve of Saint John: A Border Ballad*, 1800; *The Lay of the Last Minstrel*, 1805; *Ballads and Lyrical Pieces*, 1806; *Marmion: A Tale of Flodden Field*, 1808; *The Lady of the Lake*, 1810; *The Vision of Don Roderick*, 1811; *Rokeby*, 1813; *The Bridal of Triermain: Or, The Vale of St. John, in Three Cantos*, 1813; *The Lord of the Isles*, 1815; *The Field of Waterloo*, 1815; *The Ettrick Garland: Being Two Excellent New Songs*, 1815 (with James Hogg); *Harold the Dauntless*, 1817.

NONFICTION: *The Life and Works of John Dryden*, 1808; *The Life of Jonathan Swift*, 1814; *Lives of the Novelists*, 1825; *Lays of the Lindsays*, 1824; *Provincial Antiquities of Scotland*, 1826; *The Life of Napoleon Buonaparte: Emperor of the French, with a Preliminary View of the French Revolution*, 1827; *Religious Discourses by a Layman*, 1828; *Tales of a Grandfather*, 1828-1830 (four volumes); *The History of Scotland*, 1829-1830; *Letters on Demonology and Witchcraft*, 1830.

TRANSLATIONS: *The Chase, and William and Helen: Two Ballads from the German of Gottfried Augustus Bürger*, 1796; *Goetz van Berlichingen*, 1799 (Johann Wolfgang von Geothe).

EDITED TEXTS: *Minstrelsy of the Scottish Border*, 1802-1803 (3 volumes); *A Collection of Scarce and Valuable Tracts*, 1809-1815 (13 volumes); *Chronological Notes of Scottish Affairs from the Diary of Lord Fountainhall*, 1822.

BIBLIOGRAPHY

Allen, Emily. "Re-marking Territory: *Redgauntlet* and the Restoration of Sir Walter Scott." *Studies in*

Romanticism 37 (Summer, 1998): 163-182. A discussion of the generic politics of the Romantic literary marketplace and how the laws of genre become established; argues that *Redgauntlet* encodes an elaborate allegory of its generic history and of its forecasted reception.

Cockshut, A. O. J. *The Achievement of Walter Scott.* London: Collins, 1969. This interesting book combines a biographical sketch and a discussion of Scott's most famous and highly regarded novels—Waverley, Old Mortality, Rob Roy, The Heart of Midlothian, and *Redgauntlet.*

Cusac, Marian H. *Narrative Structure in the Novels of Sir Walter Scott.* The Hague: Mouton, 1969. The focus of this book is on structure, separating Scott's fiction into three classifications: romances, chronicles, and the mediocre hero history. Also contains helpful appendices, including classifications of novels and significant recurring elements. Includes a bibliography.

Dennis, Ian. *Nationalism and Desire in Early Historical Fiction.* New York: St. Martin's Press, 1997. Discusses Scott, James Fenimore Cooper, Jane Porter, and Lady Sydney Morgan.

Ferns, Chris. "Look Who's Talking: Walter Scott, Thomas Raddall, and the Voices of the Colonized." *Ariel* 26 (October, 1995): 49-67. Argues that although both Scott and Raddall are concerned with portraying the interaction between conflicting political and social forces within an essentially similar historical context, the manner in which they do so is very different; whereas Scott allows an unusually free interplay of voices, Raddall subordinates the dialogic interplay of voices to the monologic discourse of the narrator.

Lauber, John. *Sir Walter Scott.* Boston: Twayne, 1989. A good starting point for a study of Scott. The first three chapters provide an overview of Scott's career; the rest provide discussions of the novels; and the final chapter discusses the Waverley novels and their literary reputation. Includes a chronology and a select bibliography.

Lee, Yoon Sun. "A Divided Inheritance: Scott's Antiquarian Novel and the British Nation." *ELH* 64 (Summer, 1997): 537-567. Argues that the antiquarian mode of thought determines the historical novel's political ambivalence and provides the most effective means of understanding how this genre's popularity sprang from its literary nature.

Todd, William B. *Sir Walter Scott: A Bibliographical History.* New Castle, Del.: Oak Knoll Press, 1998. A useful tool for students of Scott. Includes bibliographical references and an index.

Zimmerman, Everett. "Extreme Events: Scott's Novels and Traumatic History." *Eighteenth-Century Fiction* 10 (October, 1997): 63-78. Discussion of extreme events in history and fiction; argues that such descriptions of extreme events are a rhetorical device to assert a perspective that remains unanalyzed, implying that analysis would erode the clear boundaries that divide humanity from the inhumane.

Mark A. Weinstein, updated by
Kimberley L. Jacobs

VARLAM SHALAMOV

Born: Vologda, Russia; July 1, 1907
Died: Moscow, U.S.S.R.; January 17, 1982

PRINCIPAL SHORT FICTION

Kolymskie rasskazy, 1978 (*Kolyma Tales*, 1980,
    and *Graphite*, 1981)

OTHER LITERARY FORMS

Varlam Shalamov was primarily a writer of short
stories, although the particular nature of the genre he
developed is unique. His stories are a blend of fiction
and nonfiction. Shalamov was also a poet, and his
only works to be published in the Soviet Union have
been poems. A collection of poems titled *Shelest
List'ev* (rustling of leaves) was published in 1964 and
Tochka kipeniia: Stikhi (boiling point: poems) appeared in Moscow in 1977. Shalamov has also written essays, in particular *Ocherki prestupnogo mira*
(n.d.; essays on the criminal world).

ACHIEVEMENTS

Varlam Shalamov's achievements cannot be measured by ordinary standards or norms. Certainly, his
greatest achievement was to stay alive during his seventeen years in what he calls the "death camps"—as
opposed to ordinary camps—in Kolyma in northeastern Siberia. He survived: Although he was indelibly
marked by the experience, it did not break him.

The quality of his short stories, which are a subtle
blend of fiction and nonfiction, is extraordinarily
high. John Glad, who translated most of the *Kolymskie rasskazy* into English in two volumes, *Kolyma
Tales* and *Graphite*, claimed in 1981 that Shalamov
was "Russia's greatest living writer." Although this
might seem excessively enthusiastic, particularly in
view of the achievements of Aleksandr Solzhenitsyn,
the claim is not to be lightly dismissed. The stories
are strikingly original in their use of the short-story
form. Solzhenitsyn himself had the highest regard for
Shalamov's talent. When he first read Shalamov in
1956, he later recalled, he felt as if he had "met a
long-lost brother" and believed that in some ways

Shalamov's experience surpassed his own. "I respect-
fully confess," Solzhenitsyn wrote, "that to him and
not to me was it given to touch those depths of besti-
ality and despair towards which life in the camps
dragged us all." Solzhenitsyn writes relatively little
about the mining camps of Kolyma in *Arkhipelag
GULag* (1973-1975; *The Gulag Archipelago*, 1974-
1978) or about the infamous "numbered" death
camps that had no names but only numbers to desig-
nate them.

The critic Grigori Svirski has well described the
shock experienced by Russian readers when
Shalamov's first stories were circulated in samizdat
form in the 1960's:

> It was truth and not perfect style that was required of
> Shalamov, and in each new story he uncovered new
> pages of truth about convict life with such power, that
> even former political prisoners who had not witnessed
> such things were struck dumb. The truth revealed by
> Shalamov shocks because it is described by an artist,
> described with such skill, as they used to say in the
> nineteenth century, that the skill is invisible.

BIOGRAPHY

Varlam Tikhonovich Shalamov was born and
reared in Vologda, a town in north-central European
Russia. Shalamov's adult life was largely spent in
prisons and camps, but ironically even his childhood
was spent in a region affected by the Russian penal
system. He has written of Vologda that "over the centuries as a result of the banishment to the area of so
many protesters, rebels, and different critics of the
tsars, a sort of sediment built up and a particular
moral climate was formed which was at a higher level
than any city in Russia." In 1919, Kedrov, the Soviet
commander of the northern front, had two hundred
hostages shot in Vologda. Little is known of
Shalamov's life, but he says in a story that one of the
hostages killed was the local chemistry teacher—as a
result, Shalamov never learned chemistry or even the
formula for water.

Shalamov was married, and in 1937, he was arrested for declaring that Ivan Bunin, the winner of the 1933 Nobel Prize in Literature, was "a Russian classic." Shalamov spent the next seventeen years in labor camps, mostly in Kolyma, in northeastern Siberia, where the prisoners worked in gold mines. The Soviet Union was the second largest producer of gold in the world, largely because of these mines, which utilized prison and slave labor; it is estimated that more than three million people died there from cold, hunger, and overwork. In *The Gulag Archipelago*, Solzhenitsyn calls Kolyma "the pole of cold and cruelty"; the British author Robert Conquest argues in *Kolyma: The Arctic Death Camps* (1978) that these killings were the conscious result of a policy of extermination.

Shalamov was released in 1954 and returned to Moscow. His stories were first circulated in manuscript form in the Soviet Union and were later published in Russian in the émigré journals *Grani* and *Novyi Zhurnal*. Some authors in the Soviet Union at the time were establishing regular contact with Western journalists and even obtaining Western lawyers to protect their rights, but Shalamov, old and ill, could do nothing to ensure more adequate publication of his works. A French version of his stories was published in 1969. It was not until 1978, however, that a complete Russian edition of the stories was brought out by Overseas Publications Interchange in London. The Soviet authorities forced Shalamov to denounce publicly the publication of his stories.

Shalamov was ill during the last decades of his life. A contemporary observer described Shalamov in Moscow: "On the speaker's rostrum stood a man with a completely fixed expression on his face. He appeared dried up and curiously dark and frozen like a blackened tree." Shalamov died on January 17, 1982.

ANALYSIS

It is natural to compare Varlam Shalamov's work to that of Solzhenitsyn; there are similarities in their subject matter, and they had great respect for each other. Solzhenitsyn was among the first to recognize Shalamov's talent in the early 1960's, when Shalamov's brief sketches of life in the Kolyma labor camps began to trickle into the embryonic network in Moscow, Leningrad, and a few other cities. Recognizing their importance, Solzhenitsyn invited Shalamov to share the authorship of The Gulag Archipelago, the multivolume "experiment in literary investigation" on which he was working. Shalamov was too ill, however, to accept Solzhenitsyn's invitation.

Unlike Solzhenitsyn, Shalamov does not aim at a panoramic view of the camp world. Also, his language is quite different from that of Solzhenitsyn. On the surface, at least, he does not appear to maintain a high pitch of passionate indignation and invective; he adheres to a deliberately cool and neutral tone. In contrast to the passionately self-righteous, not-to-be-intimidated Solzhenitsyn, with his steely courage and seemingly infinite capacity for resistance, Shalamov appears chilly, remote, preferring a miniature canvas that is fragmentary and almost incomplete. Rhetoric is left behind, the writer taking refuge in a kind of passive quietism. This first impression, however, is almost entirely false.

If Shalamov lowers his voice, it is to be even more direct, precise, and telling. His experience was quite different from that of Solzhenitsyn. Arrested in 1937, Shalamov was in Kolyma throughout World War II and observed the war only by means of the new arrivals of prisoners. Solzhenitsyn was arrested at the war's end, in 1945. Shalamov's camp experience was twice as long, and harsher; he knew no *sharashka*, or special projects camp, like that described in Solzhenitsyn's *V kruge pervom* (1968; *The First Circle*, 1968). Instead, Shalamov was designated for extermination and according to all expectations should have died.

It is difficult for the Western reader, with current notions of history and modernity, to understand Kolyma. In the United States, slavery ended with the Civil War; in Russia, the serfs were emancipated at about the same time. Though readers may think of themselves as skeptical and as not believing in unabated progress, still, old habits die hard; many realities of the contemporary world and of foreign countries appear to be impossible. In the mid-1930's, the Soviet government began to exploit its underground gold seams by means of slave labor of an unprecedented kind. Slaves, as is well known, are relatively unproductive; the People's Commissariat of Internal Affairs (NKVD), however, resolved to overcome the reluctance of their prisoners to work through the goad of hunger, by deliberately undernourishing them unless they achieved high production norms. The result was that most of the prisoners died. Then again, the NKVD paid nothing for its captives and could always replace dead ones by enslaving new people. Kolyma was the ultimate pole of this murderous system, cut off from continental Russia yet attached to it by its need for laborers.

Shalamov was arrested for calling Ivan Bunin a "Russian classic"; others were arrested for still more trifling reasons—for example, writing to a fiancé. Once in Kolyma, the captives' immediate overseers would be thieves and common criminals, officially described by the Soviet government as "friends of the people" or "socially friendly elements." In the story "Esperanto," Shalamov describes one of his jobs: "On the very first day I took the place of a horse in a wooden yoke, heaving with my chest against a wooden log." Shalamov observes wryly that man has more endurance than any other animal. In the story "Zhitie inzhenera Kipreeva" ("The Life of Engineer Kipreev"), a prisoner, Kipreev, declares that "Kolyma is Auschwitz without the ovens"; the inscription over the prison gates—strikingly similar to the German "Arbeit macht frei" at Auschwitz—is "Labor is honor, glory, nobility, and heroism." Few survived the first three years in Kolyma; the narrator observes in the story "Kusok mysa" ("A Piece of Meat"), "two weeks was a long time, a thousand years." The area contained innumerable mass graves. In the frozen taiga, dead bodies did not decompose; in the chilling story "Po Lend-licu" ("Lend Lease"), a recently arrived bulldozer—a gift from the United States government—has as its first task to cut a trench to hold a mass grave of bodies that is slowly sliding down the frozen side of a mountain.

In conditions such as these it would be unrealistic to expect a sustained attitude of vituperation like that of Solzhenitsyn. The prison conditions described by Fyodor Dostoevski in *Zapiski iz myortvogo doma*

(1861-1862; Buried Alive: Or, Ten Years of Penal Servitude in Siberia, 1881; better known as *House of the Dead*, 1915) were considered to be almost luxurious in comparison with those of the camps in Kolyma, and the same applied to Anton Chekhov's 1894 description of the penal colony on Sakhalin Island. In one of Shalamov's stories, a general, sent to Kolyma at the close of World War II, notes that the experience of the front cannot prepare a man for the mass death in the camps. One character, informed that the Soviet Union has signed the United Nations resolution on genocide in 1937, asks with caustic irony, "Genocide? Is that something they serve for dinner?" ("The Life of Engineer Kipreev"). The conditions were closer to those described by Bruno Bettelheim in *The Informed Heart: Autonomy in a Mass Age* (1960) and Eugen Kogon in his *Der SS-Staat* (1947; *The Theory and Practise of Hell*, 1950), although as Shalamov observes, "there were no gas furnaces in Kolyma. The corpses wait in stone, in the permafrost." It should be remembered that Shalamov was not there for one year, like Bettelheim, or seven years, like Kogon, but seventeen years.

"SENTENTIOUS"

The key to the unique tone in these stories can be found in the story entitled "Sententsiya" ("Sententious"), which describes a prisoner on the verge of death who gradually revives. The evolution of feelings that pass through his semiconscious mind (he is the story's narrator) is of extraordinary interest. At the beginning he is a walking dead man, one of those who were called *Musselmänner* in Nazi concentration camps, "wicks" in the Soviet camps. The narrator observes, "I had little warmth. Little flesh was left on my bones, just enough for bitterness—the last human emotion; it was closer to the bone." His greatest need is for forgetfulness and sleep. Later he improves, and he notes, "Then something else appeared—something different from resentment and bitterness. There appeared indifference and fearlessness. I realized I didn't care if I was beaten or not." As he steadily improves there is a third stage: fear. Then a fourth stage follows: "Envy was the name of the next feeling that returned to me. I envied my dead friends who had died in '38. I envied those of my neighbors who had something to chew or smoke." The narrator says bitingly that after this point, the feeling of love did not return:

> Love comes only when all other human emotions have already returned. Love comes last, returns last. Or does it return? Indifference, envy, and fear, however, were not the only witnesses of my return to life. Pity for animals returned earlier than pity for people.

The passage suggests that the evolution of feelings did not stop there, but continued. It gives a valuable insight into Shalamov's own attitudes. The narrator of the story has to learn language and individual words all over again. Each thought, each word "returned alone, unaccompanied by the watchful guards of familiar words. Each appeared first on the tongue and only later in the mind."

BITTERNESS AND HUMOR

Henceforth, this particular bitterness would stay with Shalamov as a substrate; in the foreground or almost hidden in the background, it provides his unique tone. John Gland has noted that Shalamov's tone sometimes seems neutral, distant, or passive. Yet it is never truly neutral. Usually it is closer to the bitterness described above: a dark, profoundly reverberating irony that no other author has expressed as well as Shalamov and is "closer to the bone."

Shalamov's range often goes beyond this. He can surprise with his sense of humor. His description of the visit of an American businessman, Mr. Popp, to the Soviet Union, the hasty preparation of the authorities to receive him, and his meeting with the "Commandant" of a hotel, Tsyplyakov, are as funny as Mikhail Zoshchenko at his best. The variety of people in Shalamov's stories is great. He describes naïve people such as the young peasant Fedya in "Sukhim paikam" ("Dry Rations"), the omnipresent criminals, religious fanatics, Esperantists, heroic officers from World War II such as "Pugachov" who were swept into the camps in 1945 and died attempting to escape, bureaucrats, guards, doctors, women, and the most ordinary people. Like Solzhenitsyn, he is particularly good at describing the special kind of meanness, or sadism, of one person toward another, cultivated by the totalitarian system and by the widespread presence of informers and spies. Even prisoners trying to recruit other prisoners for escape attempts were likely to be hired informers.

"AN EPITAPH"

Some of the stories are especially effective because of the variety and solidity of the characters. There is not only a single protagonist and a few other one-dimensional characters used as foils but also the unexpected breadth of real life. In the story "Nadgrobnoe slovo" ("An Epitaph"), a group of prisoners fantasize about what they will do when they leave prison and return to normal life. No two dreams are the same. One peasant wants to go to the Party headquarters, simply because there were more cigarette butts on the floor there than he had seen anywhere else: He wants to pick them up and then roll his own cigarette. The last words are given to a person hitherto silent who slowly, deliberately, expresses unrelieved hatred: "'As for me,' he said in a calm, unhurried voice, 'I'd like to have my arms and legs cut off and become a human stump—no arms or legs. Then I'd be strong enough to spit in their faces for everything they're doing to us.'"

CHEKHORIAN TRAITS

There is real artistry in these stories, and it is of an unexpected, nontraditional kind. Shalamov has been compared to Chekhov ("the Chekhov of the camps"), and although the comparison is apt there are real differences between the two writers. Both show economy, sparingly sketch in a background, and lead toward a single dramatic point or realization at the end. Shalamov's stories, however, are less obviously fictional than Chekhov's. Although Shalamov uses a variety of narrators in the stories, a majority have a speaker who resembles Shalamov himself. There is an air of casualness about the stories, both old-fashioned and at the same time extremely modern. Far more frequently than with Chekhov, the reader is unsure of the direction in which a narration is leading, although usually the story has a hidden but inexorable direction. At the end of the story "Perviy zub" ("My First Tooth"), a storyteller tries out several alternate versions of a story on a listener; the technique is similar to that used by Akira Kurosawa in his film *Rashomon* (1950). The story ends:

"I don't like that variation either," I said.

"Then I'll leave it as I originally had it."

Even if you can't get something published, it's easier to bear a thing if you write it down. Once you've done that, you can forget. . . .

As an ending this is disarming, seemingly casual, although the sharp edge of irony should not be missed. Shalamov sometimes says that he wants nothing more than to forget; often when he describes an experience he will admit that he simply did not care what would happen. Yet these attitudes are incorporated into the subject matter of the stories. Shalamov the writer, the artist, remembers and cares intensely. Western readers often miss the deeply understated irony in these passages: It is unique, subtle, and extremely powerful.

Shalamov's stories have interested many readers because of their unusual subject matter. On the verge of nonfiction, they are invaluable as documents. Their greatest value, however, is probably in their original use of form and their artistry. Stories such as the allegorical "Domino" ("Dominoes") and "Zagavor yuristov" ("The Lawyers' Plot") achieve a concentrated depth of meaning that is truly remarkable. Like Elie Wiesel, Shalamov is a survivor and a witness who also happens to be an excellent artist. By his own admission, he subordinates art to the truth of experience. Yet his art only gains from this.

OTHER MAJOR WORKS

POETRY: *Shelest List'ev*, 1964; *Tochka kipeniia: Stikhi*, 1977.

NONFICTION: *Ocherki prestupnogo mira*, n.d.

BIBLIOGRAPHY

Conquest, Robert. *Kolyma: The Artic Death Camps*. New York: Viking Press, 1978. An excellent source of background information about the Kolyma concentration camp, facilitating better understanding of Shalamov's stories. Contains frequent references to, and quotes from, Shalamov.

Glad, John. "Art Out of Hell: Shalamov of Kolyma." *Survey* 107 (1979): 45-50. Seeing Shalamov's stories in the Chekhovian tradition, Glad discusses

his struggle with the authorities and his contribution to the camp literature as a lasting document of human courage.

_____. Foreword to *Graphite*, by Varlam Shalamov. New York: W. W. Norton, 1981. Glad describes the conditions in Kolyma and the Soviet penal system. He sees the uniqueness of Shalamov's stories in their being a bridge between fact and fiction. Their artistic quality, however, especially their pantheistic surrealism, makes them true works of art.

_____. Foreword to *Kolyma Tales*, by Varlam Shalamov. New York: W. W. Norton, 1980. Similar to Glad's article in *Survey*.

Hosking, Geoffrey. "The Ultimate Circle of the Stalinist Inferno." *New Universities Quarterly* 34 (1980): 161-168. In this review of the Russian edition of *Kolyma Tales*, Hosking discusses several stories and the overall significance of Shalamov as a witness of crimes against humanity. He also compares similarities and differences between Shalamov and Aleksandr Solzhenitsyn as writers of camp literature.

Toker, Leona. "A Tale Untold: Verlam Shalamov's 'A Day Off.'" *Studies in Short Fiction* 28 (Winter, 1991): 1-8. A discussion of some aspects of Shalamov's modernist techniques, comparable to the works of Hemingway and Nabokov, as embodied in his story "A Day Off." Claims that Shalamov's work is part of the tradition that presents the darkest sides of experience against the belief in the ultimate triumph of humanist values.

_____. "Toward a Poetics of Documentary Prose— From the Perspective of Gulag Testimonies." *Poetics Today* 18 (Summer, 1997): 187-222. Places documentary genres into a nonmarginalizing perspective by constructing a paradigm of narrative modes on the basis of the ontological status of the fabula; discusses the clash between the rhetorical principles of "defamiliarization" and the "economy of effort" in documentary prose by a brief analysis of Varlam Shalamov's story "Berries."

*John Carpenter, updated by
Vasa D. Mihailovich*

IRWIN SHAW

Born: New York, New York; February 27, 1913
Died: Davos, Switzerland; May 16, 1984

PRINCIPAL SHORT FICTION
Sailor off the Bremen and Other Stories, 1939
Welcome to the City and Other Stories, 1942
Act of Faith and Other Stories, 1946
Mixed Company, 1950
Tip on a Dead Jockey and Other Stories, 1957
Love on a Dark Street, 1965
Retreat, and Other Stories, 1970
God Was Here, But He Left Early, 1973
Short Stories: Five Decades, 1978

OTHER LITERARY FORMS

Irwin Shaw wrote novels, plays, screenplays, nonfiction books, articles, and short stories. His novels *The Young Lions* (1948) and *Rich Man, Poor Man* (1970) and his plays *Bury the Dead* (1936) and *Sons and Soldiers* (1943) are well known and received critical acclaim. "Out of the Fog," "Act of Faith," "Tip on a Dead Jockey," *Two Weeks in Another Town* (1960), and *The Young Lions* have been filmed. *Rich Man, Poor Man* was the television miniseries believed by some critics to have launched America's novel-to-miniseries craze.

ACHIEVEMENTS

Irwin Shaw's forty-six-year roller coaster ride with American critics began in 1935 when Brooks Atkinson wrote of Shaw's first play, "What *Waiting for Lefty* was for Clifford Odets, *Bury the Dead* is to Irwin Shaw." Within the next four years *The New Yorker* and other top magazines published some of Shaw's best short stories, including "The Girls in Their Summer Dresses," "Second Mortgage," and the title story of his first book of short stories, *Sailor off the Bremen*. His first novel, *The Young Lions*, was hailed by some critics as the best novel to emerge from World War II, comparable to Ernest Hemingway's *A Farewell to Arms* (1929). Not all of his novels were so well received; *Lucy Crown* (1956) was

branded a soap opera. In 1970, however, *Rich Man, Poor Man* put him back on the favored son list. Critics who praised and critics who panned his novels did so by comparing them to Shaw's own brilliant short stories.

BIOGRAPHY

Irwin Shaw began professional writing for the *New Republic* after graduating from Brooklyn College. He worked as a drama critic and teacher of creative writing before serving in the army from 1942 to 1945, and during the war he spent time in Africa, England, France, and Germany. He was a member of the Author's Guild, Dramatist's Guild, and Screen Writer's Guild, and he received a National Institute of Arts and Letters grant in 1946. He was married and had one son. In 1951 he moved to Europe. In his later years, Shaw lived in Switzerland but spent his summers in Southampton, New York. On May 16, 1984, Irwin Shaw died, the result of a heart attack, in a hospital in Davos, Switzerland. He was seventy-one.

ANALYSIS

Irwin Shaw's stories have appeared in many respected magazines and are frequently anthologized in collections of short fiction. War, crime, financial disaster, adultery, and moral sterility provide major conflicts as Shaw presents a wide range of human emotions. "Sailor off the Bremen," "The Eighty-Yard Run," "Tip on a Dead Jockey," and "The Girls in Their Summer Dresses" are well-known examples of his narrative sophistication.

"SAILOR OFF THE BREMEN"

In "Sailor off the Bremen," a story of naïve revenge, an American football player learns the identity of the Nazi who disfigured his brother's face. Charley, arrogant and angry in his strength, overrules his injured brother's objections to ensnaring and punishing the offender. A series of discussions between Charley, Ernest the disfigured brother, and their friends and family develops a plot suggesting various perspectives on violence.

Irwin Shaw (Library of Congress)

In a scene centered around the brothers' kitchen table, Ernest, Preminger, and Stryker, new members of the Communist Party, disregard violence as a means for change. Charley and Ernest's wife, Sally, however, want satisfaction for their loved one's suffering. In the course of their arguments, even the strongest Communist of the three, Preminger, admits that aside from party leanings, the Nazi ought to be punished for his cruelty not merely to Ernest but to others he has sent to concentration camps. Then Stryker, although he is usually anxious and timid, agrees to help effect the revenge because he is Ernest's friend. Finally Ernest himself is resigned.

Shaw handles characterization by focusing on suggestive details that reveal much about each of the men: Ernest's face twitches almost uncontrollably; his blind eye is concealed with a dark patch. Charley's muscular hands are cleat-marked from the previous week's game. Stryker, a dentist who is attempting to replace Ernest's teeth, has a dry, raspy voice filled with doubt. Preminger, an officer aboard the *Bremen*, is cool and confident; he looks like a midwestern college boy despite his profession of espionage. In the background, Sally, patient and hospita-

ble, performs kitchen duties as the men discuss their plans.

Once the decision is made, the pace quickens. Preminger identifies the Nazi, Lueger, so that Sally, Charley, and Stryker will recognize him as they watch separately from another deck of the *Bremen*. Sally manages to arrange a date with Lueger, who is well known for his affairs with women. On the appointed evening, they see a movie, stop for a drink, and then continue along the street past a corner where Charley and Stryker are waiting.

Sally escapes when Stryker asks directions of Lueger, giving Charley the opportunity to land the first blow. In a brutal climactic scene, Stryker stands guard while Charley knocks Lueger unconscious and beats him until he has lost an eye and many teeth. Sobbing and cursing, Charley continues to beat Lueger until he is satisfied that Lueger will suffer serious injury permanently. Stryker and Charley then leave the Nazi lying in a pool of his own blood. Later, in the hospital, Preminger identifies Lueger for a questioning detective but denies any knowledge that Lueger had enemies. The eye-for-an-eye theme of the story raises questions concerning violence and morality; clearly the social and political context makes immediate answers impossible.

"The Eighty-Yard Run"

"The Eighty-Yard Run" presents another kind of social dilemma. Christian Darling, a former midwestern college football player, recalls the practice run he made that changed his football career and won for him the daughter of a wealthy manufacturer. Admired by the coaches, the students, and Louise, he appeared successful through college and afterward, when he began to manage accounts for her father in New York. As Christian muses over the long run and the intervening years, he struggles to accept the fact that he could not cope with the social and intellectual changes of the 1920's and 1930's.

Louise's father, a maker of inks, had survived the initial crash and waited until 1933 to commit suicide, leaving only debts and unbought ink behind. Christian turned to alcohol, and Louise began working for a women's magazine. Their apartment became a showcase for the sophisticated intellectuals of New

York. Unable to understand the new art or the philosophies of the new breed, Christian lost Louise's respect. Although he had attempted a succession of jobs, he had never done well at any of them, until he was hired, for his collegiate appearance, as a traveling representative for a tailoring firm. Now as Christian reflects, he realizes that while he travels, Louise dines with new, more sophisticated men and makes the social contacts that are now so important to her. Not since the eighty-yard practice run has he had any hope of his own success. Christian, visiting his old practice field, reenacts the eighty-yard run when he thinks the field is deserted. Recalling his own ease and grace at that moment, he executes perfectly the movements of fifteen years before, only to discover with embarrassment that a young couple is watching him. He leaves the field with sweat beginning to break out across his face. His situation is fixed in space and time; the story presents the effects of social and economic changes in American life as they are experienced by a particular, although representative, man.

"TIP ON A DEAD JOCKEY"

"Tip on a Dead Jockey" spotlights the lives of American expatriate flyers in Paris after the war. When Lloyd Barber, out of work and living in a shabby Parisian hotel, learns from a friend's wife that her husband, Jimmy, has disappeared for more than a month, he realizes that Jimmy must have accepted a smuggling job he himself had refused because of its risks. In this story, like "The Eighty-Yard Run," flashbacks indicate the contrast between past security and present struggle. Barber recalls, for example, the youthful beauty of Jimmy's wife, now evidencing poverty and anguish. He gives her what he can spare of his cash and reassures her that he will try to locate Jimmy.

Barber himself is depressed and lonely; he has no job but amuses himself occasionally by going to the races, where he met Bert Smith who had offered him twenty-five thousand dollars for two flights between Egypt and France, an offer which must now account for Jimmy's disappearance. Barber searches the bars and restaurants of Paris in an attempt to locate Smith, a wealthy and educated European who had enter-

tained him for weeks before revealing his intent to use Barber to smuggle money into France.

Barber's initial contact with Smith had been most profitable. As Barber continues his search through the streets of Paris, he recalls that Smith's tips on winning horses had paid off generously for the first two weeks of their acquaintanceship. On their last afternoon together at the track, however, perhaps the afternoon he decided against the smuggling job, Smith had recommended betting on a horse which fell, killing its jockey, an event Barber accepted as a bad omen. Barber had immediately refused Smith's offer and returned flight maps Smith had given him. That evening, preparing to dine alone, Barber had stumbled onto Smith and Jimmy, talking casually about racing, and Barber had thought nothing of it, underestimating Jimmy's financial need and gullibility.

Barber's search is unsuccessful. He returns to his room to find that Jimmy's wife has left a message requesting that he meet her at a nearby bar. There he finds her with Jimmy, suntanned and thin, eagerly spending the earnings of his crime. The couple asks him to go with them to dinner at an expensive restaurant, but Barber, despite his relief that Jimmy is safely home, only feels lonelier as he witnesses their happy reunion. He returns to his hotel room where a collection of letters reminds him of the emptiness of his own life: his ex-wife wants to know what to do with an old army pistol she found in a trunk belonging to him; his mother wants him to stop being foolish and come home to a regular job; a woman he does not love wants him to come and stay with her in a villa near Eze; none of the letters makes him feel less isolated. Finally, there is a letter from a boy who had flown as his waist-gunner during the war, and this letter, more than the rest, reminds him of the emptiness of expatriate life in Europe. The lonely hotel room, the evening chill, and the memory of Jimmy's reunion with his wife converge on Barber as he concludes that Europe is not the place for him, however adventurous he may have been in the past.

"THE GIRLS IN THEIR SUMMER DRESSES"

"The Girls in Their Summer Dresses" is a famous example of Shaw's skill in portraying urban life with little more than an anecdote. Michael and Frances, a young married couple, walk along Fifth Avenue in New York City on a Sunday afternoon. They decide to spend the day alone, enjoying the city, instead of visiting friends in the country as they had planned, but the husband's habit of girl-watching leads to an angry confrontation in which the beautiful women of New York become a symbol of the freedom and sexual vitality his wife resents. As a Japanese waiter cheerfully serves them drinks just after breakfast in a small bar, the husband admits his fascination with the variety of women passing daily along New York streets. Their expensive clothing, their health, and their beauty draw him like a magnet, especially as he approaches middle age.

As Frances sobs into her handkerchief, Michael finds courage to celebrate the wonderful experience of observing women, richly dressed in furs in winter or in summer dresses in warm weather. Although he reassures Frances that she is a good wife, she believes that he only wants his freedom, and he cannot convince her of his loyalty because he is not convinced of it himself. They decide to spend the rest of the day with friends after all, and as Frances walks across the bar to make a phone call, Michael cannot help admiring her figure, her legs, just as he admires the features of strangers passing along the street. Their situation is a modern one, appropriately symbolized by New York women reflecting the economic vitality of the urban setting. Although Shaw frequently stops at the surface of the modern lifestyle, his portraits of modern men and women effectively suggest the conflicts below apparent comfort and success.

OTHER MAJOR WORKS

LONG FICTION: *The Young Lions*, 1948; *The Troubled Air*, 1951; *Lucy Crown*, 1956; *Two Weeks in Another Town*, 1960; *Voices of a Summer Day*, 1965; *Rich Man, Poor Man*, 1970; *Evening in Byzantium*, 1973; *Nightwork*, 1975; *Beggarman, Thief*, 1977; *The Top of the Hill*, 1979; *Bread Upon the Waters*, 1981; *Acceptable Losses*, 1982.

PLAYS: *Bury the Dead*, pr. 1936; *Siege*, pr. 1937; *The Gentle People: A Brooklyn Fable*, pr., pb. 1939; *Quiet City*, pr. 1939; *Retreat to Pleasure*, pr. 1940; *Sons and Soldiers*, pr. 1943; *The Assassin*, pr. 1945;

The Survivors, pr., pb. 1948; *Children from Their Games*, pb. 1962; *A Choice of Wars*, pr. 1967; *The Shy and Lonely*, pr. 1986.

SCREENPLAYS: *The Big Game*, 1936; *Commandos Strike at Dawn*, 1942; *The Hard Way*, 1942 (with Daniel Fuchs); *Talk of the Town*, 1942 (with Sidney Buchman); *Take One False Step*, 1949 (with Chester Erskine); *I Want You*, 1951; *Act of Love*, 1953; *Fire Down Below*, 1957; *Desire Under the Elms*, 1958; *This Angry Age*, 1958 (with Rene Clement); *The Big Gamble*, 1961; *In the French Style*, 1963; *Survival*, 1968.

NONFICTION: *Report on Israel*, 1950 (with Robert Capa); *In the Company of Dolphins*, 1964; *Paris! Paris!*, 1977; *Paris/Magnum: Photographs, 1935-1981*, 1981.

BIBLIOGRAPHY

Eisinger, Chester E. *Fiction of the Forties*. Chicago: University of Chicago Press, 1963. In the section titled "Irwin Shaw: The Popular Ideas of the Old Liberalism," Eisinger both praises and condemns Shaw for his treatment, in the four volumes of short stories he produced between 1939 and 1950, of racial and social prejudice.

Giles, James R. "Interview with Irwin Shaw." *Resources for American Literary Study* 18 (1992): 1-21. Shaw discusses his experiences writing for movies, his reaction to being a "popular" writer, his blacklisting, and his opinion of Ernest Hemingway. Contends "Act of Faith" is an "angry" story.

_____. *Irwin Shaw*. Boston: Twayne, 1983. This book is one volume in an expanding series of literary biographies.

_____. *Irwin Shaw: A Study of the Short Fiction*. Boston: Twayne, 1991. An excellent review of Shaw's short stories.

Reynolds, Fred. "Irwin Shaw's 'The Eighty-Yard Run.'" *The Explicator* 49 (Winter, 1991): 121-123. Interprets the story as a case study in psychoneurosis in which the protagonist exhibits three symptoms of arrested development: sexual confusion, Oedipal relationships, and neurotic fixation on the past.

Shaw, Irwin. "The Art of Fiction IV." *The Paris Review* 1 (1953): 26-49. In this interview, Shaw discusses all the different forms he explored. Beginning with his earliest efforts as a script writer for the radio series *Dick Tracy*, he lays out many of his theories and techniques as playwright, novelist, and screen writer. Of the short stories he says "The form . . . is so free as to escape restrictions to any theory."

_____. "The Art of Fiction IV, Continued." *The Paris Review* 21 (Spring, 1979): 248-262. This interview is an update of the one conducted twenty-five years earlier. Shaw discusses being an expatriate writer, how he feels he has mellowed, and how dramatically his lifestyle changed when he gave up writing for the theater.

Shnayerson, Michael. *Irwin Shaw: A Biography.* New York: Putnam, 1989. A good look at Shaw's life and times.

Startt, William. "Irwin Shaw: An Extended Talent." *Midwest Quarterly* 2 (1961): 325-337. In comparing Shaw's short stories to his novels, Startt credits the shorter works with projecting more "immediacy" and a greater sense of "reality." Shaw is compared favorably with Ernest Hemingway.

Chapel Louise Petty, updated by Edmund August

LESLIE MARMON SILKO

Born: Albuquerque, New Mexico; March 5, 1948

PRINCIPAL SHORT FICTION

Storyteller, 1981 (includes prose and poetry)
Yellow Woman, 1993

OTHER LITERARY FORMS

Leslie Marmon Silko is known most widely for her novels, including *Ceremony* (1977), *Almanac of the Dead* (1991), and *Gardens in the Dunes* (1999). An early collection of poetry, *Laguna Woman* (1974), established her as an important young Native American writer, and most of the lyric and narrative poems in that book are integrated with the autobiographical writings and short stories that make up *Storyteller*. Silko has also adapted, with Frank Chin, one of her short stories into a one-act play of the same title, *Lullaby*, which was first performed in 1976. Silko has also written screenplays; in one, she adapted a Laguna Pueblo myth, "Estoyehmuut and the Kunideeyah" (arrowboy and the destroyers), for television production in 1978. Earlier, she wrote a screenplay for Jack Beck and Marlon Brando that depicted, from a Native American viewpoint, the expedition of Francisco Vásquez de Coronado in 1540 (the script was sent to Hollywood in 1977 but was not produced).

Several of Silko's critical essays and interviews provide useful insights into her short fiction, as does her correspondence with the poet James Wright, which is collected in *The Delicacy and Strength of Lace: Letters Between Leslie Marmon Silko and James A. Wright* (1986). Two particularly useful essays are "An Old-Time Indian Attack Conducted in Two Parts," published in *The Remembered Earth: An Anthology of Contemporary Native American Literature* (1979), and "Language and Literature from a Pueblo Indian Perspective," published in *English Literature: Opening Up the Canon* (1981). Silko's interviews often supply autobiographical and cultural contexts that enhance the understanding of her work; among the most insightful is the videotape *Running on the Edge of the Rainbow: Laguna Stories and Poems* (1978), which offers Silko reading from her work and is interspersed with her commentary on Laguna culture. Her nonfiction works include *Sacred Water: Narratives and Pictures* (1993) and *Yellow Woman and a Beauty of the Spirit: Essays on Native American Life Today* (1996). A collection of Silko's work and related material is housed at the University of Arizona library in Tucson.

ACHIEVEMENTS

Leslie Marmon Silko, along with Louise Erdrich, N. Scott Momaday, Simon Ortiz, James Welch, and Sherman Alexie, is regarded by critics as among the best of the more than fifty Native American writers with significant publications to have emerged since the mid-1960's. Formal recognition of Silko's fiction came quite early in her career. Her story "Lullaby" was included in *The Best American Short Stories 1975*, and "Yellow Woman" was included in *Two Hundred Years of Great American Short Stories* (1975), published to commemorate the American bicentennial. In 1974, she won the *Chicago Review* Poetry Award, and in 1977 she won the Pushcart Prize for poetry. She has also been awarded major grants from the National Endowment for the Humanities and the National Endowment for the Arts for her work in film and in fiction. In 1981, Silko received a five-year fellowship from the John D. and Catherine T. MacArthur Foundation, permitting her the freedom to pursue whatever interests she wished to develop. She received the *Boston Globe* prize for nonfiction in 1986, the New Mexico Endowment for the Humanities "Living Cultural Treasure" award in 1988, and a Lila Wallace-*Reader's Digest* Fund writers award in 1991.

BIOGRAPHY

Leslie Marmon Silko was born in Albuquerque, New Mexico, on March 5, 1948, the descendant of Laguna, Mexican, and Anglo-American peoples. Silko's mixed ancestry is documented in *Storyteller*, in which she recounts the stories of white Protestant brothers Walter Gunn Marmon and Robert G. Marmon, her great-grandfather, who, with his older brother, settled in New Mexico at Laguna as a trader, having migrated west from Ohio in 1872. Her great-grandmother Marie, or A'mooh, married Robert Marmon, and her grandmother Lillie was a Model A automobile mechanic. Both were well educated and well informed about both Anglo and Laguna lifestyles. Growing up in one of the Marmon family houses at Old Laguna, in western New Mexico, Silko inherited from these women and from Susie Marmon, the sister-in-law of Silko's grandfather Hank Mar-

mon, a treasury of Laguna stories, both mythological and historical. Indeed, "Aunt Susie" is created in *Storyteller* as Silko's source for many of the traditional stories that shaped her childhood.

Silko's early years were spent in activities that neither completely included her in nor fully excluded her from the Laguna community. She participated in clan activities but not to the same extent as the full-bloods; she helped prepare for ceremonial dances, but she did not dance herself. Attending the local day school of the Bureau of Indian Affairs, she was prohibited from using the Keresan language which her great-grandmother had begun teaching her. She had her own horse at eight, and she helped herd cattle on the family ranch; at thirteen, she had her own rifle and joined in the annual deer hunts. From the fifth grade on, Silko commuted to schools in Albuquerque. After high school, she entered the University of New Mexico, also in Albuquerque, and, in 1969, she was graduated summa cum laude from the English department's honors program. After three semesters in the American Indian Law Program at the same university, Silko decided to pursue a career in writing and teaching. For the next two years, she taught English at Navajo Community College in Tsaile, Arizona. She spent the following two years in Ketchikan, Alaska, where she wrote *Ceremony*. She returned to teach in the University of New Mexico's English department for another two years before she moved, in 1980, to Tucson, where she became a professor of English at the University of Arizona for a few years. In addition, Silko has held writing residencies in fiction at several universities and has been invited for lectures and readings at schools from New York to California. More recently, Silko returned to bookmaking, an art she enjoyed as a child, with the production of *Sacred Water: Narratives and Pictures* (1993), a collection of autobiographical vignettes. On facing pages, Silko juxtaposes verbal pictures with graphic images. Under her own imprint, Flood Plain Press, she has personally assembled, numbered, and bound every copy by hand.

ANALYSIS

While she is well read in the canonical tradition of

Anglo-American writing, having delighted particularly, at an early age, in Edgar Allan Poe, John Steinbeck, William Faulkner, Flannery O'Connor, and, later in college, William Shakespeare and John Milton, Leslie Marmon Silko brings to her own work the sensibility and many of the structures inherent in the Laguna oral tradition, creating, for example, a subtext of revisioned Laguna mythology to the more conventional aspects of her novel *Ceremony*. Although, in a manner similar to that of other American writers drawing upon an ethnic heritage, Silko chooses to place her work in the context of Laguna culture, her work appeals to diverse readers for its insights not only into the marginal status of many nonwhite Americans but also into the universal celebration of the reciprocity between land and culture.

Silko's short fiction is "told" in the context of her personal experience in Laguna Pueblo and serves as a written extension, continuation, and revitalization of Laguna oral tradition. Blurring the genre of the short story with historical anecdotes, family history, letters, cultural legacies, photographs, and lyric and narrative poems, *Storyteller* includes most of Silko's published short stories and poems. While the stories certainly stand on their own, and, indeed, many of them are included in various anthologies, Silko's matrix of thick description, conveying the mood of events as well as describing them, testifies to the essential role of storytelling in Pueblo identity, giving the people access to the mythic and historic past and relating a continuing wisdom—about the land, its animals, its plants, and the human condition—as an integral part of the natural process. About her collection, Silko has said,

> I see *Storyteller* as a statement about storytelling and the relationship of the people, my family and my background to the storytelling—a personal statement done in the style of the storytelling tradition, i.e., using stories themselves to explain the dimensions of the process.

"LULLABY"

In unifying the past and the present to illuminate the kinship of land and people, Silko's story "Lullaby," a pastoral elegy, evokes both beauty and loss. Set north of the Laguna Reservation, the story traces the life of an old Navajo couple, Chato and Ayah, from whose point of view the story is told by an omniscient narrator. While Ayah sits in the snow, presiding over her husband's death, she recalls various episodes in her own life just as if she were sharing in Chato's last memories. She is wrapped in an old army blanket that was sent to her by her son Jimmie, who was killed while serving in the army. She recalls, however, her own mother's beautifully woven rugs, themselves symbolic of stories, on the hand loom outside her childhood hogan. Again contrasting the past with the present, Ayah gazes at her black rubber overshoes and remembers the high buckskin leggings of her childhood as they hung, drying, from the ceiling beams of the family hogan.

What Ayah remembers seems better than what she has at present—and it was—but she does not escape into nostalgia for the old ways. Ayah remembers events and things as they were, for they have brought her to the present moment of her husband's death. She remembers Jimmie's birth and the day the army officials came to tell Chato of his death. She remembers how doctors from the Bureau of Indian Affairs came to take her children Danny and Ella to Colorado for the treatment of tuberculosis, which had killed her other children. Despite their good intentions, the white doctors frightened Ayah and her children into the hills after she had unknowingly signed over her custody of the children to them. When the doctors returned with reservation policemen, Chato let them take the children, leaving Ayah powerless in her protest that she wanted first to try the medicine men. Chato had taught her to sign her name, but he had not taught her English. She remembers the months of refuge in her hatred of Chato for teaching her to sign her name (and thus to sign away her children) and how she fled to the same hill where she had earlier fled with her children. She remembers, too, Chato's pride during his years as a cattle hand and how, after he broke his leg in a fall from a horse, the white rancher fired him and evicted them from the gray boxcar shack that he had provided for the couple.

As Ayah recalls these losses, she also recalls the peacefulness of her own mother, as if she were rejoining her mother, in contrast to the alienation of her own children from her after they had been away from home and learned to speak English, forgetting their native Navajo and regarding their mother as strangely backward in her ways. Now, with Chato reduced to alcoholism, senility, and incontinence, the old couple lives in the hogan of Ayah's childhood, and her routine is interrupted only by her treks to Azzie's bar to retrieve her husband. Ayah now sleeps with Chato, as she had not since the loss of Danny and Ella, because only her body will keep him warm. Fused with the heat of her body is the heat of her memory, as Ayah recalls how the elders warned against learning English: It would endanger them.

Ayah's recollection is presumably in Navajo (though Silko writes in English): The language is the story of her life and her relationship with the land on which she lived it. Place dominates her values; an arroyo and a cow path evoke precise memories, yet the evocation of her life culminates in her decision to allow Chato to freeze to death rather than see him suffer through the last days of his degradation. She wraps him in Jimmie's blanket and sings a lullaby to him which her grandmother and her mother had sung before her:

> The earth is your mother,
> she holds you.
> The sky is your father,
> he protects you.
> Sleep . . .
> We are together always
> There never was a time
> when this
> was not so.

Ayah's closing song in the story joins birth with death, land with life, and past with present. Through her story, Ayah creates an event that supersedes the oppression of the white rancher, the stares of patrons at the Mexican bar, the rejection of her acculturated children, and the apparent diminution of traditional ways: The story continues the timeless necessity of the people to join their land with the sacredness of their language.

"STORYTELLER"

In the title story of her collection *Storyteller*, an arctic allegory set in Alaska, Silko focuses even more emphatically on the power of the story to create and to sustain the life of a people. By shifting from Laguna characters to Navajo characters and, finally, by using an Eskimo context, Silko stresses the universality of storytelling among peoples who codify the world through an oral tradition. "Storyteller" seeks to explore the ramifications of divergent ways of seeing the world (or hearing it), and, at the same time, the story models the process of the oral tradition: It is not a Yupik story so much as it is one that is written as if it were a Yupik story.

"Storyteller," like "Lullaby," begins in medias res, as do many stories in any oral tradition. It, too, is told from the point of view of a woman, but the Eskimo protagonist is a young girl, anonymous though universal as the storyteller. She is in jail for killing a "Gussuck" (a derogatory term for a white person) storekeeper. According to Anglo law and logic, however, the girl is innocent. Through juxtaposed flashbacks, Silko's omniscient narrator reconstructs the events that have led to the girl's imprisonment. Moving away from the familiarity of a Pueblo context, Silko sets the story in Inuit country on the Kuskokwim River near Bethel, where she spent two months while she was in Alaska; she brings, then, her own attentiveness to the land to her fashioning of the story about attentiveness to storytelling. The imprisoned girl grew up with an old couple who lived in a shack outside the village, and she was nurtured by the stories of her grandmother. Although the girl had attended a Gussuck school, she was sent home for refusing to assimilate, having been whipped for her resistance to speaking English. Sexually abused by the old man, the girl takes the place of her grandmother in the old man's bed after her death. Before the grandmother's death, however, the girl had learned about the death of her parents, who had been poisoned with bad liquor by a trader who was never taken to court for the crime. Her grandmother had not told her the complete story, leaving much of it ambiguous and unfinished. While the girl witnesses the destruction of village life by oil drillers and listens to her "grandfather" ramble on and on, telling a story of a polar bear stalking a hunter, she recalls her grandmother's last words: "It will take a long time, but the story must be told. There must not be any lies." The girl believes that the "story" refers to the old man's bear story, but, in fact, it is the story which the girl herself will act out after the grandmother's death.

Bored by sex with the old man, the girl begins sleeping with oil drillers, discovering that they are as bestial as the old man, who sleeps in a urine-soaked bed with dried fish while he adds to his story throughout the winter. When she is about to have sex with a red-haired oil driller, he tapes a pornographic picture of a woman mounted by a dog to the wall above the bed, and then in turn mounts the girl. When she tells the old man about it, he expresses no surprise, claiming that the Gussucks have "behaved like desperate people" in their efforts to develop the frozen tundra. Using her sexuality to comprehend the strange ways of the Gussucks, the girl stalks her parents' killer as the old man's bear stalks the hunter. The Gussucks, seemingly incapable of grasping the old man's story, fail in their attention to the frozen landscape; they do not see or hear the place, the people, or the cold, blue bear of the story.

That failure to grasp the analogy of the bear story to the impending freeze of winter is what finally permits the girl to avenge the death of her parents. She lures the "storeman" from his store, which doubles as a bar, to the partially frozen river. Knowing how to breathe through her mitten in order to protect her lungs and wrapped in her grandmother's wolf-hide parka, the girl testifies mutely to the wisdom of her grandmother's stories. She knows where it is safe to tread on the ice and where it is not—she hears the river beneath her and can interpret the creaking of the ice. The storekeeper, taunted by her body, which is symbolic itself of her repository of knowledge for survival, chases her out onto the ice, trying to catch her by taking a single line to where she stands on the ice in the middle of the river. Without mittens and parka and oblivious to the warning sounds from below the ice, the storeman ignores the girl's tracks that mark a path of safety and crashes through the thin ice, drowning in the freezing river. He has had many possessions, but he lacked a story, a narrative thread, that would have saved him.

When the state police question her, the girl confesses: "He lied to them. He told them it was safe to drink. But I will not lie. . . . I killed him, . . . but I don't lie." When her court-appointed attorney urges her to recant, saying, "It was an accident. He was running after you and he fell through the ice. That's all you have to say in court," the girl, disregarding the testimony of children who witnessed the man's death, insists: "I will not change the story, not even to escape this place and go home. I intended that he die. The story must be told as it is." Later, at home under a female trooper's guard, the girl watches as the old man dies, still telling his story even as it evokes the death of the hunter; his spirit passes into the girl, who will now continue the story of the bear's conquest of the man.

Now the storyteller herself, the girl, has fused or merged with her story: The story has taken revenge on both the storeman and the old man, her first seducer, through her actions, namely the telling of the stories. The story, then, does not end, but returns to itself, the bear turning to face the hunter on the ice just as the myth of natural revenge turns the story against the storeman and the seductive power of the story turns against the storyteller, the old man. Even, however, as a new storyteller, the girl/the story has no beginning and no end: It continues as long as the people and the land continue. Indeed, the story's survival is the survival of the people; ironically, the girl's story will provide the lawyer with a plea of insanity, ensuring the survival of the story and the storyteller despite the degradation involved in charging her with madness.

YELLOW WOMAN

Silko's most celebrated story, the frequently anthologized "Yellow Woman," uses a classic Laguna legend as a structural frame for an account of a contemporary woman, whose narration recognizes parallels with a mythic figure while maintaining a wary distance from full participation in a powerful myth. From a mundane modern community where her life is drab and undistinguished, the unnamed narrator recounts a temporary excursion into the hills beyond the Pueblo village with a charismatic, confident man, a stranger whose origins and actions—while mysterious and compelling—are also dangerous and destabilizing, a crucial part of his appeal.

The beginning of the story, located in an immediate present, emphasizes the physical reality of the experience in order to establish the tangibility of the woman's adventure. "My thigh clung to his with dampness," the woman reports, before describing the impressive mountain landscape which implies a linkage between the power of the man and a supportive energy flow in the natural world surrounding the pueblo. Struck by the strangeness of the man, and by his address to her as "Yellow Woman," the familiar figure from the Laguna folk tradition, she asks "Who are you?"—a query that is never completely answered and which informs the narrative as a thematic expression of the woman's awakening desire to explore a destiny that transcends the limits of her life.

The man, whose name, Silva, is an echo of the author's and the Spanish word for "collection" or "anthology," is both a representation of the *ka'tsina* or Mountain Spirit which functions as a guiding deity for the Laguna nation and a man of an exciting moment in the woman's life. The story recalls various abduction tales across cultures but both characters are exercising choices that respect and respond to the other person's preferences. As the narration continues, the woman's thoughts move between the life she has left and to which she will inevitably return and vivid, unfolding action of passion and fulfillment. Just as she continually questions her relation to the myth, asserting "I will see someone, eventually I will see someone, and then I will be certain that he is only a man—some man from nearby—and I will be sure that I am not Yellow Woman," her willingness to respond to what she calls "the same tricks" underscores her pleasure and excitement in seeing herself involved in an incident so that ". . . someday they will talk about us, and they will say 'Those two lived long ago when things like that happened.'"

In the conclusion of the narrative, Silva is challenged by a white man with a "young fat face," the intrusive authority of the dominant world dramatized by his dismissal of Silva as a thief and cattle rustler. In accordance with the heroic dimension of the myth, Silva, his eyes "ancient and dark," sends the woman

toward safety, where, from a distance she hears "four hollow explosions that remind me of deer hunting," another connection to ancient tribal practice. Realizing that she does not have "very far to walk" to return home, the power of the adventure retreating into memory as she thinks of the mountains already "too far away now," she re-enters her ordinary life, where "my mother was telling my grandmother how to fix Jell-O and my husband, Al, was playing with the baby." The significance of the story which she has lived and which she will eventually tell is epitomized by her concluding remark that she wishes her "old Grandpa" was still alive "to hear my story because it was the Yellow Woman stories he liked to tell best," an acknowledgment of her participation in a living tradition and an indication of her awareness of the importance of storytelling as a vital means of preserving and shaping cultural identity.

While Silko's stories are about the characterization of individuals, of a culture, of the land's significance to a people and their values, and of discrimination against a people, they are most fundamentally about the oral tradition that constitutes the peoples' means of achieving identity. Storytelling for Silko is not merely an entertaining activity reminiscent of past glories but an essential activity that informs and sustains the vitality of present cultures, shaping them toward survival and bestowing meaning for the future. The people, simply put, are their stories: If the stories are lost, the people are lost.

OTHER MAJOR WORKS

LONG FICTION: *Ceremony*, 1977; *Almanac of the Dead*, 1991; *Gardens in the Dunes*, 1999.

PLAY: *Lullaby*, pr. 1976 (with Frank Chin)

POETRY: *Laguna Woman*, 1974.

NONFICTION: *The Delicacy and Strength of Lace: Letters Between Leslie Marmon Silko and James A. Wright*, 1986 (edited by Anne Wright); *Sacred Water: Narratives and Pictures*, 1993; *Yellow Woman and a Beauty of the Spirit: Essays on Native American Life Today*, 1996.

RECORDING: *Running on the Edge of the Rainbow: Laguna Stories and Poems*, 1979.

BIBLIOGRAPHY

Allen, Paula Gunn. "The Feminine Landscape of Leslie Marmon Silko's *Ceremony*." In *Studies in American Indian Literature: Critical Essays and Course Design*. New York: Modern Language Association of America, 1983. Interprets Silko's novel from a feminist perspective and sees it as divided into two kinds of characters: earth spirits in harmony with the earth and spirit destroyers. Allen says that this is a novel of feminine life forces and the mechanistic death force of witchery. The women are equatable with the land, the life force, a thesis that is central to Native American culture. Analyzes the main characters and the causes for Tayo's illness from a Jungian perspective. Gives a brief and helpful bibliography of Silko's work and of criticism about her fiction. Also discusses her poetry and the storyteller tradition that underpins her fiction.

Brumble, H. David. *American Indian Autobiography*. Berkeley: University of California Press, 1988. Gives brief biographical sketch. Compares Silko's work to N. Scott Momaday's *The Way to Rainy Mountain* (1969) and *The Names* (1976). Silko uses the traditional as well as the personal in her stories. Her fiction reflects the Native American oral culture and the traditional sense of a lifetime of stories. Says that Silko wants to convey a sense of herself as a storyteller, just as Momaday does in his fiction, and that she adopts his form and methods, which give Silko a sense of tribal identity.

Jaskoski, Helen. "From the Time Immemorial: Native American Traditions in Contemporary Short Fiction." In *Since Flannery O'Connor: Essays on the Contemporary American Short Story*, edited by Loren Logsdon and Charles W. Mayer. Macomb: Western Illinois University Press, 1987. Suggests that the narrator of "Yellow Woman" experiences the wish fulfillment of Romantic novels, playing out in a dreamlike state the fantasy of an encounter with a masterful stranger with no sense of guilt or consequence.

_____. *Leslie Marmon Silko: A Study of the Short Fiction*. New York: Twayne, 1998. A thorough critical study of Silko's short fiction, touching upon the roles of women, Native Americans, and the Southwest as they figure in her work. Includes a bibliography and an index.

Krumholz, Linda J. "'To Understand This World Differently': Reading and Subversion in Leslie Marmon Silko's 'Storyteller.'" *Ariel* 25 (January, 1994): 89-113. Discusses the role of the reader in Silko's *Storyteller*; argues that one of the central ways in which Silko challenges the representation of Native Americans is to contest their relegation to the past and to break down the oral/written distinction used to support the past/present (them/us) dichotomy.

Krupat, Arnold. "The Dialogic of Silko's *Storyteller*." *Narrative Chance: Postmodern Discourse on Native American Indian Literature*, edited by Gerald Vizenor. Albuquerque: University of New Mexico Press, 1989. Discusses *Storyteller* from the point of view of Mikhail Bakhtin and Native American autobiography.

Larson, Charles R. *American Indian Fiction*. Albuquerque: University of New Mexico Press, 1978. Views Silko as an author who is very aware of her cultural and ethnic identity and as a writer of "authentic" Native American novels. Provides an in-depth analysis of *Ceremony*, summarizes the plot, and discusses the experimental structure of the novel. Relates the story in *Ceremony* to the Grandmother Spider motif and myth. Discusses the poems included in *Ceremony*, asserting that they act as a second persona in the novel, as a medicine man. Relates Silko to N. Scott Momaday, Hyemeyohsts Storm, and James Welch.

McAllister, Mick. "Homeward Bound: Wilderness and Frontier in American Indian Literature." In *The Frontier Experience and the American Dream: Essays on American Literature*, edited by David Mogen, Mark Busby, and Paul Bryant. College Station: Texas A&M University Press, 1989. Considers the nature of the frontier in Silko's works. Compares Silko's treatment of the frontier to that of Frank Waters's *The Man Who Killed the Deer* (1942). Says that *Ceremony* and N. Scott Momaday's *House Made of Dawn* (1968) are two important American novels. All three of these books treat individuals as being spiritually disso-ciated from their homes. Says that *Ceremony* is more positive in affirming the survival of Native American values than Momaday's novel.

Palmer, Linda. "Healing Ceremonies: Native American Stories of Cultural Survival." In *Ethnicity and the American Short Story*, edited by Julie Brown. New York: Garland Publishing, 1997. Shows how the structure, image, and theme of Silko's story "Lullaby," from *Storyteller*, exemplifies the recurring Native American theme of ceremony, song, story, and memory as a means of cultural survival against the dominant society.

Ramirez, Susan Berry Brill de. "Storytellers and Their Listener-Readers in Silko's 'Storytelling' and 'Storyteller.'" *The American Indian Quarterly* 21 (Summer, 1997): 333-335. Discusses the role of the listener-reader in American Indian literature; discusses the "transformational" relationship between a storyteller and listener-readers in Silko's stories "Storyteller" and "Storytelling."

Ronnow, Gretchen. "Tayo, Death, and Desire: A Lacanian Reading of *Ceremony*." In *Narrative Chance: Postmodern Discourse in Native American Indian Literatures*, edited by Gerald Vizenor. Albuquerque: University of New Mexico Press, 1989. Provides a detailed reading of *Ceremony*, applying the perspectives of Lacanian psychology and poststructuralist literary criticism.

Salyer, Gregory. *Leslie Marmon Silko*. New York: Twayne, 1997. A critical study; subjects include women and the Laguna Indians in Silko's fiction. Includes a bibliography and an index.

Seyersted, Per. *Leslie Marmon Silko*. Boise, Idaho: Boise State University, 1980. A good critical study of Silko's work; includes a bibliography.

Silko, Leslie Marmon. "Interview." *Short Story*, n.s. 2 (Fall, 1994): 91-95. Discusses the process by which her fiction is written, its sources in the storytelling traditions of her ethnic background, how she began writing and why.

Wiget, Andrew. *Native American Literature*. Boston: Twayne, 1985. Offers an overview analysis of *Ceremony* and compares the novel to N. Scott Momaday's *House Made of Dawn* (1968). Says the book explores the death of, or threats to, traditional Native American values and ways. *Ceremony* sets the human struggle against mythic Native American legends. Examines *Storyteller*. Says that Silko successfully uses the possibilities afforded her by Native American myths and the persona of the storyteller figure to do more than provide local color: Instead Silko uses these references to develop her characters and plot. Provides a useful but brief bibliography.

Michael Loudon, updated by Melissa E. Barth and Leon Lewis

ALAN SILLITOE

Born: Nottingham, England; March 4, 1928

PRINCIPAL SHORT FICTION
The Loneliness of the Long-Distance Runner, 1959
The Ragman's Daughter, 1963
A Sillitoe Selection, 1968
Guzman Go Home and Other Stories, 1968
Men, Women, and Children, 1973
The Second Chance and Other Stories, 1981

The Far Side of the Street, 1988
Collected Stories, 1995
Alligator Playground: A Collection of Short Stories, 1997

OTHER LITERARY FORMS
Alan Sillitoe's more than three dozen published books include novels, collections of poetry, books for children, as well as travel literature, essays, and

plays. Four of his books, including *The Loneliness of the Long-Distance Runner* and *The Ragman's Daughter* have been made into films. His first novel, *Saturday Night and Sunday Morning* (1958), was also produced in a stage adaptation, and his second, *The General* (1960), carried the film title *Counterpoint*.

ACHIEVEMENTS

Alan Sillitoe's early novels and stories fall within the tradition of British working-class fiction established by Charles Dickens and Mrs. Elizabeth Gaskell in the 1840's and carried on by George Gissing, Arthur Morrison, and Walter Greenwood. *Saturday Night and Sunday Morning* won the Author's Club Prize as the best English novel in 1958, and Sillitoe's best-known story, "The Loneliness of the Long-Distance Runner," won the Hawthornden Prize in 1959 and is widely accepted as a modern classic on proletarian life. *The General*, which began as a short story in 1950, won the Nottingham Writers' Club competition in 1960. Believing the concept of class is a degradation, Sillitoe is not so political in his later work, which shows a willingness to experiment in form and style. His stories have been frequently anthologized and have been translated into more than twenty languages.

BIOGRAPHY

Born into a working-class family in the English industrial city of Nottingham, Alan Sillitoe was educated to the age of fourteen at Radford Boulevard School for Boys and worked in local factories until he joined the Royal Air Force in 1946. He served in Malaya for two years, followed by sixteen months spent in an English sanatorium recuperating from tuberculosis. During this period he read voraciously and began to write. From 1952 to 1958, he lived in France and Spain, where he became friends with Robert Graves. On the publication of *Saturday Night and Sunday Morning*, he returned to England, and he settled in Kent. He has traveled frequently and widely and has made extended visits to North Africa, Israel, and the U.S.S.R. He married the poet Ruth Fainlight in 1959 and has one son, David. His avocations are wireless telegraphy and collecting maps.

ANALYSIS

"The Loneliness of the Long-Distance Runner," the title story of Alan Sillitoe's first collection of short fiction, quickly became one of the most widely read stories of modern times. Its basic theme, that one must be true to one's own instincts and beliefs despite intense social pressure to go against them, is echoed in many of his best-known stories, including "On Saturday Afternoon," "The Ragman's Daughter," "The Good Women," and "Pit Strike." Such an attitude strikes a responsive chord in modern readers who feel hemmed in by the dictates of "official" bureaucracies and by government interference in their personal lives. It is important for Sillitoe's characters to establish their independence in a conformist world, yet at the same time they often subscribe to a class-oriented code of values which pits the disadvantaged working class against the rest of society.

"UNCLE ERNEST"

Many of Sillitoe's stories are located in urban working-class slums and reflect the environment he knew himself. In story after story these ghetto-dwellers are seen as society's underdogs, as victims of a series of injustices, real or imagined, which undermine their sense of personal dignity and self-esteem. Ernest Brown, for example, the protagonist in "Uncle Ernest," is a lonely, aging upholsterer who befriends Alma and Joan, two young schoolgirls he meets at a local café. In a series of encounters, always at the café and in public view, he buys them food and small gifts and takes pleasure in learning something of their lives. He asks nothing of the girls in return, and they come to think of him affectionately as "Uncle Ernest." After a few weeks, however, he is accosted by two detectives who accuse him of leading the girls "the wrong way" and forbid him to see them again. Unable to cope with this "official" harassment, Ernest Brown retreats into alcohol and despair.

In one sense "Uncle Ernest" is an anomaly in Sillitoe's short fiction, for although it illustrates the victimization his characters often face, it chronicles a too-ready acceptance of the larger society's interference and power. For the most part his characters remain defiant in the face of directives from those in positions of authority.

"On Saturday Afternoon"

"On Saturday Afternoon," the story of an unnamed working-class man's attempt to commit suicide, offers a sardonic example of this defiance. The man first tries to hang himself from a light fixture, but before he can succeed the police arrive and arrest him. In response to his bitter comment, "It's a fine thing if a bloke can't tek his own life," the police tell him "it ain't your life." They take him to a psychiatric hospital and unwittingly put him in a sixth floor room and fail to restrain him. That night he jumps from the window and succeeds in killing himself.

"On Saturday Afternoon" is typical of Sillitoe's stories in its assumed attitude to social authority: Although "they" interfere and place controls on an individual's right to act as he pleases, they can usually be outwitted. Here and in other stories Sillitoe's workers place great stress on "cunning," the ability to preserve individual freedom of action in a restrictive or oppressive social environment.

"The Loneliness of the Long-Distance Runner"

This attitude of cunning is well illustrated in Sillitoe's best-known story, "The Loneliness of the Long-Distance Runner." The protagonist in this story is simply called Smith, the modern equivalent of Everyman. He is a seventeen-year-old boy who has been put in a Borstal, a reform school, for theft from a baker's shop. He is also an accomplished long-distance runner and has been chosen by the Governor, or warden, to represent the Borstal in a competition for the All-England Championship. As the reader meets Smith, he is running alone over the early-morning countryside, and as he runs he considers his situation. It soon becomes apparent that he has rejected the warden's platitudes ("if you play ball with us, we'll play ball with you") and has seen through the hypocrisy of his promises as well. He recognizes the difference between his own brand of honesty, which allows him to be true to his own instincts, and the warden's, which rejects the needs of the individual in favor of social expediency. Smith's only counter to the warden's attempt to use him for his own ends is cunning. As he sees it, the warden is "dead from the toenails up," living as he does in fear of so-

cial disapproval and manipulating the inmates of his Borstal to gain social prestige. Smith, however, resolves to fight against becoming swallowed up in social convention, to be true to his own concept of honesty. Adopting such a stance means recognizing "that it's war between me and them" and leads to his decision to lose the upcoming race.

In the second part of his three-part story the reader shares Smith's reminiscences about his boyhood in a Nottingham slum. He first engages sympathy by telling how he impulsively took part in the theft for which he was sent to Borstal, and then moves quickly to describe the confrontations with police who investigated the robbery. In this section Sillitoe manages a difficult feat by maintaining support for his protagonist even though readers know the boy is guilty of theft. He does this by turning the investigation into a series of skirmishes between Smith and the authorities which allow the reader to be caught up in admiration of the boy's ability to outwit for a time a vindictive, slow-thinking policeman. Not unexpectedly, persistence pays off for the investigators, and in a highly original and amusing climax the stolen money is found and Smith is taken into custody. The facts are less important here, however, than Sillitoe's narrative skill in sustaining the reader's sympathetic involvement with his protagonist. Having manipulated the reader into becoming Smith's ally by allowing conventional notions of right and wrong to be suspended, he also paves the way for the acceptance of Smith's dramatic gesture in the final section of the story.

The third part brings the reader back to time present and the day of the race. The warden, anticipating Smith's win and the reflected glory it will bring to him, has invited numbers of influential friends to witness the competition. Ironically, none of the boys' parents is present, their invitations having been worded so that they would be likely to mistrust or misunderstand them. Details such as this add to the impression of the callousness of the Borstal authorities and help to confirm Smith's conviction that they are using the boys as pawns in a selfish social game. The purity of Smith's intentions, however, is underscored during the race by his sense of communication with the natural surroundings through which he runs and his Edenic perception of himself as "the first man ever to be dropped into this world." As he runs, his thoughts alternate between lyrical commentary on the physical satisfaction of running well and consideration of his decision to lose the race and the punitive consequences this will bring him. Nevertheless he remains firm in his decision, committed to showing the warden "what honesty means if it's the last thing I do." In the end he does lose the race and makes his point, but in much more dramatic manner than he had foreseen. Arriving at the finish line well in advance of the other runners, he is virtually forced to mark time in front of the grandstand until one of his competitors passes him and crosses the line. Smith has made his point: Like so many other of Sillitoe's protagonists, he refuses to be manipulated.

"THE GOOD WOMEN"

The fierce independence espoused by Sillitoe's working-class characters, and the rejection of what they see as unwarranted interference by society's authority figures in their personal affairs, is also evident in "The Good Women." The heroine of this story is Liza Atkin, a vital and earthy woman whom one critic called "a Nottingham Mother Courage." Liza's life, like that of Bertolt Brecht's protagonist, is plagued by economic hardship and marked by injustice and the stupidity of war. Although the story has no real plot—readers are shown a series of disconnected events which take place over a period of years—they are caught up in the problems of Liza's life and come to applaud her feisty, tough-minded manner of coping with them.

Dogged by poverty, she ekes out a precarious existence supporting her out-of-work husband and two young boys by filling a decrepit baby carriage with old rags and bits of metal from local dumps and selling them to scrap dealers, and by taking in washing from troops stationed nearby. When the means-test man attempts to deny her welfare payments because of her "business," she shouts him down so the whole street can hear. She makes her gesture of protest against war by harboring a deserter; and standing up for workers' rights in the factory where she eventually finds work, she quickly becomes known to man-

agement as "the apostle of industrial unrest." Later, when her son dies because Allied planes bombed his unit by mistake, she is devastated. She recovers, however, to become a passionate advocate of violent revolution at a time in life when most women would be settling into comfortable grandmother roles.

"The Good Women," like many of Sillitoe's stories, has strong didactic overtones. Liza Atkin, along with Smith, Ernest Brown, and the unnamed protagonist in "On Saturday Afternoon," finds herself in a world in which the dictates of society at large often contradict her personal convictions. Yet she is able to resist the pressure to conform, partly because of her strong belief in what is right (harboring the deserter to protest against war, for example), partly because she shares the habitual working-class mistrust of "them" (the authority figures who come from outside and above her own social station) and their motives. From her perspective, and from Sillitoe's, society is badly flawed, and it is up to the individual to strive for a new order in which the unjust exercise of power and the suffering it can cause are eliminated. Memorable characters such as Liza Atkin are meant to show the reader how to begin.

"PIT STRIKE"

In "Pit Strike," which was filmed for British Broadcasting Corporation Television, Sillitoe offers yet another working-class hero, a champion of fairness and integrity. Joshua, a fifty-year-old Nottingham miner, journeys to the South of England with a number of his friends to support a strike by fellow colliers. In a well-organized program of action, the men race from one coal-powered generating station to another to form picket lines and halt deliveries of coal. In a number of cases they are confronted by police whose job it is to see that deliveries are uninterrupted. Clashes between the workers, who feel they are being treated unjustly, and the police, representing the power of society as a whole, are inevitable in such circumstances. Although Joshua acts to restrain his more belligerent companions in these confrontations, he makes his own mark in a dramatic and courageous manner. When a fully loaded coal truck is seen crawling up an incline away from a picketed power station to make its delivery at another, Joshua daringly and at great personal risk runs after it and forces open the rear gate safety catches, allowing tons of coal to fall on the highway. Although he narrowly escapes death, the gesture seems worth making, and soon after this the strike is settled in the miners' favor.

Like Joshua, the characters in Sillitoe's other stories are usually agitators, passionately and defiantly reaffirming the value of the individual spirit in a world which too often encourages unthinking conformity to social norms. Sillitoe's audience may not always concur with the views his characters express, nor wish to accept the methods they use to further their aims, but their stories nevertheless touch the reader and stay tenaciously with him, disturbing, provoking, and making him more aware of the imperfect world and of himself.

OTHER MAJOR WORKS

LONG FICTION: *Saturday Night and Sunday Morning*, 1958; *The General*, 1960; *Key to the Door*, 1961; *The Death of William Posters*, 1965; *A Tree on Fire*, 1967; *A Start in Life*, 1970; *Travels in Nihilon*, 1971; *The Flame of Life*, 1974; *The Widower's Son*, 1976; *The Storyteller*, 1979; *Her Victory*, 1982; *The Lost Flying Boat*, 1983; *Down from the Hill*, 1984; *Life Goes On*, 1985; *Out of the Whirlpool*, 1987; *The Open Door*, 1989; *Leonard's War*, 1991; *Snowstop*, 1993; *The Broken Chariot*, 1998.

PLAYS: *All Citizens Are Soldiers*, pr. 1967 (with Ruth Fainlight; adaptation of a play by Lope de Vega); *Three Plays*, pb. 1978.

SCREENPLAYS: *Saturday Night and Sunday Morning*, 1960; *The Loneliness of the Long-Distance Runner*, 1961; *Che Guevara*, 1968; *The Ragman's Daughter*, 1974.

POETRY: *Without Beer or Bread*, 1957; *The Rats and Other Poems*, 1960; *A Falling Out of Love and Other Poems*, 1964; *Shaman and Other Poems*, 1968; *Love in the Environs of Voronezh and Other Poems*, 1968; *Poems*, 1971 (with Ted Hughes and Ruth Fainlight); *Barbarians and Other Poems*, 1974; *Storm: New Poems*, 1974; *Snow on the North Side of Lucifer*, 1979; *More Lucifer*, 1980; *Sun Before Departure*, 1984; *Tides and Stone Walls*, 1986; *Collected Poems*, 1993.

NONFICTION: *The Road to Volgograd*, 1964; *Raw Material*, 1972; *Mountains and Caverns: Selected Essays*, 1975; *The Saxon Shore Way: From Gravesend to Rye*, 1983 (with Fay Weldon); *Nottinghamshire*, 1986 (with David Sillitoe); *Every Day of the Week*, 1987; *Life Without Armor*, 1996.

CHILDREN'S LITERATURE: *The City Adventures of Marmalade Jim*, 1967; *Big John and the Stars*, 1977; *The Incredible Fencing Fleas*, 1978; *Marmalade Jim at the Farm*, 1980; *Marmalade Jim and the Fox*, 1984.

BIBLIOGRAPHY

Atherton, Stanley S. *Alan Sillitoe: A Critical Assessment*. London: W. H. Allen, 1979. This study primarily emphasizes the revolutionary spirit of Sillitoe's first novels, but it deals with short fiction and lesser works as well.

Hanson, Gillian Mary. *Understanding Alan Sillitoe*. Columbia: University of South Carolina Press, 1999. A useful volume of Sillitoe criticism and appreciation.

Hensher, Philip. "Radical Sentiments." *Sunday Telegraph*, July 23, 1995, p. B9. A discussion of the life and works of Sillitoe, focusing on his autobiography *Life Without Armour* and his *The Collected Stories*; discusses briefly "The Loneliness of the Long Distance Runner" and the political nature of some of Sillitoe's short stories.

Hitchcock, Peter. *Working-Class Fiction in Theory and Practice: A Reading of Alan Sillitoe*. Ann Arbor, Mich.: UMI Research Press, 1989. A good examination of the writer's themes and execution.

Leonardi, Susan J. "The Long-Distance Runner (the Loneliness, Loveliness, Nunliness of)." *Tulsa Studies in Women's Literature* 13 (Spring, 1994): 57-66. An intertextual examination of how Grace Paley's "The Long-Distance Runner" and Sara Maitland's "The Loveliness of the Long-Distance Runner" rewrite Sillitoe's "The Loneliness of the Long-Distance Runner."

Penner, Allen Richard. *Alan Sillitoe*. Boston: Twayne, 1972. A useful midcareer overview of Sillitoe's work. Penner offers a short biography and a helpful bibliography. The discussion covers Sillitoe's poetry and fiction.

Rothschild, Joyce. "The Growth of a Writer: An Interview with Alan Sillitoe." *Southern Humanities Review* 20 (Spring, 1986): 127-140. This interview sheds light on Sillitoe's career and the irrelevance of class on his artistic sensibility. Sillitoe stresses the importance of character in his fiction.

Skovmand, Michael, and Steffen Skovmand, eds. *The*

Angry Young Men. Aarhus, Denmark: Akademisk Forlag, 1975. Hans Hauge's essay on Sillitoe considers *Saturday Night and Sunday Morning* as a representative novel from an angry generation of young writers that included John Osborne, John Wain, John Braine, and Kingsley Amis.

Stanley S. Atherton, updated by
Jerry Bradley

WILLIAM GILMORE SIMMS

Born: Charleston, South Carolina; April 17, 1806
Died: Charleston, South Carolina; June 11, 1870

PRINCIPAL SHORT FICTION

The Book of My Lady, 1833
Carl Werner: An Imaginative Story, 1838
The Wigwam and the Cabin, 1845
Southward Ho!, 1854

OTHER LITERARY FORMS

William Gilmore Simms was one of the most versatile and prolific writers of his day; his eighty-two volumes include novels, short stories, poetry, plays, literary criticism, essays, biographies, and histories. Simms was also highly respected in his time as a magazine and newspaper editor.

ACHIEVEMENTS

The enormous literary output of William Gilmore Simms places him among the foremost writers of the early nineteenth century in the United States; indeed, he was the most important writer in the South at the time. His many novels are mostly historical romances in the tradition of Sir Walter Scott and James Fenimore Cooper, but they use southern settings, dialects, and heroes as their subject. His best-known novel, *The Yemassee: A Romance of Carolina* (1835), deals with the issue of Native American dispossession, a theme also common to Cooper. Simms's short

stories are often told in the tall-tale mode, which was later popularized by the Southwest humorists. In addition to his fiction, Simms wrote a number of volumes of poetry and several plays, which, like the novels, have patriotic settings and subjects. His nonfiction works include histories, biographies, and several important essays of literary criticism, one of which details the difference between romance and novel. Though often noted for the quantity rather than the quality of his work, Simms occupies an important position in American letters.

BIOGRAPHY

William Gilmore Simms was the son of an Irish immigrant tradesman. His mother died when he was two, and Simms was left in the care of his maternal grandmother when his father moved to Tennessee and later to Mississippi. Simms's formal schooling amounted to less than six years, and he was largely self-educated. At the age of twelve, he was apprenticed to a druggist but later left that trade to study law. In 1827, he was admitted to the bar in Charleston. His marriage to Anna Malcolm Giles in 1826 ended with her death in 1832. Simms's literary talents became manifest very early in his life. At nineteen, he edited the literary journal, *The Album* (1825), and two years later published his first two volumes of verse. In 1828, he cofounded and edited *The Southern Literary Gazette*. He ventured into journalism as the editor of the daily newspaper, the Charleston *City Gazette*, from 1830 until its bankruptcy in 1832. Between 1833 and 1835, he published four novels, *Martin Faber: The Story of a Criminal* (1833), *Guy Rivers: A Tale of Georgia* (1834), *The Yemassee*, and *The Partisan: A Tale of the Revolution* (1835), and established his reputation as a significant voice in American fiction. In 1836, he married Chevilette Roach and moved to her father's seven-thousand-acre plantation, "Woodlands." His newly acquired wealth freed him to pursue his literary career more fully and to venture into new avenues, such as serving, from 1844 to 1846, as a representative to the South Carolina legislature. His marriage to Roach lasted until her death in 1863 and produced fourteen children. During the period from 1836 to 1860, in addition to his many literary productions, Simms was active in the editing of several magazines, including *The Southern and Western Monthly Magazine* (1845), *The Southern Quarterly Review* (1849-1855), and *Russell's Magazine* (1857-1860), which he helped Paul Hamilton Hayne to edit. Simms's fortunes were ruined by the Civil War; in 1865, "Woodlands" was burned by stragglers from William Tecumseh Sherman's army. Reduced to poverty, Simms spent the final years of his life editing newspapers and writing to support himself and his children. He died in Charleston on June 11, 1870.

ANALYSIS

William Gilmore Simms is often viewed as the successor to Sir Walter Scott in the fostering of Romanticism. Simms was fond of asserting that his works should be viewed as romances, filled with sweeps of the imagination, bold characterization, and clearly defined moral stances. His literary works, considered as a whole, can be viewed as an epic of the South; in the epic, there are realistic elements to be sure, but Simms was interested in realism only when it served his more consuming passion for creating works of originality and vitality that portrayed the South as it was and as it aspired to be ideally. Simms's writings, too, can be associated with regionalism and the local-color movement in American letters, for he borrowed richly from the traditions and mores of his region to capture a sense of a spirit and a time.

William Gilmore Simms (Archive Photos)

"HOW SHARP SNAFFLES GOT HIS CAPITAL AND HIS WIFE"

"How Sharp Snaffles Got His Capital and His Wife," published posthumously in *Harper's New Monthly Magazine* in October, 1870, is a short story which demonstrates at a high level of quality Simms's particular and fanciful interest in local color and southern tall-tale humor. In early winter, a group of seven hunters, four professionals and three amateurs, gather around the campfire on a Saturday night after a week of hunting in the "Balsam Range" of mountains in North Carolina. Saturday night is dedicated among the professional hunters to what is called "The Lying Camp," in which mountaineers engaged in a camp hunt, which sometimes lasts for weeks at a time, are encouraged to tell "long yarns" about their adventures and the wild experiences of their professional lives. The hunter who actually inclines to exaggeration in such a situation is allowed to deal in "all the extravagances of invention; nay, he is *required* to do so." To be literal or to confine one-self to details of fact is a finable offense. The hunter is, however, required to exhibit a certain degree of art in his invented tales, "and thus he frequently rises into a certain realm of fiction, the ingenuities of which are made to compensate for the exaggerations, as they do in the 'Arabian Nights' and other Oriental romances."

The tale for the evening is told, in dialect fashion, by Sharp Snaffles to the "Jedge," the narrator of the story. Sharp tells the tale of how fourteen years ago he was in love with Merry Ann Hopson and sought to marry her. When Sharp appears at Squire Hopson's house and announces his intentions, the squire tells Sharp that he does not have the types of possessions, or capital, that would attract a woman or that would enable her to live in style. Sharp knows he must get himself some capital, but he cannot figure out how, although he spends half the night thinking and fig-uring.

The next day, Sharp sees a flock of wild geese landing on a lake. Sharp calculates that there must be forty thousand geese on the lake and considers that he could get fifty cents a head for them if he could get them to the markets in Spartanburg and Greenville. His plan is to spread a huge net across the lake, and, after the geese have landed, at a key moment pull both ends of the net in quickly and catch all the geese. The plan works perfectly, except for the fact that after reeling all the geese in, Sharp wraps the rope around his left arm and his right thigh rather than tying it to the tree in front of him. As if of one mind and body, the geese lift from the lake and carry Sharp for several miles until they hit a tree and land in its branches. Suddenly the branch on which Sharp is sitting gives way and throws him backward into the tree trunk, which is hollow and filled with honey. In the midst of his prayers for deliverance, a huge bear begins to lower himself down, bottom end first, to get to the honey. Sharp sees his chance and grabs hold of the bear's ankle; the bear is so frightened he claws his way out of the tree, taking Sharp with him. When they get to the top, Sharp pushes the bear out of the tree; the bear falls and breaks his neck.

Safely out of the tree, Sharp realizes the potential

capital available to him in the bear, the geese, and the honey. When all of his dealings are done, he has sold 2,700 geese for $1,350, the bear's hide, meat, grease, and marrow for $100, and 2,000 gallons of honey for $1,400. His wealth accumulated, Sharp then sets about the business of establishing himself as a man of capital by buying a 160-acre farm with a good house on it, furniture, and a mule for working his land. The rest of his money he has converted to gold and silver coins and loads up his pockets and his saddlebags.

As he prepares to go to Squire Hopson's, Sharp tells his friend, Columbus Mills, of the squire's talk about capital. Columbus tells Sharp that the squire has no room to talk; the squire owes Columbus a 350-dollar-note on which he has not paid a cent in three years and on which Columbus is holding the mort-gage to the squire's farm as security. Sharp asks Co-lumbus if he will sell him the squire's mortgage for the face value of the note, and Columbus agrees. Dressed in his best new outfit, Sharp then goes to Squire Hopson's house; on the way, he meets Merry Ann and tells her that they are going to be married that evening. Merry Ann thinks that he has gone slightly crazy but agrees to follow along after him and see what happens.

The squire receives Sharp coldly, but he is im-pressed by Sharp's rich clothing and his fancy new appearance. Sharp states that he has come on busi-ness and brings up the issue of the debt to Columbus Mills. The squire tells Sharp to tell Columbus he will pay him soon, and Sharp says that the squire misun-derstands Sharp's mission. The note, and conse-quently the mortgage, now belong to him, and, since he plans to be married this evening, he wants the squire to move out so that Sharp and his new bride can move in in the morning. The only way the squire can acquire any capital now and save his farm is to al-low Sharp to marry Merry Ann. At first the squire protests, but when Sharp shows him the gold and sil-ver coins in his saddlebags and his pockets he finally gives in and agrees to the wedding. Sharp fetches Par-son Stovall, and the wedding is performed that eve-ning, exactly as Sharp had promised Merry Ann. Thirteen years later, Sharp tells the Judge at the con-clusion of his tale that he and Merry Ann have a happy marriage, nine beautiful children, and more capital than Sharp ever imagined.

"GRAYLING"

Simms's passion for the wonderful and the mysterious is exemplified by "Grayling," a story which Edgar Allan Poe admired and which begins with the lamentation that the world has become so matter-of-fact lately that "we can no longer get a ghost story, either for love or money." To break the hold which "that cold-blooded demon called Science" has upon "all that concerns the romantic," the narrator proposes to tell a story that he heard as a boy from his grandmother and that involves ghosts and many things wondrous.

Set in the Carolinas in the period immediately following the Revolutionary War, the tale is of the murder of Major Lionel Spencer by Sandy Macnab. Macnab has learned that Spencer is to sail from Charleston to England to claim a large inheritance. All the Major need do to secure the estate is prove that he is Lionel Spencer. With the intention of impersonating Spencer in England, Macnab follows the Major, murders him, and throws his body in the bay.

James Grayling, a close friend of Major Spencer and an army comrade with whom Spencer camped the night before he was murdered, learns that Spencer neither has reached the tavern in the next town on his journey nor has he been seen on the road. While searching for Spencer, Grayling sees the ghost of Major Spencer, which tells Grayling that Macnab has murdered him and hidden his body in the bay. The murderer, Spencer is sure, is on his way to Charleston to sail for England. Spencer pleads with Grayling to have Macnab brought to justice, and Grayling hurriedly sets out to avenge his friend's murder.

In Charleston, Grayling's search eventually uncovers Macnab, hiding under the alias of Macleod. Macleod protests his innocence, but his guilty behavior leads the sheriff to arrest Macleod as the murderer.

Macleod secures a lawyer who files a writ of *habeas corpus*, and the judge states the case against Macleod would be stronger if the body were discovered and the murder actually proven. Grayling sets out to search the bay area, and he eventually finds Spencer's body. Macnab, alias Macleod, is found guilty and hanged.

Here ends the grandmother's tale; the narrator's father, however, suspicious of such irrationalities, tells his son the ghost was an invention of Grayling's mind and that all the supposed mysterious happenings of the tale can be accounted for by natural laws. Grayling was a bold, imaginative man. When he learned his friend had not made it to the tavern, he thought of Macnab traveling along the same road and became suspicious of foul play. He also was aware that Macnab knew Spencer was on his way to England to prove his identity and claim a large fortune. The spot where the "ghost" appeared was simply one which had already struck Grayling's keen intelligence as a perfect place for an ambush; these thoughts were in his mind as he sat down to rest by the tree. Falling asleep—or so the father contends—Grayling sees a "ghost"; you will note, however, the father states, that, although Spencer told Grayling he had been murdered by Macnab, he did not tell him how or by what weapons. Neither does he reveal what wounds he has suffered. To ride to Charleston and discover the murderer onboard the very ship Major Spencer would have sailed upon for England required no great or superior logical deduction from Grayling. "The whole story," the father tells the son, "is one of strong probabilities which happened to be verified." The son hears his father "with great patience to the end," noting that the father "had taken a great deal of pains to destroy one of my greatest sources of pleasure." The son, however, chooses to believe in ghosts and to reject his father's philosophy, saying that "it was more easy to believe the one than to comprehend the other."

"THE SNAKE OF THE CABIN"

Both "How Sharp Snaffles Got His Capital and His Wife" and "Grayling" demonstrate Simms's penchant for stories which unmask villains, reward the just and virtuous, and show the eventual triumph of good over evil. A similar pattern can be seen in the story "The Snake of the Cabin," which focuses upon the mysterious death of Ellen Ramsay, a young maiden of health and vigor who faded rapidly into sickness and death barely a year after her marriage to

Edward Stanton. At her funeral, her spurned lover, Robert Anderson, appears and accuses Stanton of using slander and witchcraft to steal Ellen away from him. Stanton is enraged, and the men have to be separated before a fight ensues. Anderson keeps up a steady vigil at Ellen's grave for several months, until he himself dies, presumably of a broken heart. Upon his death, it is discovered that he has carved matching headstones for his grave and Ellen's. Stanton, however, is adamant that the headstone is not to be erected over his wife's grave.

The tale is narrated by Mr. Atkins to a stranger who has appeared upon the scene and made inquiries about Edward Stanton. Hearing the details of the story, he tells Atkins that he has proof against Stanton which will end his claim to Ellen's estate and thus save her father, John Ramsay, the pain of having to sell several of his slaves to pay Stanton his share. The stranger is taken to Mr. Ramsay's house, where Stanton is engaged in an argument with Ramsay over how he is to receive his share of his wife's estate. The stranger listens for a while, then asks Stanton to which wife he is referring. Stanton, obviously flustered, responds that he is talking about Ellen Ramsay. The stranger responds that he thinks not, since Stanton has recently married three women in different parts of the country and claimed shares of their estates. Stanton shouts that the stranger can prove none of these charges, and the stranger reveals papers he has carried with him that substantiate his claims. Stanton is confused and shaken, and those present conclude that his behavior and the legal papers at hand reveal his guilt. The stranger unmasks himself as Henry Lamar of Georgia, the cousin and once the betrothed of a girl Stanton married and later wronged. Lamar tells Stanton he has no claim against Ellen Ramsay's estate and warns him to be out of town within forty-eight hours or Lamar will have him prosecuted.

Later that evening, Abraham, one of the slaves Stanton wanted Ramsay to sell, comes up to Ellen's brother, Jack Ramsay, and shows him a twenty-dollar bill, asking him if it is genuine. Ramsay tells him it is not and asks him where he got it. Abraham responds that he got it from Mr. Stanton, who gave Abraham

twenty dollars to convince the slaves to run away with him and achieve their freedom in the North. Ramsay decides that they will hatch a plot to seize Stanton at once, and he tells Abraham to round up Lamar, Atkins, and several others to disguise themselves as the Negro slaves and meet Stanton later that night at the designated spot. The men wait for Stanton in the woods, and when he appears, they move to capture him. He escapes and runs down the path, only to be tripped up by Abraham. In trying to escape once more, Stanton shoots at Abraham and wounds him in the arm. Abraham falls, however, and lands upon Stanton's knife, driving the blade deep into Stanton's side and killing him. For his virtuous conduct in revealing Stanton's plot to Jack Ramsay and in aiding in Stanton's capture, Abraham is provided for by the Ramsay family and becomes the official recounter of the tale of Stanton's efforts to attain gain by evil and devious means. The moral of the story is presented by Lamar, who states that evil is not an exclusive possession of the wealthy or the powerful; "the same snake, or one very much like it, winds his way into the wigwam and the cabin—and the poor silly country girl is as frequently the victim, as the dashing lady of the city and city fashions."

Simms's writings are often regarded as frivolous and criticized for their heavy Romanticism and simplistic conceptions of morality. Those who find Simms's works to be insubstantial often charge him with being a dated historical writer, one whose works must fade in significance and interest as quickly as the era they depicted passes into history and into memory. While there is some obvious merit to these charges against Simms, it cannot be denied that Simms never aspired to be anything more than a recorder of his era and its particular charms and peculiarities. More than any other writer of the Old South he achieved that aim, and his collected works remain the most sensitive, insightful, and imaginative record of the formative years of southern culture.

OTHER MAJOR WORKS

LONG FICTION: *Martin Faber: The Story of a Criminal*, 1833; *Guy Rivers: A Tale of Georgia*, 1834; *The Yemassee: A Romance of Carolina*, 1835;

The Partisan: A Tale of the Revolution, 1835; *Mellichampe: A Legend of the Santee*, 1836; *Richard Hurdis: Or, The Avenger of Blood, a Tale of Alabama*, 1838; *Pelayo: A Story of the Goth*, 1838; *The Damsel of Darien*, 1839; *Border Beagles: A Tale of Mississippi*, 1840; *The Kinsmen: Or, The Black Riders of the Congaree*, 1841 (revised as *The Scout*, 1854); *Confession: Or, The Blind Heart*, 1841; *Beauchampe: Or, The Kentucky Tragedy, a Tale of Passion*, 1842; *Helen Halsey: Or, The Swamp State of Conelachita, a Tale of the Borders*, 1845; *Count Julian: Or, The Last Days of the Goth, a Historical Romance*, 1845; *Katharine Walton: Or, The Rebel of Dorchester*, 1851; *The Sword and the Distaff: Or, "Fair, Fat and Forty,"* 1852 (revised as *Woodcraft*, 1854); *Vasconselos: A Romance of the New World*, 1853; *The Forayers: Or, The Raid of the Dog-Days*, 1855; *Eutaw: A Sequel to the Forayers*, 1856; *Charlemont: Or, The Pride of the Village*, 1856; *The Cassique of Kiawah: A Colonial Romance*, 1859.

PLAY: *Michael Bonham: Or, The Fall of Bexar, A Tale of Texas*, pb. 1852.

POETRY: *Monody on the Death of Gen. Charles Cotesworth Pinckney*, 1825; *Early Lays*, 1827; *Lyrical and Other Poems*, 1827; *The Vision of Cortes*, 1829; *The Tri-Color*, 1830; *Atalantis: A Story of the Sea*, 1832; *Areytos: Or, Songs of the South*, 1846; *Poems Descriptive, Dramatic, Legendary and Contemplative*, 1853.

NONFICTION: *The History of South Carolina*, 1840; *The Geography of South Carolina*, 1843; *The Life of Francis Marion*, 1844; *Views and Reviews in American Literature, History and Fiction*, 1845; *The Life of Captain John Smith*, 1846; *The Life of the Chevalier Bayard*, 1847; *The Life of Nathanael Greene*, 1849; *The Lily and the Totem: Or, The Huguenots in Florida*, 1850; *South-Carolina in the Revolutionary War*, 1853; *Sack and Destruction of the City of Columbia, S. C.*, 1865; *The Letters of William Gilmore Simms*, 1952-1956 (Mary C. Simms Oliphant, editor, 5 volumes).

MISCELLANEOUS: *The Centennial Edition of the Writings of William Gilmore Simms*, 1969-1975 (John C. Guilds and James B. Meriwether, editors, 16 volumes).

BIBLIOGRAPHY

Butterworth, Keen, and James E. Kibler, Jr. *William Gilmore Simms: A Reference Guide*. Boston: G. K. Hall, 1980. This very thorough bibliography lists all writings about Simms in chronological order, from 1825 to 1979. The lengthy introduction gives general background information, and the index provides an efficient means of locating books and articles on specific topics relating to Simms.

Current-Garcia, Eugene. *The American Short Story Before 1850: A Critical History*. Boston: Twayne, 1985. Current-Garcia gives a useful overview of early nineteenth century American short fiction, including a chapter on "Simms and the Southern Frontier Humorists." Several bibliographies are also included.

Guilds, John Caldwell. *Simms: A Literary Life*. Fayetteville: University of Arkansas Press, 1992. The first critical biography of Simms to appear in one hundred years, Guilds's book proceeds in a chronological fashion and emphasizes Simms's accomplishments as a novelist. Five appendices include a chart of birth and death dates for Simms's fifteen children; the will of Nash Roach, Simms's father-in-law, bequeathing the bulk of his estate to Simms and Chevillette Roach Simms, his wife; a letter written by Simms to the United States Congress in support of an international copyright bill; two elegies published in Charleston periodicals after Simms's death; and a useful list of Simms's writings appearing in book form.

_____, ed. *"Long Years of Neglect": The Work and Reputation of William Gilmore Simms*. Fayetteville: University of Arkansas Press, 1988. The twelve essays in this collection address Simms as novelist, poet, historical philosopher, humorist, lecturer, and literary critic. Mary Ann Wimsatt's essay on "The Evolution of Simms' Backwoods Humor" deals particularly with Simms's short fiction.

Guilds, John Caldwell, and Caroline Collins, eds. *William Gilmore Simms and the American Frontier*. Athens: University of Georgia, 1997. A good look at Simms's use of the frontier in his works.

Johanyak, Debra. "William Gilmore Simms: Deviant

Paradigms of Southern Womanhood?" *The Mississippi Quarterly* 46 (Fall, 1993): 573-588. Discusses the portrayal of women in Simms's fiction; claims that just as intellectual, independent, or masculinized women are repeatedly destroyed by seducers in Simms's work, readers are encouraged to view them as deviant and as contributing to their own downfall.

Mayfield, John. "'The Soul of a Man': William Gilmore Simms and the Myths of Southern Manhood." *Journal of the Early Republic* 15 (Fall, 1995): 477-500. An examination of southern men in Simms's fiction; argues that both as literary figures and as paradigms Simms's characters are failures, being stereotypes with little to offer; explores Simms's use of masks, deceits, representations, and misrepresentations as well as his introduction of the romantic rogue to reveal a subtext that provides a more realistic portrait of southern manhood.

Watson, Charles S. *From Nationalism to Secessionism: The Changing Fiction of William Gilmore Simms.* Westport, Conn.: Greenwood Press, 1993. Examines the political and social views of this southern author. Includes bibliographical references and an index.

Wimsatt, Mary Ann. *The Major Fiction of William Gilmore Simms: Cultural Traditions and Literary Forms.* Baton Rouge: Louisiana State University Press, 1989. Although Wimsatt focuses primarily on Simms's novels, this study is one of the most useful discussions of Simms's work as it reevaluates many of the misconceptions and dismissive attitudes about his fiction. Wimsatt makes use of biographical as well as historical information, and she discusses Simms's novels within the context of twentieth century critical formulations about the romance genre.

Christina Murphy, updated by
Ann A. Merrill

MONA SIMPSON

Born: Green Bay, Wisconsin; June 14, 1957

PRINCIPAL SHORT FICTION

"What My Mother Knew," 1982
"Approximations," 1983
"The Day He Left," 1983
"Lawns," 1984
"You Leave Them," 1985
"Victory Mills," 1989
"I Am Here to Tell You It Can Be Done," 1990

OTHER LITERARY FORMS

Mona Simpson's first novel, *Anywhere but Here* (1986), explores the complex relationship between mother and daughter. Her second novel, *The Lost Father* (1991), continues the story as Mayan Stevenson searches for her missing father. In *A Regular Guy* (1996) Simpson examines the relationship between a geneticist-tycoon and the illegitimate daughter he abandoned.

ACHIEVEMENTS

Mona Simpson's short stories have been selected for *Twenty Under Thirty* and the annual *The Best American Short Stories.* She was chosen as one of *Granta*'s Best Young American Novelists. In 1986 she received a $20,000 National Endowment for the Arts grant and a $25,000 award from the Whiting Foundation. In 1988 she won a John Simon Guggenheim Memorial Foundation Fellowship and Hodder fellowship, Princeton.

BIOGRAPHY

Mona Elizabeth Simpson was born in Green Bay, Wisconsin, on June 14, 1957. Her mother's great-grandparents had emigrated from Germany in the

Mona Simpson (AP/Wide World Photos)

nineteenth century and settled in Sheboygan, Wisconsin. Her grandmother moved to Green Bay, where she and her husband raised mink and ran a photoengraving business and gas stations. Simpson's father, originally from the Middle East, was a college professor; her mother was a speech therapist. As a child, Simpson attended the same school as the children of the Green Bay Packers. After her father abandoned the family, her mother moved to Beverly Hills, California, with Mona and her older brother.

Following graduation from Beverly Hills High School, Simpson earned a B.A. from the University of California, Berkeley, in 1979. She worked as a reporter for newspapers in the San Francisco area until 1981, when she won a scholarship to the graduate program in writing at Columbia University in New York City; there she earned an M.F.A. in 1983. She was accepted into Yaddo, the writers' colony at Saratoga Springs, New York, where she was able to

devote her time to writing. She married Richard Appel, a public prosecutor, who later became a writer for the television series *The Simpsons*; they would have a son, Gabriel. She taught a writing workshop in the graduate program at New York University, worked as a writing instructor at Bard College, and served as senior editor of *The Paris Review.*

ANALYSIS

Mona Simpson has earned a reputation as a writer who explores the relationships of members of families who struggle in the aftermath of divorce or other situations in which the father leaves the family. She writes about unusual family structures and problems that exist in relationships between parents and children. Her writing is filled with insights into these troubled families as she describes domestic scenes in realistic detail. She describes the characters' experiences with vivid images and stark details. Although the stories are not autobiographical in content, she draws on her own family background for feelings and insights.

In her work, Simpson combines the minimalist style of Ann Beattie with Ann Tyler's insights into family life. She portrays characters involved in real-life situations who have faced heartbreaking crises yet have found the courage to go on with their lives. Her female protagonists emerge with scars inflicted on them by incompetent or indifferent parents and manage to survive, even thrive. As she tells her stories from the first-person point of view, her young narrators show the pain they have suffered, the longing for a normal family, and finally their acceptance of their lives.

The theme of the lost father dominates Simpson's short fiction. Whether the men die, divorce their spouses, or abandon their families, in one way or another the women are left to care for themselves and their children. The mothers are often inept or poorly equipped for the responsibilities of parenting, forcing the young narrators to strike out on their own to create lives for themselves.

"WHAT MY MOTHER KNEW"

Emily, the narrator of "What My Mother Knew," is a young woman living in New York, struggling to establish a career in acting. At her mother's request, she and her brother and sister have flown to California for a visit. After her father died when Emily was a baby, her mother, Elena Hanson, struggled to support herself and her children. Her mother has always dreamed of having a beautiful home, but she could never afford one. Now, at age fifty-nine, she tells her children that she has a surprise for them and drives them to her home in Pacific Heights, a place where Emily says the rich people live. She thinks that the brick house on the hill is the most beautiful house she has ever seen.

When her children question her, Elena admits that she has leased the house for only one year. As she enjoys the view of the Golden Gate Bridge, Emily admires the music and furnishings and can see that her mother has made every attempt to create a beautiful home for this reunion. As they raise their glasses in a toast, Emily sees the secret in her mother's eyes: She is dying, and this is her last attempt to create the illusion of a happy family life. In a flashback, Emily remembers that when she was twelve years old she was looking through her mother's dresser and found evidence that her mother had been selling her blood for money. Emily finally recognizes how difficult life has always been for her mother, and the two women share an embrace of love and understanding.

"APPROXIMATIONS"

Melinda, the story's protagonist, lives alone with her mother, Carol, and has no real memories of her father. In the opening paragraph of "Approximations," Melinda, a midwestern teenager, imagines a scene in which her parents are dancing. She has cultivated this fantasy over a period of years, ever since she was four years old and learned that the man in a family photograph was her father. When Melinda finally meets her father, a waiter in Las Vegas, she is disappointed by his obvious lack of interest in her. When Carol marries Jerry, an ice-skating professional, Melinda at first refuses to accept him as a substitute father. As their relationship grows, however, Melinda replaces her dream of reunion with her father with the sense of security and stability that Jerry offers. Simpson tells the story of a girl growing from childhood to adolescence with an absent father and a

vain, immature mother who drifts along refusing to face reality. Through flashbacks, and vivid images, Simpson tells the story of a young girl learning to accept the "approximations" that make up the realities of her life and surviving in spite of the indifference and incompetence of her parents.

"THE DAY HE LEFT"

A wife and mother trying to survive after her husband leaves her is a common theme in Simpson's fiction, and here again the reader hears the story from the first-person point of view as the wife narrates the story. "The Day He Left" centers on the day a young woman's husband, Steven, leaves her and her daughter, Laura. The couple have lived together for nine years, but Steven has chosen to leave his wife and child to pursue a homosexual relationship; although he has remained on good terms with his family and plans to continue seeing his daughter, Steven wants a different life. The situation is difficult for the woman to accept because she still loves him, and they get along well together. She struggles to save the marriage, but after Steven leaves, she decides to focus her attention on making a life for herself and her daughter.

"LAWNS"

"Lawns" was included in *The Best American Short Stories 1986*, edited by Raymond Carver. First published in the *Iowa Review*, "Lawns" is the story of Jenny, a college freshman, who opens the narrative with the sentence, "I steal." Working in the mail room of her dormitory provides her with the opportunity to steal money, presents, and letters addressed to other students. On her first day on the Berkeley campus, she sees a young man, Glenn, riding a lawn mower. She sees him again that evening, the two begin spending time together, and soon she is in love. Jenny is troubled by a secret that she does not want to share with Glenn, and it influences their relationship. Through a series of flashbacks, it becomes clear that Jenny has suffered years of molestation from her father. She finally tells her mother, and her mother forces Jenny's father to leave and visits Jenny on campus to provide support. When Jenny tells her secret to Glenn, the relationship ends, and she feels that her father has cost her everything she wants from life.

It is Lauren, Jenny's roommate, who finally offers the sympathy and understanding Jenny needs to go on with her life.

"VICTORY MILLS"

"Victory Mills" appears in *Louder Than Words* (1989), a collection of stories from twenty-two writers, who each contributed a previously unpublished story the profits from which went to organizations fighting hunger, homelessness, and illiteracy. This story follows the lives of three high school friends as they move away from their hometown of Victory Mills to pursue careers in New York City: Katy, the daughter of a woman who works at the mill and a father who has abandoned the family; Tray, the handsome young man she loves; and Alex, a homosexual who has been having an affair with Whipple, an antiques dealer. Although she is a bright student, Katy is not accepted into the college of her choice and opts instead for a career as an actress. She and Alex, a graduate student, share an apartment, and Tray plays in a band. Disappointed when Tray marries Betsy, his high school girlfriend, Katy marries and has a child. As Katy becomes more famous as an actress, the three friends drift apart. Alex and Katy are reunited at the funeral of Katy's mother, June. In looking through some old papers, Katy finds a letter from her mother that shows she had her heart broken by a man named Rudy. When asked about the letter, Whipple admits that he was the man with whom June had been in love. Told from the points of view of Katy and Alex, the story alternates between the two narrators.

OTHER MAJOR WORKS

LONG FICTION: *Anywhere but Here*, 1986; *The Lost Father*, 1991; *A Regular Guy*, 1996.

BIBLIOGRAPHY

Bing, Jonathan, "Mona Simpson: Return of the Prodigal Father." *Publishers Weekly*, 243 (November 4, 1996): 50. Notes that Simpson's three novels all center on daughters neglected by incompetent parents. In the interview, Simpson says that she considers herself a minimalist and cites Raymond Carver as a writer who has influenced her work. In speaking of her own parents, Simpson says that the feelings and themes in *The Lost Father* were close to her life, but not the details.

Graham, Judith, ed. "Mona Simpson." In *Current Biography Yearbook*. New York: H. W. Wilson, 1993. Provides biographical information about Simpson's family life, education, and early career. Includes brief synopses of her novels, *Anywhere but Here* and *The Lost Father*. Describes her work as marked by striking imagery and shrewd insights into family relationships. Although much of her work seems drawn from her family history, Simpson is quoted as denying that her writing is autobiographical: "It's definitely not a memoir."

Mona (Elizabeth) Simpson. In *Contemporary Literary Criticism*. Vol. 44. Detroit: Gale, 1987. Describes Simpson's first novel, *Anywhere but Here*, as an exploration of the mother-daughter relationship and a blend of family and social themes. Includes reviews of this novel from a number of sources. In her comments to *Current Biography Yearbook* Simpson says that she wrote the first draft in one summer but spent several months revising it. The article includes an excerpt from the novel.

Judith Barton Williamson

CRITICAL SURVEY
OF
SHORT FICTION

GEOGRAPHICAL INDEX

GEOGRAPHICAL INDEX

CATEGORY INDEX

CATEGORY INDEX

SOCIAL SATIRE. *See also*
MANNERS, FICTION OF,
SOCIAL REALISM

SOUTH AFRICAN CULTURE

SOUTHERN UNITED
STATES

SOUTHWESTERN UNITED
STATES

SPANISH CULTURE

SUPERNATURAL STORIES.
See also **GHOST, GOTHIC,**
GROTESQUE STORIES,
HORROR, MAGICAL
REALISM, OCCULT,
SUSPENSE

CATEGORY INDEX

DATE DUE

HIGHSMITH 45230